RESULTS WITHOUT AUTHORITY

RESULTS WITHOUT AUTHORITY

Controlling a Project When the Team Doesn't Report to You

SECOND EDITION

TOM KENDRICK

American Management Association

New York • Atlanta • Brussels • Chicago • Mexico City • San Francisco
Shanghai • Tokyo • Toronto • Washington, D. C.

Special discounts on bulk quantities of AMACOM books are available to corporations, professional associations, and other organizations. For details, contact Special Sales Department, AMACOM, a division of American Management Association, 1601 Broadway, New York, NY 10019.
Tel: 800-250-5308. Fax: 518-891-2372.
E-mail: specialsls@amanet.org
Website: www.amacombooks.org/go/specialsales
To view all AMACOM titles go to: www.amacombooks.org

This publication is designed to provide accurate and authoritative information in regard to the subject matter covered. It is sold with the understanding that the publisher is not engaged in rendering legal, accounting, or other professional service. If legal advice or other expert assistance is required, the services of a competent professional person should be sought.

"PMI" and the PMI logo are service and trademarks of the Project Management Institute, Inc. which are registered in the United States of America and other nations; "PMP" and the PMP logo are certification marks of the Project Management Institute, Inc. which are registered in the United States of America and other nations; "PMBOK", "PM Network", and "PMI Today" are trademarks of the Project Management Institute, Inc. which are registered in the United States of America and other nations; ". . . building professionalism in project management . . ." is a trade and service mark of the Project Management Institute, Inc. which is registered in the United States of America and other nations; and the Project Management Journal logo is a trademark of the Project Management Institute, Inc.

PMI did not participate in the development of this publication and has not reviewed the content for accuracy. PMI does not endorse or otherwise sponsor this publication and makes no warranty, guarantee, or representation, expressed or implied, as to its accuracy or content. PMI does not have any financial interest in this publication, and has not contributed any financial resources.

Additionally, PMI makes no warranty, guarantee, or representation, express or implied, that the successful completion of any activity or program, or the use of any product or publication, designed to prepare candidates for the PMP® Certification Examination, will result in the completion or satisfaction of any PMP® Certification eligibility requirement or standard.

Library of Congress Cataloging-in-Publication Data

Kendrick, Tom.
    Results without authority : controlling a project when the team doesn't report to you / Tom Kendrick.—2nd ed.
        p.   cm.
    Includes bibliographical references and index.
    ISBN-13: 978-0-8144-1781-2
    ISBN-10: 0-8144-1781-7
    1. Project management.   I. Title.
    HD69.P75K463   2012
    658.4'04—dc23   2011025017

Printing number

10   9   8   7   6   5   4   3   2   1

Contents

Acknowledgments

RESULTS WITHOUT AUTHORITY benefits from the hard-earned experience of hundreds of excellent project leaders and managers who have so generously shared their experiences over the years. In particular, I need to thank Terry Ash, Ron Askeland, Ron Benton, Scott Beth, Alfonso Bucero, Craig Chatterton, Karel de Bakker, Al DeLucia, Anup Deshpande, Randy Englund, Tom Fader, Wayne Goulding, Bob Gudz, Esteri Hinman, Rosemary Hossenlopp, Nancy McDonald, Bob Montevaldo, Joe Podolsky, Patrick Schmid, Richard Simonds, Ted Slater, Jim Sloane, Jose Solera, David Straker, Arun Swamy, Peter Vogel-Dittrich, Ashok Waran, J. D. Watson, and Todd Williams, who provided examples, feedback, and encouragement throughout the process of pulling this book together. I also want to thank my long-suffering spouse, Barbara Kendrick, who repeatedly read and reread the text of this book, attacking the confusion and untangling the knots.

Although these friends (and many others) deserve a great measure of the credit for what is in this book, any errors, omissions, or unnecessary complexity are all on me. If you find any, or just want to provide feedback, please let me know.

Getting results without authority involves more than a little luck. Yet luck is what happens when preparation meets opportunity. I hope in this book you find ample guidance for your preparations, and all of your opportunities result in successful projects.

—TOM KENDRICK
SAN CARLOS, CALIFORNIA
TKENDRICK@FAILUREPROOFPROJECTS.COM

RESULTS WITHOUT AUTHORITY

CHAPTER 1

Control of Projects

PROJECTS ARE EVERYWHERE. Some of these projects succeed; others do not. Many projects fail because the project leader lacks sufficient control to keep things moving toward a successful conclusion. Insufficient project control is a result of many factors: lack of authority, geographically distributed teams, excessive project change, competing priorities, and inadequate planning—just to name a few.

Increasingly today, projects are undertaken in environments where the project leader has little formal authority. Even for project managers with formal authority, significant portions of project work are done by contributors who work for other managers, often for a different company. Projects where no one is in charge are almost certain to fail. As the leader of your project, you must assume control, whether or not you possess organizational authority. As unlikely as it may sometimes seem, any project leader can do much to establish and maintain project control. This book has many ideas for achieving project success using techniques that don't depend on organizational position or on formal authority.

▪ Who's in Charge?

In classes, workshops, and informal discussions of project management that I've been a part of, one of the most common questions is, "How can I manage my project if I have no power or authority?" This issue comes up so often that

1

I developed a list of things that project leaders can (and should) take control of, regardless of their position or power in an organization. None of these things requires any authority beyond what is implicit when you are delegated responsibility for a project, and some don't even rely on that.

Factors That Any Project Leader Can Control
- Measurement
- Reporting cycles
- Milestones
- Communication
- Project reviews
- Change management
- Rewards and recognition
- Constructive criticism
- Reciprocity and exchange
- Risk monitoring

Project leaders can use these means, along with many others in this book, to enhance their control in *any* project environment. Because the techniques outlined in the next several chapters don't rely on the command-and-control authority of the project leader, they are effective in cross-functional, agile, matrix, heavily outsourced, virtual, volunteer, and other challenging environments. In fact, even project managers with substantial authority will benefit from the practices described in this book because they avoid the potential resentment and demotivation that can result from pulling rank.

▪ Structure of This Book

The first half of this book explores three elements of project control: process, influence, and measurement. This introductory chapter introduces these elements, and Chapters 2–4 dig into the details and show how to apply them in your project environment.

The second half of the book examines when to use these three elements for control throughout the life of a typical project. The *Guide to the Project Management Body of Knowledge* (*PMBOK®* Guide), from the Project Management Institute, identifies five process groups: initiating, planning, executing, monitoring and controlling, and closing. Chapters 5–9 map these topics, describing how to better control your project from its beginning to its end. Where the *PMBOK Guide* tends to assume that a project manager has formal power, the discussion throughout this book focuses on controlling project work even when you do not have such direct authority.

Each chapter begins by outlining the principal concepts for that chapter, then explores each idea in detail using examples. Each of Chapters 2–9 concludes with a summary of key ideas, and Chapter 10 summarizes the fundamental ideas of the book and offers some final thoughts on applying them to your projects.

This book contains many ideas—far more than any single project would ever need. The advice ranges from tips useful on small projects to ideas for dealing with the complexity of large, multiteam programs. Read through the book using your own judgment to determine which ideas are the most effective and helpful for your specific situation. To get started, pick an idea or two from each section that you think will help you with your project. When you encounter a problem, use the table of contents to locate pointers to deal with it, and adapt the practices outlined there to move things back under control. Don't overcomplicate your project with processes that aren't needed; if two approaches to a project issue are equally effective, always choose the simpler one.

▪ Elements of Project Control

Every project leader has a number of levers available that increase project control. Three principal elements of control are:

1. Project processes
2. Influence
3. Metrics (measurement)

Project processes provide the structure necessary for control and can serve as an effective substitute for organizational authority. You can build *influence* in many ways, and the more you are able to sway, encourage, or win over those you are working with, the better you will be able to control your project. *Measurement* quantifies results and drives behavior, so metrics are useful for both understanding the status of your project and encouraging cooperation. With these three techniques, you can control and be successful with any type of project.

Project Processes

Some years ago, a good friend celebrated a fiftieth birthday at a bowling alley with about a hundred friends. (Names are withheld to shield the guilty.) Because most of us in attendance were of roughly the same age and few had bowled more than once in the previous three decades, the initial frames we bowled were spectacularly pathetic. In the intervening years, the gutters on either side of the lanes seemed to have developed an almost magnetic attraction for bowling balls. Some people were halfway through their initial game and still trying to knock down their first pin.

Fortunately, the alleys had bumpers on either side, which we soon flipped into position on almost all of our lanes. These bumpers ran the length of the lane over the gutters, so balls that would have otherwise fallen out of play were bounced back onto the lane. With more balls rolling toward the pins (if not exactly in the center of the alleys), scores improved dramatically.

Good processes for projects are analogous to bumpers in bowling. Well-defined processes, properly applied, keep projects from rolling off into the gutter. Project processes are a source of substantial control, and they are usually owned by project leaders because much of the work is their personal responsibility.

Early in a new project, a project leader can easily influence even project processes that others own as they are being established. Most people can recall the unpleasant results caused on projects that lacked sufficiently defined processes. Your team members, stakeholders, managers, and sponsors are all likely to agree to process discipline that addresses past problems and inefficiencies. When initiating your overall project infrastructure, work to define all processes affecting your project team, and to get them accepted by everyone in advance.

Processes permeate the project life cycle. Some are related to specific phases of project work, such as those for requirements definition, scope freeze, baseline planning, risk identification, and project review. Other processes apply throughout a project, such as those for communication and change management. Whatever their timing, clearly defined processes are bumpers that enable the project leader to keep the ball rolling toward the final objective. Project processes are the main topic of Chapter 2.

Influence

In projects, as in most situations, people tend to work on the things that they want to work on. Even when a leader's authority is absolute, ordering people to do something doesn't make them *want* to do it. Using command-and-control authority to force people to do things unwillingly leads to resentment and demotivation. Malicious compliance is also a risk; people may find ways to appear to cooperate while actually harming the project. In extreme cases, some people will fail to do as they are asked even when the personal consequences of noncompliance are severe. If generals and admirals cannot always expect automatic obedience, what chance does a project leader have?

Nevertheless, as project leader, you have a fairly good chance of gaining support if you use the correct approach. Getting cooperation is much easier when you have a two-way relationship of trust and respect with your team members. Effective project leaders create this essential foundation for influence through team-building activities, formal group events (such as project start-up workshops), and informal one-on-one interactions. The surest path to cooperation starts with establishing strong social relationships in which people don't want to disappoint each other.

Another way to enlist willing cooperation is to involve your project staff in activities *that they want to work on.* When a team member is enthusiastic about the project work, there's no trick to it; the project leader has little more to do than assign ownership and stay out of the way. When project work does not appeal to the members of your project team, however, you must work to create interest in it. The principal technique begins with an understanding that everyone's favorite call letters are *WIIFM: What's in it for me?* Leaders in any field invest the time to understand what the people they are working with really care about. Effective project leaders identify opportunities to align the project's needs with what the individuals want to do, and they assign responsibility for project activities accordingly. The tools of influence rely on *reciprocity*—an exchange of something that the individual wants for the commitment to complete work that the project requires.

Another key to influence is effective *communication.* Either project leaders are good communicators, or they are not project leaders for long. Communication is the one absolutely undisputed responsibility owned by the project leader, regardless of project type, other responsibilities, or authority. To succeed and retain control, you must manage information and always communicate effectively.

Formal project communication includes written documentation for your project, such as plans and progress reports. Using the power of your pen, you can control your project through filtering and summarizing and by deciding how best to distribute information and when.

Informal communication is also an essential component of project control. Influence and relationship building depend on frequent conversations and other casual interactions. Often you will learn about project problems much earlier through informal discussions than from formally collected project status. The earlier you can detect problems, the more options you have. Control depends on the quick resolution of issues and problems. You can also influence others by asking revealing (and sometimes embarrassing) questions. When your authority is insufficient to avoid situations that could harm your project, asking a pointed question or two at the right time can have the same effect. Your perspective as the project leader—understanding the work, the capacities of your team, and the project's priorities—enables you to guide people to rational conclusions that are consistent with project success.

Establishing and using influence for project control is explored in detail in Chapter 3.

Metrics

Control in any environment relies on measurements. Without clearly defined limits, the very concept of control lacks meaning. In addition to the obvious role of metrics in determining overall project performance, metrics also affect the behavior of the project team. As Bill Hewlett, founder of the Hewlett-Packard Company, is reputed to have said, "What gets measured gets done." Measuring a few key things on a project and publishing the results powerfully affect your project's progress.

A small set of well-defined project metrics gives the project leader a powerful tool for managing project initiation, execution, and closure. Effectively using project measurement for project control is the topic of Chapter 4.

▪ No One Ever Said That Projects Are Easy

One analogy I like to use is that running a project is like driving a vehicle down a steep hill. Control of a moving vehicle involves the use of the steering wheel, the accelerator, and the brake. Having all three is nice. With projects, however, someone else's foot is on the accelerator, and, if you brake, you will be late. You do have both hands on the steering wheel, though. So you steer with process, influence, and metrics, keeping your trajectory as true as you can. With adequate preparation, diligence, and attention to detail, you can reach your destination, exhausted but exhilarated, with no casualties and only a few scratches, dings, and minor dents here and there. Project control starts at project initiation, and it requires your full attention all the way to the end. Applying the concepts you find in this book will carry you safely to your destination: project success.

CHAPTER 2

Control Through Process

MOST MODERN PROJECTS ARE DIFFICULT. Lacking effective project management processes, most projects fall into certain chaos. Projects undertaken using practical methods have a much better chance of success, especially when the project leader has little formal authority.

The foundation of effective project management has been established for a very long time. Proposing—and gaining support for—clearly defined project processes that make sense in your environment can significantly improve control over your projects. Adopting proven project practices with your team provides structure and guidance that provides you with additional levers to use in influencing your team. When you lack (or prefer not to rely on) formal authority, employing good processes that your contributors understand and use can keep your project moving in the right direction.

This chapter outlines important processes that can be used to improve your ability to keep a project under control. We also explore the benefits of a well-defined project infrastructure and how to take advantage of a structured project office.

▪ Project Management Processes

Successfully managing a project involves at least three separate activities: achieving project objectives, managing the project processes, and leading the team. The overall objective, the most visible of the three, depends heavily on processes and leadership. The best project leaders spend much, if not most, of their time interacting with people, and productive team leadership is the main topic of Chapter 3. The focus of this chapter is on managing processes. Project leaders who collaboratively fine-tune the project processes used by their teams gain control in two ways. Using processes that project contributors and stakeholders participate in defining augments the trust and collaborative environment that successful projects depend on. In addition, getting voluntary commitment to use well-defined processes encourages appropriate behavior; it's a lot more straightforward to lead a project by helping people follow agreed-on processes than by ordering your team to do things because you say so.

Some project processes are built in; that is, your organization does things in a certain way, and you and your project team have little choice but to conform. Even when the principal processes are mandated in advance, however, some processes belong solely to the project leader, and still other project processes involving your team and project stakeholders are at least partially yours to influence and control. Gaining the necessary buy-in and commitment needed to adopt new project processes or to improve existing processes may require some effort on your part. The effort is easily justified in most cases, though, especially when defining processes that can make the difference between a project you are able to keep on track and one that tumbles into chaos. Some project processes that can help are:

- Life cycles and methodologies
- Project definition and charter
- Project planning, execution, and tracking
- Change management
- Information management
- Project management software tools
- Contract and procurement management
- Risk management
- Quality management
- Issue management
- Decision making

Before doing a lot of work defining (or redefining) processes, assess where your organization stands on project management generally. Project management processes are far more effective in organizations that place value in developing and applying project management skills and methods. High-performing project management organizations have:

- Easy access to project management training, mentoring, and support
- A process for project manager/leader selection that is orderly and that creates few accidental project managers

- Programs that reward project achievements and teamwork instead of individual heroism
- Strong standards for project documentation, with periodic meaningful review of project information
- Ongoing support and sponsorship by higher-level managers throughout projects, not just at the start

If your environment lacks these attributes, establishing effective processes is more difficult, and the processes you do adopt may be easily undermined by management or other stakeholders. Adopting well-defined processes is still worthwhile, but gaining meaningful support and commitment for them is more difficult and it may require you to exert your influence, as discussed in Chapter 3.

Although many organizations lack much of a project management culture, some organizations overdo it. In either case, periodically reviewing recent project problems at the organization level enables you to identify the root causes of issues that arise either from insufficient process focus or from excessive project overhead. All projects are unique. The process specifics that work best tend to be highly situational. Some projects benefit from elaborate, formal, *PMI PMBOK®*-influenced structures and practices. In these cases, project leaders can build a solid foundation on these processes for project control. In other organizations, more informal, agile, or adaptive methods are more appropriate, and these processes can also provide an effective framework for enhancing your control. It doesn't matter a great deal what specific processes you adopt as long as they make good business sense, have meaningful support from your team and stakeholders, and are actually used. As long as the methods you adopt for your project are well understood and consistently applied, any effective approach can enhance your overall control.

Life Cycles and Methodologies

Life cycles (or stage gates, phase reviews, or any other sequential project timing structure) and methodologies impose discipline on projects. Life cycles serve primarily to coordinate related projects and provide defined checkpoints, whereas methodologies strive to ensure consistency in how project work is done. Mandatory process aspects of either (or both) may be used to significantly enhance your project control.

Life Cycles

Nearly all projects have at least an informal life cycle that provides an overall structure and consistency for major project milestones. There are two main families of project life cycles. One is the *waterfall* type, made up of a single arc through a series of sequential phases (such as analysis, definition, design, development, testing, and release). The other is the *agile* type, in which projects are comprised of a succession of step-by-step, iterative cycles, each delivering an incremental result that approaches the final deliverable. Whatever the life cycle type, the specific details must always be customized to meet particular business, project, and customer needs. Literally thousands of variations are possible, and even within a single organization you may find significant differences. Whatever the life cycle type, the requirements for documentation, specific deliverables, and communication that are embedded in the defined milestones or reviews afford structure and implicit authority to any project leader.

The larger the project, the more likely it is that the life cycle will contain formal, explicit requirements, especially in organizations responsible for coordinating related projects running in parallel. In these cases, life cycles are set up more as management tools to assist upper-level and program managers than as processes for the project leader, and they are generally structured to determine progress at defined checkpoints, to ensure compliance with organizational standards, and to improve visibility and communications. Because life cycles of this sort are not primarily defined for the benefit of project leaders, they can represent excessive overhead that impedes progress and diverts resources from other project work. For this reason, project leaders should analyze the requirements for the chosen life cycle and seek to tailor it to improve the project's chances of success. For each requirement in the life cycle, ask two questions:

1. Why is this necessary? (If it's not, work to minimize the potential impact of any valueless overhead.)
2. How might I use or modify this particular requirement to enhance my control over the work?

Any requests or recommendations you make supported by life cycle requirements carry much more force than they would otherwise. It's much more difficult for team members to ignore things that are reviewed by managers and other outsiders, so look for opportunities to align project deliverables, documentation, and plans with the defined checkpoints and reviews that make up the life cycle. Doing so can help you to minimize control problems or at least help you identify issues early enough in your project to do something about them.

Life cycle requirements are also a powerful tool for managing potential conflicts among different functional groups with contradictory interests. The team members contributing to your project may represent many functions, such as engineering, finance, manufacturing, quality, sales, support, documentation, training, facilities, system management, and testing. If everyone commits to meeting well-defined project life cycle requirements, there will be fewer conflicts over what is due and when. Activities in the project plan arising from a life cycle are easier to control because they depend on the organizational culture behind them, not just on your personal clout (or lack of it).

Although specific life cycles vary a great deal, a project leader can use at least a few universal opportunities to eke out additional control. One example relates to managing the initial scoping process. Even agile-type project life cycles begin with an effort aimed at defining requirements and doing deliverable investigation. Completing this effort requires documentation that describes what the project is expected to produce. The more precise and thorough you can make these initial requirements, the easier it is to develop practical plans that you can use to manage the work. Up-front precision also helps in determining the consequences of later changes, and intelligently managing evolving specifications is essential to project control. Nailing down scope for a project is never easy, but you will be much more successful in achieving scope stability with the help of mandatory life cycle requirements.

A common issue with initial scoping, especially with waterfall-type life cycles, involves listing *musts* and *wants* to describe what the project will produce. Musts are fine as long as they are well justified. Wants, however, are a problem because they fail to set firm boundaries around what your project is expected to produce. The early, disciplined assessment of all wants—and either promoting them to musts or excluding them from the project—forces earlier decisions and makes the project much easier to control.

Even better is to mandate explicit boundary definitions for the project through *Is* and *Is-not* lists that make clear exactly what will and won't be produced. An effective Is-not list for a project is not a random list of silly things that would be illogical to include. It is a list of valid and, in some cases, potentially valuable requirements that you and your sponsors have *explicitly decided not to include* in the present project. All Is-not items listed will probably be considered when scoping a future project or perhaps even in a later phase or iteration of the current project. Many of these out-of-bounds features will eventually be delivered in the future—but not now, and not on your project. Failing to make an Is-not list part of project scoping increases the likelihood that different people, looking at the project from their own perspective, will make wildly varying—and dangerous—assumptions about what is in your scope.

Explicit life cycle requirements can also be useful in improving project control by ensuring that all testing, validation, and sign-off criteria are adequately specified at the same time as the requirements are set, and before any development work begins. Ultimately, the success of your project depends on acceptance of what you produce. Leaving the details of how your results will be evaluated undetermined until late in the project is extremely dangerous. As a requirement for entering the execution phase (or phases) of any life cycle, mandate a thorough plan for testing all deliverables, including measurable criteria, owners, and test participants, and any hardware or equipment that will be needed. Passing a test when you know all the questions in advance is easy. Leaving final acceptance criteria to the last minute is very risky.

You may be able to embed many other possible opportunities for enhancing your overall control in the exit criteria of a life cycle phase or iteration. Begin looking for them by identifying problems and difficulties you have had on past projects relating to the sequence or timing of key deliverables, information, and decisions. If you change nothing, past problems tend to recur, so consider ways to better or more clearly define interim project deliverables, or to schedule them earlier in the project timeline. Using compelling data from earlier problems, you should not find it difficult to get buy-in for customized exit criteria for your life cycle. Sufficiently severe past consequences may even allow you to make permanent changes to the process used throughout your organization.

Even life cycles for short-duration projects or having a series of brief incremental development phases can provide control levers for the project leader. Projects undertaken using agile management techniques involve a substantial focus on teamwork and collaboration. Structuring the work, reviews, and communication around effective practices defined by and for the team provides the project leader with a good deal to work with. By working with the team to create processes and standards that everyone buys into, a project leader can establish a robust structure to work with, especially when the team enthusiastically accepts and uses collaborative practices for close interaction. Whether the project you are working on is following an iterative, agile life cycle or a more traditional waterfall structure, working with your team to fine-tune process aspects of your life cycle requirements is a great way to gain support and build teamwork that will aid you in guiding your team. Chapter 3 offers a lot more on collaborative leadership; the following section on methodologies and other sections throughout this book provide details relating to agile methods.

Methodologies

Methodologies are similar in many ways to life cycles, though they generally go well beyond the life cycle criteria. In addition to specifying project milestone and review requirements, methodologies provide explicit guidance for how work is to be done. The process definitions generally include templates, checklists, forms, and other materials that project leaders are either required or strongly encouraged to use. Methodologies are even more specific to a single type of project than life cycles, and they generally provide a high level of detail. Product development methodologies often include specific advice on which tools and systems to use and how to use them. IT methodologies include standards for version control, documentation, and other aspects of system development. Software methodologies often have defined variations that are specific to implementations of a single vendor's system or application. Methodologies that employ iterative or cyclic phases (such as extreme programming [XP], scrum, lean development, and other agile methods) mandate processes for estimating, working in small teams, and using short-turnaround, time-boxed intervals for interim deliverables.

Methodologies are typically defined in organizations for use on all projects of a given type. Most project leaders have little choice on whether to use them. When methodologies are mandatory and carry the authority of upper management, they can be a significant source of project control for you as a project leader. When considering the effect of an aspect of a methodology, always think of how it could be used as leverage in gaining project contributors' commitments that might otherwise be problematic. If the methodology requires specific documentation to be written in a certain format during development, take full advantage of this to ensure that it is done. If the methodology provides checklists and questionnaires that can be used to highlight project issues, exploit them to improve visibility and assist you in resolving issues. Widely adopted methodologies can also facilitate your management of dependencies with other departments, suppliers, and related projects.

Structural requirements such as life cycles and methodologies can cut both ways, however. Although they can provide a solid set of well-established boundaries that you can use to keep the project moving forward, they may also consume effort and project resources doing work that may not help the project much. As with any process, you need to consider the overall benefits of any methodology and to work, when possible, to adjust the methodology wherever it fails to help your project.

Project Definition and Charter

Clear, unambiguous, high-level project documentation is essential for project control. Whether a specific document and format is defined formally for your organization or is mandated as part of an adopted methodology, developing and communicating a thorough description of your project set the stage for all subsequent work. No matter how or why you create your project definition, establish written documentation for your project that is readily available to all your project stakeholders and team members.

Project definitions take many forms and go by many different names: project charter, proposal, project datasheet, plan of record, project specification, statement of work, or even simply a project definition document. Although the name "project charter" is used here, the principles outlined in this chapter apply to any project definition document—whatever it may be called.

Project charters begin with top-down information on the desired results from the project sponsor and other stakeholders. Start your project documentation using the information you have, and wherever it is incomplete or not sufficiently clear, interview your sponsor (or others, as necessary) to learn the exact business need, problem statement, or other rationale for the project. Work to uncover any known constraints, and ask questions to understand any significant assumptions the sponsor and initial stakeholders have about the project regarding timing, staffing, and other project parameters.

Begin by assembling project charter information in an appropriate format. Use your organization's requirements for project documentation if these exist, but whether using a set format or one you have devised, be as thorough and clear as possible in the following areas:

- Project objective statement (providing in a short paragraph a high-level description of the project deliverable, the project deadline, and anticipated cost or staffing)
- Project priorities (rank ordering among scope, schedule, and resources)
- Project benefits (including a business case or return on investment analysis)
- Available information on user or customer needs
- A scope definition listing all anticipated project deliverables
- Goals for cost and timing
- Significant constraints and assumptions
- Descriptions of dependencies on other related projects
- High-level risks, new technologies required, and significant issues

Strive to include as much specific detail as you can, and, as you proceed, validate the content of your charter with the project sponsor and stakeholders.

A project charter is a living document that may grow and evolve over the course of the project, but maintaining an unambiguous, easily accessed description of the project currently approved by your sponsor and others in authority is a very powerful tool that you can use to keep your project under control. Throughout the project, the charter facilitates rejecting proposed changes that conflict with what is in the charter. Constraints that are documented in the charter, such as interim milestone deliverables or mandated compliance with published standards, are more effective as a rationale for your requests than just your say-so. A thorough charter document forms the basis for detailed scoping, planning, tracking, and periodic project reviews. Chapter 5 discusses the development and use of the project charter in initiating a project.

Project Planning, Execution, and Tracking

As a project leader, you can establish a solid basis for control by making a strong case for planning, tracking, and execution processes. Control depends on getting buy-in for these processes from your project team and then using them throughout your project.

Involving all the team members in planning and tracking activities builds buy-in and motivation. Wise project leaders encourage broad participation and include contributions from everybody in the resulting outputs from these processes. When people invest effort and see their influence on the project as it comes into focus, the project quickly shifts from someone else's project to *our project*. Controlling a project that people care about makes the project much easier and ultimately more likely to be successful than trying to manage one with an indifferent team. Using project management processes collaboratively also encourages cooperation among your team members, which also simplifies your job.

Chapter 6 includes details on using project planning processes to improve project control. Chapters 7 and 8 go into the specifics for maintaining control through the execution and tracking processes. Even for the project leader who has little or no formal authority, the disciplined use of these project management processes are essential to keeping things moving forward.

Project infrastructure decisions in all these areas are summarized later in this chapter and detailed in Appendix A. These decisions are a useful way to gain both feedback and broad acceptance of specific project management practices, and basing the decisions on team consensus enables you to enforce them without the need to pull rank.

Change Management

For projects that have initially well-defined deliverables and that are undertaken with a waterfall life cycle, one of the most difficult control problems can be managing specification changes. For projects that have high novelty and that are approached using an agile, iterative approach, change can also be problematic. In both cases, coherent processes aimed at evaluating scope modifications and accepting only those having solid business justification are essential to maintaining project control.

Phased Projects

One of the most troublesome problems for technical projects is excessive and poorly managed specification changes. When the main cause of this is a fuzzy or uncertain notion of the final deliverable, one helpful approach is to abandon the phase gate life cycle and adopt a more flexible, iterative agile approach (discussed below). If the root of your change management challenges is either beginning your work without an adequate understanding of the deliverable or stakeholders who can't seem to make up their minds (or both), solving the problem involves two things: (1) thoroughly documenting and freezing project scope when setting the project baseline and (2) adopting an effective process for managing changes throughout the remainder of the project.

Thoroughly defining scope may require a good deal of effort because you'll need to canvass all your stakeholders and work with them and your sponsor to document a consistent and coherent set of requirements that everyone can agree to. Using an Is and Is-not approach and the other ideas discussed in the preceding section on project definition is an effective way to draw clear boundaries around the scope to be delivered. When what you are and are not committing to is made clear, it significantly minimizes future changes.

Project leaders with little formal authority are also particularly dependent on a well-defined, documented process for managing scope changes; without one, *scope creep* and other general scope meanderings can easily render a project unmanageable. How formal the control process needs to be varies quite a bit, but even on trivial projects, a written process will help you avoid chasing a moving target. A project whose deliverable constantly changes is perpetually out of control.

Change management processes that contribute to your ability as leader to keep things under control have several things in common:

- Specific requirements for submitting change requests to ensure that all proposed changes (regardless of the source) provide consistent, sufficient information on each change
- A bias against accepting changes, to minimize unnecessary change
- Standards for timely response on change requests and clear, public visibility for all decisions
- A review process for changes that includes the costs and consequences of accepting a change, in addition to any potential benefits
- Unambiguous authority for the owner of the process to make final decisions, including decisions to reject changes

When you, as the project leader, are the owner of the process, then you actually have a good deal of formal authority over your project. But even if you don't have ultimate responsibility for making decisions on proposed changes, there's still hope. You can still write or at least influence the process to be used and facilitate the process to ensure that it meets the criteria you require to control project scope. You can also work to establish a strong relationship with the people who do own the process so that your inputs and opinions are used in making the final decisions.

A typical change management process flowchart appears in Figure 2-1. Simply having a process that your team, sponsor, and project stakeholders all accept is a powerful tool for overall project control. It puts people on notice that changes will be carefully examined before being accepted and establishes the hurdle of adequate documentation for changes being proposed.

A project leader can exert additional control at several key points in the change control process—namely, when ensuring that the submission is credible and when considering all options for disposition of changes.

Project leaders are among the first people to see proposed changes, and they have responsibility, or at least shared responsibility, for the proposal-complete decision point. When reviewing a change, look for a clear, compelling description of the business case for the change. If the reason for a change (the *why*) is inadequately documented, send it back to the submitter with a request for a quantitative assessment of the change's benefits. Be skeptical of change requests that specify narrowly defined technical solutions because the submitters may not be in a position to judge the best technical changes for a specific problem situation. If the requested change includes too much focus on a solu-

FIGURE 2-1. A TYPICAL CHANGE MANAGEMENT PROCESS

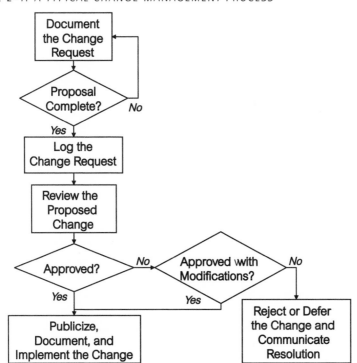

tion and too little on the actual problem, return it with a request to emphasize the business situation that inspired the requested change. Finally, ensure that the consequences of not adopting the change are credible and sufficiently detailed for analysis and that any estimates on expected impact to project timing, cost, effort, or other factors are realistic. If you disagree with any of the information provided, send the change request back to the submitter with suggested changes or specific guidance where additional or better information is needed. Give particular attention to any change that you would characterize as an enhancement because these types of changes tend to be described with exaggerated benefits and grossly underestimated consequences. The first line of defense against unnecessary change is keeping people honest.

Another point in the process when a project leader may exercise control is the accept/reject decision. Again, the main principle involves maintaining credibility. Whether they are ultimately responsible for each decision or are primary contributors of data, project leaders have two opportunities to guide the process. The first is to check the analysis information for each change to verify that it is realistic. Seek credible answers for all the following questions:

- Is the business benefit for the change well documented and believable?
- Does the proposed change represent the best available response?
- Do you have good reasons to believe that the change is feasible?
- Is the change likely to obtain the desired result?
- Will this change affect the project baseline? Are all estimates associated with the change credible? What milestones will change?
- How much additional effort will the new or changed project activities require? Do you have people willing and able to staff the work?
- Who will bear any additional expense for equipment, material, training, rework, scrap, and contractual changes?
- What are any potential unintended consequences of the change?
- Will this change affect other projects?
- Does your sponsor support the change?

Use the answers to these questions to review each change and to ensure that everyone involved in deciding how to proceed considers both the reasonably expected benefits and the costs and other consequences associated with the change. Keep in mind that the information provided to support proposed changes can be highly uncertain. Always probe for what the estimates are based on, and ask for worst and best cases or ranges for all estimates, particularly estimates of projected benefits.

The second opportunity to provide guidance for the decision process is by keeping all four potential responses visible: approval, approval with modification, deferral, and rejection. Rejection should always be the default decision, applied to all change requests for which the analysis fails to provide a compelling, credible business case. Even for beneficial changes, you can test the proposal to assess whether all the proposed change is needed right now and then counterpropose, accepting only the urgent part of a change. Acceptance with modification can effectively minimize the impact on the project while including key portions of the requested change. For desirable changes, determine the effect of delaying them to a later project. If the cost of accepting the change in the current project is larger than the estimated cost of delay, "not yet" may be your best decision. Work to approve changes sparingly and only when they are solidly supported by a strong business case.

Agile Projects

Controlling a project undertaken in small, time-boxed chunks can pose significant problems for project leaders, even those who have substantial authority. When the deliverable to be created in each work iteration is dynamically defined at the end of the previous iteration based on evaluation feedback, the lack of a solid process can result in a meandering, never-ending project that consumes time, money, and effort with little to show for it all. Managing changes and scope additions using a well-defined process is key to successfully controlling agile projects.

Before even embarking on an agile project, determine whether this approach is the best one. For projects that can define things reasonably thoroughly in advance, agile methods are always more time-consuming, expensive, and overhead-intensive. It is a bad idea to use agile methods primarily because you prefer not to define and plan things in detail up front. You need to do all this eventually anyway, and the day-at-a-time incremental approach only results in work performed out of sequence, more meetings, rework, and even doing work that was not actually necessary. Agile methods are best applied on projects that are novel, highly innovative, and when it is not feasible to define the work in advance.

Even when the flexibility of agile methods is appropriate, you must determine at least a few things in advance. Although you may not be able to determine all the specifics of your deliverable, you do need to clearly frame the problem to be solved or the overall opportunity that you are pursuing. Without a clear idea of what you are trying to accomplish, you are embarking on a fishing expedition, and your objective may never come into focus. You also need to define, at least generally, the staffing, other resources, and overall timing to be allocated to the project, and gain sponsorship to support the commitment.

The overall plan for an agile project includes specifics for the initial phase of work that:

- Defines the first increment of deliverable functionality.
- Identifies the participants in development, testing, and evaluation.
- Lays out the communication and reporting required.
- Specifies the process and duration for all subsequent phases of work.

When working without much authority, a clear process for evaluating feedback and defining the content of the next phase of work is essential. As with the criteria for changes in a phased project, the project leader is best served by a process that clearly defines how the proposed scoping for future phases will be evaluated and prioritized, using objective standards and delegating unambiguous authority for final decision making. Keep the process open, and strive for consensus decision making; the strength of agile methods relies on collaborative teamwork and cooperation. It is also good practice to develop *straw man* descriptions for several phases into the future and to adjust the work and deliverables on the horizon as you progress so that the trajectory is clear and seen by all as realistic and appropriate.

Information Management

Archiving project data serves as another foundation for project control. Information that is stored in your *project management information system* (*PMIS*), or whatever you may choose to call it, provides a solid foundation for project reference and communication. The project leader's power of the pen over the wide variety of formal documents can be a significant source of project control.

How and where the documents are stored can be equally influential. Public storage of project documents is an essential aspect of control. You can support your requests and guide decisions throughout your project using archived project documents and reports. Your documents and plans form the foundation for your project, and the project contributors and stakeholders who helped to create them and gave their approval (or at least did not object at the time) are obligated to cooperate with you in delivering on what they say. The longer that documents are available publicly, the more force and influence they have.

Project information is an essential project resource, so consider carefully where you put it and how you set up access. Some projects use Web sites, networked servers, or knowledge management systems to store key project data. For some projects, groupware applications are used both to maintain the project document archive and to provide e-mail and other services. Online electronic storage allows easy access to a single master copy of each project document that everyone associated with the project can read at any time. Updates are instantaneous, leaving minimal chance that team members will have out-of-date information. If you do implement an online PMIS, verify that all software tools, Web browsers, and other applications that team members use are up-to-date and compatible. Carefully consider any hierarchical structures you plan to use to store information, and set them up from the perspective of your team members and stakeholders. Although a structure that is oriented functionally may not be the easiest for you, it can enable team members to easily find what they need, making it far less necessary for them to come to you for project information. If your online document repository has knowledge management facilities, use them. Set up your information system to take full advantage of flexible search, key-word-in-context indexing, alias capabilities (allowing a single real document to be listed multiple places in a complex hierarchy), and other query and retrieval functions. To enhance your control without limiting people's access to information, fine-tune the security settings for individual access to permit many contributors to read the shared documents but only a few to edit them. To minimize the possibility of losing critical data, strictly limit the number of people who can delete information, and take advantage of version history archiving to retain earlier versions of project documents.

For small, co-located project teams, the PMIS might be a filing cabinet or even a notebook stored in a common area. Whatever method you select for storing project data, ensure that all project team members have adequate access at all times to at least hardcopy versions of project information. Provide current project documents in an easy-to-find place, and clearly mark or remove all out-of-date information so that it is not used for project work.

In the PMIS, set up a logical structure to store project definition documents (such as the project charter and requirements definition), project planning documents (work breakdowns, Gantt and network charts, risk registers), and project execution documents (including status reports, issue logs, and other communications). For PMIS implementations that are not online (or for emergency backup), establish a method for distributing document copies to all the places where the project contributors are located. Implement a process to keep all sites synchronized and to ensure use of only the most current project documents.

Processes involving project documentation may not be the most exciting part of a project, but, if you invest in setting up a useful, easy-to-access repository for the information that people need to have, it pays benefits throughout your project. A well-established, orderly project management information system adds immeasurably to the influence of any project leader because it is very compelling to back up your requests and actions using documents that are the product of collaborative development and review—especially documents that have been available to the whole project team for weeks or even months.

Project Management Software Tools

Project management tools are another potential source of project control for project leaders without a lot of power. Some software tools useful for project management relate to general project information, as discussed in the previous section. Other tools relate to general communication (explored in Chapter 3).

Many general-purpose project management and scheduling tools are available, and processes around them can also enhance your overall control. For large projects in which multiple people will be using scheduling tools themselves to plan and document work delegated to them, the choice of tools is where process-oriented control begins. When all the pieces of the overall plan are created using the same or at least compatible tools, the project leader's job of integrating everything into a coherent overall plan is more straightforward. Using the same tool also provides opportunities for mentoring and guidance; the leader is able to establish a position of expertise. You may also guide and influence the planning through templates that ensure thorough planning and consistent formatting.

When only the project leader or a designated planning expert is using a software tool, there are still ways to use the process to gain control. Consider the structure of the plan, and choose a work hierarchy that makes it easy for you to tailor schedule views for your subteams and individual contributors. Tips on dealing with plan complexity can be found in Chapter 6.

Also, explore the options for graphical tools outputs. Do what you can to exploit them to create easily accessed and clear images that show how your project work will proceed. Use PDF or bitmap extracts to distribute project information by e-mail, and store the information in your PMIS. Create large, poster-sized versions for meetings and common workspaces that provide visible reminders of what is planned. Carefully crafted pictures of your planned workflow can be worth many words, especially for team members who may not be very familiar with project scheduling techniques and terminology. Exactly how you use project graphics is particularly critical because it can just as easily work against you. If your project graphics prove to be too complicated or confusing, they can diminish your overall control.

Contract and Procurement Management

However much influence and authority you have within your own organization, you will probably have even less day-to-day control over project contributors who work for other companies. Although it is not always feasible, a tactic for improving your project control is to outsource as little work as possible.

If you must depend on the services of people outside your organization, you face control challenges. One way to mitigate this situation is to adhere scrupulously to the standards and requirements that your organization has for outsourced services. These processes provide you with firm boundaries and guidance that are particularly effective in initiating and executing contract project work (as well as keeping you in the good graces of your management). Before considering the use of contractors or outside consultants on a project, review your organization's overall procurement process. Identify people you can go to for help (for example, in your procurement, legal, human resources, or other departments) who have experience with setting up the required service contracts. If any part of the required process is unclear to you, have someone who has expertise explain it to you, or get that person's commitment to assist you. Identify all the functions and people who will be involved, other resources you'll need, and all the forms, approvals, and communication required. Following tried-and-true processes will enhance your project control; failing to do so will result in delay, lead to chaos, and may even get you and your organization in trouble.

Establishing a successful outsourcing relationship takes time and effort. Determine when you need to start working on it so that you have all the details in place and contracts signed in time to meet your project's deadlines. Taking shortcuts and rushing into a contractual relationship almost always leaves you with far less control than you would like.

Control begins with detailed specification of all the deliverables that you intend to outsource. Document the detailed feature specifications, measurable performance and acceptance criteria, any other relevant requirements, and the necessary timing. Ensure that the definition data is included in the contract, with all responsibilities clearly defined. Discuss these requirements with all the suppliers you may be considering throughout the process so that your expectations are clear, and make a particular effort to ensure that the supplier who is ultimately selected clearly understands the contract terms.

Establish clear-cut language in the contract for managing changes, so that all parties know the process and the consequences of any modifications. You can also improve your overall control of outsourced work by including in the contract specific incentives for early or exceptional performance and penalties for nonperformance. If-then clauses in the contract provide you with more options for control than the basic do-this-and-we-will-pay/fail-and-we-won't language that is the starting point in standard contracts. When considering the inclusion of penalty or incentive terms in your contracts, work with appropriate experts in your organization.

As you proceed with the process, present periodic updates on your progress to your project sponsor and to other stakeholders who need to approve or sign the contract. Identify any outstanding issues and correct problems as you work so that, before signing, you have both a contract that includes all that it requires and the quick approval needed to get started.

Chapter 6 provides additional specifics on negotiating and planning for improving control of outsourced work, and Chapter 8 discusses ideas for maintaining control over contract work.

Risk Management

Risk management is an important part of project planning, and much of the work required to do it well occurs during the initial analysis, scheduling, estimating, and other activities of planning. However, keeping a focus on risk throughout your project reinforces the overall goals and keeps your team's attention on the upcoming work. You can better control your project when you maintain a clear notion of what lies ahead.

Some regard risk management in projects as a discretionary activity, but a project leader with limited authority should not. The processes of risk management, in fact, enable you to do more thorough planning, highlight potential troubles and build consensus on how to deal with them, and remove (or at least mitigate) serious project problems.

To maximize the effectiveness of your risk management efforts, make risk identification a parallel activity throughout project planning. Look for incomplete understanding of project activities as you develop the work breakdown structure. Probe for risks when assigning activity ownership and developing estimates. Identify risks associated with dependencies both within and outside your project. When resources are scarce or inadequate for project tasks, or when you are dependent on a single individual for project work, note the risks. Analyze assumptions and constraints to find exposures, and encourage all who are involved in planning to consider worst-cases and potential difficulties throughout the development of the plan. Risk analysis, both qualitative and quantitative, assists you in displaying the consequences of project risks and makes your requests for modifications to the initial plans to reduce or avoid risks far more persuasive. Specifics on integrating risk processes into project planning are detailed in Chapter 6. The more robust you can make your plan, the more likely it is that you will be able to navigate through your project successfully.

Risk management also provides a lever for control throughout your project through monitoring of risk trigger events, the implementation of risk responses and contingency plans, and the periodic reexamination of the project risk list. Enhancing your control through diligent focus on risk management throughout project execution is described in Chapter 8.

▪ Quality Management

Quality management offers another set of processes that provide project structure and that can put teeth into requests from a project leader that might otherwise be ignored. Standards for quality that relate to projects are of two kinds: (1) global standards that are adopted within industries (and in some cases may be mandatory) and (2) quality standards that are unique to a specific organization or even to a single project.

Adopted Standards

If your organization has adopted or is subject to standards for quality, review what they require of you and your project team. Specific examples of such standards include organizational compliance with ISO 9000 standards, Six Sigma, and commitment to maintaining a maturity level within the Capability Maturity Model defined by the Software Engineering Institute. Use your review to identify and integrate the checklists, quality processes, and other required elements into your project planning and execution. The specific documented steps, reports, and evaluations that your project must comply with provide much more compelling motivation for team members to do things in a certain way than just your requests to do so. Because processes related to quality management can be overdone, thus adding inappropriate and expensive overhead to projects, prudent project leaders identify and emphasize processes and standards that add value, that enhance their control over the work, and that minimize overkill processes that can slow the project.

Determine who in your organization has ultimate responsibility for quality management, then ensure that the individual or group understands and approves of your approach. If quality specialists have specific responsibilities and deliverables for your project, get their commitment in advance, and don't hesitate to enlist their help when issues related to quality threaten the progress of your project. As with adopted project methodologies, quality standards convey authority to a project leader because the standards are backed up by the more influential managers responsible for their definition and compliance.

Project-Specific Quality Planning

Because quality standards, whether based on defined standards or general principles such as Total Quality Management or Six Sigma, are oriented toward consistently delivering what a customer requires, quality management is closely related to scope management. Another opportunity for better control that quality management processes offer the project leader is to align project requirements with the "voice of the customer." Strong emphasis is always added to what you say when it is clearly and directly connected to a stated customer or user need. Market research, benchmarking, and customer interviews are useful for assessing and documenting user needs and in defining the value of your project requirements. Understand what matters to your ultimate customers, and use what you learn to steer your project. Whatever you say or do will be more effective when you are acting with your customer standing behind you. This is particularly true when using agile project management methods, where there are many effective techniques for initiating and maintaining frequent customer collaboration.

Incorporate quality-related activities into your project, such as process audits, tests, reviews, inspections, and approvals. For every process that you adopt, explicitly document how the result is important to your customer. Before detailed planning commences, determine and document the final approval criteria for your project as early as possible, and review acceptance tests and evaluations that are required for scope verification with stakeholders and customers. Periodically review and update completion and evaluation criteria throughout your project, especially following approved scope changes.

Issue Management

With projects, issues inevitably arise. At the start of your project, define a process to manage project issues relating to resources, timing, priority, and other matters. Get buy-in from your team for a disciplined process to recognize, track, and resolve issues promptly. Establish an issue-tracking process that uses a visible log of current issues and includes information on each current issue, such as:

- A description of the issue
- An identifier or code associated with the issue (to facilitate communications)
- The date opened
- An assigned owner
- The current status
- The due date for closure

The process for dealing with open issues is not complicated. It defines how new items are identified and listed. It provides for a periodic review of open items (often at regularly scheduled project meetings and with adequate reporting), and it states how to deal with overdue issues. The power of an issue-tracking process for a project leader who does not have much authority comes largely from reporting on issue status and due-date information. Once an owner has accepted responsibility for an issue and committed to a resolution date, you may report on any variance and may in fact be obligated to do so. Whether the issue owner is a team member, someone from another project or organization, or even your manager, no one likes to see his or her name with a large red stoplight indicator next to it. The public nature of an issues list provides the project leader who manages it a good deal of influence and control.

For overdue issues that cannot be resolved by an owner within the team, the process should also define a time limit for escalation to someone with the authority to deal with it. Using escalation should never be the first option, though, because escalating too frequently can produce unintended consequences and erode confidence in you and your team.

Decision Making

Projects require many decisions, and making them quickly and well is essential to project control. A well-established process for group decision making is useful even when the project leader has a good deal of authority because decisions made with shared input result in more team buy-in and can be expected to deliver better results.

Decisions are rarely easy in projects, and the spectrum of opinions on a diverse project team generally makes them even more contentious and difficult. A documented process for dealing with questions and options that the project contributors have agreed to use streamlines the process and delivers decisions that everyone will accept. Work with your team early in the project to develop a process for decisions or to adopt, perhaps with modifications, an existing process. A good decision process provides powerful support for control of your project.

Your decision process should reflect the specifics of the situation, including the complexity and urgency. Regardless of the decision, the process should include the following steps:

- Develop a clear, unambiguous statement of the question that must be answered.
- Obtain team support by involving all project team members who need to be involved with the decision or who are affected by the decision; get their commitment to participate in the decision process.
- Review the problem statement and decision needed among your project team, and modify it if necessary so that everyone interprets it the same way.
- Brainstorm and generate ideas and options for the decision among your team.
- When you have an adequate number of alternatives, consider them as a team. If the decision is not complicated or the timing is urgent, work to develop group consensus using discussion, tapping into the "gut feel" of your contributors. For more complicated decisions that would benefit from in-depth analysis, use an analytical approach (such as the one described next), but even when you do this, pay attention to the initial impressions and feelings of your team. Complicated decision processes

do not necessarily result in the best decisions, and they may in fact be inferior to the instantaneous "blink" feelings that people have before they bog themselves down in a quagmire of data.

- Select with your team what you feel is the best option, striving for broad consensus. Consider the consequences of adopting the favored alternative. If there are no objections, come to closure and implement the decision.
- Document the decision, and communicate the results to others on the team and to appropriate stakeholders.
- Implement the decision and track the results. Be prepared to revisit and adjust the decision if you fail to achieve the desired results or if there are significant unintended consequences.

For complicated decisions requiring detailed analysis, approach the assessment and consideration of options using an analytical approach such as:

- Set a time limit for making a decision, and tailor the overall process to conform.
- Brainstorm and discuss potential criteria to use in making the decision (such as cost, time, usefulness, completeness, feasibility, or other considerations). Select criteria that relate to your defined goal, that are measurable, and that can be evaluated objectively by the project contributors who will assess them to make the decision.
- Work with the team to prioritize the criteria by giving each one a relative weight (where the weights of all criteria could sum to 100 percent).
- Generate as many ideas and options for the decision as possible in your allocated time. Seek to develop multiple ideas that could be acceptable to the whole team.
- Use group voting techniques, if necessary, to filter the list down to no more than about six options before considering each one in detail. Analyze the options using objective assessments of how they conform to the established decision criteria.
- Quantify any objections that come up in discussion to the ideas, adding additional criteria for the decision if necessary.
- Sequence the options using the assessments and weighted criteria.
- If the rank-ordering of your options seems wrong to anyone or if reasonable issues are voiced about the top alternative, revisit the criteria and weightings to make adjustments wherever they may be needed.

Again, even when using weighted criteria for rank-ordering and selecting preferences, keep your eyes open and ensure that the outcome is acceptable and appropriate. A "perfect" decision that lacks support may lead to more problems than another option that your team feels better about.

RUNNING A SUCCESSFUL VOLUNTEER FUNDRAISER

Bob Montevaldo has been an experienced project manager in high-tech companies for many years. However, he recently found himself with a challenge while serving on the all-volunteer board of directors for Ombudsman Services, a nonprofit organization that serves the elderly in San Mateo, California. Recent tough economic times resulted in significant funding cutbacks for the organization, and the board decided that finding additional funding sources was necessary. At the time, Ombudsman Services was also celebrating its 30th anniversary, so an event combining an anniversary celebration with a fundraiser seemed like a good plan. As the board treasurer and resident project management guru, Bob offered to start investigating such an event.

Because the undertaking needed to raise funds, it had to be an entirely volunteer activity. Bob started by enlisting the help of several people who had a long history with Ombudsman Services to hash out ideas for the event's theme, location, date, and budget. Bob documented all this in a proposal that he brought to the board for discussion. The board endorsed the proposed dinner dance concept at a local country club, and the event was approved for October, about 10 months away.

The initial group Bob had brought together had good chemistry, so he requested them to continue as the core team, each with specific responsibilities for the event. The group started meeting on a regular basis, and Bob reported their progress to the monthly board meetings. A key process Bob adopted early on was ensuring frequent communication between the board and the core team. Communication was essential because the commitment and enthusiasm of the board members were needed for obtaining auction items, securing sponsorships, and selling tickets. Bob also saw to it that the members of the core team had regular feedback from the board, and the team knew that they had continuing strong support from the board.

As the work proceeded, ideas flowed from the team to the board, and the board offered many helpful suggestions for the core team. (One board member even committed her husband's jazz band to play at the event, resulting in a significant savings.) Event planning moved forward quickly. Core team members took responsibility for sponsorship, program planning, ticket sales, event logistics, and the event auction, and Bob reported on their progress and accomplishments. Board members worked with the team to identify sponsorship prospects, solicit auction items, and make commitments for how many tickets they could sell.

As with any all-volunteer effort, there were some lapses and disappointments, but because of the overall visibility and clear documentation of assignments, they were rare. In the month prior to the event, there was much complicated activity, but the high level of communication that Bob had established paid off with commitments met and the continued enthusiasm of everyone involved. Many people even volunteered to do extra work.

One challenge the core team faced was that this was the first fundraising event of its type that Ombudsman Services had ever done. With so little organizational experience, Bob knew that a few last-minute issues and problems were bound to come up. To deal with this possibility, just before the event he set up a walk-through with all the volunteers. In this exercise, they managed to find and fix most issues that they had missed.

The event was a great success; the ballroom was filled to capacity, and ticket sales and auction results exceeded their financial goals. Many attendees asked as they were leaving when the next dinner dance would be held. In addition, an important byproduct of the event was that it raised awareness of the organization within the community, especially with local politicians and businesses.

The final thing the core team did was to hold a postmortem to document things that went especially well, and areas that could be improved before the next event. All agreed that the key success factor was keeping all volunteers engaged through effective planning, communications, documentation, and monitoring of commitments.

Good processes always matter, and never more so than when everyone on the project is a volunteer.

▪ Project Infrastructure

All projects have an infrastructure. Most have an infrastructure that is a combination of organizational standards and generally accepted defaults. Other projects have an infrastructure created by adding to or changing some key decisions that the project leader believes could materially help the current project. Establishing processes for your project sets a firm foundation for project control. Determining exactly how you apply these processes requires a framework of decisions for project planning, execution, and tracking. Documenting your decisions clarifies how you will operate and provides you with enhanced support for overall project control.

Making infrastructure decisions may require only a short team meeting for smaller projects, but you may need to make a considerably larger investment for a major program. As with most project management matters, the time spent depends on the project scale. The best time to consider infrastructure decisions is at the start of a project. Once a project is fully underway, no one has much time or inclination to think about infrastructure questions.

Key Decisions

One way to begin establishing an infrastructure for your project is to list key questions that you would like to answer, working with your project team. Your list can be one of your own making, one from an earlier project, or a template used by your organization, or it may be based on a generic template, such as the one in Appendix A. However you proceed, include questions that relate to problem areas from earlier projects, things that could become control problems for you, and issues that may lead to trouble on your current project. A few examples are:

- Planning questions (related to project initiation, plan development, outsourced work, deliverables, and planning participants and tools)
- Execution questions (related to project status and metrics, the PMIS, meetings and informal communications, team concerns, life cycles, methodologies, and quality assurance)
- Control questions (related to project reporting, scope and specification control, individual performance problems, project reviews, project cancellation, and project closure)

Detailed, specific project infrastructure decision questions for each of these areas are contained in Appendix A.

Fine-Tuning Your Infrastructure

The point is worth repeating: Take the time to develop the list of questions and decisions you would like to address with your team during project initiation, before people become overwhelmed with project deadlines. Trying to change the way you are doing things midproject is difficult—like trying to change the tire on a vehicle while it is speeding down a freeway.

Distribute the list of questions and issues to your team, and ask each person to begin thinking about options for how the project would best operate. If the team is very senior and has been involved with many projects, the list of questions alone is likely to be enough to generate ideas. For a less experienced team, some thoughts that you have on alternatives worth considering can be useful for getting the discussion going.

To make decisions, set up a meeting (or teleconference) to gather the team's thoughts and to discuss the alternatives. Set a time limit of no more than about ten minutes for each issue, and be scrupulous on timekeeping. When there is little or no disagreement, document the consensus and move on to other issues. When there is contention, you have several options:

- Extend the discussion slightly to seek closure.
- Delegate the issue to the people who are most vocal in their objections, and have them bring a proposal to a future meeting.
- Make the decision yourself, explaining your justification.

For each question that you complete, document your decision and your key assumptions. Communicate your decisions to stakeholders and to others involved in your project, and summarize the infrastructure decisions in your PMIS. Adopt the decisions to manage your project, and adjust your project processes as needed to conform to what you have decided.

Throughout your project, particularly following major changes and during project reviews, review your infrastructure decisions and consider any needed adjustments.

▪ The Project Management Office

One last process-oriented source of control is the *project management office* (*PMO*). Some organizations invest in them and others do not, but if you are in an organization that has established a project office (or a program management office, center of excellence, support team, or similar group), plan to use it to bolster your project control.

Although there may be variations, the three most common functions for a PMO are auditing, enabling, and executing. Combinations of these functions are not unusual, and the precise nature of each project office depends on the organizational needs.

- *Auditing.* Some project management offices are established to serve as process police, responsible for audits of methodologies and compliance with quality or other standards. Working closely with this type of project office potentially yields benefits similar to the adoption of the process standards discussed earlier in the chapter. However, this type of project office tends to believe that "if some is good, more is better." Use your judgment in determining how much help is appropriate, and consider carefully places where process overhead can start to make things worse.

• *Enabling.* A second type of PMO works to improve the maturity and effectiveness of project leaders throughout an organization. Using a team of internal consultants, the enabling PMO provides training, assistance in setting up organizational processes, and help in tailoring life cycles. The consultants get involved when the challenges may exceed the capabilities of a particular leader or team. This type of PMO may be useful in boosting your credibility and authority as a project leader because people tend to listen more carefully to apparently knowledgeable strangers. (One definition of an expert is someone who doesn't know any more than anyone else but is from more than 50 miles away.) In many enabling PMOs, staff is available to help with initiating, planning, and closing projects.

• *Executing.* Other PMO implementations are even more actively engaged; they are responsible for actually facilitating and doing the project work. This type of PMO has a staff of planners, administrators, and supervisors who coordinate and guide the execution of the project. For large programs, they ensure consistent planning among all the component projects. Again, the presence of outsiders who support (or even mandate) activities and processes that you need to keep your project under control can significantly enhance your apparent authority.

Potential areas where project office help can be effective are:

• Facilitating project start-up workshops
• Support for project planning efforts and help with complex software tools
• Communications and meeting planning
• Enforcement of planning standards and auditing for completeness
• Establishment of templates and checklists for common project types
• Setup of a central PMIS repository for sharing information among projects
• Organization-wide standards and reporting for change control
• Assistance with project escalations and recommendations for resolution
• Collection and analysis of organization-wide project metrics
• Assistance with the setup and execution of processes for conflict resolution, decision making, quality management, and other project processes
• Assistance with project reviews and follow-up
• Facilitation of postproject retrospective analyses and organization-wide storage of results
• Management of organizational change

Although involving staff members from a project office in your project can considerably enhance the productivity and effectiveness of your project, too much involvement can result in it no longer being your project. Sharing leadership responsibility with a PMO can end up being difficult, like sharing a banana with a gorilla.

KEY IDEAS FOR PROJECT PROCESSES

- Get team buy-in for structured project management processes, and clearly document how you will use them.
- Review past projects for problems related to structure, and work with your team to make project infrastructure decisions to resolve them.
- Take advantage of organizational expertise and project office capabilities, but resist surrendering control over your own project.

CHAPTER 3

Control Through Influence

IT IS OFTEN SAID THAT MANAGEMENT is assigned, but leadership must be earned. One aspect of earning the role of project leader is building influence both within and outside your project team. Your working style matters a great deal. Your influence with others also depends on what you have to offer them in exchange for the commitments you need and on what you can do to build and maintain relationships with your team, your sponsor, and your project stakeholders.

▪ Appropriate Leadership Styles

The introduction that most people have to project work, especially in a business context, is as a contributor. Project contributors draw on background and experience that relate to the assignments for which they are responsible. If contributors are good at what they do, sooner or later they are likely to find themselves leading a project, not just contributing to it as a team member. The transition may be gradual, such as beginning to coordinate the work of several other people on a small part of a larger project, or it may be abrupt—resulting in yet another "accidental" project manager. However it occurs, the transition comes with a pair of challenges. Moving from primarily contributing to a project to leading one requires a different set of skills, and new leaders usually have very little or no formal authority. Becoming a successful project leader means that, instead of spending most of your time with "things" and "stuff," you now spend most of your time dealing with people and communications. To do these tasks well and to be successful at leading a project when you have little power to demand or coerce commitments from people, you must establish and maintain influence over your team, stakeholders, and sponsors. This chapter outlines ideas that successful project leaders can use to get their projects going and sustain progress, without having to resort to command-and-control tactics.

An obvious difference between the typical day of a project contributor and the day of a project leader is how time is spent. For project team members, most time is dedicated to technical tasks. The guideline that's frequently used for purposes of project estimating is that about two-thirds of the time in each team member's typical workday (roughly five to six hours) can be spent doing technical work. This estimate is approximately accurate because the remaining third of each contributor's time is consumed by meetings, e-mail, telephone calls, biological imperatives, and other activities unrelated to assigned project tasks. For a project leader, though, the overwhelming majority of time is consumed by meetings and communications. A study of project managers at Hewlett-Packard some years ago found that less than 5 percent of a leader's time was dedicated to technical work, whereas 85 percent was allocated to people management and project coordination. This pattern seems to recur in projects of all types and in all companies. Successful project leaders inevitably become generalists, and over time they assume less and less personal responsibility for technical project work.

This transition can be extremely difficult because the image most people have of themselves is closely tied to what they do. Early in my project management career, I was asked to be a group supervisor and lead a team of 12 systems programmers at DuPont (which, despite the implication of the title, was not a management position). I found this transition quite painful. Particularly hard for me was delegating work to members of my team that I knew I could do faster and better. To those of us who are good at problem solving and who tend to seek the best results, delegation can be very frustrating. I knew, however, that coordinating the work of a dozen people while continuing to own significant technical responsibility would require me to do two full-time jobs: all day dealing with the team, communicating, and leading meetings, and all night catching up with my technical task commitments. Many new project leaders discover this the hard way, at the expense of their personal life and perhaps even the success of their projects. Some new project leaders never make a successful transition because they won't let go of technical responsibilities, and eventually they return to their role as a project contributor (or worse).

If this were not enough for a new project leader to deal with, the basic structure of your workday also changes. Like any knowledge workers, project contributors are most productive when they can concentrate and focus over longer periods of time. Interruptions are unwelcome and disruptive, so project contributors strive to protect sizable time blocks and to minimize outside influences. The world of a project leader does not permit this luxury; project leaders must be accessible and work effectively despite frequent interruptions. Whereas a technical contributor can get away with saying, "Leave me alone, I'm busy," any project leader with this attitude suffers escalating project problems and faces increased probability of project failure.

Exactly how you spend your time as a project leader depends on the team, the project type, and many other factors. What tends not to vary is that effective team leaders spend about 10 percent of their time per team member throughout the project. This time is spread among team meetings, one-on-one discussions, e-mail, collecting and sending status reports, telephone calls, problem solving, and other interactions. A leader of a small team of three or four certainly has the capacity to be a player/coach and to carry part of the technical load. However, a leader with 8 to 12 team members (or more) has little capacity to take on project tasks. Even though little of the leader's time spent in team management is visible in the project work breakdown structure or schedule, it is *real* project work. A project leader who invests too little time in leading, interacting, and communicating with the team slows progress and loses control.

Project control is never just a matter of allocating sufficient time for project leadership; you must also ensure that you are doing the right things. Project leaders must be very good at communicating (discussed in detail later in this chapter). Depending on the project, effective leadership may also require effort in a number of other areas that are alien to the role of project contributor, such as:

- Staffing and hiring for the project
- Communicating a project vision and representing the project as a whole
- Managing the relationships with customers, stakeholders, and sponsors
- Serving as liaison to external suppliers, contributors, and leaders of related projects
- Facilitating the project planning process
- Mastering project scheduling and other needed software applications
- Being responsible for project budgets, contracts, and other financial matters
- Managing project changes
- Escalating problems and issues when necessary

None of this is easy, and few project contributors have much relevant experience prior to becoming a project leader. Moving into the role gradually may help, and having access to formal training and mentoring available in the organization also makes a difference.

You can improve your project control by building appropriate project leadership skills in areas such as:

- Finding and using an appropriate operating style
- Facilitating productive communications
- Motivating the team

Operating Style

Project leaders need to determine what operating style or styles work best for their project teams. The best style to use depends on a lot of things: the specific needs of the team, team location (or locations), and the type of project. A leader may need to adopt a variety of styles to work effectively during different parts of a project or with separated parts of a project team.

The leadership style that you adopt will determine how members of the team perceive you. Most of the time, this perception matters more than actual authority. What team members think of you affects how they respond to your requests much more directly than your title or your position on the organization chart.

Power in organizations is of several kinds:

- Power of position
- Power to coerce
- Power to reward
- Power of expertise
- Power of personality

In most organizations, the most visible power is the power managers have because they are bosses. Formal authority grants the first two types of power: the power of position and the power to coerce. Employing using these two types of power is not possible for many project leaders because they don't have much formal authority, and for some members of the project team they may have none at all. This situation is not necessarily as hopeless as project leaders, especially new ones, assume. Even managers with a great deal of formal authority are wise to use their position and the power to threaten and punish people sparingly and only as a last resort. Overusing this kind of power through pulling rank leads to problems, including resentment, demotivation, malicious compliance, and ultimately turnover.

More effective are the other types of power. The power to reward is not the exclusive province of higher-level managers; anyone in the organization can nominate others for rewards, praise people, and do other things that are appreciated. Although the upper managers in an organization may be able to grant bigger rewards, a project leader who remains alert for opportunities can thank and reward people frequently and thoughtfully, often with rewards that are appreciated a great deal.

A primary and very effective source of project leader power derives from expertise. Power based on what you know is always effective with your sponsors, managers, and stakeholders; they did, after all, put you in charge of the project. Your technical expertise may not be a great source of power on your team because many, if not most, of your team members are probably considerably more expert in their areas than you are. Even within the team, though, you might have an edge if you are recognized as a competent generalist among a group of specialists in rather narrow fields. Your expertise in project management is also a source of power, both within your team and with your stakeholders. Finally, one type of expertise that you and you alone possess derives from your project. You are the world's foremost authority on your project, and it can be very useful to diplomatically remind people of this at appropriate times during your project.

The final source of power in the list derives from your personal relationships with others. Investing in team building, informal communication, and establishing a basis for mutual trust can also provide the project leader a good deal of power—a type that is particularly useful in times of stress and trouble. Maintaining friendly, respectful relationships with the members of your team is invaluable.

How you operate, day to day, during your project is another important part of your leadership style. Figure 3-1 shows a continuum of operating styles, with command and control on the left side and unanimous team consensus on the right. The "best" place to be in this range of options is, of course, highly situational. Regardless of the project type, in a crisis or emergency when quick action is required, the leader probably may need to act quickly without consulting the team. Similarly, faced with excessive complexity, even a five-star general or CEO with enormous authority solicits copious input before proceeding and may even decide to delegate the ultimate decision making to individuals with high levels of specialized expertise.

In your project, particularly if you have little formal authority, your options may be mostly on the right side of this operating continuum. Although this style may look like a limitation on your project control, things may not turn out that way. Using position or coercive power too often, without getting input from the team, quickly leads to rebellion and the loss of control. On the other hand, your team remains motivated if they feel that they have a say in what they are doing. When the ultimate decisions and plans that the team has contributed to are consistent with what the project requires, operating with team consensus improves your control. Because, as project leader, you gener-

FIGURE 3-1. OPERATING STYLES

How Is Project Direction Determined?

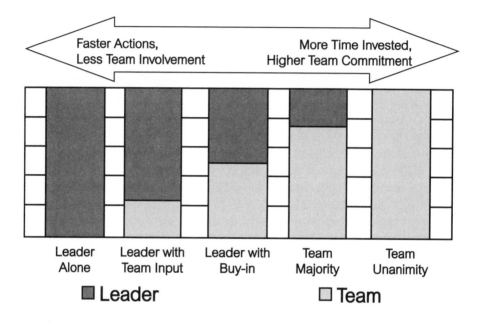

Faster Actions, Less Team Involvement · More Time Invested, Higher Team Commitment

| Leader Alone | Leader with Team Input | Leader with Buy-in | Team Majority | Team Unanimity |

■ Leader   □ Team

ally facilitate the meetings and discussions, you have ample opportunity to influence the ultimate decisions as required by the needs of the project.

In selecting how to operate day to day, you must consider a number of factors. If the team has mostly inexperienced team members who are new to the project work, your style may shift to the left and be more autocratic. With a team of experienced contributors who know what they need to do, you are probably best served by a style that involves a lot of team consensus. Collaborative planning and decision making are effective ways to increase team member ownership and buy-in. The engagement and higher motivation that result often more than compensate for the time and effort required to arrive at agreement. Agile and other project management methods that explicitly rely on cooperation and collaboration work only if everyone is fully engaged, but control on projects of any type benefits from the ongoing and meaningful engagement of all contributors.

When action must be taken quickly, shifting to the left is always an option, but be wary of doing this too often. Good project leaders usually operate somewhere in the middle of the range, balancing the need for team discussion and buy-in with timing and other project constraints.

Communication

Good communication is the foundation of effective project management, and it is also your most powerful leadership tool. To succeed, you need to influence both project communications and other communications.

Project Communications

What most people know about any project is based primarily on what they hear from the project leader. As the project leader, you collect the project status information, so you see it first. You are responsible for summarizing, filtering, and reporting the information to everyone involved with your project: to stakeholders and sponsors, to members of your team, and to the leaders of related projects. Providing clear, factual information that conveys the current status of your project is essential, and doing this well can be a source of substantial influence. When things are going well, people are impressed with your work and your team. If things are not going well, factual reporting that describes the situation and shows what you are doing to recover provides appropriate visibility and assists you when you must enlist help. To a great extent, what you say and how you say it will determine how you are perceived as a leader, particularly by your managers and peers.

The methods you use for communication also matter. Project communications can take many forms, and project leaders must use all available methods that make sense. Effective project leaders tend to overcommunicate important information. It is always worse for people connected to your project to lack data that they need than to occasionally hear something more than once. In fact, effective project leaders employ some important types of seemingly redundant communication practices—for example, following up complicated written communications with a telephone call (to clear up any potential confusion) and documenting the content of a phone call or discussion in a follow-up e-mail (to verify what was discussed and provide a permanent record). Thorough communication throughout a project is one of the most essential control tools available to a project leader.

Leadership also involves communication outside your project team. Regardless of your authority or formal position, as the project leader you are responsible for providing periodic project updates and presentations. Your communications with customers, stakeholders, and leaders of related projects provide them with a window into your work. What you report allows you to emphasize aspects of the project that you particularly want others to be aware of. Increasing the visibility of accomplishments that matter to these people raises your profile with them and improves your influence. When you need involvement from stakeholders or leaders of other projects to resolve a problem situation, clearly describing the consequences of the issue can accelerate their assistance. When things are going well, reporting good progress minimizes any potential interference or unwanted help that might otherwise be inflicted on your project. What you say and how you say it very powerfully affects your overall project community.

Communications with people you report to, such as sponsors and managers, are equally important. Your reporting permits you to build a great deal of influence with stakeholders having direct authority over your work. In addition, communication with sponsors and managers can allow you to turn the tables on those people when necessary. One key lever of control for the project leader is the assignment of task ownership (the relationship between ownership and project control is explored in more detail later in this chapter and in Chapter 6). As project leader, you have an obligation to report on the progress of each identified activity in your project, naming the individual who is assigned responsibility for it. Savvy project leaders, especially those who have minimal authority, formally assign activities such as approvals, decisions, and other responsibilities that the project leader may not be empowered to complete to their managers and sponsors—with their agreement, of course. Reporting that project progress is stalled—including a big, red stoplight indicator next to a manager's name as the reason—can be a powerful incentive for getting things unstuck. (Actually, savvy project leaders get the same result just by warning their managers and sponsors in advance what the contents of their next status report will be if there is no action.)

Other Communications

Other communications can also affect your project control. Although formal project communications provide the facts and figures about your project, building influence requires investment in informal communications. Casual conversations, informal interactions, and the increasingly ubiquitous opportunities for social networking are all central to this. Connecting with your team person to person builds the trust required to succeed with difficult projects, and being available when people need to reach you is essential to keeping a project on track. Whether you like or loathe informal interactions, ignore them only at your peril. Ideas for effective informal communications are explored in Chapter 8, where they are used to enhance control over project execution. At a high level, your influence depends on choosing communication methods that build, not degrade, overall project effectiveness.

One aspect to consider regarding informal communications is the trade-off between robust interconnections and excessive interruptions. Both too little and too much communication can be problematic, and how well your team works with you depends on how you balance this. In general, it's best to encourage team members to contact you with issues, questions, or anything at all, whenever they feel the need. You need to be approachable and responsive because, when you are not, your team assumes that you don't care. And if you don't care, why should they? Informal communications can include popping in to see you, using the phone, e-mail, and all of the growing list of instant messaging and texting facilities. If you are unfamiliar with a mode of communication popular with your contributors, figure it out and get yourself into the discussion. Wise project leaders encourage their teams to communicate directly with them without constraints.

The potential issues with excessive interruptions throughout your team are quite real, however, so it's good practice to manage your own communications (and to the extent possible, those between your team members) to minimize the amount of disruption. People work best when they can concentrate and focus on what they are doing without interruption. To protect blocks of time for effective thought and productivity, restrict your own informal communications to times when you know people are likely to be receptive: at the start or end of the day and near breaks, meals, or scheduled meetings. If everyone on the team is interrupted every few minutes with instant messages or tweets, not much work gets done. (And if you are the source, you are hurting your own project and may be generating resentment.)

Another aspect of modern informal communications that requires thought is the need to maintain sufficient security for sensitive information. You must work with your team to ensure that people do not include any proprietary information or other data in their informal communications that needs to be protected. It is becoming routine to divulge personal private information publicly as well. Sharing too much information can create a lot of future pain and problems for your project unless you discourage it and avoid doing it yourself.

Managed well, informal communications can provide an excellent foundation for robust relationships and overall control. Failing to set a good example and permitting too much, however, can convert social networking into "social not-working."

Motivation

Project leaders who lack authority assume that they cannot have much effect on team members. In reality, a team leader controls many things that can make a lot of difference. Much of the research on motivating employees builds on the work of Frederick Herzberg in the late 1950s. Subsequent research continues to support Herzberg's findings, and this is good news for project leaders who feel they have little authority. In fact, as outlined in Daniel Pink's 2009 *Drive: The Surprising Truth About What Motivates Us*, recent research indicates that not only are our personal motivating tools the most effective, but the ones that are *not* available to leaders with no authority are often counterproductive.

Herzberg's research resulted in his two-factor theory, based on which he separates motivating factors and hygiene factors in the workplace. *Motivating factors* are things that increase employee motivation and satisfaction with the work. These factors tend to be intrinsic to the work, and most are in fact things over which even low-authority project leaders can exert a great deal of influence. Herzberg's *hygiene factors*, on the other hand, have little effect on motivation when they are increased, but they can serve as powerful demotivators when they are inadequate. (Current research shows that trying to use them to motivate leads to potential ethical issues, decreased overall effort, and even eventual demotivation.)

Motivating Factors

Herzberg cited six motivating factors: achievement, recognition, the work itself, responsibility, advancement, and growth. All project leaders, regardless of their formal authority, have control (or at least significant influence) over all these factors.

The project leader is responsible for aligning the work with team members who make commitments to get it done; as such, the project leader has a lot of influence over *achievement* and delegates *responsibility* by assigning ownership for all defined project activities. An effective project leader is always on the lookout for opportunities to align skill building for team members with the needs of the project, so *growth* is another factor over which an alert leader can exercise substantial control. These factors are all integral to effective project planning, and each is explored in detail in Chapter 6.

Project leaders can also exploit *recognition*. As project leader, you write status reports and other communications in which you can name names and highlight accomplishments. You can say thank you to anyone on the team whenever acknowledgment is appropriate. (On technical projects, few leaders do this often enough.) You can celebrate accomplishments at the end of project phases, during project reviews, or anytime you choose. You also have access to established programs in your organization for reward and recognition, so you can give public awards to, or at least nominate, individuals or groups of individuals from your project team. Recognition is one of the most overlooked techniques that a project leader can use to maintain control and increase motivation. Specific ideas for rewards and recognition throughout your project are outlined in Chapter 8.

The *work itself* deserves particular attention because the project leader can influence how team members view a project, at least initially. The "vision thing" can be tricky, but when you communicate the value of the project to your contributors in terms they respond to, you enhance motivation. Projects tend to have aggressive deadlines and tight resources. They don't succeed because they are trivial or easy; they succeed because the team *cares* about them. When your team members see the project as a top personal priority, your role is simple: Provide adequate guidance and stay out of the way. Setting a vision for the project, perhaps varying the message for different members of your team, is a key element of control essential to project initiation (explored in more detail in Chapter 5).

Only *advancement* on Herzberg's list is really outside what a team leader can directly control, but even here you can exert influence through your reporting on individual performance.

Hygiene Factors

Hygiene factors tend to matter to workers only when they are unsatisfactory. Herzberg's hygiene factors are company policy and administration, supervision, relationship with supervisor, job security, working conditions, and salary. Unless people on your team are unhappy or frustrated with these factors, no one gives them much thought; they tend to fade into the background. This even includes the paycheck, which for most people rises in visibility only when it changes (especially if it decreases). If the hygiene factors seem okay, people mostly ignore them. However, when workers view these aspects of their jobs as inadequate, especially when compared with other available job opportunities, they are grumpy and uncooperative. Sooner or later, they vote with their feet and leave.

Project leaders generally can't control these factors, but that is usually not a problem because they generally contribute very little to increased motivation. Two of the factors on Herzberg's hygiene factors list—supervision and relationship with supervisor—are your responsibility (or at least partly yours). For this reason, maintaining relationships and trust with your team members is a high priority for an effective project leader.

Motivation in the Twenty-First Century

Although Herzberg's work has been heavily researched, tested, and refined over the past 50 years, it has not been modified much. Daniel Pink did a recent survey of current thinking on motivation in the workplace and elsewhere in his 2009 book *Drive: The Surprising Truth About What Motivates Us*. Pink does a good job of showing how Herzberg's motivating factors are effective, particularly when the work involved is nonroutine. He also cites literature concerning the results of trying to use money and other hygiene factors to motivate people. Ironically, attempts to use these factors as if-then rewards or bonuses not only fail to materially improve performance in nearly all environments, but, once you start down this road, you can never turn back. Even if you continue the rewards in the longer term, performance ultimately diminishes and often falls well below where it was before you started.

Pink outlines what works as the intrinsic factors of autonomy, mastery, and purpose.

- *Autonomy* is about letting people decide how to do their work. Hewlett-Packard founder Bill Hewlett was well aware of this, saying, "People do what's expected, not what's inspected." The value of process was explored in Chapter 2, and process can be very helpful at the project level. However, at the task level, contributors often know the best way to work (and you may not have a clue). Wise project leaders encourage people to use whatever methods work best for them.
- Similarly, *mastery*, encouraging and allowing people to improve their skills and knowledge, is essential to engaging a project team. Allow people to pursue mastery using training and mentoring, and support people in developing new and better abilities for the work they like to do. (Most who gravitate to project work do so because they are already good at what's required, and they genuinely enjoy doing it.)
- *Purpose* also matters to people, so work to align the project's goals with personal objectives that are meaningful to your team members.

Pink defines these intrinsic rewards for motivation as recyclable and useful in any environment. He discusses using "extrinsic" rewards (generally equivalent to Herzberg's hygiene factors) only intermittently and for routine, repetitive work. Money and other such rewards are largely ineffective in other environments.

In projects using agile methods, the intrinsic motivators are always front and center. Autonomy is embedded in the overall approach, which is based on self-organized teams who choose how best to work. Mastery is also encouraged, and the value-driven, short time-boxed deliverable cycles keep the purpose of the work front and center and the focus of frequent discussions and reviews.

▪ Getting Through Giving

Your sparkling personality and enormous talent as a project manager notwithstanding, you cannot get credible commitments for everything that your project requires simply by asking. The fundamental basis for getting what you need relies, as it always does, on exchange: giving something in return for something requested. Project leaders with little authority often think they have little to offer, so they believe that this isn't a very useful strategy for securing the necessary commitments for their projects. But, as you can see by reviewing the effective intrinsic motivating factors in the previous section, this is really not the case. Project leaders, even those with no formal authority, have a great deal to work with in the realm of exchange.

Bartering is far older than humans. The exchange of things for things or services for services is the basis for reciprocal relationships throughout all of biology. Giving and getting is such a fundamental part of how we live and conduct our lives that we sometimes don't even consciously recognize it. Even when we can secure a commitment through coercion or the exercise of power, some form of exchange is nearly always preferable. With exchange, no one feels taken advantage of, and equitable exchange serves as the foundation for trust and future interaction.

Given that exchange is a useful way to get what you need for your project, how do you go about it? One way to start building an effective strategy for yourself is to identify people in your organization who are very good at getting others to cooperate. Think about how you were convinced to lead your current project. What were you offered? Why was the approach used to get your commitment effective? People who sponsor projects and those who are effective midlevel (and higher) managers seem to have the process for negotiation and for gaining commitments embedded somewhere in their DNA.

A few things are common among successful influencers. They approach others *one on one*, as equals, leveling any differences in organizational power and authority, at least for the duration of the discussion at hand. You need to do the same. This isn't difficult when you are dealing with people who are in fact peers or who have less organizational power than you, but it can be a challenge when the situation is the other way around. To level a discussion with your sponsor or manager, or with anyone who has more position power than you have, you may need to rely on your expertise or reputation, along with the value and importance of your project.

Successful influencers also identify and use *common ground and shared interests* early. Although the two parties may begin with differing objectives and priorities, skillful questioning helps influencers to align what they need to do with something that is of value to the other party. This sounds very difficult and even unlikely, but with projects that are truly important to the organization, you can nearly always work from common ground.

Good influencers are also generally well liked. They are *friendly and helpful*. They have little difficulty initiating conversations about commitments partly because they tend to be fearless and partly because many people seem to owe them return favors. Experienced project leaders share these traits, at least the part about being owed return favors; they cooperate with requests whenever possible, especially small ones, because they know how valuable their help is likely to be in the future when they need a favor in return.

People who have a lot of success at influencing others also seem to have a knack for *closing the deal*. Anyone can learn how to do this, and even people for whom it does not come naturally can get better at it with practice. The consequences of not understanding how to effectively come to an agreement hurts you and your project more than you might think.

People who have little negotiating experience generally make their requests of others without much preamble. They assume that the other person sees things as they do and will quickly agree. In reality, other people see things from their own perspectives, which may be wildly different from yours. The response to an initial abrupt request is generally a refusal. The inexperienced requester, seeing this as illogical and inappropriate, then repeats the request, but a little louder. The other person inevitably refuses again and a little more forcefully. After a few additional rounds, the discussion can escalate to substantial unpleasantness with no prospect for ever gaining the commitment required. In addition to failing to agree on the current request, such an exchange may permanently poison any future dealings between the two people involved.

Such disasters are far from inevitable. Rather than starting with an unanticipated request with little foundation, project leaders can learn to initiate discussions with conversational questions and listen carefully. They can ask about the other person's current work and challenges to learn more about what they are doing. With sufficient knowledge of what is going on, project leaders often find it easy to secure the commitments they need by offering something in return that the other party wants or needs.

Getting commitments through giving requires negotiation, and successful negotiations depend on all parties being better off after an agreement than they were before. You generally know what you want from others to make your project successful, but you may not know in advance what they might want from you. For minor requests, a generic offering might be sufficient, such as, "Would you mind spending a few minutes reviewing my project plan to see if I have missed anything? I'd be very grateful. If you'd like, you are welcome to one of our project T-shirts." Unfortunately, not every commitment comes quite so easily, so a process for approaching more complicated situations can help a great deal.

An overall process for influencing involves ten steps:

1. Document your objective.
2. Identify who could do the work.
3. Evaluate your options, and select the best person.
4. Consider the other person's perspective.
5. List possibilities for exchange.
6. Meet with the other person.
7. Verify your assumptions, and determine what to exchange.
8. Request a commitment.

9. Document the agreement.
10. Deliver on your offer, and track the work to completion.

1. Documenting Your Objective

An overall process for negotiating begins with preparation. Clearly document what you need—in writing. Specific commitments you need to get for your project may be part of your overall project plan or details from other project documentation. In other cases it may be necessary to get out a blank piece of paper and specify the details from scratch.

2. Identifying Who Can Do the Work

Once you have a clear, written description of your needs, consider who could fulfill them. If you have several options, list each alternative, and capture the name of the person you will need to approach, along with the individual's current relationship (if any) to your project. List all possibilities; do not discount individuals who may not initially be involved with your project. The more alternatives you can generate, the greater the chance you have of securing an agreement with one of them.

3. Evaluating Your Options and Selecting the Best Person

Your primary concern in reviewing alternatives, if you have more than one, is to identify who can best provide what your project needs to be successful. Assess your options using the best available information, and write down why you think each person you listed would be a good choice to contribute to your project. Document all relevant skills, experience, and other factors that you are aware of that would be useful for the specific objective at hand and to your project as a whole. For each person, also document any concerns, issues, or risks that you know about so that you can objectively consider both the advantages and disadvantages associated with each alternative. You are doing this for at least two reasons: (1) to determine the people you should approach first and (2) to have a clear list of reasons why you are asking them to help. When you are able to convey to other people that you are aware of and respect their abilities and have confidence in them, you get their attention. Flattery may not get you everything you seek, but it may move you a lot closer than you think to agreement.

In your analysis, also consider your relationship with the people you have listed. Identify everyone on your list with whom you already have an established relationship, whether it's someone you have worked with in the past, a friend, or anyone for whom you have recently done a favor. Influencing and gaining commitments from people you know is always easier than with strangers. Reaching agreement when you lack established relationships and trust requires more effort.

4. The Other Person's Perspective

Continue your preparation by considering what you could do to improve (or to establish) your relationship with all the people you plan to approach. Consider your project from their perspective, and identify all existing connections. Document why your project matters—or at least it should matter—to each person on your list. For each situation, invest some time considering what you may have to offer that might interest the person you are approaching. Based on what you know, brainstorm options that you might use to get their attention and to obtain a credible commitment for your project. Think about what the other person does. What goals and challenges does this person face? What is important in this individual's working environment? What measures and evaluations are used? How will the other person benefit from your project when it is successful? What undesirable outcomes may the person experience if your project fails? What you ultimately agree to exchange may be quite different from what you initially come up with, but it pays to prepare in advance and to sequence the things you come up with, from the easiest to the most expensive or difficult.

5. List Possibilities for Exchange

With only a little brainstorming, most project leaders can come up with a robust list of *exchange capital* that far exceeds what they might suspect. Your list of potential exchange ideas strongly correlates to the motivating factors outlined by Herzberg, for obvious reasons. Both are based on things that people care about. To start your list of exchange ideas, consider some of these possibilities. At least some of these options will be appropriate in any given situation.

Overall Project Considerations
- *The Project Vision and Purpose.* Provide a vivid description of how the world will be better, from the other person's perspective, when the project is completed.
- *The Project's Priority.* Provide documented evidence of the strategic importance and organizational commitment to the project.
- *Sponsorship.* Name-drop when your project is strongly supported by an important, respected individual.
- *Doing the "Right Thing."* Describe the aspects of your project that appeal to the beliefs, ethics, and morals of others. If your project will resolve a

situation that currently damages or that could hurt the organization's reputation or standing, make this visible to others.

- *Doing the "Best Thing."* If your project has goals that exceed what has been done before and that will make a significant contribution, let people know. If your project will deliver exceptional quality or extraordinary reliability, or if it has other world-class characteristics, play them up.
- *Improving Customer or User Satisfaction.* Solving problems, addressing complaints, and improving customer loyalty can lead to growth, revenues, and future work.
- *Secrets.* Knowledge is power. If confidential or other aspects of your project are not generally known, consider their appeal to contributors who might like to be in the inner circle.
- *Job Security.* Projects with committed resources, particularly lengthy ones, can be a safe refuge in turbulent economic times.

Project Work Considerations

- *Ownership.* Every activity in the project needs an owner, and delegation of responsibility by name is a powerful motivator.
- *Autonomy.* When delegating work, ensure that the team members responsible have as much control over the methods, timing, and other aspects of the work as possible.
- *Preferred Work.* Whenever possible, delegate activities to the contributors who have expressed interest in them and who enjoy doing the work involved.
- *New Skills.* Every project is unique, and there are generally development opportunities for contributors to build new proficiencies.
- *New Technology.* Outline any specific areas that the project requires that are novel or that extend beyond the foundations of past projects. Particularly for projects representing new platform development, architecture, or significant innovation, sell the excitement of being on the bleeding edge.
- *New Resources and Equipment.* Emphasize any plans for upgrade and replacement of existing equipment to contributors who like to work with new toys.
- *Uniqueness.* Play up the elements of your project that differentiate it from other projects with people who value these differentiators.
- *Challenge.* Outline the risks and potentially difficult aspects of your project to contributors who thrive on a challenge and are bored with the mundane.
- *Probable Success.* For risk-averse team members who gravitate toward

the mundane, emphasize the parts of your project that are familiar territory and are likely to proceed smoothly.

- *Self-Image.* The work we do represents a large part of how we see ourselves, so play up any status element inherent in your project's activities.
- *High-Quality Help.* If your project team or support network contains particularly able people who are well known for assisting others, use their presence to influence team members who want to learn from the experts.

Recognition Considerations

- *Visibility.* For projects that get a lot of management attention, emphasize the opportunity to be noticed. For other projects, describe what you plan to do to ensure that accomplishments are acknowledged. (For the risk-averse, this two-edged sword may not have much value because, along with the potential for high-profile praise, comes the chance for intense criticism.)
- *Reputation.* Describe relevant portions of the work that are likely to be difficult and thus, when completed successfully, will result in kudos and respect. For work that is extremely difficult with a high risk of failure, point out that others will be impressed simply by the attempt.
- *Gratitude.* Although more of an ongoing tactic for enhancing control during the project, describing the recognition that individuals on the project team can anticipate can be a powerful motivator.
- *Opportunity to Mentor.* Accomplished people generally like to hear how expert they are, and many respond to sincere flattery by enthusiastically offering to share their knowledge with others.
- *Stuff.* In some cases, inexpensive items such as T-shirts, mugs, buttons, hats, or other project-related giveaway items can be useful in securing the favors and commitments necessary for your project.

Interpersonal Team and Peer Considerations

- *Trust.* Project teams that succeed build trust among the members. Getting trust begins with offering trust, and, even with people you don't know or don't know well, conducting discussions about commitments openly and honestly gets things started. For people you do know well, offer to maintain and enhance your existing relationship.
- *Contacts.* Emphasize the opportunity to get to know and work with specific team members, sponsors, managers, stakeholders, and others associated with your project, especially if any of these people are of particular interest.
- *Fast Turnaround.* Commit to quick responses to requests, problem escalations, decisions, and other project responsibilities you carry, espe-

cially if you are dealing with individuals for whom responsiveness has been a problem with other project leaders.

- *Empathy.* You and your project team are all in this together. For people who value teamwork, describe how you will work closely as a team, back each other up, and provide mutual support. Stress that acceptance and inclusion for all is automatic and will be sustained on your team for all who participate.
- *Loyalty.* Project leaders protect their teams. Although criticism of individuals may at times be necessary, an effective project leader commits to never taking action or joining in criticism before investigating and hearing out all sides. Even if fault is found, good project leaders commit to handling things one on one or within the team, minimizing any external consequences.
- *Listening.* Commit to being available to everyone on the team to talk—about anything and nearly anytime. Display active listening in all discussions, and strive to listen more and talk less in your conversations.
- *Fun.* Develop a reputation as a project leader who works hard, gets a lot done, and has a good time doing it. Use humor in meetings and in communications. Celebrate milestones and accomplishments with the team, doing things that the team as a group has endorsed. Commit to doing as much as possible to establish and maintain a sane, comfortable, and productive environment for your project team.

Interpersonal Considerations for Your Manager and Others in Authority

- *Competence.* Emphasize your capabilities and reputation for delivering on what you promise and for avoiding problems that frequently have to be managed or escalated for attention. Work to deserve the confidence your managers had in you when they asked you to lead your project.
- *Confidentiality.* Develop a reputation as someone who can be trusted to properly manage sensitive information.
- *Feedback.* Offer to provide open, honest, constructive criticism on documents and presentations where you may be more knowledgeable than your managers. Provide feedback to them quickly and directly. Be a sounding board that your managers and stakeholders can rely on for credible, useful comments.
- *Backup.* Provide coverage for your managers in their absence, and keep things under control when they are away.
- *Proactivity.* Anticipate potential problems and propose responses to organizational problems to your managers before the situations become visible and serious.

You can find additional *exchange currencies*, along with a discussion of their use in a general context, in *Influence Without Authority* by Allan Cohen and David Bradford. And you can undoubtedly add a number of additional ideas from your personal experience just by thinking about things that you have offered to others and things that have been offered to you.

The nature of projects varies enormously; you need to think in terms of your own situation and list specific ideas that are realistic for your project. Only portions of what you have to offer have appeal to each of the individuals from whom you'll need to seek cooperation. In each case, select the ideas that are most appropriate, and consider for each potential idea both the value you suspect that it has for the other person and its cost or personal consequences to you.

When you have a clear idea of what you want, a target individual to approach, and tactical ideas on how to proceed, you are almost ready to go into action. A role-play rehearsal with a trusted colleague is a good idea when you expect a high risk that you will not be successful. Risky situations might involve approaching someone who has more authority than you in your organization, someone you do not know very well, or someone you have had problems with in the past. Practice helps you gain confidence in what you need to say in these difficult cases, and it makes you more comfortable dealing with potential objections or disagreements. Whether or not you need to formally practice, review your preparations thoroughly before scheduling a discussion with the person you plan to influence.

6. Meeting with the Other Person

Schedule adequate time to discuss your project requirements with the other person—face to face, if possible. Building trust and getting a reliable agreement by telephone are possible but much more difficult. If you can't get together to meet, provide any materials that you plan to discuss in advance of the meeting, and encourage the other person to review them.

From your perspective, this meeting has one major objective—gaining the person's commitment to contribute to your project—and several preliminary smaller objectives. Your first preliminary objective is to verify that you already have a good working relationship with the other person or, when you do not, to begin establishing one.

7. Verifying Your Assumptions and Deciding What to Exchange

Your next goals are (1) to learn enough about what the other person is currently doing to validate any assumptions you made in preparing and (2) to ensure that the other person understands your project and what you need, at least in general terms. When approaching people you know well who are very likely to agree with most of your reasonable requests, these preliminary goals are often trivial. For bigger requests or when dealing with strangers, you are wise to combine these objectives with relationship building; invest the time needed to build a foundation for your request. In general, the most powerful tool you have is the open question. Asking about another person's current activities in a friendly and interested way does several things for you. Showing interest in another person is the start of a small exchange, and the other person will probably reciprocate by showing increased interest in you. This also allows people to talk about a favorite subject ("But enough about you; let's talk about me") that they know a lot about and are comfortable discussing. This type of exchange also, through subtle follow-up questions, lets you test whether your assumptions are valid about how this person sees your project, you, and the overall relationship. When the responses you get are consistent with your preparations, reaching agreement should not be difficult. When you learn things about the other person that invalidate what you expected, you probably need to consider new options for exchange.

8. Requesting a Commitment

After establishing some groundwork, you are ready to move on to the main event: requesting a commitment. In some cases, formal exchange may not even be necessary. If, through your discussions, people seem to be enthusiastic about your project, the work itself may provide sufficient incentive, and you may only need to simply ask, "How would you see yourself best contributing to this project?" If the other person's response is an offer to provide what you are seeking, accept it with thanks. Commitments that are offered by the individuals you approach are always taken much more seriously than those you request; whenever you are able to obtain an offer of what you need without asking for it, you are much better off.

When a situation requires a formal exchange and you think you have something to offer that could get you what you need, offer it, request the commitment, and shut up. Wait patiently for a response. Let the other person speak next. If the other person accepts, you are ready to move on to the hard part: getting your project done.

If the other person says no, ask why. Simply offering more in exchange might be effective, but, depending on why the other person said no, offering more may not make much difference. If you are dealing with a person who does not know you (or if for some reason does not seem to trust you), you may have to retreat a bit and revise your request to include only a small portion of what you initially requested. Starting small is an effective way to establish and build a trusting relationship, and, once people start working on something, getting a future commitment to continue is often much easier.

If the problem relates to the project or your approach to the work, try to find out how the other person might approach it. This technique may reveal options acceptable to the other person that could effectively move your project forward. The ideas that emerge from this sort of discussion may even be better than what you had in mind. Remember, you are requesting a commitment from someone who you believe is expert and may well know much more about an issue than you do. If the other person fails to come up with any other alternatives, he or she might realize that your offer is acceptable and probably the best approach available.

Often people say no because they are too busy, lack confidence or knowledge, or otherwise think that they are not able to do the work. In these cases, any specific help or guidance that you can offer may tip the balance and help you secure a commitment. Continuing the discussion in an objective, friendly way will frequently result in at least a partial commitment to what you seek.

All of the ideas for exchange (in step 5) focused on positive factors for the other person, and it is always preferable to set up agreements when both parties have something after the agreement that they see as desirable and valuable. But when positive exchanges are ineffective, you may have to explore the dark side. Negative factors may have a role in difficult situations, but focus even here on the avoidance of painful circumstances rather than on threats and punishments. You may be able to overcome resistance by outlining the consequences of your project's not succeeding. The impact of your failed project may be on the person directly, on other employees or a department the person cares about, or on the organization as a whole. Projects that are not completed successfully may affect the environment of the people we work with in many ways, and *large* failed projects can even threaten the overall health and stability of the entire company. Helping people avoid undesirable situations can be extremely persuasive.

In some cases, after much questioning and discussion, you may be forced to admit defeat and recognize that you will not secure a commitment. In these cases, trudge back to the drawing board, and look for an alternative approach that could serve your project.

If you can't come up with any acceptable alternatives, in extreme cases you might consider escalating the situation to someone with sufficient authority to coerce a commitment for your project from the other person. Although forcible coercion by others may work in the short term for your project, scorched earth tactics must always be a last resort. Establishing teamwork and trust with someone who was dragged kicking and screaming into your project is next to impossible. That person's cooperation is at best grudging, and the risks of malicious compliance—giving you something that meets the letter of your requests but that entirely misses the spirit and intent—requires you to do a great deal of surveillance and inspection. And, however the short-term situation works out, the real cost is always in the long term. It is a small world, and we all tend to work with the same folks over and over. Instead of creating a trusted colleague who makes future projects easier and more fun, escalation and coercion may create an enemy who will likely find ways to make your future projects more painful and difficult.

It is usually better to walk away when voluntary agreements prove elusive. Strive either to devise other methods for your project that do not rely on the skills of that specific individual or to seek the cooperation of others with similar talents who willingly agree to work with you.

9. Documenting the Agreement

In most cases when you prepare well, when you have a reasonable request to assist with a meaningful project, and when you are persistent, you will secure an agreement. When you have an agreement that you and the other person are both satisfied with, thank the other person and then document the agreement in writing. Some agreements result in formal contracts or amendments to contracts already in force, so this requirement is necessary anyway. Even for less formal agreements, capturing details in writing is still a good idea.

You are creating a formal version of the agreement for several reasons. In written form, you and the other party can check the agreement to ensure that it clearly says what you both had in mind and adjust it to correct any misunderstandings right at the start. Signed or not, a written summary serves as a permanent record of the commitments that you and the other person have made, which might be very useful later in the project if issues come up. Finally, written agreements carry a lot more weight than verbal ones. Commitments in writing are taken far more seriously, which is why self-help programs of all types have participants write a list of specific changes that they intend to follow through on, and that is also why we write down our New Year's resolutions. Writing down our intentions in these cases still results in a meager success rate, but goals that are only spoken (or worse yet, only thought) have a success rate of essentially zero. Writing down specific commitments, supported by meaningful exchanges, powerfully enhances your ability to control work on your project.

10. Delivering on Your Offer and Tracking the Work to Completion

An agreement without follow-through is often worthless. Follow through to ensure that others hold to their agreements with you. Deliver on what you offered, and respect both the letter and the spirit of your end of the agreement. Try to provide more than you promised, both to show your good faith and to set up future exchanges. If you committed to providing help or information once a week, do it at least that often. If you committed to specific resources, quick turnarounds on decisions, or other actions, deliver on them. Strive to provide what people really need from you on your project, not just what you promised. Thank people sincerely when they fulfill their commitments, and offer positive feedback on a regular basis to project contributors.

Project leaders who are generous with favors build up a reserve of goodwill and can maintain control in times of stress by calling in favors that they are owed. Reciprocity represents the most powerful generic contingency tool available to any project leader.

▪ Enhancing Influence

There are many other ways to build your influence in addition to reciprocity. Some methods are useful for increasing your influence within your team. Other methods are more appropriate for increasing your influence with other project leaders, stakeholders, and managers. Some people are naturally good at influencing others and, if you're one of them, you can skip this section because you use these methods all the time. Other people are very analytical and find some of these ideas alien and perhaps even vaguely dishonest. Effective project leaders are often about midway between these extremes: adept at some influencing techniques and unaware of, or at least unpracticed at, others. For most of us, consciously thinking about how better to influence others we work with is a good practice to get into. Few of us are as influential as we would like to be.

Building Influence in Your Team

At the beginning of a project you've been asked to lead, the project is your responsibility. At the start, though, there is no guarantee that the project team will look to you as a leader, cooperate with you and the other contributors, and do their part to ensure success. Even if you are the manager of every member of the project staff, you are still wise to earn their recognition as leader of the team.

You can probably think of many additional ways to go about this, but the following techniques should serve as a good starting point.

Lead by Example

On a project, you have activities and responsibilities along with everyone else on the team. Ensure that you are doing as much or more for your project as anyone else and that you are not asking others to do things that you are not willing to do (or at least try to do) yourself. Leading by example includes pitching in when someone or some part of the team needs help, putting in as many off-hours as others on the team, and providing personal support and encouragement when contributors put in extra effort. A particularly large, very important product development project at Hewlett-Packard was able to maintain its schedule despite a large number of unforeseen difficulties. The project required a substantial amount of late-evening work by most of the development team and could have completely broken the team's morale. To counter this, all the managers involved supported the extraordinary effort with a nightly competition to see who could find and deliver the best food for those working late. It turns out that very few restaurants refused takeout orders; everyone ate well, no one got tired of pizza, and motivation was never a problem.

Using Random Positive Reinforcement

When a leader provides the same recognition or thanks again and again and does so at every possible opportunity, the effort soon loses its effect. To be effective, expressions of gratitude must be (or at least seem to be) sincere. What works most effectively is positive reinforcement that's delivered randomly—praise and thanks to team members in varied forms and at unexpected times. Many are puzzled that *salary* is on Frederick Herzberg's list of hygiene factors; after all, who would come to work day after day unless they were paid? Why is a paycheck not motivating? Once in a while, a paycheck does motivate—when it goes up. The rest of the time paychecks tend to fade into the background and, if we think of them at all, we generally wonder why we are so underpaid. For most people, occasional nonmonetary rewards tend to motivate best. Rewards that do not involve money (such as various forms of recognition) are often public, whereas monetary rewards (such as your salary) are typically private. Recognition visible to peers is often deeply appreciated. To enhance your influence, be generous with your praise, but pick meaningful opportunities and don't overdo it.

Removing Barriers

Project leaders also increase their influence by being proactive. Throughout the project, be vigilant for potential problems. Ask team members, particularly team members who are having trouble with their commitments, what you might be able to do to make their work easier or to avoid future trouble. Although you can't always remove all barriers or anticipate every future problem, your influence will expand whenever you succeed in eliminating obstacles to progress, and even when you are unsuccessful your honest efforts will be appreciated.

Always Provide Reasons

Certain words have a lot more power to influence than others. The word "because" appears to lead all the lists. You always gain more cooperation if you provide reasons for your requests, particularly when the reason directly relates to something that the other person cares about. Interestingly, though, Robert Cialdini, in *Influence: Science and Practice*, cited a study of people trying to cut into long lines at a photocopier. Some said, "Excuse me, I have five pages. May I use the machine next because I have to make some copies?" Others in the study omitted the *because* and as a result were less successful than those who explicitly provided an actual reason for needing to break into the queue. When you ask anything of anybody, always formulate your request with a "because" statement, followed by a reason. And, whenever possible, find a reason that the other person responds to favorably.

Coach, Mentor, and Assist

The principle of reciprocity, of course, also works when the giving and getting are not simultaneous. Effective project leaders are as generous with their time as they can afford to be, and they frequently find opportunities to coach, mentor, and assist people on their teams as well as others. This role begins with establishing an environment where people feel free to discuss any matter or topic without fear of criticism. Encourage project team members to let you know when they lack experience or skills for their assigned activities. Provide guidance, help team members yourself if you can, and find help for them when you cannot. Be willing to teach and share your expertise with others. This is actually easier to do with people that you are not directly managing because they may be reluctant to reveal their shortcomings or ask dumb questions of their own manager. Make sure people are confident of your discretion and believe that there will be no repercussions or consequences if they reveal shortcomings to you. Assisting and mentoring others builds your influence in the short run and increases your stock of goodwill and favors owed to you over the long term.

Practice Credibility and Integrity

Influence also relies on how people perceive you. Your credibility with others depends on their believing that you mean what you say. Being straightforward and conveying information as accurately and truthfully as you are able is important, but you enhance your influence even more by showing integrity—delivering on what you say you'll do. A reputation for credibility and integrity, particularly inside your project team, significantly increases your influence.

Be Inclusive

Humans divide those they deal with into *us* and *them.* We usually listen to and like our own group (us), and we tend to ignore and mistrust strangers (them).

Effective project leaders are quick to include new contributors into the team, making them comfortable and helping them to feel like they are part of the team. Being inclusive requires you to let go of your own tendency to mistrust others and to take the first step. When you are open to building new relationships, your actions are likely to be reciprocated. This openness accelerates acceptance by all new team members and augments your influence. If new contributors resist becoming part of the team, sometimes trying harder and being persistent helps. With extreme cases, when the person continues to operate independently of the team, you may need to rely on other influence methods (or even find alternative contributors who become effective team members).

Offer Tit for Tat

Much work on collaboration since the midtwentieth century traces back to game theory and to the mathematical study of multiplayer strategy scenarios. One game in particular, the prisoner's dilemma, is relevant to the project leader. In the prisoner's dilemma, each person has an independent choice to cooperate or not, with the result for each player determined by combining their choices. The best overall outcome is when both players cooperate. If one player fails to cooperate (or *defects*), the outcome for that player is a bit worse, and the outcome for the other player is a lot worse. If both choose to defect, the outcome for each is a lot worse. The specific payouts (in most cases for this scenario, punishments) for the prisoner's dilemma may vary, but, because of the asymmetry, the best strategy that emerges from mathematical analysis is that each player should defect.

Although the choice not to cooperate works in a single instance of the prisoner's dilemma, life is not modeled best that way. We work with others over and over, so a more realistic analysis might be found in an *iterated* prisoner's dilemma, where a series of independent choices must be made. To model this case, Robert Axelrod proposed having game theory experts submit strategies for use in such situations, and he pitted each of the suggested strategies against each other in a tournament of computer-simulated prisoner's dilemmas.

Surprisingly, one of the simplest strategies won: *tit for tat*. This strategy is cooperative in the first game and thereafter follows exactly what the other player did in the previous game. This trust-but-verify approach to the game prevails over all the other more complex (and in many cases, selfish) strategies. In subsequent competitions, where all participants knew the success of the tit-for-tat strategy, it remained the overall winner. (Axelrod's *The Evolution of Cooperation* provides an excellent summary of his experiences exploring defection and cooperation.) Whether games of this sort simulated on a computer provide proof that offering trust as long as it is returned is the best course of action can be debated at length. Regardless, it is clear that a tit-for-tat approach when leading project contributors is consistent with what has always worked well for gaining and retaining cooperation of team members.

Using Referent Power (Sparingly)

Our influence also depends on who we know. Referent power—power that you have because managers or others with substantial authority support you—is another source of influence. Referent power can help you to win arguments and persuade people to do things, but using it too frequently and overtly can backfire. This kind of power is most effective when used subtly, when people know you have it and that you know that they know you have it, but you never bring it up directly. Mentioning the results of your meetings with your sponsors and others in authority and conveying any appreciation that they have expressed to the project team can be quite effective methods for keeping your team aware of your support from above. Only as a last resort should you attempt to influence others by threatening to involve others higher up in the organization. Although this may be effective in the near term, employing it too frequently damages your relationship with the people you are attempting to influence, perhaps permanently.

Effectively Building Consensus

Another effective way to improve your influence is to systematically build consensus for any ideas that you wish your team to accept. Instead of simply inflicting your desires on your team, prepare in advance to use discussion to build support for your recommendations. Consider why your idea might be attractive to each of your team members. Look at your recommendation from the team's perspective, and outline any reasons why anyone on the team might object to it. Develop responses for potential objections before you convene a team meeting. Begin your team meeting by discussing the overall situation that requires action and the consequences if you do nothing. Present a summary of your proposed response, emphasizing its main benefits and showing how your idea directly addresses the need. Invite objections and criticism, and answer any questions that arise. Respond to any objections using the information you have prepared. Encourage modifications for improvement, and adopt any beneficial suggestions. Ask for alternatives and discuss any suggestions among the team. Summarize the merits of your proposal, as well as any alternative ideas discussed, and seek consensus from the group for a single idea. If your preparation was thorough and your proposal has merit, the group will choose your idea. If your idea with modifications or some alternative has more support, it is nearly always better for the project anyway. Preparation and systematic analysis that give your idea a head start, though, adds a great deal to your influence.

Commitments in Writing

Whenever you have requested something of someone else, follow up in writing and reinforce the commitment in a tangible form. If getting the other person to document what was discussed is difficult, you should do it. Personally written commitments are the most powerful, but an e-mail from you summarizing the request and reinforcing any timing or other factors with a statement such as "Please let me know if this is not what you agreed to" can be nearly as effective. A tangible backup document increases the likelihood that the other people will follow through, and it influences their behavior.

Dressing for Success

Although it is yet another thing in life that is not fair, studies repeatedly show that, for most people, influence depends on visual cues. The advice from the 1970s best-seller *Dress for Success* is still valid: Dress for the job you want to have, not just the one you have now. How people respond to you changes depending on what you wear and how you look, so give some thought to how you wish others to see you before you come to work, meetings, and other face-to-face encounters. Dressing neatly and similarly to those in your organization with the level of formal authority that you would like to have substantially helps to close the gap between their influence and yours. If you are male, you might wear a suit or at least a tie if you work in the northeastern United States—or a clean T-shirt with no holes in it if you work in Silicon Valley. When you look the part, people may be less likely to notice that you actually have little real power.

Be Positive

Finally, be positive. People who are cheerful and use humor to good effect are much more influential than those who are grumpy, doleful, or depressing. Even on the telephone, others can always tell when you are smiling; put a smile on your face before you answer the phone. A smile in your voice makes a big difference in how other people hear what you say. Especially when you must deliver bad news, focus on the positives: what has been accomplished so far and what you are doing (and will do) together to resolve any problems. In the film *Harvey,* Jimmy Stewart's character, Elwood P. Dowd, says, "Years ago my mother used to say to me . . . 'In this world, you must be oh so smart or oh so pleasant.' Well, for years I was smart. I recommend pleasant. And you may quote me." Pleasant worked for Jimmy Stewart, and it works pretty well for everyone else too—particularly project leaders with limited authority.

Building Influence with Your Manager, Project Sponsor, and Stakeholders

To be successful, you also need to influence upward. Many of the ideas in the previous section can apply to building influence with the people that you report

to (particularly leading by example, providing reasons with requests, being helpful, practicing credibility and integrity, effectively building consensus, and being
positive). In addition, you can improve your influence with your management
by asking revealing questions and collaborating with your peers—there's strength
in numbers.

Asking Revealing Questions

Project leaders are rarely able to assert control by saying no or simply ordering
people around. Because of their role, though, project leaders can always ask
questions, and this can be equally effective. Asking revealing and even potentially embarrassing questions—questions that shine a bright light on aspects of
your project that otherwise would remain fuzzy or out of sight—allows you to
apply logic and reason to situations that might otherwise be settled using emotion, politics, or a coin flip. Project leaders bring a unique perspective to many
discussions, merging a technical, analytical viewpoint with pragmatic business
considerations. With sponsors and stakeholders, an affinity for numbers is useful when the rationale for a proposed change or other request may not be based
on much analysis. The right question, diplomatically posed at the right time,
can help you to avoid a great deal of aggravation on your projects. Specific
questions relating to project initiation are discussed in Chapter 5, and examples
useful for scope management and specification changes are explored in Chapter 8.

As project leader, you need to remain skeptical throughout the project,
verifying the information that you hear and working to understand where the
information is coming from. Some questions that can help are:

- What problem are we trying to solve? (This one shortens a lot of meet-
  ings.)
- How sure are we of the information? How can we check it?
- What is the source of the information?
- Can we quantify what we are hearing? What are the financial, timing,
  and other measurable aspects?
- Are uncertainties or data ranges associated with the information?
- What have we overlooked?
- Has this situation occurred before? How did we deal with it [or similar
  situations] in the past?
- Is this approach the only option? What other alternatives might we
  consider?
- What is the overall business case for what is being proposed?
- What are the risks associated with the proposal?
- Is the proposal consistent with our overall priorities?

- What are this proposal's benefits? How can we verify their value?
- What is the maximum tolerable project impact for this proposal?
- Are there possible unintended consequences of the proposal that could affect others?
- How will we evaluate success? Who's responsible for verifying successful closure?

A healthy skepticism and an ability to shine a bright light into the murky corners of technical projects forces people to consider things that they might prefer to overlook. Asking revealing questions within your team keeps people honest. Strategically worded questions posed to your sponsor and stakeholders can substantially increase your influence and control over your project.

Collaborating with Peers: Strength in Numbers

Another source of influence, particularly with upper-level managers, sponsors, and others responsible for the organizational infrastructure, can come through collaboration with your peers. Recommendations that come from a task force or a council of project leaders carry a good deal more weight than those that originate from just one person. You can work with others who face similar challenges to gain support for your project processes (as outlined in Chapter 2) or to change them and improve how they work. Doing this from the ground up is not easy and may take some persistence, but it is possible. There is strength in numbers. Speaking in unison with a group of like-minded project leaders, backed up with data from recent project experiences, can amplify your influence enormously.

Building influence with managers is largely about relationships; keeping your sponsor and stakeholders involved and supportive throughout your project is always a good investment of your time. Maintain the influence that you require by providing them with frequent evidence of your progress and ensuring that they remain confident in your ability to lead the project to successful completion.

Some years ago, I helped to lead a Hewlett-Packard internal task force on project management comprised of grizzled practitioners from all of HP's product groups and corporate functions. As individuals, none of us had a great deal of influence, even within our own organizations. As a Project Management Council, however, we met quarterly, discussing how to improve the effectiveness of project leaders throughout HP. Our recommendations went to directly to the CEO and other members of the HP executive committee for review and approval. Our work as a task force ultimately resulted in impressive progress in establishing better, more consistent practices for project management companywide.

▪ Maintaining Relationships

Most of your work in establishing good relationships using ideas in this chapter will be during project initiation and project planning (discussed in Chapters 5 and 6). Maintaining influence and control throughout the project depends on your ability to maintain solid relationships with all the members of your team as you execute your project. Effective communications, both formal and informal, are vital, but you can and should do much more to maintain good relationships over the course of your project.

One key to maintaining relationships is taking advantage of the things that you have in common with the people on your team. The most obvious common factor is the project itself. Even though the specific reasons for why the project matters for each person may differ, keeping the common goal of project success front and center can be a powerful unifying force.

Especially when you are working to establish a relationship with someone new, find out whether you have any colleagues or friends in common. Building your relationship through mutual acquaintances, particularly people for whom you both have respect, can result in very durable relationships.

Common experiences and educational backgrounds are another good foundation for building trust and respect. Similar past projects give you things to discuss and exchange information about, as do your academic studies, professional affiliations, and even training classes that you have attended in common.

Another effective way to connect with people, especially on a personal level, is to find common interests, hobbies, and travels. What people do with their own time is always of interest to them, and when you share interests in a type of music, sport, cinema, books, or other pastimes, you always have something to talk about. Similarly, a shared interest in a hobby (bird watching, vintage cars, photography) or an activity (cooking, sailing, raising teenagers) can create an enduring bond. Even visits to the same vacation destinations can spark interesting conversations. Uncovering things that you have in common with members of your team increases your ability to influence them (and their ability to influence you too) and supports ongoing teamwork and effective communication.

You will find a number of additional ideas and suggestions for maintaining relationships in the final section of Chapter 7 on project execution.

DEALING WITH AN OVERFLOW

In 1977, for the second time in less than 100 years, a flood ravaged Johnstown, Pennsylvania. Just as in the 1889 flood, a weakened earthen dam broke in the middle of the night in a hollow above the town, releasing a devastating wall of water, mud, debris, and death down into the city in the valley below. After the flood, all the utilities were interrupted, and response to the resulting problems was proceeding slowly and through a tangle of political and organizational conflicts. As a member of the Federal Disaster Assistance Administration, the forerunner of FEMA, Al DeLucia was assigned to assist in the recovery. Although he had no direct authority over the situation, he began investigating the cooperation problems with the utilities.

Immediately following the flood, Johnstown had no electrical power because all the underground electric lines had shorted out. Underground gas lines had settled, cracked, and leaked, so gas supplies were also turned off. When water did finally recede, both electric and gas service remained shut down for over a month, because electric sparks could ignite pockets of underground gas, and repairing the electric service required that the gas lines be repaired. In addition, even after needed repairs were completed, gas service could not be restored without a street-by-street survey of leaks. All the flooded homes needed power and hot water for cleaning and repair; unrest and political pressure increased with each day without these critical utilities. The electric and gas utilities were separate companies and had a history of noncooperation. Each utility was working independently, and work was progressing very, very slowly.

Johnstown needed a coordinated and prioritized sector-by-sector survey and repair plan quickly. Al's first idea was to talk to the mayor's office and use top-down authority to call a meeting of the utility higher-ups. As he considered this option, however, he realized that it might only make things worse. He knew that the people actually doing the work had a desire to get results—this was their town, and the problems were all close to home—and that they would respond well if he could show that he respected their knowledge and efforts. So Al instead found out who the ranking technical people were in the gas and electric companies, and he called each of them personally. He asked for their help in developing a coordinated plan and invited them to a joint meeting. Everyone readily agreed.

Al opened the first meeting by reviewing the status and outlining some broad objectives. It was quickly apparent that everyone was frustrated by the lack of progress, and all agreed to a series of daily meetings to plan a coordinated approach. Each utility sent their key people, who soon began to run the meetings. The rhythm of daily meetings quickly built trust and resulted in a smooth working relationship.

A city grid was laid out; sectors were identified and prioritized according to need, complexity, and ease of access. Together, the utilities developed a strategy where the gas company would first complete its sector survey, repair the gas mains, and then coordinate with the electric company to make electric repairs. Sector by sector, the electricity was restored, and then the gas. Al says, "Steady progress was all it took to reverse criticism in the local press. The utilities got full credit for a prompt response. Despite the slow start, Johnstown was well on its way to recovery."

Sometimes asking the right questions of the right people provides all the influence you need.

KEY IDEAS FOR INFLUENCING

- Adopt a leadership style that works with your team members, and strive to deliver on what people care about the most.
- Build your awareness and skill for influencing others.
- Use intrinsic motivating factors: ownership, recognition, mastery, overall purpose.
- Negotiate credible commitments with contributors by discovering what they want that you can offer to them and by using exchanges.
- Work to increase your influence through your actions and demeanor.
- Build and maintain relationships of trust and respect with each of your team members.
- Provide snacks.

CHAPTER 4

Control Through Project Metrics

ALL PROJECTS—ESPECIALLY LONG, complex ones—move forward little by little. Lacking metrics to demonstrate progress, the timely discovery of inadequate progress may be impossible. Even worse, if you lack adequate data, your project could be headed in the wrong direction without your knowledge.

The most commonly used measures for most projects are aimed at progress reporting. Status metrics also contribute to project control by helping you identify issues and uncover potential future problems. Project control requires timely information about resource and funding consumption, progress relative to milestones and other dates, and performance against scoping commitments. Metrics can also be used to better understand your project, to adjust the project's objectives, to improve your processes and working methods, and to motivate team members. Measures based on analysis and planning are useful for understanding the project, particularly early on. Project assessment metrics that use numerical data can show what you are getting yourself into. Typical measures for sizing a project, as well as for allowing comparison with other project opportunities and the validation of relative priorities, are:

- Resource allocations and cost estimates
- Project deliverable benefits and value assessments
- Complexity
- Forecasted volume of output

- Measures of risk and uncertainty
- Project duration

Measurement is also central to decision making. From the perspective of project control, one of the most important uses for plan-based measurements is influencing decisions concerning scoping and overall objectives. Project leaders who lack authority frequently find themselves taking on fundamentally infeasible projects, and, throughout their project, additional changes are imposed that make project success more and more unlikely. Metrics related to project size provide your first line of defense against this possibility, providing compelling data you can use to frame successful counterproposals to change unrealistic project objectives. You can use the same measurements to demonstrate the consequences of proposed project changes, allowing you to avoid unnecessary changes throughout your project.

Metrics show the effectiveness of project processes, both at review points during the project and at project completion. The measures that trigger action to review process effectiveness also guide process improvement efforts and assist you in improving your working methods in the future and on following projects.

For a project leader with little real authority over team members, measurement is also an essential tactic for motivating project contributors. Used well, such metrics are a force for good that will significantly increase your ability to keep things under control and moving ahead. Used less well, measurement aimed at motivation can backfire on you and make a shaky situation a good deal worse. For this reason, you need to carefully select and manage the measurements you adopt on your projects.

▪ Desired Behaviors

Fulfilling our objectives requires action. In a simple case, you don't need any measures. When the objectives are simple and the necessary behaviors are obvious and easily accomplished, things generally play out as hoped, as illustrated in Figure 4-1. We easily complete simple goals that consume little time or effort without any special tactics to link the objectives and the necessary actions. We can act quickly and succeed without too much forethought or intervention most of the time.

Unfortunately, we rarely work in such a trivial environment. Real environments are filled with confusing and potentially contradictory objectives, and desirable behaviors may not be very clear. Ron Benton, a colleague of many years at Hewlett-Packard who continues working as an independent consultant on these issues, recommends integrating measurement into the picture to provide guidance and to help in aligning appropriate behaviors with desired objec-

FIGURE 4-1. LINKING GOALS AND BEHAVIORS

tives. Modern projects are complex. And Ron points out that well-chosen measures that relate both to overall objectives and to the behaviors you desire can help you ensure that your team members are doing what they need to do to support overall project goals. For better or for worse, measurement always affects behavior. If you select metrics with care, they serve as a powerful tool for guiding your team that requires very little actual managerial authority.

Ron has long recommended aligning behaviors with objectives through carefully defined measures, as illustrated in Figure 4-2. Although it may be

FIGURE 4-2. GOALS AND BEHAVIORS ALIGNED THROUGH METRICS

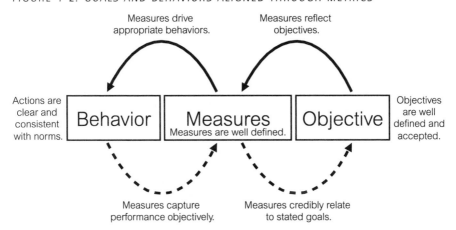

challenging to determine behaviors that support your project objectives and then to define appropriate linking measures, it is always worthwhile.

Although specific project objectives are highly variable (projects are, after all, by definition unique), some broad universal objectives can significantly contribute to your project control. These objectives should be:

- Predictable project performance versus plans
- Clearly defined, managed project scope
- Efficient and effective use of resources
- Infrequent conflicts and disagreement
- Appropriately managed risks

Behaviors that contribute to these objectives could include:

- Preference for careful planning, execution, and communication over project heroism and reactive firefighting
- Tolerating innovation and change only within appropriate, well-understood business and customer requirements
- Contributors enthusiastically moving from completed projects to follow-on projects, with rare cases of burnout
- Cooperation, with team members supporting one another and work and rewards balanced within the team
- Minimizing overall uncertainty through analysis and planning, but with people willing to accept appropriate risks (being too cautious can be risky also)

Methods for selecting measures that encourage these desired behaviors and support the objectives are discussed later in this chapter, but a few examples follow. The first of the broad objectives, performing to plan, is the genesis of many common project metrics, such as:

- Variance between actual timing versus baseline schedule
- Variance between actual costs versus baseline budgets
- Task closure rate (or earned value measurements)
- The number of "stoplight" red or yellow indicators on published status reports

For the objective of managed project scope, some selected measures are:

- Assessment measures related to deliverable definition (through assessment surveys and other means of detecting gaps and weaknesses)

- The volume of changes submitted during the project, particularly changes late in the project
- The percentage of changes accepted and implemented during the project
- Measured results from tests of project outputs

Resource usage and staffing are also measured on many projects using metrics such as:

- Cumulative overtime
- Incidents of idle time
- Comparative staffing compared with norms from earlier, similar projects
- Staff retention and turnover statistics

Metrics may also relate to encouraging cooperation and avoiding conflict. Examples are:

- Frequency of unplanned meetings
- Number of escalations
- Quantity of team rewards and recognition

Measures related to risk must track the risk tolerance that is appropriate for each project, but they can involve:

- The number of risks identified and assessed
- The number of unanticipated problems by severity (compared with norms)
- The value of delivered project results versus expectations

Setting up a system of measures that both encourage desirable behaviors and support project goals can be difficult to do for a specific project and can vary from location to location or even from contributor to contributor. Always be sensitive to context, and work to tailor your measurement goals to the people involved. For example, inflicting identical measures on teams in India, England, and California might not be a good idea. Although all three teams predominantly communicate in English and would presumably be able to understand the metric, using the same measures may result in widely divergent behaviors because of culture, background, and values. Even in the same geographical location, working across company boundaries (or even with people within your own organization soon after a merger), you may find complications arising from differences in organizational culture. Metrics can be very powerful and useful, but unless you carefully choose and test them in your specific environment, they may have unintended consequences resulting in great dysfunction and harm.

▪ Types and Uses of Project Metrics

Overall, the main reason for measurement in business organizations is to assist in achieving goals. In the context of this book, the principle business objective for measurement is good project management and control. Of the three basic types of metrics, each plays a different role in project management.

- *Predictive* project metrics are based on definition and planning information and help set realistic expectations for the project.
- *Diagnostic* metrics are based on current status and serve as indicators of progress and as timely triggers for risk response, problem solving, and decision making.
- *Retrospective* metrics assess how well the work you have completed was done and provide insight into process issues and recurring problems.

Predictive Project Metrics

Predictive project metrics are primarily used in project initiation and project planning. They serve to help you understand the project and function as a distant early-warning system for unrealistic constraints and potential project problems. These metrics use forecast information derived from analysis and planning, and they are based primarily on speculative rather than empirical data. As a result, predictive metrics are the least precise of the three metric types. Predictive project measures support project management by:

- Determining the scale of your project
- Justifying the need for revisions to the project objective
- Quantifying schedule and budget reserve requirements
- Validating cost and timing assumptions for project prioritization and value assessment

Some predictive metrics related to the overall project are explored in more detail in Chapter 5, but most predictive project metrics related to timing, resources, and setting a realistic project baseline are covered in Chapter 6.

Diagnostic Project Metrics

Based on project status information, diagnostic project metrics help you assess the current state of your project. A frog dropped into boiling water hops out promptly, but a frog set in cool water that is gradually heated sits there until he becomes consommé. Project leaders too often find themselves in hot water for similar reasons: An initially reasonable-sounding project gradually becomes impossible. This happens because of the accumulation of many small problems and incremental changes in scope, resources, and timing. If you lack an adequate set of status measures, the transition to a failed project can occur long before you realize it. Diagnostic project metrics are designed to provide real-time information about your project, and they serve as your thermometer for assessing just how hot the water is getting. Control-related uses of these metrics include:

- Identifying resource consumption and timing problems and trends
- Showing the consequences of scope changes
- Making process and staff performance issues visible
- Managing potential future problems and project risks
- Monitoring the need to revalidate the project objective for the project (or to shut it down)

Status collection and defining diagnostic metrics are the main topics of Chapter 7. Using diagnostic metrics is discussed in Chapter 8.

Retrospective Project Metrics

Retrospective metrics determine how well a process worked after it is finished. These metrics are a project's rearview mirror. Project process metrics can be assessed at the conclusion of any completed process-oriented activity throughout a project, such as during a project review (as discussed in Chapter 8). Backward-looking project-level metrics assess the overall effectiveness and efficiency of overall project processes when a project has finished (or has been canceled). Use retrospective project metrics to:

- Improve or replace existing processes.
- Evaluate long-term trends.
- Validate and improve the accuracy of predictive metrics.
- Quantify systemic project and organizational issues, risks, and problems.

Metrics related to process improvement and overall project assessment are explored in Chapter 9.

▪ Measurement Definition and Baselines

Projects are complicated, and selecting the right measures for your project may be challenging. One or two metrics are probably not enough, but committing to collection of metrics for everything that could be measured is also problematic; the overhead would be huge, and important information might be impossible to find in all the data volume. Selecting metrics for a project is about balance and utility.

The basic process steps for establishing a system of metrics are documented in Figure 4-3.

Determining Objectives and Desired Behaviors

For some project measures, determining objectives is not very complicated. We collect estimates for each activity in a project, and each estimate (whether of effort or duration) is a predictive metric based on an analysis of the work required. We collect estimates to support the overall goal of a coherent, realistic plan, and we expect that the processes we use for estimating to be supported by appropriate behaviors. If we think about the behaviors that this metric leads to, things begin to get more complicated. If inaccurate estimates are not tolerated and lead to criticism or punishment, the behaviors this metric inspires lead to padding and systemic overestimating, which undermines your objective:

FIGURE 4-3. PROCESS FOR DEFINING METRICS

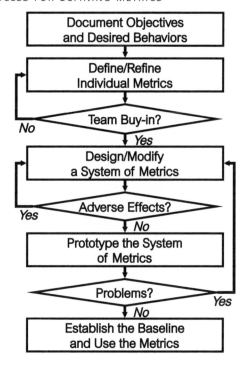

realistic plans. If we do not provide adequate time to systematically analyze the work and all estimates are rough order of magnitude or, even worse, derived from arbitrary deadline constraints, we not only fail to meet our planning objective, we also display that we do not care very much how well—or even if—this project is completed. Inevitably, this results in very undesirable behaviors for nearly all contributors.

Defining the desired behaviors and objectives before considering the question of what to measure leads to more consistent, appropriate results. Realistic plans and the desired behavior of thorough, systematic analysis may not seem very complicated, but they are in fact easily (and often) undermined as a result of too little forethought. Even in this simple case, you may need to consider several types of metrics and implement a system of measures with care and attention to how the information is collected and used.

Designing Individual Metrics

You can design individual metrics using several different approaches. Some approaches begin with objectives. Others begin with behaviors. Wherever you begin and whatever process you use initially, the final steps of the process require you to evaluate your measures for appropriateness, consistency, and potential dysfunction.

Methods for defining metrics include goal question metric, balanced scorecard, process measurement, and behavioral methods.

Goal Question Metric Approach

In the early 1990s, Victor Basili of the University of Maryland and several colleagues working with NASA developed the *goal question metric* (*GQM*) method for defining metrics. Since then, this means of definition has been widely applied, particularly for software projects, in commercial and other environments.

GQM is a systematic process based on a three-tiered hierarchy. The first tier is at the top of the hierarchy and defines the desired outputs and results. The second tier is in the middle and is composed of questions through which you can determine whether you have achieved these objectives. The third and lowest level of the hierarchy contains measures that can be used in answering the questions. Figure 4-4 shows a schematic example of a GQM hierarchy.

GQM has a very direct connection to the concept of *what's-in-it-for-me*, explored in Chapter 3 as a basis for exchange. Here, the same concept is used to anticipate the needs and interests of project sponsors and stakeholders by considering what they are going to care most about, from their perspective, when asking "How is your project going?" The best way to retain their confi-

FIGURE 4-4. A GOAL QUESTION METRIC HIERARCHY

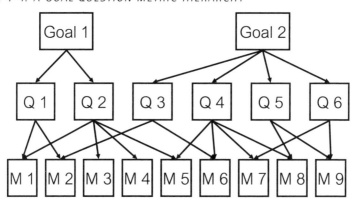

dence is to use measurable, credible data to demonstrate that you are staying on track toward achieving your agreed-upon goals. A seasoned project manager anticipates the needs of key management stakeholders and keeps relevant and objective project data current.

As an example, if one of the key goals for your project is to "improve the accuracy of project cost estimates," potential questions could include one about overall current accuracy and another about trends in accuracy over time. To quantify these questions, you need primitive metrics such as estimated and actual activity costs, along with composite metrics to determine ratios and differences. Of course, you could appear to improve estimating accuracy simply by padding all your estimates, completing the work within the effort and cost goals, and then charging additional time until the budget is used up. To guard against this, a second goal could be not to increase the overall average costs for completed work. Questions related to this goal could be about current actual costs and changes in activity expenditures over time. Some metrics may be needed to answer both questions, but other measures will likely be used uniquely by one question.

Will these two questions alone, with their metrics, actually achieve the intended overall objective of better, more realistic plans? Perhaps not, because these objectives could be undermined by undesirable team behavior such as contributors who define shorter, less costly activities in future projects. GQM is a good way to start the process of metric definition, but we still must validate the measurements and check that they are consistent with what we are using them to achieve.

Balanced Scorecard Approach

In the mid-1990s, Robert Kaplan and David Norton devised the *balanced score-card method* for defining metrics, in large part to deal with the potential for abuse and other problems that arise when measures are applied selectively. When too few measures or the wrong measures are deployed, it is possible—and in many cases likely—for the measures to look just fine even when the behaviors are undesirable and none of the objectives are being met. Kaplan devised a four-quadrant view that provides tension between the measures and helps to ensure that the metrics are less likely to result in dysfunctional behavior. The balanced scorecard method is principally aimed at the business or business-unit level, but it can be applied to projects and programs with a little creativity.

Kaplan's quadrants are *customer, finance, internal process*, and *learning and growth*. The context for these four categories is the overall strategy and vision for the organization, so the primary questions relate to how both external and internal constituencies perceive the organization, as determined using objective measures. The same type of model can be applied to projects and programs, yielding a similar system of metrics that can provide good results and minimize the possibility of overemphasis of a single dimension or dysfunctional behavior. An example of the balanced scorecard approach applied to a project is shown in Figure 4-5.

In the center of the figure is the reason the project exists, the specific technical goals and why they matter. Although the project objective is common to all perspectives, vision tends to be in the eye of the beholder and can vary considerably from quadrant to quadrant.

FIGURE 4-5. A BALANCED SCORECARD CONTEXT FOR PROJECT METRICS

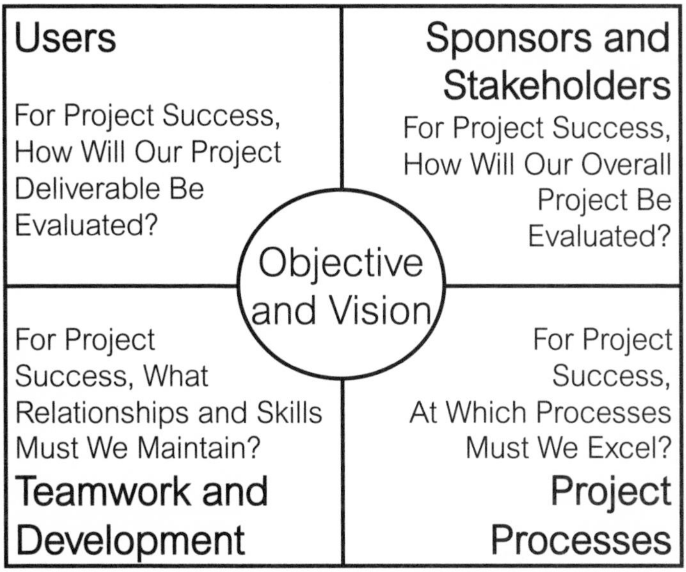

Users	Sponsors and Stakeholders
For Project Success, How Will Our Project Deliverable Be Evaluated?	For Project Success, How Will Our Overall Project Be Evaluated?
Objective and Vision	
For Project Success, What Relationships and Skills Must We Maintain?	For Project Success, At Which Processes Must We Excel?
Teamwork and Development	Project Processes

Ultimately, the end user (or customer) perspective for a project is primarily about scoping. If you can get the feature set just right, other considerations of timing and cost are much less important, particularly in the long run. Sponsors and most stakeholders tend to be more focused on timing and cost because these dimensions of a project affect what else the organization can take on, and time is money. These two perspectives are external to the project and must be balanced against internal considerations, including your need for control and survival.

The internal process view revisits themes that have figured prominently in earlier chapters. Process is one of your most important control tools, and fine-tuning the process dimension relates to execution efficiency and elements of timing and resource consumption. Teamwork and development are also central to the project and pull in the human motivation factors as well as support the team's capacity to deliver on the more challenging aspects of project scope.

Your version of a balanced scorecard for developing a set of metrics may be different from this example, but the basic idea of looking at all significant aspects of the project and setting up metrics in tension that force objective evaluation of trade-offs is a useful approach.

Process Measurement

Another approach for defining metrics rests on the ideas in Chapter 2. When you have defined a set of processes well, you have established rules and standards for performance. You can then establish expectations for performance from these rules and define metrics that show you how well the process is working. Some metrics relate to the outputs of the process, such as accuracy, quantity of omissions or defects, and degree of acceptance. Other metrics relate to the execution of the process, such as throughput, timeliness, or effort consumed.

As an example, a key process for overall project control is scope change management. Metrics of both of these types are useful in dealing with proposed specification changes. Examples of output-related measures include:

- The number of changes accepted as a percentage of those proposed
- The number of changes accepted into scope that are later modified, require significant clarification, or are subsequently dropped
- The number of initial decisions that result in escalation for reconsideration

The effectiveness of the process may also be measured by:

- How long it takes to accept submitted change proposals for review
- How much time the review process and initial decision requires
- How much effort is used in dealing with submitted changes

Defining measures as part of an overall process is a good way to provide visibility for the process and make its use more universal. Carefully selected measures let you see when a process needs revision, when it lacks appropriate priority, or when people need training or assistance. Before finalizing measures as part of a process, carefully consider whether there could be any adverse behavioral consequences. Undue emphasis on efficiency measures such as cycle time and effort consumption often lead to shortcuts, and inadequate analysis undermines the intended purpose of the process.

Behavioral Methods

Finally, of course, you can simply start where this chapter did—with behavior. Metrics tied to rewards are nearly always defined starting with a behavior that is viewed as desirable and associating monetary payment, recognition, or some potential for reward with specific behavior. (On technical projects, nonmonetary rewards are often the most effective, as discussed in Chapter 3. Ideas for rewards and motivation are explored in detail in Chapter 8.) In projects, the most universal measure, performance to schedule, is defined to encourage the project team members to do what the project plan calls for and to complete the work by the appointed time. Although not all slips on the project schedule are created equal, attention to this metric reinforces the importance of completing work on time and contributes to cooperation in keeping the overall project on track.

Because you are starting from the perspective of desired behavior, you may have some confidence that the measure will help you achieve the behaviors you are seeking. Particularly with this approach, you must validate the connection to the larger objectives in addition to driving behavior. If the "right" behaviors do not consistently deliver the results you need, metrics defined this way do not contribute much to your ability to control your project.

Documenting the Metrics

After deciding what to measure, you need to clearly define each metric and then discuss it with all the people who will affect it or be affected by it. This step further refines your understanding for each prospective metric. In addition to defining how and when information is to be collected, you need to describe how you plan to use the data. For each prospective metric, consider:

- The name and a description of the metric
- The principal objective for this metric
- The method or process used to collect the data
- The person or persons who will collect the data

- If appropriate, the person who will verify or audit the data
- The frequency for data collection (frequent enough to support your objectives, but not so often that it represents excessive overhead or generates "noise")
- For metrics that are not simple counts or ratios, specific units of measure (such as days, euros, effort-months) for reporting the data
- Where the data is stored and how it is managed
- How the information collected is reported and used
- Any barriers or potential data collection problems

As you are documenting each metric, consider the following factors:

- Is the metric unnecessarily complicated? Could you get essentially the same information more easily?
- Is the metric easy to collect? Could you learn what you need to know with less overhead?
- What will it cost to collect the data? Does your expected value for the information justify the investment?
- Is the information to be measured as timely as possible? Could we define an earlier or more leading indicator?
- Could personal information collected hurt someone? Is any part of the information proprietary or secret? How will you manage confidentiality and privacy issues?
- Is the metric objective? Will two people measuring the same thing obtain the same result?
- Can all the people who are involved clearly understand the description of the metric and the process for collecting it?
- If some people on the team speak different languages, have you verified that all translations are consistent? Have you checked for possible cultural misinterpretations?

Although this probably sounds like a great deal of effort, most of these considerations are a natural outcome of the defining process; most of the work should already be done. An example project metric is documented in Table 4-1.

Obtaining Support for Data Collection and Use

No metric is of much use if the people who are collecting the data and are affected by it do not support it. Measurement systems can be subverted in many ways. Ideas for minimizing the "gaming" of metrics and other potential barriers are explored later in this chapter, but it is better by far to establish

TABLE 4-1. METRIC DEFINITION.

Activity Closure Index	
Objective:	Provide project progress information
Normal range:	0.95 to 1.1 (higher is better)
Tension:	Output quality, deliverable cost
Calculation:	(Number of activities closed) / (Total activities) / (Percent of timeline consumed)
Data:	Activities completed, current date
Reported by:	Activity owners
Frequency:	Weekly
Tools used:	Project scheduling tool database
Potential barrier:	Performing easy, short activities first; declaring activities complete when work remains or output is unsatisfactory

metrics with broad support to start with to ensure that such problems are uncommon.

People are rarely neutral on measurement; they think that it's either a great idea or the worst thing imaginable. In general, people tend to support measurement when they think they will excel or when they think that measurement will contribute to significantly better results. Very good students look forward to report cards, and Olympic athletes have no problem with timekeepers and other scorers because they are generally pleased and validated by the measurements. We also value measurements that allow us to make better decisions or to obtain consistently better results; buyer's guides are popular with shoppers because they are full of facts and figures, and cooks rely heavily for good results on their oven's thermostat for monitoring and controlling temperature.

People dislike measurements when they suspect that they will cast what they are doing in a bad light, particularly when there are potential adverse personal consequences. One of the most common factors in failed measurement systems is using the results to punish, criticize, or increase hardship on the people who are responsible for collecting the needed data. The reliability of the collected data is suspect, at best, if project metrics are used to select projects to cancel, or if activity performance information regularly serves as the basis for personnel cutbacks. Shooting the messengers bearing bad news is a formula for project chaos and ultimate failure.

For projects, the most controversial metrics tend to be diagnostic because they are collected most frequently, are generally visible, and require the broadest input and participation. Because predictive and retrospective metrics are often primarily your responsibility and are based on information that you collect, manage, and interpret, there is generally less need to build broad support for them.

The first step in obtaining team buy-in for project status metrics is personal involvement. Team members' compliance and cooperation with any ongoing measurement effort tends to be proportionate to how much they participated in establishing it (or trust those who did set it up). As part of project initiation or planning, solicit input from your team on what status information each person thinks would be useful for the project. Before actual data collection begins, measurement usually seems like a great idea to most people, especially those who have had recent unpleasant project experiences. You can build substantial opportunities to explore (and influence) measurement options in project start-up and other planning meetings. Many examples of diagnostic project measures are in Chapter 7, with tips for reporting and other uses for them in Chapter 8. These examples—and other metrics that you and your team agree would provide useful, ongoing information for your project—are all possibilities for consensus choices.

Another aspect of buy-in is the projected use of the data. When people see that the main intended use is to improve response to problems and to support important processes, you can get their commitment and willing cooperation. If they suspect that other uses are intended, or even likely, you will encounter substantial resistance.

People support status metrics obviously aligned with better execution or process improvement. Some examples are measurements that can be used to avoid frivolous or unnecessary project change and status information useful for the identification of project problems early enough to trigger effective responses or reallocation of resources.

Gaining support for measurements that support recognition systems is also easy. And because recognition is one of the duties that you own as project leader, you can ensure that this happens. In particular, if you are able to establish with your team that you will reward accurate and timely reporting of bad results, setting up an effective system of status measures is straightforward.

The hardest part of getting buy-in for ongoing measurement is the potential for abuse, especially for information that is publicly reported. In general, the more you are able to keep visibility of your project measures internal to your team, the easier it is to gain cooperation, especially if you have established a relationship of trust and respect within the team. One possibility for minimizing public embarrassment (or worse) in broadcast reporting is to show your project measurements only in aggregate. This depersonalizes the measurement process, at least for individual members of your team. (Of course, your project measurements still reflect on you, but that's one of the reasons that project leaders have such thick skin).

Another idea for handling publicly available project information is to work with your sponsors and stakeholders to get their commitment that measurement results will be used only constructively, avoiding punitive uses of the data. For example, when progress measures are lagging on your project, you have advance commitment from your sponsor to review your staffing levels and to investigate how you might use outside or additional help to catch up. Adverse measures can also be set up as semiautomatic triggers (though some review is always prudent) that make budget or other reserves available to the project.

Discuss each metric that you intend to adopt with all affected team members. For each candidate metric, work to get consensus from the project team on the definition, the planned collection and use of the data, and the meaning of the results. One of the most effective ways to counter gaming of the metrics is to seek each person's agreement not to do it. Work to ensure that each person generating the measures willingly commits in advance to collecting or supplying accurate data.

Developing a System of Measures and Evaluating Potential Adverse Consequences

Although a single metric may encourage desired behavior and link to an important objective, for something as complicated as a project, you generally need a collection of measures. In addition, generally individual metrics by themselves can put so much emphasis on one thing that it gets too much attention (the "if some is good, more must be better" effect). Metrics assessing execution speed alone may encourage incomplete analysis or shoddy results. Too much emphasis on precision and accuracy can lead to unacceptably slow throughput and delay. The solution is to use opposing metrics together to create tension, where improvement in one measure diminishes the other one. Opposing metrics in this way forces trade-offs and results in behavior that is more appropriate than you can expect using either measurement by itself.

A system of measures should be kept lean. You can always measure many more things than are justified; your goal should be a small set of meaningful metrics. Each metric you select should pass a number of tests, in the context of the overall set of measures you are adopting. These tests include sole focus, reward and evaluation system consistency, and environment consistency.

Sole Focus

The sole focus test asks what would happen if this were the only measure you used or if the measure were emphasized substantially more than other metrics.

What potentially problematic behaviors might result? Would there be any unintended consequences to others outside your project? If so, consider modifying the metric or looking for a better alternative. If there are no particularly good alternatives, seek one or more additional metrics that provide tension to offset the undesirable effects of the metric. When adopting a metric that can lead to adverse outcomes, clearly communicate the purpose and your concern about potential abuse, and plan to monitor your project diligently to detect any problems promptly so that you can manage them.

Reward and Evaluation System Consistency

Each metric must also be consistent with your organization's reward and evaluation systems. All organizations employ some metrics to assess individual performance. These measures, however informally they may be defined, trump all others. They determine how people are paid, how secure their jobs are, and many other fundamental aspects of the employee-employer relationship. Consider carefully how people and teams are evaluated, rewarded, and recognized in your organization from the perspective of each metric you are considering. Your metric can be a problem if it encourages individual behavior that would be viewed negatively in the organization or even if it potentially interferes with more valued activities. Although you could work to modify the rewards and evaluation systems, this is generally a long-term proposition and, in any case, you may have little realistic ability to influence it. You might be able to contrast other consequences with project recognition based on the metric for which you are responsible, but if there are significant impediments, the organizational imperatives always prevail. If you face serious issues with a given metric, you can look for an alternative project measure that might be better aligned with established practices or simply choose not to use the measure.

Environment Consistency

Similarly, you also need to consider the work environment for each of your team members. Metrics expected to encourage behaviors never work when they are inconsistent with a team member's culture, traditions, or established practices. When working across international boundaries or with people from other companies, inconsistency may result in significant issues that you may not be aware of at start-up. When discussing potential measures with unfamiliar contributors, probe hard for potential problems and surface issues as effectively as you can. For example, measure differently based on geography. Imposing identical measures across parts of your team in Japan, Germany, and Canada can be perilous. Working with newly hired people in your own company or with external contractors who are working on your project may raise similar issues.

When faced with this kind of challenge, you have several options. You might be able to gain overall buy-in for your metric using your influence and working hard with all the individuals to get them to accept required changes. This solution, though, takes time and may not be practical. Alternatively, you could define an entirely different candidate metric that avoids the cultural deployment problems. You may elect to use different measures for disconnected parts of your team, but be aware that using different measures may yield inconsistent results. If a given metric appears too problematic, avoid using it.

When you have looked at each metric individually in the context of the others, examine the whole set, asking the following questions:

- Does the set of measurements reflect the aspects of your project that are most important?
- Is it missing anything that you need to include to understand and control your project?
- Is the set of measures as simple as you can make it? Have you eliminated all redundancy?
- Could a smaller or more easily collected combination of metrics provide a comparable result?
- Are your metrics defined to provide you with the timeliest, most leading indicators?
- Might the measurement goals be achieved with no impact on the desired objectives?
- Can the measurement goals be achieved without any beneficial behavior change?
- Will your use of this information make a meaningful difference, or are you collecting data just because it's there?
- Have you dropped all measures that cost more to collect than they are worth?

You should strive to define a set of metrics that represents the minimal set of information that you need to understand and control your project. Seek a set of measures that aid you in controlling your project through tension between the measures you select. As with the balanced scorecard approach, establish a set of measures that encourages appropriate overall team behavior through trade-offs in the measures.

In general, if you are unsure whether a metric will be useful but think that it probably will be, retain it in your initial list. Dropping a piece of status from your collection process later, if you find that you no longer need it, is easier than adding new overhead during a busy, stressful project.

Testing the Metrics and Resolving Problems

After you think you have a good, useful set of measures for your project, test them (or at least any that are new) to ensure that the descriptions are clear and that they will work for you. A useful set of criteria for checking the appropriateness of metrics is based on the work of quality guru J. M. Juran: Each metric should be a consensus basis for decision making, understandable, broadly applicable, interpreted uniformly, economical to use, and compatible with existing measurement capabilities.

Testing metrics requires you to set up a context and to collect the status on each. And you need to watch for some potential problems, including:

- Pockets of resistance to measurement and reporting
- Reported data that's inconsistent with expectations
- A greater-than-anticipated effort required to collect and provide the data

Find potential problems with your metrics, and resolve them by adjusting the individual metric definitions, modifying the overall set of metrics, or having a thorough discussion with team members to deal with understanding or compliance issues.

Setting a Baseline for the Measures and Establishing a Normal Range

Before starting to use a set of diagnostic metrics to control your project, validate the baseline for the measures. Only after you have a validated normal range will you be able to interpret your metrics or use them to make good project decisions. Without an established measurement baseline, you also cannot assess the effects of any process modifications or other changes that you make.

For well-established metrics, baselines may already be documented. For new measures, or for defined metrics used in a new context, you need to establish an initial data range. Although you can always start your project using an educated guess for a new metric, you need to confirm it using data from the first few cycles of status collection.

For predictive metrics, verify baselines and assumptions using corresponding retrospective metrics from earlier projects (for example, you can check your estimates against actual durations and costs from similar work done before). For retrospective metrics, you can also use the data from earlier, completed projects to set your baselines.

Using the Metrics

Once you have defined and set up a set of measures, using them is fairly straightforward, though it does require a good deal of effort and discipline.

Using predictive metrics to plan for and negotiate realistic project objectives enhances your control over a project; this topic is explored in Chapter 6. Selecting specific diagnostic measures and evaluating the data to assess the status of your project is discussed in Chapter 7. Chapter 8 includes pointers on measurement reporting, other uses for your metrics, and data archiving. Capturing lessons learned and improving processes using retrospective metrics is explored in Chapter 9.

LEARNING TO HANDLE THE TRUTH

Ron Benton, now of Ron Benton & Associates, tells of an effort he participated in some years ago at Hewlett-Packard. It inadvertently demonstrated, on a large scale, some of the unintended consequences that can occur when project metrics are imposed on project leaders with negligible authority.

HP had set a corporate-wide goal to cut project break-even times in half for R&D product development projects. Ron worked with a corporate team to develop a system of measures to help improve performance through the use of monthly actual and forecast data for schedule, resources, investment, revenue, and other project information. Everyone expected that the quarterly reports would lead to productivity improvements and support better investment and resource allocation decisions.

In one global operation with approximately 100 R&D projects under development, the group's overall R&D manager welcomed the new system and expected it to provide him with actionable insights. It took several months of extensive effort to educate project managers and the middle managers about the effort, to generate comparable historical and current data, and to get all of it entered into the system. The initial reports, consisting largely of graphs, were generated and distributed at the end of the next quarter, but they did not contain a lot of interpretation or analysis.

The most obvious issue reported was with schedule performance (measured by actual progress versus planned progress for the quarter). The reports reflected that projects across the group had slipped an average of nearly 40% (more than one month) during the past quarter, as well as in all earlier quarters. In response, the group R&D manager initiated conversations with his direct reports to understand the root cause and take action.

Despite these discussions, the second quarterly reports showed no real improvement, and the circulation of the reports was beginning to get high-level management attention. The group vice president asked, not gently, "Does this mean what I think it means?" Once verified, he sent a memorable memo to every project, middle, and general manager, making clear that continued poor project schedule performance was unacceptable and that project managers were to get it under control before the next quarter.

All knew the urgency of this demand, and the vice president and his team expected much improved schedule adherence for the next cycle. Project managers had many difficult conversations with their lab managers and general managers. At quarter end, updated project data was logged into the system, and the next reports were generated.

This time, Ron saw that the modest slips reported earlier had become much worse; schedule progress plummeted. Many projects showed slippage measured in *quarters*, not months, and the aggregate measure was literally off the chart on the bottom end. Group management was astonished and began immediately investigating what had happened. Reconstruction revealed some startling insights.

In the past, schedule slips were proposed only when all other managerial options were exhausted. Project leaders were limited because they could not increase constrained project resources, and they did not have any control over project scope. Project managers generally found it easier and less painful to conceal the full reality of their situations (while hoping for some brilliant idea or a miracle). This reaction resulted in real schedule divergence that was not reflected in the earlier reporting.

Following the vice president's memo, the past practices of reporting only the most wildly optimistic outcome were abandoned. Everyone realized they had to reveal the reality of their schedule dilemmas, which were reluctantly accepted by middle managers and passed along for reporting. Further delay in acknowledging the slippages would be even more painful.

After the dust settled, two things happened quickly. First, a genuine (and difficult) discussion started about the project review requirements that were causing the problems facing the project managers. Immediate changes led to constructive process improvement across the organization. Second, by honestly incorporating schedule reality for current projects, subsequent quarterly reports reflected schedules that were consistently and credibly on track. With these changes, the trend continued as the existing projects were completed and new ones came on-line.

▪ Potential Problems and Measurement Barriers

No set of metrics can ever be bulletproof. It is possible—some say inevitable—that any metric will be undermined. Defining metrics clearly to minimize differing interpretations and loopholes is one of your first lines of defense. You also need to understand the main reasons that metrics are gamed so that you can be vigilant and eliminate the causes for measurement dysfunction and failure.

The most common causes of gaming, more or less in order of importance, are as follows:

- Metrics are used primarily as report cards or for punishment.
- Metrics require public reporting of private or personally embarrassing information.
- Honest reporting of bad results is discouraged.
- Reporting good outcomes, even when untrue, is encouraged.
- Metrics are not aligned with rewards and recognition systems.
- The failure to report data or reporting inaccurate information has no significant consequences.
- Metrics are poorly defined or imprecise.
- Metrics are not motivating.
- Metrics have inappropriate emphasis and lack tension.

Dealing with some of these factors is part of the overall definition process, as discussed earlier in this chapter. Managing other factors requires surveillance, discipline, and a good deal of influence all through the project, particularly if your project is undertaken in an organizational context where some of these problems are common and tolerated. The topic of verifying status information throughout your project and confronting gaming behavior within your team is a major part of Chapter 7.

The best overall technique for minimizing the barriers and potential problems associated with project metrics is simple, however: Ask people not to game the measurements, and get their commitment to send you the data you need. Your part of this bargain is also not complicated, though it is very difficult at times to keep. You must treat all the people on your team fairly, thank them for the information they supply (even when it is not what you were hoping to hear), and do everything in your power to prevent others from misusing the data you collect.

KEY IDEAS FOR PROJECT METRICS

- Outline desired behaviors that you need on your team to maintain project control.
- Identify metrics that align with project objectives and desired behaviors.
- Select a small set of key measures, and obtain team support for them.
- Test the metrics, and establish a measurement baseline.
- Use the metrics to monitor and control your project.

CHAPTER 5

Control Begins with Project Initiation

TROUBLED PROJECTS FREQUENTLY have tentative beginnings. You can avoid a lot of late project anguish by asserting control as soon as the project begins, ideally with a fully engaged project team ready to hit the ground running. To do this, you need the support of your sponsor, solid documentation, and a project start-up workshop.

▪ Sponsorship

Your project sponsor has considerable organizational authority, at least enough to initiate your project. This person's authority can be useful to you, regardless of how much or how little formal authority you may have. Sponsors are the most enthusiastic and engaged at the start of a project; take full advantage of your sponsor's interest to get things off to a great start. By retaining management's attention and focus throughout your project, you can use your sponsor's authority to substantially enhance your project control.

One of the first things you can do to ensure ongoing support and attention from your sponsor and other influential stakeholders is to set expectations right away and get specific commitments. Do it while they are still enthusiastic about your project and the value of your project is fresh in their minds. In the context of this discussion, a *project sponsor* is the person who provides strategic direction, who gives formal support, and who sets the organizational priority for your project. Your sponsor also approves funding and staffing for the project and generally is the person who makes project decisions that are beyond your authority. If any of these functions are shared among several people, or if other stakeholders have influence in these matters, work to gain their support and commitments too.

In a perfect world, all sponsors would stay interested and involved until the end of every project they initiate; unfortunately, people with enough organizational authority and power to get projects and programs going have many other matters competing for their attention. Shortly after you assume responsibility for your project, use your influencing skills to extract commitments from your sponsor (and other key stakeholders) in exchange for your agreeing to lead the project. In particular, request commitments for:

- Managing the project environment
- Active involvement in project start-up
- Support for robust project management processes
- Initial validation and baseline setting (and revalidation as required throughout the project)
- Protection for the project (retaining resources, removal of barriers, prompt response to escalations, and minimization of project change)
- Organizational learning

Meaningful participation in each of these areas by higher-level managers who take interest in your project makes controlling your project a good deal easier. However, avoid getting your sponsor too involved with the day-to-day execution of your project. You want your sponsor's support, not his or her detailed involvement; after all, it's your project.

Managing the Project Environment

Your ability to control your project relies on a stable environment and advance warning of upcoming surprises. Your sponsor probably has more knowledge of what is going on in the organization than you do, so proactively get his or her commitment to inform you of any changes that could impact your project. Periodically remind your sponsor of this commitment, or use your interactions with your sponsor throughout the project to ask about upcoming organizational or other changes.

Your sponsor also needs to be the project's agent inside your organization, to serve as a liaison with even higher-level management and to be a spokesperson for the project during project portfolio analysis and overall prioritization. Ask your sponsor to describe to you why, from his or her perspective, the project is being undertaken, and capture the rationale using your sponsor's words. Offer to help your sponsor build a strong business case for the project and align the project goals with strategic business objectives. Identify significant project risks, and plan to work with your sponsor to minimize and then manage them. If your sponsor understands your project well, it will receive more attention, and the sponsor can be a more effective advocate for you. Work to get a meaningful commitment from your sponsor to monitor and manage your project's ecosystem.

In addition to specific involvement in each of these areas, request a regular time to periodically review your project with your sponsor, about an hour at least once a month. At these meetings, share accomplishments, discuss issues, and use the one-on-one opportunity to explore general matters concerning your project. Also use this time to keep your sponsor aware that you are still there.

Active Involvement in Project Start-Up

Although you may have little real organizational power, others in your organization have a good deal of authority. Your sponsor can confer status and power to you vicariously, by formally appointing you as manager (or at least leader) of the project. If your sponsor appears to be too busy to do this, you can always offer to write the memo, for your sponsor's signature, announcing the start of the project and your responsibilities.

You may also need formal involvement from your sponsor to secure commitments for staffing, funding, or other resources, particularly resources from outside organizations. If your project requires funding for travel, training, or other direct expenses, get budgetary commitments for this as well. Identify any new equipment or upgrades to existing hardware or software that you need, and begin working with your sponsor to obtain the necessary approvals. Use discussions with your sponsor to identify all the project stakeholders who can affect your project or depend on its successful completion.

Next you may need to get commitment from your sponsor to support an appropriate project start-up workshop. If your project start-up requires explicit funding approval for travel and other costs, begin building the case to justify it in your initial sponsor discussions. Sponsor involvement in your project start-up helps convey the importance of your project. Request that your sponsor participate by attending either the beginning or the close of your project start-up workshop. Specific suggestions for conducting a project start-up workshop are explored later in this chapter.

Support for Robust Project Management Processes

As discussed in Chapter 2, project management processes are an essential part of project control. If your sponsor formally supports the processes that you intend to adopt, you will have better cooperation and less resistance from your team members. For this support to be helpful, you do not necessarily need detailed, item-by-item mandates for every process step from your sponsor, and you probably won't have the time or access to arrange this anyway. High-level support from your sponsor for your overall project processes, particularly for fact-based, bottom-up planning, assists you in getting the cooperation and collaboration you need from your team for better control.

A commitment from your sponsor to review key project planning deliverables is another way to facilitate process adoption. An announcement that your sponsor will examine the *Is* and *Is not* criteria for major deliverables, inspect the high-level project work breakdown structure, or participate in periodic cycle reviews help you communicate that the processes you plan to use are mandatory, not discretionary.

If you anticipate friction in gaining support from your sponsor for key project processes, then try to help him or her understand why the processes are important and relate them to your project success. Focus particularly on getting support from your sponsor for a reality-based overall planning process for your project. Sponsors who view planning and other project management processes as frivolous overhead significantly undermine your ability to control and finish your project. If you are unable to obtain wholehearted, enthusiastic support for the processes you need, try to get a concession from your sponsor to support your approach as an "experiment," just this once, to test the value of project management processes. For some organizations, gaining meaningful support from sponsors for project processes may be a longer-term goal, but ultimately the work pays off and results in more successful, better controlled projects.

Initial Validation, Baseline Setting, and Periodic Revalidation

Two keys to overall project control are robust sponsor validation of the initial project objectives prior to planning and a meaningful commitment for revalidation following project planning, reviews, and major changes. The initial validation of objectives is to ensure alignment of the sponsor's and stakeholders' goals with the understanding that you and your team carry into the planning process. Validation by the sponsor of the project baseline, using bottom-up, fact-based planning deliverables, may require modifying the initial project goals to ensure that you are committing to a realistic, credible project objective. Project baselines that are supported only by hopes, wishes, and prayers cannot serve as a foundation for a controllable project.

Set a firm expectation with your sponsor that the initial objectives and expectations for the project are targets, not commitments, until you, working with your team, have had an opportunity to analyze the work and figure out what you need to do. Sometimes, you may find it difficult to get an advance commitment from your sponsor to consider potential project adjustments based on the results of your planning. Even in these cases, though, you still have an opportunity to show why project goals need to be adjusted and propose alternatives when you set or adjust the project baseline with your sponsor. Without an advance commitment, you are likely to encounter a good deal more resistance, but you can use your planning data to successfully negotiate project changes. (For more discussion on negotiating a credible project baseline, see Chapter 6.)

Validating an initial baseline is necessary for project control, but it is rarely sufficient. Most projects encounter change, and changes are inevitable on projects using agile methods. Following large changes, your original goals and project baseline may no longer be relevant. Unexpected problems, feedback from users, unexpected events outside your project, and myriad other things may require modifying your project objectives and result in replanning. Periodic plan modifications for projects employing agile, iterative methods and project reviews for any project that runs a year or longer also require scope adjustments and potential plan changes. In any of these cases where the overall project goals shift significantly, you need to meet with your sponsor to document the changes and to revalidate the new project baseline. Set an expectation with your sponsor to formally revalidate the project after major shifts, and provide your sponsor with as much advance notification as possible whenever a revalidation appears to be necessary. Also, incorporate process steps for revalidating the project baseline into your change control and project review processes to be used whenever appropriate.

FINDING THE RIGHT TOOL

Jim Sloane worked in aerospace for many years, and early in his career he found himself leading a project to develop a tool to be used in installing the explosive separation devices that release satellites. The deliverable was to be a one-of-a-kind tool, for which there was no precedent. Jim had picked up the project because no one had been assigned to lead it and because it was of interest to him as he had been an explosives expert in the military. Jim's role, "project lead," was not formally recognized in his test organization; he knew he would have no real authority. He also knew that it would take a lot of interpersonal skill to get the help he would need to pull off the project successfully.

Funding for Jim's project required formal approval by a control board. Before he could approach the control board for approval, though, he had to pull together specification information from potential vendors and assemble a comprehensive quotation. He had to solicit bids from contractors who specialized in applying and measuring the high-torque loads required. Jim was not an expert on any of this, so he had to cajole people into helping him get up to speed. His support equipment manager gave him a big head start, but he also needed help from QA, purchasing, mechanical engineering, and others. All these people had other important things to do, and Jim's project was small compared to their other responsibilities. To get the support he needed, Jim began by relating to each of the people he approached by asking questions about them, their families, and their jobs. Only then did he start talking about his project. Jim worked to put his colleagues at ease, and in most cases he was easily able to gain their cooperation.

In follow-up meetings and discussions with the folks he was depending on, Jim continued to build their relationships, and he was always careful to deliver on any commitments he made to them. This built their trust and helped them see Jim as a partner, not as a problem or annoyance. Jim says, "This was the single most important thing I did because these people came to trust me with their knowledge and skills. They had confidence I would perform well."

When Jim had assembled the information he needed, he set up an appointment with his control board. He came to the appointment early because he had never been through the procedure before and he wanted to understand it. When Jim arrived he found a conference room full of "gray hairs" in suits who were grilling a software engineer. They were questioning his need for a budget increase to complete his project. Not getting what they wanted from him (perhaps because the board did not understand software very well), they sent him away to "do his homework."

Jim was next and was initially pretty nervous after what he had seen happen to the control board's previous victim. However, when he put a picture of the intended tool up, there was a collective sigh of relief, and Jim overheard a soft, "Ahhhh, hardware."

Jim made his presentation, and thanks to the help he had received, it was complete and thorough. The control board was impressed. They pointed out that he would need a backup, and approved his project to purchase two from the vendor!

Although it took time, effort, and interpersonal skill, Jim was able to secure the help he needed and the approval to complete the project. Although there were elements of luck and being in the right place at the right time, Jim used his interpersonal skills to enhance his chances and to put himself in position to successfully get the high-level support and funding his project required.

Protection for the Project

Project control relies on ongoing attention and support from the project sponsor. One of the most important ongoing responsibilities for the sponsor is retaining staffing and budget for the project. Modern organizations always have many great project ideas and too few people to adequately staff them. It's always tempting to start new projects but, because people and money are always in short supply, initiating them may come at the expense of reducing what is allocated to your project. Explicit formal commitment from your sponsor to protect your resources can help. Periodically reminding your sponsor of this commitment is prudent, as is having a list of consequences ready at all times to use against threats to pull away people, funding, or other resources required by your project.

Dealing with major obstructions and barriers is also a sponsor responsibility. When you lack the authority or organizational power to resolve issues impeding your project, you can turn to your sponsor to deal with the problem. Some situations that may require sponsor assistance are:

- Arbitration and resolution for deliverables and inputs needed from other projects
- Escalations involving individual performance of cross-functional team members and other cross-organizational issues
- Decision making that is beyond your authority
- Settling differences of opinion that are blocking project progress
- Resolution of problems with outside contractors, suppliers, and partners

Set up a process with your sponsor for escalation (for use only after exhausting all other options). Get a formal commitment from your sponsor for a prompt response to escalations, a workday or two at most. Also ensure that authority for decisions is delegated to another manager (or to you) whenever your sponsor is unavailable because of business travel, vacation, or other absence.

Work with your sponsor to get a commitment to reject discretionary project changes. Your sponsor can say no to a wider range of proposed changes than you can; obtaining your sponsor's assistance in helping you to avoid unnecessary changes improves your overall ability to keep things on track. This request also helps you to close down one of the most common (and hard to manage) sources of unessential change: your sponsor. Especially for projects employing agile methods, gain agreement that all scope adjustment decisions will be based primarily on credible assessment of the value expected from the change, answering the question, "What's it worth?"

Ongoing protection of your project also requires ongoing visibility, so set up regular meetings to discuss the project status with your sponsor and provide frequent, high-level project summaries that are brief, easy to read, succinct, and to the point. (And did I mention short?)

Organizational Learning

A final area where sponsors can enhance your overall control is in providing support for process improvement, infrastructure modifications, and knowledge sharing. Commitments for setting up databases and other network repositories for organizational project data often exceed the capabilities of project leaders. Establishing facilities and better environments that support well-run, controllable projects may require higher-level sponsorship.

If your review of the infrastructure checklist in Appendix A, recommendations from your project start-up workshop, or other initial analysis raises issues requiring higher-level intervention, work with your sponsor to deal with them.

Another situation where sponsor action can be effective is in implementing recommendations made during earlier postproject retrospective analyses. If previous projects that you or your peers have completed have resulted in specific recommended changes related to control problems, raise them with your sponsor. Either get approval to make the changes or at least request permission to try a different approach. Also seek support from your sponsor to implement at least one recommended change that emerges from the postproject retrospective following your current project.

If you believe that better facilities or other major changes would afford improved control for projects throughout your organization over the long run, work through your sponsor to propose these ideas. If you are not initially successful, don't give up. Continue to collect information on the issues and plan to propose the changes again later on. Continue to work for changes that improve project control over time until they are accepted.

▪ Project Vision

There is a great deal of confusion—or at least lack of consistency—around a number of closely related project ideas. Purpose, mission, objective, vision, goal, and many other terms are used somewhat interchangeably to describe what a project is initiated to accomplish. It's useful to define these terms and make some distinctions.

Purpose is a durable part of the context for a project. Purpose is linked to organizational strategy and is shared by several, perhaps many, projects and other undertakings of your entire organization. Purpose changes slowly over time and is consistent with long-term organizational planning. Because retaining sponsorship depends on contributing to the broader goals that higher-level managers care about, controllable projects are well aligned with overall organizational purpose.

Missions, objectives, goals, and other tactical concepts relate to specific projects. These concepts describe what the project will accomplish and must be clearly and consistently defined for a project to be controllable. A project objective is best described in terms that are the same (or at least equivalent) for everyone involved, regardless of perspective. Clearly defining your overall project objective and scope is a central part of project launch (as discussed later in this chapter). Ongoing control of your project depends on managing all changes to the project objectives; change management is explored in Chapter 8.

All these concepts tend to be consistent for all team members, stakeholders, sponsors, and other project participants. The *vision* for the project may or may not be because it depends on perspective. Project vision is about why the project matters, and, although this could be the same for everyone, some aspects may be personal and unique for each individual. Creating a vision (or visions) that motivates members of your team and others you depend on is never mandatory and for short, straightforward projects the effort may not be justified. A clear objective and adequate sponsorship may be sufficient. However, for longer, more complicated projects, investing some time in "the vision thing" can be what differentiates a successful project that everyone cares about from a chaotic disaster. An inspiring project vision increases your influence, particularly during project initiation.

Projects are always difficult. They succeed because the project team cares about them and finds a way to get things done. An effective project vision that uses compelling, vivid language can help you build the commitment and perseverance you need, and it significantly assists you in controlling your project.

Value Analysis: Why Does This Project Matter?

One starting point for your project vision is your sponsor's reasons for undertaking the project. These probably include at least some broad description of the project's value. If project benefits from your sponsor's perspective are not obvious, start probing with questions such as, "What is the most important aspect of this project to you? How will things be better [or easier, or faster, or less complicated] when we are finished?" For projects undertaken for specific, known customers and uses, also ensure that you understand what *they* expect from the project. The value of a project is usually a direct consequence of why the project is being considered. Projects are initiated for a wide spectrum of reasons:

- To solve particular problems
- To respond to requests from customers or users
- To meet regulatory requirements or comply with industry standards
- To conform with organizational strategies and initiatives
- To save money or improve the performance of a business process
- To bring a product or service to market that will generate profit by meeting a perceived need
- To conduct research and exploit technical advances
- To pursue a business opportunity

Work to understand your sponsor's expectations for the project. Write down what you learn using your sponsor's words, and use active listening to paraphrase and validate what you hear. Your sponsor's motivations are the foundation for your overall project definition, and understanding the genesis of your project helps you uncover assumptions and constraints that you need to manage and control your project.

One Size Does Not Fit All

In some cases, a project vision based simply on what your sponsor or customer values is sufficiently compelling to you, to your team, and to others. But most of the time, what your sponsor values ("I will be able to run this organization with fewer people . . .") does not necessarily translate into a compelling project vision for everyone else. Sometimes you can develop an overall vision statement on your own, based on what you know about your team. In other cases, you may want to schedule some time, possibly during your project start-up workshop, to discuss the project with all the project contributors and to collect their input for a shared vision created by the entire team. Developing a vision on your own is probably faster, but it entails the risk that you may miss something, coming up with a vision that is not motivating, or worse, is demotivating. Developing a vision as a team requires some time, and some team members may resent or try to obstruct the effort, but, when done well, the process enhances trust, builds relationships, and improves cooperation. With very diverse teams, a single vision may not be feasible. You may need to develop a separate understanding of what individuals or subteams care about most.

However you proceed, your main goal is to make the ultimate success of the project align closely with the interests and concerns of your team members. Use the influencing skills from Chapter 3 to listen to your team members and to identify aspects of the project that support or connect to what they really care about. Seek words that people respond to with passion; get people excited. If your project team is incomplete or if you expect significant staffing changes during your project, discuss and revalidate the vision with new contributors as they become part of your team.

Confirm that the vision is consistent with the values of your team and your organization as a whole. Craft project vision statements that are brief, compelling, and easy to remember. Verify that you have a vision that passes the what's-in-it-for-me? test with each project contributor. Does your proposed vision inspire pride and the confidence of your team? To motivate, a vision must be accepted as credible. Is your vision statement realistic or at least plausible? Involving your team in discussing the vision and using it to build emotional buy-in for your project can substantially increase your control and influence.

GETTING THE PROGRAM GOALS RIGHT

Wayne Goulding worked for IBM for many years. When he was a beta test project manager for new hardware product releases, he faced a challenge. As a result of the consent decree mandated by the U.S. Department of Justice in the 1950s, IBM had operated for years with a strict separation of its software and hardware sales operations. IBM software product sales depended almost exclusively on the sale of IBM hardware. IBM hardware sales, however, hinged on the hardware's ability to run both IBM and third-party software. Although the software product managers had no vested interest in whether third-party software was compatible with new hardware, compatibility was very important for the hardware product managers and to IBM overall.

Wayne faced a significant constraint on his projects because his customer locations for beta tests had to be "true-blue"—that is, with no major third-party software packages. Many important customers were upset about this because they were forced to delay any deployment of new hardware until after all the relevant software vendors had an opportunity to run their tests, well after general availability of the new systems.

After hearing complaints about this for years, Wayne finally worked his way up to product launch program manager, and he was determined to fix this problem. The benefits of a fix were clear: It would remove a roadblock to early hardware sales, and it would facilitate a better structuring for the customer beta test program. Wayne had no authorization to work on this, however, and software organization told him that getting approval was impossible.

Wayne knew that he would get nowhere with a straightforward request, but he did know of something similar being done elsewhere in IBM. At the time, IBM was marketing a midsized system for which it supplied only the operating system; software development was totally open to vendor applications. To facilitate vendor testing, the product manager maintained an independent test center.

Wayne scheduled a day-long working meeting in Texas with the test center personnel, and he came away with a draft plan for support of third-party software testing. Wayne's idea was to set up a test center where any vendor could be given an isolated "virtual machine" set up for remote access. The test center would be funded by the vendors, but the IBM product manager would carry the cost of the IBM hardware/software. Test center personnel would be responsible for administering the program.

Wayne's next big challenge was to sell his plan. First were the attorneys, who needed to ensure that both the product and test center agreed with the concept and specific vendor agreements. Then it was on to the hardware product manager, who in turn moved it through the division president. Once the legal roadblocks had been removed by using an independent center and the others were in agreement, the software product manager no longer had any solid grounds for objection.

The initial implementation of Wayne's Independent Software Vendor Test Program was a hit. Five of the nine top software vendors participated, and for the first time the customers could see that IBM and the software vendors were working together for their benefit. Also, when new hardware was ready to ship, IBM could make a statement about a specific vendor software application's availability. From that point on, the hardware product launch process had been permanently changed.

Wayne concludes: "Sometimes even the best of us end up wearing blinders or don't stop long enough in the daily battles to ask whether where we are headed will get us where we need to be. The real challenge in this situation was that although the need was recognized, doing something about it seemed impossible. Overcoming resistance to do what is right takes courage and leadership, not authorization."

▪ Project Launch

With a sense of who wants the project and why, the project leader can begin defining a foundation for project control by documenting and defining the project. It would be useful if each new project emerged fully and clearly documented, and sometimes much of the information that you need is available in one form or another. Nonetheless, in the interest of control and communication, you should review and validate any available data to ensure that it is credible and appropriate through your own analysis. Careful review also uncovers any gaps so that you can work to fill them in. Some of the documentation

that you need to assemble for initial project communication are a project charter, project priorities, return on investment analysis, initial scoping, and project
staffing requirements.

Project Charter

Begin documenting your project by assembling available information. The process for project definition outlined in Chapter 2 is one of your most durable
tactics for control because it provides written information that you can use
throughout your project to keep things on track. The most common starting
point for initial project documentation is the information provided by your
sponsor or obtained through your interviews and discussion. Wherever you
obtain your information, work closely with your sponsor to verify and gain
support for your documents in order to maximize their weight and increase
their influence for controlling your project.

A project charter is one way to collect initial high-level project information. Because projects differ, even the name of this document varies, and in
some environments a comparable document may be called a project proposal,
definition document, project datasheet, system specification, plan of record, or
a statement of work.

Regardless of the name, format, or primary author, what matters most for
project control is that you capture initial project expectations in writing. Review
the information as you collect it, then validate that what you have written is
consistent with your sponsor's understanding.

Project Priorities

Documented priorities for your project help you assess trade-offs and develop
alternatives during project planning, minimize controversy over decisions
throughout the project, negotiate project changes, and support disciplined
change control for your project. The initial priorities that are part of the project
charter may or may not remain static throughout the project, but the initial
priorities are one part of the project charter that can provide leverage for influencing your sponsor. Too frequently, projects are undertaken with the sponsor
believing that any combination of scoping, time, and cost for a project can be
forced on a project leader and result in a commitment to a realistic project.
Setting priorities helps you to adjust your sponsor's expectations; it's your
chance to inform your sponsor that the initial objective may not necessarily
translate into a credible project baseline.

Setting priorities is equivalent to an old project management adage: "Fast,
cheap, good—pick two." For any given project, the triple constraint of time,
cost, and scope can be manipulated through trade-offs to conform to a wide

spectrum of possible projects. You do, however, need at least one degree of freedom available before you can start nailing down the other two parameters. Establishing and documenting priorities is an effective way to drive home to your sponsor and stakeholders that, if the deadline is firm and resources are limited, they may need to give a little on the deliverable.

Your objective in rank-ordering the parameters of the triple constraint is to determine which of the three is most critical to your sponsor and stakeholders. If you are unable to select one of the parameters using the information you have, discuss small two-way trade-offs with your sponsor to uncover preferences. Ask questions such as:

- Given the choice, would it be better to extend the project by several days or drop a feature expected in the deliverable?
- Would you prefer to add an additional staff member to this project or let the schedule slip slightly beyond the deadline?
- Would you consider a small increase to the project budget to protect the project scope?

Asking these questions early and setting credible expectations for your project is much better than having to deal with them in crisis mode late in your project.

As you explore the consequences, pain, and difficulties associated with small project changes, you begin to see the relative priorities emerge. If there is a lack of consensus among your sponsor(s) and stakeholders, initiate dialogue among them to determine which view prevails. (One colleague refers to this process as "getting all the liars in the same room.")

Document your project priorities using a three-by-three matrix. A number of formats are possible, but the message is most visible if the priorities are listed in the rows top to bottom, with each parameter of the triple constraint in a separate column, as in Figure 5-1. Place one mark in each row, showing which parameter has the highest, middle, and lowest priority for your project.

This matrix may be drawn in six ways, and each has implications for the control of your project. All three of the parameters are important to your project, and you bear the consequences of failing to meet any of them. One purpose of establishing the priorities, in addition to helping you dissuade management from prematurely constraining your project, is to reveal the relative severity of the consequences of failing to deliver on each parameter. If timing is the highest priority for your project, missing your deadline may well be career threatening. If the next priority is scope, failing to deliver part of the documented scope might be almost as dire. Failing to comply with even the lowest priority usually results in unpleasant consequences, but most of the time these are limited to verbal abuse. Project leaders tend to develop relatively thick skins, so the pros-

FIGURE 5-1. A PROJECT PRIORITY MATRIX

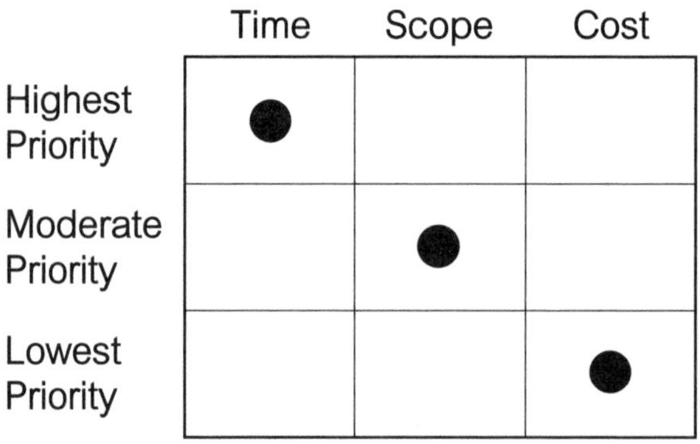

	Time	Scope	Cost
Highest Priority	●		
Moderate Priority		●	
Lowest Priority			●

pect of being yelled at for going a bit over budget in order to deliver on time is likely an acceptable outcome.

For projects using agile methods, project priorities may be considered somewhat differently, but the concept of prioritization remains. In place of scope, time, and cost, agile methods recommend using value, quality, and constraints. Value and quality are both tied to the deliverable and for most projects tend to be closely correlated. The main focus of agile projects is adjusting the scope incrementally using evaluation feedback and testing data from a succession of iterative releases. In most cases value assessment is generally given the highest priority. At the start of each successive development cycle, quality and constraints (including time and cost) are balanced against the estimated value of the features and requirements to be included in the next (and subsequent) delivery phases. Project leaders using agile methods focus on these trade-offs to make sound business decisions as their projects progress.

Keeping project priorities visible is an essential control tool. In general, whenever you find your project in difficulty, your maximum flexibility and first options to explore involve the project parameter with the lowest priority. Building a consensus early that the higher-priority parameters are more important makes it easier to avoid proposed project modifications that are in conflict with them. You can also be confident in making project decisions that protect the highest priorities, using your rank-ordered matrix to defend them.

Return on Investment Analysis

The use of predictive metrics was discussed in Chapter 4. In general, most predictive project metrics are plan based, and a number of them that are useful for project control are explored in the next chapter on project planning. The first predictive metric that you may encounter on many projects, however, involves a very early, high-level project *return on investment* (*ROI*) analysis that may have been completed even before you hear about your project.

Project ROI analysis requires two separate predictive metrics: monetary inflows and monetary outflows. All versions of ROI analysis contrast estimates of expected project benefits with preliminary cost estimates, jamming them together to derive a compound measurement showing project "goodness" that can be used to assess, compare, rank-order, and select from a portfolio of potential projects. Both of these estimates tend to be highly speculative and inaccurate, especially when the project analysis is done with no input from the project team. Because of optimism and initial project enthusiasm, benefit estimates are generally biased to be too high. Also because of optimism, coupled with a lack of information, there is a persistent bias in project cost estimates on the low side. These biases tend to be worse for very early estimates, resulting in initial ROI metrics that are unrealistic and inaccurate. Because of their prominence in many organizations, however, project leaders should be comfortable discussing ROI concepts. Influencing how the inputs are assembled and how ROI is used also helps you control your project.

Before getting too deep in the mechanics of ROI, a word about the incentives for gaming the metrics. Some incentives increase the biases inherent in the ROI process and result in less credible ROI measurements. When benefits are estimated generously and the costs are lowballed for your project, your project is more likely to be approved and funded in the first place. The higher the overall return is assessed to be, the more relative priority your project has, and this can increase your influence and organizational clout. However, when costs are significantly underestimated, your budget is likely to be set too low. With insufficient funding, you may face great difficulty finishing the work. Also, if the assessment is based on estimates of value that are impossible to realize, there is always the risk (admittedly infinitesimal, in most organizations) that someone will check later, and you will suffer the consequences of the shortfall.

As with metrics generally, in the long run the best course is to strive for accuracy for both benefits and costs. For this, you need to influence your managers and peers to strive for credible estimates (which, of course, everyone says they want to use anyway). Because early estimates for ROI are based on sparse data (or guesses), it is prudent to revisit ROI assessments for ongoing projects as better, more complete estimates become available. It is also always prudent to do a sanity check on ROI analysis using before-and-after results from recently completed projects to determine whether the information you are working with is in a realistic range.

In addition to monetary information, ROI depends on timing. There are a number of ways to combine the financial estimates and timing data, each with good and bad points. These ROI measures are calculated differently; although they all use essentially the same data, project comparisons using them can generate wildly varying results. Standard ROI calculation methods include simple payback, discounted payback, net present value, and internal rate of return.

Assessing Simple Payback

This is the easiest method for assessing ROI. It uses a running sum of costs and benefits (or returns or revenue), starting at the beginning of the project. It extends as far into the future as required for the accumulated costs (all negative cash flows from all the time periods estimated) to be balanced out by accumulated benefits (all positive cash flows for the same periods). This method for ROI is measured in months or years and provides an indication of how quickly a project pays for itself. Simple payback can be easily implemented in a spreadsheet application or even with pencil and paper.

Assessing Discounted Payback

This ROI method is similar to simple payback, but it introduces the time value of money. Future costs and benefits are discounted using an interest rate, and they affect the measure less and less the further out in the future they are. For example, if the annual interest rate used for discounting is 7 percent, a benefit one year in the future of $107 would balance a current cost of $100. Discounted payback, net present value, and internal rate of return all use a discount rate in evaluating cash flows, diminishing future values back to an equivalent present value using the formula:

$$PV = FV/(1 + i)^n$$

where PV is the present value, FV is the future value, i is the periodic interest rate, and n is the number of periods.

The discount rate used to assess discounted payback and net present value is often equivalent to a published interest rate, such as the rate at which your organization borrows money from a bank or pays on its bonds. The interest rate used for discounting is also sometimes set using your organization's goal for return on internal capital investments (which is what your project is, after all), which is generally a bit higher than the interest rate for borrowing.

Because project costs are up-front and project benefits generally do not begin until the project is completed a good deal later, the discounted payback period is always at least slightly longer than the simple payback period and is also measured in months or years.

Assessing Net Present Value

Probably the most common ROI calculation method, net present value (NPV) uses the same data as discounted payback analysis, but it also includes estimates following the project breakeven point. All expected future benefits over the life of the project deliverable are discounted back to the present, and from this all discounted project costs are deducted to give a single monetary measure. NPV can be assessed in dollars, euros, yen, or any currency.

Assessing Internal Rate of Return

The most complicated ROI metric, internal rate of return (IRR), is based on the same data as NPV, but it does not use an assumed discount rate to calculate the monetary value of the project. IRR forces the present value of each project to zero. IRR requires you to determine the interest rate needed to discount all the costs and benefits so that they balance exactly. For streams of cash flow that reverse multiple times, IRR assessment may not be unique; more than one interest rate might work. Because most projects are characterized by a stream of outlays followed by a stream of inflows, a unique IRR generally emerges. Before computers and financial calculators were widely available, IRR was not widely used because the iterative calculations used to determine the required interest rate were too tedious to make it worthwhile. Systems for assessing IRR are widely available today, and IRR is reported as a simple percentage.

Getting a Return on ROI

The assessment of a project's ROI using any of these metrics requires two series of estimates: costs for the duration of the project and returns through some or all of the expected useful life of the deliverable. The analysis required to do this well involves a good deal of effort. Even doing it poorly (which is more common) can be a lot of work. In many situations, ROI analysis on projects generates small overall benefits relative to its cost. If you have the option of avoiding extensive ROI analysis for your project, do so.

If you do not have a choice, at least strive to make the uncertainty in the input data visible and ensure that the resulting ROI (whichever version you use) is interpreted with this in mind. Early cost data, before any detailed planning is done, typically has error bars of at least ± 50 percent—mostly plus. Early estimates of financial return are based on sales projections or other speculative forecasts, and these are notoriously inaccurate for projects. Both of these arrays of estimates become even more unreliable as the amount of research and innovation required for the project increases. With this in mind, ROI analyses are most reasonably done using a number of scenarios that establish a range of possible results. One of your scenarios should be a worst case, including the highest potential costs and the lowest estimated benefits. Presenting an ROI as a range clearly communicates the level of uncertainty in the input data and can significantly improve decisions made using it. A project with a net present value of, say, "between $1.5 million and $5 million" reflects the actual precision of the ROI better than a deterministic-sounding NPV of "$4.57 million."

As projects progress, cost information improves because estimates for future project work are based on better planning data and the cost of completed work is known. Over time, you also develop greater certainty about the project completion date, and you can get additional feedback from users (or potential users) that increase your confidence in the benefit estimates. Revisiting all initial ROI assessments when you set the project baseline results in smaller ranges and a more realistic ROI for your project. On longer projects, subsequent periodic reassessment of ROI as part of a project review results in further convergence. All this helps you monitor trends and better manage project expectations.

ROI metrics are most accurate when the project is complete and you can do all the calculations using actual historical measurements. Validating ROI assessments retrospectively is one way to gauge the magnitude of your initial biases and improve your organization's processes for developing credible ROI information on new projects.

Each of the ROI calculation methods has both positive and negative aspects, summarized in Table 5-1.

Due to their differing assumptions, comparing or rank-ordering projects based on these metrics can vary widely. If your organization is using only one

TABLE 5-1. COMPARISONS OF ROI METRICS.

Metric	Positive Aspects	Negative Aspects
Simple Payback	• Easily calculated. • Retrospective auditing is straightforward and timely.	• Benefits beyond payback are ignored. • Favors short projects.
Discounted Payback	• Simple to calculate, more realistic than simple payback. • Easily audited.	• Benefits beyond payback are ignored. • Favors short projects.
Net Present Value	• Relatively easy to calculate. • Compares projects with differing time scales.	• Favors large projects. • Requires more estimates, further in the future. • Verification is not timely.
Internal Rate of Return	• Compares projects with differing sizes.	• Requires specialized financial calculations. • Requires more estimates, further in the future. • Verification is not timely.

method for ROI and it does not show your project in the best light, propose adding another metric to the analysis to your sponsor. You might also consider additionally calculating the other metrics (the same basic data is used for all of them) to find one that you can use to better illustrate your project's value.

Overall, focusing on the value of the project inherent in your vision is better than getting too wrapped up in financial ROI analysis. ROI information is never very motivating and, because it is difficult to ensure much accuracy, many people find it hard to take project ROI analysis very seriously. Many projects have justifications that are at least partially noneconomic, and some expected benefits are hard to assess in monetary terms. Projects that develop new technologies or invest in process or platform changes may have little direct benefit, but they are expected to establish foundations that generate value for an indeterminate number of future projects. Some projects are undertaken primarily to comply with legal or other mandatory requirements. If this type of indirect but nonetheless meaningful benefit is a significant factor for your project, work to ensure that it is not obscured by overemphasis on ROI analysis.

Initial Scoping

One of your most important objectives in initiating a project that you can control is to get an early, solid fix on what "done" looks like. Changes, particularly late-project changes, are the enemy of control. On most projects, much of what looks like change to you and to your project team is in reality overlooked scoping information that was available at the start of the project. To begin well, ask a lot of questions, be persistent, verify what you learn, and visibly document project scope. For your initial scoping, you need to define deliverables, verify requirements, test the limits, validate initial scoping, and get agreement on success criteria.

Defining Deliverables

If your project charter does not include a list of major project deliverables, develop one. Be as thorough as you can with your list. Brainstorm with your stakeholders, sponsor, and any team members already identified to what your project needs to produce or do. Your major deliverables list serves as the foundation for the project work breakdown structure, so whatever you fail to include can't be part of your plans. Whether you list something or not, if it is legitimately part of the reason you are taking on the project, you need to deal with it sooner or later. Knowing early and planning for the work is better than discovering things late and dealing with last-minute project crises. Even on projects undertaken using agile methods (where scope modifications are inevitable and expected), you must begin with as robust an accounting of the features expected to contribute to project value as possible. In addition to any obvious products, subassemblies, processes, services, or other deliverables, consider such deliverables as:

- Documentation (published materials, online references, and other written matter)
- Training materials and other instructional requirements
- Certification, legal, environmental, and standards compliance
- External testing needs
- Marketing or promotional collateral
- Deliverables that facilitate needed organizational changes
- Translation of written material into additional languages
- Mandatory deliverables required for your organization's life cycles or methodologies
- Logistical requirements for packaging, shipping, setup, installation, ongoing support, or other postrelease work

Develop a description for each listed deliverable or major feature to minimize the project's "fuzzy front end." For each item on your list, set completion criteria in clear and measurable terms, and specify how you plan to evaluate or test the deliverable on completion to ensure that it meets the criteria. For any deliverables that require external sign-offs or other approvals, identify the responsible individual. Document the prevailing expectations for timing and closure.

Refine your understanding of each deliverable using an *Is/Is not* list. For each deliverable, create a list with two columns, one headed "Is" and the other headed "Is not." Put all the mandatory requirements based on constraints or other imperatives into the *Is* column. If common practice for projects in your organization uses the idea of "musts and wants," all of the must requirements belong in the *Is* column. Wants are a significant enemy of project control, particularly for project leaders who lack much authority. As a starting point, list all of the wants, in the *Is not* column along with any other features and aspects of the project deliverables that are desirable but not mandatory. The *Is not* column is not for frivolous or silly requirements that no one would take seriously. It is for legitimate requirements that have value to at least some project stakeholders but that nonetheless are excluded from the current project. List these out-of-bounds requirements to set clear limits for the project and to permit you to better manage expectations and proposed changes throughout your project.

Candidates for the *Is not* list are:

- Specific things requested by users that seem inappropriately aggressive
- Lower-priority requirements that can be deferred to a subsequent project
- Items that have not been mentioned but that you anticipate might be later proposed as project changes
- Things that you or your team might wish to include that are not actually necessary, such as use of new technologies, processes, or equipment

Explicitly listing what you plan to exclude is a powerful use of communication. It often generates discussion and sometimes arguments. Some of the items you have provisionally excluded from your project may emerge as valid, high-priority requirements. When you lose an argument, the requirement moves over to the *Is* list. Items remaining on the *Is not* list remain firmly out of scope and provide you with a clear delineation between what is included and what is not, helping you maintain control throughout your project.

Even project leaders employing agile methods (for which later scoping adjustments and modifications are to be expected) find setting concrete boundaries on scope to be helpful in controlling project duration, budgets, and overall expectations.

Verifying Requirements

As part of your scoping, review the requirements until you know what you need to know to begin your project. For your defined deliverables, assess what you know about:

- Documented market analysis, verified user needs, or explicit customer agreements
- Regulatory, environmental, legal, and standards requirements
- Specific local requirements for deliverables in each place where they will be used
- Analysis of any other project options and competitive alternatives
- Core competencies and specific skills needed
- Availability of adequate project staffing
- Logistical requirements related to distribution, installation, delivery, and support
- Alignment of your project's objectives with overall organizational strategy
- Dependability and credibility of project finances
- High-level project risks
- Cross-functional dependencies and interfaces with other projects

Document what you know, and especially what you do not know, in each of these areas. Work with your sponsor and team to resolve the gaps that you discover. Take note of any missing information, and define activities for your project to deal with them. Identify all gaps you are unable to resolve, and note them as risks. What you do *not* know about your project can, and likely will, hurt you.

Testing the Limits

Initial scoping also involves reviewing and testing project constraints and assumptions. Not every identified constraint is necessarily a hard-and-fast requirement; some may be sponsor preferences, desired goals, or otherwise not really essential to the success of your project. When you probe into project assumptions, you are likely to find a number that may be relaxed, making your project more straightforward. Retaining a healthy skepticism and asking lots of questions is a great way to enhance both your project understanding and control. In the following list are some questions that can be useful for uncovering what your sponsor, customer, users, and other key project stakeholders feel most strongly about. Documenting what you learn and using it to refine the scoping for your project minimize fuzzy definitions and help you to avoid excessive changes later in the project.

- Is each requirement defined in terms that make the business problem or issue clear? (Restate any requirements that are simply summaries of a technical solution, with no indication of why.)
- Are all improvement requirements (such as performance, throughput, or efficiency) quantified? What is the present baseline, and why does the particular improvement goal matter?
- What are the ramifications of failing to fully meet a requirement? What portion of the expected value is lost if a project requirement is largely, but not entirely, achieved?
- What is the basis for the expected benefits associated with each project deliverable?
- How was the value estimated? How uncertain are the estimates, and what are the lowest and highest limits for the range?
- What additional value, if any, could be realized by exceeding any of the project requirements?
- How certain are the project assumptions? What are they based on? What are the consequences of small changes to any of them?
- If any project data seems unrealistic, where did it come from? Can you verify the information source?
- Are the requirements identified sufficient? Are potential failure modes

for the project related to possible missing requirements? Can they be safely excluded?

Validating Initial Scoping and Getting Agreement on Success Criteria

Gather your data in a high-level scope document that includes the information on all project deliverables, such as:

- Specific functions included, with reasons
- A summary of what *Is not* included
- User and interface needs
- Quantitative performance and reliability requirements
- Documentation, training, support, and any other postdelivery needs
- Acceptance tests information, including who is responsible for assessing and approving the results

Review the initial scoping with your project sponsor, customer, users, and other stakeholders as appropriate. Explain your documentation to defend what it contains when issues arise. Request and get explicit agreement that the initial scoping, when delivered as documented, represents a basis for a successful project. When necessary, modify your project scoping as appropriate to reach consensus with your sponsor and key stakeholders. Finalize the document, and communicate the detailed output objectives for your project.

Make it clear to everyone that this remains a goal, not a commitment. Scoping commitments may require modification based on project planning; further adjustments to the initial scoping may be necessary.

Project Staffing

Following your analysis of preliminary scoping (or in parallel with it), confirm your project staffing. Particularly for project leaders who do not directly manage the contributors on the project team, early identification and commitments for staffing are essential to project control.

Collect information about anyone who's already assigned to your project, Begin developing a staff roster to summarize contact information and other data. Most initial project team members are probably part of your core team and assigned primarily to your project, but your roster may also include others. Extended team members often have other responsibilities in addition to your project, and these contributors often pose significant control problems for a project leader with limited authority.

Use your project objective and scoping information to assess whether your committed staffing seems adequate for the project. Compare the skills on your existing team with the core competencies required by your initial scoping. Do a rough estimate of the number of project contributors needed for the required project roles and skill areas. Assess the overall effort that your committed project staff can supply. Inquire about anticipated time off and other commitments, and use realistic estimates. Be skeptical about the level of effort your extended team members can provide, and ask about the relative priority of your project compared with other responsibilities. Update your project roster with assigned roles that meet your staffing requirements, identifying the members of your initial team with appropriate experience and talents to take on those responsibilities.

Use this high-level analysis to identify any skill gaps or resource shortfalls; then promptly begin to work with your sponsor to locate people to resolve project staffing issues. Be clear with your sponsor about the consequences of inadequate staffing. Options for resolving project staffing issues are:

- Arranging for more time from extended project team members
- Acquiring additional staff from within the organization
- Hiring new permanent staff for the project
- Contracting for outside help
- Training existing team members to develop unavailable skills
- Changing project scope or timing to be consistent with available staffing
- Planning for overtime work by project team members (even a small dependence on this option is risky, and it diminishes your overall control)

Develop a plan to resolve the staffing issues as early in your project as possible. Be realistic about acquiring new or outside resources; getting approvals to hire or outsource can be time-consuming, and finding and adding the right people takes a lot of effort. Learning curve issues and reduced initial productivity are also factors.

Note any staffing issues you are unable to resolve with your sponsor as risks, and integrate them into your overall project risk planning.

Project work is always best done with teams of modest size, generally with ten or fewer contributors. Larger teams involve more overhead, impede relationship building and teamwork, and pose communications challenges. If your core project team is substantially larger than about a dozen people, begin considering options for subdividing it into logical subteams, each with an assigned team leader.

Use your roster to visibly identify all formal staffing commitments to your project. Once a name is added and published, the membership is real, and you can begin to build trust and good relationships with each person that you need to control your project. As you add team members, start working to learn about their personal desires and goals. Use discussions with your team members to help you secure firm, unambiguous commitments to your project.

USING COMMITMENT FOR PROJECT SUCCESS TO OVERCOME A LACK OF AUTHORITY

When Alfonso Bucero was assigned as a project manager to the General Treasury of Spanish Social Security in Spain, he learned a lot about the power of commitment. Although he was the assigned project manager, he did not have much authority for the overall project because of the structure of the project and his Hewlett-Packard project delivery organization in Spain. Alfonso was very committed to the project's success, though, and ultimately found a way to be successful.

Alfonso's project was complex, both organizationally and technically. The Data Collection Center (CENDAR) for the General Treasury of Spanish Social Security wanted to modernize the manual data entry process used to process the tremendous volume of documents—about 2 million pages per month—that were used to track and control the contributions made by employees and companies for Social Security in Spain. Increasingly, CENDAR was finding it impossible to keep up with the volume. They needed a system that would eliminate the massive flow of paper and allow for the electronic processing and storage of all the forms. They wanted a very advanced electronic document and image management system to digitize, store, and process all the forms. CENDAR published a public tender soliciting proposals, and ultimately engaged HP and Alfonso's team to implement the project.

At the beginning of the project, Alfonso made many long journeys to meet with all the members of his team. Although he lacked much formal authority, his team was relatively young (25–30 years old), and they were enthusiastic and ready to learn. He worked hard to bring together all the HP and CENDAR project team members to document a clear project definition and objectives. Effective teamwork between the customer and the HP team resulted in commitments that were fundamental to meeting the client's requirements on time, within budget, and with the expected quality level.

Further good cooperation during the solution design and implementation phases between CENDAR professionals and HP gave the customer the state-of-the-art document management system they needed. Alfonso says, "The team I created and managed in this project taught me that when all involved work together effectively, everyone achieves more." From the start of his project, Alfonso built good teamwork. Doing so was not easy because the people came from many different organizations, and they had different cultures and expectations. He believed in the project, however, and his actions support the themes of this book. Alfonso's main elements for creating a good team environment are:

- Encourage open communication and build trust.
- Address team needs, and understand that not all team members have the same needs.
- Value team members' contributions, and provide them with feedback.
- Enhance motivation through challenges and self-development.
- Recognize and reward good performance.
- Discourage criticism, and remain positive.
- Negotiate to achieve a win/win situation.
- Manage your time and your commitments.
- Involve individual team members in goal setting, decision making, planning, and risk assessment.

▪ Start-Up Workshops

There are many similar names for this event, such as project launch, Sprint planning meeting, kickoff, project planning workshop, and project initiation meeting. Whatever you choose to call it, a project start-up workshop serves to build teamwork and to establish a solid, shared understanding of what the project is about. Both the influence and control aspects of a well-run start-up workshop are substantial.

The workshop can be scheduled anytime after staffing is set and the project objectives are stated. The most common times are during project initiation, when the focus is on initial planning and team building, and toward the end of planning, when the main objectives are a shared understanding of the project baseline and integrating any new staff members into the team who will contribute to project execution. With some projects, conducting both types of project start-up workshops is useful.

Justifying the Start-Up Workshop

Workshops are most valuable when you can involve everyone on your project team in a face-to-face meeting. The most effective ones are conducted in a location that minimizes distractions and interruptions, and where sufficient time is allocated to fully discuss project information and issues. Project start-up workshops enhance your control through:

- Building relationships and trust among team members
- Building a common understanding of the project
- Establishing shared processes and terminology
- Discussing and resolving conflicts and differences among project team members
- Clarifying roles and responsibilities
- Collaborating on project planning
- Getting strong team member buy-in and commitment to the project

Despite their value, requests to hold project start-up workshops often meet with resistance. They take time, consume money and other resources, and can be difficult to coordinate and schedule. Face-to-face workshops require travel by nonlocal team members. These factors are real and must be dealt with if they become barriers to your conducting a start-up workshop.

Project contributors who claim to be too busy need to understand that the time invested is one of the best ways to deal with today's extreme time pressures. The common direction and coherent information developed in the workshop are essential for avoiding unnecessary or redundant effort and project rework. The productivity of a focused project start-up also produces a lot of results in a very short time. Most people are surprised at how much work a group can accomplish during a start-up workshop.

For sponsors who need to approve the expense and travel, the same points can be made. Overall, projects that begin well and that minimize execution problems reduce project budgets and finish more quickly. Build the business case for your workshop, and get approval from your sponsor to conduct one that is as effective as possible. The trade-off is simple: Pay a little now, or risk paying a lot later.

Traveling time, coordination, and scheduling issues are usually excuses raised by people who do not see much value in a project start-up workshop. People make time and go anywhere to take part in activities that are important to them; gaining a commitment to participate is largely about setting up a meaningful agenda and communicating the value of the workshop.

Sometimes you need to compromise on how—but never whether—you conduct your project start-up workshop. If you can't arrange a face-to-face gathering, hold your workshop via videoconference or teleconference. The important thing is to do it, using the most effective means available.

Run an Effective Workshop

Whatever the length of your project start-up workshop, define a detailed agenda. Focus the agenda on reviewing project information and appropriate planning activities, and be sure to include time for team and relationship building.

Invite your core project team and others you want to participate. Adjust the timing if necessary to confirm that all will attend. Prior to the workshop, distribute all pre-meeting materials and provide ample time for review. Arrange for adequate space to meet, off-site when possible to minimize interruptions. Prepare for the meeting well, as it sets expectations for your whole project.

When possible, get your sponsor to begin the workshop, welcome participants, and reinforce your role and the value of the project. As you begin, have each participant describe their role in the project and encourage people to interact and get to know each other. Also discuss the project's vision and why this project matters. A credible, shared project vision will draw the team together and is a very powerful tool for any project leader who lacks authority.

Use the bulk of your time to focus on the project's facts and figures, drilling into the objective, charter, scoping, major deliverables, and initial planning information. Capture workshop information as you go, and keep all notes visible. Collaborative reviews and planning activities will involve your team members and begin to convert an initial perception that the project is "yours" into the more desirable state where it is "ours." This interaction also builds the ownership and buy-in that project leaders with low authority depend upon. Projects succeed because the people who work on them care, and collaboration and open discussion lead to caring.

Another of your goals is a deep understanding of the project. Work to establish a consistent understanding of the project documents, and if time allows, begin to develop detailed planning deliverables (discussed in the next chapter), such as the project work breakdown structure, prioritized lists of features, stories, and capabilities for agile delivery, activity estimates, dependencies, and identified risks. Though you will not likely be able to complete all project planning in a typical start-up workshop, it is particularly beneficial for distributed teams who will be unable to meet face-to-face later in the project to start building a solid foundation for subsequent planning while everyone is together.

Confirming Roles

Another key portion of the workshop agenda focuses on roles and responsibilities. Detailed planning (discussed in the next chapter) includes setting individual goals and assigning ownership for all defined project activities. During the project start-up workshop, you can get a head start by beginning to delegate and identify who will be responsible for project deliverables, processes, and other requirements.

One technique, which goes by the acronym RACI, uses a two-dimensional matrix and codes for assigning individuals specific roles for project work or decisions. Responsibilities are listed in the first column of the matrix, one per row. You and the members of your project team are listed across the top, one per column. Codes defining all team member roles are added to the cells where the activities and individuals intersect. *RACI* stands for:

- *Responsible.* A responsible party makes a commitment to do the work.
- *Accountable.* The accountable party has the ultimate decision authority and bears any consequences related to the objectives. There can only be one A, and this role may be combined with R.
- *Consulted.* Any stakeholder is consulted who could participate in planning and decision making.
- *Informed.* Informed parties are regularly provided status on progress, decisions, and other information to coordinate related work and facilitate collaboration.

One reason to use a RACI chart is to delegate ownership and make responsibilities visible, which is important for motivation. Meaningful involvement of any sort reinforces connections and teamwork, though, so this process is essential for projects where the leader lacks formal authority.

During your project start-up workshop, develop a RACI chart to record roles for high-level project responsibilities such as quality management, risk analysis, training, systems management, project metrics, vendor liaison, communications, testing, and sign-off. When you complete the matrix and document it for posterity, populate the cells with the complete terms, not just a single letter, or at least incorporate a legend and definitions to minimize potential confusion by casual readers.

DOING THE PAPERWORK

The DACI model is similar to RACI, and it has an equivalent purpose. The letters stand for *driver, approver, contributor,* and *informed.* The DACI model is used at Intuit, Inc. and is effective there even for fairly small projects. Scott Beth, a senior manager with Intuit, tells this story about starting a project to converting Intuit's paper stock to recycled paper:

"After initial discussions with the sourcing manager for office and paper supplies, I asked her, 'Who's the Driver for this project?' She wasn't sure, and we realized there really was no owner for that area. I agreed to be the Approver and to be accountable for the decision to convert to recycled paper. After discussing this, I asked the sourcing manager to be the Driver, to own the responsibility for making this change. We set up milestones for reviewing progress. When we clarified the DACI for the project, we immediately started making progress and easily met all the timing and expense goals for converting to recycled paper. Defining roles and responsibilities, especially in writing, is a very effective way to secure the reliable commitments that you need to depend on to control any project."

Having Some Fun

Structure some workshop activities to have people work together in pairs or in small groups to facilitate team building. Even during shorter project start-up workshops, include at least one opportunity to engage in a suitable team-building activity. During longer workshops, activities such as a low-impact sporting event can be an effective option. (A program manager I once worked with organized a bocce match; we had a great time, and it brought the team together, even though none of us were any good at it.) Another possibility for interaction is a meal at a restaurant, providing an opportunity for people to converse and get to know one another. Even during a half-day workshop, you can set up some game or activity that gets people moving and informally interacting with one other. Have some fun during the workshop. Rarely do people become best friends in a single meeting, but that isn't the point. It's enough for people to begin to know, trust, and respect each other (and you), and to ensure that they don't become adversaries.

Capturing Issues and Closing the Workshop

The final part of the agenda is to close the workshop. As the workshop progresses, capture all the action items requiring follow-up on a posted piece of flipchart paper, on a whiteboard, or in some other visible place. At the end of the workshop, collect all the items requiring follow-up, and get owners to volunteer to manage each one and commit to an appropriate completion date. Collect final impressions, and complete the workshop on time. Strive to end on a high note, and thank all the participants for their contributions.

Following Up After the Workshop

Document the results and distribute the information to your team. In general, doing this quickly is better than spending a great deal of time making all the documents look perfect. Strive for accuracy, but get the workshop documents out to all participants and stakeholders as soon as possible. If you have captured most of the workshop information on a computer, much of it can be distributed immediately after the workshop.

Update your project management information system too, with all the project documentation that you have changed, and enter all the information you created during the workshop.

Set up time with your sponsor to discuss the results of your start-up workshop. If you generated any proposals to modify the project charter, initial scoping, or any other information you developed with your sponsor or stakeholders, schedule extra time to discuss and validate the changes.

Finally, follow up on any workshop items that you were unable to finish, and track each captured action item to completion. The initial progress you made in the workshop should carry forward into your overall project planning process.

THE 90-DAY MIRACLE

Richard Simonds, who was for many years an experienced project leader at Hewlett-Packard, shares the story of the role a project start-up workshop played in a particularly difficult project he faced:

"I was asked by my general manager to prepare a training guide for field engineers who would sell and support one of the division's soon-to-be-released products. As usual, no one on the development team had given this any thought. The new and complex product was scheduled to go to market in just three months."

Richard agreed to take on this aggressive, time-constrained project, but only after gaining a strong, high-level support commitment from his general manager. His first action was to clearly define the scope and to gain commitments for the project from eight key team members (and from their managers). This team spanned 18 time zones, from Europe to Asia, and none of the project team members was dedicated solely to this project; they all had to do it on top of their regular, full-time responsibilities. He immediately arranged for a project start-up workshop and brought all eight team members to the division's headquarters. He distributed information about the project, the workshop agenda, and other project documents in advance so that the team would arrive well prepared.

"Over the course of the three very long days we were together, we worked very hard to identify all the key elements of the project and agree on the specific assignments for each team member. We also decided how I would coordinate project activities and stay on top of progress for the eighty days we had left until the deadline. Despite the challenges of a globally dispersed team with competing commitments, the relationships and solid project planning resulting from the project start-up workshop enabled us to bring the project in on time and under budget."

At the end of the project, the division general manager called it the

90-day miracle. Richard's team had not only delivered the training guide as requested. They had also developed a training workshop to ensure that everything would be in place for the product release. The initially aggressive goal of a well-trained sales and support organization was easily met, and in the end the entire team was recognized for exemplary performance on this crash program. "The results would not have been realistic or even possible without the project start-up workshop," he concludes. "It reinforced the project's strong sponsorship, gained the commitment of the project team [and their managers], and gave me the personal leverage to be a bulldog in managing the established baseline schedule and project scope."

▪ Projects with Cross-Functional, Distributed, and Global Team Members

Initiating a project with a team made up of people from different functions or from different locations entails additional challenges. Such teams are a main reason why project leaders lack authority over their team members; managing these challenges is crucial for project success. This section contains general ideas to help you, as well as specific advice for running a long-distance project start-up workshop.

Establishing Your Team

Most of the advice for managing a *matrix team* (where contributors report in effect to more than one manager) applies, whether the team is cross-functional, multidisciplinary, distributed, or global. Initiating an effective team in these environments requires you to develop as much influence within your team as possible (as outlined in Chapter 3). Building influence, particularly with distant team members, takes a good deal of extra effort, but it pays off—and it can be the biggest difference between a well-controlled, successful project and a global, cross-functional disaster. Here are some specific ideas for increasing your influence at the start of a project:

- Identify and build on shared personal backgrounds, such as interests, hobbies, and experiences.
- Find specific, personal reasons why a successful project is important to each of your team members.
- Share pictures of distant team members, preferably pictures outside the work environment, to let people see what team members look like. (For digital pictures, reduce the file size before sending when necessary.)

- Put additional effort into informal communications. Be willing to make calls and hold meetings at times that are convenient for your team members.
- Communicate inclusively, minimizing jargon, acronyms, confusing technical language, local idioms, unusual figures of speech, and other sources of potential confusion for cross-functional teams.
- Be persistent in all communications, and always maintain a friendly tone.
- Experiment with a number of communication styles to determine what works best for individual team members.
- Reread all written communications, particularly to team members with a different native language, to ensure that what you are sending is as clear and unambiguous as possible.
- Promptly follow up conversations with written summaries and meetings with minutes.
- Follow up on complicated written materials that you distribute with at least a telephone call to verify that they have been received, read, and are not confusing.
- Whenever necessary to avoid confusion, provide translations of all project documentation into the native languages of your team members.
- Build on any past working relationships, especially previous work with your team members on successful projects.
- Discover and take advantage of personal relationships with mutually respected colleagues that you have in common with your contributors.
- Name your team, and create a shared identity.
- Reinforce team identity by using a dedicated project "war room" for a co-located team or a team Web site for a distributed team.
- Do whatever you can to bring people together for a face-to-face project start-up workshop. If distant team members are unable to travel to meet with you but you are able to travel to them, do it.
- Seek additional sponsorship for your project from the functions and locations of your team members. (Managing multiple sponsors can be tricky, but it may be necessary to influence some team members.)
- Praise each team member's specific talents and the pivotal contribution each person makes to your project.
- Personally thank team members frequently for their contributions, and copy their managers on all your communications, expressing gratitude.
- Be unflaggingly loyal to your team members, and avoid all public criticism. Keep negative feedback one on one or within your team, involving individuals' managers only as a last resort.

- Find and use all available programs for formal rewards and recognition for each of your team members.
- Get strong buy-in for collaborative planning, and always be persistent in getting each person's input and feedback.

GETTING THE PROGRAM OFF ON THE WRONG FOOT

Craig Chatterton has managed large international projects on a fee-for-service contract basis and worked in India for many years. On one large systems integration program, he found the technology was complex and the requirements (as usual) somewhat ambiguous, but these were not his biggest challenges.

He had no authority over the customer. However, because they represented another large company similar to Craig's, he believed that they held similar values. He assumed that the other company would operate in similar ways and create few problems, but unfortunately this was not the case. The incentives, culture, and politics were in fact very different and created very difficult dynamics and conflict. Within a single organization, such differences can often be bridged by common management and workarounds, but, when working with an outside company on a contract basis, you don't have those options.

Craig learned a valuable lesson and says, "Never assume others hold the same values and operate in the same way as you do. Incorrect assumptions here can do your project in. I'm not sure how things would have turned out had we known this in advance, but we would certainly have done some things very differently."

In the end, the project fell apart. Underestimating the impact of working approach differences across organizations can be disastrous.

Conducting a Long-Distance Project Start-Up Workshop

If you cannot arrange a face-to-face workshop for all the members of your team, use the best meeting technology available to you to accomplish as many of the same goals as possible. You can't use a teleconference to build the level of relationships and trust that you can establish in person, but you should be able to adequately achieve most of the goals related to project understanding.

Set up one or more short meetings with your team, each no longer than two or three hours. Longer technology-based meetings can be boring and unproductive, and shorter meetings help to minimize time-zone problems. Use the best technical tools for long-distance meetings that you have access to: videoconferencing, telephone conferencing, computer network presentation-sharing software, server-based file storage systems, and anything else you can think of. Before initial meetings, check that all the locations involved have access to compatible equipment and software. Also, resolve all access and security issues in advance, especially for participating contributors who are external to your organization.

Check that all of your team members have up-to-date versions of all the applications needed to open all documents that you attach to e-mails or save on network servers. Distribute all workshop materials well in advance of the meetings, and verify that each person has received them. Avoid the use of any networking or conferencing techniques that require a lot of bandwidth if part of your team has limited or low-speed network access.

Structure the agenda for a multipart workshop to take advantage of the time between meeting sessions for offline work. Plan for small co-located subteams or individuals to do follow-up work from earlier sessions or to prepare for the next session. Schedule the workshop segments no more than several days apart to maintain continuity. Personally contact all participants for your workshop to confirm their commitment to attend each scheduled portion of the workshop. Request that all of your team members focus full attention on the workshop during the sessions, and get acknowledgment from each of them that they will not answer e-mails, work on other tasks, or engage in recreational Web surfing during the meeting.

As preparation, assign pairs of team members who do not know each other to get in contact, and do interviews so that they can introduce the other person at the start of the meeting. Challenge each person to discover at least one interesting fact about the other person to include in the introduction. If you do not have videoconferencing available, collect a photograph of each team member to distribute before the first session or to present over the network during introductions.

Even if your project start-up workshop is not face-to-face, take full advantage of opportunities to visit and work in person with distant team members in follow-up activities or planning.

LOST IN TRANSLATION

The Pacific Ocean is immense, but not all of the distance between the western United States and Asia is geographical. Ted Slater has managed a number of complex projects involving contributors in Japan and elsewhere in Asia for Hewlett-Packard over the past several years. Before he started spending much time there, he saw the film *Lost in Translation* when it was newly released. At that time he didn't find it very funny at all. Not long ago on a business trip to Tokyo, though, Ted happened to catch it on late-night TV while he was struggling with jet lag and found himself laughing uncontrollably.

Ted learned that, for his projects to be effective, he had to meet face-to-face with the members of the core team to understand issues from their perspective. On a particularly large project, Ted used what he learned in his initial onsite meetings to convince his management to assign a technical project leader located in Hong Kong for the duration and to budget for travel so that he could participate in face-to-face meetings every six weeks in both Tokyo and Singapore. He found that he had to work hard to convince the worldwide and regional managers who were to be involved that deployment was a high priority. He did this by creating a sense of urgency by offering to provide full worldwide team support for aggressive migration following the planned release (and by helping them to understand that later migration would depend on just their own local support).

Ted describes one particularly memorable three-hour meeting in Japan: "I started the meeting with my ten-minute presentation. I then waited while the local team discussed this in Japanese. They were slowly building consensus (or so I hoped, anyway). About every 30 minutes things would quiet down and someone would turn to us and say 'Yes' or 'Okay,' but adding no other explanation. The discussions would then continue, and ultimately I secured the agreements and commitments for the project."

In working internationally, Ted has learned that patience is a virtue and that you need to interact with distant team members one-on-one as frequently as possible.

KEY IDEAS FOR PROJECT INITIATION

- Secure commitments from your sponsor for ongoing support, and begin to establish a good relationship.
- Develop a compelling project vision, and fine-tune it as needed to inspire and motivate your team.
- Thoroughly understand your objectives, and document your project charter.
- Conduct an effective project start-up workshop to get your project off to a healthy start.
- Put extra effort into building relationships and trust with your team members in distant locations.

CHAPTER 6

Building Control Through Project Planning

PROJECT INITIATION FOCUSES on where your project is going. Creating the plan for your project forces you to figure out how you are going to get there, giving you a foundation for tracking. Project planning contributes more to your overall control than just a baseline for monitoring. Planning is a collaborative process that establishes buy-in and ownership of project work and motivates your whole project team. A credible plan shows that your project is, in fact, possible. Lacking a plan, expectations for the project are based on hopes and dreams—not good foundations for building confidence or control. Your plan also provides you with predictive metrics that give you negotiating leverage with stakeholders and sponsors when your project faces unrealistic objectives.

▪ Plan Collaboratively

For project leaders who lack substantial authority, an important objective of collaborative planning is a common, shared, and coherent understanding of the work required to complete the project or, for projects using agile methods, through the next several cycles of iterative development. Collaborative planning is important on any project, but it is crucial for project leaders who do not directly manage their staff. Independent team members are much less likely to cooperate with your requests when they don't understand them or agree with them. Developing the plan as a team ensures that all the necessary commitments are based, at least in part, on choices and decisions that have been made by the contributors themselves.

Collaborative project planning builds on the project charter, initial scoping, and other documentation outlined in Chapter 5. Where initiation focuses primarily on what the project is expected to look like from the outside, planning is about seeing the project's structure and logic from the inside. This chapter's discussion is not intended to be a reiteration of project planning processes; many other books and sources describe basic planning (such as *The Project Management Tool Kit* mentioned in Appendix B). As discussed in Chapter 2, planning is a critical process for project control. Project control depends on the clear definition of the practices and methods you intend to use and on gaining support for them up front from both your sponsor and your team.

Certain planning concepts are particularly useful for increasing your influence and control. These include:

- Project infrastructure
- Breaking down the work with your team
- Individual goals and responsibilities
- Collaborative estimating
- Outsourced activities
- Interface management
- Constraints and plan optimization
- Risk identification and assessment
- Plan review

Much of this planning can be incorporated, at least for small projects, into your project start-up workshop agenda, as discussed in Chapter 5. Even for large projects, you can at least begin your collaborative planning during the workshop. If the project start-up workshop is your only opportunity to work with your team face-to-face, build the strongest case possible to lengthen the workshop and incorporate most of your planning effort into the agenda.

GETTING EVERYONE HEADED IN THE SAME DIRECTION

To underscore the importance of collaborative planning on cross-functional teams, Al DeLucia, who recently retired as the director of the Project Management Division for the U.S. Government General Services Administration (GSA) in Philadelphia, tells of a particularly challenging project he led. GSA's mission is to find and provide appropriate space for federal government "customer" agencies. This project involved establishing a new headquarters for an agency that would consolidate many functions from leased space in a number of dispersed locations into one integrated facility. Al explains:

> A cross-functional project team was created using resources from GSA and representatives from the customer agency. I was assigned the official role leading the 'source selection' process of choosing a developer. Unofficially, however, I was assigned because much animosity had developed among team members early on. This animosity was the consequence of a long history of distrust between the customer agency and GSA over the previous leased space. The team had become polarized, stalling important decisions that needed to be made to move the project forward on schedule. The customer agency kept 'gold plating' their requirements because they didn't trust the judgment of the GSA people.
>
> My job was to break this deadlock. I had recently read Jon Katzenbach's *The Wisdom of Teams* and remembered his assertion that team development requires that members work on something 'real' together. So, as a source selection official, I required the team to attend a five-day source selection training session at an off-site facility. The trainer was asked to use our project as the case study for the training, with the goal of producing the actual source selection plan.

The first day of the training, hostility was very much in evidence. Team members were reticent, and conversations were strained. Day by day, however, as the training progressed and the team worked side by side on the plan, tensions drained, people relaxed, and they began working together more and more constructively. Team spirit was bolstered even more by going out for drinks and dinner each evening. "By the end of the week," Al says, "we had a good plan that everyone had bought into, and a healthy, functioning team."

The spirit of the planning session was maintained by setting up a war room for the remainder of the project, outfitting vacant space nearby with necessary equipment and desks for each team member. "Although team members retained other workload, they were directed to work on this project in the war room and to keep all documents related to the project there," Al explains. "In this way, security and confidentiality during the source selection process were maintained, but the clear overriding benefit was the relationships established by team members by the close proximity afforded by the war room." The team posted pictures and personal items around the space in addition to the project-related materials on the walls, and it became "their" room, where they ended up spending a good percentage of their time working, talking, and just hanging out, even after hours.

"In the end," Al reports, "the project proved very successful, and team members remain friends to this day—a result of having participated together on a high-performing team."

Project Infrastructure

As the story illustrates, the environment for a project is an important place to begin establishing control for your project. Start with a quick review of post-project lessons learned from recently completed projects and your own experiences to identify problems, issues, and barriers that you may face. With your team, consider these factors and review a list of project decisions, such as the one in Appendix A. Assemble a short list of decisions from the list (or develop your own questions) by focusing on recent project problems or on specifics of your current project that you are concerned about.

Collect options and ideas from each contributor for the questions you need to answer, and discuss how you all think it would be best to run the project. Work for consensus and document the decisions as you make them. If your team is unable to reach agreement on a single approach in a reasonable time, either propose what you prefer as a way to operate (at least provisionally), skip the decision, or, as a last resort, escalate crucial decisions for resolution.

Consensus decisions on infrastructure questions are a powerful tool for project control because you can rely on what your team decided, instead of your personal authority, to back up your requests. Even if you are not successful in reaching consensus on an issue, the discussion reveals things that you need to watch out for and individuals with whom you may have difficulty. Forewarned is forearmed.

Make your infrastructure decisions visible to your stakeholders and to others involved in your project. Plan to review these decisions periodically, especially on longer projects, to keep them visible and up-to-date.

Breaking Down the Work with Your Team

A project work breakdown structure (WBS) is essentially the equivalent of a to-do list for your project. This may be called different things depending on the project type: a task list for simple, short projects, an iteration-oriented "burn down" chart when using agile methods, or functional work packages assignments for a military/defense program. A formal WBS differs from a simple list of activities in that it is organized into a hierarchy that makes the complexity of a typical project easier to understand and to deal with. A project WBS is best developed by a team that includes a wide spectrum of perspectives—the more the better for surfacing bits of essential work that may not be obvious to all. Whenver possible, include people who are not yet involved in your project but will participate later, or involve others who can represent their viewpoints. Also involve customers and users when you can, or at least people who thoroughly understand them. Control of your project demands that you get the WBS right as soon as is practical.

The top level of a project WBS is a single item, which is the entire project. The next level contains subdivisions of the project that can be aggregated to describe the project's work. Each subsequent level follows the same rules, with the elements of the lower hierarchy levels representing smaller and smaller pieces of the project that can be more clearly defined and better understood. The lowest levels of the overall breakdown comprise a list of project tasks that aggregate to the overall project's effort and are easy to describe. A project plan built using these lowest-level fragments (often called tasks, activities, or work packages) will be as inclusive and thorough as you can make it.

Some ideas for a developing a WBS collaboratively include working "up against the wall"; minimizing missing work; and documenting your results.

Up Against the Wall

At the risk of sounding like a 1960s radical, to create the most thorough WBS for your project, get up against the wall. Get your team together, give each person several pads of yellow sticky notes, and find a big chunk of blank wall (or whiteboard, collection of easel-pad sheets, or any other large, flat vertical surface). Developing a WBS is a creative, right-brain process. Posting it on a wall where everyone can see it, using pieces of paper that you can move around and easily replace, is a great way to quickly develop a sense of what you are going to need to do. Starting the effort using a computer tool is equivalent to working with blinders on. This is true even when using "right brain" computer tools that support mind-mapping or other graphical representations.

If you find it necessary to develop your WBS with a distributed team, consider initially breaking up the project by site, so most of the decomposition can be done on a wall by members of your team who are co-located. You can then use computer networking or videoconferencing to share results and stitch everything together. Even when you are unable to develop the WBS face-to-face, such long-distance methods are always far superior to trying to do it alone.

Minimizing Missing Work

Begin by reviewing several existing WBSs for similar projects. Request that each member of your team bring any plans or final task lists they have from earlier projects to help with brainstorming. Include all activities listed in any of the earlier project plans that are relevant to your project. Include activities needed to comply with legal requirements, organizational standards, and applicable life cycles or methodologies. Include "overhead" activities such as vendor and subcontractor management, special reporting, and preparation for reviews, presentations, and other meetings. Review retrospectives from recent, similar projects to identify all the things that were left out, and then scan what those projects would do differently and incorporate anything pertinent in your WBS.

For each item identified, ask: What must be done before this work can begin? Is all the prerequisite work defined? Then ask: What work logically follows this piece of the project? List any tasks you discover that are connected to those already listed. For each piece of work, capture and document your assumptions.

Consider the project WBS provisional until you have done a thorough evaluation of the whole structure with your team and have had it reviewed by at least one experienced peer project leader.

BUILDING THE CASE FOR DATA QUALITY

A few years ago, Ted Slater found himself between formal projects at Hewlett-Packard. He knew that there were ongoing issues with data quality in his business unit, and he was determined to fix them. However, he had no travel or IT budget and no project team assigned. To get the commitments needed, he planned to document the problems caused by incorrect and inconsistent data and use this to enlist the support and sponsorship he needed. Ted knew that the problems and consequences were quite serious, and the key stakeholders were, fortunately for Ted, passionate about their jobs and the quality of their work.

Ted began by developing a vision for what the project could produce. With the status quo, data quality problems had to be dealt with after the fact, which was costly and time consuming. To make matters worse, the correction methods used around the world were inconsistent and varied in their effectiveness. To deal with this, they needed better data definitions, more timely feedback for the entry process, and improvements for the overall system.

Because no one, including Ted, was formally assigned to work on this, he knew that the people he needed to cajole on to his project team would essentially be volunteering their time. To facilitate this, Ted went out of his way to accommodate their availability, frequently thanked them for their participation, acknowledged all of their contributions, and strove for consensus as they proceeded. He worked to keep everyone focused on the end state with cleaner, more consistent, and less troublesome business data. Ted also realized that holding a group of volunteers together requires that they all get along, so he also worked to ensure that everyone was very nice to each other. Throughout the project, effective communications were essential. Ted provided meeting notes that accurately reflected each contributor's words and that would be unambiguous to those who were not present.

To get a running start, Ted worked with his colleagues to collect information on the existing correction processes and business procedures so that they could be consolidated into a worldwide reference. Simply publishing and updating this information constituted a significant contribution that helped gain more sponsorship and alignment for the effort. Ted's team then began to methodically work through the information to identify differences and gaps.

Based on this effort, they identified changes that would be useful to the people who were responsible for data entry. Working within the known constraints for IT tool development, Ted's team developed a self-check analysis tool that provided feedback on data quality when it was entered. This had the potential for significantly improving the routinely reported data quality metrics, and users were self-motivated to use the tools.

Ted says: "In the end, we produced the first tools the data entry users had ever had, and the successful results for the project led to formal sponsorship and funding for a follow-on IT project. This project was difficult, and it took much longer than it would have taken with formal funding for people, IT development, and travel. But it showed that if you are determined to beg, borrow, and grovel to keep your project going, substantial results are possible."

Documenting Results

Capture the information for your project WBS immediately after you develop it. If you created it on a wall, take a digital picture or enter the items into a computer before you leave. However you initially capture the information, transfer it for posterity into a scheduling tool, a database, a document, or a *WBS dictionary*. Save it in a form that you can easily use for subsequent planning, and store it where your team members can easily find it.

The most common place to save WBS data is in a project scheduling tool, such as Microsoft Project. The structure can be displayed there or in any document using the indented outline format to show where each item falls in the hierarchy. If you prefer a tree-structured version, specialized software exists for WBS charts, or you can use any general-purpose charting or presentation tool.

How and where you store WBS data matters less for project control than how you use it. It is the foundation for your project plans, so keep it visible, current, and handy.

Individual Goals and Responsibilities

Defining the work is one challenge you face in controlling your project. Obtaining reliable commitments for each and every part of the work is the next. Your overall approach to gaining cooperation can be based on any of the ideas listed in Getting Through Giving in Chapter 3, but here we focus specifically on defining clear objectives, discovering individual preferences, delegating responsibility, and gaining two-way commitment.

Defining Clear Objectives

Begin the process of setting goals while developing the project WBS. As your project's work takes shape, determine which member of your team is the most appropriate owner for the lowest-level activities in the structure. Some assignments will be easy and obvious; some team members have specialties and expertise that directly align with work that they identify and add to the project WBS. Other work is not as simple to assign, but because each piece of the project requires an owner, you need to find a way to delegate responsibility to a willing owner. For each project task, especially any without obvious owners, verify that you have a thorough description that includes:

- A clear definition of the deliverable
- All criteria to be used in evaluating the results
- Any assumptions or constraints
- Role assignments (if the work is expected to be done by more than one person)
- Anything else that you know about how the work should be (or at least could be) done

Personal responsibility, as discussed in Chapter 3, is a powerful motivating factor. Along with the work itself, ownership can be one of your most powerful tools for getting commitments for your planned project activities. When an owner voluntarily accepts responsibility for a task with enthusiasm, most of your work is done. Document the commitment, and rely on the owner's desire to do the work to secure the deal. Ownership and the nature of the work are more than sufficient to motivate contributors for some parts of your project, satisfying the getting-through-giving requirement that a credible commitment requires.

Develop a list of all project activities, noting the commitments that emerge during the development of your WBS. Use a simple list with names, or develop a responsibility matrix, such as the RACI charts discussed in Chapter 5, listing activities one to a row with each project contributor in a separate column. To the list of activities that emerges from the WBS, add any other work that your project requires. Include all the ongoing efforts for reporting, keeping status and other project information up-to-date, and monitoring other project overhead, particularly things that you expect to delegate to members of your team.

Project leaders who lack much authority can get around the problem by identifying activities that require more organizational clout and delegating them to their project sponsor or to project stakeholders who have sufficient authority. Document this work, and either list it with all the other activities or make a separate sponsor responsibilities list.

Discovering Individual Preferences

When an activity has no obvious, eager owner, your work is cut out for you. There can be many reasons why no one seems interested in the work. Your first job is to determine, not just guess, why no one is volunteering. In some cases, the work requires a skill no one on your team has. In other cases, the work may be defined inadequately. Perhaps it is too high-profile, difficult, or risky. In still other cases, the work may appear boring, pointless, or thankless. People might avoid a commitment for other reasons: They may already have too much other work. They don't want to work with people no one likes. They want to avoid work that depends on external factors that are out of their control.

If the main reason for no enthusiasm is that everyone thinks the work isn't necessary, determine whether they're right. If the activity was listed simply because it appears on a planning template or because "we always do it," but it adds no value to the project, drop it. If the consensus is that the definition of the work is unclear, go back to the drawing board and improve the definition in the WBS. Check then to see whether the newly defined activity generates a volunteer.

Sometimes, though, you need to roll up your sleeves and play "Let's Make a Deal." The overall process for gaining commitments using reciprocity starts with understanding what the people on your team care about and want, so that you can then offer something they desire in exchange for their commitment. Chapter 3 lists many ideas about what you can offer as exchange capital, but some of the most useful are to:

- Identify team members who want to fill skill gaps or learn something new.

- Find out which activities are strongly desired by contributors, and then use them as leverage or as part of a package deal.
- Motivate contributors using project aspects they care about or a project vision statement tailored to their perspective.
- Find people on your team who thrive on challenges and who like visibility.
- Find people on your team who like predictability and hate attention.
- Identify people on your team who are overloaded doing work that you might be able to shift to others.

In your discussions with team members, be guided by the fact that people appreciate working as they choose, building expertise in fields they enjoy, and contributing to undertakings that they care about. Knowing what you can offer that might appeal to each of your team members puts you in a position to establish meaningful commitments for most, and perhaps all, of the work in your project.

Delegating Ownership and Responsibility

The next step is to close each deal. List all the known and potential project work commitments for each member of your team. On your lists, strive to find a potential owner for all the unassigned work in your WBS, and consider options that you might use to convince people to accept responsibility based on what you know about them. Request your team members to make a similar list of known and possible project commitments. Ask them also to include any other responsibilities they have outside of your project so that you can discuss their situations as a whole and verify that the commitments to your project are realistic.

Schedule a one-on-one meeting with each person on your team to discuss and confirm goals. If some particularly important unassigned activities can be assigned to more than one person on your team, sequence your discussions so that you speak with your preferred choice first. Also plan to meet with any extended team members and stakeholders who will be responsible for key project activities. Schedule a similar meeting with your sponsor last, to confirm the work you expect the sponsor to own and to explore options for dealing with project work that remains unassigned after you have met with each member of your team.

During these one-on-one meetings, begin each discussion by comparing your lists to verify commitments for all the work for which you believe the person has already accepted ownership. Add any new items for which both you and your contributor have proposed ownership, and sufficiently discuss each item listed to validate that you both have a common understanding of the work.

Work down your list of potential additional assignments, one by one, using your best influence and negotiation skills to gain enthusiastic, or at least willing, acceptance for them. Deal with resistance using open questions that probe why the person is reluctant to take on ownership. Ask your team to explain why they would rather not be responsible for the work, and explore whether something about the work could be changed to make it more desirable. Also find out whether there is any interest in taking on a portion of the work or in teaming with others who could help. If a valid alternative for the activity would be more acceptable (for example, involving more tried-and-true methods for risk-averse contributors, or a newer, innovative approach for more ambitious team members), consider it.

Be persistent, but if no realistic option surfaces to secure a commitment, note it and move on to the next item.

Gaining Two-Way Commitment

When you have discussed all the items on your list, consider all the commitments you and your contributor have jointly agreed to as a whole. Be sure that the individual sees all the commitments, combined with his or her other existing responsibilities, as realistic. List these commitments, and express your confidence in the other person's ability to get them done.

The commitments made by your team are only part of the story. Also write down any commitments that you made to your team members, and schedule any work that you need to do to deliver on them. If you do fail to deliver on what you promise, why should your team? After you have met with all of your team members, update your overall planning documents to identify all of the remaining gaps. You may be able to deal with some gaps by replanning, finding a way to make the work unnecessary. You can also potentially plug some of the holes by assigning the activities to yourself, but be careful. If you overload yourself, it will not be just a few activities at risk; it will be your entire project. Gather your information, summarizing all the work identified for your project where you have no credible owner, along with any ideas you have that might help you secure one.

Meet with your sponsor, and get commitments for any activities that you plan to delegate upward. Never be bashful. A documented commitment to make a key project decision with a specified turnaround time never seems like a big deal early in the project, and it may prove very useful later in your project. Document your sponsor's agreements, as well as any commitments you have made in exchange.

End your discussion with your sponsor by asking for help and advice on unassigned work on your project. Explore options such as:

- Allocating additional staff to your project, at least part time
- Delegating the work to others in the organization
- Outsourcing the work
- Modifying project goals so that they can be met with existing staffing

There are many other possibilities. Work to develop support from your sponsor for realistic alternatives. Be clear about the consequences to your project if you are unable to resolve your staffing issues. Propose options that you have come up with, and ask your sponsor for advice and alternatives. Determine how best to deal with each gap, and end your discussion by summarizing your decisions and the actions needed for follow-up.

Following your meeting, document all open staffing issues and any commitments where you lack confidence. Include all of this on your project risk list.

CLOSING THE DEAL

Patrick Schmid, a seasoned project leader who is managing director of PS Consulting in Germany, tells of a particularly difficult situation that he faced on one of his projects. To succeed, he had to depend on the services of an IT department team several hundred kilometers away in France. From experience, he knew that getting a positive response to his initial request would be easy, but he also knew that follow-through was very likely to be late, not quite what he required, or both. The members of the support team were well known for doing what they wanted to do, not necessarily what was needed.

"I was concerned after my initial discussions that history was going to repeat itself," he says, "so I secured approval from my management to travel and spend time with the team in France. Getting approval wasn't easy, but the consequences of potential problems gave me a potent rationale for the trip." Over the course of several meetings with the IT team, he carefully described his project and what he needed. He asked for advice on how the team, in particular his primary contact, thought it best to proceed. At the end of the day, Patrick asked his associate to join him for dinner, and during the meal they discussed a great deal, but neither of them mentioned the project.

When they met again briefly the next morning, he quickly secured an agreement for what he needed. The project was ultimately very successful, due in large part to the cooperation of the remote IT team. "In discussing it later," Patrick says, "I learned that I got cooperation because my associate did not feel that I was pressuring him; he appreciated that I gave him a say in the decision making."

Commitments offered willingly are always much more reliable than those we try to force.

Collaborative Estimating

Of all the parts of project planning, estimating seems to be the one that project teams complain about the most and find most challenging. Estimates of both duration and cost are often too optimistic, and the consequences of being wrong are severe. Estimating is one area where all the elements of control outlined in the initial chapters of this book come together. Processes and metrics matter a great deal because estimates that aren't based on a good process and measured history are just wild guesses. Also, collaborative estimating provides excellent opportunities to build teamwork and influence.

Some ideas for developing estimates that help you to understand and control your project include using your plan details, learning from history, and approaching estimating as a team activity.

Developing a Detailed View

Much of the inaccuracy in project estimating comes from two related sources: (1) estimating work too early and (2) estimating work at too high a level. Agile projects deal with this by focusing estimates on the immediate iteration and limiting the planning horizon to only a few weeks, only a bit beyond the current development cycle. All projects benefit from scrupulous standards for activity size and periodically revisiting estimates to ensure credibility.

A reliable process for estimating requires a thorough, complete WBS. If you lack enough information to develop a work breakdown structure, you cannot accurately assess the timing or cost of your work. One of the primary reasons for guidelines limiting activities at the lowest WBS level to short durations and modest effort is to join the estimation and WBS processes at the hip. If you can define the work at a sufficiently low level of granularity, you can understand it and accurately estimate it. If you can't, your estimates will most likely be optimistic. Most people are extremely bad at accurately assessing work that takes longer than about two weeks. Below this level, the single owner of the activity can take responsibility for the work and figure out what needs to be done. With estimates derived from knowledge of the work, your plan will be credible, realistic, and accurate enough to control your project.

If the estimates you develop for an activity seem to be large (more than a month in duration or in excess of 80 hours of effort), further breakdown is one way to gain higher accuracy. Some activities may appear to be difficult to decompose into smaller activities, but there are a number of ways to make things easier. One of the most straightforward is to treat the activity as a project and to apply your life cycle to it. Separate it into phases such as thinking and analysis, design and writing things down, developing and creating the deliverable, and testing and resolving problems. Other approaches include dividing the deliverable into subcomponents, thinking through a scenario for executing the work, or supporting the completion or acceptance criteria. To make your estimation credible, devise some basis for developing a solid understanding of the work, perhaps by selecting a small portion of the work and doing it.

The owners of each project activity are a good first source of duration and effort data. If their initial estimates are larger than your standards, press for further breakdown of the work to pull the estimates closer to numbers that inspire confidence. If the initial estimates you collect seem unrealistically optimistic, probe for specifics. Ask what the estimate is based on, and have the owners of project tasks describe how they plan to approach the work. Test each estimate you gather using what you know about your project's constraints and assumptions, available team skills and capabilities, staff availability and productivity, training requirements, and potential turnover. Be particularly skeptical of all estimates for project activities for which you have not yet been able to identify a named owner.

For each activity, collect an estimate of duration in workdays as well as an estimate of effort in person-days, engineer-hours, full-time equivalents, or some suitable combination of people and time. If the two estimates seem inconsistent (40 hours of effort in two days, for example), ask the activity owner to explain. Communications, meetings, and other interruptions consume time and affect the relationship between effort and duration. If the estimates you collect are based on shaky assumptions, adjust them to make them more realistic.

Finally, always probe for worst-case estimates. Get a sense of what the activity owners think might go wrong and collect this information to use in risk analysis later in your project planning. If the worst-case scenario seems very probable, revise the estimates of effort and duration accordingly.

Learning from History

Accurate estimates are always derived, one way or another, from history. Actual results for project activity cost and duration are important project diagnostic metrics, as discussed in Chapter 7. Historical measurements stored in databases or reported in the lessons learned from previous projects are good direct sources for estimating data you can use; if available, this data can help you to validate the estimates for similar work you plan to include in your project. In Extreme Programming (used for agile software development), this estimating principle is referred to as *yesterday's weather*, alluding to the fact that the statistically most accurate forecasting method predicts that today's weather will be the same as it was the previous day. It is prudent to assume that a future similar task will have roughly the same duration and cost as the last one.

Other potentially useful sources of historical information are your personal notes and recollections; consultations with experienced peers, consultants, and managers; and publicly available published information in magazines, presentations, and on the Web.

Historical information is also embedded in estimating guidelines and in parametric formulas that relate the size, volume, length, or some other aspect of a deliverable to effort and duration. All of this information is potentially valuable in verifying that your project estimates are credible and in the right range. Remain aware that, if the historical information you have is for slightly different work or involve different staffing, these estimates will only be close, not precise.

Estimating as a Team

Collaborative estimating is a well-established way to tap into the "wisdom of teams" and more deeply engage your team in the project. It is required on projects using agile methods and universally beneficial on any project, especially for work with little historical precedent or when the information may not be captured in an easily used form.

The Delphi technique is a collaborative method for estimating that provides a backdoor into historical experience. Delphi is a relatively high-overhead process, but it can generate credible estimates that your team will accept, even for activities in which the owner lacks confidence and there is no applicable historical information. Delphi works on the principle that, even when no individual is able to provide good estimates, you can rely on the team as a whole to create credible results. Delphi also involves everybody and it also enhances project motivation, buy-in, and teamwork.

Gather your team (a virtual meeting with distributed members works fairly well), including at least five people, all of whom have a good overall understanding of your project. Review what you know about each activity in your project WBS that lacks a credible estimate, but take care not to include any information or opinions on what you or others think the estimates might be. Ask each participant to provide a duration estimate, effort estimate, or both. In the first round of data gathering, ensure that each input is provided without any consultation and based only on each person's individual analysis.

Collect all the responses, and then create three groups, one each for the highest, midrange, and lowest thirds. Reveal the results, and explore with the group whether they find the average of the middle grouping to be reasonable. Also discuss the highest estimates and probe for personal experience that could credibly support these. For the lowest estimates, find out whether anyone has a clever, creative shortcut that could credibly allow the work to be done that quickly. Discuss the assumptions that outlying estimates are based on as a way to better understand them. Following the discussion, conduct more rounds of estimating, striving for convergence. For project estimating, one or two additional cycles are generally sufficient.

All collaborative estimating techniques, including Delphi, create estimates based on team inputs. Because the estimates are produced by the same individuals who will do the work, they are motivating, and contributors generally do their best to deliver on them.

Outsourced Activities

Increasingly, projects include work to be performed by consultants, contract workers, and others outside the organization. In analyzing your project, identify all the work in your WBS that is likely to be outsourced. Outsourced work is particularly difficult to manage and control, and it is one place where all project leaders, regardless of their authority, need to work primarily through influence. Planning for outsourced work includes all the normal steps with particular attention on scoping because getting it wrong can have very significant financial impact on your overall project. For better control, you also need to pay attention to your reasons for outsourcing, timing issues, sources of potential conflict and confusion (which you need to minimize), and the contractual arrangements.

Your Reasons for Outsourcing

Project work is outsourced for a number of reasons, including a lack of skills, expertise, or capacity inside your organization. It may be a strategic decision by your organization to outsource work not considered a core competency. Lower cost and a desire to build organizational partnerships are other possible reasons for outsourcing. If parts of your project are going be outsourced, or if you plan to propose including contract work, discuss your plans thoroughly with your sponsor and management to get full approval to go forward.

Identify both the benefits (such as not having to invest in building skills needed for a single project) and the risks of outsourcing for your project. If nothing else, outsourced work will probably consume more of your time per project activity because of the additional administrative requirements. With your sponsor, carefully assess the issues, timing, probable costs, and other factors. Together, make decisions to outsource project activities based on solid business criteria. Outsourcing primarily to deal with a lack of available staff weakens your project control.

Managing the Timing

Outsourcing takes time to set up, particularly if you are working with a new supplier. Review your organization's process for procurement, and discuss it with experts who know what to do. Verify that your project (and you) have adequate time to deal with filling out forms, getting approvals, communicating, and negotiating.

If you are short on time, work with your sponsor to expedite the process, or else find an alternative that better serves your project timing.

Minimizing Sources of Conflict and Confusion

Control problems with outsourced work have many causes: organizational differences, specification issues, or timing issues.

• *Organizational Differences.* Organizations have different working methods, terminology, and customs. When you are reviewing proposals and considering outsourcing options, insist on interviewing the people you will be working with. Get a sense of what the differences are between each organization and yours. If the processes and other aspects that you find are too dissimilar from yours, consider this a red flag. Building the trust and good working relationships that you need with people who think and work differently is very difficult. Seek to contract with organizations similar enough to yours to minimize the potential for misunderstandings and disagreements.

• *Specification Issues.* Because it can be both expensive and time-consuming to make changes to work that you outsource, avoid contracting out activities where the deliverables are not fully defined or could change. Carefully define detailed specifications of the deliverable, performance and measurement criteria, acceptance and testing requirements, interface specifications, standards to be followed, and all other relevant requirements. Also ensure that all contracts include clear and explicit terms defining how any changes are to be handled.

• *Timing.* Another common source of problems for outsourced work or for any work done at a distance is timing. When planning outsourced work for your project, define the work so that it includes ample opportunity for you to gather concrete evidence of progress. In addition to the ultimate deadlines, add checkpoints and milestones to review documents and prototypes and to participate in inspections, walkthroughs, and preliminary tests.

Contracting for Control

Work with the contracting experts (such as legal, purchasing, or other specialists) in your organization to set up all contracts using standard forms or formats that include all the requirements your organization requires. For each contracted deliverable, ensure that ownership and timing requirements are clearly defined. If you can, structure the contract to be fixed-price and include tight, thorough specifications to minimize risk. If the contract is not fixed-price, include a not-to-exceed limit that protects your project against excessive costs and forces renegotiation of the contract before it breaks your budget. Also consider including terms and conditions in the contract that enhance your control, such as incentives for good performance for early delivery and penalties for poor performance.

Participate in the negotiations so that you can begin to establish an open, honest relationship during contract discussions. You will carry the relationship into your project; playing hardball during contract negotiations can create great difficulties throughout the work. Finally, meet with the person who will administer the contract on the other side as you are signing the contract. Review the contract terms to ensure that all parties understand the agreement.

Interface Management

As you analyze dependencies for each activity in the WBS, pay particular attention to inputs that lie outside your project and deliverables within your project that are sent to other projects. Interrelated projects pose particular control problems, not unlike the challenges of planning outsourced work.

If you are managing a project within an elaborate hierarchy of projects that make up a large, complex program, you are likely to have many cross-project dependencies. Even in simpler situations, you probably face at least a few external inputs and dependencies.

Begin your analysis by identifying all required outside inputs to planned work in your project that could impede or halt your progress. As your project's network and timeline take shape, document all your external input requirements, including both specifications and timing.

Identify the leaders of any related projects that you believe will be responsible for producing what you need, and approach them individually to discuss your requirements. Request commitments to supply what you need in a timely manner, using the same influencing techniques discussed earlier in the chapter for securing agreement with your project contributors. Ask for a formal written agreement, including a clear summary of the specifications, timing, and completion criteria for the deliverable. Also document and get formal agreements for any other external inputs your project requires, and document any outputs needed by others where your project is responsible. Secure formal documented agreements for all interfaces and frequent status reporting even for dependencies within your own organization. Treat these memos of understanding as contracts, and use them to control and influence work outside your project.

If you encounter resistance from another project leader who is part of your same program, escalate the situation to your program manager for resolution. If you are dependent on an individual who is organizationally independent of you, discuss the situation with your sponsor. For any interface problems you are unable to resolve, you need either to develop an alternative approach or, as a last resort, to ask your sponsor to pull rank and force an agreement.

Your goal is to secure credible commitments to aid in controlling the work outside your project. If you have what seems to be an excessive number of external interfaces, consider rethinking your overall approach. If your project is a piece of a larger program, encourage the program manager to revisit the initial program decomposition, looking for a program structure with lower interdependence complexity and risk.

Constraints and Plan Optimization

Collaborative planning begins with identifying the work as a team and with building on the WBS to add information about staffing and timing. Integrating these findings into an overall plan provides a bottom-up picture of the project that can be contrasted with the original objectives. About this time in the planning process, project leaders begin to discover just how much trouble they are in. To improve project control, you must examine your critical path, consider methods for minimizing schedule complexity, resolve resource overcommitments, work to optimize your plans, and put your project *in a box.*

Critical Path

Timing is important to any project. When you combine the project activities with their initial duration estimates and presumed logical dependencies, you can determine the minimum project duration based on that information. Although you can do the analysis manually (and everyone should do this at least once, if only to understand the details), many project management scheduling tools are available, and even the least capable of these tools does a much better job than you can of analyzing a project network. The rules are basic:

- Begin with as comprehensive a list of activities as you and your team can develop.
- Establish duration estimates that are as credible as possible.
- Set up logical dependencies to link activities, avoiding fixed-date must-start-on constraints except in unusual cases.

Once entered into a scheduling tool, your network of linked activities quickly turns into a gaily colored display of red and blue bars—a Gantt chart (named after Henry Gantt, the gentleman who devised it about a hundred years ago, with no help from any computer tools). The red bars line up in sequence across the calendar, with no gaps, showing the longest sequence of planned work for your project as it is currently laid out.

A Gantt chart display of your project tells you two things about control. The end point of the final red bar tells you the earliest date that the work on your project can be expected to finish, based on your detailed planning data. If, by some miracle, the date is on or sooner than the deadline specified in your project objective, there is hope. Most of the time, though, the initial critical path for a project is well past the expected deadline. In this case, control of your project depends either on optimizing your plan and finding a credible way to make it shorter or on convincing your sponsor to adjust the deadline. Both of these topics are explored later in this chapter.

The second thing the Gantt chart shows you about your project is how much flexibility is available in your plan. This is not too useful initially, especially if the plan overshoots the deadline significantly. As your planning process approaches completion, however, you can see flexibility by comparing the relative proportion of red and blue bars on your Gantt chart. *Red bars*, by convention, are used for critical tasks and lie on the critical path. Your project can be done more quickly only if you change the estimate for one or more of these activities, one or more of their logical dependencies, or both. *Blue bars*, by convention, are used for noncritical activities—activities that can slip, at least a little bit, without lengthening the project. If most of your bars are red, you have little flexibility in your plan, and control will be very difficult. If you have a single set of red bars stretching from the project start to the finish and a much larger number of blue bars, you have a chance, because you may be able to shift the work represented by the blue bars somewhat when necessary to deal with issues and problems without delaying the overall project.

Minimizing Schedule Complexity

A potential source of confusion on projects that can threaten your control is an overly complicated plan that only you can read. You can make your project plans easier to read by judiciously inserting milestones to better show what is going on. Milestones are often used to terminate work at the end of a project phase, where dependencies fan into a decision or transition point to be synchronized before the work again fans out into many parallel streams. Milestones can be used throughout your plan to show the completion of sets of activities of any sort, and to untangle logic that would otherwise be a bewildering arrangement of network spaghetti. However, use care not to add milestones that unnecessarily increase project overhead.

For projects with multiple independent teams or with a high-level summary plan for a program, you can also make things easier on the various teams and subprojects by using milestones. Set up an initial section of the plan comprised of a set of milestones common to all the parts of the project, under a heading such as "Project Milestones." Define the milestones two to three weeks apart, and arrange them in sequence. Follow this section of your plan with a segment that contains overall work for which you are responsible, followed by additional sections breaking down the work of each team, including any external suppliers. Dependencies between activities in the same section are linked directly within that section, but dependencies to other work are all set up to link via one of the overall milestones at the top of the plan. The plan in Figure 6-1 is an example based on plans being used to manage a program responsible for a series of system deployments. The original plans contained about 400 activities, but with only one section and the milestones expanded, no more than about 60 lines are in view.

The plan can be stored with all the sections collapsed, except for the milestones cascading across the project timeline. Members of any team can easily read relevant parts of the plan simply by expanding the work for their section of the plan and the main milestones. Structuring the plan this way also simplifies tracking because the milestones gathered at the top shift and cause ripple effects throughout the plan whenever anything in the overall plan slips enough to affect one of them.

Resource Overcommitments and Leveling

Activity timing, combined with effort estimates, provides another useful view of the work. Project scheduling tools can generate histograms to show this view of the work, if you enter the effort information for each activity into the database consistently with the tool's algorithms. You can also use spreadsheet analysis or visual inspection across your Gantt chart to determine where you may have parallel work scheduled that requires more hours of effort than the individuals on your team have to offer. Identify each period during the project where your preliminary schedule requires overtime or additional staffing to support what it calls for. To have any hope of controlling your project, you need to shift the work along your timeline so that the effort required is consistent with your team's available capacity. Scheduling tools all provide an automated function to level your plan resource loads. The function may work well for you, but, before you try it, make sure you have a well-protected archive copy of your plan. The load-leveling function in most automated scheduling software is the project management equivalent of a food processor. After the software has sliced, diced, and pureed your plan, you probably won't recognize it.

Repeat your effort analysis for your whole project to see where the overall staffing is under or over what you need. This composite analysis helps you to determine whether you can manage your resource problems by shifting activi-

FIGURE 6-1. A SEGMENTED PROGRAM-LEVEL PLAN

ID	WBS	Task Name	Duration	Start	Finish	% Complete	Gantt Chart (Qtr 3: Jun Jul Aug Sep / Qtr 4: Oct Nov Dec / Qtr 1: Jan Feb Mar / Qtr 2: Apr May)
1	1	Wave N Key Milestones	199 d	Jul 4	Apr 6	0%	
2	1.1	Wave N Participants finalized	0 d	Jul 4	Jul 4	100%	
3	1.2	Wave N Participant Configurations Documented	0 d	Sep 5	Sep 5	100%	
4	1.3	Wave N Requirements Complete	0 d	Oct 10	Oct 10	100%	
5	1.4	Wave N Scope frozen	0 d	Oct 31	Oct 31	100%	
6	1.5	Wave N Scope changes prohibited	0 d	Nov 21	Nov 21	100%	
7	1.6	Wave N Design Complete	0 d	Dec 22	Dec 22	100%	
8	1.7	Wave N Construction Complete	0 d	Jan 16	Jan 16	100%	
9	1.8	Wave N System Tests Complete	0 d	Feb 6	Feb 6	0%	
10	1.9	Wave N Participant Tests Complete	0 d	Feb 20	Feb 20	0%	
11	1.10	Wave N sign off and release	0 d	Mar 9	Mar 9	0%	
12	1.11	End	0 d	Apr 6	Apr 6	0%	
13	2	Program Staff activities for Wave N	191 d	Jul 4	Mar 27	76%	
34	3	Business Process activities for Wave N	194 d	Jul 4	Mar 30	71%	
76	4	Participant activities for Wave N	199 d	Jul 4	Apr 6	67%	
121	5	System Development activities for Wave N	179 d	Jul 4	Mar 9	79%	
153	6	Output development for Wave N	180 d	Jul 4	Mar 10	77%	
170	7	Finance activities for Wave N	180 d	Jul 4	Mar 10	80%	
179	8	Testing activities for Wave N	95 d	Nov 1	Mar 13	62%	
180	8.1	Develop Wave N test plans	20 d	Nov 1	Nov 28	100%	
181	8.2	Communicate participant testing requirements	20 d	Nov 1	Nov 28	100%	
182	8.3	Develop Wave N test scenarios	15 d	Nov 29	Dec 19	100%	
183	8.4	All test data loaded	16 d	Dec 23	Jan 13	100%	
184	8.5	Test Plans for Wave N validated	16 d	Dec 23	Jan 13	100%	
185	8.6	Conduct system tests	12 d	Jan 17	Feb 1	0%	
186	8.7	Conduct participant tests	13 d	Feb 2	Feb 20	0%	
187	8.8	Retest, following defect correction	28 d	Feb 2	Mar 13	0%	
188	9	Training activities for Wave N	110 d	Nov 22	Apr 24	33%	
199	10	Support activities for Wave N	140 d	Nov 1	May 15	39%	
213	11	Release activities for Wave N	17 d	Feb 7	Mar 1	0%	

ties around or whether you need to build a case for more staff with your sponsor.

Plan Optimization and Opportunity Analysis

As your project plan detail comes into view, much of what it reveals is not good news. The initial schedule is usually too long. The staffing, resources, and budgets available are often far below what your cost analysis requires. For traditional projects, however, one potential source of relief lies on the third side of the triple constraint: scope. Following your analysis of the project and the work needed to get it done, you and your team know more about the project than anyone on earth. The project that your sponsor and stakeholders have in mind represents the best option that they are aware of, but they know less about what is possible than you do. There may be much better project possibilities than what was initially requested.

As part of your analysis, test the assumptions on scoping to explore whether superior options are available. Technical possibilities that you are aware of may allow you to far exceed the specifications originally requested. You may find that you can deliver a core set of critical functionality sooner for a small fraction of the total cost. Adopting an agile approach could allow you to quickly deliver the most critical functionality, with additional requirements phased in throughout the subsequent iterative releases. Also possible is investing in the development of reusable components that can add value to later projects or that can improve processes that will make future project work more efficient.

Spending at least a small amount of time exploring opportunities is both good business and one of your most potent levers for control, especially when your bottom-up planning significantly differs from the initial project objective. The more options you can develop for your project, particularly when the options are attractive, the more successful you are likely to be in negotiating needed changes to an infeasible project objective. Consider ways that you could add to the scope to increase your project's benefits and value, but without adding enormous additional cost or time.

Not all the options for possible alternative projects are going to be opportunities. Some realistic options reduce the overall project. For example, if you can't deliver everything envisioned in the original scope within the expected deadline and cost, extend your what-if analysis to explore what you could deliver on time and on budget. Consider possibilities for doing work in parallel (fast-tracking) to shorten the timeline. Determine whether a larger investment or staff will allow you to meet the timing and scoping goals. Once you have a plan, work to optimize it. Based on your project priorities, figure out how to meet the most important part of the scope-time-cost triple constraint by relaxing the least important factors.

Also review any intermediate milestones or target dates within your project and other constraints, such as resources available, only during specific time windows. Look for alternative plans that solve problems with minimal overall impact, by taking advantage of any identified resource undercommitments or by delaying noncritical work. Favor revisions to your plans that minimize the impact on your highest priority among scope, time, and cost.

After creating your initial plan, pushing around your assumptions to seek alternative better plans is not difficult. Your what-if analysis provides knowledge about your project that helps you control it. In addition to supporting your negotiations and discussions, developing alternate scenarios gives you information you can use to respond to project threats, and it lets you quickly and eloquently describe the adverse consequences of potential changes to your sponsor and stakeholders.

Putting Your Project In a Box

An additional way to view your project is to use your planning information to build a two-dimensional representation of your best assessment of possibilities for cost and timing. All project schedules and budgets based on planning have some measure of uncertainty. Assess this exposure using worst-case estimates of duration and effort. Determine a date range for your project, bounded by an aggressive but possible completion date (that is, supported by a bottom-up plan that is not completely ridiculous) and a worst-case timing that you think you can achieve even if a number of things go wrong. Generate a pair of budget numbers the same way: one that represents best-case project cost (assuming everything goes well) and another that has some margin for error.

Use these pairs of numbers to construct a *project box*, as shown in Figure 6-2. The space inside the box represents a continuum of credible project outcomes, ranging from barely possible in the lower left to nearly certain in the upper right. As a planning tool, the project box shows that the deterministic-looking single date associated with the final milestone on your Gantt chart is only one of many possibilities, not a guarantee. It assists you in communicating your project exposure, developing plans to manage risks, and negotiating with your sponsor.

All the points inside the shaded box need to be supported by a detailed, bottom-up plan that you and your team collaboratively create, including the best-case point on your chart. Your project's initial objective may very well lie outside the shaded region, in the infeasible space well to the left and below your box. When the best-case and worst-case points on your graph are close together, you appear to have a well-planned project with relatively low risk.

FIGURE 6-2. A PROJECT BOX

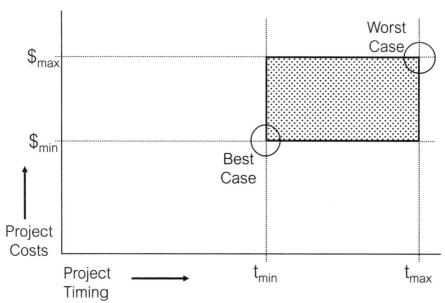

When these points are far apart, control will be difficult, and the credibility of the best-case combination is low.

The box concept can show you and your team the effects of various optimizing strategies. Compressing the project schedule by adding resources generally has two impacts: The costs (both minimum and maximum) rise and, although the minimum time drops, the time between the minimum and maximum date generally expands. It increases the overall size of the box and quantitatively shows the enlarged space of probable outcomes. Other optimizing options can similarly be compared in an objective, visual way.

The project box idea can also assist you in controlling your project through tracking trends. If you have done a good job of planning, your initial box is as large as it will ever be. Over the course of your project, as plans and expectations are replaced by actual results and refined estimates, the box contracts in size with the shrinking uncertainty. If your periodic reviews show the box contracting in place, the best-case stationary and the worst-case migrating toward it, you are well in control. If the best and worst cases shift but remain inside the original dimensions, you at least have done a thorough job of planning and analysis. If, however, the box begins drifting up and to the right, you are probably in deep trouble. Tracking the center of the box over time is a reasonable check on whether your project remains in control. Ultimately your box closes in on the single point that represents your final cost and finish date—ideally well within your original defined two-dimensional space.

Risk Identification, Assessment, and Response Planning

Throughout your project planning, maintain a list of risks that emerge. Some of these risks have been mentioned already, such as reluctant owners for activities in your WBS, worst-case estimates, and external dependencies. Others are:

- Complexity in scoping
- Inadequate specifications
- New or untried technology
- Activities lasting longer than two weeks
- Activities that depend on one key individual
- Communications or language difficulties

Risk identification, as with all of planning, is best done with your whole team. Brainstorm risks together, and let each person's concerns and potential issues prompt others to uncover related risks. Discuss project scenarios and consider what can go wrong. Problems in projects tend to recur; add to your list things that have gone badly for recent projects, including systemic organizational issues.

Again with your team, prioritize your listed risks based on their relative likelihood and potential for harm. Qualitative assessment, using ranges such as high, medium, and low for probability and impact, is generally sufficient to rank-order the list.

With the most serious potential problems at the top of your risk register, work down the list and plan around the worst of them. Avoid or mitigate risks, if possible, through planning. If you and your team come up with no obvious or viable options for preventing a risk, develop a contingency plan for it to recover as best you can from its impact.

The value of risk management for control is pretty obvious because it allows you to avoid many of the worst of your potential problems. In addition, collaborative risk planning is particularly useful for cross-functional projects because it allows your team to graphically demonstrate both the range of potential threats you all face and how painful it could get if the risks come to pass. Lack of awareness of possible exposure is a common root cause of project trouble on diverse teams; it is too easy to wander into disaster without being aware of its existence when you fail to discuss and communicate project risks.

Contingency plans are particularly useful for control because they are available at the onset of problem situations that you have identified, and they can be used to quickly recover your project. Without such plans, your project enters a crisis mode, with significant distractions and the potential for symptom-based reactive actions that may lead to further complications and problems.

Keeping risks and their consequences visible is itself an effective mitigation strategy because people tend to work to avoid serious problems if they are aware on them. Collaborative risk planning also builds teamwork, enhances interpersonal relationships, and can increase overall confidence in the project.

USING RISK MANAGEMENT TO BUILD A TEAM

Some years ago, the government of the Netherlands decided to do away with the license fees charged to Dutch television viewers that it had collected annually for over 50 years. Returning the already-collected fees to millions of households would have been difficult to manage in any circumstances, but this effort had an aggressive goal, set by the politicians involved, to get it done in 90 days. Karel de Bakker, an experienced project leader and consultant with deB Project & Risk in Groningen, helped to organize and lead a diverse team to success on this project using what he refers to as "risk-driven project management." He explains:

> The practical side of the project was not of particular interest to the ministers, MPs, or senators involved; in political decision making, the focus is rarely on efficiency or effectiveness. Nonetheless, even though the project had an adequate staff, the tight schedule meant that there wouldn't be enough time to perform all the activities necessary to deliver the required level of quality—the process had to be fully auditable.
>
> Not everybody likes taking risks, but some people really do. Perfectionists on the team were placed in charge of the production processes. Thrill seekers were asked to turn their creativity to the most uncertain project activities. Every team member became responsible for the overall project and actively looked for risks and ways to minimize them.

Karel used the differing comfort levels the project managers had with risk to align everyone with the project goal. All planning on the project was collaborative, with input from the entire team. Completing activities successfully meant reducing the project risk and improving the chances of overall success. He continues:

> In the end, the focus on managing the risks, performing at least three independent checks for every project deliverable,

and the use of extensive testing and simulation throughout the project paid off. There were fewer than 1,300 incorrect calculations out of more than 6.5 million. Our diligent risk management and use of monitoring tools resulted in payment errors that totaled far less than a tenth of one percent of the 160 million euro total, and there were no underpayments. Everybody was more than happy, and we got official approval from the external auditors.

Doing a Plan Review

Once you have completed your planning documents, examine them all together. Conduct a plan review:

- To ensure overall consistency and quality.
- To identify and add anything your review reveals as missing.
- To derive a high-level summary that you can use in discussions with your sponsor, stakeholders, and others with whom you need to discuss your project.

Involve your team in your plan review. This is another opportunity for team building, similar to a project start-up workshop, and it is an excellent way to ensure that all of your team members understand the project as a whole. Use techniques such as inspections or walkthroughs to carefully examine your project WBS, duration and effort estimates, dependencies, resource analysis, risk register and planned responses, and other project data. Search for inconsistencies, and then address them.

Bottom-up planning is about credibility. At the conclusion of your review ask each team member if the contents of the project plan are believable. Approach the issue of credibility from two perspectives:

1. Does each person have high confidence that the plan is accurate and complete?
2. Are the individuals on your team confident that the plan can achieve the stated project goals—or, if not, does the plan achieve as much of the objective as possible?

If anyone on your project team doubts the overall thoroughness or believability of your plan, probe to understand why. In some cases, a better understanding of the existing plan is sufficient to build confidence. In other cases, you may need to work further with your team to change the plan to boost its credibility. As Henry Ford said, "Whether you think you can do a thing or not, you are probably right." A team that believes in the plan finds a way to get things done; a skeptical team usually fails.

The second question is even more subjective but equally important. A credible plan that supports your sponsor's expectations is a desirable goal, but this may not always be possible. Your team members need to believe that the course of action they are choosing makes the most sense. If your plan shows that you can meet your project objective, or if the difference compared with the stated project objective is small, project control is feasible. If the differences are significant, use your planning analysis to develop at least two additional alternative projects, in addition to your team's consensus "best" version, supported by credible planning data. The more options you have that are backed up with compelling information, the more successful you are likely to be in negotiating necessary project modifications. Resolving differences between your bottom-up plans and your sponsor's top-down objectives when you commit to a project baseline is covered later in this chapter.

Conclude your project plan review by creating a high-level summary of your plans based on your detailed documents. Plan summary information should include:

- Scope (major deliverable definitions)
- Schedule (milestone charts with significant project dates)
- Cost (a budget summary)
- Staff (a project team roster with roles and responsibilities)
- Significant assumptions, issues, and risks

FLYING WITH YOUR EYES CLOSED

Reviewing information on projects is critical to catching and fixing defects and holes in a project concept before it is too late. Les Sparks (a fictitious name for a close friend who wishes to remain anonymous) is a telecommunications expert and experienced project leader with a major managed services firm. Les tells of a very complex networking project where he was asked to help create a new global digital network.

"All of the initial planning and scoping was done by only one part of the eventual team, and only from their single perspective," he recounts. "The designers failed to involve any of the network management people, so operations and manageability were never considered." To make matters worse, well into the planning, upper-level managers inflicted a disastrous change on the project. As an indirect consequence of a recent agreement unrelated to this project, the new network had to include a large amount of equipment from a specific supplier. The mandated hardware was technically inappropriate, but it was designed in anyway, doubling the costs for the project.

The project went forward over loud protests and predictions that it could not work, and the turnover on the implementation team was significant. Completion of the work took three times longer than planned, and the initial attempts to use the network were unsuccessful; the network was largely useless. Operational problems continued though 18 months of valiant but futile efforts to fix the network, and then it was abandoned.

But the company still needed the new network, and a redesign was quickly initiated. This time, there was broad cross-functional involvement in the design, and there were no inappropriate hardware constraints. The new project was completed in half the time, under budget, and the network was fully functional as soon as it was available. After his involvement leading portions of both projects, Les observes, "Wisdom is not found in just one place. Diversity is good; consensus is better. Getting opinions from more than one group and using multiple inputs results in better decisions. When you suppress dissension, the only opinion you'll get is your own."

To establish control, thoroughly review your plans with your team, and ignore what you hear at your peril.

▪ Measure Your Plan

Measurement is one of your fundamental tools for project control, as discussed in Chapter 4. Most predictive project metrics are based on planning data, and they serve as a distant early-warning system for your project. You can use predictive metrics to assess your project as a whole, identify unrealistic assumptions, uncover significant potential problems, and more clearly communicate what your project is up against. Because predictive measurements are primarily based on speculative rather than empirical data, they are generally less precise than diagnostic and retrospective metrics. Nevertheless, they can enhance your understanding and control over your project by:

- Determining project scale
- Defining completion criteria and other quantitative feature specifications
- Supporting cost-benefit and value analysis
- Validating relative project priorities
- Quantifying unrealistic constraints

- Detecting faulty assumptions
- Identifying risk management requirements
- Justifying schedule and budget reserves
- Supporting successful project objective negotiations

Defining Predictive Project Metrics

Most project predictive metrics are derived from planning information that you develop collaboratively with your team. Working by yourself or with assistance from key team members, examine the planning data to determine what it means. You should also revisit the assumptions used for predictive metrics that preceded your project planning (such as those for ROI metrics, discussed in Chapter 5), to improve their quality and accuracy. Predictive metrics help you develop a deeper understanding of your work and support efforts by your management to compare, prioritize, and select projects. A number of examples of predictive project metrics follow, grouped into several categories. No project leader would ever deploy all of these, but you can find value in at least some.

Project Scale and Scope Metrics
- Size-based deliverable analysis (such as component counts, number of major deliverables, lines of noncommented code, function or feature points, blocks on system diagrams, volume of total output)
- Project complexity (interfaces, algorithmic assessments, technical or architecture analysis)
- Total number of planned activities
- Volume of expected specification changes

Timing and Schedule Metrics
- Activity duration estimates
- Iteration or phase durations
- Feature counts
- Projected iteration counts
- Technical or design debt (overall accumulated estimates for effort or rework required to deal with effects of current system shortcomings and deficiencies)
- Project duration (schedule analysis of elapsed calendar time based on activity duration estimates—t_{min} for the project box)
- Total schedule exposure (schedule analysis based on worst-case duration estimates, contingency plans, or schedule simulations—t_{max} for the project box)
- Activity duration estimates compared with worst-case duration estimates

- Number of critical (or near-critical) paths in the project network
- Logical project complexity (the ratio of activity dependencies to activities)
- Maximum number of predecessors for any project milestone
- Total number of external predecessor dependencies
- Project independence (ratio of internal dependencies to all dependencies)
- Logical length (maximum number of activities on a single network path)
- Logical width (maximum number of parallel paths)
- Total length (sum of the durations of all activities, if they are executed sequentially)
- Total float (sum of total project activity float)
- Project density (ratio of total length to total length plus total float)

Resource and Financial Metrics
- Activity cost (or effort) estimates
- Expected cost (or effort) estimated per development iteration
- Actual iteration or phase costs
- Total cost (the sum of all activity effort estimates, or budget at completion—$\$_{min}$ for the project box)
- Total cost exposure (aggregated worst-case cost estimates, contingency costs, or budget simulations—$\$_{max}$ for the project box)
- Total effort (the sum of all activity effort estimates)
- Activity cost (or effort) estimates compared with worst-case resource estimates
- Percentages of project effort planned in each life cycle phase
- Maximum staff size (full-time equivalent team size)
- Number of unidentified activity owners
- Percentage of staff not yet assigned or hired
- Number of activity owners with no identified backup
- Anticipated staff turnover
- Number of geographically separate locations
- Value of expected project benefits
- Payback analysis (simple or discounted)
- Net present value
- Internal rate of return

General Project Metrics
- Total number of identified risks.
- Severity assessment of identified risks (percentages of your risks that fall into categories such as high, medium, and low).

- Survey-based risk assessment (summarized data collected from project staff, using a survey containing project factors).
- Adjusted total effort (project appraisal done by comparing your plan with completed similar projects and adjusting for differences).
- Cynical cartoonist correlation factor (After developing your plan, collect 30 of Scott Adams's recent Dilbert comic strips, and circulate them to your team. Ask people to mark each one that seems familiar. If your team average is below 10, control may be possible. If the average is between 10 and 20, work on your infrastructure decisions a bit more, and be very, very vigilant. If the average exceeds 20, abandon hope for your project; consider learning to draw and becoming a famous cartoonist.)

Using Predictive Metrics

Useful metrics require a baseline, and baselines for predictive metrics are best set using retrospective information and metrics from recent comparable projects. Measurement baselines are used to decide whether things are within bounds (meaning, in the case of predictive metrics, that your project is controllable) or out of range.

Use these measures to further review your plans. If the measures that you choose to evaluate for your project are supported by thorough planning and if they are consistent with completed successful projects, you are fortunate. If your planning metrics are more consistent with troubled or failed projects, changes to your project are in order. If your assessments significantly exceed what seems normal, assess the consequences of the differences. For metrics such as staff size, even relatively small increases above the norm may spell trouble. If the largest team you have previously led had 10 people, taking on a team of 12 is a big challenge. More interruptions, longer discussions, more opportunities for miscommunication, and many more two-way relationships can all get your project into trouble.

Consider options for managing the potential consequences when these measures are out of the ordinary. Rethink your infrastructure decisions and tighten up the processes you plan to use. When complexity exceeds the norm, explore older, more established alternatives for some of your work or enlist technical assistance in your planning to better understand what you need to do to succeed. You can turn down the heat on some metrics through replanning, but not without trade-offs. Consult with your contributors to enlist their help in thinking of ways to reduce problematic indicators.

If the adjustments you can make are only partially successful in resolving exposures, capture information on the remaining metrics and the consequences you anticipate. Use this data to support data-driven, principled negotiations when you discuss your project plans with your sponsor.

▪ Set a Realistic Project Baseline

If there are no substantial differences between your plans and the initial project objective, meet with your sponsor briefly to discuss your plans, commit to a baseline based on them, and skip this section.

All too often, however, even your most thorough and clever planning leaves a wide gap between what your best plans demonstrate is possible and what your sponsor originally expected. The trade-offs in planning are not unlike trying to compress a balloon full of water; when you press one side in to decrease your duration, you create corresponding outward bulges on the other sides, representing increasing costs or diminished scope. All the alternatives you devise seem to fall short in some significant respect, resulting in a no-win scenario. You have two obvious choices: Commit to the original objective, knowing that you have no credible plan to achieve it, or tell your sponsor that the project is impossible and you want nothing to do with it. Because neither option has much appeal you need to create another alternative.

In the Star Trek universe, Starfleet Academy poses a no-win scenario to cadets aspiring to command. In the Kobayashi Maru simulation, a ship full of people is stranded in space protected by a treaty. Two options are available: In one, the people are abandoned to die, and in the other, they are rescued, initiating an interstellar war.

James T. Kirk, role model for intrepid project leaders everywhere, did not like the options. He did not believe in no-win situations. So he cheated. He found a clandestine way to reprogram the simulator allowing him to win by rescuing the stranded victims and chasing off the Klingons to avert war. Your job, similarly, is to boldly find a third way, to secure a commitment to a possible project that is acceptable to your sponsor and stakeholders.

Preparing Your Information

The first steps, as described earlier in this chapter, are planning, exploring trade-offs, and developing two or more realistic project alternatives to the best team-developed plan that you can come up with. Gather your summary planning information, along with supporting detail to back it up. Focus on the quality and clarity of your summary data; too much detailed planning information can be more confusing than helpful.

For each plan, use your project box analysis, worst-case estimates, and other risk and contingency information to build a plan including an appropriate reserve for time or resources (or both). Ensure that each of your options has a reasonable chance of success and an adequate margin. This reserve in your plan is not padding to make up for bad planning or laziness; rather, it establishes a range of credible possibilities based on your assessment of the real exposures and risks your project faces. Be prepared to explain it with data from risk assessments or worst-case estimates, and be ready to defend your request with your sponsor. Successfully integrating schedule or budget reserves into your plan enhances your chances of success and provides the leverage needed by a project leader lacking authority for control. Even if you are ultimately unsuccessful in retaining a margin in your plans for risk, it is prudent to propose it in discussions with your sponsor. If you must surrender some or even all of it in your negotiations, your initial proposal provides a starting point for negotiations that makes it more probable you can set a project baseline that is not demonstrably impossible. Your initial proposals need to describe projects that are desirable to you and your team, not projects that are barely achievable.

Use your plan data and predictive metrics to build a strong case that shows why the initial expectations cannot be met. Even if you have some authority in your organization, sponsors have more; you must be very persuasive. Your best course is to assemble your facts and use principled negotiation. You can change little based on your worries, opinions, and assertions that the project will be difficult; you require factual data. Collect quantitative information about your project based on your plans. Although most predictive measurements and other planning information has a good deal of uncertainty, plausible numbers are more than adequate as long as you can explain them. Remember that the numbers your sponsor and stakeholders use are probably even less precise, having been plucked out of thin air.

If your plan shows that your project cannot be completed until a later date, document why the necessary activities cannot be executed as fast as desired. If your project needs more staff, money, or other resources than are committed, sum the aggregated specific requirements that show why. If scope changes appear necessary, document the reasons and estimate the value of the modified deliverable. In each case, summarize the consequences of not making the changes. Use monetary terms whenever possible; money is the most effective way to get the attention of your managers. In addition to financial consequences, also determine the potential impact on customer or user satisfaction, organizational reputation, or other concerns important to your sponsor and stakeholders.

Even with a strong case, you may not always prevail. If your arguments are unsuccessful with your sponsor, try refocusing the discussion on alternative opportunities. Propose your project options that may deliver demonstrably better results than those initially requested. New potential benefits are particularly useful in nudging a conversation out of a rut ("I can't deliver this! Sure you can, you're the best project leader we have"). Develop ideas that are seen as win/win. Consider opportunities that both please your sponsor and stakeholders and create more breathing room for your project. Offer to expand scope in exchange for more time or resources. Find ways to break the project into smaller, sequential projects or iterations capable of delivering results—smaller results to be sure—sooner. Any plausible proposal that whets the imagination of your sponsor can get the discussion unstuck and refocus it on the more important goal of setting up a project that is both worthwhile *and* possible.

If you are nervous or concerned about presenting a counterproposal to your sponsor, set up time with someone to practice. Rehearse what you plan to say by laying out your case for change with a colleague playing the role of your sponsor. Afterward, ask for criticism and suggestions to tighten up your arguments and improve your approach.

Negotiating

Schedule a meeting with your sponsor to set the project baseline. Request enough time to discuss your project and other issues and alternative project plans.

Begin your meeting by clearly explaining the principal reasons why the original project goals are not achievable. Then describe what you can accomplish using your executive summary of your best plan option, followed by the other alternatives you have developed. Explain that your proposals are realistic, based on solid planning and risk analysis. Highlight the value and attractiveness of each alternative.

Respond calmly and logically to sponsor demands that all the objectives are nonnegotiable and must all be met. Refer to the project priorities agreed to in the project charter, and point out that your proposed changes lean most heavily on the most flexible project parameters. Be clear and persuasive, and stand your ground.

Your influence and ability to negotiate modifications to the objective are never higher than when you are setting the project baseline; after you commit to a plan, you have little ability to alter it. Knowledge is power; remember that by now you are the world's greatest authority on your project and that many of your sponsor's assertions are based primarily on bluster. Display your enthusiasm for the project and remind your sponsor of your experience, technical knowledge, track record, and credibility. They are why your sponsor requested you to lead the project in the first place.

Try to avoid emotional or political discussions. Your sponsor is probably better at these things than you are and has more clout. Keep your project and planning data front and center in the discussions; facts and figures are the one area where you are at least on an equal footing with your management. Use principled negotiation techniques:

- Focus on interests, not positions. Emphasize the reasons the project is being undertaken, and show the value of what you can accomplish.
- Work together to brainstorm and explore options for mutual gain.
- Use active listening and open, honest communication.
- Insist on objective, fact-based criteria for discussion, analysis, and decisions.
- Focus on problem solving, not arguing about the project.

Even though detailed planning data may be a confusing and ineffective place to start your discussions with your sponsor, it does have its use. Faced with demands for faster execution or less resource consumption, hold up your detailed Gantt chart or WBS. Ask your sponsor to pick the activities you should drop in order to meet the objective. Most managers back off very quickly when confronted with such a request, and this tactic allows you to refocus the discussion on realistic adjustments. If your sponsor does start selecting activities to drop, be prepared to explain the costs and other consequences of not including those parts of your project.

Sometimes a sponsor shifts the conversation to how talented and clever you are, as if to say that you, of all people, certainly can find some way to get the project done as originally envisioned. In this case, thank your sponsor for the compliment but point out that even you cannot do what's impossible, your impressive capabilities notwithstanding. Drag the discussion back to the project.

Or the conversation may head off in the other direction. You may hear threats that your sponsor will "find someone who can do this" or demands to "do it because I say to do it." Again, stand your ground and point out that you have taken considerable time to understand the project and are working with a very capable team. What you are proposing is the best option available, and neither another project leader nor naked demands are likely to change that.

Focus on options where both you and your sponsor get a good result. When you cave in to unrealistic demands, it may appear to be a win for your sponsor, but ultimately everyone loses. You and your team are stuck trying for miracles on an out-of-control, demotivating project, and your project stakeholders and sponsor never get what they need.

Be firm, diplomatic, and persistent. Use all your influencing skills to build consensus for project goals that are credible, and do your best to justify and retain an adequate reserve in your plans so that your baseline is achievable.

If your discussion leads you to a mutual conclusion not to go forward with the project, and it might, express regret but be philosophical. Organizations always have more good project ideas than they can adequately staff. Aborting a doomed project early is much better than canceling it later, or worse, having it fail. Early termination saves money and frees resources to take on high-value, realistic projects. Find out what's next and move on.

Conclude your discussions with a review of what you have agreed to, and commit to a baseline for your project. If you got what you came for—a revised objective supported by a credible plan—thank your sponsor. If you should find yourself forced to accept a project objective that seems likely to fail, convey your reservations to your sponsor, summarizing the consequences of the decision. Either way, gather your notes and prepare to finalize your project planning documents.

Setting the Baseline

Complete your planning process by establishing the project baseline for tracking based on your agreements with your sponsor:

- Summarize and communicate the committed project deadline, budget, and deliverables for your sponsor, stakeholders, leaders of related projects, and your team.
- Revise your schedule if necessary, and set the baseline in your project scheduling tool.
- Freeze the project scope, and document all deliverable specifications.
- Make final versions of project documents available to all who need them, online if possible.
- Archive baseline planning documents in your project management information system.

GETTING THE LEAD OUT

"Get the lead out" is sometimes a command by a sponsor to speed up a project, but when Richard Simonds was a project consultant at Hewlett-Packard, he worked with one team where it had a very different meaning.

Some years ago a corporate team was charged with developing plans to convert all of HP to lead-free product manufacturing. Their initial progress was modest, so they asked Richard to help them with their project planning. "The basic plan was sound, but it was incomplete—the project was much larger than anyone had realized," says Richard. "I spent time with them reviewing the infrastructure for the project using a checklist. Much of what was missing became visible through these discussions. They made many important decisions that resulted in a much more robust project plan." (The list of questions Richard used was similar to the one in Appendix A.)

The project team presented a revised plan to the executive staff responsible for the initiative, with gratifying results: The sponsor commented on how well thought-out the plan was, the team had ready answers for every question the executives threw at them, and the project budget was nearly tripled to meet the requirements demonstrated in the plan.

The project was baselined appropriately and proceeded as planned. The team met its goals for conversion to lead-free circuit-board manufacturing at HP sites worldwide—on schedule.

▪ Use Your Plan

Once a credible plan is in place and agreed to, project control shifts to executing and tracking, which are the topics of the next two chapters. Transitioning from planning to execution primarily involves:

- Starting to collect the status on milestones and deliverables called for in the plans and issuing reports
- Reconfirming all staffing and resource commitments
- Initiating a process (similar to the one described in Chapter 2) for managing changes following scope freeze
- Ensuring that all tools and facilities to be used for communication and tracking are available and working
- Reviewing and initiating all project processes needed for execution with appropriate team members, such as for quality management, contract management, and life cycles
- Arranging ready access for all who need project documents, plans, and data
- Reviewing project infrastructure decisions for execution and control using a checklist similar to the one in Appendix A

Once you set the project baseline, maintaining control now depends on keeping your plans up-to-date and visible.

KEY IDEAS FOR PROJECT PLANNING

- Plan your project thoroughly with your team, and integrate their inputs, suggestions, and perspectives all through your planning documents.
- Use planning data to set a realistic project baseline, negotiating required changes to initial objectives with your sponsor and stakeholders.
- Begin execution of your project with a credible, understandable plan that is available to all the members of your team.

CHAPTER 7

Maintaining Control During Project Execution

PERSEVERANCE MATTERS. All projects encounter difficulty, and most undergo substantial change. Execution contributes to control through a steadfast focus on what is happening, what has been accomplished, and what is next. Dogmatic status collection sets the expectation that the 9th, 99th, and the 999th activities on the project plan are all equally important—because they are. To suspend status collection to solve a problem is to lose control; you must find a way to recover while continuing to collect the project data that you need. When using Scrum to manage an agile project, each day begins with a short stand-up status meeting, where each team member quickly recounts accomplishments in the past day, plans for that day, and any perceived impediments. This can be good practice on any project, especially when working to recover from a significant problem.

Diagnostic metrics are the basis for status collection. They provide the information you need to assess performance and progress, and their visibility ensures that barriers and issues are addressed promptly. They are the basis for ongoing communications, and they support your efforts to control your project. Control during execution also demands teamwork, which you must maintain through informal communications and personal interactions with and among your contributors.

▪ Deploying Status-Based Metrics

Initiation tells everyone what your project is doing, and planning shows how you intend to get it done. With everything clearly defined, project execution

168

ought to be straightforward. As project leader, you should be able to relax while the project progresses on autopilot, feet up, eating popcorn and patiently waiting for it to finish. Unfortunately, even the best-planned projects rarely run smoothly. Your plans are merely one prediction of the uncertain future, and to maintain control you must stay abreast of what is happening all through your project. As outlined in Chapter 4, project metrics are central to staying in control.

Diagnostic metrics in particular can show:

- Critical activity slippage
- Activities and features completed
- Activities and features discovered or added
- Excess resource consumption
- Adverse resource consumption and timing trends
- Unintended consequences of scope changes
- Staff performance problems
- Process efficiency or effectiveness problems
- Chronic issues
- The need to modify project plans or execute contingency plans
- Early signs pointing to potential future problems
- Assessment of technical or design debt
- The need to trigger risk response or other adaptive action
- When to reset the baseline for (or cancel) the project

Defining Diagnostic Metrics

Not all possibilities for measurement make sense for any given project. You need to select a small number of metrics that are likely to be useful enough to justify the effort it takes to collect them. All diagnostic metrics, even those you intend collect only infrequently, have an ongoing cost. Unlike predictive and retrospective metrics that are typically assessed only once, at the start or the end of your project respectively, diagnostic metrics require ongoing effort to obtain the information, analyze it, and then do something with it. Select your metrics carefully, choosing ones that provide useful data that you can use to guide and control your project, without inappropriate cost (or a high potential for needlessly annoying your team).

The following list is not intended to be exhaustive, but it does contain the most common types of status-based diagnostic metrics, grouped into several categories.

Timing and Schedule Metrics
- Activities finished
- Actual activity durations

- Actual activity completion dates
- Late activities and key missed milestones
- Cumulative project slip
- Early activities
- Number of added activities
- Activity closure index (the ratio of activities closed in the project so far versus the number expected)

Resource and Financial Metrics

- Actual activity costs
- Actual activity effort consumption
- Individual productivity
- Cost or effort overruns
- Cost or effort underruns
- Unplanned overtime
- Staff turnover

Earned Value Management (EVM) Metrics

- Planned value (PV), the cumulative expected cost for activities planned for execution in the project baseline by any specific date; also called budgeted cost of work scheduled (BCWS)
- Actual cost (AC), the cumulative actual cost for activities executed through any specific date; also called actual cost of work performed (ACWP)
- Earned value (EV), the cumulative expected costs associated with all the activities actually executed by any specific date; also called budgeted cost of work performed (BCWP)
- Cost variance (CV), defined as EV minus AC
- Schedule variance (SV), defined as EV minus PV
- Additional calculated metrics derived using EV, PV, and AC

Project Scope Metrics

- Number of submitted scope changes
- Number and magnitude of approved scope changes
- Features or specifications added or dropped
- Progress on feature burndown charts
- Results of tests, inspections, reviews, and walkthroughs
- Quality control statistics

General Project Metrics

- Issues opened and issues closed
- Identified risks encountered and avoided

- Risks identified after setting the project baseline
- Impact on other projects
- Impact by other projects (cost, time, scope, other)
- Communication metrics (such as volumes of e-mail and voice mail)
- Number of unanticipated project meetings

LEVERAGING YOUR DATA

Jose Solera spent many years managing projects at a major Fortune 100 company. In 1997, he found himself preparing to lead the effort to ensure that the organization would be ready for Y2K. Although he began his planning focused on just internal systems, the project quickly grew to encompass a wide range of software and products and came to involve supplier and customer readiness. Especially early on, this was a project that no one wanted; everyone just wanted it to go away. Y2K preparations would increase costs, for sure, but provide no immediate benefits. Although everyone knew that the project would avoid potential problems, this was viewed mostly as an insurance effort. Jose faced an enterprise-wide, global scope and had very few direct reports; the effort was a major challenge.

To get it going, he started with education. He worked to make everyone aware that the problem was more than just dealing with the two-digit year issue for personal computers. He communicated the issues and potential for significant and widespread damage.

Next, he began an accurate inventory of every system that could be affected and set goals so that they could measure how well they were doing and track their progress. He set his goals in terms of the percentage of the inventory that was Y2K-ready. An example goal was "25% of all critical systems would be compliant before the end of the first quarter of 1998." Rather than focus on the details of each and every project (and they numbered in the thousands), he focused on the percentages and tracked progress using these percentages as reported in his database.

Jose made a practice of calling the group leaders for the owners of all affected systems a couple of weeks before his regular reports were due to the CEO and the chairman of the board. Jose started a typical conversation saying, "I see here that the database shows that you are at 15% completion for critical systems. Our goal, due in two weeks, is 25%. What's going on?" If the response he received was an excuse for the low percentage, Jose would interrupt and point out, "I will be presenting this data to the executives. I'll be pulling what we have from the database a couple of days before the presentation, and I will report what it shows. If the information we have is not correct, please update it. If you are struggling, let me know what you need to bring your progress on track." Nine out of ten times, the issues were corrected before the presentation. For any situations that were lagging, the responsible managers had to explain the issues to the executives and how they planned to resolve them. As Jose observes, "No one wanted to do this more than once."

Control and Earned Value Management (EVM)

EVM is designed to enhance project control and, used properly, it can yield impressive results. It does entail more overhead than most other diagnostic metrics, however. Unless your organization makes use of EVM mandatory, your decision to adopt it (or any other measurements requiring significant effort) must be based on the specifics of your project. Some considerations and trade-offs to assist you in making a judgment, along with some lower-impact alternatives to EVM, are explored in this section.

Of all the diagnostic metrics, few generate more debate among project leaders than earned value. One small camp of ardent defenders cannot imagine running a project without full-bore EVM constantly in use. Another small camp of rabid detractors finds EVM a complete waste of time and energy, professing a belief that it is a high-cost effort that generates huge amounts of meaningless project data. The truth seems to lie somewhere between.

What Is EVM?

Earned value is based on a simple idea. Every planned project has a schedule and a projected budget. By the time it is finished, the project will have another plan and another budget—based on actual data from the completed project. You can use information from these two schedules and two budgets to generate compound time/cost metrics for your project. EVM works equally well using effort data instead of cost data, but the monetary version is more commonly defined and is the primary basis for the following discussion. For an effort-based equivalent, use the total effort (in person-months or some other suitable units) associated with the baseline plan and the final tally of effort consumed by the project as substitutes for the two budgets.

The two most obvious metrics are conceptually straightforward. *Planned value* (*PV*) is a curve charting the planned costs from zero at the start to the *budget at completion* (*BAC*) at the end. *Actual cost* (*AC*) is a curve on the same time scale that also starts at zero but winds its way up the two-dimensional graph based on actual expenses to eventually represent the completed project's actual outlays. (PV, like BAC, is actually a predictive metric; you can calculate it for your whole project when you set the baseline. It is often treated as a diagnostic metric, though, because it is generally calculated with the other metrics for a given date.)

The problem with these two curves is that, when they diverge, you can never know why just by looking at the graph. The difference could be due to timing problems with your activities, or it could be due to cost issues. It could even be (and usually is) a combination of the two. As long as the curves are based on entirely different schedule and budget data, you cannot tell.

Enter *earned value* (*EV*) to save the day. EV splits the difference because it is based on the planned budget combined with the actual schedule. EV is calculated by adding up the estimated costs (as with PV) for project work completed (as with AC). Now you can identify cost issues by comparing EV and AC; any differences between them are entirely due to variance between expected and actual cost. You can also identify that you have a timing issue by comparing EV and PV because the only source of difference is schedule variance. When all three basic EVM metrics have the same value for a given date, your project is considered under control—on time and on budget. The three fundamental metrics for EVM are shown in Table 7-1.

Should You Adopt EVM?

Two requirements of EVM make it controversial. The first requirement involves creating credible cost estimates for each activity or at least apportioning 100 percent of the project budget, bit by bit, among all of the lowest-level activities defined in your work breakdown structure. The second requirement is that you must collect actual cost data for each activity throughout your project. These two requirements, particularly the second one, can represent quite a bit of additional management overhead for projects where the use of this data is not already common practice or mandated. On the plus side, when using credible data, EVM reveals irreversible project cost overruns and other adverse trends very early in the project's timeline.

EVM includes a somewhat bewildering alphabet soup of calculated variances, indices, and projections for the project that are calculated using the three base metrics: EV, PV, and AC. Because the basic data used for EVM is

TABLE 7-1. BASIS OF EVM METRICS.

		Budgets	
		Planned Expense	Actual Expense
Schedules	Planned Schedule	Planned Value (PV)	(Not used)
	Actual Schedule	Earned Value (EV)	Actual Cost (AC)

primarily financial, the calculation of cost variance (CV, or EV minus AC) is the most straightforward to interpret. Because CV is the difference between the value you have *earned* (that is, the cost of the work expected by your plan) and what you have actually spent, it reveals the cumulative inaccuracy of your cost estimates for your project so far. If you begin with a thorough WBS and credible estimates, are working true to your plan, and are able to collect verifiable cost data for each activity, CV can be quite useful. This is, however, a rather long string of conditionals.

Also potentially useful is schedule variance (SV, or EV minus PV), which is the difference between the estimated costs of the work you have actually completed minus the estimated costs of the work you expected to have completed. A negative variance indicates that you are not keeping pace with your plan. Because the calculated metric is in monetary units, it can be hard to interpret. ("My project appears to be $3,000 late.") Adverse schedule variance requires further digging and root-cause analysis to pinpoint specific schedule problems. Variance analysis of metrics directly related to critical activities on your schedule is generally a more meaningful indicator of your schedule performance.

EVM also includes definitions for both schedule and cost indices. The cost performance index (CPI, or EV divided by AC) is the ratio of the cumulative estimated and actual costs for completed activities. The schedule performance index (SPI, or EV divided by PV) is also a ratio, but it is of the estimated cost of all the work completed and the estimated costs of the work you hoped to complete. As with negative values of CV and SV, values of these indices below one represent adverse variance. Additional EVM metrics continue to build on the three fundamental measures (EV, PV, and AC), using increasingly complicated formulas to calculate the estimated remaining project cost, total expected budget, expected completion date, and other project information.

EVM also includes many additional compound metrics for assessing EAC (estimate at completion), ETC (estimate to complete), TCPI (to complete performance index), and more—all potentially very useful in assessing your overall project.

The project in Figure 7-1 is about halfway to its deadline. It is significantly over budget, and it appears to be somewhat behind schedule.

Ensuring Useful EVM Results

Partly as a result of its complexity, EVM is not difficult to game, especially early in a project. Gaming is almost inevitable whenever these metrics are used primarily to criticize or punish people. EVM can be gamed by establishing a schedule that front-loads a lot of relatively easy work and associates costs with it that are overly generous. Rather than enhancing control, this results in proj-

FIGURE 7-1. GRAPH OF EVM METRICS

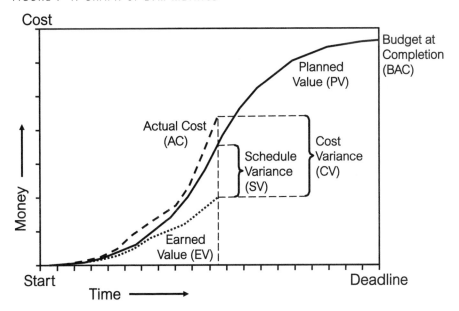

ects that, after apparently running smoothly, suddenly develop huge difficulties sometime after their midpoint. EVM can also be gamed for some projects by including all expenses for the project in what you track, not just those associated with effort. The distortion created by including nonlabor costs in some projects can be huge, and by timing them to land near the end of the project they can effectively mask a lot of problems. (This is one reason why EVM analysis based on effort rather than on money is more useful for project control. It also gives you a good reason to collect actual effort data to support future project estimating that might otherwise be lost.) Yet another way to bias the metrics is to work on things out of sequence. Starting activities early grants either 50 percent or prorated credit for EV; if you report initiating activities that are not yet scheduled, you can distort the EVM variances and indices in your favor. All these sources of bias are under the control of the project leader. Of course *you* would never consider doing this; it would be wrong. (And these gaming tactics work only in the early stages of a project anyway.)

Your team can also undermine the usefulness of EVM by misreporting costs (or effort) for activities or reinterpreting what "done" means. You can verify the data, of course, but, especially with geographically distributed teams, verification may not be easy.

The best defense against gaming with all metrics is to avoid using them for criticism or punishment. When EVM-related adverse results surface, it's best for everybody involved, including sponsors, managers, and stakeholders, to focus on resolving problems, not on affixing blame. If the cost variance is negative, the discussion should be about whether the project needs additional resources or staff. If EVM indicates a schedule variance that is an actual problem (adverse variance can be due to slippage of noncritical activities that do not threaten the project objective), discuss plan changes or adjusting the project's deadline. If the normal response to negative variance is resolution, good data is reported. When the more typical response is abuse, EVM, as with any system of metrics, exhibits garbage-in/garbage-out.

Gaming can also be minimized by asking people not to do it and by confronting data credibility problems whenever you suspect them. Also, discuss the metrics you plan to use, and get buy-in from your team in advance to minimize data quality problems.

Alternatives to EVM

EVM is fairly elaborate, consumes a good deal of your time, and can be confusing to implement. You can enhance your control with other options, similar to EVM, that require a good deal less overhead.

Agile projects employ the concept of technical debt to assess the overall work estimated to resolve issues of functional shortcomings. A burndown chart may be used to track information about the cost and rate of overall progress. Assessing these metrics within and across development iterations provides measures that are analogous to those of EVM.

For any project, you can implement a simplified version of EVM by assuming that all activities have the same cost and that they are distributed linearly across your timeline. This method surrenders a good deal of precision, especially initially. However, even fully implemented EVM is increasingly about averages and general trends as more and more of the project is completed. This simplified approach is based on an "activity closure index" (included earlier with schedule metrics). The index is based on the idea halfway through your project you should have half your activities finished. At any point, you can assess whether the fraction of the work you have completed is above, at, or below the fraction of the timeline you have consumed. This ratio approximates EVM's schedule performance index (SPI, the ratio of EV to PV). The accuracy of the activity closure index as an indicator of your project's performance improves as your project completes more and more work, and it provides a very good prediction of potential schedule overrun following the first third of your planned project duration. Determining whether the overrun is primarily due to insufficient resources or execution problems requires additional analysis, but this easily calculated index cues you to investigate.

Selecting and Setting Baselines for Diagnostic Metrics

Some of the metrics that you collect for your project are defined either by standard practices of your organization or by decisions that you made with your team in reviewing a list of infrastructure questions (see Appendix A). You may decide to add other measures, based on discussions with your team, or you may decide to measure some things about your project just for your own use to better understand how it is proceeding.

Metrics that are collected and reported publicly affect behavior. Consider the impact that the measures you intend to use could have on your project, as discussed in Chapter 4. If a metric might lead to potential adverse behavior, explore balancing it with another measure to provide tension or work to find possible alternatives.

You also need to establish a baseline for each diagnostic metric you plan to use. Without a baseline, there is a compared-to-what? problem that makes the interpretation and use of the data difficult.

Typically with diagnostic metrics, baselines are set using data from the first several collection cycles. A range based on empirical data is typically used to establish normal range for the process being measured. Use historical information to define the limits above and below which you need to act to bring things back under control. Resist making decisions and changes before determining the baseline; you cannot tell what, if anything, you have accomplished if you have no idea where you started. Individual productivity is an example of a diagnostic metric that requires baseline data. If you have a severely time-constrained project and your plans call for installing new equipment or modifying a process to improve how quickly you can get things done, begin by measuring the status quo. Measuring it again following the change lets you verify the results, to see whether your expected estimates were credible.

Not all diagnostic project metrics have baselines derived from data collection, at least not directly. Much of what you collect is compared with information from the project baseline that you set with your sponsor. If the project baseline is set using bottom-up analysis that is well grounded in historical experience, using the project baseline for your variance analysis is perfectly valid. If your project baseline is rooted more in wildly aggressive or optimistic guesses rather than in reality, variance analysis tells you more about what your sponsor does not understand than it does about how you are doing. In EVM, planned value (PV) is the baseline for both earned value (EV) and actual cost (AC). If EVM is credible, the variances and indices tell you how you are performing against reasonable norms. If PV is based on top-down demands for budget and schedule, your analysis may tell you how much trouble you are getting into, but not very much about how well you are managing your project. In general, when the baseline for a diagnostic metric is a prediction that is not supported by any data (such as a guess, a hope, or a demand), it is not very useful.

Calculated metrics have baselines derived from the baselines of the measures used to calculate them. Most variance metrics have a baseline of zero, and the index metrics have a baseline of one, including those associated with EVM.

▪ Status Collection

One of the most important and visible jobs of a project leader is communicating project status. This communication depends on a repeating cycle of information collection, analysis, response planning, and outbound reporting. The tracking and reporting cycle repeats throughout your project, typically weekly. The focus of this chapter is on surveillance and analysis, which keeps you informed. In Chapter 8, the focus shifts to the remainder of the cycle: response and reporting.

Status collection begins the cycle and involves implementing your diagnostic measures, collecting inputs, verifying the data, and using project variance information.

Implementing Your Diagnostic Measures

Most of the predictive metrics discussed in Chapter 6 are based on planning, which is primarily your responsibility. You directly control many of the inputs for the predictive measures you select. Diagnostic metrics related to project status are another story, both because using them requires ongoing work and because most of the data comes from others.

You should collect basic schedule and resource metrics routinely every tracking cycle, such as data for earned value analysis, if you plan to use it. Other metrics, such as those associated with scope, may be collected only when needed. For a typical project, collect information concerning:

- Activities started, delayed, or completed, with actual start and finish dates
- Features delivered
- Milestones completed or missed
- Effort and/or cost for completed activities
- Adjusted duration and effort estimates for problem activities
- Deliverable tests
- Data related to current issues and risks

If you are a project leader without a great deal of authority, you need to work to obtain meaningful commitments from your team to provide the information that you need. To do this, discuss with each individual on your team how the information will be used and what the benefits are. You may need to employ influencing skills to get buy-in, relying on things that you can provide as a project leader in exchange for the information you need.

For metrics you plan to collect periodically, define the frequency. Work with the members of your team to establish when you plan to collect each project metric. (Determining the frequency for data collection is included in the infrastructure checklist in Appendix A, along with other parameters of your project tracking cycle.)

Gathering status too infrequently causes serious control problems; projects move fast, and a lot can happen in a short time. Most project leaders collect routine project status about weekly, which is typically a good compromise between the currency of the data and the overhead required to assemble it. Weekly collection also allows you to establish a specific day and time that people can easily remember and become accustomed to. Your project staff members have many other things to worry about during the project, and they respond best to inquiries that they expect and understand. Collecting status more frequently is prudent on very short projects and whenever you find yourself in crisis mode, and daily status is the norm for projects using agile methods. Work with your team to determine a process and frequency for status collection that everyone accepts.

How you collect the data also matters. Devise ways to simplify the process; the easier you make it for people to respond to your status requests, the more likely it will be that you get back what you need promptly. Providing each person with a list or table of current activities that they are responsible for and including any information from the prior cycle is one way to make collection simple. If you list activities that each person owns and that are scheduled to begin in the next two weeks, you can also use your status requests to remind people of upcoming commitments. Updating a few cells in a spreadsheet or table that are well identified is quick and easy, and most people supply the information as requested. If you do decide to collect status measures in a meeting, keep the effort focused, tightly structured, and brief (15-minute stand-up meetings are held on agile projects using Scrum).

Project leaders successfully collect status using many methods. Whatever mechanism you select, do it the same way throughout your project. A very common technique is to use e-mail. E-mail provides a simple, unambiguous way to collect status, and it leaves an audit trail for your records. It works well even for distant team members, and people can send it to you at the same time that they are responding to other communications, with no need to do something unusual on their part. If the common practice in your organization is to use a Web- or server-based project tracking tool, you can also collect much of your status information by having your team members update their progress directly in the database of your scheduling tool. For cross-functional teams, though, resistance to learning a specific system and dedicating the time for weekly updates may pose insurmountable barriers. Direct online data collection also may create data integrity issues with your tracking; when more than one person enters data into a scheduling tool, inconsistencies are difficult to avoid. Other status collection methods include conversations, meetings, and online or printed forms. Any method that works for you and your team should provide what you need for project control.

You may find it necessary in some cases to use alternative methods for gleaning current status that shift more of the burden onto you. If you can't get a credible commitment from a team member to submit a regular status update, explore other options for finding out what is happening. Some of your team members may be part of other organizations or teams that routinely collect much of the data that you need, and you can collect your status by gaining access to their reports to extract what you need. If some members of your team find it easier to establish a document containing their project work that they periodically update on a server or knowledge management system, encourage them to align it with your plans and use the information on it to keep your overall status up-to-date. Consider any option that maximizes the timeliness and quality of your status information.

Collecting Inputs

Once you have determined the measures for project control and how to collect data for them, you need to routinely gather the information. Be consistent and timely in every cycle. Follow the frequency and schedule that you and your team have set as dependably as you can. If your team suspects that you are not taking status collection seriously, they begin to ignore your requests and reminders.

Provide adequate time for people to reply to your status inquiries or to update their online status documents, but establish deadlines for the status requests and follow up promptly when people fail to provide the information. Be particularly vigilant when collecting status relating to past issues or problems that may have an impact on particularly urgent current work. Managing problems requires increased intensity in status collection; it should never be a rationalization for skipping a cycle. For complex projects, out of sight is nearly always out of mind. This situation leads to small control problems cascading into much larger disasters.

One of the biggest challenges, especially for new project leaders, is dealing with bad news. When someone reports a delay, a cost overrun, or other problems, experienced project leaders clench their teeth, smile, and say, "Thank you for the information. I appreciate your letting me know promptly." Human nature in this situation is to grab a chair and break it over your team member's head, but the consequences of shooting the messenger who delivers bad news undermines your project. In a heartbeat, all the effort you have put into building trust and a good working relationship vanishes. Worse, the next time you ask for status, the reply will be, "Um, fine. Everything is going just fine. Please don't pick up that chair." Reacting to bad news with abuse or punishment, as with misusing any metrics, shuts down honest reporting and leaves you without credible project information. To control a project, you need to know what is happening. Smiling and acting grateful for bad news is something all effective project leaders learn to do.

Thank people for providing status, especially extended members of your team. Acknowledge the time and effort that it takes, at least once in a while. Ensure that people know that you care about the information, and let them see that you are using it to manage the project. If you are perceived as apathetic or just collecting data because you can, your contributors eventually stop providing it or start sending you slapped-together, inaccurate status reports.

Be persistent in collecting status inputs from distant team members and from outside contractors. If any team member fails to provide status on time, send additional requests and reminders. If all of these are ignored, call the person on the telephone to collect the status verbally. Call them when they are at work (regardless of your local time). If the problem persists, discuss the status reporting commitment that your team member made and work to resolve the problem by renewing or adjusting it. Remind any delinquent contributors that the work they are responsible for will show up in your project status report as behind or incomplete if you do not have their input; accurate reporting is your responsibility, even if it reflects badly on others. If even these measures fail to resolve the problem for some unresponsive members of your team, enlist the assistance of the individual's manager or your project sponsor, but only after you have completely exhausted all of your one-on-one options. Failure to report status can be a leading indicator of more significant performance problems (see Chapter 8), and the earlier you recognize and deal with them, the easier it is to keep your project under control.

Verifying and Analyzing Project Variance

If any of the status data seems inconsistent with other inputs or past data, too good to be true, or otherwise questionable, discuss it with the person who supplied the information. Validate the reliability of the information by asking open questions soliciting a detailed explanation of the situation.

Take all the status data you have collected in each cycle, and compare it with your project baseline. Identify all the differences you find. Most variances on projects tend to be problems, but note any good news as well. Even small adverse variances may signal major future problems, and problems are easiest to deal with while they are small.

Calculated project variances are diagnostic metrics—numbers, facts, and hard data about your project. Measured variances allow you to separate the parts of your project that are under control from the portions that are causing (or will cause) problems. Hard data for your project reveals the existence of problems, but it may not tell you much about where those problems arise or help you find a way to resolve them. Informal communication provides a second kind of status: soft data. Stories, rumors, concerns, and other nonempirical information about your project and your team help you discover the root causes behind the status you collect, as well as alerting you to potential future project trouble.

Before spending much effort working to analyze, resolve, or report on your status, investigate each variance that you do not already understand. Determine whether an unexpected status is a single event, or if it (or something similar) is likely to recur. Strive to uncover the reasons for productivity and execution problems. If other project work is interfering with your project, verify the relative priorities. Find out why delays are happening and how long they are likely to persist. Pay attention to impending changes outside your project that could impact your work, such as building construction, system upgrades, network maintenance, or changes to other services and facilities that you depend on.

In statistics, two types of errors are identified. Type-I errors are *false negative*. Investigating the underlying soft data for reported status that seems questionable may reveal apparent adverse project variances that are not really problems. Type-II errors are *false positive*, and they are more common and harder to root out. Project status reporting, especially at a distance or when the project leader has not developed much of a relationship with the team members, is potentially chock-full of this type of error. Many contributors find it much easier to report what they are expected to report, even when they are in trouble. They may fail to report problems to avoid the potential annoyance of a long conversation with you discussing what comes next.

Other motivations for unreliable reporting include:

- Expected criticism or punishment
- Inappropriate optimism ("The first half of this assignment took two weeks to complete, but I think I can finish the rest in a day or so")
- Gaming of the metrics
- Faulty assessment
- Plain dishonesty

Always be skeptical, particularly whenever you are dealing with people with whom you have not established sufficient trust. If you suspect that your status information is not reliable, follow up by seeking supporting information such as documentation, test data, or other tangible evidence of progress. Participating in reviews, tests, demonstrations, and inspections can also give you better insight into the progress of work that you can't easily monitor. Project control relies on timely, accurate information.

Having validated your status data, analyze your schedule variances. For critical delayed activities, determine the impact on your project schedule and on important intermediate milestones. For all continuing activities that are expected to finish late, determine the cause. Projects are filled with similar activities; a current delay even for a noncritical activity may reveal a problem that could impact your project significantly in the future. Also explore any positive variances, probing for possible replanning opportunities that could enhance your flexibility and chances for success.

Next, analyze any resource variances. Identify reasons for all overruns, and consider the possible impact of work scheduled later in your project. All resource overconsumption for the project is cumulative. Every little bit hurts. If you are using earned value analysis to track your project, calculate earned value, planned value, and actual cost, including work in progress. Compare any adverse variances associated with EVM (or similar tracking methods) with other project indicators, and determine the cause of any differences that you discover. Also explore opportunities to complete future work at a lower cost or effort than estimated based on any positive resource variances.

Note all other significant variances, in areas such as individual productivity, project changes, or metrics associated with your project scope or features.

Periodically, take a longer view with your analysis of status data. Examine the trends in your data at life cycle phase exits, during project reviews, or, worst case, at least once a month. If schedule or resource consumption problems are growing and you do not see a realistic way to reverse the trend, you may need to propose to your sponsor resetting the overall project objectives and baseline. Detecting the need to make adjustments to the project early makes it much easier to gain support for change proposals. If you wait until the end of your project to raise the alarm, you get little sympathy, criticism, and the probable cancellation of your project.

Saving and Using Project Variance Information

The most immediate uses of project status analysis are making adjustments to control your project and generating project reports (topics in Chapter 8). Diagnostic project metrics can also be useful for assessing and improving your processes, motivating your team, and providing real-time information about your project for meetings, presentations, and discussions.

Status metrics are also part of your project management information system (PMIS), as discussed in Chapter 2. Store the project metrics where you and your team can access them, and use them to support your project reviews, presentations, and postproject lessons learned.

MIRACLES HAPPENED ON TUESDAYS

Status collection can be a very powerful motivator. Nancy McDonald was responsible at one point for installing all of the voice and data networking for a new data center project. This data center was to be one of the largest in the eastern United States at the time, and about 30 different technology companies were involved in the massive project, including major computer systems vendors, telecommunications equipment manufacturers, and a number of networking companies.

Nancy was responsible for the hundreds of circuits in the data center, point-to-point modem connections to local and more distant sites, and a bewildering array of other requirements. She engaged a large group of suppliers and delegated the necessary implementation to them. "Due to the enormous size, the project was exceedingly complex," she says. "To be successful the project would require close cooperation between companies that were direct competitors. Each company had responsibility for installing its own equipment and services, and each had an incentive to do a good job in order to secure additional work as the already-huge data center grew."

The executive sponsor of the data center project designated the first Wednesday of the month for all 30 suppliers to report jointly on their progress and to raise any issues. Many of the suppliers initially objected to meeting in a combined session with competitors, but ultimately they all agreed to participate. With so many participants, no meeting room was sufficiently large, so the monthly meetings were held in the still empty data center itself. Nancy continues:

> At the first status meeting, using folding chairs on the data center's newly installed raised floor, the largest computer vendor highlighted an issue: Dirt under the raised floor was hampering their installation and might affect reliability. In response, a team immediately sprang into action, quickly found a contractor with a very large vacuum cleaner, and the dirt was gone. The executive sponsor of the corporation's largest-ever IT project was not about to let dust bunnies become a showstopper. The senior representative who had raised the issue was asked to inspect under the floor to verify it was clean.

All the suppliers soon saw that raising an issue at these status meetings would result in immediate action, but these actions might be embarrassing or painful. "On Mondays, two days before the Wednesday meetings, all the suppliers would call me to review their status," Nancy says. "When they asked me to assist with problems, I advised them to raise the issues at the Wednesday status meeting."

Soon, miracles began to happen on Tuesdays. Problems that were impossible to resolve on Monday were consistently being fixed by Wednesday. Because they had already discussed the issue with Nancy, the suppliers couldn't just sweep issues under the rug (or even the raised floor) and hope that no one would notice. They had to actually resolve the issue or at least have a credible plan of attack. The initially unwieldy project meetings became an extremely effective tactic for managing the overall project.

Nancy has come to realize, after many projects, that the right plans, processes, and project controls are important, but they're not enough:

> Project success always depends on the people involved. And while having the right skills is necessary, they aren't sufficient, either. For projects, you must understand the group dynamics. Multisupplier and cross-functional projects can easily deteriorate into finger-pointing and the blame game. To nip this in the bud, you have to work to establish an environment where everyone is motivated to accomplish the overall goal. This can be a consequence of everyone buying into an overarching vision, or it may simply be a desire to avoid embarrassment in front of others.

Whatever the motivation, for a project to succeed, everyone must push each other to excel—and make miracles happen.

▪ Informal Communication

Status collection and metrics are about facts and figures. Control of your project depends on more than just hard data, however. You need to know the stories behind the data, and the more you know, the better you can control your project. Communication is arguably the most important job for any project leader. This section focuses on informal communication and *soft* project status. (Project reporting, meetings, and more formal communication are addressed in Chapter 8 on project tracking.)

For project leaders who don't have a great deal of actual authority, informal communication can be substantially more critical to project control than formal communication. Whereas formal communication provides information and context, informal communication—conversations, social exchanges, even nonproject interactions—forms the basis for the trust, teamwork, and durable relationships that are essential for efficient project execution and the prompt resolution of difficulties.

For project teams composed of strangers, even a small problem may escalate into a crisis. People who don't know each other tend to be suspicious of one another, and they assume that someone must be to blame for problems. In such cases, a lot of precious time and energy can be wasted in accusations and finger-pointing. Project team members who know and like each other are much more likely to approach problems simply as problems and put their effort into resolution, not struggle to identify a scapegoat. In addition, teams with good working relationships tend to watch out for each other, and they can frequently detect and avoid potential problems before they occur. Also, many risks and problems can be detected early through informal communication, long before they become visible through formal status collection.

Management by Wandering Around

The idea of *management by wandering around* (*MBWA*) originated during the early days of Hewlett-Packard. In David Packard's book *The HP Way*, he traces the practice back to his experience as a young manager with General Electric. He found that working with people directly and getting to know them was essential to resolving difficult problems with manufacturing on the factory floor. Identifying and correcting inadequate, incomplete, and sometimes incorrect documentation required a level of interaction and trust that was impossible except through one-on-one discussion and personal involvement. The main agenda of MBWA is that it has no agenda. It is not about collecting status or solving a particular problem. It is about interacting with people and informally talking to strengthen interpersonal connections. Packard stresses the need for "frequent, friendly, unfocused, and unscheduled" interactions to seek out people's thoughts and listen to their opinions. He believed that anyone could do it; you just have to make the time for it and do it willingly.

Project leaders who have little power or authority depend heavily on social relationships to get things done, and MBWA is one of the most effective ways available to build and enhance these relationships. In fact, even if you have power, social connections may be more effective. As Dan Ariely, a behavioral economist at MIT, says in his book *Predictably Irrational*, "Money, it turns out, is very often the most expensive way to motivate people. Social norms are not only cheaper, but more effective as well."

MBWA can be done remotely, using the telephone, but it is much more effective face-to-face. The same principles apply to remote MBWA as for in-person interactions; it is about building a long-lasting relationship based on trust, openness, and mutual respect. Some people begin or extend telephone calls to inquire generally about the other person and to catch up. Others prefer to call periodically just to talk, but this can be difficult for busy people, particularly with global teams. MBWA can also rely on technology, all the way from exchanging casual notes, pictures, and postcards to using full-motion video-conferencing. Even with all the technology available these days, relationships between people who are co-located and interact directly are deeper, more meaningful, and more durable. Work to take full advantage of any time available during trips or meetings where you can meet face to face with remote team members, even if only for a short time.

These principles help you use MBWA effectively:

- Be unpredictable and spontaneous. If spontaneity isn't natural for you, leave yourself reminders.
- Ask general, open questions instead of yes-or-no questions. (Examples: "What do you like best about your work? What have you done recently that you are most pleased with? Are there any changes that you would like to see? How is your family/pet/hobby/club?")
- Listen attentively. Let the discussion go wherever it goes and allow the other person to do most of the talking.
- Avoid confrontation or arguments. Foster an open, trusting environment.
- Focus on matters that have nothing to do with your company, organization, or project. Get to know your team members personally.
- Wander even if you are shy. Practice makes it easier over time.
- Seek out all of your team members equally, not just the people who are easiest to find or with whom you are already friends.
- Wander without any specific objectives, armed only with a few general questions to use if necessary.
- Wander often. MBWA is not a waste of time.

Joe Podolsky, who was an experienced manager for many years at HP, summed this up: "In the end, we each instinctively know that our most precious asset is our time. Investing that asset in face-to-face contact will always be appreciated as our most sincere and visible sign of caring."

Conversations

Conversation is a central part of management by wandering around and of informal communication in general. Overdoing conversation is easy; if you initiate conversations too frequently, productivity drops. You also undermine your control if you interrupt contributors doing urgent work, so keep your visits brief. In general, though, you should always be available for interruption from your team members. Project leaders who fail to suspend what they are doing when team members need to talk do so at their own peril. Responding promptly when team members have something they need to discuss is one of your primary responsibilities, and it's an important source of your influence within the project.

As with all communication, conversations are most effective when they are face-to-face. Studies vary on the precise breakdown, but the general consensus is that about half of the meaning we convey in conversation is nonverbal: body language, facial expressions, posture, and so forth. Roughly another third of meaning is carried in intonation, leaving a small minority of meaning (less than 10 percent, by some accounts) left for the basic words to convey. Because formal communication is almost entirely written, it is usually less influential and meaningful than person-to-person informal communication. Conversing regularly and effectively is key to project success. Exploit every opportunity available to meet and converse face-to-face with distant team members. It takes additional effort to overcome the barriers and disadvantages that your project faces when distance makes one-on-one interaction infrequent or impossible.

Conversing well is a critical skill, particularly for project leaders who have little formal authority. In effective conversations:

- Each person's ideas are heard in the context of a two-way dialogue.
- Questions arise naturally out of the discussion and active listening. Questions intended to lead to predetermined answers are avoided.
- All parties show genuine interest in what each speaker is saying and wait until thoughts are complete without interrupting.
- Each person speaks a roughly equal amount of time.

The environment for effective conversation also matters, and it includes location, timing, and other factors. Conversations that take place in the office, or "turf," of one person, especially when that person has more organizational power, can be intimidating and may limit what people are willing to say. The best environment for conversation is neutral, not belonging to anyone in the conversation. The setting for effective conversation needs to be comfortable and allow people to face each other on the same level. If some participants are sitting, all should be seated, facing one another in the same type of furniture. Overly formal settings can constrain conversations; choose a casual environment that allows open, friendly discussions.

On the telephone, timing is important. Conversation is best when the participants are awake, alert, and not distracted. Be sensitive to time-zone is-

sues when setting up telephone meetings and teleconferences, and avoid conflicts with mealtimes, any other commitments you are aware of, and the middle
of the night. Unfortunately for you, project leaders have more influence and
get better feedback when calling others to talk with them during their business
day. Even if it falls at an awkward or inconvenient time for you, adjust your
schedule to theirs. (Project leaders tend to lose sleep to 5:30 A.M. and 11:00
P.M. meetings, at least occasionally.)

It is easy to see how conversations or any information delivered through
speaking can lead to misunderstandings. Referring to Figure 7-2, each original
idea that you convey begins as a thought inside your head and must be translated into a message in spoken language. The words you choose can be many
or few, and regardless of how you choose to construct your message, it always
seems perfectly clear and complete—to you. The spoken message is then
launched into the no man's land between you and the person you are speaking
with. In addition to the words, your message includes your nonverbal communication (such as emphasis and body language), some of which you aren't even
aware of. Listeners who receive the message repeat the process in reverse,
reassembling the idea using the verbal and nonverbal bits that they happen to
be paying attention to.

The original idea and the message that you create are both products of
your own unique perspective, so portions of it may be completely opaque to
your listener. The perceived message is a product of the listener's perspective,
and it may be subject to selective editing; listeners tend to hear what they

FIGURE 7-2. COMMUNICATION OF IDEAS

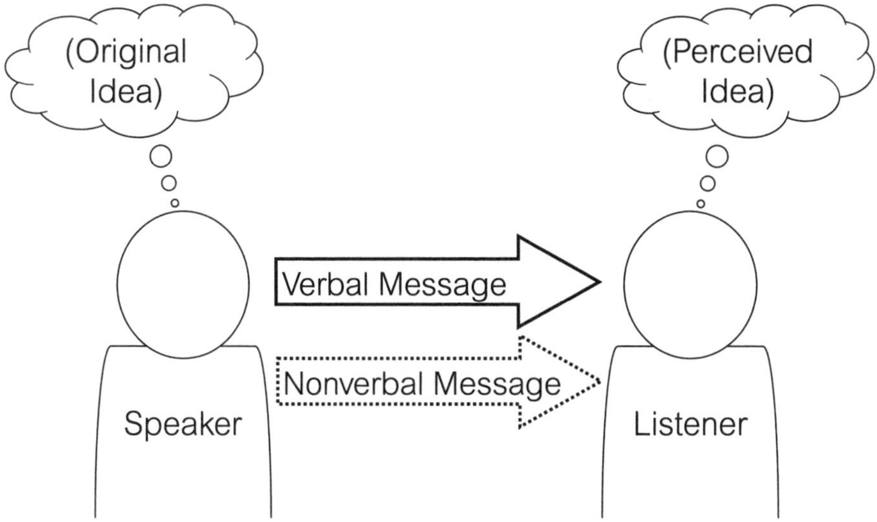

want to hear. (People who live together for a long time are well aware of this phenomenon. Their perspectives generally converge through shared experiences and mutual regard, but the selective editing of spoken messages seems to increase over time.) The chances are low that the original idea that the speaker had and the idea that the listener perceives will align exactly.

You can improve the odds by carefully considering what you say and how you say it. Avoiding jargon, idioms, acronyms, and other potentially confusing terminology helps. Speaking slowly and clearly, particularly when on the telephone or speaking to people who are not native speakers of the language being used, is also a good practice.

Active listening is also a valuable technique for detecting and correcting misunderstandings. Active listening requires listeners to paraphrase the idea in their own words, reversing the communications process. If there are differences between what the speaker had in mind and what the listener conveys using different words, the chances are good that it can be detected and corrected. Use active listening to ensure that what you think you are hearing from team members is in fact what they mean. When you are conveying important, complicated ideas through conversation, ask the people you are speaking with to express back to you what they heard you say. Do not simply ask, "Is that clear?" For critical project information that you communicate verbally, following up in writing to reinforce your message is also a good idea.

Conversations are carried on differently around the world. In North America and Northern Europe, conversational etiquette is for speakers to take turns, speaking when the other person finishes. In Latin America and southern Europe, conversational patterns are similar, but speakers tend to overlap, with transitional periods when both people are speaking. In Asia, there is often a respectful pause after one person speaks before the next person begins to talk. When conversing with people from the same cultural background, this all works fine, most of the time. But when people with different conversational patterns converse, the interaction can result in frustration or, worse, be perceived as rude. The safest course of action for project leaders is to do their best to fall into the pattern of the other person, with some bias in favor of the Asian model. Speaking too soon after another person completes a thought can be a result of not really listening. Some conversations are little more than two monologues— each delivered in spurts, interrupted by the other—with neither person paying much attention to what the other is saying. Project leaders need to listen well, a practice that others appreciate and that helps to build a relationship of trust and respect.

Informal Notes, E-Mail, and Social Media

Your informal written communications are also important for building influence on your project. Even though you typically scribble notes and create and send e-mails, text, and instant messages quickly, you need to take enough care with each of them to avoid problems. Few things erode your influence faster than creating confusion. Don't force your correspondents to guess what you mean; state things clearly, and avoid sending incomplete information that forces people to seek clarification.

Although some informal written communication is essential, both too little and too much of it can hurt your project. Discuss preferences with your team members one-on-one to tailor your interactions and make them more effective. With social media, instant messaging, and even e-mail, consider when the best times are to communicate. Before sending messages that could break your team's concentration and decrease productivity, consider the urgency of your communications.

Your influence improves when you communicate well. Always reread what you have written before you send it (or scrawl and leave it stuck to a computer screen). Check for possible misunderstandings, mistakes, or anything that could be read differently than you intend. If someone has asked you a question that has two options ("Would you rather meet on Tuesday or Wednesday?"), don't just respond "Yes." Consider each message from the perspective of the recipient, keeping your eyes open for comments that could imply unintended criticism or statements that could be wrongly interpreted as complaints. Take full advantage of spell-check software, but don't put all your trust in it. One of the most common errors in hastily written notes is omitting the word "no" or "not"—with potentially catastrophic results. Carefully reread what you write to make sure it actually says what you mean.

Written communication is flat; there are no good ways to incorporate the equivalent of nonverbal spoken language. You can use typographical conventions such as use of capitals, bold, or italics to indicate emphasis, but there is no guarantee that the reader will pick up the emphasis you intended. Emoticons like the smiley face (☺) might help, but again the exact meaning may not always be clear to the reader, and many people find them silly. Always follow up any written news that is complex or might have negative connotations with a conversation to ensure that your message is not misinterpreted. Better yet, have the conversation first and then follow up with a written confirmation.

Tailor your written communications, particularly messages that you send to only one recipient, by including a personal sentence or two at the start or the end. Make your informal written communication part of your management-by-wandering-around strategy, building your relationships with those you work with and reinforcing personal connections. Even though it is more effort, for important messages and requests, consider sending individual notes that include a personalized comment or two instead of a single standardized e-mail message to a long distribution list. This tactic makes it much more likely that your message is read.

Informal communication on projects invariably includes a lot of ad hoc electronic message exchanges that may volley back and forth for quite a few cycles in a small group. If the ongoing discussion at some point requires new participants, you do everyone a favor by untangling the story by providing a short, high-level summary of the exchanges to date in the note you forward to anyone new.

Informal communications can also create security issues, so consider the implications of the communications modes you employ and discourage the use of any that are not consistent with your organization's policies. Monitor your team's communications that may be visible to people outside your project, and work to eliminate any project information that must remain confidential.

Finally, be careful to scan all e-mail notes you create and eliminate, or at least tone down, any potentially personal information that should not be widely circulated. Double-check the distribution list before you reply to all, and avoid blanket replies entirely when sending your note to a subset of the distribution would be more appropriate. When, for any reason, you need to communicate sensitive or private information by e-mail, make it as clear as possible to all recipients that the information is for their use only and not to be shared. If you are upset by an e-mail or other communication you receive, never reply immediately. Let some time pass. Write your response, and then file it away for at least an hour, better yet a day, and go do something else. When you return to the note, decide whether what you have written is likely to make things better or worse. Edit the note to ensure that your response does not damage your project, your relationship with any of your stakeholders or team members, or your overall influence. Remaining calm and rational (or even appearing to be calm and rational) when everyone else is stressed and begins to panic invariably increases your control of your project. Electronic messages can live forever and they are very easy to forward; be vigilant about what you write and send.

A BLINDING FLASH OF INSIGHT

Informal communications are often what separate a frustrated project leader with a failing project from a successful one. Peter Vogel-Dittrich, who was a manager and consultant for many years with Hewlett-Packard in Germany, tells of a large cross-functional project called *Insight* that he was part of some years ago to revamp a program for new first-level managers worldwide. The team was global, with assignments for people in India, Europe, the United States, and other countries. He remembers, "In the three months leading up to the pilot for the program, rigorous weekly telephone meetings were used to discuss progress and deliverables, and the program manager based in the United States kept things on track by being perceived as tough."

During the pilot in Spain, many of the members of the virtual team met face-to-face for the first time. In the preceding months, most of the interactions among the team had been somewhat stiff and formal, and the impression many had formed of the program leader was that she was "all business." In person, she and everyone else relaxed, and as issues arose during the pilot they were quickly resolved. There was a great deal of flexibility and cooperation. Cultural issues and differences, which were central to the success of this program, could be seen and felt, not just described.

Subsequently, after the pilot, there was an entirely different environment within the project. People operated differently following their interactions in person, and they had much more positive perceptions of one another compared with the first phase of the work, when the team was just virtual. Peter credits the solid relationships that were formed for the success of the program (and the dinners in Spain probably didn't hurt, either). As the program was being established, the open sharing and interaction among the members of the distributed team were essential to gaining acceptance and widespread success of their efforts.

▪ Maintaining Relationships

Establishing good relationships with your project team depends a great deal on your ability to exert influence (the topic of Chapter 3). Establishing trust and a good relationship with each of your contributors is one of your main objectives during project initiation and planning, as discussed in the previous two chapters.

Continued influence and control depend on your ability to maintain those solid relationships with all the members of your team throughout project execution. You can and should do a number of things to maintain good relationships with your team for the remainder of your project. Some methods include building on common interests, using team activities, tailoring your interactions, staying positive and loyal, interacting socially, and using humor.

Building on Common Interests

Some of your informal communication in your MBWA should concern topics other than your project. You may share many possible interests with your team members, including your academic background, professional affiliations, hobbies, sports, literature, movies, travel, food, earlier projects, or other employers.

Identifying what you have in common with your team members gives you things to discuss and solidifies your relationships and ongoing teamwork.

Using Team Activities

Successful project teams function together effectively and secondarily focus on individual concerns. Use team-oriented activities throughout your project to encourage and sustain effective teamwork. You can also foster collaboration by establishing a communal space for the team to call its own, either an actual room (such as a war room) or a virtual space such as a Web site. Even for distributed, global, and virtual teams, it is useful to bring people together in person at the start of the project and again about every six months throughout the project.

The most effective way to begin a new project is to assemble the team for a project start-up workshop (discussed in Chapter 5). When people know each other, they tend to like and trust each other, and they can work together smoothly. It is human nature for people who have never met to be suspicious and to quarrel with each other, especially when they come from different backgrounds. Start-up workshops are most effective when conducted face-to-face. If this proves impossible, schedule at least a teleconference meeting to allow all your team members to interact with each other at the same time.

One way to strengthen interpersonal connections right at the beginning of a project is to work as a team to name your project. Forging a project identity draws the team together by providing an easy, shorthand way to refer to the project as a whole. If you decide to select a project name with your team, ensure that the name makes sense and that it is culturally appropriate for everyone on the team. (But don't, in an attempt to please, name it after your sponsor's dog. Dogs don't live forever, and it's hard to run a project named for a dead pet.)

Throughout project planning, the entire project team has many opportunities to work together. Take full advantage of planning activities to reinforce and maintain effective teamwork. Agile projects require this, and all projects benefit from it mightily.

There are many opportunities to work as a team throughout the execution of a project. Structure your work so that all team members, including contributors who are geographically distant, have integration, interfacing, and coordination requirements that ensure collaboration at least once a month during the project. Other chances to work as a team are variance analysis and replanning, change management, risk monitoring and review, conflict and issue management, collaborative problem solving, evaluating test and evaluation results, and project reviews. More details on collaborative approaches for these activities are outlined in Chapter 8.

The final opportunity for teamwork on most projects is capturing lessons learned during a postproject retrospective meeting. This is done primarily to improve processes for future projects by uncovering things that went well and should be repeated and things that did not go well that need to be changed. However, the meeting also serves to bring the project to an orderly conclusion and recognize the team's successes. A retrospective is also an excellent opportunity to reinforce relationships developed during the project. Building teamwork on a project that is ending might seem like an odd thing to invest time in, but it's a small world and people who have worked together once are very likely, sooner or later, to work together again. Chapter 9 further explores the subject of capturing lessons learned from your project.

Tailoring Your Interactions

Each of the people on your project team has individual preferences for how he or she likes to work, communicate, and interact. These unique preferences result from all of each person's experiences, learning, culture, and background. When you share a substantially similar history with one of your team members, you should have little difficulty interacting in ways that you both find familiar and comfortable. However, on today's project teams, the backgrounds of team members from different cultures, educational backgrounds, parts of the world, and age groups vary a great deal. Discussing communications options when reviewing the decisions for your project infrastructure, as described in Chapter 2, is a useful way to set expectations and to establish appropriate methods for interacting.

Some people may be naturally team-oriented and accustomed to working closely with others within a defined, structured hierarchy. Other people may be more independent and a good deal more comfortable working in an environment where they have a high degree of autonomy. Cultural differences even affect how time and deadlines are perceived. Some people are scrupulous about making and meeting time commitments; others have a less precise approach to deadlines. Preferred communication styles vary a great deal, with some people preferring informal interactions to be verbal, others favoring more distance and communications in writing, and still others comfortable with frequent texting, instant messaging, and other informal interactions.

Uncovering these preferences is an important part of establishing a relationship with each of the members of your team. This can be a challenge, especially when the interpersonal differences between you and a contributor are significant or the team member is located far away. Nonetheless, to the best of your ability, you need to minimize the effects of your personal cultural and other preferences. This is easier said than done, but one tactic that helps is never to pass up a chance to visit distant team members, to see for yourself where and how they work. You can learn the most if you journey alone. Traveling with co-workers creates a "bubble" of your own culture that is a barrier to understanding the places and people you visit. Also, whenever your attention is on your traveling companions, it is not on the people you are visiting. Study may help you understand other cultures; many references and classes are available on languages and cross-cultural relations. The most effective way to understand others and build relationships, however, is through personal interaction, which is, after all, your main objective. Some communication preferences on your team may take you out of your comfort zone, but you need to strive to do the best you can to get into sync with each of member of your team. In most cases, simply trying to meet people partway is rewarded with significantly increased cooperation and improved relations.

To some extent, it may also be effective to partition project work in ways that minimize the need for frequent interactions, making differing preferences for communication and variations in working styles less significant to the project. Even when this solution is helpful, though, you remain responsible for the project as a whole and must interact regularly with everyone on the team. The burden falls squarely on your shoulders for conforming to styles, time frames, and modes of communications that are effective for each member of your team.

BUILDING A HEALTHY PROGRAM TEAM

Rosemary Hossenlopp is an experienced project management consultant who works with organizations in Silicon Valley and elsewhere. She has successfully helped build many effective program teams and tells of a recent experience working with a Silicon Valley market leader. There were a number of issues, but she was quickly able to gain the attention she needed, build support, and show results.

One of the first things Rosemary noticed was that program priorities were not well aligned. Large programs have many stakeholders, and typical organization charts show each functional area at the same level. This arrangement makes it appear that all work streams are equal, but in reality they never are. To realign priorities, she worked with the program team to identify the key focus areas required for the upcoming tollgate review meeting. A key item that she was responsible for, involving a cross-functional offsite meeting, was running behind schedule. Rosemary had other pressing work, but she was able to delegate the planning to another person on the team, who jumped in and fleshed out the overall framework. With this momentum, others began to contribute. A senior member of the team created the format needed for presenting information on key focus area deliverables, actions, and risks. By highlighting the need and getting the work started, Rosemary was able to get things back on track by delegating the work to others who had been there longer and who served as effective change advocates.

She also noted a reluctance to report status as red when programs were significantly behind in meeting milestones. Reporting program health accurately is essential to control, so she set up one-on-one meetings with executive leadership to discuss the situation. Behind closed doors, they developed consensus on how to proceed. They set up an extended core team meeting to improve the accuracy of cross-functional sharing of key program information.

Rosemary also noted that people were more focused on the program itself and less focused on why the program was important. She needed to better align overall program priorities with the expected business value expected by senior leadership. To move in this direction, she recommended identifying the work not by functional area (such as marketing or development), but instead by the specific benefits to be delivered (for example, customer adoption, delivery readiness, or platform enablement). The measurements and reporting related to these deliverables helped in coordinating the work of all involved, regardless of their function.

At the start, the program had great activity and many people working on it, but there were obvious issues with coordination and communication. Reviewing the documents in the online program repository, Rosemary found extensive meeting notes, organization charts, and presentations, but there was no clear sense of project health. Dealing with this required lots of person-to-person communication, clarification of the priorities and objectives, and better definition of the key metrics related to overall performance.

Rosemary summarizes:

> Program improvements are hard won by hard work, but program managers can be more confident that the process they set in motion will gain results if they focus on the value of the business deliverables, priorities for key focus areas, and metrics aligned with those key focus areas. During this program, the issues were complex, and the work was intense. There was continuous pressure to deliver results visible in every meeting. With the changes made, however, the overall status moved toward green in three months. Being honest about program health meant that the successes were real, and over time the program team developed a spirit of sincere camaraderie. Prospects for success were no longer in doubt.

Soon after this, Rosemary began helping with an even larger program in the same organization.

Staying Positive and Loyal

When everything on your project is going well (don't laugh—it happens), it's easy to be positive. But even when things aren't going very well, good project leaders remain resolutely positive. Depressed, unhappy project leaders who are convinced that their projects are doomed invariably infect their teams with this belief. Pessimism is contagious, and it is disastrous to projects. Giving the impression that the project is a death march quickly derails the good relationships you have worked so hard to establish among your team members.

An essential tool for maintaining trust and team cohesion is unflagging loyalty. Your loyalty to each team member must be unwavering throughout the project. As things go wrong on your project (and they will), you start to hear complaints and criticisms of your team members from outside your project. You may even be tempted to be critical of team members yourself when discussing your project with others. Publicly criticizing members of your team can be extremely corrosive to team cohesion. You must listen to complaints, problems, and issues, and commit to looking into them, while steadfastly expressing support for your team members until you can investigate further.

Loyalty, trust, and good relationships within your team are essential, and your team members will tend to follow your lead on loyalty to others on the team and to the project. Throughout the project, as difficult as it may be at times, strive to serve as a good example. Remaining loyal to your team contributes much to team success.

In the midst of problems, work to keep the focus on problem solving and recovery, not on personal attacks and "blame-storming." Don't focus on problem areas to the complete exclusion of things that are going well; always mention things that are on schedule and going well in project discussions. Remember to thank people frequently for their efforts and acknowledge accomplishments. When reporting on problems, focus on the progress you are making toward recovery.

Interacting Socially and Feeding People

Team cohesion is about more than just the project. Non-project-related activities, such as going to a movie, a sporting event, or some other type of outing, can be a significant boost to building team relationships. This tactic works best when the activities are selected by the team and are not too frequent. The context of a face-to-face meeting such as a start-up workshop or project review provides a good opportunity to schedule some kind of event that will involve the whole team, including distant team members.

Armies are said to travel on their stomachs, and so do most project teams. One thing that all humans have in common is eating. Common interests tend to draw us together and help in team building. Sharing a meal fills this need, and it also serves as a socializing event. With a little research and creativity, you can find edibles that can be enjoyed by even the most diverse team members. Teams can share snacks of some kind in the course of normal meetings. They can share meals together before or after a meeting or work, or they can integrate food into special events. One project team I worked with was particularly fond of dark chocolate. This global team held twice-yearly meetings that were attended by participants from all over the world. During these meetings, a competition developed where all attendees were challenged to bring local chocolates or something made with chocolate to the next meeting. During the breaks, we all gorged on chocolate. It was the best kind of competition, because in the end, everyone won.

Take advantage of the power of social events and food to build camaraderie, but do it in ways that your team responds to, and in moderation.

Using Humor and Having Fun

Projects can be difficult, long, and stressful. Breaking away from a monomaniacal, relentless focus on the work, at least occasionally, helps everyone survive.

Likeable project leaders have more influence over their teams and more control over their projects. Cultivating an appropriate sense of humor is a good way to increase your likability. You don't need to be a natural-born comedian to share a short, humorous story appropriate to a meeting or to include a relevant cartoon in a presentation or an e-mail. Getting people to laugh or at least smile is an excellent stress reliever and can be of great help in maintaining morale and working through difficult situations. Showing you are not overly serious all the time is a good way to connect better with your team and improve relationships. Use humor in moderation, and work to stay within the boundaries of decorum, taste, and cultural sensitivity.

CREATING TRUST ACROSS A GLOBAL TEAM

Emphasizing the importance of maintaining good relationships, J. D. Watson, a manager with many years of experience at DuPont, shared this story about a project critical to divesting a part of his organization that was being sold to another company. The project involved establishing a new global telecommunications infrastructure for a hundred locations in 65 countries. In addition to the significant costs, the project team had to manage all the technical difficulties, including application changes and data center consolidations, on the very tight timetable required by the divestiture agreement.

Quickly, all the telecommunications managers involved realized they would not succeed without face-to-face meetings. In person, language and cross-cultural difficulties shrank, turf battles were avoided, and problems were much easier to resolve. E-mail and teleconferences were also frequent across all time zones, but ultimately the face-to-face meetings proved essential for ensuring that none of the hundreds of the necessary tasks would be overlooked. J. D. observes: "Success for this complex global project was dependent on thousands of details, many of which only came to light through the individual discussions and interactions made possible by our face-to-face meetings.

He continues:

> The nature of project team relationships is increasingly ephemeral. When I worked major projects in the past, relationships with internal experts and external contractors were well established and long lasting. These days, you're lucky if there are any people you know on your team; the group you work with from Texas on one project may be from India on the next, and from Guangzhou for the one after that. Because people don't trust people that they don't know, it is more and more essential to meet in person.

▪ Keeping Your Team Focused

The modern project is surrounded by distractions. An effective project leader understands this, and works to minimize them and retain a tight focus on the project. Results depend on team members working steadfastly on project activities and retaining a clear understanding of the project's purpose.

The Myth of Multitasking

These days, most people are convinced that they can do several things simultaneously and do them all well. For nearly everyone this belief is demonstrably untrue; the human brain is not set up to do more than one thing requiring conscious concentration at a time. Complex knowledge work involves deep concentration, and dealing with frequent interruptions results in inefficiency, errors, and stress. Recovering from a single disruption during intense concentration—figuring out where you were before the intrusion and then coming back up to full mental speed—takes about 20 minutes. When people are evaluated while trying to do two things at once (such as reading and listening), results consistently show—often to their surprise—that they do neither very well.

For most project work, progress depends on people having substantial blocks of time to work without distraction. Do what you can to establish an environment where your contributors have protection from needless noise and interruptions. When possible, minimize how often people check their e-mails, instant messages, and other social media, and take care not to contribute to the load of distractions yourself. Interpersonal interaction builds teamwork, but excessive communications erode productivity.

One of the most prolific users of Twitter, the English comedian and actor Stephen Fry, has completely dropped off at least twice, saying in his "farewell tweet" in January 2010, "I need peace, absolute peace, an empty diary and zero distraction. I enter a kind of writing purdah, an eremitical seclusion in which there is just me, a keyboard, and abundant cups of coffee, all in a room whose curtains have been drawn against the light." (Eremitical means "like a hermit"; I looked it up.) Getting results requires quiet, no matter how much we may believe otherwise.

Refreshing the Project Vision

Even if you are able to minimize chaos, you can't ensure productivity unless people remain motivated to work on the project. In Chapter 3, project purpose was one of the key motivating factors for engaging people. Beginning a project with a compelling vision is a good way to ensure that team members care about the project. Project beginnings are generally enthusiastic and high energy, and early commitments are often not much problem. However, as projects proceed—especially lengthy ones—people can become bored, disinterested, and ready to move on to something new. One way to retain energy and engagement is to keep a motivating vision front and center.

Not every contributor is equally motivated by the overall vision your sponsor has when initiating the project; you may find it necessary to adjust what you include or emphasize depending on the person you are speaking with. Some team members are most interested in the work that they are responsible for and motivated by what they are learning and the expertise they are building. Others may be motivated by the effective teamwork and the control they have over how and when they do their work. For most people, at least some aspect of the project deliverable matters: its value to the organization or to a customer, the quality or novelty of what you are creating, or some other unique characteristic.

Effective project leaders keep the overall purpose of the project visible, and use compelling language to remind the team frequently why what you are all working on matters.

CLEARING A TECHNICAL DEBT

Anup Deshpande is an experienced project manager in Silicon Valley who recently joined a dynamic company as engineering program manager. In his first week, he started to discover piles and piles of issues that had been shoved out of sight but were causing a lot of trouble. He knew that he had been hired with a charter to turn around the organization's effectiveness and to help it deliver software with predictable quality, schedule, and performance.

What he was finding revealed major communications failures among the organization's cross-functional teams. There were big disconnects between the product management, engineering, QA, upper management, and other parts of the organization. The result was a substantial backlog of technical debt and unrealized customer expectations. A lot of hard work was going on, but productivity was hindered by a lack of cohesion, and the chaos resulted in inadequate product quality.

Anup gathered information on the situation and started working on his game plan. As the program manager, he had some influence, but he did not have any *carrots* or *sticks* to resolve any of the problems by force. To get results, he knew that he would need upper management buy-in for some radical changes.

Anup gathered a few knowledgeable folks to seek advice to help him with planning. All agreed that starting small to get a few easy wins, biting off a little at a time was better than trying to eat an entire elephant all at once. He proposed this to his management and got their buy-in.

To get started, Anup started providing training to a few teams. He introduced the concepts of lean and agile methods, focused on once-a-month delivery of incremental, clearly defined deliverables. He worked with the product management team to lay out a roadmap for the entire year, with the understanding that it would be adjusted as they progressed based on changing market demands, the competition, and management decisions. Every month, the product manager selected a modest number of the top-ranking items from the project backlog to assign to the monthly release cycles. The development and QA teams started taking ownership of the items in these smaller buckets, provided helpful feedback and questions prior to each release cycle, clarified all delivery requirements, and pushed back any incomplete proposed items to product management. Anup dedicated time each month to analyze the current technical debt and worked to minimize the ongoing quality issues. Schedule predictability increased substantially, and quality improved quite a bit. Stress began to decrease, and mutual respect rose among cross-functional teams.

Crisp communication and demonstrable progress, Anup recognized, are essential for long-lasting success.

KEY IDEAS FOR PROJECT EXECUTION

- Define diagnostic project metrics that enhance control of your project; then get buy-in for them from your team.
- Be dogmatic and disciplined in collecting project status.
- Use informal communication to collect soft data, and work to maintain relationships and trust within your team.
- Work to retain motivation, focus, and engagement.

CHAPTER 8

Tracking and Monitoring for Project Control

MOST STATUS CYCLES bring at least some unwelcome news. Sorting out the problematic from the merely annoying is the first step in maintaining overall control. Seeking ways to adapt or shift the plan to deal with bad news means recovering from problems, not succumbing to them. To do this you need to have a full complement of techniques for control of schedule, cost, quality, and other potential problems. Managing scope changes is essential to project control, as are dealing with individual performance problems, managing issues, and monitoring risks. To control long-duration projects and programs, you need to rely on periodic project reviews to ensure that the objectives continue to make good business sense and to make needed plan adjustments. On occasion, control actions also may require, as a last resort, canceling the project.

▪ Scope and Specification Change Management

Project control depends heavily on scrupulously managing scope for your deliverables. Failing to control scope is about the most common reason projects fail to achieve their objectives. When scope is allowed to meander, the results aren't good. The old adages are true:

- Projects quickly get to 80 percent complete, then stay there forever.
- The first 90 percent of a project takes 90 percent of the time. The remaining 10 percent takes the other 90 percent.

This performance is not due to laziness or stupidity. It results from unconstrained scope change. When the rate of specification change exceeds your rate of progress, you can never reach your moving target. Nailing down project scope relies on freezing your scope when you set the project baseline, as discussed in Chapter 6. Avoiding unnecessary changes through the remainder of the project requires an effective process for managing proposed scope changes that empowers you to say *no* most of the time. Even on agile projects, scope is fixed for the current development iteration, and it is specified in detail for subsequent cycles. Changes on agile projects, although expected, must always be justified based on value. Although specifics of the change process vary with the specific project, for overall control it needs to operate much like the general change control process described in Chapter 2.

If you don't have a great deal of formal authority, a robust process for managing scope changes may be all that stands between you and complete chaos. If a good process exists in your organization, adopt it and use it. If not, write one and get your team to provide feedback on it. Draft a process that has a default answer of *reject* for changes, with all changes treated as unnecessary until proven otherwise. Also include explicit criteria to be used in making a decision for each change. The more specific you make the criteria, the more useful they are in helping you to control project scope. Develop and include a criterion for characterizing each change as either mandatory (addressing an execution problem, regulatory or legal changes, shifts in relevant standards, new competitive offerings) or nonmandatory (enhancements, new technology, opportunities, meddling management). Design your process to strongly discourage changes that are not mandatory or lack significant credible value.

Your team can be one of your most insidious sources of scope creep, so asking for and implementing their advice when you establish your change control process is essential to securing their buy-in and support. You also need to get approval from your sponsor and key stakeholders, because they are also fertile sources of frivolous change.

Before you set your project baseline, get everyone who you think might come up with project changes to sign off on a well-defined, documented change management process. Most people you approach willingly offer support if you ask early enough in your project. If you wait until they have a change in mind, however, their enthusiasm for the management process drops quickly.

Whatever the specifics of your exact process, work diligently to minimize inappropriate project changes. During the initial consideration of any change, quickly assess its consequences on your project objectives. Focus particularly on any expected impact on your highest priority. If you have a severely time-constrained project and a change would inject a significant delay, point this out. If resources are strictly limited and the change requires additional effort or expense, let people know.

Always answer two questions about every proposed change:

1. What does it cost?
2. What is it worth?

Be thorough with the first question, and remember that only you and your team are really in a position to assess the impact of proposed changes. It's your project, after all. Be very skeptical of answers to the benefit question, especially for changes that seem to be enhancements rather than proposals aimed at resolving legitimate project problems or better addressing legitimate project needs. Seek verifiable evidence for all value estimates, and determine uncertainty by requesting range information. If the cost of a change appears to exceed its potential value, that's a good argument against the change.

Finally, always consider all four possible decisions for any change: rejected, approved, approved with modifications, and deferred for future consideration. When you are unable to muster an outright *no*, answering *not yet* is almost as good. When you are not able to avoid changes, be thorough in exploring any alternatives that might meet the need with lower impact. Validate each aspect of each change that appears inevitable, and strip out anything superfluous before approval. A disposition of "Okay, in part" may allow you to avoid much of a change's impact on your project.

When changes are approved, communicate them. Notify your team and others who need to know, and promptly update all affected project plans and documents. On agile projects, adjust your features backlog list, and revise the content that future iterations are expected to deliver. For projects of any type, keep your scoping documentation visible and available to all stakeholders.

A VIEW FROM THE EDGE

With large, multisystem programs, even managers with substantial authority sometimes have too little. Ron Askeland has long worked as an R&D master engineer with the Hewlett-Packard Inkjet Products Group in San Diego, where scoping problems frequently cross organizational boundaries. The complexity arises because different HP businesses are responsible for the printer, the ink cartridges that carry and eject the ink for printing, and various printing media for specialized applications. The differing charters and motivations of these businesses make resolving technical problems particularly difficult; a solution that fixes a problem for one division can, and often does, create problems for the other divisions involved.

Shortly before the end of one new printer project, serious integration problems arose. Changes were going to be required to meet the scheduled introduction date for the printer. No single project team working alone would be able to own the entire problem, and the lowest-level manager that everybody reported to was on the corporate executive committee. Clearly, they needed to quickly find a pragmatic solution that considered the system as a whole. Ron says:

> To deal with this situation, we developed the concept of a "seam team." We established a cross-divisional work group chartered to develop the best overall resolution, considering all trade-offs within the system as a whole. Led by a senior engineer, with core team members from all of the affected businesses and functions, the seam team was set up to facilitate rapid development and streamline the normal build/test/fix cycle. The engineers were given decision authority and asked to develop a system solution while ensuring that no important issues fell between the cracks.

Working together, ink chemists, pen designers, system test engineers, media chemists, and printer design engineers made rapid progress on the problem, taking into account all the components of the overall system. The team got this problem resolved in the required time, including obtaining approvals for modifications in nearly all the subsystems.

Seam teams are responsible for evaluating problems and optimizing solutions at the system level, exploring all options without regard to where the ideas originated. They are led by engineers, not managers, to give the teams independence and to avoid tying them too closely to the priorities of a specific division. To move quickly to closure, seam teams have both the authority and responsibility to address their issues. Seam team recommendations carry weight because the management of all the affected organizations is committed in advance to accept their decisions. All seam team recommendations are communicated widely and put into effect with very little interference or debate.

Ron observes: "These projects lived and died by their seam teams. Seam teams are essential for promptly resolving difficult issues in parallel."

▪ Overall Control

Project scope control involves the element of choice. Managing it requires a specialized decision process. Most other project control issues are a result of unavoidable circumstances or events that have already occurred. Depending on the severity of the problem, maintaining project control can involve anything from some minor planning adjustments to substantial changes to the overall baseline and objectives.

To stay under control, effective project leaders use variance analysis to detect control problems. Early detection is essential to control because problems uncovered while they are small can often be resolved with minor adjustments. You can easily arrange such actions as working late, shifting the timing of a noncritical activity, or having other team members pitch in to help someone who is having difficulty. Easy fixes may not always work, though. Tactics that bring your project back into control need to focus broadly on the entire remaining portions of your project. Your highest priority is delivering on your commitments. If the action required to restore a credible likelihood of overall success involves making changes to parts of your project not directly related to the immediate problem, then that's the action you need to take. Always work to understand and deal with the root causes of project issues, not just their symptoms.

Regardless of the source or magnitude of a control problem, approach resolution using the Deming *plan-do-check-act cycle*:

- *Plan.* Using the variance analysis of your project status or other information about a situation that you need to control, work with your team to develop options for response. Consider the costs, other impacts, possible unintended consequences, and risks associated with each proposed response. Review all proposed ideas for consistency with your project infrastructure decisions. Conclude your planning by using a decision process (such as the one outlined in Chapter 2) to select the best option.
- *Do.* Get any approvals needed from your sponsor, management, or other project stakeholders. For proposals that impact project scope, get approval through your scope change process. For any major changes that affect your project's goals, work with your project sponsor to renegotiate and reset the project baseline. Update all affected project plans or documents, and implement your chosen action.
- *Check.* Use status metrics and other information to verify either that you have resolved the problem or that a control problem persists. Check for unintended consequences and impact on other work or projects.
- *Act.* Loop back to the plan phase for situations that require further attention. If you have successfully resolved your control problem, take any steps necessary to minimize recurrence later in your project or in the future. Document your actions and results in your project management information system (PMIS), for later project reviews and analysis of lessons learned.

Common project control problems fall into many categories, including performance problems, schedule control, cost control, quality control, issue management, decision making, outsourcing and contract administration, risk monitoring and control, losing a project sponsor, and taking over a project. Specific ideas for dealing with each of these are explored in the following sections.

Performance Problems

In planning, you assigned ownership of all project responsibilities and all of the lowest-level activities in your work breakdown structure to some individual on your team (or, by default, to yourself). Whenever you identify a variance from your plan or other problems, there is always some chance that the individuals doing the work could be at fault. When investigating the source of a variance, start with the assigned owner. Meet with the individual, face-to-face if possible, to explore the situation. Discuss the consequences to the project (in terms of additional cost, schedule slippage, or other issues) of missing a commitment. Emphasize aspects that affect your contributor personally.

Work to understand why your team member failed to follow through. Some reasons may be:

- Your team member does not know how to do the work.
- Delegation of ownership was not clear.
- Conflicting priorities represent more work than your contributor can finish.
- Your team member requires help or more resources.
- A required input for the work is delayed.
- Your contributor has too little authority to do the work.
- Necessary information for the work is unavailable.
- The individual was directed to do something else.
- Your contributor sees little personal benefit or reward in achieving the goal.

Don't guess what the reasons might be or jump to conclusions. Ask your contributor to describe the reasons in his or her own words. Probe to uncover the root cause, not just an excuse.

Ask your team member for possible solution suggestions. If the root cause is something that the individual needs but does not have, consider options for obtaining it. Situations where, for example, your contributor needs help or training are opportunities to employ your influence. Arranging for a mentor, coaching, or training may solve the problem while strengthening your relationship. Don't promise what you can't deliver, but do commit to removing barriers and helping in any way you can.

When a possible resolution requires additional project expense that you may not be in a position to approve, approach your sponsor or other manager to request and secure the money. If you need a way to justify the training, consider this story: Responding to a training request, the approving manager observed that it would be expensive and asked, "What if I approve this request and he quits?" The project leader replied with another question, "What if you don't approve it and he stays?" The manager promptly approved the training expense.

With your team member, look for solutions that address the root cause of the problem. Examples include a problem escalation to expedite a delayed input or a discussion with your sponsor to resolve a resource shortage. After your team member has made proposals for resolution, bring up any ideas you have as well. (You will find suggestions for specific types of project control problems further along in this section.) Work together to select and document the path forward that appears best to both of you. Ask for a commitment to follow through, and express your confidence that your contributor will be successful.

For performance problems that persist despite your repeated attempts at one-on-one resolution, involve the individual's manager, your sponsor, a manager responsible for personnel problems, or others who can help in these situations. Turn things over to those with experience in handling chronic performance cases to protect your organization, the individual, and yourself. Unless you are the individual's direct manager, limit your role in dealing with serious performance problems to that of a concerned participant.

WALKING IN SOMEONE ELSE'S SHOES

Ashok Waran, a long-time veteran of many complex projects, recalls a performance issue he encountered in Bangalore when he was working for a small company that manufactured computer devices for the public sector in India. This was before the economic liberalization in India when all of the components they used were made locally. He remembers:

"I was a project manager working on developing data terminals, statistical multiplexers, and word processors, among other devices. I was a young manager then and had not learned much about influencing my coworkers.

"For one particular project, I was a designer, developer, and manager rolled into one. I believed that everyone involved with my project would do whatever it took to get the job done—just as I would have. One of my responsibilities was to get the electronics working and tested, and that was easy. I had people I had worked with before for that, and of course I could do that by myself, if needed.

"I was also responsible for getting the final product out of the factory. We had a workshop that did the sheet metal and fiberglass work, and they were responsible for getting all the components assembled and ready to ship. The factory workers were very skilled in their own areas, but different in their behavior and approach from the engineers who were responsible for the electronics.

"As a project manager, my job included bringing everything together—the electronics, the power supply, and the final assembly. Everything else was proceeding well, but I had a great deal of trouble motivating the factory workers. They ignored some of my orders. Others they would pretend to obey, but then produce only what they wanted to. They were intelligent people, but they didn't look at the world the way I did. The packaging—the metal cages, the fiberglass covers—all had to be made by hand, then painted and finished. I could never predict when this work would be finished. This made my overall task of bringing everything together very difficult, and I was frustrated.

> This is when I began to visit with the factory workers to get to know things more intimately. I spent time and energy at the workshop getting to understand what it took to do their work and learning about their work environment. Most important, I got to know the people. I couldn't do any of what they did myself, but I was there with them when they had problems and showed interest in trying to solve them. I found that my work with them earned me such huge gratitude that after a short time, they would have done the impossible for me. As a result, we easily achieved our desired results and met the delivery schedule that I had been so concerned about.
>
> This experience taught me humility, and it taught me a lot about people and giving them respect. The big difference between the factory workers and the engineers [like me] was complete loyalty: They wouldn't even hesitate to lay their lives on the line, had I asked for it. I was moved beyond words for who they were and what they could do. I learned to respect them enormously. My approach to project work was profoundly influenced by those folks. It made me a better manager, far better than I might have been otherwise.

Schedule Control

Most schedule problems are detected during the plan variance analysis portion of your project tracking cycle. Determine the impact on your project's key milestones and completion date. Investigate the reason for each variance, initially with the activity's owner. Determine whether the timing problem is a single event or the result of something chronic. For problems that are likely to recur, assess the potential impact on later project work.

As with all planning, the more brains and perspectives the better; always involve your project contributors in brainstorming approaches that could restore your project schedule. Focus on addressing root causes, particularly with potentially recurring problems. Consider alternatives such as:

- Using responses that have been effective in similar past situations
- Consuming schedule reserve (if you negotiated some)
- Implementing a contingency plan developed as a risk response
- Delaying the start of one or more noncritical activities to let other team members assist in catching up
- Revising the sequence of remaining project work
- Decomposing future project activities for faster parallel execution
- Shifting resources away from activities where you can tolerate longer durations
- Personally helping out, when you can, with slipping activities
- Identifying innovative shortcuts for remaining project work
- Borrowing resources temporarily from other projects or organization efforts
- Working overtime or on nonworkdays
- Proposing removal of lower-priority requirements from the project deliverable
- Getting approval from your sponsor for the resources and expense required to crash upcoming project activities
- Documenting a compelling case and using it to negotiate a later deadline with your sponsor
- Proposing other major changes to the project baseline

Test rescheduling ideas you are considering using a copy of your baseline schedule. Explore possible *what-if* scenarios thoroughly, looking for realistic possibilities for getting back on track. For each schedule problem you encounter, also consider whether future project work could run into similar difficulties. Treat these as new project risks, and modify your schedule as necessary to minimize later problems.

The earlier you deal with significant threats to your deadline, the less painful it will be. If you get to the scheduled end of your project and a great deal of work remains, no one will be happy with you or your team. At that point, cancellation is more likely than approval for a timing adjustment, with dire consequences to your career and reputation. Be proactive and address problems as soon as you detect them, and, if a scheduling problem requires escalation, don't procrastinate.

Cost Control

Like schedule problems, most budget problems surface while assessing variance in your tracking cycle. Financial variance is cumulative; every adverse variance affects your project budget. Use root-cause analysis to understand why your costs are too high, initially through discussion with the activity's owner. Determine whether each variance might be a recurring problem or part of a dangerous trend. For chronic problems, determine the expected overall impact on the rest of your project.

Brainstorm with members of your team to develop approaches to deal with project costs.

Many of the same tactics that applied to schedule control, including pitching in yourself, applying contingency plans, and using solutions that have worked in the past, may lower overall expenses. Consider as well alternatives such as:

- Consuming budget reserve (if you negotiated some)
- Locating people you can temporarily borrow without cost from other projects or organization efforts
- Leveling resources
- Lengthening the schedule
- Documenting a compelling case and using it to negotiate additional resources or funding with your sponsor, or proposing other major changes to the project baseline

Verify that your ideas address your expense and budget problems, either by bringing overall expected expense in line with your plans or through a well-documented proposal for a larger budget. The earlier you can address a cost overrun situation, the less painful it will be. If problems accumulate and you run out of money well before your project is complete, you will get little sympathy, and your proposals for adjustment are unlikely to be approved.

Quality Control

Scope-related variances may also arise from your analysis of project status. Begin your diagnosis of the situation through discussions with the owner of the activity, test, inspection, walkthrough, or other source of the problem metrics. A cause-and-effect analysis (or fishbone diagram) helps you to understand the root causes. When needed, involve the rest of your project team in uncovering process issues or other potential problem sources.

Quality control begins with planning. It's often said: "Quality is planned in, never inspected in." Quality planning is tightly coupled to the scope planning and deliverable definition processes discussed in earlier chapters. Reliability, performance, usability, and other aspects of your deliverable that are critical to your project's success all must be reflected in your requirements and defined acceptance criteria. Structure your plans to deliver what is needed. Quality management also generally involves industry standards and specific policies adopted by your organization.

Project quality control and quality assurance are tightly linked. Examining work results throughout your project to detect quality control problems shows you whether your quality assurance processes are providing adequate structure and guidance to achieve your goals. Quality problems you may detect in your status metrics include deliverable-related measurements that are outside the defined limits, nonrandom in unexpected ways, or exhibiting adverse trends. You can use statistical tools such as Pareto charts, scatter diagrams, control limit graphs, and histograms to help you to diagnose problems and resolve them.

If you can solve a quality problem by adjusting a process that you and your team own, improve the process. Other situations may result from hardware or equipment problems, requiring recalibration, replacement, or repair. If scope changes are required, document and submit them. If the process that you need to improve is beyond your authority, document what the owner of the process needs, then use your data and influencing skills to sell your sponsor on the need for a change. Offer to help with any necessary modifications.

Significant quality problems may also involve escalation, and you may not be able to resolve some quality problems. Projects are unique, and you may learn that the quality your project has achieved is the best that it can deliver. If so, document the situation and meet with your sponsor and important stakeholders to explain the constraints you have discovered. Quality problems can be showstoppers; if the differences between what you can deliver and your goals are too great, project cancellation may be an inevitable result. However, if the project quality that you are able to achieve does deliver sufficient value, negotiate project changes, update your project scoping documents, adjust your acceptance criteria, and get on with your project.

Issue Management

Issues arise throughout projects. Your control relies on visibility and prompt resolution. Managing issues is important for project control, and it requires a process similar to the one outlined in Chapter 2. To maintain control:

- Recognize issues promptly.
- List issues with owners and expectations for resolution, and keep them visible.
- Escalate, but only when all else fails.

Issues are problems that don't yield to trivial resolution. They can arise from a significant project variance, a meeting action item, a risk that has occurred, or many other sources. Be proactive; monitor your status data, and use informal communication to detect project issues as soon as possible. Controlling an issue begins with catching it while it is small and resolving it before its effects become unmanageable. Ignoring issues and hoping that they go away is never healthy for your project.

Increase the visibility of current issues for your team by creating a list and maintaining it in a public place. A list that is part of your PMIS that you regularly review with your team is usually sufficient. On the list, assign an issue identifier, note the date you opened the item, and unambiguously describe the issue. Work with your team to identify an appropriate owner and a target completion date to each item. Include a status indicator for each item, such as open (unresolved), done (resolved), obsolete (resolution is no longer required), or replaced (superseded by a newer item).

Project team meetings are a good opportunity to review open items and to discuss owners and dates. For urgent items, however, you must initiate action as soon as you uncover the problem without waiting for the next meeting. Use a process for setting goals, like the one described in Chapter 6, to get a commitment from the assigned owner of each issue and an agreement to the resolution deadline. Track open issues and follow up on items on your list that are approaching (or past) their due dates. Use issue status reporting to publicly recognize prompt resolutions and to highlight any delays. Publicizing a lack of follow-through can be a very effective motivator.

As a last resort, when resolving an issue is beyond your team's capacity, prepare to escalate to someone outside your team who has sufficient authority to deal with the issue. Develop a detailed summary of the problem, including your attempts to deal with it. Outline possible approaches for resolution that might be used by others with more authority than you have, and document the costs and other consequences of each alternative. Before you escalate, also quantify the consequences of failing to resolve the issue quickly. Inform your sponsor (or another decision maker that you have identified for this escalation) that you have an issue. With this person, review the escalation process you established during project initiation, and get a firm ownership commitment from them and a due date for resolution.

Continue to track the status of escalated issues in your list with the new owner, and include its status in your project reporting, explicitly assigned to the decision maker. Track the issue through to resolution. If it looks like the resolution will be late, warn that you plan to report the status with a big, red stoplight indicator. If that doesn't bring things promptly to closure, issue your report and name names.

Sometimes, many project issues arise simultaneously. After listing all of them, use the principles of medical triage to avoid becoming overwhelmed. Sort the issues into three groups using the following categories:

- Problems you must address immediately
- Problems you must address soon
- Problems you will be unable to solve (if there are any)

If you have significant issues in the third "hopeless" category, thoroughly document them and discuss the situation with your project sponsor. For the remaining items, focus on the most urgent issues first, and then establish owners, dates, and plans for dealing with the rest.

GAINING AUTHORITY WHEN YOU HAVE THE SKILLS, BUT NO ASSIGNMENT

Some years ago, Todd Williams was assigned to audit a recently classified troubled project and report the findings to management. Todd did so, but the manager he reported to spent little time on the project and did nothing to solve its problems. Todd saw that the project manager was ineffective and his team had lost respect for him, but he was told that, as an auditor, his job was to report problems, not solve them. With a total lack of authority, he chose to work through a third party—the project manager—to implement corrective actions.

On his own, Todd initiated a deeper investigation into the ills of the project. What he found were two primary issues: The project manager was not holding the customer accountable for its deliverables, and one team member was failing to complete his tasks. To deal with this, he adopted a three-step approach. First, he would work to build a relationship with the team to garner its support. Next, he would find and resolve a major issue to gain the team's respect. Finally, he planned to work as a liaison between the project manager and the team—effectively managing both.

To build a relationship with the extended team, Todd needed to understand what was going on. He met with and patiently listened to their complaints and proposed solutions, which was in stark contrast to the existing project manager's style. He explains, "The team members quickly saw that I was not just 'someone from corporate' who would do nothing. They realized I could make a difference and would support them in completing the project."

To gain respect, Todd picked a problem to solve that was frustrating the entire team. The issue he chose involved writing a series of equipment interface specifications. Todd selected it because he had experience doing the task and it would highlight other problems. Specifically, using the specifications, he planned to expose the excuses of the nonperforming team member and break the logjam that the person was creating. The team was excited to be making progress, management was pleased to see results, and the project manager was grateful.

Todd says, "Having gained the respect of the project manager, I continued to make suggestions based on the team's inputs. We focused on other problem areas, and the pace of the project picked up. I basically was working as a surrogate project manager. Although I never had any actual authority, I was the genesis of nearly all the decisions."

Decision Making

From beginning to end, projects are riddled with decisions. Many decisions can and should be delegated to individuals (including yourself) and are an important element of activity ownership and motivation. Others, though, may be far-reaching and affect your entire project. Making good decisions promptly is essential to project control.

Effectively making and implementing significant decisions when you lack authority always requires team input and collaboration. Include all the members of your team and other stakeholders who are affected by such decisions in the overall process, and employ a well-defined process such as the one described in Chapter 2. For complicated decisions, spend adequate time discussing the situation to understand the issues and the question that you are answering before you begin considering options. Encourage all team members to ask questions and contribute to the deliberations, and solicit opinions from each person.

As you begin considering possible options, pay attention to how people feel about each alternative. Favor decisions that people on your team are comfortable with. Complicated analytical decision processes employing weighted evaluations of decision criteria don't necessary result in better decisions, and consensus decisions increase team cohesion and teamwork. Move to make decisions without delay.

After implementing a project-wide decision, monitor the results to ensure that it is effective and that there are no serious unintended consequences. If issues arise with any of your decisions, work to resolve them or go back and revisit your decision. Remaining in control of your project often requires prompt action, sometimes without as much information as you would prefer, and a willingness to make further changes and adjustments as you proceed.

Outsourcing and Contract Administration

Most of what applies to any other control issue applies to work done on a fee-for-service basis. Schedule problems are not uncommon, and they often occur without much warning after a long series of doing-just-fine status reports. Precision, performance, and quality issues can also arise without much warning. Depending on the contract terms, cost problems can also quickly spin out of control.

If you detect a problem that relates to the terms of the contract, escalate the issues to specialists in your organization promptly, and work through them to implement changes or adjustments needed.

For execution issues that are within the terms of the agreement, contact your contract liaison or meet with the external contributors on your team to discuss the situation. Response and resolution ideas include all those listed previously; explore options with your contract team members that will result in a credible commitment to get things back on track. Seek to resolve or at least to minimize the project impact from any variances. For timing problems, arrange for expedited execution of upcoming work whenever possible to get back on schedule.

If the contract includes penalty clauses, consider using them for leverage. Price reductions and other adjustments that may be built into the contract do not generally help you successfully complete your project, though. So most of the time you are a lot better off if you are able to resolve problems by working together instead of invoking penalty clauses.

When you encounter scoping changes that affect team members who are working on contract, there could be significant cost issues. Before initiating a change that would modify any contract terms, discuss the proposed changes with both your sponsor and your supplier liaison. Review the terms of the contract regarding amendments, and get an estimate of what the financial or other impact of the change would be to the contract. Avoid amending the contract if possible, but when contract changes are unavoidable, work to minimize the incremental expense or other adverse consequences. For all contract changes, quickly amend or rewrite the contract, get all parties to approve it, and get your project back on track.

HOLDING YOUR HEAD HIGH IN THE FACE OF ADVERSITY

At the end of some successful projects, over half the people working on them will lose their jobs. What crazy, upside-down type of projects are these? Outsourcing projects.

Nancy McDonald managed a number of these projects while a consultant for Accenture, and learned a lot about getting them done. Typically with information technology (IT) projects, a company decides to have its formerly in-house IT infrastructure operated by an outside company. Before assuming responsibility for the work previously done by in-house staff, the outsourcing firm must bring its team up to speed on all operations.

This is very challenging because there are usually a lot of custom-built, poorly documented legacy application systems. To quickly master them, the outsourcing team is dependent on the current in-house staff for training, most of whom will soon be losing their jobs. To make matters worse, the in-house people must also continue to do their current jobs in parallel with training their replacements. Although none of the in-house systems teams report to the project manager for the outsourcing company, the project manager must somehow gain their cooperation.

For this sort of project, both organizations expect to benefit, but the current staff, including many who have worked there for many years, will not. There is no point in trying to pretend that an outsourcing project will be a win/win for everyone. Gaining cooperation begins with acknowledging that the company has made the decision to outsource the work and that these decisions are rarely about the quality of the work performed by the in-house personnel.

Nancy says, "I also learned that it was essential to acknowledge the emotional roller coaster that the in-house staff would be experiencing. When events like this happen to people, it is critical to find ways to give them some control over their own destiny. That means helping people to see they have choices, even if their first choice (keeping their current job), is not an option." In some cases, there may be retention bonuses offered to key personnel who stick around and cooperate, so those people can decide either to earn that retention bonus or forgo it and resign to start looking for another job right away.

Even when no bonuses are offered, there are still options. Employees can opt to behave in ways that express their anger, disappointment, frustration, or fear, or they can try to make the best of an unpleasant situation and demonstrate their true professionalism. Although managing outsourcing projects was not Nancy's first choice, she had a job to do and wanted to do it well. She says:

> As project manager I stressed that the only thing an individual has complete control over is his or her own behavior. I asked all the people involved with the project to be sensitive to the feelings of others, and most important, to behave in a way that would allow each person to feel good about themselves.

I asked everyone to figure out what was right for them. Different people made different decisions about staying with their employer, or not, during the transition of the in-house work. Having a choice, and choosing to hold your head high in the face of adversity, is a powerful motivator.

Nancy managed a number of very successful outsourcing projects, and nearly everyone acted incredibly professionally and did their jobs well. Ultimately, though, she decided to follow her own advice about making choices, and she changed careers. She says, "As with many involved in outsourcing projects, my success led to the termination of my job. Although the change resulted in a significant cut in pay, I feel good about my decision. In the end, feeling good about myself is what motivates me."

Risk Monitoring and Control

Risk control is a bit different from the other items in this section, which all deal with issues, problems, and other project certainties. Risks are tied to future probabilities, so there may or may not be much to do at any given time.

Risk monitoring has three aspects that relate to control. One is ongoing surveillance of the trigger events associated with each risk on your risk register. The second is regular review of project risks in order to identify new risks and to reevaluate the identified items on your risk register. The third is periodic review of contingency plans, schedule reserves, and budget reserves to determine whether any changes are needed.

Ongoing monitoring means regularly scanning project status to detect risk trigger events or thresholds. You also need to be on the lookout for overall risk and to ensure that team members who own the risk response plans remain alert. Status-cycle monitoring is usually sufficient for minor risks, and it also reveals unanticipated risks that may arise. For more significant risks, the risk owners need to diligently monitor for trigger events so that they can react promptly with their contingency plans. Many risks identified have specific time windows when they are most likely to occur. Be particularly vigilant during any times of maximum exposure. When you detect a problem that is a result of a risk you have not foreseen, or if your established contingency plans prove ineffective, deal with project risks using appropriate schedule and cost control techniques. If a risk represents a material change to your project baseline, discuss the situation with your project sponsor and appropriate stakeholders. When facing the consequences of a major risk, escalate promptly; risk-related problems tend to go from bad to very bad in a hurry. Some risk responses may even require renegotiating a new project baseline.

Every day of your project, you learn more and realize new things. At least once a month, get out your risk register and review it in light of your new knowledge. Add any new risks that are now apparent. New risks arise from changes in or around your project; consider anything that has shifted since your last review. You may also discover additional risks by reviewing recent and upcoming work, looking for previously invisible exposures that may now be obvious. Assess the impact and probability of all new risks, and reconsider your assessments for all the risks already listed. As you reassess existing risks, remove any that no longer represent a threat or that have already occurred. Using the new and revised assessments, reprioritize your risk register. Develop and implement mitigation and avoidance strategies, where possible, for significant new risks, and establish owners, triggers, and contingency plans for all significant risks that you are not able to prevent. After each review, circulate a summary of your work. Between reviews, store the risk register where it can be easily accessed, discuss new risks in project team meetings, and work to keep the most significant identified risks visible to your team.

As your project progresses, changes occur. Work with those monitoring key risks to review contingency plans periodically. Ensure that your planned risk responses remain your best options. Periodic review also serves to keep the risks and their consequences more visible. Monitor trends in your status data for signs of overall project risk exposure. Earned value and other diagnostic metrics can reveal how your project is progressing, and these measures may provide early warnings of upcoming project-level problems.

Not all project risks are listed on your risk register. Some risks are unknown, arising from external factors or from unique aspects of your project. The only effective mitigating technique for unknown risk is establishing management reserve for your project: schedule reserve to deal with unanticipated timing problems and/or budget reserve to deal with expense overruns. If you have established reserve for your project, monitor how much of it is consumed by your contingent actions and unexpected problems. If your project is half done and 80 percent of your reserve is used up, discuss the need for additional reserve (or other project changes) with your sponsor.

Throughout your project, archive the risk registers. Track your risk history in your PMIS for future planning, project reviews, and analysis of lessons learned at project completion.

Losing a Project Sponsor

If you find yourself in midproject with no sponsor (due to reorganization, retirement, a medical problem, or other circumstances), work to find a new one.

Projects without a sponsor—particularly projects managed by project leaders with limited authority—are very likely to encounter difficulties that they may not be able to recover from. Resources can be endangered, you may have no one to escalate problems to or seek help from, and you might have a hard time getting stakeholders, your team, and others to take your project seriously.

Make finding a new sponsor a high priority. Consider managers in your organization that would be good candidates. One option is to identify the person in your organization (besides you, of course) who would suffer the most if your project is not successful. Another option is to find the lowest-level manager above you in your organization who is capable of canceling your project. Whether you can convince this person to assume sponsorship or not, at least ensure that this manager has a good impression of your work.

Before you make an approach, investigate what your prospective new sponsor cares about. Develop a presentation that connects the value of your project—and the potential consequences of failure—to interests that are relevant to your potential sponsor. Use your influencing skills to sell your project, and reestablish the management support your project requires.

Taking Over a Project

Almost as traumatic as losing a sponsor is the loss of the project leader. If you are asked to assume leadership for a project that has already begun, proceed with caution. Although the plans, team, and infrastructure could be excellent, don't assume so. Follow the maxim "Trust but verify." Use the existing plans to monitor ongoing work as you begin to sort through all the available information for the project and get to know the team. As with any project, control and success depend on understanding and preparation. Even good documentation cannot help you much until you understand the project.

Treat any project you inherit in much the same way you would a new one. Validate the charter and scoping documents, and thoroughly review or rewrite the project plan. If the project plan you develop fails to meet the stated objective, approach the sponsor and propose a more realistic baseline. You can't take a great deal of time to do this, but for your own sake, do it. (The original project leader did leave for some reason, and it may or may not be exactly what you were told.) You have at least a little initial leverage; the project sponsor does need to get a commitment from someone to run the project.

A change of project leader is a good time to schedule a project review, using a process such as the one discussed later in this chapter. Most of the planning you need to do can be integrated into the review, and it can be a good place to start building the relationships and trust you need for project control.

STEPPING INTO A DEEP PUDDLE

As a naive young project leader, I learned all this the hard way. I was leading a team of about a dozen systems programmers who were extremely good at what they did, which was remotely managing a few dozen midsize systems at sites throughout the United States. They worked together well, and as a team we were very productive. One day, while we were minding our own business, I was told that we were to apply what we knew to the installation and support of a major mainframe system. The system was already configured and the hardware was on the way, and they handed me a plan. I was assured that experts had reviewed the details and signed off on it; we were told to expect little difficulty. Even with my inexperience, I was skeptical, but who was I to question the experts?

The more we got into the project, the more I realized that the planning had been done primarily by salespeople who knew almost nothing about how this particular system would be used. In fact, much of the installation was unique, and *no one* knew much of anything about it. We were flying blind without anyone we could approach for advice or help. We continually ran into problems and roadblocks, and progress was slow and erratic. One critical element of the system we had to configure was a specialized interface unit. After several hours of unsuccessful attempts to get it running, I noticed a half dozen people in navy blue suits, white shirts, and striped ties watching us from the edge of the data center. When I asked why they were there, I was told that they wanted to watch the installation because we were the first team in the world to install their hardware in production.

Long days, weekends, and holidays were consumed getting things set up and running. Ultimately we were able to get the system operational, more or less on schedule. Despite this achievement, the project was hardly a success. The teamwork we had worked so hard to build was frayed by the pressure, resulting in many arguments and short tempers throughout the project. Shortly after we finished, one way or another, all the contributors found their way into different responsibilities.

All this angst did indelibly impress on me that I should never rely on a plan that I had not verified personally.

▪ Formal Communication

Control throughout most of your project depends heavily on the tracking cycle of information flowing inward through data collection, the analysis of project metrics, plans for response, and outbound reporting to inform people what is happening in your project. The first two portions of this process cycle—status collection and variance analysis—were explored in Chapter 7. Control strategies for response are found earlier in this chapter. Outbound formal communications are the final step of your repeating tracking cycle, including project status reports, project meetings, and presentations.

Project Status Reports

Status reporting pulls together all three strategies for control outlined in this book. Reporting is a central part of your information management process. Done effectively, it enhances your influence, and it is the primary conduit for conveying project diagnostic metric analysis.

Maintaining control of your project requires that you be seen as the leader. When you have little formal authority, being the source of project information gives you crucial leverage. When no one on the project has specific formal authority, whoever takes the initiative to manage the flow of project information is seen as the leader by default, and serving as the principal source of project information can be an effective substitute for formal authority.

At least weekly, issue project status reports with the frequency you committed to in setting up your communications infrastructure. Never skip cycles when there are problems; you might even need to intensify your status collection and reporting frequency to regain control. If you say that you will send a project report every Friday, send one every Friday. Distribute a detailed status report every cycle to your team, and at least a summary to your sponsor, key stakeholders, and the managers of related projects.

One of your most powerful control levers is the power of the pen. When you collect status information from your contributors, work to summarize, clarify, and emphasize what you want and need people to know. Always begin your project status reports with a short executive summary, containing about five to seven main points that you want to emphasize. Focus on important accomplishments, current issues, and significant next steps.

After the summary, include more detailed information in sequence of declining importance. Never issue reports that simply concatenate individual reports from your team members; such reports bury important information in a confusing mass of data. Make it easy for people to find what they need, and format your reports so items are in the same place every cycle. Set the sequence of information in your reports to lead with accomplishments and emphasize the positive. First impressions are lasting, and you increase the impact of your reports if the people reading them clearly understand what you and your team have achieved. Leading off with problems, issues, and other negative news can cause a loss of confidence in you and your team and severely interfere with your future influence.

Clear language increases your influence. Monitor your writing to eliminate any confusion that might erode it. In written reports, avoid jargon, acronyms, and any potentially ambiguous or confusing terminology. Never assume that all recipients understand everything about your project. Project teams are dynamic, and your reports could be forwarded to almost anyone. Particularly with global teams, avoid idioms; they often don't translate across cultures. (My wife had a European colleague who was hurt to learn that a request for his opinion was worth only "two cents.")

Your power of the pen also involves making decisions about what to include or exclude. For periodic status reports it is neither necessary nor appropriate to put in everything that you know. It's not helpful to include excessive project detail in reports that will be broadly distributed; in fact, its presence may obscure important information. There is always a trade-off between demonstrating your professionalism and diligence on the one hand and scaring the pants off your managers and sponsors on the other. Filter what you communicate to maximize the visibility of the most essential information.

Not all project news is good. You also need to report situations that are not going well. Reporting on issues and problems can even be an opportunity to expand your influence, as long as you consistently include recovery plan information showing that you are in control. In your reports, always pair the descriptions of problems with explicit responses showing how you plan to resolve them, or at least how you plan to minimize the impact.

After writing a report, set it aside while you do something else. Your project status report underpins your control; before you send it, read it over—carefully. Proofread it for errors, but also focus on your message. Try to misinterpret what you wrote. If parts of your report can be read with more than one meaning, rewrite to make them unambiguous. Remove any unnecessarily pessimistic or negative thoughts, because what you think about your project is contagious. If you communicate confidence, people will share it. If you communicate doubts, people will become depressed and start looking for a cliff to jump off. Also remove all personal information or criticism concerning your team members. Confine your broadcast status reporting to verifiable facts about your project; deal with interpersonal and performance problems privately.

Finally, in all written communications, never miss a chance to recognize contributions by individuals and teams of contributors, both within and outside your team. Recognition is motivating. Naming names and making contributions visible can substantially improve your chances of getting cooperation and commitments for the remainder of your project and beyond.

FLATTERY CAN GET YOU ANYWHERE

Earlier in my career, I was part of a large program created to consolidate hardware into a new state-of-the-art data center being established in a new European headquarters building in Geneva, Switzerland. We were to gather computer systems and other equipment from a half-dozen older sites all over the city, and my part of the program was to manage moving all the telecom equipment and packet-switching hardware used for worldwide data communications—while ensuring, of course, uninterrupted network access to all systems over the several months that it would take to relocate all the computers.

A central part of the new data center design was a massive patch panel through which all the internal and external communications were to be routed. As the time to begin installing my networking hardware approached, I grew concerned that the patch panel was behind schedule. The empty panel frame had been erected in the data center, but the hardware that would fill it up was still sitting in the manufacturer's boxes. To no avail, I dropped hints a few times to the team responsible for assembling this hardware. On a program like this, there are always many competing priorities and tasks.

A week before my first installation was scheduled, I approached the leader of the patching hardware installation team. Rather than complaining about the looming deadline, I asked him to show me how the panel worked, asking him to help me verify that everything was compatible. Together, we started opening boxes, and he showed me how the parts fit together. I continued asking questions and opening boxes while he started snapping things together and screwing the components in place. After about 45 minutes, he had installed about a dozen connections and wired them up. I was able to test my cables and fittings and verify there were no mechanical mating problems or electrical faults. I thanked him for his help, and we both returned to other work.

Although I was grateful that some of the hardware I depended on was now installed, my real motive was to collect data for my weekly status report. In my summary for the beginning of my next report, I mentioned that I was now confident we would meet our schedules, based on the capable and effective efforts of my partner project leader. I praised his cooperation and expertise and publicly thanked him for his efforts.

Because of the attention the status report generated, the patch panel infrastructure was fully installed in plenty of time. In addition, throughout the rest of my project, whenever I saw the other team leader in the data center, he always asked whether I needed anything done.

Project Meetings

Meetings are another important type of formal project communication. Controlling your meetings is crucial to controlling your project, because most people assume, with justification, that if you cannot run a meeting well, you probably cannot run a project either. If it is run well, your regular project meeting—whether weekly, daily, or other frequency—serves as one of your most useful control tools.

Unfortunately, on many projects the status meeting does not accomplish much, is only sporadically attended, and is primarily a time sink. Avoid this by setting a detailed agenda for all meetings, and focus only on discussions that are important to all contributors.

An effective project meeting should focus on three things: (1) noting significant accomplishments and recognizing the people who were responsible; (2) conducting a quick review of what lies ahead for the project; and (3) summarizing any expected issues or barriers. For agile projects using Scrum, the daily 15-minute stand-up meeting is strictly confined to collecting only these three items from each contributor.

Even with a formal agenda, important side topics arise. Although sometimes the urgency is high enough to justify hijacking your meeting, usually the best course is to capture such issues as action items and then address them in a separate follow-up meeting.

Your team will find project meetings useful and attend them willingly if you begin meetings on time and keep them short, and end them early whenever possible. Although a project with no meetings is unrealistic, most projects can be easily managed with fewer. Enhancing your control through meetings requires that you carefully consider the reason for each meeting and to avoid calling a meeting whenever you have other effective options. Keep the meetings that you do hold efficient, organized, and as short as possible.

MINUTES TO PROVIDE CONTINUITY (AND SAVE HOURS)

Terry Ash, who for many years was an IT director at Hewlett-Packard, is a veteran of many worldwide projects and virtual teams. "When running a global project," he says, "one of the most important things is communication, and I've found that it's impossible to overcommunicate. You need to communicate more than you think is necessary." He uses periodic teleconferences at workday-friendly times for all the time zones involved. The calls are weekly when his projects are running well; when in crisis mode, he holds teleconferences daily. Terry explains:

> One key to doing these teleconferences successfully is making sure to take good notes, document the action items and con-

firm them over the telephone, and then follow up with an e-mail to ensure that everybody has understood them the same way. This is especially important when dealing with different cultures and team members whose native language is different from the language used by the project team. Reflective listening, and double-checking what you heard and what is being committed to, is key to avoiding confusion. When you come around to the next meeting, be it the next day or next week, you immediately use your meeting minutes as a reference point to get started. That way you can measure your progress since the last teleconference before moving on to any new issues you have.

For Terry, dealing with distant team members is all about disciplined, frequent interaction. "Communicate, as much as you can. Think of every way possible to get messages and information back and forth between separated teams."

Presentations

Formal communication also includes project presentations. Presentations are often opportunities to directly capture the attention of your sponsor and stakeholders, and by influencing them you can improve your overall project control and keep your project vision front and center.

Determine which stakeholders will attend any formal project presentations, and be thoroughly prepared to address the aspects of your project that matter to each of them. Never assume that everyone knows as much about the work as you do, and translate complicated project information into clear, understandable language. Always include updates on your progress, accomplishments, and next steps to demonstrate the competence of your team and your effectiveness as the project leader. In presenting information about remaining project work, be positive, and use the information to motivate and renew enthusiasm and support for your project.

▪ Rewards and Recognition

Recognition and, when appropriate, rewards for your team make controlling your project during execution a good deal easier. The principal of reciprocity—giving and getting—operates throughout your project; you can increase your influence by using public recognition of successfully completed work and secure commitments in exchange for specific rewards.

The easiest and cheapest (and most underused) form of reward and recognition is the simple thank-you. Contributors on complicated technical projects complete difficult work all the time, and often the only thing that they hear is, "Good! Here's more work." When team members do a good or even a satisfactory job on a project activity, don't miss the chance to express your appreciation. Personal thanks improve your relationships with your team and provide an excellent excuse to manage by wandering around (or by telephoning around). Including thanks to individuals or teams working on your project in status reports can be very motivating. Thanking people for their work in an e-mail and copying their managers when they do not report to you also are powerful tools for strengthening your project influence and control. And, of course, a thank-you is something you should do anyway; you should be genuinely grateful for every piece of your project that you can put behind you, putting you one step closer to successful completion.

Project leaders who don't have a great deal of authority may feel that they aren't able to do much about formal rewards and recognition. Even so, you can always request, propose, cajole, and use your influence to recommend these things to the people who can do something. This is a case where trying is appreciated almost as much as succeeding. Whatever might come of a suggestion that you make for rewards, at least the individuals involved appreciate your efforts.

Rewards and recognition work best when you confine them to things your team appreciates. Public recognition can be either motivating or demotivating, depending on the individuals involved, cultural factors, and other factors. Public team rewards can do more for your project control than individual rewards in most cases because they avoid the inevitable consequence of identifying one winner and, by implication, many losers. Individual rewards, particularly those with significant value, may be of more help to your project when kept private.

Rewards and recognition fall into two broad categories, tangible and intangible. Although granting tangible rewards may require more authority than you have as a project leader, intangible rewards are fair game for anyone.

Intangible Rewards and Recognition

Many ideas for recognizing contributions cost nothing but a little of your time and perhaps a negligible expense. These ideas work best when used unexpectedly. If you become predictable and your behavior begins to look insincere, your efforts may reduce overall morale and team cohesion.

- Thank people personally. Write them a note, and send a copy to their managers.

- Print out an e-mail thank-you note, then handwrite a (legible) personal comment and sign it. Give or send it directly to the person.
- Highlight individual and team results in team meetings, and include them in the meeting minutes.
- Give credit where credit is due. Use team members' names in your presentations, reports, reviews, and other project documents when discussing project accomplishments. Be specific about results, and describe why their contributions matter.
- Ask your project sponsor or other high-level manager to personally thank individuals on your team. (And thank *them* for doing it.)
- Communicate with the managers of your team members. Thank them for their cooperation and support for your project. Also give them feedback on individual performance, particularly for each individual's annual performance appraisal.
- Organize brief gatherings for self-congratulation (always with snacks) when you pass significant milestones. Find a way to involve distant team members in a similar celebration at their location.
- Recognize significant accomplishments of people and teams in public meetings (but only when you know such recognition is welcome and culturally appropriate).
- Put up a big sign that everyone at your location can see when you complete your project or achieve a major milestone.
- Take individuals to lunch or send them a small, unique, and edible gift. (Be careful of food items that melt, though.)
- Offer project team members an opportunity to attend meetings with your sponsor, management, or key stakeholders.
- Delegate more responsibility for project work.
- Provide time off for work that requires personal sacrifice.
- Devise awards to acknowledge performance: small items such as buttons or a trophy that circulates among the team to recognize the Star of the Week. Keep a public list, perhaps with pictures, and find plausible reasons to ensure that all team members are included sooner or later.

Tangible Rewards and Recognition

Use tangible rewards with care, especially if they are given in public. When rewards or recognition are inconsistent with personal preferences or are unwelcome, they can become de-motivating. Most monetary rewards are private, and, as with any positive reinforcement, they are most effective when awarded randomly. If monetary incentives become expected, they are no longer seen as rewards and may even become counterproductive. Know what tangible rewards are available, and consider employing (or proposing) some of these ideas:

- Events and celebrations planned with members of your team
- The nomination of individuals or teams for award programs, either internal or external to the organization
- Approval to attend desired training or professional conferences
- Performance awards that have monetary value, such as gift certificates
- Promotion or explicit expansion of responsibilities
- Salary increases
- Bonuses or stock options

You can doubtless come up with your own long list of possibilities. Be creative, and discuss anything that you are considering with your team to ensure that it is welcome and motivating. No one enjoys forced merriment or being embarrassed.

▪ Project Reviews for Lengthy Projects

If you have a car, you probably don't do very much for it most weeks except add more fuel and perhaps wash it, look at the oil level, and check the air in your tires. While this works fine in the short run, if you never do more than this, the car will soon fail. Automobiles need periodic maintenance to run properly, so it's a good idea to take it in about twice a year to have it thoroughly checked. After six months you need to replace the oil and repair anything that is wearing out, to restore it to good working order.

Longer projects present a similar challenge. The planning horizon for most complex projects is about three to six months, so a periodic review is useful to ensure that you have the information you need to control the next parts of your project. In addition, keeping the work on a very long project fresh and interesting is a challenge. As mentioned in the last chapter, revitalizing the vision for lengthy projects is essential to maintaining team motivation, and reviews are also a good way to reinforce your role as project leader. On lengthy projects, schedule reviews at least every six months, generally synchronized with life-cycle or stage-gate transitions, other significant milestones, completion of a major deployment, a substantial project change, or the close of a fiscal period.

Plan a project review to be similar to a project start-up workshop, focused on project planning and reinvigorating team relationships. In a project review you'll also have the opportunity to look backward, so it will let you schedule a celebration. (Long projects never seem to have enough parties.) Reviews held at the end of each development iteration for projects using agile methods are both more frequent and less formal, and their agendas will exclude some of these items. Nonetheless, they serve essentially the same purposes.

Prepare well for a review by assembling current project documents and plans. Set a date when the people you want to attend are available and schedule sufficient time to dig into your project. Get a firm commitment from each team member to participate, via teleconference if necessary.

Begin your project review with a summary of major accomplishments and recognize specific accomplishments by individuals and teams. Spend time reminding people why your project matters, to revitalize your team and maintain motivation. Throughout your review, use the collaborative planning ideas from Chapter 6 to involve your whole team in updating schedules, estimates, dependencies, any scope adjustments, and other project data using your best current information. During the review, use all opportunities you can find to reward and recognize your team, and consider including a team celebration of some sort. At the end of the review, collect all information and close the review with a recap of all the action items, with due dates and commitments from owners for each one.

▪ Project Cancellation

Some projects that seem like excellent ideas, even through initiation and planning, ultimately prove not to be. As you progress, you learn more and more. Barriers, risks, and challenges that were hidden at the outset emerge from the shadows to threaten your project. When the obstacles prove to be too great, cancellation may be unavoidable.

Projects are canceled for many reasons. Some are stopped because they are unable to meet their goals. Watch for trends in your status metrics showing:

- Quality or other scope issues that fail to meet requirements
- Inadequate schedule progress
- Excessive resource consumption
- Inadequate staffing or other resource shortfall

Before you conclude that you should abandon your project, do at least a quick project review to verify the magnitude of your problems. Revisit the expected benefits, and consider whether the business case for continuing your project is credible. If your project's current costs, timing, and value no longer make sense, investigate other options for scoping; opportunities that you were not aware of initially may now be apparent. Just because your project cannot achieve its original objectives does not necessarily mean that you should recommend canceling it. If you believe that your project is viable with modifications, discuss it with your team and stakeholders, set up a meeting with your sponsor, and negotiate a realistic new baseline.

If it becomes clear, however, that the current prognosis for your project is dire, or if you are unsuccessful in setting a new baseline, prepare to bring your project to an end. One of the worst reasons to continue a project that extends well beyond its deadline or runs over budget is, "We're almost done." Throwing good money after bad, especially on projects with a history of chronic problems, is rarely a good business decision.

Healthy projects are also sometimes terminated, generally for reasons external to the project, such as:

- Loss of interest by the sponsor
- Shifts in business strategy or organizational priorities
- Actions by competitors or changes in market demand or user requirements
- Recognition, by the organization, that the projects running are exceeding capacity

In these cases, you may not be able to do much about the decision. It's still useful, though, to verify assumptions and to discuss alternatives for continuing with your management. Know the value and vision for your project, either as it is or with modifications. New sponsorship, reprioritization, a major shift in scoping, or other changes might be a better proposition than cancellation.

However, when it's clear that your project must be canceled, accept it. Don't prolong the process. The longer a project runs, the more invested everyone gets in it. No matter when you pull the plug, it is difficult, demotivating, and stressful, but it is far less so after only a few months than after everyone has invested a year of their lives in the project.

When your project clearly cannot be rescued, verify the decision to cancel with your sponsor, and report it in writing to your team, your management, and your stakeholders. Write a final status report, summarizing the situation and describing any alternatives that were considered. Let people know the results that your project achieved, recognize your team's contributions, and include a summary of your plans for project closure.

Complete the shutdown of your project by updating your documents in the project management information system. If the project might be revived in the future, leave sufficient information to make continuing the work as easy as possible. Work with the specialists in your organization to terminate any project contracts, according to the terms set out in the contract. Document all the work completed under contract, and determine any financial or other consequences of early termination. Complete any paperwork required for ending the contract, and approve final payments that are due, including any penalties.

Complete your other project closure activities, as outlined in Chapter 9, particularly the postproject analysis of lessons learned. Generally, you learn a lot more from things that go wrong than from things that succeed. Strive to keep things as positive as you can. Focus your retrospective analysis on what went well and on things to change, minimizing recriminations, blame-storming, and personal attacks. Thank people sincerely for their work, and help everyone transition with enthusiasm from the project to whatever they do next.

▪ Control Challenges

Projects of all types encounter barriers, and many are challenged partway through to do more with less. Project leaders also face conflicts in matrix, distributed, cross-functional, and global teams caused by separation. It is easy to work with and gain the cooperation of people with whom we are friendly and we know well. From a distance, whether literal, intellectual, functional, cultural, or some other type, the situation reverses. People don't trust others they don't know.

To meet these challenges, you need to use your influence to establish relationships and trust with your team members, as described in Chapter 3, and maintain good team cohesion through your loyalty, personal interactions, good humor, and other ideas, as outlined in Chapter 7. Because most control problems are easiest to resolve (and to avoid in the first place) face-to-face, meet one-on-one with your contributors as frequently as practical. On longer projects, bring distributed teams together at least twice a year for project reviews or other collaborative activities. Mistrust develops over time between virtual team members who have little or no personal contact with each other. To remain in control, you also need to manage barriers, resource challenges, and conflicts.

Dealing with Barriers

Project teams often face barriers that block progress, such as inadequate re-sources, timing conflicts, or insufficient priority. Individuals on your team may face difficulties in their work that they cannot control, and often these issues are beyond your control. You need to confront and manage the obstacles.

Team cohesion depends on a one-for-all/all-for-one attitude across the whole team, starting with you as the project leader thinking about each team member's problems as your own. If a problem is a result of a failure to fulfill some earlier written commitment, you may be able to resolve it by intervening, reminding the others of the promise, and mentioning that you would prefer not to have to widely circulate a detailed summary of the situation in your next status report. Communication (or even threatened communication) can be an effective way to deal with a wide range of issues and project problems.

In other situations, you can use your planning and other project data to clearly show the consequences of not resolving an issue to the people responsi-ble for the problem. A compelling, data-driven case may provide sufficient le-verage to get things in your project back on schedule.

You may be unable to resolve some barriers solely through your own efforts. However, in more extreme cases, you need to escalate to get help from your project sponsor or others with more authority. If you have successfully maintained good relationships with your sponsor and stakeholders, escalation generally leads to a quick resolution (which is one reason, among many, to keep your project sponsors involved and supportive). Use escalation only as a last resort, though, after exhausting all the options you have to influence and resolve the situation on your own. Frequent escalations annoy your sponsor, undermine your reputation, alienate the people that you need to work with, and make project control more difficult.

Doing More with Less

Even if you begin your project with adequate funding and staff, you may encounter new budget constraints partway through the work. For any given project, only some combinations of scope, time, and cost are actually feasible. If resources drop, you will need to successfully negotiate project adjustments to compensate for the smaller resources.

Start this process by investigating whether the resource cutbacks are inevitable. Ask questions about the overall project assumptions and restrictions, and verify all current project constraints with your sponsor and key stakeholders. Explore the value expected from your project, comparing your previously committed resource requirements with the anticipated benefits. Also inquire about your project's overall priority, especially if it appears inconsistent with proposed funding reductions. If there is a strong business case in favor of not reducing your project budget, make it.

If it appears that funding reductions are unavoidable, use scenario-based questions to revalidate the relative priorities of time, scope, or cost with your sponsor. For example, ask, "Would it be better in the face of these restrictions for our project to be a week late or to accept a minor scope reduction?" Keep digging until you know which constraints are truly essential and which are negotiable.

Using this information, work with your team to explore plan changes consistent with a smaller budget that best preserve what's most valuable about your project. Use what-if analysis to adjust your project plans to meet the highest priorities by rearranging dependencies, shortening durations through staffing changes, or other adjustments. Create several plan variations, and strive to come as close as possible to meeting the most important project objectives. Plan for negotiations with your sponsor by preparing summaries of several credible alternative projects.

Meet with your sponsor to discuss adjustments to your project objectives and baseline. Begin with the plan variation that you believe is your best option, even if it falls significantly short of the original project goals. Use data to show that your proposal is consistent with past similar projects and is based on solid, thorough analysis. If your best alternative differs appreciably from the current constraints, present additional plan-based project options.

In discussions with your sponsor, use principled negotiation based on facts and data. Your sponsor has more organizational clout and influence than you do, but keep in mind that, even if you have little authority or power, you are still the world's leading expert on your project. When negotiating adjustments to unrealistic constraints, use what you know. Citing solid evidence of what is and is not possible, you should be able to engage your sponsors and stakeholders in collaborative problem solving, not posturing.

If, despite your best efforts, you are initially unsuccessful in getting agreement for project changes, discuss the consequences of proceeding with unrealistic funding. Although it may be desirable to attempt to do more with less, realistically it may be possible only to do less with less. No one wins when a project has an impossible goal: You lose because your project fails. Your team loses because they have had an unsuccessful, depressing experience. Your sponsor and management lose too because they presumably need what the project is expected to produce. If it fails, they lose too. Work together with your sponsor and management to agree on credible objectives and a baseline for your project that is consistent with evolving constraints.

Resolving Team Conflicts

Sometimes the barriers arise within your own team, where one team member's progress is impeded by another. Because interpersonal conflicts can be so corrosive, dealing with them quickly is essential. The best approaches for dealing with conflicts among team members rely on confrontation and compromise.

Other techniques for conflict resolution include autocratic forcing of your preferred solution, ignoring the situation by withdrawing and hoping that the conflict will diffuse, and smoothing over the situation by encouraging team members to be nice to each other. For project teams that need to cooperate over the course of a lengthy project, forcing, withdrawing, and smoothing over are not effective because they fail to deal with the conflict's root cause, which is likely to recur and cause bigger troubles later in the project. Confrontation, pulling the issues causing the conflict into the open, and compromise provide a basis for long-term solutions that everyone involved will be able to live with.

Interpersonal conflicts are common in projects with cross-functional, virtual, or geographically dispersed teams, especially when the project leader has limited authority. Work with your team members to establish consensus for a conflict resolution process for diffusing disagreements throughout the project.

Whenever a conflict arises among team members, work collaboratively to resolve it promptly within your team by:

- Reviewing documented information for the project and resolving all portions of the disagreement that you can, using defined, validated data
- Setting up a face-to-face meeting (or a conference using a suitable technique) that includes all the people involved
- Establishing an environment where everyone treats others with respect and is comfortable discussing matters openly
- Verifying that everyone wants to resolve the conflict
- Taking each issue of the conflict one at a time, starting with the ones that seem easiest
- Probing for information using open-ended questions and active listening, seeking to understand the source of the disagreement
- Letting people present their side of each issue
- Allowing everyone to ask questions of each speaker, but discouraging criticism and negative comments
- Avoiding outbursts of emotion and personality by maintaining a focus on facts and data
- Quantifying the matters discussed in terms of time, money, or other numerical units that permit objective comparisons
- Brainstorming alternatives and combinations of ideas to find resolutions that are win/win, allowing all to agree with, or at least accept, a common solution
- Confirming closure of each issue as you reach agreement and documenting what you decide in writing

If a consensus solution proves impossible, you may find it necessary to pull rank and impose your decision. If so, support your position with as solid and logical a case as you can develop. Ensure that everyone understands why you believe your decision is best for the project, and begin working to repair any bruised relationships.

Despite your best efforts, some conflicts within your team may be impossible for you to resolve. In these more serious cases, escalate the situation to your project sponsor or to others with more authority. Problem escalation should always be your last resort, but sometimes a solution imposed from outside the team may be the only option possible. As with all escalations, use this tactic sparingly; it can generate resentment and malicious compliance on your team that can undermine your control.

PERSEVERANCE PAYS

David Straker is a veteran of many large projects in the United Kingdom. On a recent job, as quality manager for a big government program, he found himself with no direct authority and under huge pressure to deliver on time. Because the program was publicly funded and had a very visible delivery date, if it was even a day late it would have been all over the front pages of the national newspapers. In addition, questions would be asked in Parliament, and heads would roll (as they had in the past). For this effort, David was responsible for documenting processes well enough to survive a significant change in staffing because the program was about to move to another city and many currently working on it were expected to leave. He says: "Unsurprisingly, the move plans didn't help much with overall motivation. Many people just wanted just to complete what they were doing and then move on. Documenting the program processes in that environment was a big challenge."

David did a great deal to succeed with this daunting project, including:

- Getting each team to allocate a person who would be responsible for knowledge capture within that team
- Naming these leaders *knowledge project managers* (KPMs) so that they felt responsible and would see the work as a serious part of the program
- Meeting weekly with all of the KPMs to keep them engaged, to keep them up-to-date, and to promote sharing
- Developing a comprehensive toolkit of methods, templates, and checklists, and training the KPMs to use it
- Helping the KPMs and their teams to analyze the state of progress and to plan for knowledge capture work
- Working one-on-one with the KPMs to coach them and to help them work effectively with their teams
- Building knowledge transition into the HR processes so that people who left would hand over their work in an orderly way
- Meeting regularly with the managers of all the teams to ensure their active and committed ongoing sponsorship
- Meeting regularly with the overall program manager to keep him up-to-date and to encourage him to prod people when necessary
- Collecting and maintaining progress metrics and reporting them regularly at the program meeting where all the managers of the teams met, naming and shaming as appropriate
- Setting up a centralized repository for knowledge capture and badgering people to submit completed work there
- Reviewing all work as it was finished to ensure that it was thorough and complete

David summarizes:

> In other words, I planned, helped, nagged, chased, escalated, and did whatever it took to make people realize that I wasn't going to go away. When people realized I wasn't going to give up, they found it easier to play along than to play hooky. Successful completion on all of this was never a straight road, and I encountered many objections, delays, and other games. Through it all, though, I just kept smiling, cajoling, and nudging everyone along. By the end I had managed to assemble pretty much everything we needed.

KEY IDEAS FOR PROJECT TRACKING AND MONITORING

- Manage scope changes with a disciplined process that accepts only mandatory, business-justified modifications.
- Develop and take adaptive actions promptly whenever problems arise.
- Use reports and other formal communication to keep people in sync with your project and aware of its progress.
- Motivate your team using frequent thanks and recognition, and rewards when appropriate.
- Periodically review longer projects to validate objectives and plans and to revitalize the project vision.
- Deal with barriers to progress and promptly resolve project conflicts.

CHAPTER 9

Enhancing Overall Control Through Project Closure

CLOSING A PROJECT WELL involves some time and work, but it is essential to the control of future projects. Getting agreement from your sponsor and from all your stakeholders that your work was satisfactorily completed is necessary before you can transition to new projects. Retrospective metrics contribute to longer-term control by guiding needed process improvements and validating predictive project metrics. Archiving your completed project documents provides information necessary for defining and planning similar future projects.

And speaking of future projects: It's a small world, and it's safe to assume that you will work again with at least some of the people on your current project. Because of this, you need to plan two final things with your team. The first is to reinforce your relationships by celebrating your accomplishments and recognizing and rewarding the contributions of your project team. The second is to conduct a postproject retrospective analysis, which improves your control of future work through standardizing the practices that worked well and by improving processes that did not.

▪ Delivering Your Results and Getting Sign-Off

As important as staying in control is throughout your project, even more essential is bringing everything to a successful conclusion. The whole point of your project is to deliver an appropriate result that gains final approval. Getting written acknowledgment that you have delivered a satisfactory result is always a good idea, but it is particularly important for project leaders who lack much authority because you may need it later.

If you defined your scope well during project initiation, including clear, quantified acceptance criteria, and if you were able to minimize scope changes throughout your project, ensuring that your deliverable meets the required specifications should be straightforward. Most projects undergo some scope change; when using agile methods, you may have many adjustments. Whenever you accept any significant scope changes as you proceed through your project, make any necessary adjustments to your acceptance criteria, to your testing plans and processes, and to any equipment you need for testing. Before requesting final customer certification that the work is satisfactory, complete an even more stringent evaluation with your project team. Work to design your tests and checks so that what you produce exceeds, at least slightly, all the stated requirements. If your team's tests reveal defects or problems, develop plans to resolve them before user acceptance tests.

Deliver what you have produced as planned, and then inform your sponsor. Work with those who will approve your results to verify that you have met your project goals. Obtain approval for each in-scope requirement, one by one. If all requirements are accepted, get a formal sign-off and notify your sponsor and other stakeholders. Sign-off varies for projects of different types, but it is generally coordinated with a project milestone event such as final life cycle phase transition, release to shipping or manufacturing, customer or user acceptance, or final test. If your project was done under contract, initiate the final customer billing promptly.

If your project fails to meet one or more requirements, document them and address any deficiencies by:

- Extending your project to accommodate the additional work necessary
- Renegotiating project scope to be consistent with what you produced
- Obtaining conditional sign-off and committing to resolution at a future date

Even in cases with residual deficiencies, get a written acknowledgment of what you have delivered. Distribute a summary of the results of acceptance testing in your next project status report, and archive it with the outcome of each of your tests in your project management information system.

▪ Employing Retrospective Project Metrics

In general, the role of retrospective metrics is to evaluate a process following execution. Retrospective measurements are especially useful for a project leader with limited power and authority. These measures can provide the additional data you need to successfully negotiate with your managers and future sponsors on matters where you were unpersuasive in the past. These metrics are also useful on projects in determining how efficiently and effectively you worked during the project. Whether your project ends successfully, with difficulty, or even if it is canceled, backward-looking project measurements reveal much about what you did well and what you need to improve. Specific uses of retrospective project metrics include:

- Validating the accuracy of predictive metrics
- Adjusting phase or iterative development durations and completion standards
- Deciding when to improve or replace current project processes
- Providing guidance for fine-tuning your project processes (such as estimating)
- Assessing the effectiveness of your scope and change management
- Identifying significant individual or team accomplishments
- Uncovering new sources of risk and recurring problems
- Empirically forecasting the magnitude of *unknown* project risk
- Establishing standards for schedule reserves and budget reserves
- Tracking long-term trends

Defining Retrospective Project Metrics

Many retrospective metrics are after-the-fact actual measurements that correspond to plan-based predictive metrics. Others relate to the efficiency and effectiveness of your processes or other quantitative data for evaluating your project and comparing it with similar projects. Retrospective metrics assist you in diagnosing your overall project. They also help you to detect trends over time, both positive trends that you wish to continue and negative trends that you need to reverse. All of these objectives—setting better baselines for predictive project measures, improving project processes, and tracking overall trends—equip you with the information you need to improve your control over future projects that you undertake. Examples of retrospective project metrics, grouped into several categories, are listed here. No project leader finds it useful or even necessarily possible to evaluate each of them, but you will find value in at least some of them.

Project Scale and Scope Metrics
- Actual size of the project deliverable (such as component counts, number of major deliverables, lines of noncommented code, function or feature points, blocks on system diagrams, or volume of total output)
- Stability of initial scoping

- Number of submitted changes
- Number of accepted changes
- Number of defects (classified by severity)
- Final performance and quality measures for deliverables compared to project objectives

Timing and Schedule Metrics
- Actual activity durations
- Actual phase or iteration durations
- Actual project duration
- Number of missed major milestones
- Assessment of duration estimation accuracy
- Performance to standard duration estimates (for standardized activities)
- Number of new unplanned activities

Resource and Financial Metrics
- Actual activity costs (or effort)
- Actual total expense at project completion
- Total project effort
- Final earned value assessments, such as cost variance (CV) and schedule variance (SV), or other evaluation of effort or cost estimation accuracy
- Cumulative project overtime
- Added staff
- Staff turnover
- Actual phase or iteration costs
- Actual life cycle phase or iteration effort percentages
- Performance to standard effort estimates (for standardized activities)
- Variances in travel, communications, equipment, outsourcing, or other expense subcategories
- Measured value of the delivered benefits

General Project Metrics
- Late project defect correction effort, as a percentage of total effort
- Number of project risks encountered
- Project issues tracked and closed
- Actual measured return on investment (ROI)

Deploying and Using Retrospective Metrics

Baselines for retrospective metrics are often based on retrospective measures from similar past projects and trend assessments. Be wary of making changes to processes based on the measures from only a single project. Another common issue with retrospective metrics is the compared-to-what problem. Some adverse-looking variances and indices may derive more from unrealistic initial assumptions than from anything in your overall project process. (These measures may provide you with ammunition to better highlight faulty assumptions and to better manage expectations on future projects, however.)

As with predictive metrics, most of the data collection falls to you. The choice of which metrics you evaluate, in addition to any that are required within your organization, is largely your personal choice. Reasonable places to start are metrics that relate to particularly problematic forecasts (such as project estimates), processes that you are concerned about, and aspects of your project infrastructure that need improvement.

Retrospective measures are a significant source of information for post-project lessons learned, and periodic preliminary assessment of these metrics should be a key focus of your project reviews. Process improvement is an important use of backward-looking measures. Retrospective metrics have a role (along with trends in diagnostic metrics) as a trigger for initiating a focused effort to modify poor processes; they are also your primary means of evaluating process changes. Retrospective measurements from your previous, inadequate process can be compared with retrospective measurements from your modified process to verify that you have met your process improvement goals. If you have not, the measurements tell you that you need to seek other modifications, and the specific numbers may help you find the best opportunities to investigate.

▪ Administrative Closure

Closing out a project involves several administrative activities to finish up the project paperwork and say thank-you to your team. These steps include closure (if necessary) for any outsourced work and issuance of final project reports.

Closing Outsourced Work

If some of your contributors are working under contract, verify that all their work is satisfactory and that you have received all deliverables, documentation, reports, and other outputs. Review the contract to ensure that all parties, including you, have met the terms of the agreement, including any approved revisions or amendments.

If you find any deficiencies, discuss them with your contractors or the supplier liaison for that contract. Whenever possible, resolve all variances involving project requirements by successfully getting the work completed. If any part of the work under contract can't be finished, determine any consequences, such as penalties or payment adjustments. If there are any other significant differences between the terms of a contract and the actual performance of your contractors, determine what you need to do to deal with them. If necessary, escalate to others with sufficient authority and contracting expertise to resolve all outstanding contract issues.

Complete the financial obligations of each contract by reviewing the payment history and approving all final payments required by the terms of each contract. Also complete all of the paperwork and reports required by your organization to account for contracted work, and promptly finish all the necessary project accounting you are responsible for. After all final payments are made, terminate the contract, or at least the portion of the contract that relates to your project.

As a final step, evaluate the overall performance of each service supplier you worked with during your project. If any of your contract work was terminated before the end of your project, thoroughly document the situation, especially if the termination was due to performance issues. Add the document to your project information archive, along with all accounting reports, contract communications, status project reports, contract change history, and other relevant documents. Forward a copy of your supplier evaluation information to your peers who are responsible for similar project work because they may want to consider using comparable services in the future.

Final Project Reports

Write a final project report, including all the information that is customarily reported at project end within your organization. Use your final report to communicate to your team, your sponsor, and your stakeholders that the project is over. A final project report is generally very similar in structure to the periodic status reports that you send throughout your project, but it focuses on the project as a whole, not just on current events. It also is an excellent place to recognize specific accomplishments achieved by your entire project team and to formally highlight significant contributions made by individuals and by groups of contributors to your project.

As with all of your project status reports, begin your final report with a high-level summary, a small number of points that include your project's most significant accomplishments. Also, explicitly thank all your contributors. Structure the rest of the report to supply details and project retrospective metrics on important aspects of your project. If you have completed your postproject analysis of lessons learned by the time you issue your report, include your most important recommendations, placing them near the beginning of your report. Add your final report to your project information archive.

▪ Celebration and Team Rewards

One of the best (and certainly the easiest and least expensive) things that project leaders can do to motivate people and reinforce their influence is to thank team members for their contributions to the project. Express sincere gratitude to each of your team members for their help, support, and hard work throughout the project. Thank people face-to-face if possible. For distant team members, at least make a personal telephone call. Find at least one thing in particular to comment on for each individual as a way to reinforce your appreciation. Also express your thanks in writing. For any contributors who do not report to you, send copies of your notes to their managers. Chances are that you will work with at least some of the people again who were on your team, and how you exit this project makes a difference when you meet again. (And even if you don't ever work together again, thanking people is still the right thing to do. It never hurts, and it often helps.)

Rewards and other types of recognition (as covered in Chapter 8) are another important way to positively reinforce the contributions of individual contributors and groups of people on your team. Be generous in giving credit for project accomplishments to your team members in presentations, discussions with management, and in other conversations.

As project leader, you have another final task: arranging to commemorate the end of your project with some sort of event. If your project was highly successful and if you can get approval to hold a party or take your team out to dinner, find out what your team would prefer and then organize it. If you are not able to do anything significant that might involve additional expense, at least set up a small get-together to end your project on a positive note. Even if your project didn't end exactly as planned or there were problems along the way, at least identify a few achievements that you can all be proud of. Effective celebrations don't need to be elaborate; simply getting together to share some snacks that you provide or having a potluck meal, with food contributed by everyone on your team, can be a great way to end a project. If your team is distributed across several sites, consider options that allow each location to have a comparable event. Find a way to let everyone join the party.

USING CLOSURE FOR INFLUENCE AND MOTIVATION

Randy Englund, a very experienced program manager, author, and principal of Englund Project Management Consultancy, shares a story about how failing to get complete closure after a project affects the results and the motivation of its participants. A few years ago, Randy volunteered to help lead a major symposium on project management by serving as the content and program director for the event, which was mounted by several Project Management Institute chapters in northern California. Randy says:

> As you might expect, this effort followed most of the steps required of a well-managed project management process: We created a vision and agreed upon it, invited speakers who had compelling messages that fit with the event's theme, enlisted sponsors, extensively promoted the event, and held weekly status meetings including all project participants. We collected key documents centrally, and drafted a 'day in the life of' scenario that allowed us to step through all the details and ensure nothing was forgotten. Enthusiasm was high and the event was a smashing success, with attendance at maximum capacity for the site.
>
> The problem in my mind came after the event was over. Many volunteers put a great deal of time into the project, but after it ended there was essentially no follow-up. The event was evidently a big financial success, but final financial details were never shared. All the volunteers wanted closure—clear reasons for our project success, acknowledgement of goals met, and recognition for their hard work. The team never even saw a summary of the attendee surveys that were collected.

After the event, this large team of resourceful and productive volunteers simply disbursed. No lessons learned or best practices were captured; future events were unable to replicate key factors that made this event successful.

Randy continues:

> I was able to influence the upfront design of this project, such as running a single track so all messages were heard by all participants and inviting known speakers with known messages instead of putting out a call for papers, but I was not able to get the project manager and sponsoring organizations to schedule a follow-on project review. Everyone was busy with other things after the event. We failed to include an explicit review as part of our original plan, so it never happened. The result was that many volunteers saw the experience as incomplete, and that all their hard work went for naught.

People want closure, especially after a successful project. Randy concluded:

We learned from each other and had fun together, but in retrospect I sense that some involved do not share the same level of high regard that I felt. There was no forum for bringing everything to a coherent close and where feelings could be shared. It appears that in this case, no news is bad news. We lost the opportunity to generate a longer term impact on our community and build upon messages generated by the event. As a consequence, I am now less willing to participate in other projects for this organization.

Randy summarizes:

As a project team member, I have to accept some accountability for our lack of closure, but I also see how dependent we were on the overall project leader to guide us through this stage. We needed someone to urge us through the final unfinished tasks. This example underscores for me how influential the project leader is throughout a project, from beginning to end. If the ending is not complete, team members will be left with unexplored feelings, and willingness to give their best efforts going forward is disrupted as everyone's attention shifts to the next activity. Effective project leaders exert significant effort into ensuring thorough closure. Failure to do so is a huge lost opportunity to influence perceptions, ensure good future working relationships, reward people for their best efforts, acknowledge the importance of the project to the organization, and learn together how to apply the experiences to future projects.

▪ Capturing Lessons Learned

Some project teams break up and scatter immediately; the only chance to meet and reflect on the project as a whole is right at the end of the work. If that's your only chance to capture lessons learned, take it. Schedule time with your entire team that coincides with delivering your results. However, if you can wait a week or so after your project work completes and schedule a separate activity for this purpose, you generally get a more useful outcome. Waiting gives people a chance to reflect on the project as a whole, rather than just on the last part of the work, which tends to be stressful and adversely affects how people feel about the project. Never delay more than two weeks, though, because you may have difficulty getting people to participate, and memories, especially bad memories, can fade quickly. Whenever you decide to meet, a postproject retrospective analysis provides you an opportunity to discuss all aspects of the project and allows you and your team to put it securely in the past and move on to whatever is next. If you have difficulty persuading any of your team members to participate, then tell them it's an opportunity to bring things to emotional closure and to give voice to their feelings about the project, both good and bad. This perspective may entice them to attend.

The overall process is structurally very similar to a project review, except that the focus of a review is primarily forward looking, designed to address the remaining project work, whereas a retrospective analysis is, as the name suggests, primarily backward looking. Your tasks are to prepare for the retrospective, to meet to review project results and processes, and then to document and follow up on recommendations.

Preparing for the Retrospective

The value of a retrospective relates to improving long-term project control, and you accomplish that by identifying good practices to keep and bad practices to change. Benefiting from effective practices is not very difficult and is probably well within your authority as a project leader. The second part, implementing changes, can be somewhat tricky because change is difficult and recommendations from postproject analyses are often ignored.

In some organizations that faithfully do retrospectives, project after project reports the same problems. The documents are written, distributed, and filed—but nothing changes. Remember, one definition of insanity is doing the same thing again and again, hoping for a different result. Commitment to change is the only way to break the cycle. For a retrospective analysis to be worth the time and effort, you need a commitment to take action on the results. In advance, request support from your management to implement one or more of the recommendations produced by your analysis. If your organization has a PMO, involve its staff in planning for the retrospective meeting, and work with them to help ensure that the analysis is used. A meaningful commitment for change can also be a compelling motivation for your team members to participate.

Decide how best to facilitate the discussions. If you run the meeting, you may find it hard to fully participate. Consider using a PMO staff member, another project leader, or someone else from outside your project team to lead the meeting.

Before the meeting, send each participant a template or survey to get them thinking about the overall project. Collect information about your project in categories such as project management processes, project infrastructure, communications and information management, and tools and techniques. Solicit thoughts about what went well and what could use improvement, and challenge people to develop recommendations to address anything that they do not believe went as well as it might have. Collect the input in advance, especially from any participants you invited who won't be able to attend. Compile all the input you collect to seed your discussions.

Arrange to have the current project documents and retrospective metrics available for reference during the retrospective analysis meeting, including your final project report, if it is complete. Plan an agenda for the meeting in advance, working with your outside facilitator if you use one. Include:

- Discussion of things that went well in the project
- Identification of processes or other project aspects that need improvement
- Prioritization of recommendations
- Action plans and summarization of lessons learned
- Thoughts about the project from each contributor

Meeting to Review Project Results and Processes

A retrospective analysis is just a meeting; structure it to be an effective one. Start the meeting promptly, review the agenda, come to agreement on ground rules (especially one prohibiting personal criticisms), and assign a recorder to keep track of what happens. Open the discussion with a focus on what went right, for two reasons: This starts things off on a positive note and, if you fail to discuss the good outcomes first, you may never get to them. Keep track of processes that were particularly effective and of any useful things that your project did differently from earlier projects. When you have listed and discussed most of the positive things people have identified (including all observations you collected from those unable to attend), begin to identify potential changes.

For changes, look for processes to modify or eliminate, practices to simplify, and opportunities to standardize work or develop a new process. Focus on the work and processes used. Avoid "blame-storming," and discourage hunting for scapegoats for things that did not go well on the project. Use measurements from your project to quantify the need for changes. If arguments arise concerning what happened during the project, resolve them using your project reports and other documents. When you have identified specific suggestions for areas of improvement, prioritize your list and focus on the top two or three items.

Use root-cause analysis to discover the source of each item, and brainstorm process changes that could address each identified situation. Consider all the recommendations as a team, and select the best options available.

If you can implement a recommendation working with your team, identify an action item and plan to do it. If any recommendations require authority exceeding yours, assign yourself an action item to develop a proposal and take it to your sponsor or other management.

As you close your meeting, collect all the issues and action items, and verify the owners and due dates. Summarize what you have learned, and ask all participants to write down something that they plan to do differently on the next project. End the meeting by offering each person a chance to quickly comment on the project and to share personal plans for future work. End with yourself, and use the opportunity to reinforce your thanks to everyone for their contributions.

Documenting and Following Up on Recommendations

Document your retrospective meeting and summarize the recommendations you and your team have made. Include the details of the meeting, such as the lists of what went well and what should change. Send your summary to the members of your team who participated in the analysis, and add it to your project management information system.

Circulate your key findings to other project leaders. If your organization has a PMO, provide it with a copy of your analysis. For large projects, consider scheduling a formal project presentation to share your key lessons learned.

Follow up on your key recommendations. Implement the changes recommended where you can, and work to convince your management to approve more significant changes using metrics, your project team's input, and other supporting data. For process changes that you implement, use metrics to verify that you have achieved the results you expect, and carefully watch out for unintended consequences.

MEASURING SUCCESS

When projects encounter trouble, postproject analysis usually turns up the same issues that plagued other, earlier projects: "We didn't fully understand the requirements" or "We didn't spend enough time planning" are the common reactions. Esteri Hinman, an experienced program manager at Intel Corporation, relates a different story from an experience from a time before she joined Intel, when she participated in a project retrospective analysis for a project:

My personal experience has taught me the value of thorough planning. A former manager of mine 'bet his career' on project planning. He was convinced that by applying more rigor to our processes, particularly the up-front processes, he would gain high productivity dividends. For his software development project, he did everything by the book, with a great deal of discipline. His team was still defining user needs when parallel projects in the same program were closing up their requirements. When everyone else was well into coding, his team was still meeting weekly with the customer to validate output, walk through an exhaustive list of business cases, and define usage models. His team started coding when everyone else had already begun unit testing.

But his team's coding went quickly because of their thorough analysis, and they began system tests around the same time the rest of the teams went to quality assurance and customer acceptance test. His team continued to accelerate through all the testing phases and finished ahead of the rest of the other projects—with a significantly lower bug rate and a more successful customer acceptance test than any of the other teams.

At the project retrospective, we learned that his project team was 439 percent more productive than any other team in the program. His team accomplished with ten people what similar teams would have needed more than forty people to do. The principal reasons were reduced rework, a clearer understanding of the business needs, a better customer relationship, and superior overall project management.

The results of this retrospective are a compelling basis for continuous improvement of the planning process.

Esteri uses this example to overcome resistance to thorough project planning. She observes, "Project teams want to get going, and planning never seems very much like 'real project work.' People need to feel that they are accomplishing something." She deals with this by employing a "plan for the plan" to guide her teams through the initial analysis and planning phases for her projects. "This approach fills several needs," she says. "First, it gives the team a sense of accomplishment as they complete the planning deliverables. Second, it shows that the planning process, which few enjoy but everyone understands is necessary, will in fact soon come to a close and we can begin project execution. I have found that with teams using this approach we can produce higher quality, more thorough plans, and have far more successful projects."

KEY IDEAS FOR PROJECT CLOSURE

- Finish your work, and get formal acceptance for your deliverables.
- Complete final project documentation.
- Thank your team, and celebrate what you accomplished.
- Capture and apply the lessons learned.

CHAPTER 10

Conclusion

IF YOU ARE ASKED TO LEAD A PROJECT, someone believes that you are capable of doing it. If you believe it too, then you are both probably correct.

Project control begins with an understanding of the overall process of project management, figuring out what your project requires to be done, and then gaining commitments from the team members to do the work. The rest of control involves work: keeping up with all the effort, analyzing the status you collect, developing responses to deal with variances, and communicating project status. All of this is possible if you set the right foundation.

The first half of this book outlines three essential elements for control:

- Processes for ensuring consistency and alignment
- The influence needed for gaining cooperation and establishing teamwork
- The metrics required for assessing the state of your project and driving behavior

The second half explores using these elements to control your project, starting with initiation, through planning, execution, and tracking, and finally ending with closure. Although many ideas and examples are included in this book, projects come in all shapes and sizes. Determining exactly what is most likely to help you control your project is a judgment that you must make. Rather than becoming overwhelmed with every single detail, pick a few ideas relating to aspects of your recent projects that should have gone better. Select a few practices from the book that you believe may help, and then tailor them to use in your project. Apply them as you proceed, and pick some additional ideas for your next project.

Managing a project with limited authority is difficult, and it can be discouraging. If a problem arises during your project, review the material here for possible responses, and use them to help manage your way back into control. Involve your team in problem solving. Work with colleagues who can act as mentors and sounding boards to support you when things are not going well and can help you deal with obstacles.

Teamwork always makes a difference, because a high-performing, close-knit project team tends to find a way around most project difficulties, even seemingly insurmountable ones. Whatever else you do, work to establish and maintain a solid relationship of trust and respect with each member of your project team.

No matter how thorough your plans and regardless of how proactive you are in detecting and dealing with problems, situations inevitably arise that you can't manage within your team. Throughout your project, keep your sponsor aware of your progress and issues and, when you do encounter barriers or problems you are unable to resolve, escalate promptly. Make your sponsor's job in helping you as easy as possible by providing a clear summary of what you are facing, an outline of the consequences of failing to deal with the situation, and at least one credible option for resolution. A cooperative sponsor is your ultimate control tool. If you escalate only to deal with the most severe project obstacles and showstoppers, your tactic of last resort can restore your control.

This suggestion works effectively only when sponsors behave properly, and sometimes they don't. Sponsors who act badly create project problems that lead to failure, and they may be completely unaware of what they are doing. Patrick Schmid, managing director of PS Consulting in Germany, once presented his list of surefire methods for sponsors to ensure project failures at a project management conference. I call this useful list "Maximum Strength Projecticide." You have Patrick's full permission to use his list in any way that might encourage your sponsors to act in the best interests of their projects.

How to Guarantee That Every Project Will Fail
- Always select projects using only *gut feel.*
- Never share project selection criteria with the project team; it's none of their business.
- Avoid accountability for the project by claiming you're not the only decision maker.
- Always demand stretch-goal results that are unachievable.

- Enlist additional sponsors to provide the project leader with conflicting objectives.
- Hold back allocated resources for more important things until the project is in crisis.
- Never waste time talking with project leaders; you have important things to do.
- Ignore environment changes, and focus only on your daily activities.
- Make changes to projects at least weekly to keep everybody on their toes.
- Never make even small decisions without demanding more information and a detailed investigation.
- Discourage any analysis of postproject lessons learned, because everything will be different the next time anyway.

Ultimately, succeeding with any project is all about gaining the cooperation of all the people involved. Marketing guru and motivational speaker Zig Ziglar says, "You can get everything in life you want if you help enough other people get what they want." Controlling projects when you have little authority comes down primarily to aligning your project activities and goals with those of your sponsor, your team, and your stakeholders—getting by with a little help from your friends.

Appendix A
Example Project
Infrastructure Decisions

THESE SAMPLE QUESTIONS may be useful in drafting your own list. There are many more questions here than any single project would ever find useful; only select the critical few decisions that will really make a difference. After many projects, you will probably find that you have given attention to most of these questions.

Planning Questions

Project Initiation
- Who is the sponsor of this project? What is the stated business purpose of the project?
- How will the project charter be developed? Who will write it?
- Who will review and approve the project charter?
- How will the initial project scoping be defined and documented?
- Who is responsible for validating the proposed initial project scope?
- What departments, functions, and external organizations will be involved in this project?
- Who are the key stakeholders for this project? For the project, what is the interest or connection for each stakeholder?
- How will the project be staffed? Who is responsible for resolving all open staffing decisions? What is the timing for closure?
- If hiring is required, how will it be done? Who will be responsible?

- For project team members who report to other managers, how will staffing commitments be documented? What ongoing role in the project will the managers in the other organizations play?
- What are the roles and responsibilities of each team member?
- Who is responsible for defining and managing the development, training, and skill building (if any) needed for each contributor to the project?

Project Plan Development
- What life cycle applies to this project? Will any modifications be needed? What phases or iterations are defined for this project?
- Will the project employ iterative development cycles or phases to deliver a sequence of incremental outputs? At what frequency? At what level of detail will subsequent iterations or phases be planned?
- What activities are mandated at life cycle phase-exits, development iteration reviews, checkpoints, stage gates, or milestones?
- Will a project methodology be used? Will this project need to get any exceptions or changes approved?
- What process will you use to develop the plan?
- What level of planning detail is appropriate for this project?
- What are the agenda and timing for a project start-up workshop? Where and when will it be held? What approvals will you need for the meeting?
- How will you capture and document project assumptions and constraints?
- How will you identify, analyze, and plan for project risk?
- What planning meetings will you hold?
- When and how will you conduct the planning meetings?
- How will you identify, document, and manage dependencies between related projects?
- How will you and your team conduct a review of the plan documents?
- What is the process for establishing the plan as a project baseline? When will the baseline be set?
- What process will you use if you must make changes or adjustments to the project objectives or baseline plan?
- Who approves the decision to freeze or to make adjustments to the baseline plan?
- Do you plan to conduct periodic plan reviews for this project? How frequently?

Outsourced Work
- How will you determine whether you will need to outsource project work? Who in your organization must be involved in the outsourcing process?

- Before outsourcing project work, what approvals will you require? What support will you need, and who will provide it?
- Who will thoroughly document all work that is to be outsourced to an external supplier? Who will create the request for proposal (or other document) that will be distributed to potential suppliers?
- Who will manage communications with potential suppliers and collect their proposals? Who will evaluate each proposal? With what process?
- Who will select suppliers for outsourced work? Who will negotiate the terms for the contracts and obtain all needed signatures and approvals?
- Who on your project team will be responsible for managing the relationship with each supplier while the contracts are in force? In each case, will the same person track progress, approve payments, and serve as a liaison?

Planning Deliverables
- What format is required for each planning component?
- What information is needed in the project charter?
- What are your standards and format for the project scope documentation?
- What deliverable testing documentation will be needed? Who will verify planned tests and evaluations for completeness? Who will review and approve them?
- At what level of detail will you document your work breakdown structure (WBS)?
- What information must be defined for each project activity?
- How will you develop, verify, and capture duration and effort estimates?
- What cost budgeting information does your project require?
- What level of detail will you use in your resource and staffing plans?
- What quality planning is necessary? Will you require a formal quality plan?
- What contracts and documents will be needed for outsourced work?
- How will you document and track project risks?
- What will be in your communications plan?
- What additional project planning documents, if any, are mandated by your life cycle, methodology, or organization?
- Where will project documents be stored?
- How will project information be distributed? How will you manage any security considerations on access to project data?
- Will it be necessary to provide any project planning documents in more than one language? If so, who is responsible for translation into each relevant language? How will you verify consistency between versions?

Planning Participants
- In addition to the project leader, who will contribute to planning the project?
- What are the roles for the participants in the planning process? What are their responsibilities?
- How will you involve remote team members in project planning?
- Who will review the overall project plan?
- Who will validate and sign off on each project document?
- What are the roles of the project sponsor and other stakeholders in project planning?
- Who will be responsible for representing the customers and users of the project deliverable in planning?
- Who is responsible for the final decision to set the project baseline and objective?

Planning Tools
- What techniques will you use for project planning and scheduling?
- Will you use a software application for project scheduling and tracking? Which product and version? Are related projects using the same tools?
- Who will enter the information into and use any software tools for planning? Will the same person be responsible for tool use in tracking?
- Will you use an automated tool for issue management, change control, resource and budget tracking, risk analysis, project communications, or other purposes? If so, which products and versions?
- Will other software (such as programs for database management, spreadsheet analysis, word processing, presentations and graphics, or knowledge management) be needed? What applications and versions will you use?
- Do you have all the equipment, capacity, and performance to operate the software you will use? When will all needed hardware and upgrades be available?
- If you need to share information with others who are using different software products or versions, how will you resolve compatibility issues?
- What tool training will be needed?
- What support will you need? Who will support your planning tools?

Planning Metrics
- What plan-based predictive metrics will you define for this project?
- Who will document and evaluate the plans for these measures?
- How will you use these measures for your project?

Execution Questions

Project Status
- What status information will you collect for the project? What level of planning detail will serve as your basis for status requests?
- How frequently will you collect project status? On what day (or days)? At what time?
- What method will you use to collect project status from team members? Will you use different methods for remote contributors?
- How will you validate status data?
- Who will compare the status with project plans to uncover variances and assess project impact?

Status Metrics
- What status-based diagnostic measures will you use for this project?
- Are all metrics clearly defined and documented?
- Does each measure have a validated baseline or other realistically defined control limits?
- Are all measures understood by the people who will collect and report them? Have all people involved willingly agreed to participate?
- How will you minimize the gaming of project metrics?
- Will all metrics be collected in each status cycle? Who will collect any measures that are gathered on a different frequency? How will these measures be collected?
- What process will you use to evaluate the measures?
- How will you use diagnostic measures on your project?
- What trends will you track for the diagnostic metrics? Are responses defined for metrics that drift outside defined control limits? Who will take action?
- In addition to routine project status reports, what other reporting will you do using diagnostic project metrics? How frequently?

Project Management Information System (PMIS)
- Where will status data and other diagnostic metrics data be archived?
- Who is responsible for establishing the PMIS? How will information be organized?
- Who will maintain and have change access for the PMIS? If multiple people can update the PMIS, who has authority to resolve any inconsistencies or information conflicts?
- Which project contributors and stakeholders, if any, will be restricted to read access to the PMIS?
- For project data stored online, how will you manage access security?
- What specific documents and other information will be in your PMIS?

- Will all documents in the PMIS be in the same language? For any documents in a different language, how will you handle translation? If some documents will be translated into one or more additional languages, how will you ensure content consistency?
- How long do you need to retain project data in the PMIS following the project?

Project Meetings

- What regular meetings will be scheduled for this project? What are the stated objectives for these meetings?
- On what day and time will regular meetings be held? Where?
- If relevant, how will remote team members participate in the meetings? Will multiple meetings or periodic time shifts be necessary?
- Does each routine meeting have a well-defined standard agenda?
- Who is responsible for managing any changes or additions to the agenda for specific meetings, and who will distribute reminders, including the current agenda, before each meeting?
- Is the length of each meeting as short as practical, considering the agenda?
- Who will lead the meetings? Will the same person facilitate all the meetings?
- Who is responsible for taking notes during the meeting? Who will document the meeting and distribute meeting minutes to all attendees, appropriate stakeholders, and others?
- What documented ground rules do you use for project meetings?
- What other meetings, if any, will be required for this project? Where and when will they be scheduled? What are the purpose and agenda for these meetings, and who will lead them?

Team Concerns

- How will you and your project team make collaborative decisions? If you are unable to reach consensus, how do you come to closure?
- What process will you use to track project issues and problems?
- Where will issues and action items be logged and managed?
- How frequently will you update and communicate issue status?
- How will you manage conflicts between team members?
- How long will you spend trying to resolve decisions, issues, or conflicts within your team before escalating the situation? What other criteria will you consider before escalating a team problem to someone with more authority?
- Who will you escalate problems to, as a last resort? Does that person have sufficient authority to make final decisions?

- What team-building activities will you schedule during the project? What else will you do to enhance teamwork?
- What team member training or development will be necessary for your project? What approvals, support, and funding will be required for this training?
- For this project, what periodic rewards and recognition will be available for team members? How do you plan to take advantage of all appropriate opportunities? Does your recognition process include notification of the managers of team members who report to others?
- How frequently will you meet one-on-one with each team member? Do you plan to provide specific feedback on performance and results at least monthly? Typically, how much of your discussions with individuals will concern nonproject matters?
- How frequently is the job performance of each team member formally evaluated? What will you do to ensure that your inputs are included in each project contributor's performance appraisal?

Informal Communications
- How frequently do you plan to *manage by wandering around* with the members of your team?
- What will you do to encourage frequent interactions and informal conversations among project team members?
- What will you do to enhance relationships and trust between yourself and remote team members?
- What communication methods will you use for your project?

Life Cycles, Methodologies, and Other Organizational Requirements
- What specific deliverables are mandated by your organization at phase-exits, development iteration reviews, stage gates, or other project transition points?
- When are the deliverables due, and how much lead time should you allow normally for preparation of these documents, reports, and other items?
- Who will be responsible for preparation of the information needed?
- What other deliverables, if any, must you supply to your organization (or others) to comply with a project methodology, published standards, laws, regulations, or other requirements? When are they due? Who will be responsible for creating these deliverables?

Process Management and Quality Assurance
- Are key processes relating to consistent execution of project work and ensuring the quality of your deliverable well documented, understood, and routinely used?

- How frequently do you conduct process audits or reviews to ensure that the processes continue to serve their need? Alternatively, what diagnostic metrics with control limits will you monitor for these processes to trigger reviews?
- What is your procedure for evaluating a process and proposing process improvements? If the process affects other projects or teams, how do you manage modifications?
- What reporting or other communications, if any, are you required to provide during this project on your project processes?

Control Questions

Project Reporting

- What routine project reporting will be required?
- What format will be used for regular project status reporting?
- Who is responsible for creating reports? How often?
- Who will distribute the reports? Who will receive the reports?
- Will status reports in more than one language be necessary? If so, who is responsible for translation?
- Will summary or specialized reporting be needed for the project sponsor or key stakeholders? Who will create it? How frequently?
- In addition to periodic status, will separate reports for issue tracking, scope changes, plan adjustments, risk management, or other project aspects be required for this project? Who will create them? How frequently?
- What criteria will be used to determine if problem or exception reports need to be generated? What distribution will be required on nonroutine reporting?

Scope and Specification Control

- What is the process for setting project scope? Will your project scope be frozen with the setting of a project baseline, determined one development iteration at a time, or using some other method? Who approves project scope? How will the accepted project scope be documented?
- What scope change management process will you use? Where is it documented? Have all team members, your sponsor, and all relevant stakeholders (especially customers) agreed to the process?
- How will you document, log, and track all proposed changes or adjustments?
- What criteria will you use in separating routine changes from urgent requests that must be dealt with as soon as possible?
- How will you analyze proposed changes or scoping adjustments? How will you verify expected value, benefits, or results for each change? How

will you estimate the cost, resource, timing, and other impact to the project? How will you assess potential risks and unintended consequences associated with each proposed change?

- Who needs to be involved in analyzing proposed changes?
- How frequently will you consider nonurgent changes?
- How quickly will decisions on routine changes be made?
- What process will be used to determine the disposition of each change?
- Who will be involved in making decisions to accept or reject requested changes for your project? What is the role of each person? If the group fails to reach consensus on a particular change, who makes the final decision?
- How will you communicate change decisions?
- For each accepted change or adjustment, who is responsible for updating the plans and other project documents? How will you obtain commitment from your team members to follow through and implement each accepted change or adjustment?
- For major changes that impact the project baseline and objectives, what is the process for making a change? Who needs to approve project baseline modifications?

Overall Control
- Who in addition to the project leader is involved in assessing project progress? What is each person's role?
- How will you assess schedule progress?
- How much deviation from the baseline schedule will you accept before involving your project team in planning for a response?
- How much time slippage will you accept before escalating to management, either to request assistance for or to reset the project objective and modify the project baseline?
- How will you assess cost and resource usage?
- How much deviation from the planned project effort and expense estimates will you accept before exploring response options with your project team? Is overtime (particularly unpaid overtime) acceptable on this project? How much?
- How much effort or financial overrun can you tolerate before escalating to management to change the project baseline to approve more funding or obtain more staff?
- What metrics related to deliverable quality are relevant for this project? When the measures are outside acceptable ranges, how will you respond?
- How will you assess progress for outsourced work? What interim deliverables, early tests or inspections, or other evidence of progress are

available? What remedies and responses do you have for addressing inadequate performance? What escalation processes have you established? What alternatives, if any, are available that could substitute for the outsourced effort?

- How frequently will you reassess project risks? How do you document and communicate newly uncovered potential problems?
- How will you monitor trigger events associated with identified risks? How often will you review the overall risk profile for your project? How much risk will you and your sponsor and stakeholders accept before considering project changes or cancellation?
- What will you do if you lose your sponsor because of reorganization, resignation, health problems, or just loss of interest in your project? How will you reacquire adequate sponsorship to sustain progress?

Individual Performance Problems
- If analysis of a project performance problem appears to be due to inadequate performance by a project contributor, how will you proceed in investigating the situation and determining the cause?
- How will you confront the individual and work together to resolve the performance problem?
- If the individual reports to another manager, how will you involve this manager in your discussions?
- How will you renew the team member's commitment, document agreement, and work to resolve the project problem? What criteria will you use to determine when a situation cannot be resolved and you need to find other alternatives?

Project Reviews and Baseline Management
- How often will this project require plan reviews?
- Who will schedule and plan these reviews?
- Which project team members need to participate in reviews?
- Will the sponsor or other stakeholders participate in reviews?
- What is your project review agenda?
- Who will lead the reviews?
- If all necessary people are unable to meet in the same location, how will you involve remote participants?
- Who will take notes during project reviews?
- How will review results be documented? To whom will the results be distributed?
- Who will review data in the PMIS?
- How will any changes, proposals, or other results of the review be presented to the project sponsor and other stakeholders?

- Who will follow up and ensure that all actions assigned in the review are closed promptly?

Project Cancellation
- What criteria will be used in determining whether to stop the project?
- Who has ultimate responsibility to decide whether to change the project baseline or to cancel the project?
- What process will you use to close a canceled project? What activities and deliverables are required?

Project Closure
- What process is required for testing, deliverable evaluation, and scope verification?
- What sign-offs and approvals do you need? Who must validate successful project completion?
- When will you conduct the postproject retrospective analysis to determine lessons learned? Who will participate?
- What end-of-project reports are required? Who will write them? Who will receive them?
- What process will you use to close out the contracts used for outsourced project work?
- How will you commemorate the conclusion of the project with your project team (for example, with a celebration or party)?
- What rewards and recognition are possible for individuals and teams who contributed to the project? What will you do to ensure that all appropriate rewards are used and that you personally thank each contributor?

Retrospective Metrics
- What postproject measures will you assess for this project?
- Are all retrospective metrics unambiguously defined and documented?
- Who will collect postproject measures for this project? How do you plan to collect and validate these measures?
- What process will you use to evaluate the measures?
- How will you use retrospective measures to improve your next project?

Appendix B
Selected References

ALTHOUGH THERE ARE HUNDREDS OF BOOKS on project management, influence, and metrics, the few listed here are a good starting point for further exploration of the topics covered in this book.

Books on Project Management

Kendrick, Tom. *The Project Management Tool Kit: 100 Tips and Techniques for Getting the Job Done Right*, 2nd ed. AMACOM, 2010. Short process descriptions of essential project management processes.

Kerzner, Harold. *Project Management: A Systems Approach to Planning, Scheduling, and Controlling*, 10th ed. John Wiley & Sons, 2009. This sizable volume is thought by many to be the bible on project management.

Project Management Institute. *A Guide to the Project Management Body of Knowledge*, 4th ed. Project Management Institute, 2008. The PMBOK® *Guide* is an overview of a wide range of project management topics. It provides a vocabulary and high-level descriptions but lacks specifics on what to do and how to do it.

Wysocki, Robert. *Effective Project Management: Traditional, Agile, Extreme*, 6th ed. John Wiley & Sons, 2011. A thorough book covering a range of project management approaches.

Books on Influence

Cialdini, Robert B. *Influence: Science and Practice*, 5th ed. Prentice Hall, 2008. A systematic exploration of how influence operates.

Cohen, Allan R., and David L. Bradford. *Influence Without Authority*, 2nd ed. John Wiley & Sons, 2005. A very complete and thorough book on exchange and reciprocity.

DeMarco, Tom, and Tim Lister. *Peopleware: Productive Projects and Teams.* Dorset House, 1999. Insightful essays on the human side of project management.

Englund, Randall, Bob Graham, and Paul Dinsmore. *Creating the Project Office: A Manager's Guide to Leading Organizational Change.* Jossey-Bass, 2003. Thoroughly explores the process of effecting organizational changes using project management.

Pink, Daniel. *Drive: The Surprising Truth About What Motivates Us.* Riverhead Books, 2009. A good survey of traditional and current thinking on motivation in the workplace.

Books on Metrics

Austin, Robert D. *Measuring and Managing Performance in Organizations.* Dorset House, 1996. A useful book that explains why measurement so often leads to organizational dysfunction.

Grady, Robert B. *Successful Software Process Improvement.* Prentice Hall PTR, 1997. Describes using metrics for sustainable process improvements.

Kaplan, Robert S., and David P. Norton. *The Balanced Scorecard: Translating Strategy into Action.* Harvard Business Press, 1996. Defines a process for establishing a system of compatible business metrics.

Index

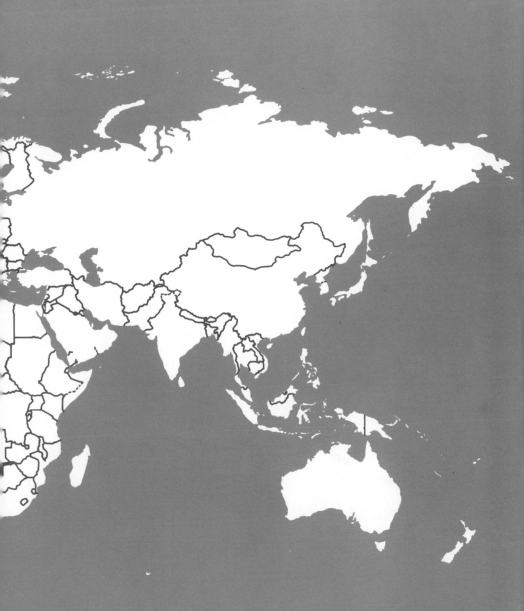

Angola
a country study

Federal Research Division
Library of Congress
Edited by
Thomas Collelo
Research Completed
February 1989

On the cover: Portion of a fresco depicting revolutionary
scenes at the Karl Marx Institute of Education in Luanda

*DT
1269
.A54
1990*

Third Edition, First Printing, 1991.

Library of Congress Cataloging-in-Publication Data

Angola : a country study / Federal Research Division, Library of
Congress ; edited by Thomas Collelo. — 3d ed.
   p. cm. — (Area handbook series) (DA pam ; 550-59)
  "Supersedes the 1979 edition of Angola : a country study,
edited by Irving Kaplan"—T.p. verso.
  "Research completed December 1988."
  Includes bibiliographical references (pp. 277-295) and index.
  Supt. of Docs. no. : D 101.22:550-59/990
  1. Angola. I. Collelo, Thomas, 1948- . II. Kaplan, Irving.
III. Library of Congress. Federal Research Division. IV. Series.
V. Series: DA pam ; 550-559.
DT1269.A54   1990   90-3244
967.3—dc20   CIP

#21409136

Headquarters, Department of the Army
DA Pam 550-59

For sale by the Superintendent of Documents, U.S. Government Printing Office
Washington, D.C. 20402

107329

Foreword

This volume is one in a continuing series of books now being prepared by the Federal Research Division of the Library of Congress under the Country Studies—Area Handbook Program. The last page of this book lists the other published studies.

Most books in the series deal with a particular foreign country, describing and analyzing its political, economic, social, and national security systems and institutions, and examining the interrelationships of those systems and the ways they are shaped by cultural factors. Each study is written by a multidisciplinary team of social scientists. The authors seek to provide a basic understanding of the observed society, striving for a dynamic rather than a static portrayal. Particular attention is devoted to the people who make up the society, their origins, dominant beliefs and values, their common interests and the issues on which they are divided, the nature and extent of their involvement with national institutions, and their attitudes toward each other and toward their social system and political order.

The books represent the analysis of the authors and should not be construed as an expression of an official United States government position, policy, or decision. The authors have sought to adhere to accepted standards of scholarly objectivity. Corrections, additions, and suggestions for changes from readers will be welcomed for use in future editions.

Louis R. Mortimer
Acting Chief
Federal Research Division
Library of Congress
Washington, D.C. 20540

Acknowledgments

The authors wish to acknowledge the contributions of the following individuals, who wrote the 1979 edition of *Angola: A Country Study,* edited by Irving Kaplan: H. Mark Roth, "Historical Setting"; Irving Kaplan, "The Society and Its Physical Setting"; Margarita Dobert, "Government and Politics"; Eugene K. Keefe, "National Security"; and Donald P. Whitaker, "The Economy." Their work provided the organization and structure of the present volume, as well as substantial portions of the text.

The authors are grateful to individuals in various government agencies and private institutions who gave their time, research materials, and expertise to the production of this book. The authors also wish to thank members of the Federal Research Division staff who contributed directly to the production of the manuscript. These people include Richard F. Nyrop, who reviewed all drafts and served as liaison with the sponsoring agency, and Marilyn L. Majeska and Andrea T. Merrill, who managed book production. Vincent Ercolano and Sharon Schultz edited the chapters, and Beverly Wolpert performed the final prepublication review. Also involved in preparing the text were editorial assistants Barbara Edgerton and Izella Watson. Shirley Kessel compiled the index. Linda Peterson of the Library of Congress Composing Unit set the type, under the direction of Peggy Pixley.

Invaluable graphics support was provided by David P. Cabitto, who reviewed all the graphics and designed the artwork on the cover and title page of each chapter; Kimberly A. Lord, who prepared all the maps except the topography and drainage map, which was prepared by Harriett R. Blood; and Sandra K. Ferrell, who prepared the charts. In addition, Carolina E. Forrester reviewed the map drafts, and Arvies J. Staton supplied information on ranks and insignia.

Finally, the authors acknowledge the generosity of the individuals and public and private agencies who allowed their photographs to be used in this study. The authors are indebted especially to those persons who contributed original work not previously published.

Contents

List of Figures

Preface

Like its predecessor, this study is an attempt to treat in a concise and objective manner the dominant social, political, economic, and military aspects of Angolan society. Sources of information included scholarly journals and monographs, official reports of governments and international organizations, foreign and domestic newspapers, and numerous periodicals. Up-to-date data from Angolan sources for the most part were unavailable. Chapter bibliographies appear at the end of the book; brief comments on some of the more valuable sources suggested as possible further reading appear at the end of each chapter. Measurements are given in the metric system; a conversion table is provided to assist those readers who are unfamiliar with metric measurements (see table 1, Appendix A). A glossary is also included.

Place-names follow a modified version of the system adopted by the United States Board on Geographic Names and the Permanent Committee on Geographic Names for British Official Use, known as the BGN/PCGN system. The modification is a significant one, however, in that some diacritical markings and hyphens have been omitted.

Terminology and spelling sometimes presented problems. For example, after independence Angola's ruling party was known as the Popular Movement for the Liberation of Angola (Movimento Popular de Libertação de Angola—MPLA). In 1977, however, in asserting its commitment to the principles of Marxism-Leninism, the MPLA added to its nomenclature "Partido de Trabalho." The term is translated in this book as "Workers' Party" but is elsewhere often seen as "Labor Party." Furthermore, because the spelling of the names of ethnic groups occasionally varies, in some cases alternate spellings are given in parentheses. Finally, many Angolan officials who fought in the liberation struggle against the Portuguese acquired noms de guerre; these officials are often referred to in press accounts by their nicknames. When such officials are cited in the text, their noms de guerre are given in parentheses after their surnames.

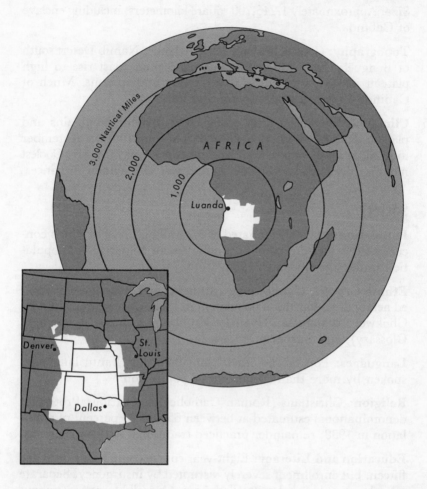

AFRICA

3,000 Nautical Miles

2,000

1,000

Luanda

Denver

St.
Louis

Dallas

Country

Formal Name: People's Republic of Angola.

Short Form: Angola.

Term for Citizens: Angolans.

Date of Independence: 1975, from Portugal.

Geography

Size: Approximately 1,246,700 square kilometers, including enclave of Cabinda.

Topography: Coastal lowland along Atlantic; Namib Desert south of Benguela; hills and mountains paralleling coast rise to high plateau in east, divided by many rivers and streams. Much of Cabinda Province coastal plain and hills.

Climate: Hotter and drier along coast than in mountains and plateau. Rainy season in northern part of country from September to April; in southern part from November to about February. Coolest months July and August. Warm and wet in Cabinda Province.

Society

Population: In 1988 estimated at 8.2 million, most of which concentrated in western half of country. About 46 percent of population under age fifteen in 1986.

Ethnic Groups: Ovimbundu, Mbundu, and Bakongo constituted nearly three-fourths of population in 1988. Other groups Lunda-Chokwe, Nganguela, Nyaneka-Humbe, Ovambo, *mestiço* (see Glossary), and European.

Languages: Portuguese official language, but Bantu languages spoken by more than 95 percent of population.

Religion: Christians (Roman Catholics and various Protestant denominations) estimated at between 65 and 88 percent of population in 1988; remainder practiced traditional African religions.

Education and Literacy: Eight-year course compulsory until age fifteen, but enrollment severely disrupted by insurgency. Separate school system in rebel-controlled areas. Overall literacy rate about 20 percent in 1987.

Health and Welfare: Very poor health care because of years of insurgency. High prevalence of infectious diseases; 20,000 to 50,000 amputees. Large number of foreign, especially Cuban, medical personnel in country. Life expectancy in 1987 forty-one for males and forty-four for females.

Economy

Gross Domestic Product (GDP): Approximately US$4.7 billion in 1987; US$600 per capita.

Extractive Industries: Oil most important sector of economy. Contributed 30 percent of GDP in 1985. Concentrated in areas offshore of Cabinda Province. Diamond mining in northeast disrupted by fighting.

Agriculture: In steep decline as result of insurgency. Contributed only 9 percent of GDP in 1985. Coffee principal export crop.

Manufacturing: Stagnant in late 1980s because of insurgency and lack of spare parts. Contributed 16 percent of GDP in 1985. Main industries food processing, construction, and textiles.

Exports: Oil revenue nearly 90 percent of total export earnings in 1988.

Imports: Foodstuffs, military equipment, and inputs to petroleum industry most important imports.

Currency: In December 1988, official rate of kwanza was Kz29.3 to US$1, but United States dollar traded on parallel market at up to Kz2,100.

Fiscal Year: Calendar year.

Transportation and Telecommunications

Railroads: Three lines with total of 3,075 kilometers of track ran from coast to hinterland. Benguela Railway, longest line, severely damaged by insurgency.

Roads: Total of about 70,000 kilometers of roads, of which 8,000 kilometers paved.

Ports: Three major ports (Luanda, Lobito, and Namibe) and several smaller terminals.

Inland Waterways: Nearly 1,300 kilometers of navigable rivers.

Airports: International airport at Luanda; thirteen other major airports.

Telecommunications: Fairly reliable system included microwave, troposcatter, and satellite links.

Government and Politics

Government: Marxist-Leninist government based on 1975 Constitution (later revised) but dominated by Popular Movement for the Liberation of Angola-Workers' Party (Movimento Popular de

Libertação de Angola-Partido de Trabalho—MPLA–PT). Government composed of executive branch led by president, who appointed Council of Ministers and Defense and Security Council. Legislative branch consisted of People's Assembly. As of late 1988, because of inability to hold elections, People's Assembly had been appointed. Justice system composed of Supreme Court, Court of Appeals, people's revolutionary courts, and series of people's courts.

Politics: Real power resided with MPLA–PT, whose chairman was president of republic. Political Bureau most important body in party. Central Committee, although subordinate to MPLA–PT party congress, wielded greater influence over party policies. No legal opposition parties, but beginning in 1976 National Union for the Total Independence of Angola (União Nacional para a Independência Total de Angola—UNITA) waged devastating insurgency from bases in southeast and elsewhere.

Foreign Relations: Government relied on Soviet Union and its allies, especially Cuba, for military support. United States and other Western nations played important economic roles. South Africa, which has supported UNITA, most important regional threat. December 1988 regional accords with South Africa and Cuba—which provided for cessation of South African support for UNITA, withdrawal of Cuban troops from Angola, and independence for Namibia—may change complexion of regional politics and foreign relations.

International Organizations: Member of African Development Bank, Council for Mutual Economic Assistance (observer status), Customs Cooperation Council, Group of 77, International Telecommunications Satellite Organization, Nonaligned Movement, Organization of African Unity, Southern African Development Coordination Conference, United Nations and its agencies, and World Federation of Trade Unions.

National Security

Armed Forces: Active-duty strength consisted of army of 91,500, air and air defense force of 7,000, and navy of 1,500; reserve personnel of 50,000. At end of 1988, armed forces supported by nearly 50,000 Cuban troops and a few thousand Soviet and East German advisers. Army supported by 50,000-member Directorate of People's Defense and Territorial Troops, a kind of reserve militia. Two years of universal and compulsory conscription.

Combat Units and Major Equipment: Army organized into more than seventy brigades in ten military regions. Operated about 1,100 Soviet-manufactured tanks and armored fighting vehicles. Air force organized into three regiments (fighter-bomber, transport, and helicopter). Combat aircraft included MiG-23 and MiG-21 fighters. Navy used three ports and had guided missile fast patrol boats and torpedo boats.

Military Budget: Amounted to US$1.3 billion in 1986 (in constant 1980 dollars)—more than 40 percent of government expenditures and about 30 percent of GNP.

Paramilitary and Internal Security Forces: Largest group was People's Vigilance Brigades, a lightly armed citizens' militia with strength of from 800,000 to 1.5 million. In 1988 about 7,000 border guards and 8,000 police officers (supported by force of 10,000).

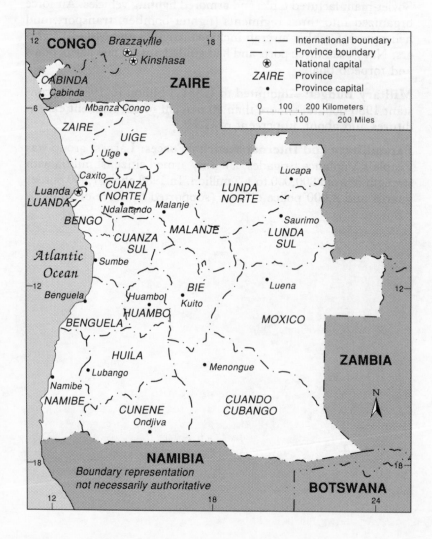

Figure 1. Administrative Divisions of Angola, 1988

Introduction

AN IMPORTANT SYMBOLIC EPISODE in the course of Angolan history took place on June 22, 1989, in the remote Zairian town of Gbadolite. On that date, Angolan president José Eduardo dos Santos shook the hand of Jonas Savimbi, leader of the antigovernment movement, the National Union for the Total Independence of Angola (União Nacional para a Independência Total de Angola—UNITA). This friendly gesture occurred at the end of a meeting attended by representatives from seventeen African nations and held under the auspices of Zairian president Mobutu Sese Seko. Accompanying the handshake was a communiqué calling for a cease-fire between government forces and UNITA rebels, national reconciliation, and direct negotiations; specific provisions were to be arranged later. But like many other incidents in Angolan history, this promising event soon became a disappointment as the parties failed to make progress along the path to peace. And so, scarcely two months after the so-called Gbadolite Declaration, UNITA announced the end to the cease-fire. As the internal turmoil resumed, Angolans once again became victims in a civil war that by 1989 had lasted for fourteen years.

Clearly, turmoil, victimization, and disappointment are themes that have pervaded Angola's history, especially since the arrival of Europeans in the fifteenth century. Although the Portuguese crown initially sent to Angola teachers to educate and priests to proselytize, Portugal eventually came to view the area mainly as a source for slaves, especially for Brazil, its colony across the Atlantic Ocean. In the several centuries during which the slave trade flourished, scholars estimate that 4 million Africans from the Angola region were taken into slavery. Of this number, perhaps half died before reaching the New World.

During its five centuries of colonization, Portugal treated Angola mostly with indifference or hostility. Although Angolans were often responsible for enslaving other Africans, Portuguese traders provided the impetus and the market for slaving. By raising small armies, Portuguese fought their way into Angola's interior, disrupting as they went kingdoms having sophisticated civilizations. Less alluring to Portuguese settlers than Brazil, Angola generally attracted poorer immigrants, a great many of whom were *degredados* (see Glossary), or exiled convicts. Portugal's exploitation of Angola did not cease even after slavery had been legally abolished in Angola in 1858. Lisbon spent the last part of the nineteenth century engaged in wars against the African kingdoms that it had not yet conquered and in consolidating its hold on territories awarded to it at the Berlin Conference of 1884 during the so-called scramble for Africa.

In the twentieth century, and particularly after 1926 and António Salazar's rise to power in Portugal, Lisbon exploited Angola's agricultural and mineral wealth. Salazar facilitated this exploitation by inducing greater numbers of Portuguese to settle in Angola to manage plantations and mines and by enacting labor laws that forced Angolans to work for Portuguese. He also ensured that Africans could not easily participate in or benefit from the colonial administration.

In the 1950s and 1960s, as most other African colonies were winning their independence, many Angolans, especially educated *mestiços* (see Glossary) and *assimilados* (see Glossary), came to resent the continued oppressiveness of the Salazar regime, which steadfastly refused to consider granting independence to its African holdings. As a consequence, in the early months of 1961 a rebellion erupted in the northern part of the colony. This event sounded the opening shots of Angola's war of liberation, a conflict that dragged on until 1974. In that year, a military coup d'état in Lisbon toppled the government of Marcello Caetano (who had replaced Salazar in 1968). The generals who assumed power had fought the anticolonialists in Africa and were weary of that battle. And so, soon after the coup they announced plans for the independence of all of Portugal's African possessions.

Unlike other Portuguese African colonies, the transition to independence in Angola did not proceed smoothly. During the 1960s and 1970s, the three most important liberation movements were the Popular Movement for the Liberation of Angola (Movimento Popular de Libertação de Angola—MPLA), the National Front for the Liberation of Angola (Frente Nacional de Libertação de Angola—FNLA), and UNITA. When these groups could not resolve peacefully their differences about the leadership and structure of a unified government, they turned their guns on each other; the FNLA and UNITA eventually formed a loose coalition to oppose the MPLA, the movement that finally prevailed. The subsequent chaos, however, induced most Portuguese to repatriate, leaving Angola critically deficient in skilled professionals such as managers, teachers, and technicians.

The resultant civil war had domestic, regional, and international dimensions. Domestically, the movements tended to be divided along ethnic lines: the MPLA came to be identified with the Mbundu, the FNLA with the Bakongo, and UNITA with the Ovimbundu. In the late 1980s, ethnicity was still a sensitive issue.

Regionally, Zaire came to the aid of the FNLA by supplying bases and some combat troops. South Africa, concerned about communist expansion in southern Africa, invaded Angola from neighboring Namibia. Internationally, the Soviet Union backed the MPLA with matériel and advisers, while Cuba supplied thousands of combat troops. The United States sided with the FNLA by providing financial assistance and by helping to hire mercenaries.

By mid-1976 most of the fighting had died down. The South Africans had withdrawn, and, for the most part, the FNLA and UNITA had been routed, thanks primarily to the effectiveness of Cuban forces. Consequently, the MPLA was able to legitimize its claim of control over the government. Nonetheless, despite its legitimization and the recognition of its claim by most African states and many other countries and international organizations, the MPLA still was confronted with an insurgency. Leading this insurgency from the southeast part of the country was Savimbi's UNITA, which had regrouped with the assistance of South Africa, and, after 1985, with aid from the United States. By 1989 this conflict, which many believed was merely an extension of the civil war, had claimed an estimated 60,000 to 90,000 lives, had exacted hundreds of thousands of casualties, and had forced about 700,000 people from their homes.

During the 1980s, the strains of the conflict were everywhere apparent. A significant portion of Angola's young populace (median age 17.5 years in 1988), estimated at 8.2 million in 1988, was moving westward away from the principal battlegrounds. Between 1975 and 1987, cities such as Luanda, Huambo, and Benguela witnessed an almost unchecked population explosion. But as the cities filled, the countryside emptied. The consequences of this rural-to-urban migration were devastating to the nation's welfare. The cities were unable to absorb such masses so quickly; the government could not provide adequate services, such as medical care and education; and jobs and housing were in short supply. Most important, with agricultural workers leaving their farms, the cities could not obtain enough food for their residents. By the late 1980s, Angola, once a food exporter, was importing more than half of its grain requirements. Moreover, thousands of those who could not reach cities settled in displaced persons camps, many of which were funded and operated by international relief organizations. Unrecorded as of 1989 were the psychological effects on the populace of leaving the relatively stable, traditional environment of the country for the uncertain, modern society of the city.

Exacerbating these demographic strains was the economy's poor performance in the 1980s in relation to its vast potential. The

xxiii

production of coffee, sisal, sugar, iron ore, and diamonds either declined or stagnated. Furthermore, the closure by UNITA insurgents of the Benguela Railway, which linked the rich mining regions of Zaire and Zambia with Atlantic ports, denied transit fees to the government. As a result, the economy became almost exclusively dependent on petroleum. Production of oil had begun in 1956, and by the late 1980s, with the financial and technical assistance of Western companies, oil sales accounted for nearly 90 percent of export earnings. Most Angolans, however, failed to benefit from these earnings. To finance the war against UNITA, the government in 1986 allocated more than 40 percent of its budget to defense expenditures, leaving relatively little for pressing social needs.

Several other factors contributed to economic weaknesses. First, because of the lack of foreign exchange, imported consumer goods were scarce, especially in state-run stores. This scarcity generated a widespread parallel market in which goods were frequently bartered rather than sold because Angola's unit of currency, the kwanza (for value of the kwanza—see Glossary), was virtually worthless. And because of commodity shortages, graft and pilfering (particularly at points of entry) became government concerns. National production also suffered because industrial workers and agricultural laborers were reluctant to work for kwanzas; as a result of the shortage of goods, the government often could not even barter for the services of workers or the output of farmers.

The UNITA insurgency and its associated disruptions notwithstanding, the government itself was responsible for some economic ills. Critics of the government claimed that mismanagement in centralized planning, state-run companies, and state-owned farms contributed significantly to the nation's economic decline. The government, in fact, seemed to agree in 1987, at which time President dos Santos announced plans to restructure the economy, calling for greater commercial liberalization and privatization of enterprise.

But while the government was willing to concede the economic shortcomings of Marxism-Leninism, it was resolutely opposed to accepting the notion of sweeping changes in political ideology. Since the First Party Congress in December 1977, when the MPLA became a "workers' party" and added "PT" (for Partido de Trabalho) to its acronym, Angola's leadership had followed a course that some observers have described as "Moscow oriented." Despite this characterization and the fact that Angola's enmeshed party-government structure resembled that of the Soviet Union, the dos Santos regime was notably more moderate than the regime of his predecessor, Agostinho Neto. In the late 1980s, however, political power remained in the hands of dos Santos and his small inner circle.

For the most part, Angola's goal of installing a functioning socialist state had not been attained. Although millions of Angolans had been mobilized into mass organizations or defense forces, political debate was narrowly constrained. The party, with a membership of only about 45,000, dominated the government. As of 1989, the People's Assembly—nominally the highest state organ—was largely an appointed body, unrepresentative of the constituents it was designed to serve. Likewise, the MPLA–PT was controlled primarily by the eleven-member Political Bureau (led by its chairman, dos Santos) and secondarily by the Central Committee; the party congress, the MPLA–PT's theoretical supreme body, in practice was subordinate to the other organs. In addition, reflecting the nation's precarious security situation, many serving in party and government positions were military officers.

Angola's foreign relations wavered in the 1980s. Within black Africa, Luanda's relations with other states generally were good. Those with Zaire, however, fluctuated from normal to poor because of Kinshasa's sponsorship during the 1970s of the FNLA and because of Angola's support during the same period of an anti-Mobutu armed movement. In addition, although Zaire denied aiding UNITA, most observers agreed that during the 1980s Kinshasa allowed Zairian territory to be used to support Savimbi's movement, creating another bone of contention between the two neighbors. Angola's principal antagonist in the region, however, was not Zaire but South Africa. Since its invasion of Angola in 1975 and 1976 during the war of independence, Pretoria has frequently violated Luanda's sovereignty, either in pursuit of members of the South West Africa People's Organization (SWAPO—a group fighting for Namibian independence) or in support of UNITA forces.

In the late 1980s, Angola's ties to the superpowers were in a state of flux. Although Luanda was closely aligned with the Soviet Union and its allies, this relationship generally was considered an outgrowth of Angola's security predicament. In economic concerns, the MPLA–PT often turned to the West, particularly in matters relating to the oil sector but also for trade and commerce and in other areas. Reportedly, the Soviet Union prodded the Angolan government into participating in the December 1988 regional accords, but in late 1989 it was uncertain how the reforms being carried out in the Soviet Union under Mikhail S. Gorbachev would affect the policies and practices of the MPLA–PT government. The other superpower, the United States, also played an important role in the accords. After their signing, however, United States president George P. Bush affirmed American support for the UNITA rebels and vowed to continue backing Savimbi's movement until the MPLA–PT and UNITA reached an accommodation.

The MPLA's independence struggle and subsequent conflict with UNITA and South Africa compelled the government to develop the People's Armed Forces for the Liberation of Angola (Forças Armadas Populares de Libertação de Angola—FAPLA). Comprising a ground force, air and air defense force, and navy, FAPLA was one of the largest and most heavily armed militaries in Africa. In 1988 experts estimated its strength at 100,000 active-duty personnel, 50,000 reservists, and many hundreds of thousands more in a variety of militias and internal security units. Bolstering this force in the late 1980s were about 50,000 Cuban troops, who provided logistical and combat support.

FAPLA was armed and trained by the Soviet Union and its allies. Its major equipment included MiG-21 and MiG-23 aircraft, T-62 and T-72 main battle tanks, and an assortment of air defense, field artillery, and naval assets. Although this arsenal and the assistance of Cuban troops and Soviet and East European advisers had prevented a UNITA victory, by 1988 Luanda had incurred an external debt estimated at almost US$4 billion, most of which was owed to Moscow for military matériel and assistance.

In late 1989, Angola's economic and political prospects appeared less bleak than they had only a year or two earlier. The economic restructuring program, together with other austerity measures, convinced the International Monetary Fund (IMF—see Glossary) to admit Angola as a member in June 1989 (over the objection of the United States). This event opened the door for greater financial assistance. Furthermore, the December 1988 regional accords, which provided for the staged withdrawal of Cuban troops, the cessation of South African support for UNITA, and the independence of Namibia, augured well for Angola's future. Observers reasoned that as the Cuban troops departed (and by mid-1989 more than 10,000 had left), Luanda's payments to Havana for military aid would drop; with South Africa's cutoff of support to UNITA, that organization's ability to disrupt the economy would decline and perhaps push it closer to accepting a peace plan; and with independence for Namibia, the threat of South African aggression would diminish substantially. Carrying this logic one step further, reporters argued that if the peace process begun at Gbadolite in June 1989 could be revitalized and an agreement between the MPLA–PT and

UNITA achieved, Angolans stood a chance of reversing the pattern of turmoil, victimization, and disappointment that had plagued the country for the previous 500 years.

October 18, 1989

* * *

A few significant events occurred in Angola after the completion of the research and writing of this manuscript. By mid-1990 it became clear that Angola, Cuba, and South Africa, the signatories of the December 1988 regional accords, were intent on faithfully executing the provisions of the agreement. Since the signing, more than 37,000 Cuban troops had departed Angola, and the remaining 13,000 Cubans, most of whom were stationed near Luanda, were to be brought home by mid-1991. As promised, South African forces withdrew from Angolan territory, and Pretoria ceased aid to UNITA. Finally, Namibia held elections and, as planned, celebrated its independence on March 21, 1990.

These positive developments notwithstanding, most Angolans enjoyed little improvement in their quality of life, and, for many, conditions deteriorated. The primary reason for this decline was that the MPLA–PT and UNITA had failed to make much progress on the path to peace. Each side of the dispute held a different interpretation of the Gbadolite Declaration. Analysts suggested that Mobutu, the mediator of the Gbadolite talks, may have presented varying versions of the agreement to each side. In any case, warfare persisted from mid-1989 to mid-1990 as FAPLA and UNITA troops battled each other for control of the southeastern town of Mavinga. Government forces captured the town in early February 1990, but intense fighting continued in the region for several months. Following a heavy engagement, FAPLA retreated from Mavinga in early May, and UNITA reoccupied it.

In addition to the combat that raged in Angola's southeast, UNITA reportedly made inroads in the country's northwest. This success allegedly was accomplished through Zairian operational support and United States assistance. According to some sources, the Zairian government was resupplying UNITA forces there via cargo flights from Kinshasa. The United States, using this Zairian air bridge, reportedly provided UNITA with matériel and other assistance worth an estimated US$45 million to US$60 million annually. By mid-1990 UNITA forces sabotaged water facilities and electric power lines to Luanda and generally disrupted the economic life of the nation.

Despite the on-going military situation, there appeared to be some softening of political positions. In April 1990, government and UNITA representatives met in Portugal for negotiations. As a result, UNITA recognized the Angolan state with President dos Santos as its head. UNITA, however, also called for the replacement of the single-party state with a multiparty government chosen in free elections. Observers saw a coincidence of interests here because the MPLA–PT had pledged to hold elections in which nonparty candidates—including members of UNITA—could run for seats in the People's Assembly. The single-party versus multiparty issue was to be debated at the Third Party Congress, scheduled for December 1990.

Regardless of the outcome of this congress, however, observers believed that UNITA's battlefield successes might encourage Savimbi to hold out for a total military solution. With the continued United States commitment to UNITA, at the same time that Cuban troops were withdrawing and the Soviet Union's interest in supporting the MPLA–PT government was weakening, some analysts reasoned that a UNITA victory in Angola, whether on the battlefield or at the polls, was merely a question of time.

September 9, 1990   Thomas Collelo

Chapter 1. Historical Setting

A village near Pungo Andongo, formerly Pungu-a-Ndondong, the capital of the Ndongo Kingdom in the sixteenth century

IN NOVEMBER 1975, after nearly five centuries as a Portuguese colony, Angola became an independent state. By late 1988, however, despite fertile land, large deposits of oil and gas, and great mineral wealth, Angola had achieved neither prosperity nor peace—the national economy was stagnating and warfare was ravaging the countryside. True independence also remained unrealized as foreign powers continued to determine Angola's future.

But unattained potential and instability were hardships well known to the Angolan people. They had suffered the outrage of slavery and the indignity of forced labor and had experienced years of turmoil going back to the early days of the indigenous kingdoms.

The ancestors of most present-day Angolans found their way to the region long before the first Portuguese arrived in the late fifteenth century. The development of indigenous states, such as the Kongo Kingdom, was well under way before then. The primary objective of the first Portuguese settlers in Angola, and the motive behind most of their explorations, was the establishment of a slave trade. Although several early Portuguese explorers recognized the economic and strategic advantages of establishing friendly relations with the leaders of the kingdoms in the Angolan interior, by the middle of the sixteenth century the slave trade had engendered an enmity between the Portuguese and the Africans that persisted until independence.

Most of the Portuguese who settled in Angola through the nineteenth century were exiled criminals, called *degredados* (see Glossary), who were actively involved in the slave trade and spread disorder and corruption throughout the colony. Because of the unscrupulous behavior of the *degredados*, most Angolan Africans soon came to despise and distrust their Portuguese colonizers. Those Portuguese who settled in Angola in the early twentieth century were peasants who had fled the poverty of their homeland and who tended to establish themselves in Angolan towns in search of a means of livelihood other than agriculture. In the process, they squeezed out the *mestiços* (people of mixed African and white descent; see Glossary) and urban Africans who had hitherto played a part in the urban economy. In general, these later settlers lacked capital, education, and commitment to their new homelands.

When in the early 1930s António Salazar implemented the New State (Estado Novo) in Portugal, Angola was expected to survive on its own. Accordingly, Portugal neither maintained an adequate

3

social and economic infrastructure nor invested directly in long-term development.

Ideologically, Portugal maintained that increasing the density of white rural settlement in Angola was a means of "civilizing" the African. Generally, the Portuguese regarded Africans as inferior and gave them few opportunities to develop either in terms of their own cultures or in response to the market. The Portuguese also discriminated politically, socially, and economically against *assimilados* (see Glossary)—those Africans who, by acquiring a certain level of education and a mode of life similar to that of Europeans, were entitled to become citizens of Portugal. Those few Portuguese officials and others who called attention to the mistreatment of Africans were largely ignored or silenced by the colonial governments.

By the 1950s, African-led or *mestiço*-led associations with explicit political goals began to spring up in Angola. The authoritarian Salazar regime forced these movements and their leaders to operate in exile. By the early 1960s, however, political groups were sufficiently organized (if also divided by ethnic loyalties and personal animosities) to begin their drives for independence. Moreover, at least some segments of the African population had been so strongly affected by the loss of land, forced labor, and stresses produced by a declining economy that they were ready to rebel on their own. The result was a series of violent events in urban and rural areas that marked the beginning of a long and often ineffective armed struggle for independence.

To continue its political and economic control over the colony, Portugal was prepared to use whatever military means were necessary. In 1974 the Portuguese army, tired of warfare not only in Angola but in Portugal's other African colonies, overthrew the Lisbon regime. The new regime left Angola to its own devices—in effect, abandoning it to the three major anticolonial movements.

Ideological differences and rivalry among their leaderships divided these movements. Immediately following independence in 1975, civil war erupted between the Popular Movement for the Liberation of Angola (Movimento Popular de Libertação de Angola—MPLA) on the one hand and the National Front for the Liberation of Angola (Frente Nacional de Libertação de Angola—FNLA) and the National Union for the Total Independence of Angola (União Nacional para a Independência Total de Angola—UNITA) on the other hand. The MPLA received support from the Soviet Union and Cuba, while the FNLA turned to the United States. UNITA, unable to gain more than nominal support from China, turned to South Africa. Viewing the prospect of a Soviet-sponsored

MPLA government with alarm, South Africa invaded Angola. The Soviet and Cuban reaction was swift: the former provided the logistical support, and the latter provided troops. By the end of 1976, the MPLA, under the leadership of Agostinho Neto, was in firm control of the government. Members of UNITA retreated to the bush to wage a guerrilla war against the MPLA government, while the FNLA became increasingly ineffective in the north in the late 1970s.

The MPLA, which in 1977 had declared itself a Marxist-Leninist vanguard party, faced the task of restoring the agricultural and production sectors that nearly had been destroyed with the departure of the Portuguese. Recognizing that traditional Marxist-Leninist policies of large-scale expropriation and state ownership would undermine redevelopment efforts, Neto permitted private involvement in commercial and small-scale industry and developed substantial economic relations with Western states, especially in connection with Angola's oil industry.

After Neto's death in 1979, José Eduardo dos Santos inherited considerable economic difficulties, including the enormous military costs required to fight UNITA and South African forces. By the end of 1985, the security of the Luanda regime depended almost entirely on Soviet-supplied weaponry and Cuban troop support. Consequently, in the late 1980s Luanda's two main priorities were to end the UNITA insurgency and to make progress toward economic development. By late 1988, a United States-sponsored peace agreement held out some hope that, given time, both priorities could be achieved.

Precolonial Angola and the Arrival of the Portuguese

Although the precolonial history of many parts of Africa has been carefully researched and preserved, there is relatively little information on the region that forms contemporary Angola as it was before the arrival of the Europeans in the late 1400s. The colonizers of Angola, the Portuguese, did not study the area as thoroughly as British, French, and German scholars researched their colonial empires. The Portuguese, in fact, were more concerned with recording the past of their own people in Angola than with the history of the indigenous populations.

The limited information that is available indicates that the original inhabitants of present-day Angola were hunters and gatherers. Their descendants, called Bushmen by the Europeans, still inhabit portions of southern Africa, and small numbers of them may still be found in southern Angola. These Khoisan speakers lost their predominance in southern Africa as a result of the southward expansion of Bantu-speaking peoples during the first millennium A.D.

The Bantu speakers were a Negroid people, adept at farming, hunting, and gathering, who probably began their migrations from the rain forest near what is now the Nigeria-Cameroon border. Bantu expansion was carried out by small groups that made a series of short relocations over time in response to economic or political conditions. Some historians believe that the Khoisan speakers were peacefully assimilated rather than conquered by the Bantu. Others contend that the Khoisan, because of their passive nature, simply vacated the area and moved south, away from the newcomers.

In either case, the Bantu settled in Angola between 1300 and 1600, and some may have arrived even earlier. The Bantu formed a number of historically important kingdoms. The earliest and perhaps most important of these was the Kongo Kingdom, which arose between the mid-1300s and the mid-1400s in an area overlapping the present-day border between Angola and Zaire (see fig. 2). Other important kingdoms were Ndongo, located to the south of Kongo; Matamba, Kasanje, and Lunda, located east of Ndongo; Bié, Bailundu, and Ciyaka, located on the plateau east of Benguela; and Kwanhama (also spelled Kwanyama), located near what is now the border between Angola and Namibia. Although they did not develop a strong central government, the Chokwe (also spelled Cokwe) established a significant cultural center in the northeast of present-day Angola.

The precolonial kingdoms differed in area and the number of subjects who owed allegiance, however nominal, to a central authority. The kings might not directly control more land or people than a local ruler, but they were generally acknowledged as paramount. Kings were offered tribute and were believed to possess substantial religious power and authority. A king's actual secular power, however, was determined as much by his own personal abilities as by institutional arrangements.

The African kingdoms tended to extend their lines of communication inland, away from the Atlantic Ocean. Until the arrival of the Europeans, Africans regarded the sea as a barrier to trade. Although the sea might supply salt or shells that could be used as currency, the interior held the promise of better hunting, farming, mining, and trade.

Kongo Kingdom

In the middle of the fifteenth century, the Kongo Kingdom was the most powerful of a series of states along Africa's west coast known as the Middle Atlantic kingdoms. Kongo evolved in the late fourteenth century when a group of Bakongo (Kongo people) moved south of the Congo River into northern Angola, conquering the people they found there and establishing Mbanza Kongo (now spelled Mbanza Congo), the capital of the kingdom. One of the reasons for the success of the Bakongo was their willingness to assimilate the inhabitants they conquered rather than to try to become their overlords. The people of the area thus gradually became one and were ruled by leaders with both religious and political authority.

By the middle of the fifteenth century, the *manikongo* (Kongo king) ruled the lands of northern Angola and the north bank of the Congo River (present-day Congo and Zaire). Kongo was the first kingdom on the west coast of central Africa to come into contact with Europeans. The earliest such contact occurred in 1483 when the Portuguese explorer Diogo Cão reached the mouth of the Congo River. After the initial landing, Portugal and Kongo exchanged emissaries, so that each kingdom was able to acquire knowledge of the other. Impressed by reports from his returning subjects, Nzinga Nkuwu, the *manikongo,* asked the Portuguese crown for missionaries and technical assistance in exchange for ivory and other goods.

The ruler who came to power in 1506 took a Christian name, Afonso. He too admired European culture and science, and he called on Portugal for support in education, military matters, and the conversion of his subjects to Christianity. Many historians, in fact, maintain that Afonso behaved more like a "Christian" than most of his teachers. Afonso, therefore, soon came into conflict with Portuguese bent on exploiting Kongo society. The most insidious and lasting aspect of this exploitation was the slave trade.

Not long after Afonso became king, Portugal began to turn its attention to the exploration of Asia and the Americas. As Portugal's interest in another of its colonies, Brazil, increased, its interest in Africa declined. Over time, the Portuguese crown came to view Kongo primarily as a source of slaves. Slaves were used first on the sugar plantations on nearby Portuguese-claimed islands but later were sent mainly to Brazil. Once Kongo was opened to the slave trade, halting or limiting it became impossible. Afonso's complaints to the Portuguese crown about the effects of the trade in his lands were largely ignored. By the 1520s, most of the missionaries had returned to Portugal, and most of the remaining whites were slave traders who disregarded the authority of the *manikongo.*

In addition to the slave trade, Kongo faced other challenges in the sixteenth century. After the death of Afonso in the 1540s, the kingdom endured a period of instability that culminated in an upheaval in 1568. This rebellion was long attributed by Portuguese sources and others to the invasion by a group of unknown origin

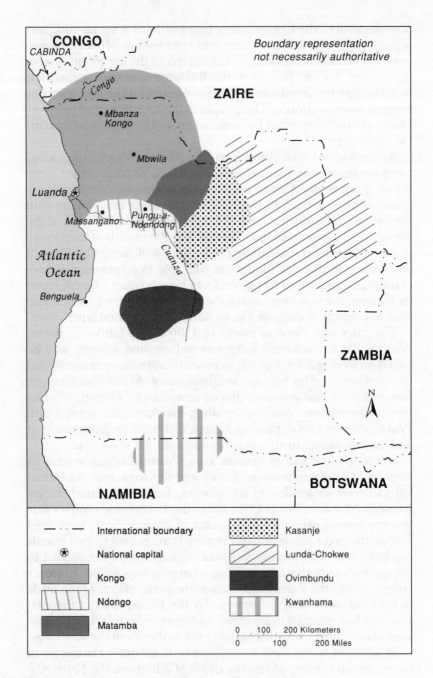

Figure 2. *Major Angolan Kingdoms, 1200–1900*

called the Jaga. Others, however, believed that the attack was probably launched by a Bakongo faction opposed to the king that may
have been joined or aided by non-Bakongo seeking to gain control
over the Kongo slave trade and other trading routes. In any case,
the assault on the capital (which had been renamed São Salvador)
and its environs drove the king, Alvaro I, into exile. The Portuguese
governor of São Tomé, responding to pleas from Alvaro I, fought
the invaders from 1571 through 1573, finally ousting them and occupying the area until the mid-1570s.

A few years earlier, Sebastião, the Portuguese king, had granted the area south of the Bakongo as a proprietary colony to Paulo
Dias de Novais, an associate of Portuguese Jesuits and an experienced explorer of the West African coast. In 1576, in effective
control of the countryside and facing no organized Kongo opposition, the Portuguese founded the town of Luanda, in effect establishing the colony of Angola. Other African leaders, however,
continued to resist the Portuguese, and the Europeans only managed
to establish insecure footholds along the coast. Concerned that African attacks might impede the stream of slaves to Brazil and Portugal, in 1590 the crown assumed direct control of the colony.

Alvaro I and his successor, Alvaro II, brought stability to the
Kongo Kingdom by expanding the domain of their royal authority while keeping at bay encroachment by the Portuguese, whose
colony during the late years of the sixteenth century remained confined to the area south of Kongo. But after the death of Alvaro
II in 1614, conflicts over access to cultivable land between Kongo
and the Portuguese colony of Angola soured formerly amicable
relations, and in 1622 the Portuguese governor of Angola launched
an attack on Kongo. Although not entirely successful from the Portuguese point of view, the war had a number of lasting effects. First,
the colony captured a large number of slaves, which demonstrated how rewarding slave raiding could be. Second, the Portuguese
came out of the war convinced of the existence of silver and gold
mines in Kongo, a belief that encouraged a series of conflicts between the colonists and the Kongo Kingdom for the next half century. The war also created a xenophobia among the Bakongo of
the interior, who drove away many Portuguese. Because the trading system depended largely on the Bakongo, commerce was greatly
disrupted, with effects on the Angolan colony as great as those on
the Kongo Kingdom.

Adding to Kongo's troubles in the early 1600s was a general dissatisfaction among the Bakongo with their rulers, some of whom
were greedy and corrupt. Consequently, conflicts arose over succession to the throne, and more and more sections of the kingdom

gained substantial degrees of autonomy and established local control over the trade that had so enriched the monarchy in earlier years.

Ndongo Kingdom

Shortly after Cão made his initial contact with the Kongo Kingdom of northern Angola in 1483, he established links farther south with Ndongo—an African state less advanced than Kongo that was made up of Kimbundu-speaking people. Their ruler, who was tributary to the *manikongo,* was called the *ngola a kiluanje.* It was the first part of the title, its pronunciation changed to "Angola," by which the Portuguese referred to the entire area.

Throughout most of the sixteenth century, Portugal's relations with Ndongo were overshadowed by its dealings with Kongo. Some historians, citing the disruptions the Portuguese caused in Kongo society, believe that Ndongo benefited from the lack of Portuguese interest. It was not until after the founding of Luanda in 1576 that Portugal's exploration into the area of present-day Angola rivaled its trade and commerce in Kongo. Furthermore, it was only in the early seventeenth century that the importance of the colony Portugal established came to exceed that of Kongo.

Although officially ignored by Lisbon, the Angolan colony was the center of disputes, usually concerning the slave trade, between local Portuguese traders and the Mbundu people, who inhabited Ndongo. But by mid-century, the favorable attention the *ngola* received from Portuguese trade or missionary groups angered the *manikongo,* who in 1556 sent an army against the Ndongo Kingdom. The forces of the *ngola* defeated the Kongo army, encouraging him to declare his independence from Kongo and appeal to Portugal for military support. In 1560 Lisbon responded by sending an expedition to Angola, but in the interim the *ngola* who had requested Portuguese support had died, and his successor took captive four members of the expedition. After the hostage taking, Lisbon routinely employed military force in dealing with the Ndongo Kingdom. This resulted in a major eastward migration of Mbundu people and the subsequent establishment of other kingdoms.

Following the founding of Luanda, Paulo Dias carried out a series of bloody military campaigns that contributed to Ndongo resentment of Europeans. Dias founded several forts east of Luanda, but—indicative of Portugal's declining status as a world power—he was unable to gain firm control of the land around them. Dias died in 1579 without having conquered the Ndongo Kingdom.

Dias's successors made slow progress up the Cuanza River, meeting constant African resistance. By 1604 they reached Cambambe,

A Roman Catholic church in Luanda, built by the Portuguese
Courtesy Richard J. Hough

where they learned that the presumed silver mines did not exist. The failure of the Portuguese to find mineral wealth changed their outlook on the Angolan colony. Slave taking, which had been incidental to the quest for the mines, then became the major economic motivation for expansion and extension of Portuguese authority. In search of slaves, the Portuguese pushed farther into Ndongo country, establishing a fort a short distance from Massangano, itself about 175 kilometers east of Angola's Atlantic coast. The consequent fighting with the Ndongo generated a stream of slaves who were shipped to the coast. Following a period of Ndongo diplomatic initiatives toward Lisbon in the 1620s, relations degenerated into a state of war.

The Defeat of Kongo and Ndongo

The Portuguese imposed a peace treaty on the Bakongo. Its conditions, however, were so harsh that peace was never really achieved, and hostilities grew during the 1660s. The Portuguese victory over the Bakongo at the Battle of Mbwila (also spelled Ambuila) on October 29, 1665, marked the end of the Kongo Kingdom as a unified power. By the eighteenth century, Kongo had been transformed from a unitary state into a number of smaller entities that recognized the king but for all practical purposes were independent. Fragmented though they were, these Kongo states

11

still resisted Portuguese encroachments. Although they were never again as significant as during Angola's early days, the Bakongo played an important role in the nationalist and independence struggles of the twentieth century.

The Ndongo Kingdom suffered a fate similar to that of Kongo. Before the Dutch captured Luanda in 1641, the Portuguese attempted to control Ndongo by supporting a pliant king, and during the Dutch occupation, Ndongo remained loyal to Portugal (see The Dutch Interregnum, 1641–48, this ch.). But after the retaking of Luanda in 1648, the *ngola* judged that the Portuguese had not sufficiently rewarded the kingdom for its allegiance. Consequently, he reasserted Ndongo independence, an act that angered the colonists. In 1671 Ndongo intransigence prompted a Portuguese attack and siege on the capital of Pungu-a-Ndondong (present-day Pungo Andongo). The attackers killed the *ngola,* enslaved many of his followers, and built a fort on the site of the capital. Thus, the Ndongo Kingdom, which had enjoyed only semi-independent status, now surrendered entirely to Portugal.

Matamba and Kasanje Kingdoms

As Portugal became preoccupied with the Ndongo Kingdom as a source of slaves, two inland Mbundu states—Matamba and Kasanje—prospered. Little is known of Matamba before the seventeenth century, but in 1621 Nzinga (called Jinga by the Portuguese), the sister of the *ngola a kiluanje,* convinced the Portuguese to recognize Ndongo as an independent monarchy and to help the kingdom expel the Imbangala people from its territory. Three years later, according to some sources, Nzinga poisoned her brother and succeeded him as monarch. Unable to negotiate successfully with a series of Portuguese governors, however, she was eventually removed. Nzinga and many of her followers traveled east and forged alliances with several groups. She finally ascended to the throne of the Matamba Kingdom. From this eastern state, she pursued good relations with the Dutch during their occupation of the area from 1641 to 1648 and attempted to reconquer Ndongo. After the Dutch expulsion, Nzinga again allied with the Portuguese. A dynamic and wily ruler, Nzinga dominated Mbundu politics until she died in 1663. Although she dealt with the Europeans, in modern times Nzinga has been remembered by nationalists as an Angolan leader who never accepted Portuguese sovereignty.

After Nzinga's death, a succession struggle ensued, and the new ruler tried to reduce Portuguese influence. Following their practice with the Ndongo, the Portuguese forced him out and placed their own candidate, Kanini, on the throne. Kanini coveted the nearby kingdom of Kasanje—peopled by Mbundu but ruled by Imbangala—for its role in the slave trade. Once he had consolidated power, in 1680 Kanini successfully moved against Kasanje, which was undergoing a succession crisis of its own. Kanini's defeat of the Kasanje state made his Portuguese benefactors realize that as his empire expanded, Kanini was increasingly threatening their own slaving interests. Subsequently, Kanini defeated a Portuguese military expedition sent against him, although he died soon after. In 1683 Portugal negotiated with the new Matamba queen to halt further attempts to conquer Kasanje territory and, because of mounting competition from other European powers, convinced her to trade exclusively with Portugal.

Lunda and Chokwe Kingdoms

The Lunda Kingdom lay east, beyond Matamba and Kasanje. It developed in the seventeenth century, and its center was in present-day Zaire's western Shaba Region (formerly Katanga Province). The Lunda Kingdom expanded by absorbing the chiefs of neighboring groups in the empire, rather than by deposing them. The Lunda consolidated their state by adopting an orderly system of succession and by gaining control of the trade caravans that passed through their kingdom.

The Portuguese hoped to deal directly with the Lunda for slaves and thus bypass the representatives of the Matamba and Kasanje, who acted as intermediaries. Apparently entertaining similar ideas, the Lunda attacked Matamba and Kasanje in the 1760s. The Lunda, however, proved no more successful than the Portuguese at totally subduing these Mbundu kingdoms.

The Chokwe, who, according to oral accounts, migrated from either central Africa or the upper reaches of the Kasai River in present-day Zaire, established themselves as trading intermediaries in eastern Angola in the middle of the nineteenth century. With guns that they obtained from the Ovimbundu, they attacked and destroyed the Lunda Kingdom in 1900. The Chokwe rapidly expanded their influence in the northeast and east, replacing the Lunda culture with their own language and customs.

Ovimbundu and Kwanhama Kingdoms

Between 1500 and 1700, the Ovimbundu peoples migrated from the north and east of Angola to the Benguela Plateau. They did not, however, consolidate their kingdoms, nor did their kings assert their sovereignty over the plateau until the eighteenth century, when some twenty-two kingdoms emerged. Thirteen of the kingdoms, including Bié, Bailundu, and Ciyaka, emerged as powerful entities, and the Ovimbundu acquired a reputation as the most successful traders of the Angolan interior. After the Portuguese conquered most of the Ovimbundu states in the late nineteenth century, the Portuguese colonial authorities directly or indirectly appointed Ovimbundu kings.

The Kwanhama, belonging to the Bantu-speaking group, established a kingdom early in the nineteenth century in the vicinity of the border with present-day Namibia. Kwanhama kings welcomed trade with Europeans, especially with Portuguese and German gun dealers. Feared even by the Portuguese, the well-armed Kwanhama developed a reputation as fierce warriors. Their kingdom survived until 1915, when a large Portuguese army invaded and defeated them.

The Dutch Interregnum, 1641–48

During the first half of the 1600s, when Portugal became involved in a succession of European religious and dynastic wars at the insistence of Spain, the Portuguese colonies were subjected to attacks by Spain's enemies. Holland, one of Spain's most potent enemies, raided and harassed the Portuguese territories in Angola. The Dutch also began pursuing alliances with Africans, including the king of Kongo and Nzinga of Matamba, who, angered by their treatment at the hands of the Portuguese, welcomed the opportunity to deal with another European power.

When it rebelled against Spain in 1640, Portugal hoped to establish good relations with the Dutch. Instead, the Dutch saw an opportunity to expand their own colonial holdings and in 1641 captured Luanda and Benguela, forcing the Portuguese governor to flee with his fellow refugees inland to Massangano. The Portuguese were unable to dislodge the Dutch from their coastal beachhead. As the Dutch occupation cut off the supply of slaves to Brazil, that colony's economy suffered. In response, Brazilian colonists raised money and organized forces to launch an expedition aimed at unseating the Dutch from Angola. In May 1648, the Dutch garrison in Luanda surrendered to the Brazilian detachment, and the Dutch eventually relinquished their other Angolan conquests. According to some historians, after the retaking of Luanda, Angola became a de facto colony of Brazil, so driven was the South American colony's sugar-growing economy by its need for slaves.

Angola in the Eighteenth Century

Slave Trading in the 1700s

Slave trading dominated the Portuguese economy in eighteenth-century Angola. Slaves were obtained by agents, called *pombeiros,* who roamed the interior, generally following established routes along rivers. They bought slaves, called *peças* (pieces), from local chiefs in exchange for commodities such as cloth and wine. The *pombeiros* returned to Luanda or Benguela with chain gangs of several hundred captives, most of whom were malnourished and in poor condition from the arduous trip on foot. On the coast, they were better fed and readied for their sea crossing. Before embarking, they were baptized en masse by Roman Catholic priests. The Atlantic crossing in the overcrowded, unsanitary vessels lasted from five weeks to two months. Many captives died en route.

During the sixteenth century and most of the seventeenth century, Luanda had been the main slave port of the Portuguese, but toward the end of the 1600s they turned their attention to Benguela. Although the first efforts at inland expansion from Benguela failed, the Portuguese eventually penetrated the Ovimbundu kingdoms and subjected their people to the same treatment that had earlier befallen the Mbundu. By the end of the eighteenth century, Benguela rivaled Luanda as a slave port.

According to historian C.R. Boxer, African slaves were more valued in the Americas than were American Indian slaves because Africans tended to adjust more easily to slavery and because they were less vulnerable to the diseases of Europeans. Boxer also suggests that Jesuits in the New World opposed the notion of using Indians as slaves, whereas they were less resistant to the use of Africans as slaves. Many of these African slaves were sent to Spanish colonies, where they brought a higher price than they would have if sold in Brazil.

From the late sixteenth century until 1836, when Portugal abolished slave trafficking, Angola may have been the source of as many as 2 million slaves for the New World. More than half of these went to Brazil, nearly a third to the Caribbean, and from 10 to 15 percent to the Río de la Plata area on the southeastern coast of South America. Considering the number of slaves that actually arrived, and taking into account those who died crossing the Atlantic or during transport from the interior to the coast for shipping, the Angola area may have lost as many as 4 million people as a result of the slave trade.

By the end of the eighteenth century, it became clear that Lisbon's dream of establishing a trading monopoly in its colonies had not been achieved. Competition from foreign powers contributed significantly to Portugal's inability to control the slave trade, either in Angola's interior or on the coast. In 1784, for example, the French expelled a garrison that the Portuguese had established a year earlier in Cabinda. Portugal was also concerned about the northward expansion of Dutch settlers from the Cape of Good Hope area. Moreover, at this time the British, Dutch, and Brazilians, not the Portuguese, were contributing most of the capital and vessels used in the slave trade. Furthermore, many of the European goods arriving at Angolan ports were coming from nations other than Portugal.

Portuguese Settlers in Angola

The Portuguese authorities and settlers in Angola formed a motley group. The inhabitants resented the governors, whom they regarded as outsiders. Indeed, these officials were less concerned with the welfare of the colony than with the profit they could realize from the slave trade. But governing the small colony was difficult because any central administrative authority had to deal with a group of settlers prone to rebellion. Because Brazil was the jewel of Portugal's overseas territories, Portuguese who immigrated to Angola were frequently deserters, *degredados,* peasants, and others who had been unable to succeed in Portugal or elsewhere in the Portuguese-speaking world.

Owing principally to the African colony's unsavory reputation in Portugal and the high regard in which Brazil was held, there was little emigration to Angola in the 1600s and 1700s. Thus, the white population of Angola in 1777 was less than 1,600. Of this number, very few whites were females; one account states that in 1846 the ratio of Portuguese men to Portuguese women in the colony was eleven to one. A product of this gender imbalance was miscegenation; for example, the *mestiço* population in 1777 was estimated at a little more than 4,000.

Besides exporting them, Europeans in Angola kept slaves as porters, soldiers, agricultural laborers, and as workers at jobs that the Portuguese increasingly considered too menial to do themselves. At no time, however, was domestic slavery more important to the local economy than the exporting of slaves.

The 1800s: Turmoil in Portugal, Reform and Expansion in Angola

The Early Nineteenth Century

The nineteenth century ushered in a period of crisis for Portugal. The invasion by Napoleon's armies in 1807 forced the Portuguese court into exile in Brazil. In 1820 the regency was overthrown, and a conflict began between constitutionalists and monarchists that did not end until 1834. Many of these changes were echoed in Angola, where there were uprisings and an army mutiny that toppled the colony's governor.

The instability in Europe in the first three decades of the nineteenth century removed Portugal, Britain, France, and Holland from the Angolan slave market. But this turn of events allowed Angolan traders access to other markets. Unfettered trade with Brazilians, Cubans, and American southerners enabled the Portuguese slave dealers to enjoy a period of great prosperity, while the Angolan kingdoms suffered increased depopulation. After the constitutionalist triumph in Portugal in 1834, a provisional junta took charge in Luanda.

Abolition of the Slave Trade

In the early 1830s, the Portuguese government appointed a progressive prime minister, the Marquês de Sá da Bandeira, whose most important reform was the abolition of the slave trade in 1836. The decree, however, could not be enforced adequately, and it took Britain's Royal Navy to put an end to the activity in the middle of the nineteenth century.

In 1858 slavery was legally abolished in Angola. Government slaves had already been freed in 1854, but the 1858 proclamation declared that all slavery should cease by 1878. Legislation was passed to compensate owners and to care for the freed people. But many of the colonists found ways to circumvent the decree, so that the actual conditions of labor did not change significantly.

Expansion and the Berlin Conference

The abolition of the slave trade coincided with increased Portuguese expansion in Angola. Expansion began in 1838 with the conquest and establishment of a fort at Duque de Bragança (renamed Calandula), in an area east of Luanda. By mid-century the Portuguese had extended their formal control still farther east to the Kasanje market near the Cuango River (see Matamba and Kasanje Kingdoms, this ch.). In 1840 the Portuguese founded the town of Moçâmedes (present-day Namibe) on the coast south of Benguela. The Portuguese also attempted to gain control of the coast from Luanda north to Cabinda through military occupation of the major ports. Because of British opposition, however, they were unable to complete this attempt and never gained control of the mouth of the Congo River.

The cost of military operations to secure economically strategic points led in 1856 to the imposition on Africans of a substantially increased hut tax, which for the first time had to be paid with currency or trade goods rather than with slaves. As a result, many

Africans either refused to pay or fled from areas controlled by the Portuguese. By 1861, therefore, the Portuguese lacked the resources for continued military expansion or economic development, and most of the interior remained in the control of African traders and warriors.

From the late 1870s through the early 1890s, Portugal renewed expansion into the interior. Part of the impetus came from the Lisbon Geographical Society, founded in 1875 by a group of industrialists, scholars, and colonial and military officials. This society stimulated a popular concern for the colonies in Portugal. In reaction to the activities of the society and the growing interest among Europeans in colonial adventure, the Portuguese government allotted large sums for public works in Africa and encouraged a minor revival of missionary work.

An advisory commission to Portugal's Ministry of the Navy and Colonies formed an expedition in the 1870s to link Angola on the Atlantic coast with Mozambique on the Indian Ocean coast. The Portuguese government supported this expedition because it aspired to control a solid strip of territory across the central part of the continent. Nonetheless, Portugal was unable to gain control of the hinterland.

Aware of French and Belgian activities on the lower Congo River, in 1883 the Portuguese occupied Cabinda and Massabi north of the Congo River, towns that Portugal had long claimed. In the same year, Portugal annexed the region of the old Kongo Kingdom. Seeking to uphold these claims against French and Belgian advances in the Congo River Basin, Portugal negotiated a treaty with Britain in 1884; the other European powers, however, rejected it. Portugal's subsequent demands for an international conference on the Congo fell on deaf ears until German chancellor Otto von Bismarck seized on the idea as an opportunity to diminish French and British power.

At the Berlin Conference of 1884, the participants established in principle the limits of Portugal's claims to Angola, and in later years, treaties with the colonial powers that controlled the neighboring territories delineated Angola's boundaries. But because other, more powerful European states of the nineteenth century had explored central Africa, they, not Portugal, determined Angola's boundaries. The west coast territory Portugal acquired included the left bank of the Congo River and the Cabinda enclave, an acquisition whose value to the state was demonstrated in later years by the discovery there of oil. Britain, however, forced Portugal to withdraw from Nyasaland (present-day Malawi) and Rhodesia (present-day Zimbabwe and Zambia).

Portugal and Belgium concluded several agreements between 1891 and 1927, establishing a complex border generally following natural frontiers. Cabinda's boundaries with the French Congo and the Belgian Congo were delimited in 1886 and 1894, respectively, and by the end of the nineteenth century, Portugal had staked out most of its claims in Angola.

As far as Europe was concerned, Angola was in the Portuguese sphere of influence, and its status was not subject to further deliberations. Considering its diminished stature in relation to other European powers, Portugal had done well to hold onto as much territory as it had. But the fact that Angola was recognized as a Portuguese possession did not mean that it was under Portuguese control. The work of conquest took the better part of twenty-five years, and in some remote areas even longer.

Settlement, Conquest, and Development
The Demographic Situation

As the spheres of interest in the African interior became clarified, European nations turned to fulfilling the obligation imposed by the Berlin Conference of effectively occupying all territories claimed. For Portugal, meeting this obligation involved not only the conquest of the independent African kingdoms of the interior but also an attempt to settle Portuguese farmers.

Immigration in the late nineteenth century was discouraged by the same conditions that had deterred it earlier: a difficult climate and a lack of economic development. Although there were fewer than 10,000 whites in Angola in 1900 (most of whom were *degredados*), there was a substantial increase in white female immigration; the male-to-female ratio that year was a bit more than two to one. Concomitantly, there was a drop in the ratio of *mestiços* to whites; whereas *mestiços* had outnumbered whites in 1845 by more than three to one, in 1900 this ratio was reversed. Africans still constituted more than 99 percent of the population in 1900. Their numbers reportedly declined from an estimated 5.4 million in 1845 to about 4.8 million in 1900, although scholars dispute these figures. Whites were concentrated in the coastal cities of Luanda and Benguela. In addition to farming and fishing, Europeans engaged in merchant activities in the towns and trade in the bush. In the south, colonies of farmers who had settled earlier in the century had dwindled into small outposts, as many settlers returned to Luanda.

In the late nineteenth century, Africans controlled trade in the plateaus of the interior, despite Portuguese expansion. The Ovimbundu proved highly successful intermediaries on the southern trade route that ran from the Bié Plateau to Benguela. The Ovimbundu were more competitive than the *sertanejos* (people of the frontier, as Europeans and their representatives in the rural areas were called), who often had to pay tribute and fines to African chiefs through whose territory they traveled. By the mid-1880s, the Ovimbundu by and large had replaced the *sertanejos*. The Chokwe and Imbangala also took advantage of their positions in the interior to extend their control over the region's trade. Nonetheless, by the late 1800s Portuguese encroachments and the imposition of European rule limited the political freedom of these Africans and diminished their prosperity.

Military Campaigns

After the Berlin Conference, the Portuguese military was preoccupied with the subjugation of the African inhabitants of the hinterland, and by 1915 it secured the colony for Portugal. Before African resistance was broken, intensive military action was necessary in several areas. One campaign took place in the southern region in response to a request from the Boer settlement near Humbe that was threatened by the Kwanhama. Sporadic campaigning included several serious reverses for the Portuguese. The Portuguese were able to bring the Kwanhama under control only with the assistance of field artillery and the establishment of a series of fortified garrisons. One of the most difficult Portuguese military campaigns was waged against the Dembos, a Kimbundu-speaking people who lived less than 150 kilometers northeast of Luanda. The Portuguese attacked the Dembos repeatedly over a period of three years before the Dembos were finally subdued in 1910. Because of difficult conditions, including the tropical climate, the Portuguese did not complete their occupation of Dembos land until 1917.

Administration and Development

Portuguese colonial policies toward civil administration were first formulated in Mozambique, where in the 1890s António Enés, former minister of colonies, advocated close control and full use of African labor, administrative reorganization, and colonization schemes. In 1899 Paiva Couceiro, who had been with Enés in Mozambique, published a volume in which he advocated white colonization, decentralization of administration from Lisbon, and the necessity of inculcating in the Africans the "habit of work." As governor general of Angola between 1907 and 1910, Couceiro prepared the basis of civil administration in the colony. Military officers were to oversee administrative divisions, and through them European civilization was to be brought to the Africans. Many of Couceiro's reforms were incorporated in legislation in 1914 that brought, at least in theory, financial and administrative autonomy to the colony.

There was considerable progress toward the development of an economic infrastructure during the first quarter of the twentieth century. New towns sprang up in the interior, and road construction advanced. The key to development, however, was the Benguela Railway, which would become Angola's largest employer and which linked the mines of the Belgian Congo's Katanga Province (in present-day Shaba Region in Zaire) to the Angolan port at Lobito.

In the 1920s, the Diamond Company of Angola (Companhia de Diamantes de Angola—Diamang), an exclusive concessionaire in Angola until the 1960s, initiated diamond mining. As the employer of more Africans than any other industry, Diamang deeply affected the lives of its 18,000 African workers through extensive investment and the provision of social services.

The Portuguese, however, were generally unable to provide Angola with adequate development capital or with settlers. Trade had fallen off sharply when the rubber boom ended just before World War I, and the war itself produced only a brief revival of foreign trade. At the end of what is commonly referred to as Portugal's republican era (1910–26), the finances of the colony were in serious difficulty.

Angola under the Salazar Regime

Angola under the New State

The right-wing Portuguese military coup of May 1926, which ended the republican era, led to the installation of a one-party regime in Portugal and the establishment of what came to be known as the New State. A young professor of economics, António Salazar, became minister of finance in 1928, and by 1930 he was one of the most prominent members of the government. He held the post of prime minister from 1932 until 1968, when he was incapacitated by a stroke. During his tenure in office, he left a lasting impression on events in Angola.

The most important changes introduced into Angola by the new regime were embodied in the Colonial Act of 1930. This act brought Angola's economy into line with economic policies that the new regime was implementing at home. But Portugal's application of strict financial controls over the colony also halted the drift toward political autonomy in Angola.

Portugal's policies toward Angola in the 1930s and 1940s were based on the principle of national integration. Economically, socially, and politically, Angola was to become an integral part of the Portuguese nation. In line with these policies, Portugal renamed African towns, usually after Portuguese heroes. Still later, in the early 1950s, Portugal withdrew the currency, known as the *angolar,* and replaced it with the Portuguese escudo.

Portugal integrated its economy with that of Angola by erecting protective trade tariffs and discouraging foreign investment capital, except in the construction of the Benguela Railway and in the exploitation of diamonds. In this way, Portugal sought to make Angola self-supporting and, at the same time, to turn it into a market for Portuguese goods. But despite a certain degree of success, Angola enjoyed no real prosperity until after World War II, when higher coffee prices brought enormous profits to Angolan producers. The consequent economic success of the coffee plantations, owned primarily by newly arrived Portuguese settlers attracted by the colony's increasing wealth, continued until independence in 1975, when the Portuguese exodus and civil war severely disrupted the Angolan economy.

Salazar's Racial Politics

Until 1940 Portuguese constituted less than 1 percent of Angola's population, and it was not until 1950 that their proportion approached 2 percent. This increase in the number of Europeans and the continuation of forced labor (not abolished until 1962) and other labor abuses led to an intensification of racial conflict. Before 1900 *mestiços* had been engaged in a variety of commercial and governmental roles, but as the white population came to outnumber them, the status of *mestiços* declined. In the first two decades of the twentieth century, laws and regulations requiring a certain level of education to hold some government positions effectively excluded *mestiços* from access to them. In 1921 the colonial administration divided the civil service into European and African branches and assigned *mestiços* and the very few African *assimilados* to the latter, thereby limiting their chances of rising in the bureaucratic hierarchy. In 1929 statutes limited the bureaucratic level to which *mestiços* and *assimilados* could rise to that of first clerk, established different pay scales for Europeans and non-Europeans in both public and private sectors, and restricted competition between them for jobs in the bureaucracy. Given this legal framework, the immigration of increasing numbers of Portuguese led to considerable disaffection among *mestiços,* who had hitherto tended to identify with whites rather than with Africans.

Beginning in the 1940s, the system of forced labor came under renewed criticism. One particularly outspoken critic, Captain Henrique Galvão, who had served for more than two decades in an official capacity in Angola, chronicled abuses committed against the African population. The Salazar government responded by arresting Galvão for treason and banning his report. Despite the introduction of some labor reforms from the late 1940s through the late 1950s, forced labor continued.

Legislation that was passed in Portugal between 1926 and 1933 was based on a new conception of Africans. Whereas Portugal previously had assumed that Africans would somehow naturally be assimilated into European society, the New State established definite standards Africans had to meet to qualify for rights. The new legislation defined Africans as a separate element in the population, referred to as *indígenas* (see Glossary). Those who learned to speak Portuguese, who took jobs in commerce or industry, and who behaved as Portuguese citizens were classified as *assimilados*. In accepting the rights of citizenship, *assimilados* took on the same tax obligations as the European citizens. Male *indígenas* were required to pay a head tax. If they could not raise the money, they were obligated to work for the government for half of each year without wages.

The colonial administration stringently applied the requirements for assimilation. In 1950, of an estimated African population of 4 million in Angola (according to an official census that probably provided more accurate figures than previous estimates), there were fewer than 31,000 *assimilados*. But instead of elevating the status of Africans, the policy of assimilation maintained them in a degraded status. The colonial administration required *indígenas* to carry identification cards, of major importance psychologically to the Africans and politically to the Portuguese, who were thus more easily able to control the African population.

The authoritarian Salazar regime frequently used African informants to ferret out signs of political dissidence. Censorship, border control, police action, and control of education all retarded the development of African leadership. Africans studying in Portugal—and therefore exposed to "progressive" ideas—were sometimes prevented from returning home. Political offenses brought severe penalties, and the colonial administration viewed African organizations with extreme disfavor.

Rise of African Nationalism

In the 1940s and 1950s, African acquiescence to Portuguese colonization began to weaken, particularly in the provinces bordering the Belgian Congo and in Luanda, where far-reaching changes in world politics influenced a small number of Africans. The associations they formed and the aspirations they shared paved the way for the liberation movements of the 1960s.

The colonial system had created a dichotomy among the African population that corresponded to that of the Portuguese social structure—the elite versus the masses. Within the context of the burgeoning nationalist struggle, competition developed between the small, multiracial class of educated and semi-educated town inhabitants and the rural, uneducated black peasantry that formed the majority of Angola's population. At the same time, black Angolans identified strongly with their precolonial ethnic and regional origins. By the 1950s, the influence of class and ethnicity had resulted in three major sources of Angolan nationalism. The first, the Mbundu, who inhabited Luanda and the surrounding regions, had a predominantly urban, elite leadership, while the Bakongo and Ovimbundu peoples had rural, peasant orientations. The major nationalist movements that emerged from these three groups—the MPLA, the FNLA, and UNITA—each claimed to represent the entire Angolan population. Before long, these movements became bitter rivals as the personal ambitions of their leaders, in addition to differences in political ideology and competition for foreign aid, added to their ethnic differences (see Ethnic Groups and Languages, ch. 2).

Roots of Discontent

Portugal's assimilationist policy had produced a small group of educated Africans who considered themselves Portuguese. But as this group recognized that it was not fully respected by the Portuguese and as it became increasingly aware of its alienation from its traditional origins, some members began to articulate resentment, both of their own ambiguous social and cultural situations and of the plight of the nonassimilated majority of Africans. From among their ranks emerged most of the first generation of liberation movement leaders.

The influx of rural Africans to towns also bred anticolonial resentment. In the 1950s, the population of Luanda almost doubled, and most of the growth was among Africans. Lured by the expectation of work, Africans in towns became aware of the inequality of opportunities between Europeans and Africans. The compulsory labor system that many had experienced in rural areas was regarded as the most onerous aspect of Portuguese rule. More than any other factor, this system, which was not abolished until 1962, united many Africans in resentment of Portuguese rule.

*Under the Salazar regime,
Angolans who neither spoke
Portuguese nor behaved as
Europeans, like this mother
and child, were classified
as* indígenas.
Courtesy Richard J. Hough

The Salazar government's settlement policies contributed to the spread of anticolonial resentment, especially after 1945. These policies resulted in increased competition for employment and growing racial friction. Between 1955 and 1960, for example, the government brought from Portugal and the Cape Verde Islands more than 55,000 whites. Induced to emigrate by government promises of money and free houses, these peasants settled on *colonatos* (large agricultural communities). Many immigrants to the *colonatos* were unskilled at farming, often lacked an elementary education, or were too old for vigorous manual labor. Consequently, many of them were unsuccessful on the *colonatos* and, after a time, moved to towns where they competed with Africans, often successfully, for skilled and unskilled jobs. The Portuguese who held jobs of lower social status often felt it all the more necessary to claim social superiority over the Africans.

External events also played a role in the development of the independence movements. While most European powers were preparing to grant independence to their African colonies, the Salazar regime was seeking to reassert its grasp on its colonies, as witnessed by the effort it expended in the ill-fated *colonato* system.

There were two basic patterns in the rise of nationalism in Angola. In one case, African *assimilados* and other urban Africans with some education joined urban *mestiços* and whites in associations based on the assumption that their interests were different

25

from, and perhaps in competition with, those of the majority of the African population still attached to their rural communities. Angolans also formed organizations based on ethnic or religious groupings that encompassed or at least sought to include rural Africans, although the leaders of these organizations often had some education and urban experience.

African Associations

The beginnings of African associations, to which the liberation movement traced its roots, remained obscure in 1988. Luanda was known to have had recreational societies, burial clubs, and other mutual aid associations in the early 1900s. After the Portuguese republican constitution of 1911 increased freedoms of the press, opinion, and association in the African colonies, a number of African associations were formed, including the Lisbon-based African League in 1919. Sponsored and financed by the Portuguese government, partly in response to pressure from the League of Nations with which African League leaders had established contacts, the African League was a federation of all African associations from Portuguese Africa. Its avowed purpose was to point out to the Portuguese government injustices or harsh laws that ought to be repealed. In 1923 the African League organized the second session of the Third Pan-African Congress in Lisbon.

Assimilados (*mestiço* and African) dominated most associations, and their membership seldom included uneducated Africans. Because the associations were under close Portuguese control, their members were unable to express the full extent of their discontent with the colonial system. As a result, extralegal, politically oriented African associations began to appear in the 1950s. Far-reaching economic and social changes, the growth of the white settler population, increased urbanization of Africans, and the beginnings of nationalist movements in other parts of Africa contributed to the growth of anticolonial feeling. In 1952 some 500 Angolan Africans appealed to the United Nations (UN) in a petition protesting what they called the injustices of Portuguese policy and requesting that steps be taken to end Portuguese rule.

The Popular Movement for the Liberation of Angola

The earliest anticolonialist political group in Angola, founded about 1953, was the Party of the United Struggle of Africans of Angola (Partido da Luta Unida dos Africanos de Angola—PLUA). In December 1956, the PLUA combined with other organizations in Luanda to form the MPLA, whose aim was to achieve independence for Angola by means of a united front of all African interests.

After many of its leaders were arrested in March 1959, the party moved its headquarters to Conakry, Guinea. The MPLA's first leader, Mário de Andrade, an educated *mestiço* and a poet, gave the party a reputation for representing primarily the interests of urban intellectuals rather than the indigenous masses.

The MPLA traces its Marxist-Leninist origins to its ties with the clandestine Portuguese Communist Party (Partido Comunista Português—PCP). The initial MPLA manifesto called for an end to colonialism and the building of a modern society free of prejudice, a goal that could be realized only after a lengthy period of political preparation followed by a revolutionary struggle. The MPLA leadership sought a definite direction and a set of objectives for the independence struggle, in contrast with the broad nationalist approach of its greatest rival for supremacy in the struggle, the FNLA. Thus, the MPLA's program, outlined in a policy document in the 1960s, avoided a stated commitment to socialism or Marxism-Leninism, but it clearly alluded to the movement's adherence to Marxist-Leninist principles and the Nonaligned Movement. The organization's leftist orientation attracted the support of the Soviet Union and China, both of which envisioned prospects for a foothold in Africa provided by a ruling Marxist-Leninist vanguard party.

The National Front for the Liberation of Angola

The FNLA was founded in 1954 as the Union of Peoples of Northern Angola (União das Populações do Norte de Angola—UPNA). Founded to advance the interests of the Bakongo rather than to promote independence, the UPNA petitioned the UN in 1957 for restoration of the Kongo Kingdom, an objective shared by the Alliance of Bakongo (Alliance des Bakongo—Abako) in the Belgian Congo (present-day Zaire; see Kongo Kingdom, this ch.). Because of important ties to the Bakongo in the Belgian colony and because of the difficulties of operating in Angola, the UPNA was based in Léopoldville (present-day Kinshasa, capital of Zaire). In 1958, acknowledging the futility of its quest, the UPNA adopted the title Union of Angolan Peoples (União das Populações de Angola—UPA) and the aim of independence for all of Angola.

Organizational Weaknesses

The Angolan African organizations active before 1961 were disorganized and lacked resources, membership, and strong leadership. There were a number of reasons for these weaknesses. First, their members were not prepared for either a political or a military struggle during the 1950s, however attractive they may have found nationalist ideals. Second, they were divided socially as well as ethnically. There were gulfs between the *mestiços* and the *assimilados,* on the one hand, and the *indígenas,* on the other hand, that frequently resulted in the pursuit of different goals. Third, although a substantial proportion of the white community also wanted Angola to break away from Portuguese domination, it hoped to perpetuate the colonial regime in every aspect except its control by Lisbon.

Finally, there was a critical lack of capable black leaders in the 1950s. The newly developing elite was not large enough to run a nationalist movement, and traditional leaders, focused on ethnic issues, were not prepared to lead such a movement. Church leaders, who might have been capable as national movement leaders, did not enter the struggle unless disaffected or until they became targets of police repression.

Beginning of Revolution

After 1959, as several African states won their independence, anticolonial sentiment intensified in Portugal's overseas territories. The Portuguese met this sentiment with stiffening opposition characterized by increasing surveillance and frequent arrests. In December 1959, the Portuguese secret political police, the International Police for the Defense of the State (Polícia Internacional de Defesa de Estado—PIDE), arrested fifty-seven persons in Luanda who were suspected of being involved in antigovernment political activities. Among those arrested were a few Europeans, *assimilados,* and other Africans. After this incident, the Portuguese military in Angola reinforced its position, particularly in the northwestern provinces, and became increasingly repressive.

In the first months of 1961, tensions came to a head. A group of alleged MPLA members attacked police stations and prisons in an attempt to free African political prisoners. Then, a group of disgruntled cotton workers in Malanje Province attacked government officials and buildings and a Catholic mission. In the wake of further sporadic violence, many wealthy Portuguese repatriated. They left behind them the poor whites who were unable to leave on short notice but who were ready to take the law into their own hands.

The violence spread to the northwest, where over the course of two days Bakongo (thought by some to have been UPA members) in Uíge Province attacked isolated farmsteads and towns in a series of forty coordinated raids, killing hundreds of Europeans. Also involved in the rural uprisings were non-Bakongo in parts of Cuanza Norte Province. During the next few months, violence spread northward toward the border with the former Belgian Congo as the

Portuguese put pressure on the rebels. Although it had not begun that way, as time passed the composition of the rebel groups became almost exclusively Bakongo.

The Portuguese reacted to the uprising with violence. Settlers organized into vigilante committees, and reprisals for the rebellion went uncontrolled by civilian and military authorities. The whites' treatment of Africans was as brutal and as arbitrary as had been that of the Africans toward them. Fear pervaded the country, driving an even deeper wedge between the races.

The loss of Africans as a result of the 1961 uprisings has been estimated as high as 40,000, many of whom died from disease or because of famine; about 400 Europeans were killed, as well as many *assimilados* and Africans deemed sympathetic to colonial authorities. By summer the Portuguese had reduced the area controlled by the rebels to one-half its original extent, but major pockets of resistance remained. Portuguese forces, relying heavily on air power, attacked many villages. The result was the mass exodus of Africans toward what is now Zaire.

In an effort to head off future violence, in the early 1960s the Salazar regime initiated a program to develop Angola's economic infrastructure. The Portuguese government increased the paved road network by 500 percent, stimulated the development of domestic air routes, provided emergency aid to the coffee producers, and abolished compulsory cotton cultivation. To reestablish confidence among Africans and among those who had been subject to reprisals by white settlers, the military initiated a campaign under which it resettled African refugees into village compounds and provided them with medical, recreational, and some educational facilities.

The uprisings attracted worldwide attention. In mid-1961 the UN General Assembly appointed a subcommittee to investigate the situation in Angola, and it produced a report unfavorable to Portuguese rule. The events also helped mobilize the various liberation groups to renewed action.

Angolan Insurgency

The rebels who had coordinated the 1961 uprisings later began to undertake effective military organization. The several nationalist organizations set up training camps and attracted external military aid. In the summer of 1961, for example, the UPA, which had strong support among the Bakongo, formed the National Liberation Army of Angola (Exército de Libertação Nacional de Angola—ELNA), a force of about 5,000 untrained and poorly armed troops. Subsequently, groups of Angolans went to Morocco and Tunisia to train with Algerian forces, then fighting for their own nation's independence. After winning its independence in 1962, Algeria supplied the ELNA with arms and ammunition.

In March 1962, the UPA joined with another small Kongo nationalist group, the Democratic Party of Angola (Partido Democrático de Angola—PDA) to form the FNLA. The FNLA immediately proclaimed the Revolutionary Government of Angola in Exile (Govêrno Revolucionário de Angola no Exílo—GRAE). The president of the FNLA/GRAE, Holden Roberto, declared his organization to be the sole authority in charge of anti-Portuguese military operations inside Angola. Consequently, he repeatedly refused to merge his organization with any other budding nationalist movement, preferring to build the FNLA/GRAE into an all-Angolan mass movement over which he would preside.

By 1963, with training and arms from Algeria, bases in Zaire, and funds from the Organization of African Unity (OAU), the FNLA/GRAE military and political organization was becoming formidable. Still, it made no significant territorial gains.

Meanwhile, the MPLA, which had been behind the initial uprisings in Luanda in February 1961, had suffered a great deal from Portuguese reprisals, with many of its militant leaders dead or in prison. The rebuilding of the MPLA was substantially aided in 1962 by the arrival of Agostinho Neto, an assimilated Mbundu physician who had spent several years in jail for expressing his political views and had recently escaped from detention in Portugal. Neto attempted to bring together the MPLA and Roberto's FNLA/GRAE, but his efforts were thwarted by Roberto's insistence that his organization represented all Angolans.

Initially based in Kinshasa, as was the FNLA/GRAE, in 1963 the MPLA shifted its headquarters to Brazzaville (in present-day Congo) because of Roberto's close ties to Zairian president Mobutu Sese Seko. From Brazzaville, the MPLA launched small guerrilla operations in Cabinda, but the movement was militarily far weaker than the FNLA. Moreover, it lacked an operations base from which it could reach the densely populated north and center of Angola.

As it dragged on into 1964 and 1965, the conflict became stalemated. Hampered by insufficient financial assistance, the insurgents were unable to maintain offensive operations against a fully equipped Portuguese military force that had increased to a strength of more than 40,000. The FNLA settled into a mountain stronghold straddling the border of Uíge and Zaire provinces and continued to carry on guerrilla activities. The insurgents found it increasingly difficult to sustain the cohesion they had achieved after 1961 and 1962. Between 1963 and 1965, differences in leadership, programs, and following between the FNLA and the MPLA led to open hostilities that seriously weakened each group's strength and effectiveness.

Ascendancy of the MPLA

In 1964 the MPLA reorganized and increased its efforts to reinforce its units fighting in the Dembos areas. The improved efficiency of the movement's political and military operations attracted support from other African countries, the OAU, and several non-African countries, all of which had previously scorned the MPLA because of its internal problems.

The growing military success of the MPLA in the mid-1960s was largely the product of support from the governments of Tanzania and Zambia, which permitted the organization to open offices in their capitals. More important, Tanzania and Zambia allowed the transport of Chinese and Soviet weapons across their territories to the Angolan border. Because of the influx of weapons, in 1965 the MPLA was able to open a military front in eastern Angola, from which it launched a major offensive the following year. By this time, the MPLA had become a greater threat to Portugal's colonial rule than the FNLA.

In June 1966, the MPLA supported an unsuccessful coup against President Marien Ngouabi of Congo, whereupon activities of all guerrilla groups in Brazzaville were curtailed. After the MPLA moved its headquarters to Lusaka, Zambia, in 1968, it conducted intensive guerrilla warfare in the Angolan provinces of Moxico and Cuando Cubango.

Beginning in 1969, attacks in Lunda and Bié provinces forced the Portuguese to resettle many inhabitants of these areas in fortified villages. Wherever MPLA guerrillas were in control, they created new political structures, mainly village action committees. Politically indoctrinated MPLA guerrillas, some of whom had received military training in Eastern Europe, ranged all over eastern Angola. By 1968 the MPLA was able to hold regional party conferences inside the country.

The MPLA had a political advantage over the FNLA because of the links of MPLA leaders to the international ideological left. Its multiracial, Marxist-Leninist, and nationalist (versus ethnic or regional) views appealed to liberals in Europe and North America. Because of his radical orientation, however, Neto failed to get help from the United States. During the mid-1960s, the MPLA's ties to the communist world intensified as MPLA military cadres traveled to the Soviet Union, Czechoslovakia, and Bulgaria. Beginning in 1965, the MPLA began to receive training from Cuban forces.

Emergence of UNITA

The MPLA and FNLA faced a third competitor beginning in 1966 with the emergence of UNITA. UNITA first came to international attention when, in December 1966, a group of its guerrillas attacked the town of Vila Teixeira de Sousa (renamed Luau), succeeding in interrupting the Benguela Railway and stopping Zambian and Zairian copper shipments for a week. The new organization was formed by Jonas Savimbi, the former foreign minister and main representative of the Ovimbundu within the FNLA/GRAE, whose disagreements with Roberto over policy issues led to Savimbi's resignation in July 1964. Savimbi had traveled to China in 1965, where he and several of his followers received four months of military training and became disciples of Maoism. Perhaps the strongest impact of Maoism on UNITA has been Savimbi's insistence on self-sufficiency and maintenance of the organization's leadership within Angolan borders. Upon his return to Angola in 1966, Savimbi turned down an invitation from the MPLA to join its organization as a rank-and-file member and moved UNITA into the bush, where the organization began its guerrilla war with a small amount of Chinese military aid transported via Tanzania and Zambia.

Although UNITA lacked educated cadres and arms, it attracted the largest following of the three movements from the Ovimbundu, who comprised about one-third of the population. And, unlike the MPLA and FNLA, UNITA enjoyed the benefits of a unified and unchallenged leadership directed by Savimbi. Moreover, in contrast to the *mestiço*-dominated, urban-based MPLA, Savimbi presented UNITA as the representative of black peasants. UNITA's constitution proclaimed that the movement would strive for a government proportionally representative of all ethnic groups, clans, and classes. His Maoist-oriented philosophy led Savimbi to concentrate on raising the political consciousness of the peasants, most of whom were illiterate and widely dispersed. Savimbi preached self-reliance and founded cooperatives for food production and village self-defense units. He set up a pyramidal structure of elected councils grouping up to sixteen villages that—at least in theory—articulated demands through a political commissar to a central committee, whose thirty-five members were to be chosen every four years at a congress.

In the early 1970s, UNITA began infiltrating the major population centers, slowly expanding its area of influence westward beyond Bié. There, however, it collided with the eastward thrust of the MPLA, which was sending Soviet-trained political cadres

Agostinho Neto, Angola's first president, delivers a speech on independence day.
Courtesy United Nations (J.P. Laffont)

to work among the Ovimbundu and specifically with the Chokwe, Lwena, Luchazi, and Lunda, exploiting potential ethnic antagonisms (see Ethnic Groups and Languages, ch. 2).

On the eve of independence, UNITA controlled many of the rich, food-producing central and southern provinces and was therefore able to regulate the flow of food to the rest of the country. At the time, it claimed the allegiance of about 40 percent of the population.

Liberation Movements in Cabinda

Several movements advocating a separate status for Cabinda were founded in the early 1960s, all of them basing their claims on their own interpretation of Cabindan history. The most important of these was the Movement for the Liberation of the Enclave of Cabinda (Mouvement pour la Libération de l'Enclave de Cabinda—MLEC), led by Luis Ranque Franque, which had evolved out of various émigré associations in Brazzaville. In December 1961, a faction of the MLEC headed by Henriques Tiago Nzita seceded to form the Action Committee for the National Union of Cabindans (Comité d'Action d'Union Nationale des Cabindais—CAUNC). A third group, Alliance of Mayombe (Alliance de Mayombe—Alliama), led by António Eduardo Sozinho, represented the Mayombe (also spelled Maiombe), the ethnic minority of the enclave's interior. The three groups resolved their differences and united in 1963 as the Front for the Liberation of the Enclave of Cabinda (Frente para a Libertação do Enclave de Cabinda—FLEC). When the MPLA began its military incursions into Cabinda in 1964, it encountered hostility not only from coastal members of FLEC who were living in and near the town of Cabinda but also from Mayombe peasants, whose region near the Congo frontier MPLA guerrillas had to cross.

Emulating the FNLA, FLEC created a government in exile on January 10, 1967, in the border town of Tshela in Zaire. Reflecting earlier divisions, however, the faction headed by Nzita established the Revolutionary Cabindan Committee (Comité Révolutionnaire Cabindais) in the Congolese town of Pointe Noire.

Portuguese Economic Interests and Resistance to Angolan Independence

Portugal's motivation to fight Angolan nationalism was based on economic factors. Salazar had instituted an economic system in 1935 that was designed to exploit the colonies for the benefit of Portugal by excluding or strictly limiting foreign investments. But by April 1965, Portugal faced increasing defense expenditures in order to resist the growing military strength of the nationalist movements, the MPLA in particular. This turn of events forced Salazar to permit the influx of foreign capital, which resulted in rapid economic growth in Angola.

One of the most lucrative foreign investments was made by the Cabinda Gulf Oil Company (Cabgoc), a subsidiary of the United States-based company Gulf Oil (now Chevron), which found oil in the waters off Cabinda. Other economic concerns included iron, diamonds, and the manufacturing sector, all of which experienced an enormous increase in production from the mid-1960s to 1974 (see Background to Economic Development, ch. 3). By this time, Angola had become far more valuable economically to Portugal than Mozambique or any of its other colonies. Consequently, Angola's economic growth reinforced Portugal's determination to refuse Angolan independence.

One of the most far-reaching and damaging features of the Portuguese counterinsurgency was the implementation of a resettlement program in 1967. By grouping dispersed Africans into large villages organized by the military in eastern and northwestern Angola, the Portuguese hoped to achieve organized local defense against guerrilla attacks and to prevent insurgent infiltration and mobilization among peasants. Outside the fighting zones, the

Portuguese used resettlement villages to promote economic and social development as a means of winning African support. The Portuguese further controlled the African population by establishing a network of spies and informers in each resettlement village.

By 1974 more than 1 million peasants had been moved into resettlement villages. The widespread disruption in rural Angola caused by the resettlement program, which failed to stop the insurgency, had profound and long-term effects on the rural population. The breakdown in the agricultural sector in particular was so pervasive that rural reconstruction and development in independent Angola had, as of 1988, never really succeeded.

The Portuguese armed forces gained an advantage over the insurgents by the end of 1973 through the use of napalm and defoliants. The MPLA suffered the most from counterinsurgency operations, which were concentrated in the east, where the MPLA had its greatest strength. The MPLA's military failures also caused further conflicts between its political and military wings, as guerrilla commanders blamed the MPLA political leadership for the organization's declining military fortunes. In addition, the Soviet Union's support for Neto was never wholehearted.

The FNLA, which fought from Zairian bases, made little progress inside Angola. Furthermore, the Kinshasa government, reacting to a 1969 Portuguese raid on a Zairian border village that the FNLA used as a staging base, shut down three border camps, making it even more difficult for the FNLA to launch actions into Angola. Moreover, internal dissent among FNLA troops exploded into a mutiny in 1972; Mobutu sent Zairian troops to suppress the mutiny and save his friend Roberto from being overthrown. Although the Zairian army reorganized, retrained, and equipped FNLA guerrillas in the aftermath of the mutiny, the FNLA never posed a serious threat to the Portuguese.

UNITA was also suffering from a variety of problems by the end of 1973. Militarily it was the weakest nationalist movement. The organization's military arm lacked sufficient weaponry. Many of its Chokwe members, who did not have the ethnic loyalty to the organization felt by the Ovimbundu, went over to the better-armed FNLA and MPLA.

The Portuguese Coup d'Etat and the End of the Colonial Era

During the early 1970s, its African wars—including fierce nationalist struggles in Mozambique and Guinea-Bissau—were draining Portugal's resources. By 1974 the Portuguese had lost 11,000 military personnel in Africa. On April 25, 1974, a group of disillusioned military officers, led by the former governor and commander in Guinea-Bissau, General António de Spínola, overthrew the Lisbon government.

On July 14, Spínola acceded to the wishes of officers who favored independence for the Portuguese territories in Africa and promised to take steps toward their freedom. At the end of July, Spínola appointed Admiral Rosa Coutinho as head of a military council formed to oversee Angola's independence. Also during this time, UNITA and the MPLA signed cease-fire agreements with Portugal; the FNLA initially moved military units into northern Angola, but later it too signed a cease-fire. The liberation movements set up offices in the major population centers of the country, eager to mobilize support and gain political control.

The approximately 335,000 whites in Angola, who had no political experience and organization under years of Portuguese authoritarian rule, were unable to assert a unilateral independence. In addition, their security was severely threatened as the new Spínola government began releasing political prisoners and authorized Angolans to organize, assemble, and speak freely. In July 1974, white frustration exploded into violence as Luandan whites rioted, pillaged, and massacred African slum dwellers. The Portuguese army quickly suppressed the riot, but when the Portuguese government announced that it intended to form a provisional Angolan government that would include representatives of both the nationalist movements and the white population, further rioting by whites erupted in Luanda.

Coalition, the Transitional Government, and Civil War

In the wake of the coup in Portugal, there remained a wide split in the Angolan nationalist movement. Lisbon was anxious to relinquish power to a unified government and took an active role in bringing about a reconciliation of the three liberation movements. In addition, at the urgings of the OAU, Neto, Roberto, and Savimbi made several attempts to form a common front. At a meeting in Kenya in early January 1975, they recognized their parties as independent entities with equal rights and responsibilities, agreed that a period of transition was necessary before independence could be achieved (during which they would work with the Portuguese to lay the foundation for an independent Angola), and pledged to maintain Angolan territorial integrity. They also agreed that only their three organizations would be included in a unity government. FLEC, with its goal of a Cabindan secession, did not support territorial integrity and was excluded. In addition, an MPLA splinter group led by Daniel Chipenda was not considered a legitimate nationalist movement, and it too was excluded.

Angolans celebrating independence in the streets of Luanda,
November 1975
Courtesy United Nations (J.P. Laffont)

Meeting in Alvor, Portugal, on January 10, the Lisbon government and the nationalist movements produced an agreement setting independence for November 11, 1975. Under the Alvor Agreement, a transitional government headed by a Portuguese high commissioner was formed; it included the MPLA, UNITA, and the FNLA.

One factor that influenced these agreements was the role of Admiral Coutinho. His pro-MPLA proclivities threatened the delicate balance that the liberation movements had achieved. Angered by his activities, Spínola removed him at the end of January 1975.

On January 31, 1975, the transitional government was sworn in, but the coalition, based on a fragile truce, had serious difficulties, as the leaders of its three member organizations bickered over a number of issues, including personal power. Within days, localized conflicts between MPLA and FNLA forces were renewed. Moreover, on February 13 the MPLA attacked the Luanda office of Chipenda's faction, after which Chipenda joined the FNLA and became its assistant secretary general.

Foreign Intervention

During the transition period, foreign powers were becoming increasingly involved as the situation in Angola rapidly expanded into an East-West power struggle. In late January, a high-level United States government policy-making body authorized a grant of US$300,000 to the pro-Western FNLA, which at the time seemed to be the strongest of the three movements. In March the Soviet Union countered by increasing arms deliveries to the MPLA, and by mid-July that group had become appreciably stronger militarily. Alarmed, the United States increased funding to the FNLA and, for the first time, funded UNITA. Cuba, which had been aiding the MPLA since the mid-1960s, sent military instructors in the late spring of 1975. By early October, more Cuban military personnel had arrived, this time primarily combat troops; their total then probably reached between 1,100 and 1,500.

In April the presidents of Zambia, Tanzania, and Botswana decided to support Savimbi as leader of an Angolan government of national unity, believing that UNITA attracted the widest popular support in Angola. Savimbi also had the support of some francophone states and of Nigeria and Ghana. Some of these countries later withdrew that support when the OAU pleaded for reconciliation and adherence to the Alvor Agreement.

Collapse of the Transitional Government

Inevitably, the delicate coalition came apart as the leaders of the three movements failed to resolve fundamental policy disagreements or control their competition for personal power. Although the OAU brought Neto, Roberto, and Savimbi together in June 1975 for negotiations that produced a draft constitution, heavy fighting broke out in early July and spread swiftly throughout the country. Within a week, the MPLA had forced the FNLA out of Luanda, while the FNLA had eliminated all remaining MPLA presence in the northern towns of Uíge and Zaire provinces. UNITA formally declared war on the MPLA on August 1, 1975. A year earlier, the MPLA had created its military wing, the People's Armed Forces for the Liberation of Angola (Forças Armadas Populares de Libertação de Angola—FAPLA), which became the core of the postindependence army (see Armed Forces, ch. 5). The FNLA and UNITA, recognizing that their separate military forces were not strong enough to fight the MPLA, formed an alliance and withdrew their ministers from the provisional government in Luanda, heralding full-scale civil war. The United States Central Intelligence Agency (CIA), meanwhile, initiated a covert program to have American and European mercenaries fight with the FNLA.

On August 14, 1975, the transitional government collapsed. Portugal ordered the dissolution of the coalition government and announced the assumption of all executive powers by the acting Portuguese high commissioner in Angola. In reality, MPLA officials filled those ministries abandoned by the FNLA and UNITA, thereby allowing the MPLA to extend its political control throughout the Luanda government.

South African Intervention

South Africa's interest in Angolan affairs began during the Portuguese colonial period, especially after 1966 when the insurgency spread to the east. South Africa's military and intelligence services cooperated closely with those of Portugal. South Africa and Portugal opened a joint command center in Cuito Cuanavale in southeast Angola in 1968, and from there South African troops participated in actions against Angolan nationalist guerrillas as well as against southern Angola-based guerrillas of the South West Africa People's Organization (SWAPO), the Namibian group fighting for independence from South African rule.

The collapse of Portugal's empire and the prospect of black rule in Angola (and Mozambique) caused enormous concern in Pretoria. Especially troubling to the South African government was the leftist orientation of several of these nationalist movements. Thus, in August 1975 South African military forces came to the aid of the FNLA-UNITA alliance and occupied the Ruacaná hydroelectric complex and other installations on the Cunene River. On October 23, a force of 300 South African troops, assisted by about 3,000 South African-trained Angolans, invaded Angola. They advanced rapidly north for nearly 1,000 kilometers and came within 100 kilometers of Luanda. This force was later increased to as many as 10,000, but most of these troops were Angolans under South Africa's military command.

The South African invasion had several international consequences. It prompted a massive increase in the flow of Soviet military supplies to the MPLA and caused Cuba to send thousands of men to Angola in defense of the government. Moreover, because the United States was supporting the same factions as the South African regime, the United States involvement drew harsh criticism from the international community. Furthermore, many African countries that until then had opposed the MPLA, including Nigeria, Tanzania, Ghana, and Sudan, reversed themselves and recognized the MPLA government.

Independence and the Rise of the MPLA Government

Unlike Portugal's other African possessions, which had made relatively peaceful transitions to independence months earlier, by November 11, 1975, Angola was in chaos. In the absence of a central government to which Portuguese officials could relinquish control, Portugal refused to recognize any faction; instead, it ceded independence to the people of Angola. The MPLA subsequently announced the establishment of its government in Luanda and called the territory it controlled the People's Republic of Angola.

The FNLA and UNITA announced a separate regime with headquarters in the southern city of Huambo and called their territory the Democratic People's Republic of Angola. But because of continuing hostility between them, the FNLA and UNITA did not set up a government until December 1975, nor did they attempt to fuse their armies. Moreover, the FNLA–UNITA alliance received no formal recognition from other states, mostly because of its South African support. In general, the international community, particularly other African states, viewed South African involvement in favor of the FNLA and UNITA as a legitimization of Soviet and Cuban support for the MPLA.

By January 1976, with the support of some 10,000 to 12,000 Cuban troops and Soviet arms worth US$200 million, it was clear that the MPLA had emerged as the dominant military power. By February 1976, the FNLA and its mercenaries had been defeated in northern Angola; under international pressure, South African troops had withdrawn into Namibia; and the MPLA was in control in Cabinda. Furthermore, United States assistance to the FNLA and UNITA ceased following the passage by the United States Senate of the Clark Amendment, which prohibited all direct and indirect military or paramilitary assistance to any Angolan group. The OAU finally recognized the MPLA regime as Angola's official government, as did the UN and Portugal and more than eighty other nations.

Transformation into a Marxist-Leninist Party and Internal Dissent

Although Marxist influences were evident before independence, Marxism-Leninism had not been the MPLA's stated ideology. But during a plenum of the MPLA Central Committee in October 1976, the party formally adopted Marxism-Leninism. The plenum also resulted in several major organizational decisions, including the creation of a secretariat, a commission to direct and control the Department of Political Orientation, and the Department of Information and Propaganda. The National Party School, founded in February 1977, trained party cadres to fill national and provincial party positions, and at the First Party Congress in December 1977, the MPLA transformed itself into a vanguard Marxist-Leninist party to be called the Popular Movement for the Liberation of Angola-Workers' Party (Movimento Popular de Libertação de Angola-Partido de Trabalho—MPLA–PT).

The estimated 110,000 members of the MPLA–PT had widely diverse backgrounds and political ideas, which made factionalism inevitable. The Neto regime soon faced problems generated by independent left-wing organizations and militant workers. Neto made the first public reference to internal dissent on February 6, 1976, when he denounced a demonstration that had protested the termination of a popular radio program that had been critical of the new government and that had demanded rule by workers and peasants. The government arrested some of the demonstrators and launched a major crackdown on opposition elements. One of these was the so-called Active Revolt, a faction founded in 1973 that comprised intellectuals of varying political orientation and included the MPLA's first president, Mário de Andrade, and other prominent MPLA leaders. Another opposition element was the Organization of Angolan Communists (Organização dos Comunistas de Angola—OCA), a Maoist movement founded in 1975 that attacked the MPLA as a bourgeois party, condemned Soviet imperialism, and called for the withdrawal of all Cuban forces.

Shaba Invasion and the Nitista Plot

Several incidents in the mid- to late 1970s contributed to the MPLA regime's reliance on Soviet military aid and the presence of Cuban troops. The first incident occurred on March 8, 1977, when the National Front for the Liberation of the Congo (Front National pour la Libération du Congo—FNLC), a political opposition group hostile to Zaire's President Mobutu, launched an attack from Angola on Zaire's economically vital Shaba Region. Although the Zaire government halted the invasion with the aid of Moroccan troops, Mobutu accused the MPLA of having instigated the attack. In return, Neto charged Mobutu with harboring and militarily supporting both the FNLA and FLEC. The MPLA government, faced with continuing border violations and engaged in recriminations with the Mobutu regime, requested and received an increase in the number of Cuban troops.

Another incident brought factionalism in the MPLA leadership into sharp focus. Two ultraleftists, minister of interior and Central Committee member Nito Alves and Central Committee member José Van Dúnem, had become critical of the government's economic policies, which both men considered too moderate. They also criticized the government leadership for its heavy representation of whites and *mestiços*. In October 1976, the MPLA condemned Alves for factionalism and abolished his ministry. The government set up a commission of inquiry that investigated reports that Van Dúnem and Alves had purposely caused food shortages to stir up discontent. The commission found the men guilty and expelled them from the Central Committee in May 1977. Later that month, Alves and Van Dúnem led an uprising in the capital and called for mass demonstrations outside the presidential palace. The uprising failed, but Alves, Van Dúnem, and their followers seized a number of senior government leaders, whom they later killed.

The Neto regime, already alarmed by party factionalism and the number of members who did not actively support the party's Marxist-Leninist objectives, conducted a massive purge. It reorganized the party and the mass organizations, many of which had supported Alves and Van Dúnem. The commissars and directing committees in eight provinces, appointed by Alves when he had been minister of interior, were removed. Thousands of Alves supporters, referred to as Nitistas, were dismissed from their positions and detained. All mass organizations were made subordinate to the MPLA. Finally, to achieve these changes, national and provincial restructuring committees were set up. By December 1980, the party had shrunk from 110,000 members to about 32,000 members.

Strengthening Ties with the Soviet Union and Its Allies

The Nitista plot shook the Neto regime severely and was a stark

After independence, an MPLA soldier stands on an armored vehicle in front of a Portuguese statue that has been deliberately covered with a cloth. Courtesy United Nations (J.P. Laffont)

reminder of the young government's vulnerability in the face of internal factionalism and South African destabilization efforts. In the aftermath of the failed coup attempt, the government came to the realization that its survival depended on continued support from the Soviet Union and its allies. Consequently, the government's reliance on Soviet and Cuban military support increased, as did its commitment to Marxist-Leninist ideology.

A new phase of Angola's formal relationship with the Soviet Union had already begun in October 1976, when Neto signed the Treaty of Friendship and Cooperation with the Soviet Union pledging both signatories to mutual military cooperation. The treaty was significant in global terms in that it gave the Soviet Union the right to use Angolan airports and Luanda harbor for military purposes, enabling the Soviet Union to project its forces throughout the South Atlantic region.

For the Soviet Union, its intervention in Angola was a major foreign policy coup. Soviet leaders correctly judged that the United States, because of its recent Vietnam experience, would be reluctant to intervene heavily in a distant, low-priority area. Conditions would thus be created in which the Soviet Union could exert its influence and gain a firm foothold in southern Africa. In addition, South African involvement in Angola convinced most members of the OAU that Soviet support for the Angolan government was a necessary counterweight to South African destablization efforts.

Furthermore, United States support for UNITA during the civil war had tainted the United States in the eyes of the OAU and many Western governments, which perceived a South African-American link.

Beginning in 1978, periodic South African incursions into southern Angola, coupled with UNITA's northward expansion in the east, forced the Angolan government to increase expenditures on Soviet military aid and to depend even more on military personnel from the Soviet Union, the German Democratic Republic (East Germany), and Cuba.

The Angolan government's relationships with the Soviet Union and Cuba were linked in some ways but distinct in other respects. Clearly, the Soviets and Cubans were both attracted to the Angolan government's Marxist-Leninist orientation, and Cuba generally followed the Soviet Union's lead in the latter's quest for international influence. Nonetheless, Cuba had its own agenda in Angola, where Cuban leader Fidel Castro believed that by supporting an ideologically compatible revolutionary movement he could acquire international status independent of the Soviet Union.

Although Soviet and Cuban interests in Angola usually converged, there were also disagreements, mostly because of the factionalism within the MPLA-PT. On the one hand, the Soviet Union seemed to have favored Minister of Interior Alves's more radical viewpoints over those of Neto and probably supported the Nitista coup attempt in 1977. The Cubans, on the other hand, played an active military role in foiling the coup attempt and increased their troop presence in Angola shortly thereafter in support of the Neto regime.

Economic Problems and Implementation of Socialist Policies

One of the priorities of the Neto regime after independence was to repair the country's infrastructure, which had been shattered by the liberation struggle and the civil war (see Background to Economic Development, ch. 3). There had been extensive damage to bridges, roads, and transport vehicles, and most undamaged vehicles had been taken out of the country by the Portuguese. With no means of transporting food and other essential supplies to many areas of the country, the distribution system collapsed. Furthermore, a good part of the economy disintegrated when most of the Portuguese settlers, including skilled workers and government and economic development administrators, left the country at independence.

Perhaps more in response to the economic emergency than as a result of the party's long-term commitment to a planned socialist economy, the government created a large state sector as stipulated in a resolution passed during the October 1976 party plenum (see Role of the Government, ch. 3). Earlier that year, the government allowed state intervention in the management of private companies that had suffered most from the Portuguese withdrawal and passed the Law on State Intervention in March 1976, which provided for the formal nationalization of private companies. As a result, a large part of the economy, including abandoned commercial farms, the mining industry, and the banking sector, became publicly owned. The government, however, acknowledging the massive reconstruction task it faced, continued to encourage and support the private sector and to welcome foreign investment.

The MPLA leadership gave urgent priority to the revival of the agricultural sector, which employed about 75 percent of the economically active population. But the government's rejection of market incentives, the massive dislocations caused by warfare, the disorganization of the new bureaucracy, and hostility among the peasants to imposed collectivization of their land doomed most government efforts. Once a food exporter, Angola was forced to import an ever-increasing amount of food.

Although the agricultural sector barely continued to produce, the Angolan economy survived because of the oil produced by and sold to Western private enterprise (see Oil, ch. 3). The honest and straightforward approach of the Angolan government toward its Western investors earned it the admiration of its partners and resulted in the inflow of capital not only in the oil industry but also in mining and fishing.

The UNITA Insurgency and the South African Threat

In addition to severe economic disruptions, in the late 1970s the Angolan government was also challenged by the UNITA insurgency. UNITA was able to survive after the war for independence, first, because of the continued loyalty of some of its traditional Ovimbundu supporters, but, more important, because of military and logistical support from South Africa. Pretoria established its relationship with UNITA for several reasons. Vehemently anticommunist, South Africa felt threatened by the MPLA's turn toward the Soviet Union and its allies. The South Africans also wished to retaliate for Luanda's support of SWAPO. Furthermore, by helping UNITA shut down the Benguela Railway, which linked the mining areas of Zaire and Zambia to Atlantic ports, Pretoria made these two countries more dependent on South Africa's transportation system and thus more responsive to South African wishes.

In support of UNITA leader Savimbi, the South African Defense Force (SADF) set up bases in Cuando Cubango Province in southeastern Angola. Savimbi established his headquarters in Jamba and enjoyed air cover provided by the South African air force from bases in Namibia (see fig. 16). The SADF also trained UNITA guerrillas in Namibia and provided UNITA with arms, fuel, and food. On occasion, South African ground forces provided direct support during UNITA battles with FAPLA.

Damaging though the UNITA assaults were, the greatest threat to Angola's security in the late 1970s was posed by the SADF. Following its withdrawal from Angola in mid-1976 after its involvement in the war for independence, the SADF routinely launched small-scale incursions from Namibia into southern Angola in pursuit of SWAPO guerrillas. The first large-scale South African incursion into Angola took place in May 1978, when the SADF raided a Namibian refugee camp at Cassinga and killed hundreds of people. By the end of 1979, following the SADF bombing of Lubango, the capital of Huíla Province, an undeclared border war between South Africa and Angola was in full force.

The Final Days of the Neto Regime

By the late 1970s, Angolan head of state Agostinho Neto had reached a better understanding of the motivations behind the 1977 Nitista coup attempt. Accordingly, he sought a more pragmatic approach to balancing the diverse personalities and schools of thought within the government and party. In December 1978, Neto began a series of government and party reorganizations designed to increase the powers of the president, purge both ruling structures of incompetent and corrupt officials, and balance ethnic, racial, and ideological elements. By abolishing the offices of prime minister and deputy prime minister, Neto was able to deal directly with his ministers rather than through intermediaries. The reorganization also resulted in the dismissal or reassignment of a large number of senior party officials. Neto effected the most dramatic change in the MPLA–PT Political Bureau, which had been dominated by *mestiços* and Mbundu. He reorganized the Political Bureau by appointing officials, including three Bakongo and two Cabindan members, who gave it a broader ethnic representation (see Structure of Government, ch. 4). These reorganizations were accompanied by a partial amnesty that included the release from prison and return from exile of members of the Active Revolt, many of whom Neto reintegrated into the party. Furthermore, Neto welcomed back to Angola a number of FNLA members and, according to some sources, even made friendly overtures to Chipenda. By 1979 Neto had largely succeeded in molding the MPLA–PT into a cohesive organization of carefully selected cadres.

Neto also pursued a foreign policy designed to weaken external support for UNITA (and what was left of the FNLA and FLEC) and to secure friendly relations with as many states as possible for both security and economic reasons. Included in this last goal was a July 1979 foreign investment law that provided more attractive benefits for foreign investors and that Neto designed primarily to encourage further Western investment in oil exploration.

The Dos Santos Regime

When Neto died in September 1979 in a Moscow hospital, he was still in the process of consolidating his power and reconciling with former opponents. To his credit, the internal party cohesion that he fostered allowed a smooth transfer of power to José Eduardo dos Santos, a Soviet-educated Mbundu who had served as first deputy prime minister and then as minister of planning following the December 1978 reorganization.

Despite his student years in the Soviet Union, dos Santos was a moderate with a pragmatic outlook, not unlike that of Neto. He soon expressed his preference for a mixed economy with an important role for the private sector. The direction in which he guided the MPLA–PT was especially telling. He pushed for the promotion to the Central Committee of four moderates—Manuel Alexandre Rodrigues (nom de guerre Kito; Mbundu), Kundi Paihama (southern Ovambo), Paulo Jorge (*mestiço*), and Roberto de Almeida (*mestiço*). The ethnic backgrounds of these four men also demonstrated the new regime's continuing commitment to broadened representation in the top party leadership. Nonetheless, no Ovimbundu—the largest ethnic group and the one to which Savimbi belonged—was a member of the Political Bureau. Dos Santos defended this omission by explaining that there were no politically educated Ovimbundu who could fill top party positions. The promotion of Minister of Foreign Relations Jorge to full membership in the Central Committee was especially significant because, during the Neto regime, Jorge had initiated contact with the West and maintained the flexible foreign policy that characterized that regime, despite Soviet objections. Minister of Domestic and Foreign Trade Almeida, also promoted to full Central Committee membership, was an active participant in the fostering of Angola's economic ties with the West as well.

Steps Toward a Stronger Party and Political Discord

The party unanimously confirmed dos Santos as its president during the MPLA–PT's First Extraordinary Party Congress held in December 1980. The congress also increased the number of Central Committee members from fifty-eight to seventy, and it took a decisive step toward creating a greater role for the party in running the nation and a diminished role for the government. A major constitutional change that had been enacted earlier paved the way for the formation of the national People's Assembly. Provincial assemblies, elected by the public, then elected assembly members, who in turn elected a twenty-five-member permanent commission that included the president and the entire Political Bureau. Thus, the People's Assembly, which replaced the government's Council of the Revolution, became an organ primarily of the party rather than the government.

During a meeting in March 1981, the Central Committee further reinforced the MPLA–PT's primacy over the government by assigning to itself increased responsibility for the job of orienting and supervising the work of the Council of Ministers. A government reorganization followed the meeting, and several ministers left the government to take on senior party positions, where they had greater opportunities to gain power. Because most of the ministers who remained in the Council of Ministers were technocrats, the bureaucratic skills of government officials improved, and the reorganization further differentiated government and party functions.

Dos Santos's efforts to secure the supremacy of the party over the government, however, created sharp divisions within the government and party elites along political and racial lines. On one side were the Africanists, or nationalists, who were mostly black and held most of the senior positions in the government and ministries. The Africanists, for the most part, were known as pragmatists and favored improved relations with the West and a rapprochement with UNITA. On the other side were the ideologues, mostly *mestiços* and whites, who dominated the party and adhered adamantly to the Soviet Marxist-Leninist line. Although these divisions caused bitter schisms and numerous policy-making problems, they were not unusual for a government that dealt with both the Soviet Union and its allies (in the military sphere) and the West (in the economic sphere).

The Namibia Issue and Security Threats in the 1980s

In the early 1980s, the status of Namibia evolved into a

complex international issue involving principally the governments of the United States, Angola, South Africa, and Cuba. The United States, troubled by the growing Soviet and Cuban presence in Angola, sought to reduce this influence by becoming directly involved in negotiations for a withdrawal of Cuban troops from Angola and for Namibian independence. For its part, Angola claimed that if the SADF threat were removed from its southern border, it could safely reduce the number of Cuban troops and Soviet advisers. The most obvious way this could be done was if South Africa granted independence to Namibia. South Africa, already preoccupied with the leftist regime in Angola, was reluctant to relinquish control of Namibia and allow free elections because of the possibility that these elections would bring its traditional nemesis, SWAPO, to power.

In 1977 Britain, Canada, France, the Federal Republic of Germany (West Germany), and the United States formed an informal negotiating team, called the Contact Group, to work with South Africa to implement a UN plan for free elections in Namibia. The South African government, however, was fundamentally opposed to the UN plan, which it claimed was biased in favor of the installation of a SWAPO government in Namibia. Pretoria continued to attend negotiating sessions throughout the early 1980s, always prepared to bargain but never ready to settle.

By the beginning of 1981, South Africa's undeclared war with Angola and its support for an increasingly effective UNITA had become the focus of the dos Santos regime. After the failure in January 1981 of the UN-sponsored talks on the future of Namibia, South African military aggression escalated and became directed as much against Angolan targets as against SWAPO guerrillas. In August 1981, the SADF launched Operation Protea, in which several thousand troops and accompanying equipment penetrated 120 kilometers into southwestern Angola. This invasion marked the beginning of a different kind of war, one in which South Africa no longer pretended to restrict its incursions to the pursuit of SWAPO units but openly intensified its assaults on Angolan economic targets and began to occupy Angolan territory, particularly in Cunene Province. Furthermore, SADF support for UNITA in 1982 and 1983 increased to the extent that the South African Air Force (SAAF) participated in UNITA operations against FAPLA.

The rapid escalation of South African military aggression in Angola was matched by the massive infiltration of the countryside by UNITA forces. This activity far exceeded UNITA's previous hit-and-run operations aimed primarily at the Benguela Railway. But perhaps the most detrimental effect of the UNITA insurgency was the disruption of the economy, particularly the agricultural sector. By the end of 1985, fighting between UNITA and FAPLA had forced hundreds of thousands of peasants to flee from the fertile central highlands. The result was a precipitous drop in food production. UNITA guerrillas also frequently mined roads and railroads, blew up electric power transmission lines, and attacked dams, mining facilities, and coffee plantations. Moreover, they began taking foreign technicians hostage in the hope of gaining publicity for the UNITA cause.

Second Party Congress

The Second Party Congress of the MPLA–PT, held in December 1985, focused on two main themes: greater economic efficiency and improved defense capabilities. The party had little to celebrate in view of the deplorable conditions that then prevailed. Politically, the party lacked sufficiently educated cadres, and economically, the government was forced to import 80 percent of its food and had become dependent on Western oil companies to keep the economy afloat. The large number of party members attending the congress who were also military officers (about a quarter of all party delegates) exemplified the MPLA–PT's emphasis on the defense sector. The Central Committee report to the congress projected that more than one-third of the government budget would go to defense and security over the next five years.

During the congress, party officials expressed their dissatisfaction with economic policies patterned on Soviet models that had failed to revive Angola's agricultural sector. In fact, the most significant results of the congress were a purge of Soviet hardliners and an influx of well-trained nationalists with more pragmatic viewpoints. Within the party's senior ranks, many leading ideologues were demoted, as were a number of *mestiços;* they were replaced with younger black technocrats and the president's closest supporters.

An unexpected change involved one of the most prominent members of the pro-Soviet group, Lúcio Lára, who had been considered the second most powerful figure in the MPLA–PT. Lára lost his position in the Political Bureau and ended up with the largely honorary position of first secretary of the People's Assembly. Overall, the most notable outcomes of the congress were the enhanced prestige and authority of dos Santos and a more professional and loyalist party leadership, in which the armed forces were heavily represented.

By the late 1980s, Angola had far to go in its quest to become a viable, sovereign state. More than 50,000 Cuban troops remained in the country to provide security; UNITA and the SADF launched attacks with impunity; the oil sector—and hence the treasury— suffered grievously from the worldwide slump in petroleum prices; and hundreds of thousands of Angolans, in the countryside as well as in the increasingly crowded cities, were malnourished. Yet, in late 1988 there were a few reasons for optimism. United States-sponsored negotiations were finally successful, opening the door for a settlement of the Namibia dispute, the withdrawal of Cuban forces from Angola, and an accord between the MPLA–PT and UNITA—in short, the conditions necessary for Angola to resume the process of nationbuilding and to prepare a better future for its people (see Regional Politics, ch. 4).

* * *

Sources emphasizing the early history of the Africans in Angola are Jan Vansina's *Kingdoms of the Savanna,* Douglas L. Wheeler and René Pélissier's *Angola,* and Joseph C. Miller's *Kings and Kinsmen.* The best accounts of Portuguese expansion in Angola are Gerald J. Bender's *Angola under the Portuguese* and Lawrence W. Henderson's *Angola: Five Centuries of Conflict,* both of which deal extensively with the brutality of Portuguese colonial policies and institutions. Other useful works are Malyn Newitt's *Portugal in Africa,* C.R. Boxer's *Race Relations in the Portuguese Colonial Empire, 1415-1825,* and John Sykes's *Portugal and Africa.*

By far the most complete and valuable account of the Angolan nationalist struggle is John A. Marcum's *The Angolan Revolution.* This work is divided into two volumes: *The Anatomy of an Explosion, 1950-1962* and *Exile Politics and Guerrilla Warfare, 1962-1976.* Keith Somerville's *Angola: Politics, Economics, and Society* is an exhaustive and well-written account of the MPLA's institutions and policies.

A wealth of material exists on Angola's security problems and the escalation of Soviet and Cuban military support. Some of the best sources are Tony Hodges's *Angola to the 1990s,* a special report published by the Economist Intelligence Unit; John A. Marcum's paper prepared for the United States Information Agency titled "Radical Vision Frustrated: Angola and Cuba"; Gerald J. Bender's article in *Current History* titled "The Continuing Crisis in Angola"; two chapters by John A. Marcum titled "UNITA: The Politics of Survival" and "A Quarter Century of War" in *Angola, Mozambique, and the West,* edited by Helen Kitchen; two articles by Gillian Gunn titled "The Angolan Economy" and "Cuba and

Angola,'' also in Helen Kitchen's edited volume; and Arthur Jay Klinghoffer's *The Angolan War*.

Documentation of Angola's recent history can be found in the annual *Africa Contemporary Record* and various issues of *Africa Confidential,* as well as many periodicals dealing with Africa. (For further information and complete citations, see Bibliography.)

Chapter 2. The Society and Its Environment

A young Angolan celebrates during a carnival.

IN LATE 1988, ANGOLAN SOCIETY still bore the scars inflicted by five centuries of colonial rule and by a thirteen-year-long insurgency that had drained the national treasury and frustrated the government's efforts to implement Marxist-Leninist policies. Complicating the study of contemporary Angolan society was the limited information available to researchers. During the period of turmoil that began in 1975, few Western observers had been allowed access to government-controlled areas. Furthermore, the Angolan press was closely controlled by the government and prone to propagandistic reporting; antigovernment sources were equally slanted.

Despite these limitations, certain features of Angolan society could be outlined, if not clearly discerned. In 1988 Angola had an estimated population of 8.2 million, the great majority of whom lived in the western half of the country. Nearly 7 million Angolans lived in government-controlled areas. The remainder, an estimated 1.25 million, resided in rebel-held regions. Most Angolans inhabited rural areas, although there had been a significant trend since the 1970s toward urban growth. By 1988 about a third of the population was living in towns and cities. Most of the urban areas were in the more populous western half of the country.

Scholars often divided the population into a number of ethnolinguistic categories, but in many cases these categories had been devised by others, both Portuguese and Africans. Physical boundaries based on these categories had been established by the Portuguese for use in census taking and related activities. Although they acquired a certain meaning for the people included in them in the course of the colonial period and during the nationalist struggle, these categories were neither fixed nor internally homogeneous, and they were subject to change under shifting historical conditions.

The three largest categories—the Ovimbundu, the Mbundu, and the Bakongo—together constituted nearly three-quarters of Angola's population. *Mestiços* (persons of mixed European and African ancestry; see Glossary), at less than 2 percent of the population, had played an important role in the ruling party since independence, mostly because they were fairly well educated in a society in which educated persons were relatively few. They had, however, been the target of much resentment, a consequence of their former identification with the Portuguese and, often, of their expressions of superiority to Africans. The regime of José Eduardo dos Santos, who became president in 1979, sought to dissipate this resentment by replacing high-ranking *mestiço* party and government officials with individuals of other ethnic backgrounds.

Little is known of the actual workings of indigenous social systems as modified during the colonial period. The most persistent of groupings and institutions, such as clans or tribes, were based on descent from a common ancestor, in most cases a common female ancestor, and were traced through females. (With rare exceptions, however, authority lay in male hands.) As enduring as these had been, such groupings and institutions were showing signs of losing their significance toward the end of the colonial era. In many instances, they were further disrupted by the devastating effects of the insurgency waged by the National Union for the Total Independence of Angola (União Nacional para a Independência Total de Angola—UNITA), which caused massive displacement of much of the rural population, particularly from the eastern provinces.

The Portuguese-imposed national structure was almost totally destroyed by the Marxist-Leninist institutions established after independence in 1975. There have been significant changes, however, in the ideology of the country's leaders in the mid- to late 1980s. Although the ruling party, the Popular Movement for the Liberation of Angola-Workers' Party (Movimento Popular de Libertação de Angola-Partido de Trabalho—MPLA–PT), inveighed against what it called petit bourgeois tendencies, its leaders accepted private enterprise and a more tolerant attitude toward personal gain as means of coping with the country's massive economic and administrative problems.

Despite its opposition to religion, the Marxist-Leninist government did not prohibit the existence of religious institutions. Many Angolans were Roman Catholics or Protestants, and missionaries had been instrumental in providing education to Angolans during the colonial era when schooling had been largely denied to Africans by the colonial authorities. Nonetheless, the government was suspicious of large organized groups that could threaten its stability, particularly the Roman Catholic Church, because it had not overtly opposed Portuguese colonialism. There was less hostility toward the Protestant churches, which had not maintained particularly close ties to the Portuguese colonial authorities. Indigenous religions continued to influence the lives of a large segment of the population, even though some of these people also belonged to Christian denominations.

In the late 1980s, there was a tremendous need for educated Angolans in both the economic and the governmental sectors, especially in technical fields. Although the government had made steady progress in providing education at the primary and secondary school levels, there were still severe teacher shortages, mostly in rural areas, and vast problems in reaching those children living in areas where UNITA military actions were most frequent.

There were also shortages of trained Angolan personnel in the health field, which had forced the government to bring in hundreds of foreign health care personnel to meet the needs of the population as well as to train Angolans in health care practices. Nonetheless, the high infant mortality rate and proliferation of diseases, exacerbated by poor sanitation and malnutrition, attested to the government's insufficient progress in this area.

Physical Setting

A total area of 1,246,700 square kilometers (including Cabinda Province) makes Angola the seventh largest state in Africa, but it is also one of the most lightly populated (see fig. 1). The country is bordered to the north and east by Zaire, to the east by Zambia, and to the south by Namibia. The 7,270-square-kilometer enclave of Cabinda, which is separated from the rest of Angola by a strip of Zairian territory, is bordered on the north by Congo.

Terrain

Angola has three principal natural regions: the coastal lowland, characterized by low plains and terraces; hills and mountains, rising inland from the coast into a great escarpment; and an area of high plains, called the high plateau (*planalto*), which extends eastward from the escarpment (see fig. 3).

The coastal lowland rises from the sea in a series of low terraces. This region varies in width from about 25 kilometers near Benguela to more than 150 kilometers in the Cuanza River Valley just south of Angola's capital, Luanda, and is markedly different from Angola's highland mass. The Atlantic Ocean's cold, northward-flowing Benguela Current substantially reduces precipitation along the coast, making the region relatively arid or nearly so south of Benguela (where it forms the northern extension of the Namib Desert), and quite dry even in its northern reaches. Even where, as around Luanda, the average annual rainfall may be as much as fifty centimeters, it is not uncommon for the rains to fail. Given this pattern of precipitation, the far south is marked by sand dunes, which give way to dry scrub along the middle coast. Portions of the northern coastal plain are covered by thick brush.

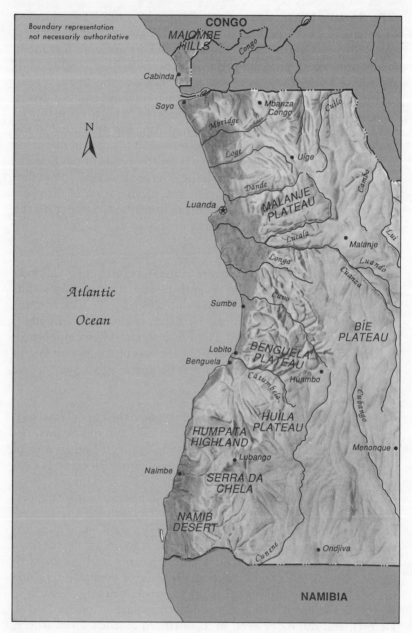

Figure 3. Topography and Drainage

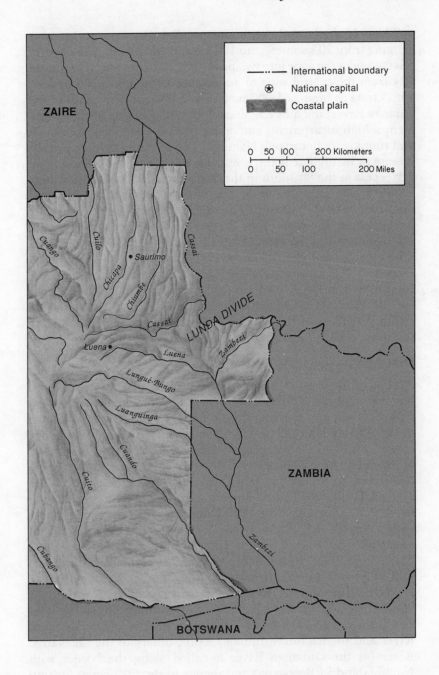

The belt of hills and mountains parallels the coast at distances ranging from 20 kilometers to 100 kilometers inland. The Cuanza River divides the zone into two parts. The northern part rises gradually from the coastal zone to an average elevation of 500 meters, with crests as high as 1,000 meters to 1,800 meters. South of the Cuanza River, the hills rise sharply from the coastal lowlands and form a high escarpment, extending from a point east of Luanda and running south through Namibia. The escarpment reaches 2,400 meters at its highest point, southeast of the town of Sumbe, and is steepest in the far south in the Serra da Chela mountain range.

The high plateau lies to the east of the hills and mountains and dominates Angola's terrain. The surface of the plateau is typically flat or rolling, but parts of the Benguela Plateau and the Humpata Highland area of the Huíla Plateau in the south reach heights of 2,500 meters and more. The Malanje Plateau to the north rarely exceeds 1,000 meters in height. The Benguela Plateau and the coastal area in the immediate environs of Benguela and Lobito, the Bié Plateau, the Malanje Plateau, and a small section of the Huíla Plateau near the town of Lubango have long been among the most densely settled areas in Angola.

Drainage

Most of the country's many rivers originate in central Angola, but their patterns of flow are diverse and their ultimate outlets varied. A number of rivers flow in a more or less westerly course to the Atlantic Ocean, providing water for irrigation in the dry coastal strip and the potential for hydroelectric power, only some of which had been realized by 1988. Two of Angola's most important rivers, the Cuanza and the Cunene, take a more indirect route to the Atlantic, the Cuanza flowing north and the Cunene flowing south before turning west. The Cuanza is the only river wholly within Angola that is navigable—for nearly 200 kilometers from its mouth—by boats of commercially or militarily significant size. The Congo River, whose mouth and western end form a small portion of Angola's northern border with Zaire, is also navigable.

North of the Lunda Divide a number of important tributaries of the Congo River flow north to join it, draining Angola's northeast quadrant. South of the divide some rivers flow into the Zambezi River and thence to the Indian Ocean, others to the Okavango River (as the Cubango River is called along the border with Namibia and in Botswana) and thence to the Okavango Swamp in Botswana. The tributaries of the Cubango River and several of the southern rivers flowing to the Atlantic are seasonal, completely dry much of the year.

Climate

Like the rest of tropical Africa, Angola experiences distinct, alternating rainy and dry seasons. In the north, the rainy season may last for as long as seven months—usually from September to April, with perhaps a brief slackening in January or February. In the south, the rainy season begins later, in November, and lasts until about February. The dry season (*cacimbo*) is often characterized by a heavy morning mist. In general, precipitation is higher in the north, but at any latitude it is greater in the interior than along the coast and increases with altitude.

Temperatures fall with distance from the equator and with altitude and tend to rise closer to the Atlantic Ocean. Thus, at Soyo, at the mouth of the Congo River, the average annual temperature is about 26°C, but it is under 16°C at Huambo on the temperate central plateau. The coolest months are July and August (in the middle of the dry season), when frost may sometimes form at higher altitudes.

Population Structure and Dynamics

As of late 1988, the last official census in Angola had been taken in 1970. As a result, most population figures were widely varying estimates based on scanty birth and death rate data. According to the United States Department of Commerce's Bureau of the Census, Angola's 1988 population was about 8.2 million. The United States Department of State gave a 1986 figure of 8.5 million, while the United Nations (UN) Economic Commission for Africa estimated the mid-1986 population at 8.9 million. The Angolan government estimated the 1988 population at almost 9.5 million (see table 2, Appendix A). The government figure, however, may have included Angolan refugees in neighboring countries. According to the U.S. Committee for Refugees, a private agency, in mid-1987 more than 400,000 Angolan refugees resided in Zaire and Zambia. There were about 50,000 Cuban soldiers and civilians and about 2,000 military and civilian advisers and technicians from the Soviet Union and the German Democratic Republic (East Germany) stationed in Angola. There were also about 10,000 South African refugees, most associated with the antigovernment African National Congress (ANC); 70,000 Namibian refugees, most associated with the South West Africa People's Organization (SWAPO); and 13,200 Zairian refugees. There was no officially reported immigration or emigration.

In spite of warfare, poor health care, and the large number of Angolans in exile, the population was growing steadily in the late 1980s. Like population estimates, however, growth rate

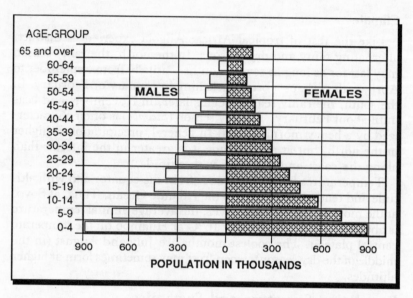

Source: Based on information from *African Statistical Yearbook, 1986,* Pt. 3, Addis Ababa, 1986.

Figure 4. Population Distribution by Age and Sex, Mid-1986

calculations varied considerably. According to a 1987 estimate by the United States Central Intelligence Agency (CIA), the growth rate was 3.6 percent. The UN 1986 estimate of 2.7 percent was a good deal lower, while the government, whose demographic estimates typically exceeded those of Western governments and international organizations, announced a 1986 growth rate of almost 4.9 percent. The CIA figured the infant mortality rate in 1987 at 167 per 1,000, and the United States Bureau of the Census calculated the death rate at 21 per 1,000.

According to UN figures, Angola had a very young population. In 1986 the UN estimated that about 46 percent of the population was under age fifteen (see fig. 4). At the other end of the age scale, only 4.8 percent of the population was sixty years of age or older. The government estimated the median age at 17.5 years. Life expectancy in 1987, according to United States government sources, was forty-one for males and forty-four for females.

The 1970 census showed the most densely settled areas of Angola to be the plateau, those coastal zones including and adjacent to the cities of Luanda, Lobito, Benguela, and Moçâmedes (present-day Namibe), and the enclave of Cabinda. The most densely settled province in 1970 was Huambo. The other large area of relatively dense settlement included much of Cuanza Norte Province and the southern part of Uíge Province. This area was the major center for coffee cultivation and attracted a number of Europeans and migrant workers. Except for Zaire Province in the far northwest, the most thinly populated areas of Angola lay in its eastern half.

Since the start of the independence struggle in the early 1960s, an almost continuous process of urbanization has taken place. This process was accelerated in the 1980s by the UNITA insurgency, which induced hundreds of thousands of Angolans to leave the countryside for large towns. Angola's urban population grew from 10.3 percent in 1960 to 33.8 percent in 1988 (according to government statistics). Much of the growth occurred in Luanda, whose population more than doubled between 1960 and 1970, and which by 1988 had reached about 1.2 million. Other towns had also acquired larger populations: Huambo grew from fewer than 100,000 residents in 1975 to almost 1 million in 1987, and Benguela's population increased from 55,000 to about 350,000 over the same period.

After independence in 1975, there were a number of changes in the structure of the population. The first was the exodus of an estimated 350,000 white Portuguese to their homeland. Yet, by 1988 there were an estimated 82,000 whites (representing 1 percent of the population), mostly of Portuguese origin, living in Angola.

The second change was brought about by large-scale population movements, mostly among the Ovimbundu who had migrated in the 1950s and 1960s to work on coffee plantations in northwestern Uíge Province. Panic-stricken by the onset of civil war in 1975, most Ovimbundu workers fled to their ethnic homelands in the central provinces. Another large-scale population movement occurred as many of the Bakongo who had fled to Zaire during the nationalist struggle returned to Angola (see Coalition, the Transitional Government, and Civil War, ch. 1).

The third and most striking population shift, most notable in the late 1970s and 1980s, had been the flight of increasing numbers of internal migrants out of the central provinces, where the effects of the UNITA insurgency had been most destructive. Most of this massive migration had been toward urban areas. From 1975 to 1988, millions of rural civilians were displaced, including more than 700,000 forced from their villages since 1985 by armed conflict. Many of these migrants relocated to ramshackle displacement camps, many of which were run by West European private voluntary organizations. Although these camps were less vulnerable to attacks by UNITA guerrillas, conditions in them were poor. Food and water were in short supply, and health care was limited.

Many of the displaced persons living in Benguela Province were Ovimbundu from the plateau regions of eastern Benguela and Huambo provinces. The officially registered displaced population of 21,478 in Benguela Province (1988 figure) lived in nine camps and one transit center, but there were probably thousands more living with family members in the province's urban areas, including Lobito and Benguela. The estimated 116,598 displaced persons living in several camps in Cuanza Sul Province had been forced to flee from the province's eastern rural areas or from the plateau regions of Benguela, Huambo, and Bié provinces because of intense guerrilla activity. Because access to many rural areas was limited and sometimes impossible, most of these displaced persons were forced to rely on other local populations and some limited and sporadic outside assistance. Most displaced persons fled from the more fertile and wetter highlands to the less hospitable coastal zone and would be expected to return to their homes when the security situation improved.

In 1988, however, the majority of displaced persons had become integrated into the larger urban population, especially around Luanda. Many displaced persons who sought refuge in urban areas did so through family or other relations to circumvent government registration procedures and so avoid taxation, conscription, or forced resettlement. Consequently, the exact numbers of these people could not be computed. In Luanda much of the destitute population, estimated at 447,000 and mostly consisting of displaced persons, lived in vertical shantytowns (large apartment blocks in the center of the city with inadequate or nonexistent water sources or sanitary facilities) or in huge, maze-like neighborhoods known as *musseques,* the largest of which housed an estimated 400,000 people.

Ethnic Groups and Languages

Although Portuguese was Angola's official language, the great majority of Angolans (more than 95 percent of the total population) used languages of the Bantu family—some closely related, others remotely so—that were spoken by most Africans living south of the equator and by substantial numbers north of it.

Angola's remaining indigenous peoples fell into two disparate categories. A small number, all in southern Angola, spoke so-called Click languages (after a variety of sounds characteristic of them) and differed physically from local African populations. These Click speakers shared characteristics, such as small stature and lighter skin color, linking them to the hunting and gathering bands of southern Africa sometimes referred to by Europeans as Bushmen.

Displaced persons walk to a camp in Cuanza Sul Province.
Courtesy Richard J. Hough

The second category consisted of *mestiços,* largely urban and living in western Angola. Most spoke Portuguese, although some were also acquainted with African languages, and a few may have used such a language exclusively.

The Definition of Ethnicity

Bantu languages have been categorized by scholars into a number of sets of related tongues. Some of the languages in any set may be more or less mutually intelligible, especially in the areas where speakers of a dialect of one language have had sustained contact with speakers of a dialect of another language. Given the mobility and interpenetration of communities of Bantu speakers over the centuries, transitional languages—for example, those that share characteristics of two tongues—developed in areas between these communities. Frequently, the languages of a set, particularly those with many widely distributed speakers, would be divided into several dialects. In principle, dialects of the same language are considered mutually intelligible, although they are not always so in fact.

Language alone does not define an ethnic group. On the one hand, a set of communities lacking mutually intelligible dialects may for one reason or another come to share a sense of identity in any given historical period. On the other hand, groups sharing a common language or mutually intelligible ones do not necessarily constitute a single group. Thus, the Suku—most of them in Zaire but some in Angola—had a language mutually intelligible with at least some dialects of the Bakongo. However, their historical experience, including a period of domination by Lunda speakers, made the Suku a separate group.

Although common language and culture do not automatically make a common identity, they provide a framework within which such an identity can be forged, given other historical experience. Insofar as common culture implies a set of common perceptions of the way the world works, it permits individuals and groups sharing it to communicate more easily with one another than with those who lack that culture. However, most Angolan groups had, as part of that common culture, the experience and expectation of political fragmentation and intergroup rivalry. That is, because one community shared language and culture with another, political unity or even neutrality did not follow, nor did either community assume that it should. With the exception of the Bakongo and the Lunda, no group had experienced a political cohesion that transcended smaller political units (chiefdoms or, at best, small kingdoms). In the Bakongo case, the early Kongo Kingdom, encompassing most Kikongo-speaking communities, had given way by the eighteenth century to politically fragmented entities. In the Lunda case, the empire had been so far-flung and internal conflict had become so great by the nineteenth century that political cohesion was limited (see Kongo Kingdom; Lunda and Chokwe Kingdoms, ch. 1).

Very often, the name by which a people has come to be known was given them by outsiders. For example, the name ''Mbundu'' was first used by the Bakongo. Until such naming, and sometimes long after, the various communities or sections of a set sharing a language and culture were likely to call themselves by other terms, and even when they came to use the all-encompassing name, they tended to reserve it for a limited number of situations. In virtually all colonial territories, Angola included, the naming process and the tendency to treat the named people as a discrete entity distinct from all others became pervasive. The process was carried out by the colonial authorities—sometimes with the help of scholars and missionaries—as part of the effort to understand, deal with, and control local populations. Among other things, the Portuguese tended to treat smaller, essentially autonomous groups as parts of larger entities. As time went on, these populations, particularly the more educated among them, seized upon these names and the communities presumably covered by them as a basis for organizing to improve their status and later for nationalist agitation. Among the first to do so were *mestiços* in the Luanda area. Although most spoke

Portuguese and had a Portuguese male ancestor in their genealogies, the *mestiços* often spoke Kimbundu as a home language. It is they who, in time, initiated the development of a common Mbundu identity.

In general, then, the development of ethnic consciousness in a group encompassing a large number of communities reflected shifts from the identification of individuals with small-scale units to at least partial identification with larger entities and from relatively porous boundaries between such entities to less permeable ones. But the fact that these larger groups were the precipitates of relatively recent historical conditions suggests that they were not permanently fixed. Changes in these conditions could lead to the dissolution of the boundaries and to group formation on bases other than ethnicity.

In any case, ethnic identities are rarely exclusive; identification with other entities, new or old, also occurs in certain situations because not all sections of a large ethnic group have identical interests. It remained likely that earlier identities would be appealed to in some situations or that new cleavages would surface in others. For example, descent groups or local communities were often involved in competitive relations in the precolonial or colonial eras, and the conditions similar to those giving rise to such competition might still prevail in some areas. In other contexts, younger members of an ethnic group may consider their interests to be different from those of their elders, or a split between urban and rural sections of an ethnic entity may become salient.

In Angola, the displacement of hundreds of thousands of people, especially in the late 1980s, had significant repercussions on ethnic identification. For example, many of those forced to abandon rural areas and traditional ethnic communities for urban dwellings no longer engaged in agricultural activities and the small town life that defined their communities. Instead, they were forced to become urban laborers in ethnically mixed surroundings. Many were compelled by their new circumstances to learn new languages and give up traditional life-styles in order to survive in their new environment.

Ethnolinguistic Categories

Caveats notwithstanding, a listing of the more commonly used ethnic rubrics and an indication of the dimension of the categories they refer to is useful as a preliminary description of Angola's peoples. The 1970 census did not enumerate the population in ethnic terms. The most recent available count, therefore, is based on projections of the 1960 census. Most projections assume that the

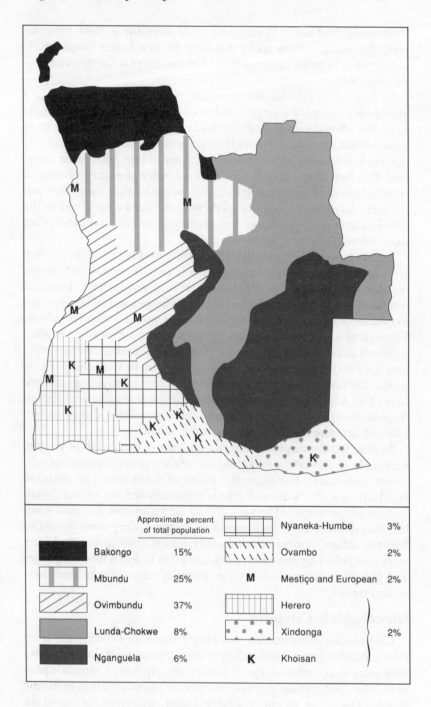

Approximate percent
of total population

Bakongo 15%

Mbundu 25%

Ovimbundu 37%

Lunda-Chokwe 8%

Nganguela 6%

Nyaneka-Humbe 3%

Ovambo 2%

M Mestiço and European 2%

Herero

Xindonga 2%

K Khoisan

Figure 5. Ethnolinguistic Groups, 1988

rank order of the major ethnolinguistic categories did not change, although the proportions may have done so. In particular, a fairly large segment of the Bakongo of the northwestern provinces of Zaire and Uíge were already refugees in 1970 and were not included in the 1970 census. Although it is not clear how many Bakongo subsequently returned to Angola, it may be assumed that many of them returned and that their relative status as the third largest group was unchanged. The same is true of other ethnic groups whose members fled to Zaire and Zambia in the late 1980s when the insurgency intensified in Angola's border regions. This category would include many Ovimbundu, who fled central Angola to Zambia, and many Lunda and Chokwe (also spelled Cokwe), who fled to Zaire from eastern and northern Angola.

Ovimbundu

The largest ethnolinguistic category, the Ovimbundu, were located in west-central Angola, south of Mbundu-inhabited regions (see fig. 5). In 1988 the United States Department of State estimated that they constituted 37 percent of the population. The language of the Ovimbundu was Umbundu.

The core area of the Ovimbundu kingdoms was that part of the Benguela Plateau north of the town of Huambo. Expansion continuing into the twentieth century enlarged their territory considerably, although most Ovimbundu remained in that part of the plateau above 1,200 meters in elevation.

Like most African groups of any size, the Ovimbundu were formed by the mixture of groups of diverse origin (and varying size). Little is known of developments before the seventeenth century, but there is some evidence of additions to the people who occupied the Benguela Plateau at that time. Over time, a number of political entities, usually referred to as kingdoms, were formed (see Ovimbundu and Kwanhama Kingdoms, ch. 1). By the eighteenth century, there were twenty-two kingdoms. Thirteen were fully independent; the other nine were largely autonomous but owed tribute to one of the more powerful entities, usually the kingdom of Bailundu, but in some cases Wambu or Ciyaka. By the beginning of the second decade of the twentieth century, effective occupation by the Portuguese had caused a fairly rapid decline in the power of the heads of these kingdoms, but Ovimbundu continued to think of themselves as members of one or another of the groups based on these political units after World War II.

In addition to the groups that clearly spoke dialects of Umbundu, there were two on the periphery of Ovimbundu distribution: the Mbui, who seemed to straddle the linguistic boundary between

69

the Ovimbundu and the Mbundu; and the Dombe living to the west near the coast, whose language was closely related to Umbundu, although not a dialect of it. The Dombe and several other groups, including the Nganda and the Hanya (who, according to one account, spoke Umbundu dialects) relied on cattle raising, as did their southern neighbors, the Herero and the Ovambo. Still others, typically the old tributary kingdoms, came to speak Umbundu relatively recently.

Until the Portuguese established firm control over their territory, the Ovimbundu—particularly those of the major kingdoms of Bailundu (to the northwest), Bihe (to the northeast), and Wambu (in the center)—played important roles as intermediaries in the slave, ivory, and beeswax trades, acting as carriers, entrepreneurs, and raiders. With the decline of the slave trade in the last decades of the nineteenth century, the entrepreneurs among the Ovimbundu turned to the rubber trade, abandoning the warfare and raiding that had hitherto been integrally related to their economic activities. The rubber slump at the beginning of the twentieth century, the end of the de facto autonomy of their kingdoms not long after, and the displacement of Ovimbundu traders by the Portuguese forced these people to turn to cash-crop agriculture. (The men had hitherto had little involvement with cultivation; in fact, the women continued to be responsible for the cultivation of subsistence crops.)

The introduction of cash crops, particularly coffee, led to a series of changes in settlement patterns and social arrangements (see Structure of Society, this ch.). But after a time, soil exhaustion, lack of support of African agriculture by the colonial authorities, incursions of Portuguese settlers who took over valuable property in the highlands, and a number of other factors contributed to a decline in the success of Ovimbundu cash-crop agriculture. By the early 1960s, up to 100,000 Ovimbundu, estimated at one-quarter of the group's able-bodied adult males, were migrating on one-year and two-year labor contracts to the coffee plantations of Uíge and Cuanza Norte provinces; another 15,000 to 20,000 sought work in Luanda and Lobito; and roughly the same number worked in the industrial plants of Huambo or for European farmers in the Benguela Plateau. In most cases, remuneration was low, but these migrant workers had little alternative. This pattern continued through the remainder of the colonial period, except for those males who were involved in nationalist activity (usually with UNITA).

In the 1940s, the Ovimbundu organized what was probably the most closely knit Angolan community of the colonial era. With the financial and ideological aid of North American Christian missionaries, they established a network of Christian villages, each with its own leadership, schools, churches, and clinics. They were thus able to maintain the Ovimbundu culture while providing educational and social amenities for their children. The generation that emerged out of this structure became the disciples of Jonas Savimbi and the basis for UNITA, which in the 1980s used the same concepts to maintain Ovimbundu cohesiveness within UNITA-controlled areas.

Given the degree of change in Ovimbundu society and the involvement of the Ovimbundu with UNITA, it was difficult to determine their long-range role in Angolan politics. Just how long Ovimbundu solidarity would persist under changing circumstances could not be predicted.

Mbundu

Just north of Ovimbundu territory lived the Mbundu, the second largest ethnolinguistic category, whose language was Kimbundu. In 1988 they made up an estimated 25 percent of the Angolan population. In the sixteenth century, most of the groups that came to be known as Mbundu (a name apparently first applied by the neighboring Bakongo) lived well to the east of the coast in the plateau region (at a somewhat lower altitude than the Ovimbundu); a few groups in the far northeast lived at altitudes below 700 meters. In general, the outlines of the area occupied by the Mbundu had remained the same. The major exception was their expansion of this area to parts of the coast formerly occupied by Bakongo and others.

Although most of the boundaries of Mbundu territory remained fairly firm, the social and linguistic boundaries of the category had shifted, some of the peripheral groups having been variably influenced by neighboring groups and the groups close to the coast having been more strongly influenced by the Portuguese than were the more remote ones. Moreover, the subdivisions discernible for the sixteenth century (and perhaps earlier) also changed in response to a variety of social and linguistic influences in the colonial period. The Mbundu in general and the western Mbundu in particular, located as they were not far from Luanda, were susceptible to those influences for a longer time and in a more intense way than were other Angolan groups.

There were a number of Kimbundu dialects and groups. Two, each incorporating Portuguese terms, gradually became dominant, serving as lingua franca for many Mbundu. The western dialect was centered in Luanda, to which many Mbundu had migrated over the years. The people speaking it, largely urban, had come to call themselves Ambundu or Akwaluanda, thus distinguishing themselves from rural Mbundu. The eastern dialect, known as Ambakista, had its origins in the eighteenth century in a mixed Portuguese-Mbundu trading center at Ambaca near the western edge of the plateau region, but it spread in the nineteenth century through much of eastern Mbundu territory. Another Kimbundu-speaking group, the Dembos, were generally included in the Mbundu category. Living north of Luanda, they had also been strongly influenced by Kikongo speakers.

By the late 1960s, the Mbundu living in the cities, such as Luanda and Malanje, had adopted attributes of Portuguese life-style. Many had intermarried with Portuguese, which led to the creation of an entirely new class of *mestiços*. Those who received formal education and fully adopted Portuguese customs became *assimilados* (see Glossary).

The Mbundu were the MPLA's strongest supporters when the movement first formed in 1956. The MPLA's president, Agostinho Neto, was the son of a Mbundu Methodist pastor and a graduate of a Portuguese medical school. In the 1980s, the Mbundu were predominant in Luanda, Bengo, Cuanza Norte, Malanje, and northern Cuanza Sul provinces.

Bakongo

The Kikongo-speaking Bakongo made up an estimated 15 percent of the Angolan population. In 1988 the Bakongo were the third largest ethnolinguistic group in Angola. Concentrated in Uíge, Zaire, and Cabinda provinces, where they constituted a majority of the population, the Bakongo spilled over into the nation of Zaire (where they were the largest single ethnic group) and Congo. Although the Angolan city of São Salvador (renamed Mbanza Congo) was the capital of their ancient kingdom, most of the Bakongo were situated in Zaire.

Their former political unity long broken, the various segments of the ethnolinguistic category in Angola experienced quite different influences in the colonial period. The Bashikongo, living near the coast, had the most sustained interaction with the Portuguese but were less affected by participation in the coffee economy than the Sosso and Pombo, who were situated farther east and south. All three groups, however, were involved in the uprising of 1961. The Pombo, still farther east but close to the Zairian border, were much influenced by developments in the Belgian Congo (present-day Zaire), and a large contingent of Pombo living in Léopoldville (present-day Kinshasa) formed a political party in the

Children playing ware,
a traditional game
Courtesy UNICEF
(Maggie Murray-Lee)

early 1950s. The Solongo, dwelling on the relatively dry coastal plain, had little contact with the Portuguese. They and the Ashiluanda of the island of Luanda, to the south, were Angola's only African sea fishermen.

The Mayombe (also spelled Maiombe) of the mountain forests of Cabinda spoke a dialect of Kikongo but were not part of the ancient kingdom. That part of the Mayombe living in Zaire did join with the Zairian Bakongo in the Alliance of Bakongo (Alliance des Bakongo—Abako) during the period of party formation in the Belgian Congo, but the Cabindan Mayombe (and other Kikongo-speaking groups in the enclave), relatively remote geographically and culturally from the Bakongo of Angola proper, showed no solidarity with the latter. Instead, in 1961 the Mayombe formed a Cabindan separatist movement, the Alliance of Mayombe (Alliance de Mayombe—Alliama), which merged with two other Cabindan separatist movements in 1963 to form the Front for the Liberation of the Enclave of Cabinda (Frente para a Libertação do Enclave de Cabinda—FLEC).

One of the first major revolts of the nationalist struggle was instigated by Bakongo in March 1961 in the northwest. The Portuguese crushed the peasant attack, organized by the Bakongo group, the Union of Angolan Peoples (União das Populações de Angola—UPA), on their settlements, farms, and administrative outposts. Subsequently, 400,000 Bakongo fled into Zaire. In 1962 the UPA formed the National Front for the Liberation of Angola (Frente Nacional de Libertação de Angola—FNLA), which became one of the three major nationalist groups (the other two being the MPLA and UNITA) involved in the long and bloody war of independence. Most of the FNLA's traditional Bakongo constituency fled into exile in Zaire during the war. Following independence, however, many Bakongo exiles returned to their traditional homesteads in Angola. They had since retained their ethnolinguistic integrity.

Lunda-Chokwe

The hyphenated category Lunda-Chokwe constituted an estimated 8 percent of the Angolan population in 1988. As the hyphenation implies, the category comprises at least two subsets, the origins of which are known to be different, and the events leading to their inclusion in a single set are recent. The Lunda alone were a congeries of peoples brought together in the far-flung Lunda Empire (seventeenth century to nineteenth century) under the hegemony of a people calling themselves Ruund, its capital in the eastern section of Zaire's Katanga Province (present-day Shaba Region). Lunda is the form of the name used for the Ruund and for themselves by adjacent peoples to the south who came under Ruund domination. In some sources, the Ruund are called Northern Lunda, and their neighbors are called Southern Lunda. The most significant element of the latter, called Ndembu (or Ndembo), lived in Zaire and Zambia. In Angola the people with whom the northward-expanding Chokwe came into contact were chiefly Ruund speakers. The economic and political decline of the empire by the second half of the nineteenth century and the demarcation of colonial boundaries ended Ruund political domination over those elements beyond the Zairian borders.

The Chokwe, until the latter half of the nineteenth century a small group of hunters and traders living near the headwaters of the Cuango and Cassai rivers, were at the southern periphery of the Lunda Empire and paid tribute to its head. In the latter half of the nineteenth century, the Chokwe became increasingly involved in trading and raiding, and they expanded in all directions, but chiefly to the north, in part absorbing the Ruund and other peoples. In the late nineteenth century, the Chokwe went so far as to invade the capital of the much-weakened empire in Katanga. As a consequence of this Chokwe activity, a mixed population emerged in parts of Zaire as well as in Angola, although there were virtually homogeneous communities in both countries consisting of Chokwe, Ruund, or Southern Lunda.

The intermingling of Lunda (Ruund and Southern Lunda) and Chokwe, in which other smaller groups were presumably also caught up, continued until about 1920. It was only after that time that the mixture acquired the hyphenated label and its members began to think of themselves (in some contexts) as one people.

The languages spoken by the various elements of the so-called Lunda-Chokwe were more closely related to each other than to other Bantu languages in the Zairian-Angolan savanna but were by no means mutually intelligible. The three major tongues (Ruund, Lunda, and Chokwe) had long been distinct from each other, although some borrowing of words, particularly of Ruund political titles by the others, had occurred.

Portuguese anthropologists and some others accepting their work have placed some of the peoples (Minungu and Shinji) in this area with the Mbundu, and the Minungu language is sometimes considered a transitional one between Kimbundu and Chokwe. There may in fact have been important Mbundu influence on these two peoples, but the work of a number of linguists places their languages firmly with the set that includes Ruund, Lunda, and Chokwe.

Economic and political developments in the 1970s affected various sections of the Lunda-Chokwe differently. Substantial numbers of them live in or near Lunda Norte Province, which contains the principal diamond mines of Angola. Diamond mining had been significant since 1920, and preindependence data show that the industry employed about 18,000 persons. Moreover, the mining company provided medical and educational facilities for its employees and their dependents, thereby affecting even greater numbers. How many of those employed were Lunda-Chokwe is not clear, although neighboring villages would have been affected by the presence of the mining complex in any case (see Extractive Industries, ch. 3). In the intra-Angolan political conflict preceding and immediately following independence, there apparently was some division between the northern Lunda-Chokwe, especially those with some urban experience, who tended to support the MPLA, and the rural Chokwe, particularly those farther south, who tended to support UNITA. In the 1980s, as the UNITA insurgency intensified in the border areas of eastern and northern Angola, Lunda-Chokwe families were forced to flee into Zaire's Shaba Region, where many remained in 1988, living in three sites along the Benguela Railway. The impact of this move on the ethnolinguistic integrity of these people was not known.

A somewhat different kind of political impact began in the late 1960s, when refugees from Katanga in Zaire, speakers of Lunda or a related language, crossed the border into what are now Lunda Sul and northern Moxico provinces. In 1977 and 1978, these refugees and others whom they had recruited formed the National Front for the Liberation of the Congo (Front National pour la Libération du Congo—FNLC) and used the area as a base from which they launched their invasions of Shaba Region (see National Security Environment, ch. 5). In the 1980s, these rebels and perhaps still other refugees remained in Angola, many in Lunda Sul Province, although the Angolan government as part of its rapprochement with Zaire was encouraging them to return to their traditional homes. The Zairian government offered amnesty to political exiles on several occasions in the late 1980s and conferred with the Angolan government on the issue of refugees. In 1988, however, a significant number of Zairian refugees continued to inhabit Lunda-Chokwe territory. The significance for local Lunda-Chokwe of the presence and activities of these Zairians was not known.

Nganguela

Nganguela (also spelled Ganguela) is a term, pejorative in connotation, applied by the Ovimbundu to the peoples living east and southeast of them. The essentially independent groups constituting what was no more than a Portuguese census category was split by southward penetration of the Chokwe in the late nineteenth century and early twentieth century. Only two groups in the western section of the territory accepted the name Nganguela; the others carried names such as Lwena (or Lovale), Mbunda, and Luchazi—all in the eastern division. The Lwena and Luchazi, roughly equal in number, constituted about a third of the census category of Nganguela, which in 1988 accounted for an estimated 6 percent of the Angolan population.

Unlike the farming peoples who numerically dominated the larger ethnolinguistic categories, the groups in the western division of the Nganguela were cattle raisers as well as cultivators. Those in the eastern division near the headwaters of the Zambezi River and its tributaries also relied on fishing.

All the groups included in the Nganguela ethnolinguistic category spoke languages apparently related to those spoken by the Ruund, Southern Lunda, and Chokwe. Lwena and Chokwe, although not mutually intelligible, were probably more closely related than Chokwe was to Ruund or Lunda. Except for sections of the Lwena, during the time of kingdoms most of these peoples were outside the periphery of Lunda influence, and some (in the western division) were affected by Ovimbundu activity, including slave raiding.

Of the ethnolinguistic categories treated thus far, the Nganguela have had the least social or political significance in the past or in modern times. For the most part thinly scattered in an inhospitable territory, split by the southern expansion of the Chokwe, and lacking the conditions for even partial political centralization, let alone unification, the groups constituting the category went different ways when nationalist activity gave rise to political movements based in part on regional and ethnic considerations. The western division, adjacent to the Ovimbundu, was most heavily represented in the Ovimbundu-dominated UNITA. Some of the groups in the eastern divisions were represented in the MPLA–PT, which Mbundu and *mestiços* dominated, although the Lwena, neighbors of and related to the Chokwe, tended to support UNITA.

In the 1980s, the spread of the UNITA insurgency into the Nganuela-inhabited area adjacent to the Zambian border led to the flight of many Nganguela families into Zambia. The extent of this flight and its effects on the ethnolinguistic integrity of the Nganguela were unknown.

Ovambo, Nyaneka-Humbe, Herero, and Others

In far southwestern Angola, three categories of Bantu-speaking peoples have been distinguished. Two of them, the Ovambo and the Herero, were more heavily represented elsewhere: the Ovambo in Namibia and the Herero in Namibia and Botswana. The Herero dispersion, especially that section of it in Botswana, was the consequence of the migration of the Herero from German South West Africa (present-day Namibia) after their rebellion against German rule in 1906. The third group was the Nyaneka-Humbe. Unlike the other groups, the Nyaneka-Humbe did not disperse outside Angola. In 1988 the Nyaneka-Humbe (the first group is also spelled Haneca; the latter group is also spelled Nkumbi) constituted 3 percent of the population. The Ovambo, of which the largest subgroup were the Kwanhama (also spelled Kwanyama), made up an estimated 2 percent of the Angolan population. In the second half of the nineteenth century, the Kwanhama Kingdom of southern Angola was a powerful state involved in a lucrative trade relationship with the Portuguese, who, together with the Germans, occupied Kwanhama territory in the early twentieth century. In the 1980s, the Ovambo were seminomadic cattle herders and farmers. The Herero constituted no more than 0.5 percent of the population in 1988. Traditionally, the Herero were nomadic or seminomadic herders living in the arid coastal lowlands and in the mountainous escarpment to the east in Namibe, Benguela, and Huíla provinces. Many Herero migrated south to Namibia when the Portuguese launched a military expedition against them in 1940 following their refusal to pay taxes.

In the southeastern corner of the country, the Portuguese distinguished a set of Bantu-speaking people, described on a map prepared by José Redinha in 1973 as the Xindonga. The sole linguistic group listed in this category was the Cussu. The *Language Map of Africa,* prepared under the direction of David Dalby for the International African Institute, noted two sets of related languages in southeastern Angola. The first set included Liyuwa, Mashi, and North Mbukushu. These languages and other members of the set were also found in Zambia and Namibia. The members of the second set, Kwangali-Gcikuru and South Mbukushu, were also found in Namibia and Botswana. The hyphen between Kwangali and Gcikuru implies mutual intelligibility. Little is known of these groups; in any case, their members were very few.

All of these southern Angolan groups relied in part or in whole on cattle raising for subsistence. Formerly, the Herero were exclusively herders, but they gradually came to engage in some cultivation. Although the Ovambo had depended in part on cultivation for a much longer time, dairy products had been an important source of subsistence, and cattle were the chief measure of wealth and prestige.

The southwestern groups, despite their remoteness from the major centers of white influence during most of the colonial period, were to varying degrees affected by the colonial presence and, after World War II, by the arrival of numbers of Portuguese in such places as Moçâmedes (present-day Namibe) and Sá da Bandeira (present-day Lubango). The greatest resistance to the Portuguese was offered by the Ovambo, who were not made fully subject to colonial rule until 1915 and who earned a considerable reputation among the Portuguese and other Africans for their efforts to maintain their independence. In the nationalist struggle of the 1960s and early 1970s and in the postindependence civil war, the Ovambo tended to align themselves with the Ovimbundu-dominated UNITA. Many also sympathized with the cause of SWAPO, a mostly Ovambo organization fighting to liberate Namibia from South African rule.

Hunters, Gatherers, Herders, and Others

Scattered throughout the lower third of Angola, chiefly in the drier areas, were small bands of people. Until the twentieth century, most of them were nomadic hunters and gatherers, although some engaged in herding, either in addition to their other subsistence activities or as their chief means of livelihood. Those who survived turned, at least in part, to cultivation.

The bands living a nomadic or seminomadic life in Cuando Cubango Province (and occasionally reaching as far east as the upper Cunene River) differed physically and linguistically from their sedentary Bantu-speaking neighbors. Short, saffron-colored, and in other respects physically unlike the Nganguela, Ovambo, and Nyaneka-Humbe, they spoke a language of the !Xu-Angola or Maligo set of tongues referred to as Khoisan or Click languages (the exclamation point denotes a specific kind of click), whose precise relations to each other are not yet fully understood by observers.

Several other hunting and gathering or herding groups, the members of which were taller and otherwise physically more like the local Bantu speakers, lived farther west, adjacent to the Ovambo and Herero. These people spoke Bantu languages and were less nomadic than the Khoisan speakers, but they were clearly different from the Ovambo and Herero and probably preceded them in the area.

Mestiços

In 1960 a little more than 1 percent of the total population of Angola consisted of *mestiços*. It has been estimated that by 1970 these people constituted perhaps 2 percent of the population. Some *mestiços* left at independence, but the departure of much greater numbers of Portuguese probably resulted in an increase in the proportion of *mestiços* in the Angolan total. In 1988 *mestiços* probably continued to number about 2 percent of the Angolan population.

The process of mixing started very early and continued until independence. But it was not until about 1900, when the number of Portuguese in Angola was very small and consisted almost entirely of males, that the percentage of *mestiços* in the population exceeded the percentage of whites (see The Demographic Situation, ch. 1).

After a number of generations, the antecedents of many *mestiços* became mixed to the extent that the Portuguese felt a need to establish a set of distinctions among them. Many *mestiços* accepted this system as a means of social ranking. One source suggests that the term *mestiço* used alone in a social context applied specifically to the offspring of a mulatto and a white; the term *mestiço cabrito* referred to the descendant of a union between two mulattos; and the term *mestiço cafuso* was applied to the child of a union between a mulatto and a black African. It is possible that an even more complex set of distinctions was sometimes used.

Most *mestiços* were urban dwellers and had learned to speak Portuguese either as a household language or in school. Although some of the relatively few rural *mestiços* lived like the Africans among whom they dwelt, most apparently achieved the status of *assimilados,* the term applied before 1961 to those nonwhites who fulfilled certain specific requirements and were therefore registered as Portuguese citizens.

With some exceptions, *mestiços* tended to identify with Portuguese culture, and their strongly voiced opposition over the years to the conditions imposed by the colonial regime stressed their rights to a status equivalent to that of whites. Before World War II, only occasionally did *mestiço* intellectuals raise their voices on behalf of the African population. Thus, despite the involvement of *mestiços* in the nationalist struggle beginning in 1961 and their very important role in the upper echelons of the government and party, significant segments of the African population tended to resent them. This legacy continued in the late 1980s because *mestiços* dominated the MPLA–PT hierarchy.

Starting in the late 1970s, an average of 50,000 Cuban troops and civilian technical personnel (the overwhelming majority of whom were male) were stationed in Angola. As a result, a portion of the nation's younger population was undoubtedly of mixed African and Cuban descent. This new category of racial mixture, however, had not been described by researchers as of late 1988, and no figures existed on how many Angolans might fall into this category.

Structure of Society

The most pervasive influences on the structure of Angolan society in the late 1980s were the Marxist-Leninist policies of the government and increased militarization to counter the UNITA insurgency. Based on the principle that the party, the working class, and the worker-peasant alliance played a leading role in society, Marxist-Leninist policies were applied in the late 1970s to every sector of society and the economy, affecting the lives of urban and rural inhabitants alike. Direct military actions had the greatest effect on those living in the central and southern provinces, causing large displacements of whole groups of people and the creation of a substantial refugee population in Zambia and Zaire. Moreover, thousands of young men and women were conscripted into the Angolan armed forces, while many thousands of older citizens served in militias and civil defense units (see War and the Role of the Armed Forces in Society, ch. 5). In regard to the direct effects of war, press reports in 1988 estimated that since 1975 the insurgency had claimed from 60,000 to 90,000 lives and had orphaned an estimated 10,000 children. The U.S. Committee for Refugees reported that by 1988 about 20,000 Angolans, mostly women and children, had been crippled by mines buried in rural fields and roads.

Social Structure in Rural Communities

The crucial social units in rural systems were villages (or other forms of local community) and groups based on common descent, actual or putative. These were basic entities, even if subject to change in form and function in the period preceding the Portuguese incursion and during the centuries when Portugal exercised only indirect influence in the interior. Throughout these hundreds of years, changes in the structure of rural political and economic systems had their impact on rural communities and kin groups, but rural community organization and the organization of kin groups, often linked, remained the most significant elements in the lives of ordinary Africans.

In general, the connection between a rural community and a descent group (or some other kin-based set of persons) lay in the fact that the core of each community consisted of a descent group of some kind. Others in the community were tied to the members of the group by marriage or, in an earlier period, by a slave or client relationship, the effects of which may well have survived the formal abolition of slavery, as they have elsewhere. Typically, neighboring villages were tied together either because their core groups were made up of members of related descent groups (or different segments of a larger descent group) or, in some cases, by fairly frequent intermarriage among members of a limited set of villages.

Traditionally, descent groups in Angola are matrilineal; that is, they include all persons descended from a common female ancestor through females, although the individuals holding authority are, with rare exceptions, males. In some cases, junior males inherit from (or succeed to a position held by) older brothers; in others, males inherit from their mother's brother. Patrilineal descent groups, whose members are descended from a male ancestor through males, apparently have occurred in only a few groups in Angola and have been reported only in conjunction with matrilineal groups, a comparatively rare phenomenon referred to as a double descent system.

It must be emphasized that even where double descent systems did not exist, kin traced through the father were important as individuals in systems in which group formation was based on matrilineal descent. In some cases, the Bakongo for example, an individual would be tied through his father to the latter's matrilineage, appropriate members of which have an important say in aspects of that individual's life.

Broadly speaking, matrilineal descent groups alone have been reported for the Bakongo (but are well described only for some of the Zairian Bakongo), the Mbundu, the Chokwe, and the Ovambo, but their occurrence is probable elsewhere. A double descent system has been reported for Angola's largest ethnolinguistic group, the Ovimbundu, and might also be found among some of the southern groups.

The structure and workings of the double descent system of the Ovimbundu had not been adequately described as of 1988. In any case, ethnographic studies made in the middle of the twentieth century suggest that patrilineal groups as such (as opposed to links with the father and some of his kin) had virtually disappeared and that matrilineal groups had, by and large, lost most of their significance as a result of major changes in patterns of economic activity.

Descent groups vary in size, degree of localization, function, and degree of internal segmentation. In the kinds of groups commonly called clans, the links between a putative common ancestor and the living cannot be traced, and no effort is made to do so. Such groups are larger in scope than the units into which they are divided, although they need not have many members in absolute terms. They are rarely localized, and their members may be widely dispersed. Clans have not been widely reported in Angola. The only large ethnic category in which they have been said to exist is the Bakongo. Even among the Bakongo, the clans do not seem to have had political or economic functions.

More typical of traditional Angolan communities have been the kinds of descent groups usually called lineages, in most cases matrilineages. Among such descent groups, the common ancestor is not so remote, and genealogical links can be traced to her. Structurally, lineages of greater depth (for example, those five to seven generations in depth from ancestor to most recent generation) may be further segmented into shallower lineages (perhaps three to four generations in depth), lineages at each level having different functions. This structure seems to have been the case among the Bakongo. There, the deeper unit controlled the allocation of land and performed tasks connected with that crucial function, whereas shallower lineages controlled matters such as marriage.

Another important aspect of rural community life was the role of traditional leaders. After the outbreak of African opposition to colonial rule in the early 1960s, most local leaders were, if not loyal to the Portuguese, reluctant to support the nationalist movements.

The MPLA, in particular, was urban based and therefore had little contact with local leaders in rural areas. Following independence, however, and most markedly in the 1980s, the government recognized the necessity of gaining the support of rural peasants to counter the spreading influence of UNITA. Thus, party officials began appointing local leaders to district or local committees, thereby reassigning to them a significant role in the local political hierarchy.

Ovimbundu Social Structure

Before the twentieth century, neither matrilineage nor patrilineage dominated Ovimbundu society. Economic matters, such as property rights, seem to have been linked to the matrilineage, while political authority was passed through the patrilineage. The lineage system declined in the twentieth century, as more and more Europeans settled on the highly arable plateau. The results were land shortage and commercialization that loosened the control either lineage system might have over what had become the primary resource in the Ovimbundu economy. By the mid-1950s, terms formerly used for the patrilineal and matrilineal descent groups were still heard, but they no longer referred to a cohesive group. They were applied instead to individual patrilineal and matrilineal relatives. Significantly, the Portuguese term *família* had also come into use by this time.

The development of cash-crop agriculture and changes in land tenure, in combination with inadequate soils and Ovimbundu agricultural techniques, led to soil depletion and the need by nuclear families for increasingly extensive holdings. Nucleated villages, consequently, became less and less feasible.

Increasingly, particularly in the coffee-growing area, the homestead was no longer part of the nucleated village, although dispersed homesteads in a given area were defined as constituting a village. The degree of dispersal varied, but the individual family, detached from the traditional community, tended to become the crucial unit. Where either Protestants or Roman Catholics were sufficiently numerous, the church and school rather than the descent group became the focus of social and sometimes of political life. In at least one study of a section of the Ovimbundu, it was found that each entity defined as a village consisted almost exclusively of either Protestants or Roman Catholics (see Christianity, this ch.).

But given the problems of soil depletion and, in some areas, of land shortage, not all Ovimbundu could succeed as cash-crop farmers. A substantial number of them thus found it necessary to go to other regions (and even other countries) as wage workers. Consequently, some households came to consist of women and children for long periods.

In 1967 the colonial authorities, concerned by the political situation east of the Ovimbundu and fearing the spread of rebellion to the plateau regions, gathered the people into large villages to control them better and, in theory at least, to provide better social and economic services (see Angolan Insurgency, ch. 1). The Ovimbundu, accustomed to dispersed settlement, strongly resented the practice. Among other things, they feared that the land they were forced to abandon would be taken over by Europeans (which in some cases did happen).

By 1970 compulsory resettlement had been abolished in part of Ovimbundu territory and reduced elsewhere. Then the Portuguese instituted a rural advisory service and encouraged the formation of what they called agricultural clubs. The old term for matrilineal descent group was sometimes applied to these organizations, which were intended to manage credits for Ovimbundu peasants. These units, however, were based on common interest, although traces of kin connections sometimes affected their operation, as did the relations between ordinary Ovimbundu and local rulers. Moreover, conflict within the group often took the form of accusations of sorcery. The effects on these units of independence, the stripping away of the advisory service, and the early years of the UNITA insurgency were unknown. It is unlikely, however, that the Ovimbundu took to enforced cooperation or collectivization easily.

The effects of the UNITA insurgency on Ovimbundu life were extensive and frequently devastating. Much of the fighting between government troops and UNITA forces, especially in the 1980s, took place on Ovimbundu-occupied territory. Largely dependent on agriculture, Ovimbundu village life was seriously disrupted, and large numbers of Ovimbundu were forced to flee, abandoning their traditions along with their homes.

As UNITA gained control over a growing area in southeast Angola, however, the organization tried to preserve the integrity of Ovimbundu life-style and customs (see fig. 16). UNITA established a series of military bases throughout the southeast that served as administrative centers for the surrounding regions. Under Ovimbundu leadership, the bases provided educational, social, economic, and health services to the population, operating much like the village system on the central plateau. To what extent this system preserved at least some aspects of Ovimbundu traditional life in the late 1980s was unknown.

Mbundu Social Structure

Among the Mbundu, the matrilineage survived centuries of change in other institutions. Membership in and loyalty to it was

Villagers pumping water from an uncontaminated well
Courtesy UNICEF (Maggie Murray-Lee)

of great importance. The lineage supported the individual in material and nonmaterial ways because most land was lineage domain, access to it required lineage membership, and communication between the living and their ancestors, crucial to traditional religion, was mediated through the lineage.

The Mbundu lineage differed from Bakongo and Ovimbundu groups in its underlying theory; it consisted not of individuals but of statuses or titles filled by living persons. In this system, a Mbundu could move from one status to another, thus acquiring a different set of relationships. How, in fact, this theoretical system affected interpersonal relationships between biological kin has not been described, however.

The Mbundu matrilineage was in some respects a dispersed unit, but a core group maintained a lineage village to which its members returned, either at a particular stage in their lives or for brief visits. Women went to the villages of their husbands, and their children were raised there. The girls, as their mothers had done, then joined their own husbands. The young men, however, went to the lineage village to join their mothers' brothers. The mothers' brothers and their sisters' sons formed the more or less permanent core of the lineage community, visited from time to time by the women of the lineage who, as they grew old, might come to live the rest of their lives there. After a time, when the senior mother's brother

85

who headed the matrilineage died, some of the younger men would go off to found their own villages. A man then became the senior male in a new lineage, the members of which would be his sisters and his sisters' sons. One of these younger men might, however, remain in the old village and succeed the senior mother's brother in the latter's status and take on his role completely, thus perpetuating the older lineage. According to one account, the functioning lineage probably has a genealogical depth of three to four generations: a man, his sister's adult sons, and the latter's younger but married sister's sons. How this unit encompasses the range of statuses characteristic of the matrilineage in Mbundu theory is not altogether clear.

Social Structure in Urban Areas

Whatever the kind and degree of change in the workings of lineage and community in rural Angola, research in the *musseques* of Luanda showed that the lineage system had little significance there. *Musseques* are settlements in and around Luanda (and some of the other big towns) in which many of the urban poor live. Residents of the settlements in Luanda were predominantly of Mbundu origin. In the 1980s, the settlements became the refuge of hundreds of thousands of displaced persons.

Some of the inhabitants of the *musseques* worked regularly in manual jobs, but others were employed only intermittently, and still others would go jobless for long periods. The variation in the material circumstances of males in particular affected the composition of the households. Ideally, and often in fact, the household consisted of a man and a woman, living in a union legally or otherwise sanctioned, and their children. Occasionally, another kinsman or kinswoman was part of the unit. In the 1980s, with the influx of the rural displaced, additional kin or acquaintances were probably also becoming part of many of the family units.

The man was expected to assume the primary responsibility for supporting the household and to provide, if possible, for the education of the children, although others sometimes contributed. Given the economic circumstances of most of these men, the burden sometimes became overwhelming, and some men reacted by leaving the household. This reaction accounted, with some exceptions, for the presence of female heads of households.

In the 1980s, an important effect of extended kinship ties was the expectation of migrants from rural areas that they could turn first to their kin already in place for at least temporary housing and other aid. The tendency was to look to heads of households who were of the same matrilineage, but that practice was not universal. Moreover, it did not signify that the matrilineage had been transplanted to the *musseques*. The relationship between the head of the household and the newly arrived migrant was that between two individuals. The urban situation did not provide the conditions for the functioning of the matrilineage as a social, political, and economic unit.

Given the combination of the nuclear family household, the absence of matrilineages, and the relative ethnic homogeneity of the *musseques* of Luanda, the organization of permanent or temporary groups engaged in social or political activity and the formation of interpersonal relationships were likely to be based directly on economic concerns or on other common interests arising out of the urban situation. Elsewhere, such concerns and interests were often mediated by or couched in terms of considerations of ethnicity or kinship.

Effects of Socialist Policies

Beginning in late 1977 with the First Party Congress of the MPLA, at which the conversion of the MPLA to a vanguard party was announced, party leaders attempted to define the kind of society and economy they wished to develop. The process of definition was by no means systematic and often simply drew on Marxist-Leninist clichés borrowed from the Soviet model. Nevertheless, from time to time statements of either purpose or criticism focused on specific features and problems of Angolan society as these leaders saw them. Sometimes, the solutions offered appeared to have conflicting implications.

Running through the statements of leaders and editorials in Angola's largest newspaper, *Jornal de Angola,* and other party and state publications were frequent and strong references to the need to eliminate all signs of ethnicity, regionalism, and racism. On several occasions, the statements and editorials asserted that ethnicity and regionalism were not the same, but their differences were not spelled out. Because there is a link between ethnolinguistic category and location, the differential effects on behavior of ethnicity and regionalism are often difficult to determine.

At the same time that the party cautioned against racism (the reference is to *mestiços* and to those Portuguese who remained in Angola after independence), it also discouraged attitudes of superiority. Presumably, this was an allusion not only to the preindependence attitudes of Portuguese and *mestiços* but also to those of urban, educated Africans, who would in former times have been called *assimilados*. In fact, it is unlikely that the Portuguese in the party would act in the style of the Portuguese colonial official or settler,

87

but some *mestiços,* uncommitted ideologically, might act in such a way; educated Africans, secure in their racial situation, were even more likely to exhibit a sense of superiority to ordinary Africans. The sensitivity of the party to popular perceptions about racism and attitudes of superiority was partly responsible for attempts in the 1980s by the dos Santos regime to remove from the top party echelons a number of *mestiços,* who dominated the party structure, and replace them with a more ethnically diverse group (see Political Environment, ch. 4).

In the 1980s, there was a significant shift of attitude on the part of government and party officials toward private enterprise and what the party had previously labeled "petite bourgeoisie." In the 1970s, the term was widely and pejoratively used to discourage individuals from activities in which they could accumulate personal wealth. Although self-aggrandizement was still discouraged, the party recognized that economic and agricultural centralization had failed as development strategies and that movement toward private enterprise would be necessary to boost domestic production, increase the supply of goods available to the Angolan population, and generally improve the economic picture.

The implications of these policy changes for the structure of society, including economic support for individual peasant farmers and an increase in the role of private traders, were extensive. Where the party once discouraged the existence of an entrepreneurial bourgeoisie both in urban and in rural Angola, some observers believed that efforts to develop the country and come to grips with its economic and technical problems might generate not only a bureaucratic middle class and elite but also a business middle class less amenable to control than a salaried state bourgeoisie.

Policies Affecting Rural Society

Prior to independence, most peasants engaged in subsistence farming and cattle herding, whereas commercial farms and plantations, which produced most of the cash crops, were owned and operated primarily by Portuguese settlers. Although most farmers and herders consumed most of what they produced, those who did market some of their output depended on Portuguese bush traders. A barter system developed through which agricultural produce was exchanged for agricultural supplies and consumer goods from the cities. This entire system collapsed with the sudden departure of the Portuguese farmers and bush traders at independence.

The government acted immediately by transforming the abandoned commercial farms into state farms, all of which were large

Homeless children on a street in Luanda
Courtesy UNICEF (Maggie Murray-Lee)

and understaffed. The lack of personnel with managerial and technical skills, the breakdown of machinery, and the unwillingness of peasants to work for wages soon eroded the experiment in nationalization, and by the early 1980s much of the land was appropriated for individual family farming.

The government proceeded cautiously in its dealings with the peasants, recognizing that productivity had to take priority over ideology. Thus, instead of immediately collectivizing land, the government formed farming cooperatives, but this too failed because of the government's inability to replace the function of the Portuguese bush traders, despite the establishment of a barter system managed by two state companies (see Agriculture, ch. 3). By the early 1980s, most peasants, having never received from the state any promised goods, returned to subsistence farming and their traditional way of life.

A shift in agricultural policy began in 1984 that may have provided the basis for a fundamental change in rural life in the future. The goal was to restore a flow of farm surplus products to urban areas and reduce dependence on imports. Along with the dissolution of the state farms, the government began setting up agricultural development stations to provide assistance to farmers in the form of technical advice, equipment, and seeds and fertilizer. In 1988 these measures were gradually reversing the decline

89

in agricultural production for the market in the few provinces unaffected by the UNITA insurgency.

Policies Affecting Urban Society

Many of the difficult economic conditions existing in Angola's cities and towns were the result of the UNITA insurgency, including the almost total disruption of the transportation system necessary to carry produce from rural to urban areas. However, by the late 1980s the government had recognized that much could be blamed on the cumbersome and ineffective mechanisms of the centralized economy (see Role of the Government, ch. 3). In 1988 the government, faced with the continuing decline of the manufacturing sector, began to move away from state-controlled companies and promised to enact new laws that would make private ownership possible.

The impact of the changes in economic policy were not immediately apparent in Luanda in 1988. The only two sources of goods for the capital's population were rationed and poorly stocked state stores and the parallel market, where the local currency was accepted at only a fraction of its face value. Many foreign businesses were giving their Angolan employees credit at a government supermarket where they could buy food. Some foreign businesses set up their own stores in which their employees could shop. The largest parallel market operation in Luanda, Roque Santeiro, was only one of many that depended on European shipments for products such as clothing, watches, medicine, and tape players, as well as food. There was some indication that goods were also bought by insiders at state stores and resold at many times the price in the parallel market. Despite official rhetoric, the government recognized its inability to provide basic goods to the population and seldom interfered with parallel market activities.

Physical living conditions in Luanda were deplorable in 1988. The elegant marble apartment buildings that lined the city's downtown streets during the colonial era had become slums with neither running water nor electricity. Even most of those able to afford luxuries were living without basic conveniences or amenities; evening activities, such as cultural events or dining out, were rare. And because of a lack of spare parts, there were few taxis or other means of transportation.

Role of Women and Children

Almost no research existed on the role of women and children in Angolan society in the late 1980s, but a few generalities could be drawn. In rural Angola, as in many African economies, most of the population engaged in agricultural activities. Women performed much of the agricultural labor, as did children of both sexes. Marriage generally involved family, political, and economic interests as well as personal considerations. The household was the most important unit of production and was usually composed of several generations. The women grew and prepared most of the food for the household and performed all other domestic work. Because of their major role in food production, women shared relatively equal status with men, who spent much of their time hunting or tending cattle.

Many women and children belonged to two mass organizations: the Organization of Angolan Women (Organização da Mulher Angolana—OMA) and the Popular Movement for the Liberation of Angola-Youth Movement (Juventude do Movimento Popular de Libertação de Angola—JMPLA). Before independence, the OMA and JMPLA were instrumental in mobilizing political support for the MPLA among thousands of Angolan refugees. After independence, and especially after the creation of the MPLA–PT in 1977, the mass organizations came under the strict control of the party and were given the role of intermediaries between the MPLA–PT and the population.

In 1987 the OMA had a membership of 1.3 million women, most of whom lived in rural areas. Among the many contributions of OMA's members were the establishment of literacy programs and service in health and social service organizations (see Mass Organizations and Interest Groups, ch. 4). Most OMA members, however, were poor and unemployed. In 1988 only 10 percent of MPLA–PT members were women, although more women were finding jobs in teaching and professions from which they had been excluded in the past.

The JMPLA, which claimed a membership of 72,000 teenagers and students in 1988, became the only route to party membership after 1977. JMPLA members were required to participate in the Directorate of People's Defense and Territorial Troops, formerly the People's Defense Organization (Organização de Defesa Popular—ODP), and political study groups. The relatively small size of the organization, however, was indicative of the difficulty the government faced in recruiting young people from rural areas.

Effects of the Insurgency

The UNITA insurgency had a far greater impact on Angola's social fabric than the government's socialist policies. Hundreds of thousands of displaced persons were forced not only to seek refuge in towns and military protected resettlement areas but also to disrupt traditional life-styles. Intensive military recruitment drained urban and rural areas of much of the young adult male population as well. UNITA frequently reported avoidance of government military conscription and battlefield desertions, and its spokespersons also claimed in late 1988 that large numbers of teachers in rural areas had been recruited by the government, depleting the schools of trained instructors. It was not clear to what extent, if any, this disruption changed the social order in families, or if village social structures remained intact.

Another significant influence on the population caused by the UNITA insurgency was the emphasis on defense. Two militia forces were created: the ODP in 1975 (renamed the Directorate of People's Defense and Territorial Troops in 1985), and the People's Vigilance Brigades (Brigadas Populares de Vigilância—BPV) in 1984 (see War and the Role of the Armed Forces in Society; Internal Security Forces and Organization, ch. 5). The Directorate of People's Defense and Territorial Troops, operating as a back-up force to the Angolan armed forces, had both armed and un-armed units dispersed throughout the country in villages to protect the population from UNITA attacks. Although the Directorate of People's Defense and Territorial Troops had an estimated 50,000 official members in 1988, as many as 500,000 men and women may have been participating in reserve functions. The BPV, organized more as a mass organization than as a branch of the armed forces, had an estimated 1.5 million members in 1987. Designed to function in urban areas, the BPV had broader responsibilities than the Directorate of People's Defense and Territorial Troops, including political and military training of the population and detection of criminal activities.

The consequences of war-related economic failure also disrupted Angolan society profoundly. The government had been compelled to expend enormous economic and human resources to fight UNITA, denying the population basic goods and services as well as diverting those with the skills badly needed for national development into military positions. The toll was heaviest among children, who suffered the most from substandard health conditions and the underfunded and understaffed school system. The insurgency also contributed heavily to underproduction in the agricultural sector, resulting in dangerous food shortages, especially in rural areas, and in the country's dependence on external food sources.

Religious Life

The attitude of the Angolan government toward religion was inconsistent. The MPLA–PT's strong commitment to Marxism-

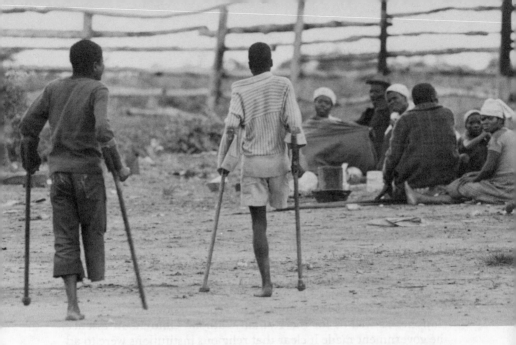

Young victims of the insurgency
Courtesy International Committee of the Red Cross (Yannick Müller)

Leninism meant that its attitude toward religion, at least officially, corresponded to that of the traditional Soviet Marxist-Leninist dogma, which generally characterized religion as antiquated and irrelevant to the construction of a new society. The government also viewed religion as an instrument of colonialism because of the Roman Catholic Church's close association with the Portuguese. Furthermore, because membership in the party was the road to influence, party leaders and many of the cadres were likely to have no formal religious commitment, or at any rate to deny having one (even though most of Angola's leaders in the 1980s were educated at Catholic, Baptist, or Congregational mission schools). Nonetheless, the government acknowledged the prevalence of religion in Angolan societies and officially recognized the equality of all religions, tolerating religious practices as long as the churches restricted themselves to spiritual matters. The state, however, did institute certain specific controls over religious organizations, and it was prepared to act quickly when it felt that it was challenged by the acts of a specific group. Thus, in early 1978 the MPLA–PT Political Bureau ordered the registration of "legitimate" churches and religious organizations. Although priests and missionaries were permitted to stay in the country as foreign residents and although religious groups or churches could receive goods from abroad, further construction of new churches without a permit was forbidden.

A conflict developed in the late 1970s between the government and the Roman Catholic Church. In December 1977, the bishops of Angola's three archdioceses, meeting in Lubango, drafted a pastoral letter subsequently read to all churches that claimed frequent violations of religious freedom. Their most specific complaint was that the establishment of a single system of education ignored the rights of parents. They also objected to the government's systematic atheistic propaganda and its silencing of the church's radio station in 1976. In response to charges of government meddling in religious affairs, President Neto issued a decree in January 1978 stating that there was complete separation between church and religious institutions. In addition, *Jornal de Angola* printed an attack on the bishops, accusing them of questioning the integrity of the Angolan revolutionary process.

The outcome of the conflict had repercussions for Protestant churches as well as for the Roman Catholic Church. In essence, the government made it clear that religious institutions were to adhere to government and party rulings regarding nonreligious issues.

In the late 1980s, there was a slight change in the government's policy toward religion. The president and others in the government and party elites, recognizing that political opposition had not coalesced around religious leaders, became less fearful of religious opposition and therefore more tolerant of religious groups in general. One exception was the Our Lord Jesus Christ Church in the World, an independent Christian sect founded in 1949 by Simon Mtoko (also spelled Simão Toco). Mtoko, a Protestant from Uíge Province, fashioned the sect after the Kimbanguist movement (not to be confused with traditional *kimbanda* practices, which had arisen in the Belgian Congo in the 1920s; see Indigenous Religious Systems, this ch.). The government had been especially suspicious of the Mtokoists because of their strong support in Benguela Province, most of whose residents were Ovimbundu, the principal supporters of UNITA. Mtokoists also were involved in riots in the Catate region of Bengo Province and in Luanda at the end of 1986, and they attacked a prison in Luanda in 1987 in an attempt to free fellow believers who had been arrested in the 1986 riots. As a result, the government banned the sect, claiming that its members had used religion to attack the state and had therefore lost their legitimacy. Subsequently, however, as part of the general relaxation of its policy on religion, the government softened its position on the sect and in March 1988 declared it a legal religion.

Christianity

Religious affiliation in Angola was difficult to define because many who claimed membership in a specific Christian denomination also shared perceptions of the natural and supernatural order characteristic of indigenous religious systems. Sometimes the Christian sphere of the life of a community was institutionally separate from the indigenous sphere. In other cases, the local meaning and practice of Christianity were modified by indigenous patterns of belief and practice.

Although Roman Catholic missions were largely staffed by non-Portuguese during the colonial era, the relevant statutes and accords provided that foreign missionaries could be admitted only with the approval of the Portuguese government and the Vatican and on condition that they be integrated with the Portuguese missionary organization. Foreign Roman Catholic missionaries were required to renounce the laws of their own country, submit to Portuguese law, and furnish proof of their ability to speak and write the Portuguese language correctly. Missionary activity was placed under the authority of Portuguese priests. All of this was consistent with the Colonial Act of 1930, which advanced the view that Portuguese Catholic missions overseas were "instruments of civilization and national influence." In 1940 the education of Africans was declared the exclusive responsibility of missionary personnel. All church activities, education included, were to be subsidized by the state. In reality, Protestant missions were permitted to engage in educational activity, but without subsidy and on condition that Portuguese be the language of instruction (see Education, this ch.).

The important Protestant missions in place in the 1960s (or their predecessors) had arrived in Angola in the late nineteenth century and therefore had been at work before the Portuguese managed to establish control over the entire territory. Their early years, therefore, were little affected by Portuguese policy and practice. Before the establishment of the New State (Estado Novo) in Portugal in 1926, the authorities kept an eye on the Protestant missions but were not particularly hostile to them (see Angola under the New State, ch. 1). Settlers and local administrators often were hostile, however, because Protestant missionaries tended to be protective of what they considered their charges. In those early years and later, Protestant missionaries were not only evangelists but also teachers, healers, and counselors—all perhaps in a paternal fashion but in ways that involved contact with Africans in a more sustained fashion than was characteristic of Roman Catholic missionaries and local administrators.

Protestant missionaries worked at learning the local languages, in part to communicate better with those in their mission field, but above all in order to translate the Old Testament and the New Testament into African tongues. Protestant missionaries were much more likely than administrators and settlers to know a local language. Roman Catholic missionaries did not similarly emphasize the translation of the Bible and, with some exceptions, did not make a point of learning a Bantu language.

Because specific Protestant denominations were associated with particular ethnic communities, the structure of religious organization was linked to the structure of these communities. This connection was brought about in part by the tendency of entire communities to turn to the variety of Protestantism offered locally. The conversion of isolated individuals was rare. Those individuals who did not become Christians remained to a greater or lesser extent adherents of the indigenous system; unless they migrated to one of the larger towns, persons of a specific locality did not have the option of another kind of Christianity. Those members of a community who had not yet become Christians were tied by kinship and propinquity to those individuals who had. On the one hand, indigenous patterns of social relations affected church organization; on the other hand, the presence of Christians in the community affected the local culture to varying degrees. Christians who could quote Scripture in the local tongue contributed phrases to it that others picked up, and the attributes of the Christian God as interpreted by the specific denomination sometimes became attached to the high god of the indigenous religious system and typically made that deity more prominent than previously.

The involvement of the Protestant churches in the languages of their mission areas, their medical and other welfare activity, and their ability to adapt to local structures or (in the case of the Methodists among the Mbundu) to be fortuitously consistent with them gave Protestants much more influence than their numbers would suggest. For example, the leaders of the three major nationalist movements in the 1970s—the MPLA, UNITA, and the FNLA—had been raised as Protestants, and many others in these movements were also Protestants, even if their commitment may have diminished over time.

Estimates of the number of Roman Catholics in Angola varied. One source claimed that about 55 percent of the population in 1985 was Roman Catholic; another put the proportion in 1987 at 68 percent. Most Roman Catholics lived in western Angola, not only because that part of the country was the most densely populated but also because Portuguese penetration into the far interior was comparatively recent and Roman Catholic missionaries tended to follow the flag. The most heavily Roman Catholic area before independence was Cabinda Province, where most of the people were Bakongo. Bakongo in Angola proper were not quite so heavily

Roman Catholic, and Protestantism was very influential there. There was a substantial proportion of Roman Catholics among the Mbundu in Luanda and Cuanza Norte provinces. Less heavily Catholic were the Ovimbundu-populated provinces of Benguela and Huambo, although the city of Huambo had been estimated to be two-thirds Catholic. In the southern and eastern districts, the proportion of Roman Catholics dropped considerably.

The proportion of Protestants in the Angolan population was estimated at 10 percent to 20 percent in the late 1980s. The majority of them presumably were Africans, although some *mestiços* may have been affiliated with one or another Protestant church.

The government recognized eleven Protestant denominations: the Assembly of God, the Baptist Convention of Angola, the Baptist Evangelical Church of Angola, the Congregational Evangelical Church of Angola, the Evangelical Church of Angola, the Evangelical Church of South-West Angola, the Our Lord Jesus Christ Church in the World (Kimbanguist), the Reformed Evangelical Church of Angola, the Seventh-Day Adventist Church, the Union of Evangelical Churches of Angola, and the United Methodist Church.

In the late 1980s, statistics on Christian preferences among ethnic groups were unavailable, but proportions calculated from the 1960 census probably had not changed significantly. According to the 1960 census, about 21 percent of the Ovimbundu were Protestants, but later estimates suggest a smaller percentage. The sole Protestant group active among the Mbundu was the Methodist Mission, largely sponsored by the Methodist Episcopal Church of the United States. Portuguese data for 1960 indicated that only 8 percent of the Mbundu considered themselves Protestants, but Protestant missions had considerable success among the Dembos. As many as 35 percent of the Bakongo were considered Protestants by the official religious census of 1960, with Baptists being the most numerous.

In addition to the Protestant churches directly generated by the missions and continuing in a more or less orthodox pattern, there were other groups, which stemmed at least in part from the Protestant experience but expressed a peculiarly local tendency and which were dominated entirely by Africans. The number of Angolans identifying with such African churches is not known, but it is reasonable to assume that many Angolans were attached to them.

Indigenous Religious Systems

There were as many indigenous religious systems in Angola as there were ethnic groups or even sections of ethnic groups. Two or more ethnic groups might share specific elements of belief, ritual, and organizational principle, but the configuration of these elements would be different for each group or section. Nevertheless, certain patterns were widespread.

Most traditional African religions claim the existence of a high god, but this deity's attributes vary. For example, some groups emphasize the high god's role as a creator, while others do not. Specific events in the human world are not usually explained by reference to this god, nor is a cult addressed to it.

The active entities in indigenous religious systems are ancestral and nature spirits. Ancestral spirits are considered relevant to the welfare of a descent group or its members, and nature spirits are considered relevant to the welfare of a community in a given location. However, specific individuals may be directly affected by one of the nature spirits resident in rocks or trees or in natural forces such as wind or lightning.

Ancestral spirits, especially those of recently deceased kin, must be honored with appropriate rituals if they are expected to look favorably on the enterprises of their descendants. Only some of these rituals are performed by the descent group as a whole. More frequently, they are performed by and on behalf of a segment of the group or an individual.

In theory, nature spirits are not generally considered to have led a human existence, but there are exceptions. Occasionally, the spirits of local rulers or others are detached from specific descent groups or are considered to have the characteristics of other nature spirits in that they are resident in features of the landscape.

The spirits of the ancestors of a kin group are looked to for assistance in economic and social matters, and some misfortunes—famine, poor crops, personal losses—are ascribed to failure to have performed the appropriate rituals or to having misbehaved in some other way. Not all misfortunes are attributed to ancestral or nature spirits, however. Many people believe that magical powers inhere in things and that these powers, though usually neutral, may be used malevolently to afflict others or to prevent others from dealing with affliction, particularly illness and death. It is further thought that individuals, sometimes unconsciously and without the use of material or technical means, can bring illness or other affliction to human beings. Such persons, usually called witches, are thought to be marked by the presence of a substance in the stomach or other organ. The terms *witch* and *sorcerer* have been applied to those who use their power malevolently, and the distinction between the two is based in part on whether the power is inherited (witch) or acquired in exchange for something of value (sorcerer), whether the power is mystical or technical, and whether the power is used on one's (the witch's) own behalf or on behalf of others, at a price. In fact, this distinction is made only in some societies and may be linked to certain features of community social structures and associated with patterns of accusation—whether kin by blood or marriage or non-kin are held to be responsible.

Individual difficulties are attributed to witchcraft, sorcery, or the acts of ancestral or nature spirits. The determination is usually made by a diviner, a specialist whose personal power and use of material objects are held to be generally benevolent (although there are cases in which a diviner may be accused of sorcery) and whose sensitivity to patterns of stress and strain in the community help him or her arrive at a diagnosis. A diviner—widely called a *kimbanda*—may also have extensive knowledge of herbal medicine, and at least part of the work of the *kimbanda* is devoted to the application of that knowledge.

The *kimbanda* is said to have inherited or acquired the ability to communicate with spirits. In many cases, the acquisition of such power follows illness and possession by a specific spirit. The proficiency and degree of specialization of diviners varies widely. Some will deal only with particular symptoms; others enjoy broad repute and may include more than one village, or even more than one province, in their rounds. The greater the reputation of the *kimbanda,* the more he or she charges for services. This widespread term for diviner/healer has entered into local Portuguese, and so central is the role of the *kimbanda* to the complex of beliefs and practices characterizing most indigenous religions that some sources, such as the *Jornal de Angola,* have applied the term *kimbandism* to indigenous systems when cataloging Angolan religions.

In general, the belief in spirits (ancestral or natural), witches, and sorcerers is associated with a worldview that leaves no room for the accidental. Whether events are favorable or adverse, responsibility for them can in principle be attributed to a causal agent. If things go well, the correct ritual has been performed to placate the spirits or invoke their help. If things go badly, the correct ritual has not been performed, or a spirit has been otherwise provoked, or malevolent individuals have succeeded in breaching whatever protective (magical) measures have been taken against them. This outlook often persisted in Angola among individuals who had been influenced by Christianity or secular education. With some changes in particulars, it seemed to pervade urban areas, where a *kimbanda* rarely lacked clients.

Education

Conditions Before Independence

African access to educational opportunities was highly limited for most of the colonial period. Until the 1950s, facilities run by the government were few and largely restricted to urban areas. Responsibility for educating Africans rested with Roman Catholic and Protestant missions (see Religious Life, this ch.). As a consequence, each of the missions established its own school system, although all were subject to ultimate control by the Portuguese with respect to certain policy matters.

Education beyond the primary level was available to very few Africans before 1960, and the proportion of the age-group that went on to secondary school in the early 1970s was still quite low. Nevertheless, primary school attendance was growing substantially. Whether those entering primary schools were acquiring at least functional literacy in Portuguese was another matter. Primary school consisted of a total of four years made up of a pair of two-year cycles. Portuguese statistics do not indicate how many students completed each of the cycles, but it is estimated that far fewer completed the full four years than entered the first cycle. Similarly, there seems to be general agreement among observers that a great number of those who entered secondary school did not complete it. In general, the quality of teaching at the primary level was low, with instruction carried on largely by Africans with very few qualifications. Most secondary school teachers were Portuguese, but the first years of secondary school were devoted to materials at the primary level.

Conditions after Independence

The conflict between the Portuguese and the various nationalist movements and the civil war that ensued after independence left the education system in chaos. Most Portuguese instructors had left (including virtually all secondary school staff), many buildings had been damaged, and the availability of instructional materials was limited.

A report of the First Party Congress published in December 1977 gave education high priority. The report emphasized Marxism-Leninism as a base for the education system and its importance in shaping the "new generation," but the objectives of developing national consciousness and respect for traditional values were also mentioned. The training at all levels of persons who would be able to contribute to economic development was heavily stressed.

The government estimated the level of illiteracy following

independence at between 85 percent and 90 percent and set the elimination of illiteracy as an immediate task. Initiated in November 1976, the literacy drive gave priority to rural peasants who had been completely ignored by the Portuguese education system. The priorities for education were, in order of importance, literacy, primary education, secondary education, and intermediate and university education. The government established the National Literacy Commission (under the leadership of the minister of education) to administer the literacy campaign.

The government reported that in the first year of the literacy campaign (November 1976 to November 1977) 102,000 adults learned to read and write; by 1980 the figure had risen to 1 million. By 1985 the average rate of adult literacy was officially estimated at 59 percent; United States government sources, however, estimated literacy at only 20 percent. In late 1987, Angola's official press agency, Angop, reported that the provinces with the most newly literate people included Huíla, Huambo, and Benguela and that 8,152 literacy teachers had participated in the campaign since its inception.

At independence there were 25,000 primary school teachers, but fewer than 2,000 were even minimally qualified to teach primary school children. The shortage of qualified instructors was even more pronounced at the secondary school level, where there were only 600 teachers. Furthermore, secondary schools existed only in towns.

101

The First Party Congress responded to this problem by resolving to institute an eight-year compulsory system of free, basic education for children between ages seven and fifteen. Four years of primary education, provided free of charge, began at age seven. Secondary education, beginning at age eleven, lasted a further six years.

School enrollment, which rose very slowly considering Angola's youthful population, reflected the dire effects of the insurgency. In 1977 the government reported that more than 1 million primary school students were enrolled, as were about 105,000 secondary school students, roughly double the numbers enrolled in 1973. What proportions of the relevant age-groups these students constituted was not known, but in the case of the primary school students it may have been almost two-thirds, and in that of secondary school students, perhaps a tenth to an eighth. Official government statistics released in 1984 showed that primary school enrollment had declined to 870,410, while secondary school enrollment (including vocational school and teacher training students) had increased to 151,759. This made for combined primary and secondary school enrollment consisting of 49 percent of the school-age population. By 1986 the primary school enrollment had increased to 1,304,145. Luanda's Agostinho Neto University, the country's only university, had an enrollment of 4,493 students in 1984, which had declined to 3,195 by 1986. A total of 72,330 people were enrolled in primary adult education programs in 1986.

The government began implementation of its education plan in close cooperation with its allies, particularly Cuba. Between 1978 and 1981, Cuba sent 443 teachers to Angola. According to an Angolan source, in 1987 an estimated 4,000 Angolan students, representing one-fourth of all foreign students from Africa, Asia, Latin America, and the Caribbean studying in Cuba, were attending Cuban elementary, middle, and college preparatory schools, as well as polytechnical institutes and the Superior Pedagogical Polytechnic Institute. Also in Cuba, assisting in the education of their compatriots, was a group of twenty-seven Angolan teachers. In addition, the Soviet Union participated in Angolan education programs. More than 1,000 Angolan students had graduated from intermediate and specialized higher education programs in the Soviet Union by the end of 1987, at which time 100 Soviet lecturers were teaching at Agostinho Neto University, the Luanda Naval School, and the Institute of Geology and Cartography in the Angolan capital. By mid-1988 United States sources reported that 1,800 Angolan students were studying in the Soviet Union.

A number of Angolan organizations become active during the 1980s in the quest for better educational facilities. In 1987 the

JMPLA launched a special campaign to recruit 1,000 young people to teach in primary schools in Luanda Province. The groups targeted by the campaign included secondary school and higher education graduates, as well as some workers. The OMA not only sponsored programs to teach women to read and write but was also involved in programs to reduce infant mortality and promote family planning. Even the military formed a special group in 1980, the eighth contingent of the Comrade Dangereux Brigade, whose basic function was to teach primary school; 6,630 brigade members were reported to have taught 309,419 students by 1987.

Despite the government's efforts, the UNITA insurgency prevented the construction of a new education system on the remains of that inherited from the Portuguese. The demands of the war had drained funds that could otherwise have been applied to building schools, printing books, and purchasing equipment. In 1988, according to the United States Center for Defense Information, the Angolan government spent more per capita on the military (US$892) than on education (US$310). The war in the southern and central regions of the country also prevented the spread of the school system; the consequences of the fighting, including UNITA attacks on schools and teachers and the massive displacement of rural populations in those areas, disrupted the education of hundreds of thousands of school-age children. Further damaging to Angola's future was the fact that many of those studying abroad had either failed to complete their courses of study or had not returned to Angola.

Education in UNITA-Claimed Territory

By the mid-1980s, UNITA had gained control over a large part of Angola's southeast and claimed to have gained the allegiance of more than 1 million Angolans. As an integral part of his strategy to win over the hearts and minds of the populations in the occupied area, UNITA leader Jonas Savimbi established a state within a state, complete with a system of schools and hospitals to meet the needs of the local populations. The town of Jamba, UNITA's stronghold in southern Cuando Cubango Province, had a population of between 10,000 and 15,000, all of whom claimed loyalty to UNITA and Savimbi.

Although much of the information released by UNITA was propagandistic, it provided a rough outline of the educational situation in UNITA areas. UNITA claimed that its complex system consisted of nearly 1,000 schools, in which almost 5,000 teachers taught more than 200,000 children. A Portuguese reporter who visited UNITA-claimed territory in late 1987 reported that the

UNITA education system consisted of two years of kindergarten, four years of primary school, and seven years of high school. Upon completion of high school, the brightest students were given scholarships to study at universities in Britain, Côte d'Ivoire, France, Portugal, and the United States. Others attended middle-level technical courses in agriculture, nursing, primary school teaching, and typing in Jamba's Polytechnical Institute. UNITA's academic organization closely resembled that of Portugal, with Latin an important part of the curriculum.

Another Portuguese source reported in mid-1988 that there were ninety-eight Angolan scholarship students studying in Portugal under UNITA sponsorship. Because Portuguese institutions did not recognize the courses taught in Jamba, UNITA-educated students were required to take the examinations from the fourth class level up to university entrance examinations, losing two or three years of their UNITA education in the process. In other European countries, however, UNITA-sponsored students took only the examinations required for admission to the education level for which they wanted to enroll. Nevertheless, UNITA preferred to send its students to Portugal because of the common language. UNITA-sponsored students generally studied agronomy, engineering, and medicine.

Health and Welfare

In general, the civil war had degraded the quality and availability of health care since independence. Logistical problems with supply and distribution of equipment as well as the lack of physical security impeded the provision of health care throughout the country, and public health services existed only in areas under government control. The rest of the country depended on international and private relief organizations, although UNITA provided a fairly extensive health care system of its own in rebel-controlled areas. Poor even by African standards, health conditions in Angola were made even worse by the failure of government health programs to reach much of the population and by the movement of a significant part of the population out of war-ravaged regions. The country remained heavily dependent on foreign medical assistance because instruction in Angolan medical schools had progressed slowly.

Prior to independence, only urban inhabitants, many of whom were Portuguese, had access to health facilities. One of the MPLA's priorities when it came into power was to provide health care to the entire population through a network of health facilities overseen by the National Health Service, an organization subordinate to the Ministry of Health. In theory, basic health workers determined the level of care required by each patient. In rural areas, village dispensaries and health stations were staffed by a nurse, and district health centers provided outpatient services, a pharmacy, and up to twenty beds. District health centers referred patients to provincial hospitals when necessary. In reality, health care was limited and often unavailable in rural areas because of the lack of resources and the absence of government control throughout much of the country. The government claimed, however, to run 700 health posts and 140 health centers in rural areas in the late 1980s. UNITA, as part of its general goal of disrupting government services, impeded and often prevented the movement of health care personnel and medical equipment in many areas of the country, including regions outside its immediate control. Reports from various sources, mostly appearing in the Portuguese press, alleged that UNITA forces had attacked and destroyed rural medical facilities.

The OMA, the National Union of Angolan Workers (União Nacional dos Trabalhadores Angolanos—UNTA), and the Angolan Red Cross were also involved in promoting health care through the provision of health education, vaccination campaigns, and surveillance of health conditions. Particularly prominent was a primary health care program provided by the Angolan Red Cross in urban shantytowns. Most health-related programs, however, were administered by foreign and international organizations with the cooperation of the Angolan government. Most of these programs, primarily the International Committee of the Red Cross (ICRC) and various UN agencies, provided emergency relief aid to those affected by the UNITA insurgency. The ICRC operated mostly in the provinces of Huambo, Bié, and Benguela, administering projects for improving nutrition, sanitation, and public health, with a total staff of some 70 people, assisted by about 40 physicians, nurses, technicians, and administrators from foreign Red Cross societies and an estimated 800 Angolan relief workers.

Infectious and parasitic diseases were prevalent among most of the population. These diseases flourished in conditions of inadequate to nonexistent environmental sanitation, poor personal hygiene habits, substandard living conditions, and inadequate to nonexistent disease control programs. These conditions caused a cholera epidemic in 1987 and 1988 that killed almost 2,000 people in twelve provinces.

Conditions worsened in the 1980s, primarily because the UNITA insurgency had resulted in the creation of a massive internal refugee population living in tent camps or urban shantytowns. The most frequent causes of death included gastrointestinal diseases, malaria, respiratory infections, and sexually transmitted diseases, all of which were aggravated by endemic malnutrition. The most prevalent diseases included acute diarrhea, cholera, hepatitis, hymenolepiasis, influenza, leprosy, meningitis, onchocerciasis, schistosomiasis, tuberculosis, typhoid, typhus, yaws, and yellow fever. In addition, in 1989 approximately 1.5 million Angolans were at risk of starvation because of the insurgency and economic mismanagement. The United Nations Children's Fund (UNICEF) estimated that Angola had the world's fourth highest mortality rate for children under the age of five, despite a program launched in 1987 by UNICEF to vaccinate children against diphtheria, measles, polio, tetanus, tuberculosis, and whooping cough. UNICEF claimed to have vaccinated 75 percent of all Angolan children under the age of one.

If statistics provided by the chief of the Department of Hygiene and Epidemiology in Angola's Ministry of Health were accurate, the incidence of acquired immune deficiency syndrome (AIDS) in Angola was fairly low by African standards—0.4 percent of blood donors in Luanda and 2 percent to 4 percent of adults in Cabinda tested positive for the AIDS virus. The highest percentage of cases was in the northeast region bordering Zaire. There were indications, however, that the actual number of AIDS cases was significantly higher; the United States-based AIDS Policy Research Center claimed a high incidence of the disease among Cuban troops based in Angola and Angola-based African National Congress members. The biggest problems in determining the extent of the epidemic were inadequate communications systems and the lack of modern blood testing or computers to tabulate the death toll in rural areas. In cities controlled by the government, the World Health Organization helped initiate an information and testing campaign in 1988 that included the distribution of condoms.

Another prevalent health concern centered on the tens of thousands of people, many of them women and children, crippled by land mines planted by UNITA insurgents and, according to foreign relief organizations, by government forces. Estimates on the number of amputees ranged from 20,000 to 50,000. Foreign relief organizations operated orthopedic centers in both government-controlled and UNITA-occupied areas, providing artificial limbs and physical therapy. The largest facility was the Bomba Alta Orthopedic Center in Huambo, Angola's second largest city, which was operated by the ICRC. Designed essentially to manufacture orthopedic prostheses and braces for paralytics and to provide physical rehabilitation, in 1986 the center treated 822 patients, of whom 725 were adults and 97 were children. In 1987 the center was

*Women washing clothes in an irrigation canal,
a breeding ground for insects that spread parasitic diseases
Courtesy UNICEF (Maggie Murray-Lee)*

staffed with twenty-one Angolan and three foreign medical personnel, ten of whom specialized in orthopedic prostheses for the lower limbs. The center provided 1,260 patients with prostheses in 1988.

Most of Angola's estimated forty-five hospitals, all government operated, were located in urban areas (see table 3, Appendix A). Conditions in the hospitals, however, were often deplorable. Poor sanitation, a lack of basic equipment, and disruptions in water and electrical services were common. Trained medical personnel were in chronic short supply; in the late 1980s, Angola had only 230 native-born doctors, and only 30 percent of the population had access to health services. Most physicians, nurses, technicians, and national health advisers were foreigners—principally Cubans, East and West Europeans, and South Americans. In 1986 there were about 800 physicians in Angola (1 per 10,250 people—a very low ratio even by African standards) and somewhat more than 10,500 nurses. A Western source reported in February 1989 that 323 physicians, or 41 percent of the total number of doctors in government-controlled areas, were Cubans.

The government had placed a high priority on health and medical training programs, requiring that all foreign medical personnel teach classes in medicine, in addition to performing their clinical duties. There were two physician training programs in the country (in Luanda and Huambo) and more than twenty nursing schools, staffed primarily by Angolan, Cuban, and Soviet teachers. Most of the instructors in all medical training programs were foreign (primarily Cuban, Yugoslav, Soviet, and East German), and Angolan students attended medical training programs in Cuba, East Germany, and Poland.

According to a Portuguese source, health care in UNITA-controlled Angola was well organized and effective. The rebels operated a hospital in Jamba, which was staffed by Portuguese-trained medical personnel assisted by several French personnel from the volunteer organization Doctors Without Borders. Jamba's hospital was highly specialized, with the capability to meet most of the needs of the surrounding population; the only unavailable treatments were neurosurgery and cardiothoracic surgery. The hospital was apparently well equipped (probably by South Africa) with both instruments and medicines. Although tropical diseases were prevalent, war casualties were often the reason for hospitalization, with most of the wounded having first been treated at field hospitals established along the military fronts.

*   *   *

108

Sections of this chapter dealing with preindependence subjects and general discussions of the structure of society are based on parts of larger studies. Such studies include Hermann Pössinger's "Interrelations Between Economic and Social Change in Rural Africa," Lawrence W. Henderson's "Ethnolinguistic Worlds," Douglas L. Wheeler and René Pélissier's *Angola,* and Joseph C. Miller's *Kings and Kinsmen,* which includes a discussion of the complex character of Mbundu matrilineages.

Much of the more recent information has been culled from books, studies, and translations of foreign publications provided by the United States Joint Publications Research Service. Keith Somerville's *Angola: Politics, Economics, and Society* provides an excellent overview of the government's policies on education and religion; Linda M. Heywood's "The Dynamics of Ethnic Nationalism in Angola" contains a detailed analysis of UNITA's aspirations among the Ovimbundu as well as Ovimbundu life in present-day Angola; and Angola's official press agency, Angop, has provided detailed items pertaining to issues of health and education. Also of great value are articles in the *Washington Post* and *New York Times* by foreign correspondents such as Blaine Harden and James Brooke dealing with the effects of the UNITA insurgency on the rural and urban populations.

Two valuable sources on the grave conditions in which most Angolans live are the U.S. Committee for Refugees' *Uprooted Angolans* and the final report of the United States Private Voluntary Agency and the United States Government Assessment Team to Angola. (For further information and complete citations, see Bibliography.)

Chapter 3. The Economy

Women cultivate a field belonging to a farmers' association.

IN 1988 OBSERVERS OFTEN mentioned Angola's need to rehabilitate and revive its economy. Since independence in 1975, most economic production had deteriorated, and the country had become almost totally dependent on the export of oil for revenues. In the wake of the war for independence, the flight of trained personnel and foreign capital had left the country without the means to continue production. Furthermore, the prolonged insurgency, which still affected much of the country in late 1988, had undermined those enterprises that were still functioning. Although the political and military situation undoubtedly contributed to these economic problems, the Angolan economy had never been very strong, and most economic successes were of recent and precarious origins.

By the late 1980s, the economic potential of Angola had not been reached. Existing transportation networks, including railroads, roads, and ports, serviced only a fraction of the traffic they were built to accommodate. Likewise, manufacturing industries, such as textiles, cement, vehicle assembly, and food processing, all operated well below their productive capacities. Moreover, vast areas that had been cultivated for both cash and subsistence crops lay idle, and Angola was forced to import food. Indeed, even the local labor force, which had worked on the large agricultural estates, was unemployed and subsisted in displacement camps or in the cities on foreign aid. The only exceptions to the general regression in productivity were in the oil, electric power, telecommunications, and air transportation industries. While these sectors were expanding, most of Angola's economic production was shrinking.

Background to Economic Development

The Angolan economy has been dominated by the production of raw materials and the use of cheap labor since European rule began in the sixteenth century. The Portuguese used Angola principally as a source for the thriving slave trade across the Atlantic; Luanda became the greatest slaving port in Africa (see Slave Trading in the 1700s, ch. 1). After the Portuguese Empire abolished the slave trade in Angola in 1858, it began using concessional agreements, granting exclusive rights to a private company to exploit land, people, and all other resources within a given territory. In Mozambique, this policy spawned a number of companies notorious for their exploitation of local labor. But in Angola, only the

113

Diamond Company of Angola (Companhia de Diamantes de Angola—Diamang) showed even moderate success. At the same time, Portuguese began emigrating to Angola to establish farms and plantations (*fazendas*) to grow cash crops for export (see Agriculture, this ch.). Although these farms were only partially successful before World War II, they formed the basis for the economic growth that shaped Angola's economy in the late 1980s.

Before World War II, the Portuguese government was concerned primarily with keeping its colonies self-sufficient and therefore invested little capital in Angola's local economy. It built no roads until the mid-1920s, and the first railroad, the Benguela Railway, was not completed until 1929. Between 1900 and 1940, only 35,000 Portuguese emigrants settled in Angola, and most worked in commerce in the cities, facilitating trade with Portugal. In the rural areas, Portuguese settlers often found it difficult to make a living because of fluctuating world prices for sugarcane and sisal and the difficulties in obtaining cheap labor to farm their crops. As a result, they often suspended their operations until the market prices rose and instead marketed the produce of Angolan farmers.

But in the wake of World War II, the rapid growth of industrialization worldwide and the parallel requirements for raw materials led Portugal to develop closer ties with its colonies and to begin actively developing the Angolan economy. In the 1930s, Portugal started to develop closer trade ties with its colonies, and by 1940 it absorbed 63 percent of Angolan exports and accounted for 47 percent of Angolan imports, up from 39 percent and 37 percent, respectively, a decade earlier. When the price of Angola's principal crops—coffee and sisal—jumped after the war, the Portuguese government began to reinvest some profits inside the country, initiating a series of projects to develop infrastructure. During the 1950s, Portugal built dams, hydroelectric power stations, and transportation systems. In addition, Portuguese citizens were encouraged to emigrate to Angola, where planned settlements (*colonatos*) were established for them in the rural areas. Finally, the Portuguese initiated mining operations for iron ore, manganese, and copper to complement industrial activities at home, and in 1955 the first successful oil wells were drilled in Angola (see Extractive Industries, this ch.). By 1960 the Angolan economy had been completely transformed, boasting a successful commercial agricultural sector, a promising mineral and petroleum production enterprise, and an incipient manufacturing industry.

Yet by 1976, these encouraging developments had been reversed. The economy was in complete disarray in the aftermath of the war of independence and the subsequent internal fighting of the liberation movements. According to the ruling Popular Movement for the Liberation of Angola-Workers' Party (Movimento Popular de Libertação de Angola-Partido de Trabalho—MPLA–PT), in August 1976 more than 80 percent of the agricultural plantations had been abandoned by their Portuguese owners; only 284 out of 692 factories continued to operate; more than 30,000 medium-level and high-level managers, technicians, and skilled workers had left the country; and 2,500 enterprises had been closed (75 percent of which had been abandoned by their owners). Furthermore, only 8,000 vehicles remained out of 153,000 registered, dozens of bridges had been destroyed, the trading network was disrupted, administrative services did not exist, and files and studies were missing.

Angola's economic ills can also be traced to the legacy of Portuguese colonial development. Although the Angolan economy had started to show strong signs of growth by 1960, most developments had originated recently and precariously. Many of the white settlers had come to Angola after 1950 and were understandably quick to repatriate during the war of independence. During their stay, however, these settlers had appropriated Angolan lands, disrupting local peasant production of cash and subsistence crops. Moreover, Angola's industries depended on trade with Portugal—the colony's overwhelmingly dominant trade partner—for both markets and machinery. Only the petroleum and diamond industries boasted a wider clientele for investment and markets. Most important, the Portuguese had not trained Angolans to operate the larger industrial or agricultural enterprises, nor had they actively educated the population. Upon independence Angola thus found itself without markets or expertise to maintain even minimal economic growth.

As a result, the government intervened, nationalizing most businesses and farms abandoned by the Portuguese. It established state farms to continue producing coffee, sugar, and sisal, and it took over the operations of all factories to maintain production. These attempts usually failed, primarily because of the lack of experienced managers and the continuing disruptions in rural areas caused by the National Union for the Total Independence of Angola (União Nacional para a Independência Total de Angola—UNITA) insurgency. Only the petroleum sector continued to operate successfully, and by 1980 this sector had helped the gross domestic product (GDP—see Glossary) reach US$3.6 billion, its highest level up to 1988 (see fig. 6). In the face of serious economic problems and the continuing war throughout the countryside, in 1987 the government announced plans to liberalize economic policies and promote

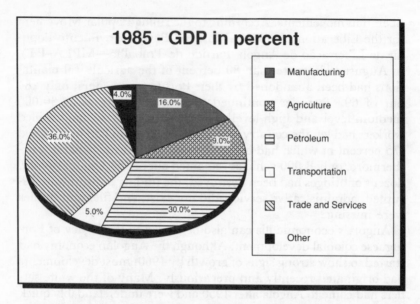

1985 - GDP in percent

- ■ Manufacturing
- ▨ Agriculture
- ☰ Petroleum
- ☐ Transportation
- ▨ Trade and Services
- ■ Other

16.0%
4.0%
9.0%
36.0%
30.0%
5.0%

Source: Based on information from Tony Hodges, *Angola to the 1990s*, London, 1987, 43.

Figure 6. Gross Domestic Product (GDP) by Sector, 1985

private investment and involvement in the economy. But most observers believed that the key to Angolan economic success rested only partially with the privatization of production. Even if peace were achieved, the economy would still have great difficulties in reaching its full potential.

Structure of the Economy

Since independence, the economy has been dominated by the oil export industry and drained by the need to carry on the war against the UNITA insurgents. Because of the collapse of the cash-crop economy, particularly the cultivation of coffee by large-scale plantations, in 1988 the economy depended totally on the oil sector to generate funds. As a result of increased oil production, GDP had risen steadily from Kz109.4 billion (for value of the kwanza—see Glossary) in 1982 to Kz144.9 billion in 1985.

Unfortunately, however, as the war against UNITA continued, most revenue from oil sales was quickly spent on the nation's defense forces. The relationship between oil profits and defense requirements became most acute in 1986 when the price of oil dropped, reducing government revenues and resulting in a jump in the percentage of government spending on defense.

At the same time, the war has also wreaked havoc in the already suffering agricultural sector, forcing the government to use precious foreign exchange to import food. Once a food exporter, Angola by the late 1980s was importing half of its grain requirements to compensate for reduced production in the war-torn rural areas.

Although the war has caused much rural-to-urban migration, industries based in the cities have been unable to harness this potential work force. Most of the Angolans coming into the cities have little education or training, partly because education in the rural areas has been disrupted by the war. Furthermore, the industries in the cities have been hurt by the lack of raw materials, including grain, timber, sugarcane, and cotton, normally produced in the rural areas. Consequently, industries have come to depend on high-priced imported materials. The frequent unavailability of industrial inputs, particularly during 1986 when the government severely restricted imports to protect foreign exchange reserves, has led to underproduction and underuse in the manufacturing sector (see Industry, this ch.).

As a result of the general dislocation in the economy, particularly in the transportation and distribution systems, many goods were unavailable in the 1980s. Thus, the black market (also called the parallel market, or *kadonga*) had come to dominate trade and undermine government efforts to impose order on domestic production. Consequently, the value of the kwanza also dropped, making it increasingly difficult for the government to attract wage earners to either agricultural or manufacturing enterprises. Furthermore, pilfering and graft in most economic enterprises had become common, as workers recognized that goods used in barter were more valuable than wages paid in kwanzas. As a result, inflation was high, goods were scarce, worker absenteeism was widespread, and productivity was low.

Role of the Government

The government, under the control of the MPLA–PT Central Committee, directly controlled most of the economy (see Structure of Government, ch. 4). Government-owned enterprises took the place of private enterprises and businesses. Because most Portuguese owners of manufacturing concerns and agricultural plantations fled the country at the time of independence, the new government was forced to nationalize factories and farms to keep them operating. The government also intervened directly to protect the country's wealth from foreign exploitation by creating companies to control Angola's mineral and petroleum wealth. State-owned companies in the oil industry have negotiated attractive terms of operation with the foreign companies that pump the oil, keeping a large percentage of the profits inside the country. The government's economic policies thus have combined ideology with necessity to fill the gap left by the Portuguese, without emulating the economic system created under colonialism.

But in the mid-1980s, Angola's centralized economy had fallen on hard times. Despite a 21.5 percent rise in the volume of oil production in 1986, government oil receipts fell to only 45 percent of the budgeted level because of the serious drop in worldwide oil prices that year. As a result, government revenues were barely half of the level budgeted for 1986 (see table 4, Appendix A). The government responded by cutting overall expenditures by 5.5 percent, mostly for items related to economic development, although expenditures for social services rose by 14 percent. The war against UNITA compounded the effect of lost oil revenue—defense expenditures rose to a record 40.4 percent of the 1986 budget (see War and the Role of the Armed Forces in Society, ch. 5).

Weak economic performance since independence has led government planners to reorient economic ideology, endorsing programs to liberalize many state policies and return some state functions to the private sector. In December 1986, the government decreed the liberalization of agricultural marketing, allowing for some free trade of agricultural goods to motivate farmers to produce more for the local market. Since the departure in 1975 of the Portuguese traders, who traditionally had monopolized rural trading, the inefficiency of the National Company for the Marketing and Distribution of Agricultural Products (Emprêsa Nacional de Comercialização e Distribuição de Produtos Agrícolas—Encodipa) and the scarcity of basic consumer goods and manufactured agricultural inputs have discouraged peasants from producing surpluses (see table 5, Appendix A). Most peasants have retreated to a purely subsistence form of farming. Similar inadequacies by the state livestock marketing company have resulted in serious overstocking in the cattle-raising southwestern region of Angola. Since 1984 the government has also been dissolving the state farms established on land formerly owned by Portuguese commercial farmers and has been turning the land over to the workers. Agricultural development stations have been set up to provide these farmers with services such as mechanized plowing. Furthermore, local peasant associations and cooperatives have been established throughout the country to organize production and consolidate resources.

On August 17, 1987, President José Eduardo dos Santos announced plans to restructure the economy. These reforms, called the Economic and Financial Rectification (Saneamento Económico e

Financeiro—SEF), put the economy in line with the policy guidelines approved by the Second Party Congress in December 1985. In his speech, the president listed several factors affecting the economy, including the steep fall in oil prices in 1986, the "excessive centralization of socialist planning methods," the poor management of state enterprises, and corruption. The SEF program mandated a strong move toward the private sector domestically and abroad, including membership in the International Monetary Fund (IMF—see Glossary) and World Bank (see Glossary). The foreign investment law was therefore being reviewed, and an office was to be established to promote investment and reduce negotiating costs. The SEF program also called for the privatization of nonstrategic state enterprises, ending budget subsidies to the remaining state enterprises, shifting from state farms to the peasant sector, raising prices, enacting monetary reforms, and devaluing the kwanza. The president noted that because the state had tried to enter so many different areas of economic activity, it had been unable to prevent the deterioration of the services for which it was traditionally responsible, such as education, health services, police, and civil administration. One area that the government was unlikely to relinquish to the private sector, however, was control over imports (see Foreign Trade and Assistance, this ch.).

In addition to the general liberalization of economic policies that the government proposed, the MPLA–PT Central Committee also launched a campaign against graft and the parallel market. The parallel market offered at exorbitant prices a full range of goods normally unavailable inside Angola. By June 1987, forty-two work teams had been established to oversee government efforts to end this illegal trade, and the provincial authorities had ordered the closing of all parallel markets. In addition, the government directed the military to supervise more closely the movement of goods at the intraprovincial and interprovincial level. The government also started an educational campaign of "consciousness raising" on farms and in factories to discourage the theft and pilfering that fed goods to the parallel market.

These efforts notwithstanding, in 1988 sources estimated that approximately 40 percent of the goods imported through Luanda never reached their intended destinations because of theft. Moreover, because the purchase of basic foodstuffs required ration cards, in 1988 the parallel market was thriving.

Foreign Trade and Assistance

Because of the overall decline in productivity after independence, Angola has become increasingly dependent on foreign trade and assistance to meet its domestic needs. It has also become dependent on oil export earnings to fund imports. Traditionally, the most important imports have been machinery items, especially equipment for the oil industry. By the mid-1980s, however, military equipment and food were becoming Angola's most important imports. The country continued to export most of its oil to the West, in particular the United States. The Soviet Union, as the country's arms supplier, and France and the United States, as suppliers of oil equipment, were the country's major import partners. Assistance from individual foreign countries and international organizations was also becoming increasingly important to Angola because of its mounting food crisis.

Only by severely limiting imports has the government been able to prevent a serious crisis in the balance of payments account. In the 1980s, the Ministry of Planning, in consultation with the National Bank of Angola (Banco Nacional de Angola—BNA), the Ministry of Domestic and Foreign Trade, and other ministries drew up an annual foreign trade budget as part of the annual national plan. This plan set ceilings for categories of imports in each sector of the economy, and import quotas were then allocated to individual companies. For each foreign order, the importing company was required to submit invoices and apply to the Ministry of Domestic and Foreign Trade for an import license. Most imports were brought in by state foreign trade companies and new regional import-export companies. However, the oil companies enjoyed foreign exchange autonomy and imported their equipment directly.

Foreign Trade

Until the dramatic fall in world oil prices in 1985 and 1986, the most dominant feature of the external economy since independence had been the large increase in oil export earnings (see table 6, Appendix A). By 1985 crude oil exports were more than eight times their 1973 level. At the same time, however, there was a precipitous drop in other exports, most notably coffee and diamonds, leaving Angola almost completely dependent on oil for export earnings. In 1988, for example, oil revenue represented nearly 90 percent of total export earnings. Nevertheless, the strong performance of the oil sector, combined with stringent import controls, resulted in continuing trade surpluses, which by 1985 had risen to US$740 million.

The country's principal trading partners, except for the Soviet Union, continued to be Western nations. The United States has been the main market for oil and thus the leading importer by far of Angolan goods since at least 1980. Angola's other main Western markets were Spain, Britain, Brazil, and the Netherlands. Spain, in particular, substantially increased its trade with Angola by importing a record US$300 million worth of goods in 1985, ten times the 1980 level. Angola's principal Western sources of goods were the United States, France, and Portugal (suppliers of oil industry equipment), but an increasing amount of goods came from Brazil. The Soviet Union, because of the large amount of arms it supplied, emerged as the major source of imports. Angola has also developed close trade ties with Zimbabwe, importing maize for local consumption and blankets to use as items of barter in rural marketing campaigns.

Since 1979 Angola has imported an increasing amount of foodstuffs from Western nations. In particular, it has imported wheat from the European Economic Community (EEC) and Canada, increasing from 83,000 tons in 1980 to 205,000 tons the following year and dropping to an average of 160,000 tons per year from 1982 to 1986. Likewise, Angola imported meat (100,000 tons in 1985) and milk (400,000 tons in 1985) from the West.

Because of the sharp drop in oil prices in 1986, imports were severely limited by the government. The government suspended the issue of import licenses except when importers obtained credit abroad or had their own foreign exchange. Capital goods imports were slashed, as were consumer goods, spare parts, and some industrial inputs. Military purchases were not cut, however, nor were imports of food, pharmaceuticals, goods for rural marketing campaigns, and oil industry equipment.

Foreign Assistance

Since 1980 foreign assistance grants have increased because of Angola's agricultural crisis and the drop in oil export earnings. In 1984 gross official development assistance from multilateral institutions rose to US$33 million, nearly double the figure for 1979 (see table 7, Appendix A). Foreign aid was likely to increase in the late 1980s as a result of Angola's accession to the Lomé Convention (see Glossary) in April 1985, making the country eligible for funding under the Lomé III Agreement, which was to remain in effect until 1990.

Because of the mid-1980s crisis in local agricultural production, food imports were essential to feed the population, and Angola had to appeal for more than US$100 million in food aid. Nevertheless, such aid did not meet food requirements, and in 1986 the country experienced a cereal shortfall of more than 100,000 tons. In addition, Angola appealed for US$21 million in nonfood aid in 1987, most of which was earmarked for relief and survival items.

Most direct aid was provided by Western organizations, and Angola was trying to improve its relations with several individual Western countries to negotiate for further assistance. In addition to assistance provided by the United Nations (UN) World Food Programme (WFP), in the late 1980s the EEC was providing assistance through the Lomé III Agreement as well as through the European Investment Bank. Furthermore, Angola regularly received aid from Sweden for various small-scale development projects, and France provided some assistance tied to the purchase of French equipment. Angola has improved relations with the Federal Republic of Germany (West Germany) and succeeded in reaching an agreement in 1987 with that country for 3,600 tons of food aid. Likewise, Portugal agreed in 1987 to provide US$140 million in credits toward the recovery of Angolan companies hurt by the exodus of Portuguese settlers after independence and to cooperate in some joint economic ventures with the Angolan government.

Angola also received significant assistance from the Soviet Union and East European nations. In 1977 Angola and the Soviet Union established an intergovernmental commission for technical, scientific, and trade cooperation. Projects addressed by this commission have included the design of a hydroelectric station, rural electrification, assistance in the petroleum and fishing industries, the supply of industrial equipment and physicians, and the training of Angolan technicians. The commission agreement was to run to the year 2000 and included plans for Soviet technical assistance in the petroleum industry, in light industry, and in livestock production. Angola has similar technical assistance agreements with Hungary (for the pharmaceutical and automobile industries), with Yugoslavia (for the petroleum industry and for agriculture), and with Bulgaria (for urban planning). Yugoslavia also built a large department store in Luanda to market Yugoslav-made goods, and trade between the countries has increased. And in October 1986, the government signed a cooperation agreement with the Council for Mutual Economic Assistance (Comecon or CMEA), the common market for the Soviet Union, its East European allies, and a few other countries. Under Comecon a joint commission on cooperation was to be established to determine future forms of cooperation and assistance between the nations.

Labor Force

Before independence the economy employed a labor force of unskilled Angolans and trained Portuguese. Since independence there has been little change in the overall composition of the work force, although in the 1980s there was a shortage of both skilled and

Semiskilled laborers work in a plastics factory.

unskilled workers. Most foreign workers fled the country at independence, but some have returned as contract workers, called *coopérants* by the government. Many unskilled workers in the rural areas—primarily plantation laborers—migrated to the cities in the wake of the 1975–76 fighting and the exodus of the plantation owners and managers. In the 1980s, most of the work force, even in the cities, remained illiterate and untrained for work in the manufacturing sector. By 1980 the labor force still conformed to its preindependence distribution: roughly 75 percent of all workers were engaged in agricultural production, 10 percent in industry, and 15 percent in services.

Calling itself a socialist workers' state, Angola was committed to protecting the rights of its workers and providing them with a reasonable wage. In the 1980s, all workers therefore belonged to the National Union of Angolan Workers (União Nacional dos Trabalhadores Angolanos—UNTA) and received a minimum wage. In addition, there were incentive programs at some factories, and UNTA promoted a "socialist emulation" program in which workers won bonuses for exceptional productivity. Nevertheless, the government has become dissatisfied with worker productivity, especially at the state-run enterprises, and has proposed to tie all wages to performance.

Foreign workers have also posed a problem for the government because of their high salaries and because they contradict the party's ideological commitment to the use of Angolan labor. The government, however, was forced to use foreign workers in many crucial positions after the departure of the Portuguese. These positions included those held by physicians, teachers, engineers, and technicians. Most came from Portugal, Cuba, Eastern Europe, Italy, France, Spain, Scandinavia, and Brazil. By 1984 the salaries of these foreign workers accounted for more than US$180 million, despite government attempts to force a reduction in this work force.

In pursuit of Angolanization (that is, the goal of having an upper-level work force that is at least 50 percent Angolan), in 1985 the government began initiating some training programs. In November of that year, it reached agreement with the German Democratic Republic (East Germany) on a training program for Angolan financial analysts. The greatest success occurred in the petroleum sector, however, in which by the end of 1985 more than 50 percent of the workers were Angolans with some technical training. This success was the result of actions taken by the government and the National Fuel Company of Angola (Sociedade Nacional de Combustíveis de Angola—Sonangol), which employed about half of the workers in the petroleum industry, to substitute Angolans for foreign workers. The 1982 Angolanization law (Decree 20/82) established a special fund for training activities. Consequently, intensive training courses and seminars in the petroleum field increased from 66 in 1982 to 151 in 1985. Sonangol participated in financing various training efforts, including scholarship grants. Furthermore, Sonangol closely cooperated with Angolan universities to introduce fields of study related to the petroleum industry. In the early 1980s, two training programs, one for geologists and geophysicists and the other for petroleum engineers, were instituted in the schools of science and engineering at the University of Angola. At the same time, the university's school of engineering began an equipment engineer training program. The training of middle-level technicians was undertaken by the National Petroleum Institute, at Sumbe in Cuanza Sul Province; the institute's teachers and administrators were *coopérants* from Italy (see fig. 1). The institute trained between fifty and sixty production specialists per year, some of whom were from countries belonging to the Southern Africa Development and Coordination Conference (SADCC).

By the beginning of 1986, the government claimed some success in its Angolanization program. According to the minister of industry, 44 percent of senior-level and middle-level management in industry were Angolans. Nevertheless, after the drop in oil prices in 1986, the government sought to reduce the number of foreign workers even further and enacted the Statute on the Coopérant

Worker. This law established the principle that *coopérants* must train Angolan workers in their jobs and pay taxes based on Angolan labor regulations. To increase the ranks of Angolan workers, the government even encouraged the return of Angolan exiles who had formerly opposed the MPLA. These included former members of the National Front for the Liberation of Angola (Frente Nacional de Libertação de Angola—FNLA), the Organization of Angolan Communists (Organização dos Comunistas de Angola—OCA), and UNITA (see Political Opposition, ch. 4). The response to this encouragement has been somewhat meager, however, because of Angola's ongoing instability.

Extractive Industries

The petroleum industry dominated the extractive industries and, indeed, the entire economy. Since the dramatic increase in oil prices in 1973 and 1974, petroleum had assumed growing importance. The petroleum industry was so important, in fact, that the MPLA for the most part allowed foreign oil companies to import as much machinery as they needed and made only modest demands for the Angolanization of the work force. Thus, petroleum has remained the most successful sector in the economy, despite the 1986 price drop, and has provided the government with most of its revenues. In contrast, mining of diamonds and iron ore, commodities that once ranked as major exports, has almost ceased because of disruptions from the war. Either through direct attacks on diamond mines or through the disruption of iron ore transport, in the 1980s it had become nearly impossible to continue operating these mineral industries. Diamond production started to revive in 1987, but only in areas patrolled by government troops.

Oil

As of December 1984, the country's total proven recoverable reserves of crude oil were estimated by Sonangol at 1.6 billion barrels. This amount was considered sufficient to maintain production at 1986 levels until the end of the century. Most Angolan oil is light and has a low sulfur content. As the only oil producer in southern Africa, Angola has promoted cooperation in energy matters on behalf of SADCC.

The first oil exploration concession was granted by the Portuguese authorities in 1910, but commercial production did not begin until 1956 when the Petroleum Company of Angola (Companhia de Petróleos de Angola—Petrangol) started operations in the Cuanza River Basin (see fig. 3). The company later discovered oil onshore in the Congo River Basin and became the operator for most of

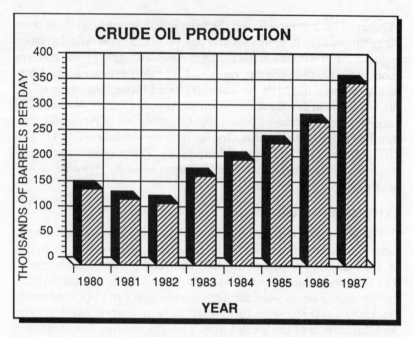

CRUDE OIL PRODUCTION

Source: Based on information from United States, Central Intelligence Agency, *International Energy Statistical Review*, November 27, 1984, 1; and September 27, 1988, 1.

Figure 7. Crude Oil Production, 1980–87

the onshore fields in association with Texaco, an American company, and Angol (a subsidiary of Portugal's SACOR). At about the same time, a subsidiary of the American-based Gulf Oil, the Cabinda Gulf Oil Company (Cabgoc), began explorations in the Cabinda area in 1954 and started production in 1968. Production rose from 2.5 million tons in 1969 to 8.2 million tons in 1973, while exports nearly quadrupled in volume. Because of the added benefit of the 1973 oil price increase, the value of oil exports was almost twelve times higher in 1973 than in 1969, and oil finally surpassed coffee as the principal export. Crude oil production in the early 1980s dipped somewhat as a result of decreased investments. By 1983, however, production had rebounded and thereafter continued to set new output records (see fig. 7).

Postindependence Exploration and Production

Following independence, the new government enacted sweeping changes in the oil industry and claimed sole rights over all of the petroleum deposits in the country. Under the Petroleum Law No. 13/78, enacted on August 26, 1978, the government established Sonangol as the exclusive concessionaire of the state's hydrocarbon resources. The company was divided into several directorates, including one for the development of hydrocarbons and another for the distribution of byproducts on the domestic market. The hydrocarbons directorate was responsible for reaching agreements with private companies for the development of local resources. In 1978 it divided Angola's offshore area (except for Cabinda) into thirteen blocks of approximately 4,000 square kilometers each for development by private companies (see fig. 8). By 1981 exploratory drilling had been conducted on Blocks 1 through 4, and production began in Blocks 2 and 3 in 1985.

Sonangol was empowered to enter into two types of agreements with foreign companies: joint ventures, in which Sonangol and its private partners shared in investments and received petroleum produced in the same proportion (51 percent Sonangol, 49 percent foreign); and production-sharing agreements, in which the foreign company served as a contractor to Sonangol, made the necessary investments, and was compensated by receiving a share of the oil produced. Sonangol also could stipulate a price cap in the production-sharing agreements that would allow windfall profits to accrue to Sonangol and not to the foreign companies. In practice, all of the new areas opened up for exploration and production since independence have been subject to production-sharing agreements, while the areas previously under production—primarily in Cabinda—were joint-venture operations between Sonangol and foreign companies. In addition, Sonangol also participated in joint-venture companies that provided services and supplies to the oil exploration and production companies.

Except for Cabinda, production in the offshore fields started after independence. In offshore Block 1, the first seismic work began in May 1982, and the first drilling commenced in December of that year. Activity in Block 2 began in 1980, and by 1985 two fields were producing (Cuntala and Essungo) a total of 11,700 barrels per day (bpd—see Glossary). In addition, oil was discovered by the end of 1985 in the West Sulele formation in Block 2. Sonangol had started construction in Block 2 of the Kwanda operational base to provide support for operators in Blocks 1, 2, and 3. Block 3 also started exploration activity in 1980, and by 1986 at least six wells there were considered commercial. A major development project was being initiated in Block 3 for the Palanca and Pacaca fields and for a sea-loading terminal. The other blocks in exploration were 4, 5, 6, 7, and 9; Blocks 8, 10, 11, and 12 had not been opened by the government as of the end of 1985 (see table 8, Appendix A).

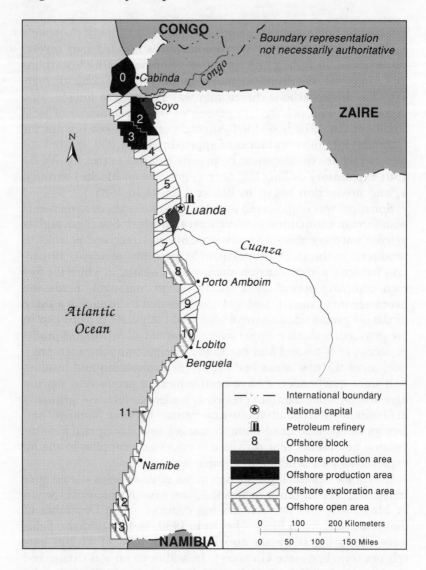

Source: Based on information from Tony Hodges, *Angola to the 1990s,* London, 1987, 54.

Figure 8. Oil Exploration and Production Areas, 1986

Oil was also produced in onshore fields in the Cuanza and Congo river basins. There were forty-six wells in the Cuanza River Basin, near Luanda, where production began in 1959. In 1986 Sonangol estimated that the field had a life of another five to six years at then-current levels of production. Being an old field, it had very low production costs. The oil fields in the Congo River

Basin, however, were far more productive, yielding nearly eight times the amount raised in the Cuanza River Basin. From 1981 to 1985, between 30,700 bpd and 34,900 bpd were produced in the Congo River Basin, but an average of only about 4,200 bpd was produced in the Cuanza River Basin.

In addition to its production agreements, Sonangol has actively invested in the development of production capabilities and in exploration and distribution projects. In 1979 the company compiled the available data on the sedimentary basins and carried out a seismic survey program on the continental platform, upon which the subsequent division of the continental shelf platform was based. Furthermore, the company has made major investments in expanding its ability to distribute petroleum at home and abroad since it assumed direct responsibility in 1977 for marketing Angolan oil (Cabgoc marketed Cabinda oil, which accounted for almost half of Angola's oil production). Some of Sonangol's other major investments included gas injection facilities in Cabinda; development of the Takula, Lumueno, Quinfuquena, Quinguila, Essungo, and Cuntala fields and the offshore Cabinda fields; construction of the Kwanda oil field service base; and construction of the Quinfuquena oil terminal.

New arrangements have also been made for the future development of several production areas. Financing totaling US$350 million has been secured for the development of the Takula fields in Cabinda, owned jointly by Sonangol and Cabgoc, from an international consortium of banks. Cabgoc has also signed three new joint-venture contracts on oil research and exploration in Cabinda. Under the terms of these contracts, Cabgoc was to be responsible for the total cost of the research operations and was to be reimbursed by Sonangol only if commercially viable oil was discovered.

As a result of the many joint-venture and production-sharing agreements reached by the government in the late 1970s, by 1985 US$798 million had been invested in exploration and US$1.2 billion in development. The largest investors were Cabgoc and Sonangol in Cabinda and the French firm Elf Aquitaine and its partners in Block 3. This increased investment has led to higher production. For example, production in Cabinda more than doubled between 1980 and 1985.

Marketing

Exports of crude oil have outpaced exports of refined oil because refining facilities have not been expanded at the same rate as crude oil output. In the late 1980s, all of the oil produced offshore

129

(in Cabinda and Block 3) was exported, while the crude oil found onshore was refined domestically.

Petrangol's output was about 32,000 bpd in 1985, sufficient to meet domestic demand for most products except butane and jet fuel, while a large surplus of fuel oil was produced for export (585,900 tons in 1985). The facilities for bottling propane and butane were also expanded at a cost of US$7 million. The capacity of the Petrangol oil refinery on the outskirts of Luanda was increased to 1.7 million tons a year in 1986. In 1987 Sonangol was exploring the possibility of having some of its crude petroleum refined in Portugal.

The supply of petroleum products for the domestic market was controlled by Sonangol and increased 8 percent between 1980 and 1985. Initially, Sonangol shared the market with Shell and Mobil, but Sonangol bought out the Angolan subsidiaries of these companies in 1981 and 1983. Subsequently, Sonangol also purchased two Portuguese companies that bottled gas, gaining a monopoly over the distribution of refined products. Among these products, butane gas accounted for 65 percent of the total gas consumed locally and was used primarily in homes in urban areas. In addition, Sonangol distributed gasoline, gas oil, and lubricating oils. Its greatest distribution problems were the lack of storage facilities throughout the country and problems associated with the domestic transportation network.

In response to the fall in oil prices in 1986, the Angolan government began considering regional cooperation to protect the interests of oil suppliers. In that year, Angola was invited to join the Organization of Petroleum Exporting Countries (OPEC). Although it declared its willingness to act in concert with OPEC members to avert the growing crisis in oil prices, Angola joined the African Petroleum Producers' Association, which included four OPEC members (Algeria, Gabon, Libya, and Nigeria) and three non-OPEC oil producers (Cameroon, Congo, and Benin). Together, these eight countries produced 188 million tons of oil in 1986, equivalent to about one-fifth of OPEC's production and 6.4 percent of world production.

In the late 1980s, the major foreign oil companies operating in Angola were American. Chevron, which had taken over Gulf, owned 49 percent of the shares in the offshore Cabinda blocks, Angola's largest production area, where output was fairly stable in 1986 and 1987 at about 200,000 bpd. In 1986 President Ronald Reagan's administration pressured American oil companies and equipment suppliers to withdraw their interest in the Angolan oil industry to protest the presence of Cuban troops in Angola.

Oil exploration off the coast
of Cabinda
Courtesy United Nations
(J.P. Laffont)

Chevron therefore withdrew 20 percent of its interests from Cabgoc and sold its shares to the Italian firm Agip. Conoco, however, rebuffed this pressure and became the third American oil company to begin operations in Angola in offshore Block 5. Texaco, another major operator in Angola, operated in offshore Block 2, near Soyo, where it held a 40 percent interest in a production-sharing consortium. It also had a 16 percent interest in some of the onshore fields in the Congo River Basin.

The United States Congress also banned new Export-Import Bank lending and credit insurance for sales to the Angolan oil industry, putting American suppliers at a major disadvantage in this market. British suppliers waiting to come into the market have been delayed because of the reluctance of British banks to offer long-term or medium-term credits for such sales. However, France has entered the market, granting exceptional credit facilities for oil-related sales.

Diamonds

Diamond mining began in 1912, when the first gems were discovered in a stream in the Lunda region in the northeast. In 1917 Diamang was granted the concession for diamond mining and prospecting, which it held until independence. Control over the company was obtained by the government in 1977. In April 1979, a general law on mining activities (Law 5/79) was enacted and gave

131

the state the exclusive right to prospect for and exploit minerals. Accordingly, a state diamond-mining enterprise, the National Diamond Company (Emprêsa Nacional de Diamantes—Endiama), was founded in 1981 and acquired the government's 77 percent share in Diamang. UNITA, which selected the diamond mining industry as a principal target, soon crippled mining efforts, and by the beginning of 1986 the two foreign companies involved in servicing and operating the industry pulled out of Angola. By mid-1986 Diamang was formally dissolved, leaving large outstanding debts.

Attacks by UNITA on mining centers, disruption of transport routes, and widespread theft and smuggling caused diamond sales to fall to US$33 million by 1985 and to an estimated US$15 million in 1986. In late 1986, Roan Selection Trust (RST) International, a subsidiary of the Luxembourg-registered holding company ITM International, began mining in the Cafunfo area, along the Cuango River, the site of Angola's most valuable alluvial diamond deposits (see fig. 9). Mining had been halted there for more than two years after UNITA attacked the mining camp in February 1984, kidnapping seventy-seven expatriate workers and severely damaging the mining equipment. After the subsequent kidnapping of a British expatriate in November 1986, defense forces in the area were strengthened, allowing the resumption of mining operations. In 1987 production there averaged 60,000 carats, and about 120,000 carats were produced in the other two mining areas, Andrada and Lucapa. By 1987 diamond production had risen to 750,000 carats, compared with less than 400,000 carats produced in 1986. The 1987 figure, however, was still not much more than 1985 production and only a little over half of 1980 output (see table 9, Appendix A).

This increase in production has benefited from the rise in the price per carat received for Angolan diamonds. The resumption of mining in the area along the Cuango River and a decline in theft of stones of higher value in the Andrada and Lucapa areas have increased the value of output. Furthermore, Endiama, which was responsible for overseeing the industry and for holding monthly sales, has benefited from a general improvement in the world diamond market as well as dealers' willingness to pay higher prices in the hope of securing favored treatment in the future. As a result, average carat value established by the monthly sales in 1987 exceeded US$110, more than twice as much as in 1985 (US$45) and at its highest level since 1981 (US$119).

In 1987 Endiama signed a two-year mining contract with the Portuguese Enterprises Corporation (Sociedade Portuguêsa de

Empreendimentos—SPE), a Portuguese company that has retained a large number of Portuguese technicians previously employed by Diamang. Former Diamang shareholders founded SPE in 1979 after Diamang was nationalized. The precise terms of the contract were not made public, but it was thought that the company would undertake new prospecting, which had been at a virtual standstill since independence. Through a subsidiary, the SPE also was to help Endiama with diamond valuation, which a British company had been carrying out. In December 1987, Angola also signed an agreement with the Soviet Union to cooperate in mining diamonds and quartz. Under the terms of the agreement, the Soviet Union was to participate in mining enterprises and was to draw up a detailed geological map of Angola.

In 1987 the government also began to revise the 1979 mining law to encourage new companies to invest in the diamond-mining industry, in particular to resume prospecting. Among the companies believed to be considering investing in 1988 was Britain's Lonrho conglomerate, which had taken an increasingly active interest in Angola in the late 1980s. The South African diamond-mining giant DeBeers was also interested after it lost its exclusive marketing rights for Angolan diamonds at the end of 1985 because of government suspicions that DeBeers had devalued Angolan diamonds. DeBeers has expressed interest in studying the kimberlite pipes (deep, subsurface deposits), which, because of the depletion of the alluvial deposits, were thought to represent the future of the Angolan diamond industry.

Iron Ore

Once one of the country's major exports, iron ore was no longer mined in the late 1980s because of security and transportation problems. From the mid-1950s until 1975, iron ore was mined in Malanje, Bié, Huambo, and Huíla provinces, and production reached an average of 5.7 million tons per year between 1970 and 1974. Most of the iron ore was shipped to Japan, West Germany, and Britain and earned almost US$50 million a year in export revenue. After independence, the government established a state company, the National Iron Ore Company of Angola (Emprêsa Nacional de Ferro de Angola—Ferrangol), for the exploration, mining, processing, and marketing of iron ore. Ferrangol contracted with Austromineral, an Austrian company, to repair facilities and organize production in Cassinga. Production began to slow in 1974 as a result of technical problems at the Cassinga mine in Huíla Province and stopped completely in August 1975. The area fell under foreign control after South African forces invaded in 1975.

133

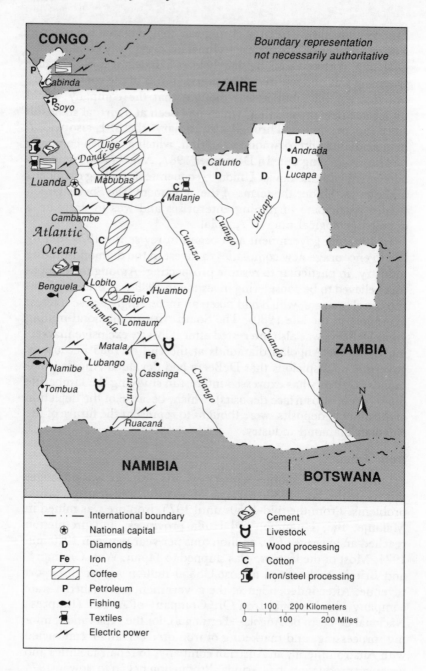

CONGO

Boundary representation not necessarily authoritative

P

Cabinda

P Soyo

ZAIRE

D

•Andrada

D

Lucapa

Uíge

Dande

Cafunfo

D

D

Luanda

D

Mabubas

C

Malanje

Fe

Chicapa

Cambambe

Atlantic Ocean

C

Cuanza

Cuango

Benguela

Lobito

Huambo

Biópio

Catumbela

Lomaum

Cuando

ZAMBIA

Matala

Fe

Lubango

Cassinga

Cubango

Cunene

Namibe

Tombua

N

Ruacaná

NAMIBIA

BOTSWANA

	International boundary		Cement
⊛	National capital		Livestock
D	Diamonds		Wood processing
Fe	Iron	C	Cotton
▨	Coffee		Iron/steel processing
P	Petroleum		
◄	Fishing	0 100 200 Kilometers	
▮	Textiles	0 100 200 Miles	
⚡	Electric power		

Figure 9. Economic Activity, 1988

Although South Africa withdrew its troops in early 1976, as of 1988 mining had not resumed in the area.

By 1988 the Cassinga mines had a production capacity of approximately 1.1 million tons per year. However, the railroad to the port of Namibe (formerly Moçâmedes) needed extensive repair, and since it was located only 310 kilometers north of the Namibian border, security against South African attacks could not be ensured. Furthermore, UNITA was active in the area and posed a threat to the rail line if it were repaired. Even if these problems could be resolved, production of iron ore at Cassinga would be costly in view of the depressed state of the world steel market in the late 1980s.

Other Minerals

In addition to diamonds and iron ore, Angola is also rich in several other mineral resources that had not been fully exploited by the late 1980s. These include manganese, copper, gold, phosphates, granite, marble, uranium, quartz, lead, zinc, wolfram, tin, fluorite, sulfur, feldspar, kaolin, mica, asphalt, gypsum, and talc. The government hoped to resume mining in the southwest for crystalline quartz and ornamental marble. It has been estimated that 5,000 cubic meters of marble could be extracted annually over a period of twenty years. A state-owned company mined granite and marble in Huíla and Namibe provinces and in 1983 produced 4,450 cubic meters of granite and 500 cubic meters of marble. Since then, the company has ceased production to re-equip with modern machinery. Quartz production, however, was suspended indefinitely because of the military situation in the areas close to the extraction sites in Cuanza Sul Province.

The government established a company in 1980 to exploit phosphate deposits located in the northwest. There were 50 million tons of deposits in Zaire Province and about 100 million tons in Cabinda. Although studies of the deposits in both locations have been made by Bulgarian and Yugoslav companies, as of 1988 production had not started at either site.

Agriculture

By the end of the colonial period, a variety of crops and livestock was produced in Angola. In the north, cassava, coffee, and cotton were grown; in the central highlands, maize was cultivated; and in the south, where rainfall is lowest, cattle herding was prevalent. In addition, there were large plantations run by Portuguese that produced palm oil, sugarcane, bananas, and sisal. These crops were grown by commercial farmers, primarily Portuguese, and by peasant farmers, who sold some of their surplus to local Portuguese traders in exchange for supplies. The commercial farmers were dominant in marketing these crops, however, and enjoyed substantial support from the colonial government in the form of technical assistance, irrigation facilities, and financial credit. They produced the great majority of the crops that were marketed in the cities or exported.

After independence, the departure of Portuguese farmers and traders in the rural areas undermined agricultural productivity. In response, the government set up state farms on land formerly owned by the Portuguese and established the National Company for the Marketing and Distribution of Agricultural Products (Emprêsa Nacional de Comercialização e Distribuição de Produtos Agrícolas—Encodipa) to maintain the rural trading system. Neither body, however, was successful, and by 1984 the government started phasing out the state farms and turned production over to individual farmers. In December 1985, the government also put most rural trade back into private hands. To help peasant farmers, the government established agricultural development stations and provided bank credits for small-scale agricultural projects. Several hundred state farms were to be turned over to associations of tenant farmers as an embryonic form of cooperative. The association was to buy or rent tools for shared use, share marketing initiatives to strengthen prices, and share transport. By the end of 1985, the Directorate of Farm Marketing controlled 4,638 farm cooperatives and 6,534 farmers' associations; but of these, only 93 cooperatives and 71 associations were operational.

In the late 1980s, the country faced serious problems in resuscitating agricultural production. By 1988 the departure of the Portuguese, rural depopulation, and the physical isolation of the farming areas had almost totally halted commercial production of such cash crops as coffee and sisal, as well as the subsistence production of cereals. Production was stagnating because of marketing and transport difficulties; shortages of seed, fertilizer, and consumer goods for trade with peasant farmers; and the impact of the war on planting, harvesting, and yields. Land mines and fear of attacks had forced peasants to reduce the areas under cultivation, especially fields distant from villages, and to abandon hopes of harvesting some planted areas. Moreover, the internal migration of peasants to safer areas had resulted in the overcultivation of lands and decreased yields.

Despite these obstacles, there were some successes. The relatively secure Huíla Province maintained a fair level of production, and the reorientation of government policy away from inefficient state

136

farms and toward peasant producers promised to provide services to and boost production by peasant farmers. By the end of 1987, there were twenty-five development stations providing services to peasant producers in ten provinces, and four more were being set up.

Coffee

Nowhere has the decline in agricultural production been more dramatic than in the coffee sector. Formerly Angola's leading export, by 1985 coffee exports had dropped to 8 percent of their 1973 level (see table 10, Appendix A). Under colonial rule, about 2,500 large commercial farms and 250,000 peasants were involved in growing coffee. During the 1975–76 fighting, the owners, managers, and skilled technicians, as well as most of the migrant work force, abandoned the coffee estates, which were then nationalized. Suffering from a lack of skilled management and shortages of available labor in the rural areas, these coffee farms have continually posted losses. By 1985 the thirty-four state coffee companies produced only 8,890 tons of coffee and depended on government subsidies to stay in business. The government marketed only 4,700 tons from peasant producers in that year.

In 1983 the government adopted an emergency program to revive the coffee industry. Local coffee companies, rather than the National Coffee Company (Emprêsa Nacional de Café—Encafe), were given the responsibility to run the state coffee farms, and, to encourage greater efficiency, the area under cultivation was reduced to less than one-fifth of the area abandoned by the large commercial coffee growers at independence. Aid for these efforts has been obtained from the French Central Board for Economic Cooperation (Caisse Centrale de Coopération Economique—CCCE) and two UN organizations, the WFP and the Food and Agriculture Organization (FAO). The WFP was furnished with US$14.3 million on a five-year (1983–87) plan to pay coffee workers in food rather than in local currency to discourage worker absenteeism, one of the industry's most serious problems. In addition, the government, as part of its program of economic liberalization, was in the process of turning over the marketing of coffee to local, rather than national, organizations.

Despite these efforts, however, by 1985 the state coffee farms had only about 50 percent of the required work force because of the general drain of people from the rural areas and the unattractive wages that were paid in nearly worthless kwanzas. Moreover, the industry was still plagued by the UNITA insurgency, whose attacks had inflicted over US$4 million worth of damage on coffee plantations by 1985. Other problems encountered on the coffee plantations mirrored the general deterioration of the economic infrastructure. High charges for transportation of coffee and machinery and lack of facilities for hulling the coffee slowed and made more expensive the entire production process. Furthermore, some plantation managers complained that their workers were not productive, not only because of absenteeism but also because of their advanced age.

The decline in coffee exports in the mid-1980s resulted largely from the depletion of stocks that had earlier cushioned exports as production declined. Exports to members of the International Coffee Organization (ICO) have remained fairly stable since 1983, but exports to non-ICO members, of which East Germany has been by far the most important market in the late 1980s, have declined. The fall in sales to the non-ICO market has eroded coffee earnings because these sales have traditionally been at substantially higher prices than those to ICO members. Exacerbating the decline in production and exports has been the depressed world market for coffee. From February 1986 to August 1987, ICO indicator prices dropped by more than 20 percent.

Food Crops and Livestock

The decline in marketed food crop production and the rapid growth of the urban population have caused a food crisis in the cities. By the mid-1980s, urban dwellers depended almost entirely on cereal imports, and the approximately 600,000 rural displaced persons were completely dependent on food aid from foreign donors. Local production of cereals met only half the national requirement in 1986 and totaled only about 300,000 tons—about 60 percent of the yearly average in the mid-1970s. Decreased production was the result of general problems associated with the war, including deteriorating transportation and a lack of market incentives for peasant producers. By the late 1980s, malnutrition was widespread.

Similarly, livestock production has declined. Both cattle and pigs are raised, but production fell from 36,500 tons slaughtered in 1973 to only 5,000 tons in the early 1980s. This tremendous decrease was the result of a combination of factors, including the departure of the commercial farmers, increasing disruption from the war (in this case from South African forces in the southern part of the country), and the deterioration of facilities and services, especially vaccinations, crucial for livestock production. During their occupation of Cunene Province in 1975, the South African troops allegedly destroyed some 1,500 water holes for cattle, severely damaging livestock production in that region.

A laborer holds a basket of freshly picked coffee beans.
Courtesy United Nations (J.P. Laffont)

Timber

Timber production also declined dramatically after independence. Production of logs dropped from 555,000 cubic meters in 1973 to below 40,000 cubic meters in 1981 and 1982. Nonetheless, the government was interested in promoting production to supply local manufacturing. Some valued woods, such as mahogany, grow in the rain forests in Cabinda, where there are also eucalyptus, pine, and cypress plantations. A new state forestry company was established in 1983 with aid from Cuba to revive the industry in Cabinda, and by 1985 log production had risen to 113,000 cubic meters. In 1986 the Panga-Panga enterprise of Cabinda, which manufactured pressed wood, exported 123 million square meters of sheets to Italy.

Fishing

Fishing was a major industry before independence. In the early 1970s, there were about 700 fishing boats, and the annual catch was more than 300,000 tons. Including the catch of foreign fishing fleets in Angolan waters, the combined annual catch was estimated at 1 million tons. Following independence and into the late 1980s, however, the local fishing industry had fallen into disarray, the result of the flight of local skilled labor and the return of the fishing boats to Portugal. By 1986 only 70 of the 143 fishing boats in Namibe, the port that normally handled two-thirds of the Angolan catch, were operable. Furthermore, most of the fish-processing factories were in need of repair. Once an exporter of fish meal, by 1986 Angola had insufficient supplies for its own market.

Some of the foreign fishing fleets operating in Angolan waters were required by the government to land a portion of their catch at Angolan ports to increase the local supply of fish. Fishing agreements of this kind had been reached with the Soviet Union, which operated the largest number of boats in Angolan waters, and with Spain, Japan, and Italy. Spain also agreed to help rehabilitate the Angolan fishing industry in exchange for fishing rights. In other cases, the government allowed foreign fleets to export their entire catch in exchange for license fees.

In the mid-1980s, the government began rehabilitating the fishing industry, especially in Namibe and Benguela provinces. The first priority was to replace and repair aging equipment. To accomplish this goal, the government was receiving a significant amount of foreign assistance. In 1987 the EEC announced plans to provide funds to help rebuild the Dack Doy shipyards and two canning plants in Tombua. Spain sold Angola thirty-seven steel-hull boats for US$70 million, and fourteen modern fishing boats were on order from Italy.

Industry

Under the Portuguese, the manufacturing sector grew rapidly because of the substantial increase in the size of the white settler population, the creation of a large domestic market for goods, and the strict exchange controls imposed in 1962 that encouraged investment in local industry. The manufacturing sector was dominated by light industries that produced consumer goods, especially the food-processing industry, which accounted for 46 percent of the value of manufactured output in 1973. In contrast, heavy industries accounted for only 22 percent of output. When the settlers fled, most small manufacturing firms were left without their clerical work force, their managers, and even their owners; in 1976 only 284 out of 692 manufacturing businesses were operating under their old management. In reaction to the decline in the manufacturing sector, in March 1976 the MPLA government enacted the Law on State Intervention and nationalized all of the abandoned businesses. However, by 1985 industrial production was only 54 percent of its real value in 1973.

In the years immediately following independence, the government spent large sums to put plants back into operation, but its plans were overly ambitious, and it overestimated the state's capacity to keep factories supplied with necessary materials and inputs. In the early 1980s, investment was cut drastically, as the government sought to control expenditures and the foreign exchange deficit. Because of limited funding, projects were more carefully selected, and there was clearer recognition of the need for simultaneous restructuring in other sectors, particularly those supplying raw materials for manufacture. By 1986 approximately 180 companies were operating in the manufacturing sector, and their output was equal to about 13 percent of GDP. Of that amount, state-run companies accounted for 56 percent.

Among the most acute problems for industrial rehabilitation were shortages of raw materials, unreliable supplies of water and electricity, and labor instability. The decline in domestic production of many raw materials has been especially critical in the decline in local manufacturing. For example, by 1986 only a small fraction of the 8,000 tons of cotton needed annually by the textile industry was supplied locally, while during the early 1970s Angola exported raw cotton. The deterioration of the water supply system has also damaged many industries, especially breweries, as have cutoffs in electricity supply. Furthermore, labor problems, a consequence of a shortage of skilled workers and disincentives to work for wages in an inflated economy, have depleted the local work force. Foreign exchange constraints have also prevented many industries from importing the necessary raw materials.

Electric Power

Angola is especially well endowed with potential sources for the production of electricity, both hydroelectric (estimated in 1986 at 7,710 megawatts potential capacity) and thermal (using locally produced oil). By 1986, however, a total of only 367 megawatts of generating capacity existed at the country's main power stations. Power stations on four rivers traditionally supplied most of the electricity consumed in the main urban areas: the Cambambe station on the Cuanza River and the Mabubas station on the Dande River provided electricity to the capital and the north, the Biópio and Lomaum stations on the Catumbela River supplied cities in the central provinces, and the Matala station on the Cunene River was the main source of power in the south. The Ruacaná station, also on the Cunene River near the border with Namibia, was under South African control during much of the 1980s. In addition, thermal stations in Luanda, Namibe, Cabinda, Huambo, Biópio, Uíge, and Lubango supplied power. However, these regional power systems were not connected. Furthermore, there were separate local grids in Cabinda and in the diamond-mining area of Lunda Norte Province.

Repairs were needed on the electrical system because of deteriorating equipment and the sabotage of stations and distribution lines. The central system has been hit repeatedly by UNITA, which in the 1980s put the Lomaum station and a substation at Alto Catumbela out of commission. Many of the power lines in the central area and in the northwest have also been cut by UNITA. Therefore, many businesses have installed their own generators and produce approximately 20 percent of the total electricity generated in Angola. In the late 1980s, the government was going ahead with plans to build a 520-megawatt hydroelectric station on the Cuanza River at Capanda to augment the northern system. The government had also reached an agreement with Brazil and the Soviet Union for financial and technical assistance in building the station for an estimated US$900 million.

Food Processing

The food-processing industry suffered not only from the general economic constraints in Angola but also from government-

*Workers build drying racks at a small
government-run fishing village.*

imposed import restrictions. By 1988 the industry depended almost entirely on imports for its raw materials. By 1985 food processing had reached only 37 percent of its 1973 level. The most successful branches of the industry were maize processing (84 percent of the 1973 level), wheat milling (57 percent), and brewing (55 percent). Since independence, there have been some major investments in brewing and soft drinks, sugar processing, baking and flour milling, and vegetable oil production. The government controlled the bread-making industry and operated eight bakeries. Considerable improvements have been made in factory equipment to boost production; nevertheless, production came to a standstill twice in 1985 because of a lack of wheat flour.

War and the sudden departure of Portuguese technicians in 1975 adversely affected sugar production. The main problems were a decline in cane production and a deterioration in the quality of cane. Formerly grown on large Portuguese-owned plantations, cane was produced in the 1980s by state-run organizations assisted by Cuban technical advisers. After the Portuguese abandoned the plantations, most of the sugarcane plants were not maintained. The sucrose content in Angolan sugarcane dropped from a pre-1975 average of 9.5 percent to an average of only 3.5 percent in 1987, making it necessary to grow nearly three times as much cane to produce the equivalent amount of sugar. Among many other problems that aggravated sugar production were the shortage of water for irrigation, lack of equipment and fertilizers, theft, and poor drainage in the cane fields. Furthermore, there has been a large decline in the area cultivated, inappropriate cane varieties have been introduced, and machinery in the sugar mills has become dilapidated. Although some sugar was exported at the end of the colonial period (18,303 tons in 1973), an average of about 55,000 tons a year was imported from Cuba between 1979 and 1986.

Light Industry

By 1986 light industry, which included textiles, clothing, tobacco, soaps, matches, and plastic and wood products, had almost been restored to its preindependence level of production. The largest investments in light industry have been in two large textile projects: the Africa Têxtil plant in the city of Benguela (US$15 million), completed in 1979, and the Textang-II plant in the city of Luanda (US$45 million), completed in 1983. They each had a production capacity of more than 10 million square meters of cloth per year but have produced far less because of shortages of cotton. Other notable investments have been in wood processing (US$12 million), with projects in Cabinda and Luanda.

*Assembling chairs and
finishing wood
at a small furniture factory*

The state-owned National Textile Company (Emprêsa Nacional de Têxteis—Entex) has also suffered from a shortage of cotton. Founded in 1980, Entex had factories throughout the country and the capacity to produce 27 million square meters of cloth per year. By 1987, however, the company was turning out only 12 million square meters. Likewise, the production capacity of blankets was nearly 1.7 million per year, but only 900,000 were produced in 1986. Adding to Entex's problems, one of its major factories, Textang-I, was shut down in 1986 because of a lack of treated water and damage from mud. By 1987 no stocks of raw materials or spare parts had been replaced.

Similarly, plastics production under a state-run company was only about half of installed capacity. Operating factories abandoned by the Portuguese after 1976, the state agency suffered from a lack of materials and from aging equipment. It employed foreign technical assistants but had also been training Angolan workers at home and overseas.

Heavy Industry

By 1985 heavy industry was producing only 35 percent of its 1973 output. The main branches of this sector were the assembly of vehicles; production of steel bars and tubes, zinc sheets, and other metal products; assembly of radio and television sets; and manufacture of tires, batteries, paper, and chemical products. There have been large investments to rehabilitate steel production. Nevertheless, although imports of steel dropped from more than 58,000 tons in 1980 to 35,000 tons in 1986, Angola still imported most of its finished steel goods, including tubes, sheets, and plates.

In 1983 the government established a company to process scrap metal. The Northern Regional Enterprise for the Exploitation of Scrap Metal, located in Luanda, had the capacity to process 31,000 tons of scrap metal and produced 7,125 tons of processed scrap metal in 1985, its first year of operation. The government claimed that the efforts of this enterprise had saved US$1.4 million that would have been spent on importing scrap metal. The government planned to establish another company in Lobito, with the financial support of the United Nations Development Programme (UNDP) and the United Nations Industrial Development Organization (UNIDO).

The government also controlled the automobile assembly industry through a company founded in 1978 after a Portuguese firm had been nationalized. The company consisted of a factory that assembled light vehicles; a plant, possibly at Viana, that assembled buses and heavy trucks; and a factory at Cunene that built the chassis for all these vehicles. The light vehicle factory was particularly affected by the cutback in imports in 1982, and its output fell in 1983–84 to only 20 percent of capacity. Likewise, the bus and truck plant has experienced shutdowns because of a lack of parts. Inputs for the automobiles came from state-owned companies that produced paint, plastic seats, metal tubing, and rubber tires.

Construction Materials

Despite official support for the construction materials industry, by 1985 production of building materials still fell far short of government hopes. In 1988 the government was rehabilitating the Angolan Cement Company (Emprêsa de Cimento de Angola—Cimangola), which accounted for 90 percent of Angolan production. Cimangola was founded in 1954 and was declared a mixed enterprise after independence, with part-Danish ownership. In 1973 Cimangola produced 582,300 tons of cement, but in 1985 it produced only 183,600 tons. In 1988 the government was planning to double the production capacity of the Cimangola plant on the outskirts of Luanda through the installation of another kiln, bringing production capacity up to 750,000 tons.

Transportation and Telecommunications

Roads

The Portuguese left Angola with a relatively well-developed road network that totaled about 70,000 kilometers, 8,000 of which were paved. Since 1975, however, many bridges have been blown up, many vehicles have been destroyed, and many roads have been subject to attack by UNITA guerrillas, necessitating military convoys for road transportation. In the late 1980s, roads and railroads were still exposed to sabotage and ambush. Rural-urban trade and supply bottlenecks limited most inland industries, and transport and communications services suffered from labor shortages. The highest priority has been given to repairing the bridges linking the provincial capitals.

Railroads

In the 1980s, three different 1.067-meter gauge rail systems ran from the hinterland to major ports on the Atlantic Ocean (see fig. 10). The longest line (1,394 kilometers) was the Benguela Railway. It linked the port of Lobito with the central African rail system that served the mining regions of Shaba (Zaire) and the Zambian Copperbelt. The Benguela Railway had a rail spur to Cuima, near Huambo. In late 1988, it was operating only between Lobito and Benguela. In the south, the 899-kilometer Namibe

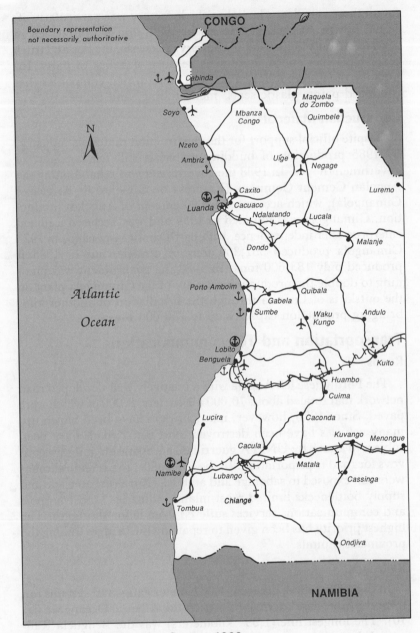

Figure 10. Transportation System, 1988

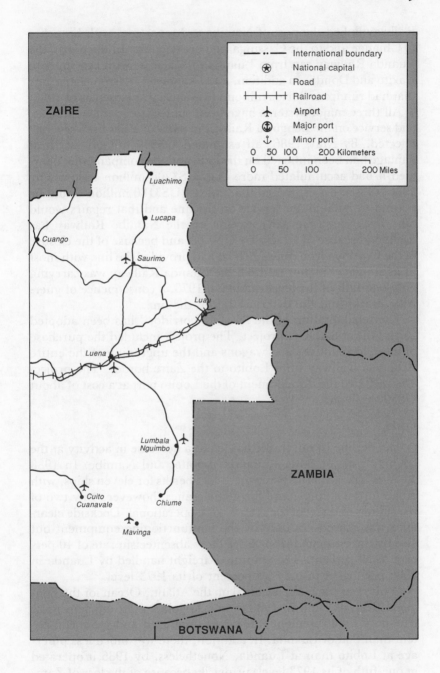

Railway linked the port of Namibe to Menongue, with branches to Chiange and to the Cassinga iron ore deposits. In the north, the Luanda Railway ran from Luanda to Malanje, with rail spurs to Caxito and Dondo. In addition, a 123-kilometer, narrow-gauge line that had run from Porto Amboim to Gabela was closed as of 1987.

All three major systems have been subject to guerrilla attacks, and service on the Benguela Railway in particular has been severely affected. By May 1986, an estimated US$69 million worth of damage had been inflicted on the line, and the company that operated it had accumulated more than US$200 million in losses by 1986. Observers estimated that at least US$180 million would be needed to rehabilitate service on the line and that repairs would take five years. Similarly, traffic on the Namibe Railway has declined because of attacks by UNITA and because of the closure of the Cassinga iron mines, which had provided the line with most of its freight. Finally, by 1986 the Luanda Railway was carrying only one-fifth of the level carried in 1973, a consequence of guerrilla attacks and the deterioration of the line.

The rehabilitation of the ''Lobito corridor'' has been adopted as an official SADCC project. The project included the purchase of more locomotives and wagons and the upgrading of the entire Benguela Railway from Lobito to the Zaire border. The project also included the development of the Lobito port at a cost of about US$90 million.

Ports

The decline in rail traffic has led to a decrease in activity at the country's major ports—Luanda, Lobito, and Namibe. In 1988 Luanda's port was in disrepair. It had berths for eleven ships, with adjacent rail sidings, and forty-one cranes; however, only two of the sidings and few of the cranes were operational. Dockside clearance was slowed not only by the nonfunctioning equipment but also by the estimated labor force daily absenteeism rate of 40 percent to 50 percent. The volume of freight handled by Luanda in 1986 had fallen to only 30 percent of its 1973 level.

Lobito was the main terminal on the Atlantic Ocean for the Benguela Railway, and in 1988 it was Angola's most efficient port. The port's management was better organized and more competent than that of Luanda. In addition, there was much less pilferage at Lobito than at Luanda. Nonetheless, by 1986 it operated at one-fifth of its 1973 level, primarily because of the loss of Zambian and Zairian traffic on the Benguela Railway.

Namibe, too, was hampered by inoperable equipment and loss of traffic. The volume of cargo handled there dropped sharply after the halt of iron ore exports, leaving the ore terminal idle.

In addition to minor general cargo ports at Ambriz, Benguela, Porto Amboim, Sumbe, and Tombua, there were major petroleum-loading facilities at the Malongo terminal in Cabinda Province and at the Soyo-Quinfuquena terminal at Soyo. In the late 1980s, some of the minor ports were taking on greater importance as road transportation became increasingly disrupted by UNITA ambushes.

To help rectify some of these transportation problems, the government had contracted with West German and Danish companies to improve port operations and to establish repair and storage facilities. The government was also involved in training pilots, sailors, and mechanics and also sent students to Portugal, Cuba, and the Soviet Union to study merchant marine subjects.

Air Transport

In contrast to other transport methods, air transport has grown, partly in response to the difficulties of land transport. The state-run national airline, Angola Airlines (Linhas Aéreas de Angola—TAAG; formerly known as Transportes Aéreos de Angola), has been highly profitable and in 1984 posted pretax profits of US$12.7 million. The airline benefited from high passenger and cargo load on its flights, the low price of jet fuel in Angola, and the low wages paid to employees. In 1988 TAAG was planning to refurbish its fleet of Boeing 737s and 707s. Because of United States opposition to the sale of American aircraft to Angola, TAAG was expected to purchase its new aircraft from Airbus Industrie of France.

Domestic service linked Luanda with Benguela, Cabinda, Huambo, Lubango, Malanje, Negage, and Soyo. Because of unrealistically low fees, demand for domestic flights was heavy. Boarding a flight, even with a confirmed reservation, was often problematic, and flight schedules were undependable. Although it operated only domestic flights before independence, TAAG has since established an extensive international route network based at the country's major airport at Luanda. TAAG offered service from Luanda to the African countries of Zaire, Zambia, Mozambique, Cape Verde, São Tomé and Príncipe, and Congo. The company's international routes served Havana, Lisbon, Moscow, Paris, and Rome.

Telecommunications

Telecommunications in Angola have also improved since independence. The number of telephone subscribers has grown from 24,500 in 1974 to 52,000 in 1986. Luanda was estimated to have two-thirds of all telephones. Two state bodies were responsible for telecommunications: the National Telecommunications

Company (Emprêsa Nacional de Telecomunicações—Enatel) for domestic service, and the Public Telecommunications Company (Emprêsa Pública de Telecomunicações—Eptel) for international service. Enatel included twenty automatic and thirty-six manual telephone exchanges and three telex centers. Eight of the eighteen provincial capitals had automatic local and interurban services; interurban links were provided by microwave and troposcatter systems. International Telecommunications Satellite Organization (Intelsat) links were provided via an earth station at Cacuaco. In December 1986, Angola resumed contacts with Intersputnik, the Soviet-sponsored international space telecommunications organization, and planned to incorporate the station at Cacuaco into the Intersputnik system. To ensure continuous international communications, in 1986 the government announced plans to install a second earth station at Benguela.

Balance of Payments, Finances, and Foreign Debt

Balance of Trade and Payments

Despite generally large trade surpluses, the national current account has been in deficit since statistics were first published in 1978. Trade surpluses have been outweighed by large deficits on "invisibles"—primarily interest and profits, transport costs, and technical assistance payments. The largest part of the outflow for interest and profits was accounted for by the payments of state-run petroleum companies abroad for amortization of their loans (see table 11, Appendix A).

By 1988 the medium-term and long-term capital account had been positive for many years because of large inflows from loans, most of which were granted by the Soviet Union on concessional terms. The centralized planning system strictly controlled external borrowing, and each year the Ministry of Planning set a ceiling on borrowing, following consultations with the National Bank of Angola (Banco Nacional de Angola—BNA).

Most of Angola's debt has been contracted on concessional terms. The effective rate of interest on medium-term and long-term debt was only 4.9 percent in 1985, and the average loan maturity was about seven years. Out of a total of US$3.25 billion in disbursed and undisbursed debt, US$2.06 billion was owed to the Soviet Union for military purchases. This amount carried very attractive terms: an annual interest rate of 3 percent and repayment over ten years, including a three-year grace period. In contrast, only 11.5 percent of loans from creditors outside Comecon were granted on a concessional basis.

*Cranes unloading cargo
at Lobito
Courtesy Richard J. Hough*

*A dock at the port in Luanda
Courtesy Richard J. Hough*

153

The government has taken steps to reverse the growth in imports of services, proposing new programs to train Angolans to provide key technical assistance. At the Second Party Congress in December 1985, the government proposed several steps to give priority to national companies when awarding building contracts; to cut less essential services, such as transport expenditures and international telephone and telex usage; and provisionally to suspend private transfers abroad. In particular, in March and June 1986 the government placed severe restrictions on salary transfers abroad by foreign resident workers and foreign aid workers.

Finances

Banking was a monopoly of the state-run BNA, which controlled currency, loans, and foreign debts for the private and state sectors. Reflecting the general liberalization of state economic policies adopted in 1986, the BNA has provided credit for foreign investors and has tried to encourage foreign banks to establish operations inside Angola. The BNA handled all government financial transactions and played an important role in setting fiscal policy, especially regarding permissible foreign loans and the establishment of annual ceilings on imports. The bank has been notably unsuccessful, however, in halting the decline of the kwanza, which in late 1988 traded on the parallel market for up to 2,100 per United States dollar—barely one-seventieth of its theoretical value. In fact, because the local economy was based more on barter than on monetary exchange, the BNA's primary impact has been in the area of foreign loans, which have become increasingly important to the economy.

Foreign Debt

Angola's total disbursed external debt, much of which was owed to the Soviet Union and its allies for arms purchases, totaled about US$4 billion in mid-1988. There was only a 0.3 percent rise in medium-term and long-term debt in 1986, but the buildup of arrears after the crash in oil prices resulted in a 145 percent increase in short-term debt. Arrears accounted for US$378 million, including US$224 million owed to Western countries. In 1986 the Soviet Union (Angola's largest creditor), Brazil (the second largest), and Portugal agreed to reschedule debt payments.

By the end of 1986, some debt payments were running seven to eight months late, and some Western export credit agencies denied Angola most medium-term and long-term credits. The depreciation of the United States dollar, to which the Angolan kwanza was tied, has added to the balance of payments pressure.

This situation existed because Angola's oil sales were denominated in United States dollars, while many of its imports were priced in relatively stronger European currencies. By 1987 Angola's accumulated arrears (US$378 million) and its debt-service obligations (US$442 million of principal and US$196 million of interest) equaled nearly half of its exports of goods and services.

The government in 1987 attempted to put together a financial arrangement to repay its external debts over a fifteen-year period. The minister of finance proposed raising US$1 billion on the international capital market through the issue of fifteen-year, floating-rate notes to pay off its arrears to Western creditors, to prepay principal due on nonpetroleum-related debts, and to provide approximately US$125 million in revenue. The Paris Club (see Glossary), however, turned down the proposal because of its complexity, uncertainty over its success, and the cost implications for the creditor countries. To provide an alternative, the Europeans advised Angola that they would consider debt rescheduling if the government would seek membership in the IMF. Subsequently, President dos Santos announced in August 1987 that his government intended to apply for membership in the IMF and the World Bank.

* * *

Information on Angola continues to be difficult to obtain. For many years, government policies and the ongoing insurgency discouraged visits by international organizations, journalists, and scholars. By the late 1980s, however, more information was becoming available. The most comprehensive source on the economy is Tony Hodges's *Angola to the 1990s*. Specific material on economic background can be gleaned from Malyn Newitt's *Portugal in Africa* and Gerald J. Bender's *Angola under the Portuguese*. Publications of multilateral organizations, such as the UN and the World Bank, are helpful for data on various aspects of the economy. Useful periodicals include the Economist Intelligence Unit's quarterly *Country Report, Jeune Afrique, West Africa, Jornal de Angola, Africa Economic Digest, Africa Research Bulletin, Marchés tropicaux et méditerranéens, Afrique-Asie,* and *Africa Hoje.* (For further information and complete citations, see Bibliography.)

Chapter 4. Government and Politics

Angolans march at a political rally.

AFTER THIRTEEN YEARS of guerrilla warfare, Angola finally escaped from Portuguese colonial rule in 1975, but with few of the resources needed to govern an independent nation. When an effort to form a coalition government comprising three liberation movements failed, a civil war ensued. The Popular Movement for the Liberation of Angola (Movimento Popular de Libertação de Angola—MPLA) emerged from the civil war to proclaim a Marxist-Leninist one-party state. The strongest of the disenfranchised movements, the National Union for the Total Independence of Angola (União Nacional para a Independência Total de Angola—UNITA), continued to battle for another thirteen years, shifting the focus of its opposition from the colonial power to the MPLA government. In late 1988, the social and economic disorder resulting from a quarter-century of violence had a pervasive effect on both individual lives and national politics.

Angola's 1975 Constitution, revised in 1976 and 1980, ratifies the socialist revolution but also guarantees some rights of private ownership. The ruling party, renamed the Popular Movement for the Liberation of Angola-Workers' Party (Movimento Popular de Libertação de Angola-Partido de Trabalho—MPLA-PT) in 1977, claimed the power of the state. Although formally subordinate to the party, the government consolidated substantial power in its executive branch. The president was head of the MPLA-PT, the government, the military, and most important bodies within the party and the government. In his first nine years in office (1979–88), President José Eduardo dos Santos further strengthened the presidency, broadening the influence of a small circle of advisers and resisting pressure to concentrate more power within the MPLA-PT. His primary goal was economic development rather than ideological rigor, but at the same time dos Santos considered the MPLA-PT the best vehicle for building a unified, prosperous nation.

Among the first actions taken by the MPLA-PT was its conversion into a vanguard party to lead in the transformation to socialism. Throughout the 1980s, the MPLA-PT faced the daunting task of mobilizing the nation's peasants, most of whom were concerned with basic survival, subsistence farming, and avoiding the destruction of the ongoing civil war. Only a small minority of Angolans were party members, but even this group was torn by internal disputes. Factional divisions were drawn primarily along

159

racial and ideological lines, but under dos Santos influence within the MPLA–PT gradually shifted from *mestiço* (see Glossary) to black African leadership and from party ideologues to relative political moderates.

Mass organizations were affiliated with the party in accordance with Marxist-Leninist dogma. In the face of continued insurgent warfare and deteriorating living standards, however, many social leaders chafed at party discipline and bureaucratic controls. Dos Santos worked to build party loyalty and to respond to these tensions, primarily by attempting to improve the material rewards of Marxist-Leninist state building. His greatest obstacle, however, was the destabilizing effect of UNITA and its South African sponsors; Angola's role as a victim of South Africa's destructive regional policies was central to its international image during the 1980s.

In December 1988, Angola, South Africa, and Cuba reached a long-sought accord that promised to improve Luanda's relations with Pretoria. The primary goals of the United States-brokered talks were to end South Africa's illegal occupation of Namibia and remove Cuba's massive military presence from Angola. Vital economic assistance from the United States was a corollary benefit of the peace process, conditioned on Cuba's withdrawal and the MPLA–PT's rapprochement with UNITA. Despite doubts about the intentions of all three parties to the accord, international hopes for peace in southwestern Africa were high.

Background

Political units in southwestern Africa evolved into complex structures long before the arrival of the first Portuguese traveler, Diogo Cão, in 1483. The Bantu-speaking and Khoisan-speaking hunters the Portuguese encountered were descendants of those who had peopled most of the region for centuries. Pastoral and agricultural villages and kingdoms had also arisen in the northern and central plateaus. One of the largest of these, the Kongo Kingdom, provided the earliest resistance to Portuguese domination (see Kongo Kingdom, ch. 1). The Bakongo (people of Kongo) and their southern neighbors, the Mbundu, used the advantage of their large population and centralized organization to exploit their weaker neighbors for the European slave trade.

To facilitate nineteenth-century policies emphasizing the extraction of mineral and agricultural resources, colonial officials reorganized villages and designed transportation routes to expedite marketing these resources. Colonial policy also encouraged interracial marriage but discouraged education among Africans, and the resulting racially and culturally stratified population included people of mixed ancestry (*mestiços*), educated Angolans (*assimilados*—see Glossary) who identified with Portuguese cultural values, and the majority of the African population that remained uneducated and unassimilated (*indígenas*—see Glossary). Opportunities for economic advancement were apportioned according to racial stereotypes, and even in the 1960s schools were admitting barely more than 2 percent of the school-age African population each year.

Portugal resisted demands for political independence long after other European colonial powers had relinquished direct control of their African possessions. After unsuccessfully seeking support from the United Nations (UN) in 1959, educated Luandans organized a number of resistance groups based on ethnic and regional loyalties. By the mid-1970s, four independence movements vied with one another for leadership of the emerging nation (see African Associations, ch. 1).

The MPLA, established by *mestiços* and educated workers in Luanda, drew its support from urban areas and the Mbundu population that surrounded the capital city. The Union of Peoples of Northern Angola (União das Populações do Norte de Angola—UPNA) was founded to defend Bakongo interests. The UPNA soon dropped its northern emphasis and became the Union of Angolan Peoples (União das Populações de Angola—UPA) in an attempt to broaden its ethnic constituency, although it rebuffed consolidation attempts by other associations. The UPA, in turn, formed the National Front for the Liberation of Angola (Frente Nacional de Libertação de Angola—FNLA) in 1962, when it merged with other northern dissident groups.

A variety of interpretations of Marxist philosophy emerged during the 1950s and 1960s, a period when Western nations refused to pressure Portugal (a member of the North Atlantic Treaty Organization—NATO) to upgrade political life in its colonies. The Portuguese Communist Party (Partido Comunista Português—PCP) helped organize African students in Lisbon and encouraged them to press for independence. A campaign of arrests and forced exile crushed most Angolan nationalist leadership, but in Portugal underground antifascist groups were gaining strength, and Angolan liberation movements flourished. The MPLA established its headquarters in Léopoldville, Belgian Congo (present-day Kinshasa, Zaire), and in 1962, after a period of exile and imprisonment, Agostinho Neto became head of the MPLA.

Neto, a physician, poet, and philosopher, strengthened the MPLA's left-wing reputation with his rhetorical blend of socialist ideology and humanist values. He also led the group in protests against enforced cotton cultivation, discriminatory labor policies, and colonial rule in general. MPLA and UPA leaders agreed to cooperate, but long-standing animosities led members of these two groups to sabotage each other's efforts. Within the MPLA, leadership factions opposed each other on ideological grounds and policy issues, but with guidance from the Soviet Union they resolved most of their disputes by concentrating power in their high command. Soviet military assistance also increased in response to the growing commitment to building a socialist state.

In April 1974, the Portuguese army overthrew the regime in Lisbon, and its successor began dismantling Portugal's colonial empire. In November 1974, Lisbon agreed to grant independence. However, after centuries of colonial neglect, Angola's African population was poorly prepared for self-government: there were few educated or trained leaders and almost none with national experience. Angola's liberation armies contested control of the new nation, and the coalition established by the Alvor Agreement in January 1975 quickly disintegrated (see Coalition, the Transitional Government, and Civil War, ch. 1).

Events in Angola in 1975 were catastrophic. Major factors that contributed to the violence that dogged Angola's political development for over a decade were the incursions into northern Angola by the United States-backed and Zairian-backed FNLA; an influx of Cuban advisers and, later, troops providing the MPLA with training and combat support; South African incursions in the south; UNITA attacks in the east and south, some with direct troop support from Pretoria; and dramatic increases in Soviet matériel and other assistance to the MPLA. Accounts of the sequence of these critical events differed over the next decade and a half, but most observers agreed that by the end of 1975 Angola was effectively embroiled in a civil war and that growing Soviet, Cuban, South African, and United States involvement in that war made peace difficult to achieve.

International recognition came slowly to the MPLA, which controlled only the northern third of the nation by December 1975. A small number of former Portuguese states and Soviet allies recognized the regime, and Nigeria led the Organization of African Unity (OAU) in granting recognition. The FNLA and UNITA attempted unsuccessfully to establish a rival government in the Angolan town of Huambo, but no one outside Angola recognized their regime. By the end of 1976, Angola was a member of the UN and was recognized by most other African states, but its domestic legitimacy remained in question.

A view of Lobito, one of Angola's largest cities
Courtesy Richard J. Hough

MPLA leader Neto had avoided ideological labels during the struggle for independence, although the MPLA never concealed the Marxist bias of some of its members. Neto viewed Marxist-Leninist orthodoxy as a means of unifying and organizing Angola's diverse society and of establishing agricultural growth as the basis for economic development. He also hoped to avoid disenfranchising urban workers or encouraging the growth of a rural bourgeoisie, while maintaining crucial military support from the Soviet Union and Cuba.

One of the MPLA's many slogans, "people's power" (*poder popular*), had won broad support for the group before independence, especially in Luanda, where neighborhood self-help groups were formed to defend residents of poor and working-class neighborhoods against armed banditry. This movement was quickly curtailed by the police, but people's power remained a popular symbol of the demand for political participation. After independence, despite constitutional guarantees of people's power, the slogan became a symbol of unrealized expectations. President Neto, despite his democratic ideals, quickly developed an autocratic governing style. He introduced austerity measures and productivity campaigns and countered the resulting popular discontent with an array of security and intelligence operations.

Industrial workers, who were among the first to organize for people's power, found their newly formed unions absorbed into the

163

MPLA-controlled National Union of Angolan Workers (União Nacional dos Trabalhadores Angolanos—UNTA), and the party began to absorb other popular organizations into the party structure. Students, laborers, and peasant farmers agitated against what they perceived as a *mestiço*-dominated political elite, and this resentment, even within the ranks of the MPLA itself, culminated in an abortive coup attempt led by the former minister of interior, Nito Alves, in May 1977.

In the aftermath of the 1977 Nitista coup attempt, the MPLA redefined the rules for party membership. After the First Party Congress in December 1977 affirmed the Central Committee's decision to proclaim its allegiance to Marxist-Leninist ideals, the MPLA officially became a "workers' party" and added "-PT" (for "Partido de Trabalho") to its acronym. In 1978 its leaders began a purge of party cadres, announcing a "rectification campaign" to correct policies that had allowed the Nitista factions and other "demagogic" tendencies to develop. The MPLA–PT reduced its numbers from more than 100,000 to about 31,000, dropping members the party perceived as lacking dedication to the socialist revolution. Most of those purged were farmers or educated *mestiços,* especially those whose attitudes were considered "petit bourgeois." Urban workers, in contrast to rural peasants, were admitted to the MPLA–PT in fairly large numbers.

By the end of the 1970s, the ruling party was smaller, more unified, and more powerful, but it had lost standing in rural areas, and its strongest support still came from those it was attempting to purge—educated *mestiços* and *assimilados.* Progress was hampered by losses in membership, trade, and resources resulting from emigration and nearly two decades of warfare. The MPLA–PT attempted to impose austerity measures to cope with these losses, but in the bitter atmosphere engendered by the purges of the late 1970s, these policies further damaged MPLA–PT legitimacy. Pursuing the socialist revolution was not particularly important in non-Mbundu rural areas, in part because of the persistent impression that *mestiços* dominated the governing elite. National politicians claimed economic privilege and allowed corruption to flourish in state institutions, adding to the challenges faced by dos Santos, who became MPLA–PT leader in 1979.

Structure of Government
The Constitution

Adopted in November 1975, independent Angola's first and only Constitution dedicates the new republic to eliminating the vestiges of Portuguese colonialism. The Constitution provides numerous guarantees of individual freedom and prohibits discrimination based on color, race, ethnic identity, sex, place of birth, religion, level of education, and economic or social status. The Constitution also promises freedom of expression and assembly.

Constitutional revisions in 1976 and 1980 more clearly establish the national goal of a revolutionary socialist, one-party state. As revised, the Constitution vests sovereignty in the Angolan people, guaranteed through the representation of the party, and promises to implement "people's power." It also emphasizes the preeminence of the party as policy-making body and makes the government subordinate to it. Government officials are responsible for implementing party policy. Economic development is founded on socialist models of cooperative ownership.

Other constitutional guarantees include health care, access to education, and state assistance in childhood, motherhood, disability, and old age. In return for these sweeping guarantees, each individual is responsible for participating in the nation's defense, voting in official elections, serving in public office if appointed or elected, working (which is considered both a right and a duty), and generally aiding in the socialist transformation.

Despite its strong socialist tone, the Constitution guarantees the protection of private property and private business activity within limits set by the state. National economic goals are to develop agriculture and industry, establish just social relations in all sectors of production, foster the growth of the public sector and cooperatives, and implement a system of graduated direct taxation. Social goals include combating illiteracy, promoting the development of education and a national culture, and enforcing strict separation of church and state, with official respect for all religions.

The Constitution also outlines Angola's defense policy. It explicitly prohibits foreign military bases on Angolan soil or affiliation with any foreign military organization. It institutionalizes the People's Armed Forces for the Liberation of Angola (Forças Armadas Populares de Libertação de Angola—FAPLA) as the nation's army and assigns it responsibility for defense and national reconstruction. Military conscription applies to both men and women over the age of eighteen (see Armed Forces, ch. 5).

Executive Branch

The President

Executive authority is vested in the president, his appointed ministers, and the Defense and Security Council (see fig. 11).

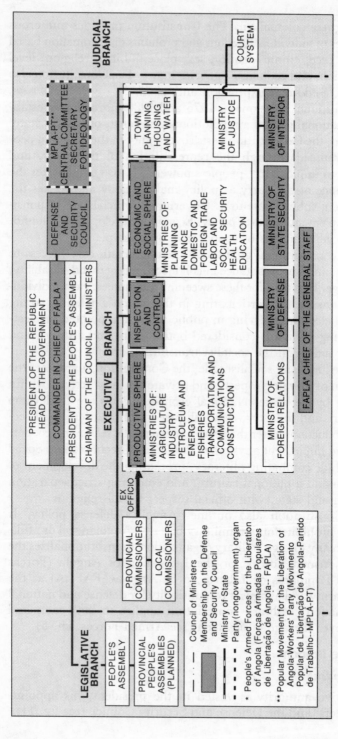

Source: Based on information from Tony Hodges, *Angola to the 1990s*, London, 1987, 12.

Figure 11. Structure of the Government, 1988

The president is selected as head of the MPLA–PT by the Political Bureau. His authority derives first from his status as head of the MPLA–PT and then from his preeminence in government. President dos Santos, like his predecessor, had wide-ranging powers as the leading figure in politics and the military. He was commander in chief of the armed forces and chairman of the Council of Ministers. He was also empowered to appoint and dismiss a wide variety of national and provincial officials, including military officers and provincial commissioners. The president could also designate an acting president from among the members of the MPLA–PT Political Bureau, but if he died or were disabled, his successor would be chosen by the Central Committee.

Council of Ministers

In late 1988, the Council of Ministers comprised twenty-one ministers and ministers of state. The seventeen ministerial portfolios included agriculture, construction, defense, domestic and foreign trade, education, finance, fisheries, foreign relations, health, industry, interior, justice, labor and social security, petroleum and energy, planning, state security, and transport and communications. Ministers were empowered to prepare the national budget and to make laws by decree, under authority designated by the national legislature, the People's Assembly, but most of the ministers' time was spent administering policy set by the MPLA–PT.

In February 1986, dos Santos appointed four ministers of state (who came to be known as "superministers") and assigned them responsibility for coordinating the activities of the Council of Ministers. Their portfolios were for the productive sphere; economic and social spheres; inspection and control; and town planning, housing, and water. Twelve ministries were placed under superministry oversight; the ministers of defense, foreign relations, interior, justice, and state security continued to report directly to the president. This change was part of an effort to coordinate policy, reduce overlapping responsibilities, eliminate unnecessary bureaucratic procedures, and bolster the government's reputation for efficiency in general. Most ministers and three of the four ministers of state were also high officials in the MPLA–PT, and their policy-making influence was exercised through the party rather than through the government.

Defense and Security Council

In May 1986, the president appointed eight respected advisers to the Defense and Security Council, including the ministers of defense, interior, and state security; the ministers of state for the economic and social spheres, inspection and control, and the productive sphere; the FAPLA chief of the general staff; and the MPLA–PT Central Committee secretary for ideology, information, and culture. The president chaired the council and gave it a broad mandate, including oversight and administration in military, economic, and diplomatic affairs. He strengthened this authority during the council's first five years by treating the council as an inner circle of close advisers. By 1988 the Defense and Security Council and the Political Bureau, both chaired by the president, were the most powerful decision-making bodies within the government and party, respectively.

Legislative Branch

The principle of people's power was enshrined in the 223-member People's Assembly, which replaced the Council of the Revolution as the nation's legislature in 1980. The primary purpose of the People's Assembly was to implement some degree of participatory democracy within the revolutionary state and to do so outside party confines. People's Assembly delegates did not have to be party members, and many were not. The planned electoral process was the election of 203 delegates to three-year terms by an electoral college. The electoral college, in turn, would be elected by universal suffrage. The remaining twenty delegates were to be elected by the Central Committee of the MPLA–PT. During the 1980s, implementation of this plan was obstructed by security problems and bureaucratic snarls. In 1980 the Central Committee elected all People's Assembly members. In 1983 the government's lack of control over many rural areas, combined with a dearth of accurate census data, prompted dos Santos to postpone the elections. The 1986 elections, actually held in 1987, consisted of mass meetings at which the names of nominees were presented on a list prepared by the existing People's Assembly. A few names were challenged and removed, but these lengthy public discussions did not constitute the democratic process required by the Constitution.

The People's Assembly met every six months to approve the national budget and development plan, enact legislation, and delegate responsibilities to its subcommittees. It also elected the twenty-five-member Permanent Commission to perform assembly functions between sessions. The president headed the Permanent Commission, which was dominated by members of the MPLA–PT Political Bureau. The subordination of the People's Assembly to the MPLA–PT was ensured by including high-level party officials among the former's appointed members and by frequent reminders of the preeminence of the party. The government's intention was to create people's assemblies at all levels of local administration in order to establish a government presence in remote areas and promote party-government contacts. The planned assemblies were an important symbol of people's power, although they were also intended to be controlled by the party elite.

Judicial System

The Ministry of Justice oversaw the nation's court system, which comprised the Supreme Court, the Court of Appeals, people's revolutionary courts, and a system of people's courts. High-level judges were appointed by the minister of justice. The Supreme Court and the Court of Appeals heard cases involving national officials and appeals from lower courts. People's revolutionary courts heard accusations related to national security, mercenary activity, or war crimes. They presided over both military and civilian cases, with senior military officers serving in a judicial capacity in military cases (see Conditions of Service, Ranks, and Military Justice, ch. 5). Appeals were heard by appellate courts in each provincial capital.

People's courts were established in the late 1970s by the National Court Administration of the Ministry of Justice as part of a nationwide reorganization along Marxist-Leninist lines. The people's court system comprised criminal, police, and labor tribunals in each provincial capital and in a few other towns. The MPLA–PT Political Bureau appointed three judges—one professional and two lay magistrates—to preside over each people's courtroom and assigned them equal power and legal standing. Although the professional judges had substantial legal training, lay judges were appointed on a rotating basis from among a group of citizens who had some formal education and several weeks' introductory legal training. Some were respected leaders of local ethnic groups. No juries were empaneled in either civil or criminal cases, but judges sometimes sought the opinion of local residents in weighing decisions.

Local Administration

As of late 1988, Angola was divided into eighteen provinces (*províncias*) and 161 districts (*municípios*) (see fig. 1). Districts were further subdivided into quarters or communes (*comunas*), villages (*povoações*), and neighborhoods (*bairros*). Administration at each level was the responsibility of a commissioner, who was appointed by the president at the provincial, district, and commune levels and elected at the village and neighborhood levels. The eighteen provincial commissioners were ex-officio members of the executive branch of the national government. The supreme organ of state power was the national People's Assembly. Provincial people's assemblies comprised between fifty-five and eighty-five delegates, charged with implementing MPLA–PT directives. People's assemblies were also envisioned, but not yet operational in late 1988, at each subnational level of administration.

In 1983 the president created a system of regional military councils to oversee a range of local concerns with security implications. High-ranking military officers, reporting directly to the president, headed these councils. Their authority superseded that of other provincial administrators and allowed them to impose a state of martial law within areas threatened by insurgency. The boundaries of military regions and the provinces did not coincide exactly. Until 1988 ten regional military councils were in operation. In early 1988, however, the Ministry of Defense, citing this structure as inadequate, announced the formation of four fronts (see Constitutional and Political Context, ch. 5).

Popular Movement for the Liberation of Angola-Workers' Party

Background

During the 1960s, the MPLA established its headquarters at Kinshasa, Zaire, and then at Lusaka, Zambia, and Brazzaville, Congo. The MPLA's scattered bases and diverse constituent groups contributed to disunity and disorganization, problems that were exacerbated by personal and ideological differences among party leaders. The first serious split occurred in 1973, when Daniel Chipenda led a rebellion, sometimes termed the Eastern Revolt, in protest against the party's *mestiço*-dominated leadership and Soviet interference in Angolan affairs. Chipenda and his followers were expelled from the MPLA, and many joined the northern-based FNLA in 1975. Then in 1974, about seventy left-wing MPLA supporters based in Brazzaville broke with Agostinho Neto. This opposition movement became known as the Active Revolt. Shortly after independence, a third split occurred within the party, culminating in the 1977 coup attempt by Nito Alves. Later in 1977, the MPLA transformed itself into a Marxist-Leninist vanguard party and launched a lengthy rectification campaign to unify its membership, impose party discipline, and streamline decision-making processes.

In 1980 Angola was governed by a new head of state under a newly revised Constitution. The nation's first legislature, the

People's Assembly, served as a symbol of people's power, but state organs were clearly subordinate to those of the party. Within the MPLA-PT, channels for political participation were being narrowed. Both government and party leaders established a hierarchy of organizations through which they hoped to mobilize rural populations and broaden political support. At the same time, MPLA-PT leaders launched programs to impose party discipline on the party's cadres and indoctrinate all segments of society in their proper role in political development.

Overall goals were relatively easy to agree upon, but poverty and insecurity exacerbated disagreements over specific strategies for attaining these objectives. By the mid-1980s, the party had three major goals—incorporating the population into the political process, imposing party discipline on its cadres, and reconciling the diverse factions that arose to dispute these efforts. Some MPLA-PT officials sought to control political participation by regulating party membership and strengthening discipline, while others believed the MPLA-PT had wasted valuable resources in the self-perpetuating cycle of government repression and popular dissent. President dos Santos sought to resolve disputes that did not seem to threaten his office. However, much of the MPLA-PT's political agenda, already impeded by civil war and regional instability, was further obstructed by these intraparty disputes.

Structure

The Political Bureau reported in 1988 that the MPLA-PT had more than 45,000 members. Its social composition, an important aspect of its image as a popular vanguard party, consisted of approximately 18 percent industrial workers, 18 percent peasants, 4 percent agricultural wage earners, and 60 percent described by the Political Bureau as "other classes and social strata interested in building socialism." However, the fact remained that many party members were still government employees, members of the petite bourgeoisie the MPLA had denounced so loudly in the 1970s.

The central decision-making bodies of the MPLA-PT included the Political Bureau, Central Committee, and the party congress, each headed by the president as party chairman (see fig. 12). A hierarchy of committees existed at the provincial, district, and village levels; the smallest of these, the party cell, operated in many neighborhoods and workplaces. The MPLA-PT's organizing principle was democratic centralism, which allowed participants at each level of the organization to elect representatives to the next higher

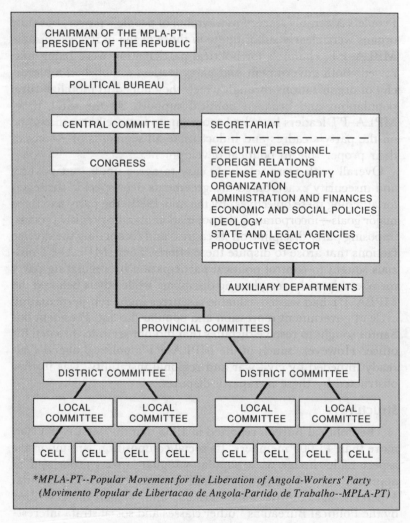

MPLA-PT--Popular Movement for the Liberation of Angola-Workers' Party
(Movimento Popular de Libertacao de Angola-Partido de Trabalho--MPLA-PT)

Source: Based on information from Keith Somerville, *Angola,* Boulder, 1986, 88–89; and
Popular Movement for the Liberation of Angola-Workers' Party, *Angola: Trabalho
e luta,* Paris, 1985, 68.

Figure 12. Structure of the MPLA-PT, 1988

level. MPLA–PT policy guaranteed open discussion at each level,
but majority decisions were binding on the minority, and lower-
level bodies were bound by higher-level decisions. Party hierarchies were incomplete in most areas, however, because of low
literacy rates, poverty, and security problems. Many lower-level
party functionaries therefore had roles in both party and government.

Political Bureau

The Political Bureau's eleven full members and two alternates were elected from among Central Committee members to assume the responsibilities of the committee between its sessions and to control the policy direction of the party. This small group wielded substantial power within the MPLA–PT, and its authority and membership overlapped that of the Central Committee Secretariat. In late 1988, the Political Bureau and the Defense and Security Council were the most influential bodies in the party and government, respectively.

Central Committee

Although the Central Committee was formally subordinate to the MPLA–PT party congress, in late 1988 the ninety Central Committee members wielded greater influence over party policy. The Central Committee assumed control between sessions of the party congress, and members of the Central Committee were influential in setting the congressional agenda.

Central Committee actions were implemented under the direction of its Secretariat, which in late 1988 consisted of nine department heads elected from the Central Committee. The Secretariat was responsible for directing day-to-day party work, collecting and analyzing information, preparing guidelines, and recommending courses of action in accordance with party congress policy.

Subordinate to the Central Committee Secretariat were seventeen specialized auxiliary agencies, which in late 1988 included the departments of administration and finance, agriculture, culture and sports, defense and security, economic and social policies, education, energy and communications, executive personnel, foreign relations, industry, information and propaganda, legal system, mass and social organizations, organization, policy and ideology, public welfare, and state agencies. These departments worked in cooperation with provincial and lower-level party organizations to implement Central Committee directives.

Party Congress

Theoretically the supreme body within the MPLA–PT, the party congress was actually controlled by top party officials. Following its first regular session in 1977 and an extraordinary session in 1980, the party congress was expected to convene once every five years. Most of the 630 delegates to the 1985 Second Party Congress were elected from among provincial committees, with most members of the Central Committee and all members of the Political Bureau as delegates. The party congress was responsible for setting the party's overall policy direction, confirming the Political Bureau's choice of party chairman and president, and electing the Central Committee members, who retained the decision-making authority of the party congress between sessions.

Regional Organization

The basic unit of the party was the cell, which consisted of between three and thirty members within a workplace or small neighborhood. Each cell elected a sector committee, which in turn elected a rural village committee or urban neighborhood committee, as appropriate. These committees, in turn, elected district and provincial committees. Higher-level committees were supposed to meet every two years and elect executive functionaries to set their agendas and retain minimal authority between meetings. An important task in each committee was the election of a party control commission to combat factionalism and promote cooperation among party functionaries within the region. At each level, control commission members were confirmed by the next higher level body before assuming office.

Operations

In addition to a chronic shortage of cadres, the MPLA–PT faced numerous obstacles in its first decade as a ruling body. By late 1988, the MPLA–PT party structure had not yet matured enough to respond temperately to criticism, either from within or from without. Party leaders dealt harshly with their critics, and political participation was still carefully controlled. Impeded by civil war, insurgency, economic problems, and the perception of elitism within its party ranks, the MPLA–PT campaign to mobilize grass-roots support remained in its early stages. Party membership was a prerequisite for effective political action, but channels of entry into the MPLA–PT were constricted by the party's entrenched leadership and centralized authority structure. Critics of the MPLA–PT, in turn, felt that after a quarter-century of warfare, they were being underserved by a large government apparatus that was preoccupied with internal and external security.

Factionalism also slowed the implementation of MPLA–PT programs. Rather than a strong, unified, vanguard leadership, the MPLA–PT presented an elite cadre torn by racial and ideological differences. Racial stratification, the legacy of colonial rule, permeated the party and society, providing a continuous reminder of economic inequities. The MPLA–PT had not established a reputation as a leader in the struggle to end racial discrimination,

*Villagers in Benguela Province showing support for the government
at an impromptu rally
Courtesy Richard J. Hough*

in part because of its roots among student elites selected by colonial officials. Many early party leaders were *mestiços* who had studied in Europe; some had married whites and were removed from the cultural background of their African relatives. Moreover, some Angolans still identified Marxist philosophy with European intellectuals rather than African peasants.

Ideological splits also grew within party ranks during the first nine years of dos Santos's regime, overlaying racial divisions. Divergent views on the role of Marxism in Angola produced clashes over domestic and foreign policy. Some African MPLA–PT leaders placed nationalist goals ahead of ideological goals, such as the radical transformation of society, and one of their nationalist goals was the elimination of *mestiço* domination.

The lines between racial and ideological factions tended to coincide. On the one hand, strong pro-Soviet views were often found among the party's *mestiço* leaders, who were inclined to view Angola's political situation in terms of revolutionary class struggle. In their eyes, ethnic, regional, and other subnational loyalties were obstacles to political mobilization. Black African party militants, on the other hand, often viewed racial problems as more important than class struggle, and they hoped to shape the MPLA–PT into a uniquely Angolan political structure. For them, Soviet intervention brought new threats of racism and foreign domination. Traditional ethnic group leaders were, in this view, vital to grassroots mobilization campaigns. Race and ideology did not always coincide, however. A few staunch ideologues were black Africans, while a small number of *mestiços* espoused moderate views and favored nonaligned policies.

Political Environment

In many Third World states, the president was the paramount leader, and in this regard Angola was no exception. Its president, José Eduardo dos Santos, combined strong party loyalty with political pragmatism. This loyalty had political and personal bases. Dos Santos owed much of his success to the MPLA, which he had joined in 1962 at the age of nineteen. The party sponsored his study at Baku University in the Soviet Union from 1963 to 1970. In 1974 MPLA leader Neto appointed dos Santos to the Central Committee, which elected him to its elite Political Bureau; this group elected him to succeed Neto, who died in 1979. Dos Santos traveled to the Soviet Union a few weeks later to confirm his revolutionary agenda as president.

Dos Santos's loyalty to Marxism-Leninism was founded in his student years in the Soviet Union, where he also married a Soviet citizen (who later returned to her homeland). There, he developed his belief in the vanguard party as the best strategy for mobilizing Angola's largely rural population. At the same time, however, he professed belief in a mixed economy, some degree of decentralization, an expanded private sector, and Western investment. Like many African leaders, he did not equate political eclecticism with internal contradiction, nor did he view Angola's political posture as an invitation to Soviet domination.

Dos Santos did not embrace Marxism for its utopian appeal; his view of Angolan society after the envisioned socialist transformation did not lack internal conflict. Rather, he viewed Marxist-Leninist organizational tenets as the most practical basis for mobilizing a society in which the majority lacked economic and educational opportunities. A small vanguard leadership, with proper motivation and training, could guide the population through the early stages of national development, in his view, and this approach could improve the lives of more people than capitalist investment and profit making by a small minority. During the 1980s, because trade with the Soviet Union and Eastern Europe failed to develop and because Western technical expertise appeared vital to Angola's development, dos Santos favored improved political relations with the West as a step toward peace and greater prosperity. Although he had scorned his predecessor's shift in the same direction in the late 1970s, dos Santos denied that his move signaled a weakening commitment to Marxism.

Despite his strong party loyalty, in the late 1980s dos Santos was known as a political pragmatist. He sometimes spoke out against the MPLA-PT's most extreme ideologues and took steps to limit their influence. He openly criticized the results of the rectification campaign of the late 1970s, which, in his view, had removed too many loyal members from the party's rolls. He also recognized that the campaign had alienated much of the nation's peasant majority, that they remained indifferent toward party programs in the late 1980s, and that they had not benefited from many MPLA-PT policies.

Political pragmatism was not to be confused with a liberal style of governing. In response to security crises and public criticism, dos Santos ordered arrests, detentions without trial, and occasional executions. He concentrated power in his office and narrowed his circle of close advisers. He enlarged the executive branch of government by appointing new ministers of state to coordinate executive branch activity and convinced the MPLA-PT Central Committee to entrust him with emergency powers. Dos Santos also persuaded party leaders to empower him to appoint regional military councils that had sweeping authority over civilian and military affairs in unstable regions of the country and that were answerable only to the president.

Dos Santos further consolidated his hold on executive authority in April 1984 by establishing the Defense and Security Council (see Executive Branch, this ch.). In 1985 he enlarged the party Central Committee from sixty to ninety members and alternates, thus diluting the strength of its staunch ideological faction.

Undermining potential opponents was not dos Santos's only motivation for consolidating power within the executive branch of government. He was also impatient with bureaucratic "red tape," even when justified in the name of party discipline. Accordingly, the primary qualification for his trusted advisers was a balance of competence, efficiency, and loyalty. Rhetorical skills, which he generally lacked, were not given particular priority; ideological purity was even less important. His advice for economic recovery was summed up as "produce, repair, and rehabilitate." The direct, relatively nonideological governing style exemplified by this approach earned dos Santos substantial respect and a few strong critics.

Economic and security crises worsened during the first nine years of dos Santos's presidency, draining resources that might have been used to improve living standards and education. The president rejected advice from party ideologues, whose primary aim was to develop a sophisticated Marxist-Leninist party apparatus. Rather than emphasize centralized control and party discipline, dos Santos embraced a plan to decentralize economic decision making in 1988. He then appointed Minister of Planning Lopo do Nascimento to serve as commissioner of Huíla Province in order to implement this plan in a crucial region of the country.

The 1985 Second Party Congress assented to the president's growing power by approving several of his choices for top government office as party officials. Among these was Roberto de Almeida, a member of the Defense and Security Council in his capacity as the MPLA–PT secretary for ideology, information, and culture and one of dos Santos's close advisers. Party leaders elected Almeida, a *mestiço,* to both the MPLA–PT Central Committee and the Political Bureau.

Demoted from the top ranks of the party were the leading ideologue, Lúcio Lára, and veteran *mestiço* leaders Paulo Jorge and Henrique Carreira (nom de guerre Iko). The split between ideologues and political moderates did not render the party immobile, in part because of dos Santos's skill at using Angola's internal and external threats to unite MPLA–PT factions. The ever-present UNITA

*A utility crew in Luanda
fixes a street lamp.*

*Maintenance workers surface a
length of road.*

insurgency provided a constant reminder of the frailty of the nation's security.

Mass Organizations and Interest Groups
Mass Organizations

Three mass organizations were affiliated with the MPLA–PT in 1988—the Popular Movement for the Liberation of Angola-Youth Movement (Juventude do Movimento Popular de Libertação de Angola—JMPLA), the Organization of Angolan Women (Organização da Mulher Angolana—OMA), and the UNTA. Each was founded as an anticolonial social movement during the 1960s and transformed into a party affiliate when the MPLA–PT became a vanguard party in 1977. Although these groups were formally subordinate to the party in accordance with Marxist-Leninist doctrine, they continued to operate with relative autonomy. Strict party ideologues objected to this independence and sometimes treated organization leaders with contempt. The resulting tensions added to public resentment of party discipline and became a political issue when Neto accused leaders of the JMPLA, the OMA, and the UNTA of supporting the Nitista coup attempt of 1977. Alves, the coup leader, had criticized MPLA–PT leaders for bourgeois attitudes and racism, and many people in these organizations supported Alves's allegations.

In the late 1970s, mass organizations became an important target of the rectification campaign. Their role in society was redefined to emphasize the dissemination of information about party policy and the encouragement of participation in programs. Throughout most of the next decade, MPLA–PT officials continued to criticize the lack of coordination of organizational agenda with party needs. The mass organizations became centers of public resentment of MPLA–PT controls, but these groups were not yet effective at organizing or mobilizing against MPLA–PT rule.

Popular Movement for the Liberation of Angola-Youth Movement

The JMPLA was founded in 1962 and converted into a training ground for MPLA–PT activists in 1977. It claimed a membership of 72,000, mostly teenagers and students, in 1988. The JMPLA conducted military exercises and political study groups, measuring success within the group primarily by an individual's commitment to the socialist revolution. The Second Congress of the JMPLA was held on April 14, 1987, a date that was also celebrated as National Youth Day.

Despite the symbolic and practical importance of the political role of the nation's youth, MPLA-PT officials generally had a derisive attitude toward JMPLA leaders during the 1980s. At the MPLA-PT congresses of 1980 and 1985, party officials criticized youth leaders for their failure to encourage political activism. They also remonstrated against youth group officials for the bourgeois attitudes, materialism, and political apathy they detected among children and teenagers. One measure of these problems was the continued urban influx among young people, which impeded MPLA-PT efforts at rural mobilization.

MPLA-PT leaders assigned the JMPLA the task of guiding the national children's organization, the Agostinho Neto Organization of Pioneers (Organização dos Pioneiros Agostinho Neto—OPA). The goal of the OPA was to educate all children in patriotic values, socialism, and the importance of study, work, and scientific knowledge. Founded as the Pioneers in 1975, the group took the name of the nation's first president at its second conference in November 1979, following Neto's death. JMPLA leaders generally viewed the OPA as a recruiting ground for potential political activists.

National Union of Angolan Workers

The UNTA was organized in 1960 in the Belgian Congo (present-day Zaire) to assist refugees and exiled MPLA members in their efforts to maintain social contacts and find jobs. Managing the UNTA became more difficult after independence. The UNTA headquarters was transferred to Luanda, where the shortage of skilled workers and personnel for management and training programs became immediately evident. UNTA leaders worked to transform the group from an adjunct to a national liberation army to a state labor union, but encouraged by the "people's power" movement, many workers thought the MPLA victory entitled them to assume control of their workplace. UNTA leaders found that workers' rights were sometimes given a lower priority than workers' obligations, and at times industrial workers found themselves at odds with both the government and their own union leadership. These tensions were exacerbated by the demands of militant workers who favored more sweeping nationalization programs than those undertaken by the government; some workers opposed any compensation of foreign owners.

During the early 1980s, Cuban advisers were assigned to bring industrial workers into the MPLA-PT. With their Angolan counterparts in the UNTA, Cuban shop stewards and union officials undertook educational programs in technical and management training, labor discipline and productivity, and socialist economics. Their overall goal was to impart a sense of worker participation in the management of the state economy—a difficult task in an environment characterized by warfare and economic crisis. By late 1988, the Cubans had achieved mixed success. Some of the UNTA's 600,000 members looked forward to the prosperity they hoped to achieve through MPLA-PT policies; many others felt their links to the government did little to improve their standard of living, and they were relatively uncommitted to the construction of a socialist state. UNTA officers did not aggressively represent worker interests when they conflicted with those of the party, and the fear of labor unrest became part of Angola's political context.

Organization of Angolan Women

The OMA was established in 1963 to mobilize support for the fledgling MPLA. After independence, it became the primary route by which women were incorporated in the political process. Its membership rose to 1.8 million in 1985 but dropped to fewer than 1.3 million in 1987. The group attributed this decline to the regional destabilization and warfare that displaced and destroyed families in rural areas, where more than two-thirds of OMA members lived. In 1983 Ruth Neto, the former president's sister, was elected secretary general of the OMA and head of its fifty-three-member national committee. Neto was reelected secretary general by the 596 delegates who attended the OMA's second nationwide conference on March 2, 1988.

During the 1980s, the OMA established literacy programs and worked to expand educational opportunities for women, and the government passed new legislation outlawing gender discrimination in wages and working conditions (see Conditions after Independence, ch. 2). MPLA-PT rhetoric emphasized equality between the sexes as a prerequisite to a prosperous socialist state. At both the First Party Congress and the Second Party Congress, the MPLA-PT Central Committee extolled contributions made by women, but in 1988 only 10 percent of MPLA-PT members were women, and the goal of equality remained distant. Through the OMA, some women were employed in health and social service organizations, serving refugees and rural families. More women were finding jobs in teaching and professions from which they had been excluded in the past, and a very small number occupied important places in government and the MPLA-PT. However, most Angolan women were poor and unemployed.

In addition to leading the OMA, Ruth Neto also served on the MPLA-PT Central Committee and as secretary general of the

*The government has had difficulty mobilizing support
from peasant farmers.*

Pan-African Women's Organization (PAWO), which had its headquarters in Luanda. The PAWO helped sponsor Angola's annual
celebration of Women's Day (August 9), which was also attended
by representatives from neighboring states and liberation movements in South Africa and Namibia.

Interest Groups

Peasant Farmers

In the early 1970s, rural volunteers were the backbone of the
MPLA fighting forces, but after independence few peasant fighters were given leadership positions in the party. In fact, most farmers were purged from the party during the rectification campaign
of the late 1970s for their lack of political commitment or revolutionary zeal. Criteria for party membership were stricter for farmers
than for urban workers, and a decade later MPLA–PT leaders
generally conceded that the worker-peasant alliance, on which the
socialist transformation depended, had been weakened by the rectification campaign. When debating the reasons for this failure,
some MPLA–PT members argued that their urban-based leadership had ignored rural demands and implemented policies favoring urban residents (see Effects of Socialist Policies, ch. 2). Others
claimed that the party had allowed farmers to place their own

183

interests above those of society and that they were beginning to emerge as the rural bourgeoisie denounced by Marxist-Leninist leaders in many countries.

Policies aimed at rural development in the early 1980s had called for the establishment of state farms to improve productivity of basic foodstuffs in the face of shortages in equipment and technical experts. Cuban and Bulgarian farm managers were put in charge of most of these farms. These advisers' objectives were to introduce the use of mechanization and chemical fertilizers and to inculcate political awareness. By the mid-1980s, however, the salaries of foreign technical experts and the cost of new equipment far outweighed revenues generated by these state enterprises, and the program was abandoned.

Many farmers reverted to subsistence agriculture in the face of the spreading UNITA insurgency and what they often perceived as government neglect. Convincing them to produce surplus crops for markets presented formidable problems for party leaders. UNITA forces sometimes claimed crops even before they were harvested, and urban traders seldom ventured into insecure rural areas. Even if a farmer were able to sell surplus crops, the official price was often unrealistically low, and few consumer goods were available in rural markets even for those with cash (see Agriculture, ch. 3).

In response to the apparent intransigence of some rural Angolans, the MPLA–PT attempted another strategy for mobilizing political support by creating farmers' cooperatives and organizing them into unions to provide channels of communication between farmers and party leaders. In late 1988, these unions represented only a small percentage of the rural population, but some party leaders still expected them to succeed. Rural resentment of the urban-based MPLA–PT leadership was still fairly widespread, however, and this resentment contributed to the success of UNITA in Angola's southern and eastern provinces.

Traditional Elites

In the late 1980s, President dos Santos was working to strengthen his support among the nation's traditional leaders. Every few weeks, he would invite delegations of provincial and local-level representatives to meet with him, and Angop would headline these meetings with "the chiefs." Their discussions focused on regional economic and social concerns and served the important political purpose of demonstrating the government's desire to avoid confrontation and to secure support in rural areas.

The MPLA had a neutral relationship with traditional elites before independence, in part because the urban-based party had little contact with ethnic group leaders, whose following was strongest in rural areas. After independence, in its determination to improve the national economy and infrastructure, the MPLA called on people to rise above ethnic and regional loyalties, labeling them impediments to progress in the class struggle. Early MPLA rhetoric also condemned many religious practices, including local African religions. Such policies provoked the contempt of some traditional leaders.

Crises were dampened somewhat by the party's often confrontational relationship with the civil service during the early 1970s. Civil servants, as representatives of the colonial regime, had often clashed with traditional leaders or had otherwise subverted their authority. The MPLA, in contrast, condemned the elitist attitudes of bureaucrats who were employed by the colonial regime, thus gaining support from traditional rulers. At the same time, however, the party drew much of its support from the petite bourgeoisie it condemned so loudly, and much of the civil service remained intact after independence.

By 1980 MPLA–PT efforts to consolidate support in outlying regions were evident. Party officials appointed ethnic group leaders to participate in or lead local party committees in many areas. Merging traditional and modern leadership roles helped strengthen support among rural peasants who would have otherwise remained on the periphery of national politics. Although success was limited to a few areas, this program allowed dos Santos to maintain a balance between national and regional interests. Even some party ideologues, initially inclined toward strict interpretations of Marxist-Leninist dogma, voiced the belief that populist elements might be appropriate for a Marxist regime in an African context.

Religious Communities

The MPLA–PT maintained a cautious attitude toward religion in the late 1980s, in contrast to its determination in the late 1970s to purge churchgoers from the party. A 1980 Ministry of Justice decree required all religious institutions to register with the government. As of 1987, eleven Protestant institutions were legally recognized: the Assembly of God, the Baptist Convention of Angola, the Baptist Evangelical Church of Angola, the Congregational Evangelical Church of Angola, the Evangelical Church of Angola, the Evangelical Church of South-West Angola, the Our Lord Jesus Christ Church in the World (Kimbanguist), the Reformed Evangelical Church of Angola, the Seventh-Day Adventist Church, the Union of Evangelical Churches of Angola, and the United Methodist Church (see Christianity, ch. 2). Roberto de Almeida, the MPLA–PT Central Committee secretary for ideology, information, and culture, admonished church leaders not to perpetuate oppressive or elitist attitudes, and he specifically warned that the churches would not be allowed to take a neutral stance in the battle against opponents of the MPLA–PT regime.

The official attitude toward religion reflected the ideological split in the party leadership. Staunch party ideologues, who had purged almost all churchgoers during the rectification campaign of the late 1970s, opposed leniency toward anyone claiming or recognizing moral authority outside the regime. But as they had done in regard to traditional leaders, the president and his close associates weighed the balance between ideological purity and political necessity and soon moderated their antireligious stance. Political opposition had not coalesced around religious leaders, and, in general, the fear of religious opposition was weakening in the late 1980s.

Employing Marxist-Leninist diatribes against the oppression of the working class, only the most strident ideologues in the MPLA–PT maintained their opposition to religion. The Roman Catholic Church was still strongly identified with the colonial oppressor, and Protestant missionaries were sometimes condemned for having supported colonial practices. More serious in the government's view in the late 1980s was the use by its foremost opponent, Jonas Savimbi, of the issue of religion to recruit members and support for his UNITA insurgency. Savimbi's Church of Christ in the Bush had become an effective religious affiliate of UNITA, maintaining schools, clinics, and training programs.

Small religious sects were annoying to MPLA–PT officials. The ruling party suspected such groups of having foreign sponsors or of being used by opponents of the regime. To the government, the sects' relative independence from world religions was a gauge of their potential for political independence as well. Watch Tower and Seventh-Day Adventist sects were suspect, but they were not perceived as serious political threats. However, the Jehovah's Witnesses were banned entirely in 1978 because of their proscription on military service.

During the late 1980s, security officials considered the small Our Lord Jesus Christ Church in the World to be a threat to the regime, despite the fact that the Mtokoists, as they were known, were not particularly interested in national politics (see Internal Security, ch. 5). Their founder, Simon Mtoko (also known as Simão Toco), had been expelled from Angola by the Portuguese in 1950 for preaching adherence to African cultural values. He returned to Angola in 1974 but soon clashed with MPLA leaders over the regime's authority over individual beliefs. He opposed the party's

Marxist rhetoric on cultural grounds until his death in 1984. After his death, officials feared the group would splinter into dissident factions. The church was legally recognized in 1988 even though Mtokoists clashed with police in 1987 and 1988, resulting in arrests and some casualties.

Political Opposition

After thirteen years of national independence, Angola's armed forces, FAPLA, remained pitted against UNITA in a civil war that had erupted out of the preindependence rivalry among liberation armies. The FNLA and the Front for the Liberation of the Enclave of Cabinda (Frente para a Libertação do Enclave de Cabinda—FLEC) lost popular support during the first decade of independence, and, as a result, in 1988 UNITA remained the only serious internal threat to the dos Santos regime. Few Angolans expected either UNITA or government forces to achieve a military victory, but the political impact of the UNITA insurgency was substantial nonetheless (see The Enduring Rival: UNITA, ch. 5).

Jonas Savimbi established UNITA in 1966. Leading a group of dissident members from the northern coalition that included the FNLA, he established a rival liberation movement that sought to avoid domination by Holden Roberto and his Bakongo followers (see Angolan Insurgency, ch. 1). UNITA recruits from Savimbi's Ovimbundu homeland and from among the Chokwe (also spelled Cokwe), Lunda, Nganguela (also spelled Ganguela), and other southern Angolan societies sought to preserve elements of their own cultures (see Ethnic Groups and Languages, ch. 2). Some southerners also maintained centuries-old legacies of distrust toward northern ethnic groups, including the Bakongo and the Mbundu.

Savimbi's legitimacy as a dissident leader was acquired in part through the reputation of his grandfather, who had led the Ovimbundu state of Ndulu in protest against Portuguese rule in the early twentieth century. From his father, Savimbi acquired membership and belief in the United Church of Christ, which organized Ovimbundu villages into networks to assist in mission operations under colonial rule. One of these networks formed the Council of Evangelical Churches, a pan-Ovimbundu umbrella organization that united more than 100,000 people in south-central Angola. They were served by mission schools, training centers, and clinics, with near-autonomy from colonial controls. Local leaders, who staffed some of these establishments, voiced their demands for greater political freedom, and colonial authorities moved to suppress the Council of Evangelical Churches as pressures for independence mounted in the 1960s.

The territory in southeastern Angola controlled by UNITA in the late 1980s included part of the area that had been administered by the Council of Evangelical Churches before independence (see fig. 16). Here, many people supported Savimbi's struggle against the MPLA–PT as an extension of the long struggle for Ovimbundu, not Angolan, nationhood. UNITA-run schools and clinics operated with the same autonomy from Luandan bureaucratic control as their mission-sponsored counterparts had before independence.

Ethnic loyalties remained strong in the southeast and other UNITA-controlled areas of rural Angola. Class solidarity, in comparison, was an almost meaningless abstraction. Savimbi was able to portray the class-conscious MPLA–PT in Luanda in terms that contrasted sharply with models of leadership among the Ovimbundu and other central and southern Angolan peoples. He described party leaders as a racially stratified elite, dominated by Soviet and Cuban advisers who also provided arms to suppress the population. The MPLA–PT's early assaults on organized religion reinforced this image. Many rural Angolans were also keenly aware that the party elite in Luanda lived at a much higher standard than did Savimbi's commanders in the bush. And they carefully noted that people in rural areas under MPLA–PT control still lived in poverty and that the government bureaucracy was notoriously inefficient and corrupt.

UNITA's regimented leadership, in turn, presented itself as the protector of rural African interests against outsiders. Through Savimbi's skilled public relations efforts, his organization became known as a local peasant uprising, fighting for political and religious freedom. Savimbi had no headquarters in other countries and took pride in the humble life-style of his command in Jamba, well within UNITA-held territory. On this basis, he won some support in the south and east, gained volunteers for UNITA forces, and slowed government efforts to extend MPLA–PT control into the countryside. In the late 1980s, however, international human rights organizations accused UNITA of human rights abuses, charging that UNITA was intimidating civilians to force them to support UNITA or to withhold support for the MPLA–PT.

For the government, the ever-present threat of the UNITA insurgency served a number of useful purposes. It helped rally support for party unity in the capital and surrounding areas. The government was able to capitalize on the reputation for brutality that grew up around some UNITA commanders and the destruction of rural resources by UNITA forces. Young amputees in Luanda and other towns provided a constant reminder of the several thousand land mines left in rural farmland by Savimbi's troops.

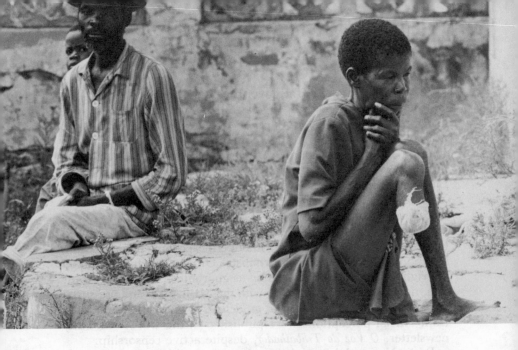

In the late 1980s, amputees such as these could be found
in towns and villages throughout the country.
Courtesy International Committee of the Red Cross (Yannick Müller)

UNITA activity also provided an immediate example of the party ideologues' stereotype of destabilization sponsored by international capitalist forces. These forces were, in turn, embodied in the regional enemy, South Africa. The UNITA insurgency also enabled the MPLA–PT government to justify the continued presence of Cuban troops in Angola, and it helped maintain international interest in Angola's political difficulties.

The regional accord reached in December 1988 by Angolan, South African, and Cuban negotiators did not address Angola's internal violence, but in informal discussions among the participants, alternatives were suggested for ending the conflict (see Regional Politics, this ch.). Western negotiators pressured the MPLA–PT to bring UNITA officials into the government, and even within the party, many people hoped that UNITA representatives—excluding Savimbi—would be reconciled with the dos Santos government. Savimbi, in turn, offered to recognize dos Santos's leadership on the condition that free elections, as promised by the 1975 Alvor Agreement, would take place after the withdrawal of Cuban troops.

Mass Media

The government nationalized all print and broadcast media in

1976, and as of late 1988 the government and party still controlled almost all the news media. Angola's official news agency, Angop, distributed about 8,000 issues of the government newsletter, *Diário da República,* and 40,000 copies of *Jornal de Angola* daily in Luanda and other urban areas under FAPLA control. Both publications were in Portuguese. International press operations in Luanda included Agence France-Presse, Cuba's Prensa Latina, Xinhua (New China) News Agency, and several Soviet and East European agency offices.

Under the scrutiny of the MPLA–PT, the media were limited to disseminating official policy without critical comment or opposing viewpoints. The Angolan Journalists' Union, which proclaimed the right to freedom of expression as guaranteed by the Constitution, nonetheless worked closely with the MPLA–PT and pressured writers to adhere to government guidelines. Views differing slightly from official perceptions were published in the UNTA monthly newsletter, *O Voz do Trabalhador,* despite active censorship.

Rádio Nacional de Angola broadcast on medium-wave and short-wave frequencies in Luanda and eighteen other towns. Radio broadcasts were in Portuguese and vernacular languages, and there were an estimated 435,000 receivers in 1988. In the late 1980s, people in central and southern Angola also received opposition radio broadcasts from the Voice of Resistance of the Black Cockerel, operated by UNITA in Portuguese, English, and local vernaculars. Limited television service in Portuguese became available in Luanda and surrounding areas in 1976, but by 1988 there were only about 40,500 television sets in the country.

Angop maintained a cooperative relationship with the Soviet news agency, TASS, and Angola was active in international efforts to improve coordination among nonaligned nations in the field of communications. Information ministers and news agency representatives from several Third World nations were scheduled to hold their fifth conference in Luanda in June 1989—their first meeting since 1985, when they met in Havana. The Angop delegation was to serve as host of the 1989 conference, and Angolan information officials in the government and party were to chair the organization from 1989 to 1992.

Angola was also a leader among Portuguese-speaking nations of Africa. Students from these nations attended the Interstate Journalism School in Luanda, which opened May 23, 1987, with support from the Yugoslav news agency, Tanyug. In September 1987, journalists from these five Lusophone nations held their third conference in Bissau, Guinea-Bissau. A major goal of this group was to coordinate cultural development based on their common language, but an important secondary goal was to demonstrate support for

Angola in its confrontation with South Africa. By 1990 they hoped to celebrate the Pan-African News Agency's opening of a Portuguese desk in Luanda.

Foreign Relations
Policy Making

Angola's foreign relations reflected the ambivalence of its formal commitment to Marxism-Leninism and its dependence on Western investment and trade. Overall policy goals were to resolve this dual dependence—to achieve regional and domestic peace, reduce the need for foreign military assistance, enhance economic self-sufficiency through diversified trade relations, and establish Angola as a strong socialist state. MPLA–PT politicians described Angola's goal as geopolitical nonalignment, but throughout most of the 1980s Angola's foreign policy had a pronounced pro-Soviet bias.

Two groups within the MPLA–PT and one council within the executive branch vied for influence over foreign policy, all under the direct authority of the president. Formal responsibility for foreign policy programs lay with the MPLA–PT Central Committee. Within this committee, the nine members of the Secretariat and the five others who were members of the Political Bureau wielded decisive influence. The Political Bureau, in its role as guardian of the revolution, usually succeeded in setting the Central Committee agenda.

During the 1980s, as head of both the party and the government, dos Santos strengthened the security role of the executive branch of government, thereby weakening the control of the Central Committee and Political Bureau. To accomplish this redistribution of power, in 1984 he created the Defense and Security Council as an executive advisory body, and he appointed to this council the six most influential ministers, the FAPLA chief of the general staff, and the Central Committee secretary for ideology, information, and culture. The mandate of this council was to review and coordinate the implementation of security-related policy efforts among ministries. The Ministry of Foreign Relations was more concerned with diplomatic and economic affairs than with security matters.

Southern Africa's regional conflict determined much of Angola's foreign policy direction during the 1980s. Negotiations to end South Africa's illegal occupation of Namibia succeeded in linking Namibian independence to the removal of Cuban troops from Angola. The Cuban presence and that of South West Africa People's Organization (SWAPO) and African National Congress (ANC) bases in Angola bolstered Pretoria's claims of a Soviet-sponsored onslaught against the apartheid state. On the grounds that an independent Namibia would enlarge the territory available to Pretoria's enemies and make South Africa's borders even more vulnerable, South Africa maintained possession of Namibia, which it had held since World War I. Pretoria launched incursions into Angola throughout most of the 1980s and supported Savimbi's UNITA forces as they extended their control throughout eastern Angola.

The MPLA–PT pursued its grass-roots campaign to mobilize peasant support, and UNITA sought to capitalize on the fear of communism to enhance its popularity outside rural Ovimbundu areas. Many Angolans accepted MPLA–PT condemnations of the West but balanced them against the fact that Western oil companies in Cabinda provided vital revenues and foreign exchange and the fact that the United States purchased much of Angola's oil. Moreover, in one of Africa's many ironies that arose from balancing the dual quest for political sovereignty and economic development, Cuban and Angolan troops guarded American and other Western companies against attack by South African commandos or UNITA forces (which were receiving United States assistance).

Regional Politics

Most African governments maintained generally cautious support of the Luanda regime during most of its first thirteen years in power. African leaders recognized Luanda's right to reject Western alignments and opt for a Marxist state, following Angola's long struggle to end colonial domination. This recognition of sovereignty, however, was accompanied by uncertainty about the MPLA–PT regime itself, shifting from a concern in the 1970s that spreading Soviet influence would destabilize African regimes across the continent to a fear in the 1980s that the MPLA–PT might be incapable of governing in the face of strong UNITA resistance. The large Cuban military presence came to symbolize both Angola's political autonomy from the West and the MPLA–PT's reliance on a Soviet client state to remain in power. By 1988 the party's role in the struggle against South Africa had become its best guarantee of broad support across sub-Saharan Africa.

Pretoria's goals in Angola were to eliminate SWAPO and ANC bases from Angolan territory, weaken MPLA–PT support for Pretoria's foes through a combination of direct assault and aid to UNITA, and reinforce regional dependence on South Africa's own extensive transportation system by closing down the Benguela Railway (see fig. 10). At the same time, however, South Africa's

*Having fled the UNITA insurgency, these youngsters faced
malnourishment in a displacement camp.
Courtesy Richard J. Hough*

right-wing extremists relied on Marxist rhetoric from Angola and Mozambique as evidence of the predicted communist onslaught against Pretoria. The political ties of Angola and Mozambique to the Soviet Union also bolstered South Africa's determination to strengthen its security apparatus at home and provided a rationale for continued occupation of Namibia. Knowing this important prop for Pretoria's regional policies would diminish with the Cuban withdrawal from Angola, South Africa actually prolonged Angola's dependence on Soviet and Cuban military might by derailing negotiations for Namibian independence.

In 1984 South Africa and Angola agreed to end support for each other's rebels and work toward regional peace. This agreement, the Lusaka Accord, was not implemented, however, as Pretoria continued incursions into Angola, partly in response to new arrivals of Cuban forces.

Regional Accord

On December 22, 1988, after eight years of negotiations, Angola, Cuba, and South Africa concluded a regional accord that provided for the removal of Cuban troops from Angola. In a series of talks mediated by the United States, the three parties agreed to link Namibian independence from South African rule to a staged withdrawal of Cuban troops from Angola. Both processes were to begin in 1989. Cuban troops were to move north of the fifteenth parallel, away from the Namibian border, by August 1, 1989. All Cuban troops were to be withdrawn from Angolan territory by July 1, 1991 (see Appendix B).

The December 1988 regional accords did not attempt to resolve the ongoing conflict between Angolan forces and UNITA. Rather, it addressed the 1978 UN Security Council Resolution 435, which called for South African withdrawal and free elections in Namibia and prohibited further South African incursions into Angola. The United States promised continued support for UNITA until a negotiated truce and power-sharing arrangement were accomplished.

The December 1988 regional accords created a joint commission of representatives from Angola, Cuba, South Africa, the United States, and the Soviet Union to resolve conflicts that threatened to disrupt its implementation. However, immediate responsibility for the accord lay primarily with the UN, which still required an enabling resolution by the Security Council, a funding resolution by the General Assembly, and a concrete logistical plan for member states to establish and maintain a Namibian peacekeeping force as part of the UN Transition Assistance Group (UNTAG) called for by Resolution 435.

Angola's participation in the regional accords was pragmatic. The accords promised overall gains, but not without costs. They entailed the eventual loss of Cuban military support for the MPLA–PT but countered this with the possible benefits of improved relations with South Africa—primarily an end to South African-supported insurgency. The accords also suggested possible benefits from improved regional trade, membership in the World Bank (see Glossary) and International Monetary Fund (IMF—see Glossary), and loans for development purposes. President dos Santos intended to reduce Angola's share of the cost of the Cuban presence, to reduce social tensions in areas where Cuban military units were stationed, and to weaken UNITA's argument that the MPLA–PT had allowed an occupation force to install itself in Angola. The MPLA–PT also hoped to gain a friendly SWAPO government in neighboring Namibia and an end to sanctuary for UNITA forces in Namibian territory. (This goal was complicated by the fact that Ovambo populations in southern Angola and Namibia provided the core of SWAPO, and, at the same time, many Ovambo people supported UNITA.)

As the first Cuban troops planned to withdraw from Angola, most parties to the accords still feared that it might fail. Angolan leaders worried that the UNITA insurgency would intensify in the face of the Cuban withdrawal; that UNITA leaders might find new sources of external assistance, possibly channeled through Zaire; and that South African incursions into Angola might recur on the grounds that ANC or SWAPO bases remained active in southern Angola. South African negotiators expressed the fear that the Cuban troop withdrawal, which could not be accurately verified, might not be complete; that Cuban troops might move into Zambia or other neighboring states, only to return to Angola in response to UNITA activity; or that SWAPO activity in Namibia might prompt new South African assaults on Namibian and Angolan territory. SWAPO negotiators, in turn, feared that South Africa or some of Namibia's 70,000 whites might block the elections guaranteed by UN Resolution 435, possibly bringing South African forces back into Namibia and scuttling the entire accords. These and other apprehensions were evident in late 1988, but substantial hope remained that all regional leaders supported the peace process and would work toward its implementation.

Relations with Other African States

Angola was wary of attempts at African solidarity during its first years of independence, an attitude that gave way to a more activist role in southern Africa during the 1980s. President Neto rejected an offer of an OAU peacekeeping force in 1975, suspecting that OAU leaders would urge a negotiated settlement with UNITA. Neto also declined other efforts to find African solutions to Angola's instability and reduce the Soviet and Cuban role in the region. A decade later, Angola had become a leader among front-line states (the others were Botswana, Mozambique, Tanzania, Zambia, and Zimbabwe) seeking Western pressure to end regional destablization by Pretoria. Luanda also coordinated efforts by the Southern African Development Coordination Conference (SADCC) to reduce the front-line states' economic dependence on South Africa.

Angola's relations were generally good with other African states that accepted its Marxist policies and strained with states that harbored or supported rebel forces opposed to the MPLA–PT. The most consistent rhetorical support for the MPLA–PT came from other former Portuguese states in Africa (Cape Verde, São Tomé and Príncipe, Guinea-Bissau, and Mozambique).

Nigeria, which led the OAU in recognizing the MPLA–PT regime in 1975, went on to seek a leadership role in the campaign against South Africa's domination of the region, but Nigeria never forged very close ties with Angola. Nigeria's own economic difficulties of the 1970s and 1980s, its close relations with the West, and other cultural and political differences prevented Luanda and Lagos from forming a strong alliance.

Zaire's relations with Angola were unstable during the 1970s and 1980s. Zairian regular army units supported the FNLA in the years before and just after Angolan independence, and Angola harbored anti-Zairian rebels, who twice invaded Zaire's Shaba Region (formerly Katanga Province). But Zaire's President Mobutu Sese Seko and President Neto reached a rapprochement before Neto's death in 1979, and Zaire curtailed direct opposition to the MPLA–PT. Nonetheless, throughout most of the 1980s UNITA operated freely across Zaire's southwestern border, and Western support for UNITA was channeled through Zaire (see National Security Environment, ch. 5). Complicating relations between these two nations were the numerous ethnic groups whose homelands had been divided by the boundary between Zaire and Angola a century earlier. The Bakongo, Lunda, Chokwe, and many smaller groups maintained long-standing cultural, economic, and religious ties with relatives in neighboring states. These ties often extended to support for antigovernment rebels.

Zambia, which had officially ousted UNITA bands from its western region in 1976, voiced strong support for the MPLA–PT at the same time that it turned a blind eye to financial and logistical support for UNITA by Zambian citizens. Without official approval, but also without interference, UNITA forces continued to train in Zambia's western region. Lusaka's ambivalence toward Angola during the 1980s took into account the possibility of an eventual UNITA role in the government in Luanda. Both Zambia and Zaire had an interest in seeing an end to Angola's civil war because the flow of refugees from Angola had reached several hundred thousand by the mid-1980s. Peace would also enable Zambia and Zaire to upgrade the Benguela Railway as an alternative to South African transport systems.

Elsewhere in the region, relations with Angola varied. Strained relations arose at times with Congo, where both FNLA and Cabindan rebels had close cultural ties and some semi-official encouragement. Senegal, Togo, Malawi, and Somalia were among the relatively conservative African states that provided material support to UNITA during the 1980s. Throughout most of the decade, UNITA also received financial assistance from several North African states, including Morocco, Tunisia, and Egypt, and these governments (along with Kuwait and Saudi Arabia) pressured their African trading partners and client states to limit their support of the MPLA–PT.

Communist Nations

The Soviet Union supported the MPLA–PT as a liberation movement before independence and formalized its relationship with the MPLA–PT government through the Treaty of Friendship and Cooperation and a series of military agreements beginning in 1975. Once it became clear that the MPLA–PT could, with Cuban support, remain in power, the Soviet Union provided economic and technical assistance and granted Angola most-favored-nation status (see Foreign Trade and Assistance, ch. 3).

The support of the Soviet Union and its allies included diplomatic representations at the UN and in other international forums, military hardware and advisers, and more direct military support in the face of South African incursions into Angola. Civilian technical assistance extended to hydroelectric projects, bridge building and road building, agriculture, fisheries, public health, and a variety of educational projects. Technical assistance was often channeled through joint projects with a third country—for example, the Capanda hydroelectric project entailed cooperation between the Soviet Union and Brazil.

Soviet-Angolan relations were strained at times during the 1980s, however, in part because Angola sought to upgrade diplomatic ties with the United States. Soviet leadership factions were divided over their nation's future role in Africa, and some Soviet negotiators objected to dos Santos's concessions to the United States on the issue of "linkage." The region's intractable political problems, and the cost of maintaining Cuban troop support and equipping the MPLA–PT, weakened the Soviet commitment to the building of a Marxist-Leninist state in Angola.

Angolan leaders, in turn, complained about Soviet neglect— low levels of assistance, poor-quality personnel and matériel, and inadequate responses to complaints. Angola shared the cost of the Cuban military presence and sought to reduce these expenses, in part because many Angolan citizens felt the immediate drain on economic resources and rising tensions in areas occupied by Cuban troops. Moreover, dos Santos complained that the Soviet Union dealt with Angola opportunistically—purchasing Angolan coffee at low prices and reexporting it at a substantial profit, overfishing in Angolan waters, and driving up local food prices.

For the first decade after independence, trade with communist states was not significant, but in the late 1980s dos Santos sought expanded economic ties with the Soviet Union, China, and Czechoslovakia and other nations of Eastern Europe as the MPLA– PT attempted to diversify its economic relations and reduce its dependence on the West. In October 1986, Angola signed a cooperative agreement with the Council for Mutual Economic Assistance (Comecon or CMEA), a consortium dedicated to economic cooperation among the Soviet Union and its allies.

As part of the Comecon agreement, Soviet support for Angolan educational and training programs was increased. In 1987 approximately 1,800 Angolan students attended institutions of higher education in the Soviet Union. The Soviet Union also provided about 100 lecturers to Agostinho Neto University in Luanda, and a variety of Soviet-sponsored training programs operated in Angola, most with Cuban instructors. Approximately 4,000 Angolans studied at the international school on Cuba's renowned Isle of Youth. More Angolan students were scheduled to attend the Union of Young Communists' School in Havana in 1989. Czechoslovakia granted scholarships to forty-four Angolan students in 1987, and during that year Czechoslovakia and the German Democratic Republic (East Germany) also provided training for about 150 Angolan industrial workers.

Cuba's presence in Angola was more complex than it appeared to outsiders who viewed the Soviet Union's Third World clients as little more than surrogates for their powerful patron. The initiative in placing Cuban troops in Angola in the mid-1970s was taken by President Fidel Castro as part of his avowed mission of "Cuban internationalism." Facing widespread unemployment at home, young Cuban men were urged to serve in the military overseas as their patriotic duty, and veterans enjoyed great prestige on their return. Castro also raised the possibility of a Cuban resettlement scheme in southern Angola, and several hundred Cubans received Angolan citizenship during the 1980s. Cuban immigration increased sharply in 1988. In addition to military support, Cuba provided Angola with several thousand teachers, physicians, and civilian laborers for construction, agriculture, and industry. Angolan dependence on Cuban medical personnel was so complete that during the 1980s Spanish became known as the language of medicine.

China's relations with Angola were complicated by Beijing's opposition to both Soviet and United States policies toward Africa. China supported the FNLA and UNITA after the MPLA seized power in Angola, and China provided military support to Zaire when Zairian troops clashed with Angolan forces along their common border in the late 1970s. China nonetheless took the initiative in improving relations with the MPLA–PT during the 1980s. The two states established diplomatic ties in 1983.

United States and Western Europe

Angola's relations with the United States were ambivalent. The United States aided the FNLA and UNITA before independence. During most of 1976, the United States blocked Angola's admission to the UN, and in late 1988 the two nations still lacked diplomatic ties. United States representatives pressured Luanda to reduce its military reliance on Cuba and the Soviet Union, made necessary in part by United States and South African opposition to the MPLA–PT and support for UNITA. In 1988 Angola's government news agency quoted Minister of Foreign Relations Afonso Van Dúnem (nom de guerre Mbinda) as saying the United States had a "Cuban psychosis" that prevented it from engaging in talks about Namibia and Angola. Nevertheless, after the December 1988 regional accords to end the Cuban military presence in Angola, United States officials offered to normalize relations with Angola on the condition that an internal settlement of the civil war with UNITA be reached.

Political and diplomatic differences between the United States and Angola were generally mitigated by close economic ties. American oil companies operating in Cabinda provided a substantial portion of Angola's export earnings and foreign exchange, and this relationship continued despite political pressures on these companies to reduce their holdings in Cabinda in the mid-1980s. The divergence of private economic interests from United States diplomatic policy was complicated by differences of opinion among American policymakers. By means of the Clark Amendment, from 1975 to 1985 the United States Congress prohibited aid to UNITA and slowed covert attempts to circumvent this legislation. After the repeal of the Clark Amendment in 1985, however, trade between Angola and the United States continued to increase, and Cuban and Angolan troops attempted to prevent sabotage against United States interests by UNITA and South African commandos.

Western Europe, like the United States, feared the implications of a strong Soviet client state in southern Africa, but in general European relations with the MPLA–PT were based on economic interests rather than ideology. France and Portugal maintained good relations with the MPLA–PT at the same time that they provided financial assistance for UNITA and allowed UNITA representatives to operate freely in their capitals. Portugal was Angola's leading trading partner throughout most of the 1980s, and Brazil, another Lusophone state, strengthened economic ties with Angola during this period.

* * *

John A. Marcum's two-volume series, *The Angolan Revolution*, analyzes historical trends in Angolan politics and society from the early colonial struggle through the early years of independence. Marcum also views the postwar environment and its political implications in ''Angola: Twenty-five Years of War,'' and he analyzes obstacles to the socialist transformation in ''The People's Republic of Angola.'' Keith Somerville's *Angola: Politics, Economics, and Society* provides an extensive discussion of Angola's variant of Marxism-Leninism and raises the question of its implications for the rural majority of Angolan people. Kenneth W. Grundy's ''The Angolan Puzzle'' assesses Angolan prospects for peace in 1987 in the context of the regional struggle.

Gerald J. Bender analyzes Angola's contemporary predicament from a historical perspective in ''American Policy Toward Angola'' and ''The Continuing Crisis in Angola.'' Catherine V. Scott, in ''Socialism and the 'Soft State' in Africa,'' compares 1980s political developments in these two Marxist states in southern Africa. Tony Hodges's *Angola to the 1990s*, essentially an economic analysis, also contains insight into political trends. Fred Bridgland's ''The Future of Angola'' and *Jonas Savimbi* provide critical views of MPLA–PT rule, while Fola Soremekun's chapter on Angola in *The Political Economy of African Foreign Policy*, edited by Timothy M. Shaw and Olajide Aluko, and *Angola's Political Economy* by

M.R. Bhagavan view Angola's 1980s leadership from a more favorable perspective. (For further information and complete citations, see Bibliography.)

Chapter 5. National Security

An elderly member of the People's Vigilance Brigades

IN THE LATE 1980s, ANGOLA was a nation at war, still struggling to escape the legacy that one standard history has characterized as "five centuries of conflict." Since the 1960s, Angola had experienced, sometimes simultaneously, four types of war: a war of national liberation, a civil war, a regional war, and the global struggle between the superpowers. Angola had won its independence from Portugal in 1975 after a thirteen-year liberation struggle, during which the externally supported African nationalist movements splintered and subdivided. However, independence provided no respite, as the new nation was immediately engulfed in a civil war whose scope and effects were compounded by foreign military intervention. Although the Popular Movement for the Liberation of Angola (Movimento Popular de Libertação de Angola—MPLA) eventually won recognition as the legitimate government, it did so only with massive Soviet and Cuban military support, on which it remained heavily dependent in late 1988.

Despite the party's international acceptance and domestic hegemony, Angola in the late 1980s remained at war with itself and its most powerful neighbor, South Africa. The insurgency led by the National Union for the Total Independence of Angola (União Nacional para a Independência Total de Angola—UNITA), bolstered by growing foreign support, spread from the remote and sparsely populated southeast corner of the country throughout the entire nation. South African interventions on behalf of UNITA and against black South African and Namibian nationalist forces in southern Angola also escalated. Luanda's reliance on the Soviet Union, Cuba, and other communist states for internal security and defense increased as these threats intensified. Intermittent diplomatic efforts since the late 1970s had failed to end the protracted war; indeed, each new initiative had been followed by an escalation of violence.

Nonetheless, a turning point in this history of conflict may have been reached in 1988. After the warring parties clashed in the early part of that year at Cuito Cuanavale, in Africa's largest land battle since World War II, the exhausted parties succeeded in negotiating a regional peace agreement brokered by Chester A. Crocker, the United States assistant secretary of state for African affairs. On July 13, representatives of Angola, Cuba, and South Africa initialed an agreement on a "set of essential principles to establish the basis for peace in the southwestern region of Africa."

They signed a cease-fire agreement on August 22, to be overseen by their Joint Military Monitoring Commission. Finally, their trilateral accord of December 22 provided for South African military withdrawal and cessation of assistance to UNITA; the phased removal of Cuban forces from Angola over a twenty-seven-month period ending on July 1, 1991; termination of Angolan assistance to African National Congress (ANC) exiles in the country; and South African withdrawal from Namibia coupled with independence for that territory under United Nations-supervised elections (see Appendix B). Although UNITA was not a party to this historic regional peace agreement, it was hoped that internal peace based on national reconciliation would also ensue. Whether the trilateral accord would be honored and whether Angolans would make peace among themselves were crucial issues in late 1988. History suggested that this would be but a brief respite from endemic conflict, but the promise of a future free of conflict may have provided the impetus to break with the burden of the past.

National Security Environment

Although Angola's boundaries with neighboring states were not disputed, the country's geopolitical position heavily affected national security. Luanda enjoyed fraternal relations with Congo and Zambia, but sporadic antagonism characterized the regime's relations with Zaire. Since Pretoria's intervention in the civil war of 1975–76, an undeclared state of war had existed with South Africa, which occupied Namibia, the territory to the south of Angola (see fig. 1).

Relations with Zaire, with which Angola shares its longest border, had been punctuated by hostility since the 1960s, when Zaire's President Mobutu Sese Seko sponsored and provided sanctuary to an MPLA rival, the National Front for the Liberation of Angola (Frente Nacional de Libertação de Angola—FNLA), and to the separatist Front for the Liberation of the Enclave of Cabinda (Frente para a Libertação do Enclave de Cabinda—FLEC). Although there had been no conflicts over the positioning of the border itself, the direct intervention of regular Zairian forces in Angola on behalf of the FNLA in September 1975 exacerbated the three-way civil war and attendant intrusions by South African, Soviet, and Cuban forces.

Despite a February 1976 accord in which the Angolan and Zairian governments renounced further hostilities, Zaire not only continued to provide sanctuary and assistance to the FNLA, which made periodic raids into Angola, but also facilitated FLEC attacks on Angola's oil-rich Cabinda Province. Aircraft based in Zaire also violated Angolan airspace, occasionally bombing villages on the northern border. In retaliation, in 1977 and 1979 Luanda allowed Katangan dissidents based in Angola to invade Zaire's Shaba Region (formerly Katanga Province), from which they were repelled only after the intervention of Egyptian, Moroccan, French, and Belgian forces (see Angola as a Refuge, this ch.).

Having apparently evened their scores, Angola and Zaire normalized relations in 1978, and the two erstwhile antagonists entered into a nonaggression pact with Zambia in 1979. In February 1985, Luanda and Kinshasa signed a security and defense pact including mutual pledges not to allow the use of their territory for attacks on each other; the two governments also set up a joint defense and security commission to develop border security arrangements. In July 1986, Angola and Zaire set up joint working groups and regional commissions to implement their pledges, and in August 1988 they signed a border security pact.

Despite normalization and border security agreements, Angolan-Zairian relations remained strained and fraught with inconsistencies in the late 1980s. The two countries could not effectively control their 2,285-kilometer border, which UNITA forces continued to cross freely. Furthermore, Kinshasa continued indirect support of UNITA, particularly after 1986, by permitting United States use of the Kamina airbase in Shaba Region to deliver military aid to the insurgents and to train them in the use of new weapons. Despite numerous diplomatic and media reports of Zaire's involvement in logistical support of UNITA, Kinshasa persisted in denying the charges.

Zaire's erratic behavior did not constitute a direct threat to Angola. The activities of South Africa, however, were another matter. Whereas Zaire had limited itself to using its strategic location to support insurgencies against the Angolan government, Pretoria had the means to sponsor guerrilla resistance and to wage protracted war. In order to defend the 1,376-kilometer Angolan border with occupied Namibia against infiltration by South West Africa People's Organization (SWAPO) guerrillas based in Angola, South African forces cleared a one-kilometer-wide strip along nearly half the border's length. The Ovambo people, SWAPO's main base of ethnic support, straddled the border, facilitating SWAPO's movements and recruitment efforts (see Ethnic Groups and Languages, ch. 2).

Starting in the late 1970s, South Africa had engaged in an escalating series of air and ground raids and prolonged operations in southern Angola against SWAPO and in defense of UNITA. The South African Defense Force (SADF) occupied parts of southern Angola between August 1981 and April 1985. During and after that period, it undertook frequent air and ground attacks, hot pursuit operations, preemptive raids against SWAPO bases, and major interventions against Angolan armed forces on behalf of UNITA. In fact, large-scale South African air and ground attacks on Angolan government forces in 1985, 1987, and 1988 reversed the momentum of Luanda's offensives and saved UNITA from almost certain defeat. South Africa finally withdrew its troops from Angola in September 1988 under the terms of the United States-brokered peace plan. South Africa had also provided UNITA with massive arms and logistical support, which was to be terminated under the tripartite regional peace accord (see Regional Politics, ch. 4).

To bolster its regional position, Luanda sought to regularize and strengthen its security ties with neighboring states. In addition to its nonaggression and border pacts with Zaire, Angola employed regular consultation, coordination, and cooperation with Botswana, Mozambique, Tanzania, Zambia, and Zimbabwe in an effort to enhance regional security. These ties were reinforced through bilateral defense accords with Tanzania and Mozambique signed in May 1988 and July 1988, respectively. A defense pact with Zambia was also reported to have been signed in March 1988, but this report was denied by the Zambian government.

Evolution of the Armed Forces
Background

Throughout history, relationships based on conflict, conquest, and exploitation existed among the Angolan peoples as well as between Angolans and their Portuguese colonizers. Following the initial contacts in the 1480s between Portugal and the Kongo and Ndongo kingdoms, relations were peaceful. However, by the early sixteenth century Angolans were enslaving Angolans for the purpose of trading them for Portuguese goods. This commerce in human beings stimulated a series of wars (see Precolonial Angola and the Arrival of the Portuguese, ch. 1). The Portuguese eventually intervened militarily in the kingdoms' affairs and subsequently conquered and colonized Kongo and Ndongo. Whereas warfare among Africans traditionally had been limited in purpose, scale, intensity, duration, and destructiveness, the wars of slavery and Portuguese conquest were conducted with few restraints.

Intra-African and Portuguese-African warfare continued from the seventeenth to the nineteenth century, as the slave and firearms trade penetrated the hinterland and Portugal attempted to extend its territorial control and mercantile interests. War and commerce were the principal occupations of the Portuguese settlers, who represented the worst elements of their own society. Portugal was the first European nation to use deported convicts (*degredados*—see Glossary) to explore, conquer, and exploit an overseas empire. But unlike other European penal exiles, who were mostly impoverished petty criminals, these Portuguese exiles were the most serious offenders. By the mid-seventeenth century, virtually all non-African army, police, and commercial activities were dominated by the *degredados*. Indeed, until the early twentieth century the great majority of Portuguese in Angola were exiled convicts (see Settlement, Conquest, and Development, ch. 1).

During the nineteenth century, the *degredados* expanded and consolidated their hold on the political, military, and economic life of the territory. In 1822 *degredado* renegades joined garrison troops in Luanda in revolting against the Portuguese governor and setting up a junta. The *degredados* comprised the bulk of the Portuguese resident military and police forces, both of which engaged in plunder and extortion. In the 1870s, there were about 3,600 Portuguese officers and men stationed in Angola, and this number increased to 4,900 by the turn of the century. These were supplemented by African soldiers, auxiliaries, and Boer immigrants.

In contrast to the earlier pattern of episodic military campaigns with transient effect, the early twentieth century brought systematic conquest and the imposition of direct colonial rule. Taxation, forced labor, and intensified military recruitment were introduced. Although Portuguese policy officially permitted the assimilation of Africans, virtually all officers and noncommissioned officers remained white or *mestiço* (see Glossary). During the dictatorship of António Salazar (1932–68), the Portuguese army in Angola was 60 percent to 80 percent African, but not a single black Angolan achieved officer rank (see Angola under the Salazar Regime, ch. 1).

Independence Struggle, Civil War, and Intervention

When the African nationalist revolt erupted in early 1961, the Portuguese army in Angola numbered about 8,000 men, 5,000 of whom were African. The colonial forces responded brutally, and by the end of the summer they had regained control over most of the territory. The human cost, however, was enormous: more than 2,000 Europeans and up to 50,000 Africans died, and about 10 percent of Angola's African population fled to Zaire. By early 1962, the Portuguese army in Angola had grown to 50,000 and thereafter averaged 60,000 into the mid-1970s. About half of this expansion was achieved by conscription in Angola, and most conscripts were Africans. The Portuguese established a counterinsurgency program of population resettlement throughout the country. By the mid-1970s, more than 1 million peasants had been relocated into strategic settlements, and 30,000 males had been impressed into service in lightly armed militia units to defend them.

The thirteen-year Angolan war for independence, in which three rival nationalist groups fought the Portuguese to a stalemate, ended after the April 1974 military coup in Portugal. At that time, the MPLA and the FNLA had an estimated 10,000 guerrillas each, and UNITA had about 2,000. Within a year, these groups had become locked in a complex armed struggle for supremacy. By November 1975, when independence under a three-way coalition government was scheduled, the MPLA and the FNLA had built up their armies to 27,000 and 22,000, respectively, while UNITA had mustered some 8,000 to 10,000. Further complicating the situation was a substantial foreign military presence. Although the Portuguese forces numbered only 3,000 to 4,000 by late 1975, some 2,000 to 3,000 Cubans had arrived in support of the MPLA, from 1,000 to 2,000 Zairian regulars had crossed the border to aid the FNLA, and 4,000 to 5,000 SADF troops had intervened on behalf of UNITA. The civil war was soon decided in favor of the MPLA by virtue of the massive influx of Soviet weapons and advisers and Cuban troops.

The Development of FAPLA

In the early 1960s, the MPLA named its guerrilla forces the People's Army for the Liberation of Angola (Exército Popular de Libertação de Angola—EPLA). Many of its first cadres had received training in Morocco and Algeria. In January 1963, in one of its early operations, the EPLA attacked a Portuguese military post in Cabinda, killing a number of troops. During the mid-1960s and early 1970s, the EPLA operated very successfully from bases in Zambia against the Portuguese in eastern Angola. After 1972, however, the EPLA's effectiveness declined following several Portuguese victories, disputes with FNLA forces, and the movement of about 800 guerrillas from Zambia to Congo.

On August 1, 1974, a few months after a military coup d'état had overthrown the Lisbon regime and proclaimed its intention of granting independence to Angola, the MPLA announced the formation of the People's Armed Forces for the Liberation of Angola (Forças Armadas Populares de Libertação de Angola—FAPLA), which replaced the EPLA. By 1976 FAPLA had been transformed from lightly armed guerrilla units into a national army capable of sustained field operations. This transformation was gradual until

Government recruits learning the mechanics of an AK-47 assault rifle
Courtesy United Nations (J.P. Laffont)

the Soviet-Cuban intervention and ensuing UNITA insurgency, when the sudden and large-scale inflow of heavy weapons and accompanying technicians and advisers quickened the pace of institutional change.

Unlike African states that acceded to independence by an orderly and peaceful process of institutional transfer, Angola inherited a disintegrating colonial state whose army was in retreat. Although Mozambique's situation was similar in some respects, the confluence of civil war, foreign intervention, and large-scale insurgency made Angola's experience unique. After independence, FAPLA had to reorganize for conventional war and counterinsurgency simultaneously and immediately to continue the new war with South Africa and UNITA. Ironically, a guerrilla army that conducted a successful insurgency for more than a decade came to endure the same kind of exhausting struggle for a similar period.

Armed Forces

Constitutional and Political Context

The Angolan Constitution provides a framework for both international and national security policies. Article 16 establishes the country's official policy of military nonalignment and prohibits the construction of foreign military bases on Angolan territory. Reflecting its concern for territorial unity and the status of Cabinda

211

Province as an integral part of the national homeland, Article 4 also provides that "any attempt to separate or dismember" any territory will be "forcefully combated." The president, under Article 6, is designated commander in chief of the armed forces and in Article 53 is also given extraordinary powers to declare a state of emergency or a state of siege, to declare war, and to make peace.

The government's organization for security and defense reflected both ideological and national security considerations in its interlocking network of party, government, and military officials. The Council of the Revolution, which performed both executive and legislative functions before 1980, included the minister of defense, the chief of the general staff, and regional military commanders. In the first national People's Assembly (national legislature), which in 1980 replaced the Council of the Revolution as the supreme organ of state, defense and security personnel constituted 10 percent of the membership (see Structure of Government, ch. 4).

Since the early days of the liberation struggle, the MPLA had recognized the need for firm political direction of FAPLA. Political control was established and maintained by two complementary means: political indoctrination and institutional penetration and subordination. Political education was an integral part of FAPLA's military training, and political commissars were attached to guerrilla units to ensure compliance with party directives.

MPLA politicization and controls were formalized and expanded after the transformation of FAPLA into a conventional army during 1975 and 1976. Many of the independence leaders continued to hold concurrent positions in the party, government, and military establishment. At the regional level, the overlaying of military and political leadership was also common, as many of the provincial commissars were both MPLA Central Committee members and FAPLA lieutenant colonels. Within the armed forces, political commissars in each unit reported not to the military chain of command but to the political leadership of the region or province.

Extensive politicization of the military by institutional means did not preclude the possibility of military intervention in politics. In 1977 Nito Alves led an abortive coup in which several MPLA and FAPLA leaders were killed. In the aftermath, Alves's supporters were executed or purged, and the top military and political posts in the armed forces were assigned to loyalists: David António Moises was appointed FAPLA chief of the general staff, and Julião Mateus Paulo (nom de guerre Dino Matross) became FAPLA national political commissar.

The interpenetration of the MPLA and FAPLA was maintained throughout both organizations' hierarchies. In 1983, six years after the MPLA had designated itself a "workers' party" (Partido de Trabalho; henceforth the party was known as the MPLA–PT), a series of party committee seminars for the political organs of the defense and security forces was inaugurated by Paulo, then Central Committee secretary for defense and security. The purpose of these seminars was to review the implementation of party directives and structures within the armed forces. In 1985 seminar members recommended that the party's provincial departments of defense and security implement the 1984 directive to award membership to armed forces veterans and disabled soldiers and that the local party and the Popular Movement for the Liberation of Angola-Youth Movement (Juventude do Movimento Popular de Libertação de Angola—JMPLA) participate more actively in defense and security. For its part, FAPLA had a political directorate that maintained party liaison and supervision.

In the 1980s, the need for total mobilization and coordination of the nation's resources to combat the escalating UNITA insurgency and South African intervention led to reorganizations of both the central and the provincial governments. President José Eduardo dos Santos created the Defense and Security Council under his chairmanship in April 1984 to plan and coordinate national security policy. Originally, the council included the ministers of defense, state security, and interior; the FAPLA chief of the general staff; and the party Central Committee secretary for ideology, information, and culture as an ex officio member. In May 1986, the Defense and Security Council expanded to include the ministers of state for inspection and control, for the productive sphere, and for economic and social spheres, posts that had been created in a February 1986 government reorganization. In effect, the Defense and Security Council became the standing body of the Council of Ministers when the latter was not in session. The Defense and Security Council met in two sessions: a weekly meeting on defense and security matters, and a biweekly meeting on economic issues.

In July 1983, the MPLA–PT Political Bureau decided to form regional military councils as an "exceptional and temporary measure" to coordinate political, military, economic, and social leadership in areas "affected by armed acts of aggression, vandalism and banditry." The councils reported directly to the president as FAPLA commander in chief, who was empowered to determine which areas warranted such councils and to appoint council members. The councils were authorized to requisition and restrict the movement of people and goods, and their newly created military tribunals tried crimes "against state security, economic sabotage, speculation and disobedience of directives from the regional military councils, as well as those who may damage or endanger the interests of collective defense and security" (see Criminal Justice System, this ch.). Eleven of Angola's eighteen provinces were immediately made subject to regional military councils, whose chairmen were FAPLA colonels.

Before 1988 FAPLA's areas of operations were divided into ten military regions (see fig. 13). In early 1988, however, calling this structure inadequate, the Ministry of Defense announced the formation of northern, eastern, southern, and central fronts. The northern front encompassed Zaire, Uíge, Malanje, Cuanza Norte, and Bengo provinces. The eastern front covered Lunda Norte, Lunda Sul, and Moxico provinces. No official information on the other fronts was available in late 1988, but presumably the southern front included Cuando Cubango, Cunene, Huíla, and Namibe provinces, and the central front may have comprised Bié, Huambo, Benguela, and Cuanza Sul provinces. There was no information on the status of Cabinda and Luanda provinces, but perhaps they remained separate regions because of their strategic importance and small size. Because of the uncertain boundaries of these fronts, most news accounts referred to the military regions when describing FAPLA's areas of operation.

Armed Forces Organization and Mission

The minister of defense served under both the political and the military authority of the president in his dual role as head of government and FAPLA commander in chief. Because defense and security matters were of extreme urgency, the minister of defense was considered second in importance only to the president. The minister was responsible for the entire defense establishment, including the army, air force, navy, and local militias. The commanders of the three major military services each held the title of vice minister of defense. Colonel Henrique Carreira (nom de guerre Iko), the first minister of defense, held the post from 1975 to 1980; as of late 1988 Pedro Maria Tonha (nom de guerre Pedalé) had been minister of defense since July 1980 (see fig. 14).

The Angolan armed forces were collectively known as FAPLA. The army was officially termed the People's Army of Angola (Exército Popular de Angola—EPA). The government and most press reports, however, referred to the army as FAPLA. The triple mission of the military was to protect and defend the authority of the party and government from internal subversion, to defend the country from external attack, and to assist regional allies in meeting their internal and external security needs. Accordingly, FAPLA was organized and equipped to fight both counterinsurgency and conventional wars and to deploy abroad when ordered; it had engaged in all these tasks continuously since independence. Its main counterinsurgency effort was directed against UNITA in the southeast, and its conventional capabilities were demonstrated principally in the undeclared war with South Africa. FAPLA first performed its external assistance mission with the dispatch of 1,000 to 1,500 troops to São Tomé and Príncipe in 1977 to bolster the socialist regime of President Manuel Pinto da Costa. During the next several years, Angolan forces conducted joint exercises with their counterparts and exchanged technical operational visits. The Angolan expeditionary force was reduced to about 500 in early 1985. It is probable that FAPLA would have undertaken other "internationalist" missions, in Mozambique for example, had it not been absorbed in war at home.

In 1988 the strength of the Angolan armed forces was estimated at 100,000 active-duty and 50,000 reserve personnel, organized into a regular army and a supporting militia, air and air defense force, and navy. The active-duty forces had expanded greatly since independence as UNITA's insurgency spread throughout the country and South African interventions increased in frequency and magnitude. As of late 1988, Lieutenant General António dos Santos Franca (nom de guerre Ndalu) was FAPLA chief of the general staff and army commander. He had held these positions since 1982.

Ground Forces

The regular army's 91,500 troops were organized into more than seventy brigades ranging from 750 to 1,200 men each and deployed throughout the ten military regions. Most regions were commanded by lieutenant colonels, with majors as deputy commanders, but some regions were commanded by majors. Each region consisted of one to four provinces, with one or more infantry brigades assigned to it. The brigades were generally dispersed in battalion or smaller unit formations to protect strategic terrain, urban centers, settlements, and critical infrastructure such as bridges and factories. Counterintelligence agents were assigned to all field units to thwart UNITA infiltration. The army's diverse combat capabilities were indicated by its many regular and motorized infantry brigades with organic or attached armor, artillery, and air defense units; two militia infantry brigades; four antiaircraft artillery brigades; ten tank battalions; and six artillery battalions. These forces were concentrated most heavily in places of strategic importance and

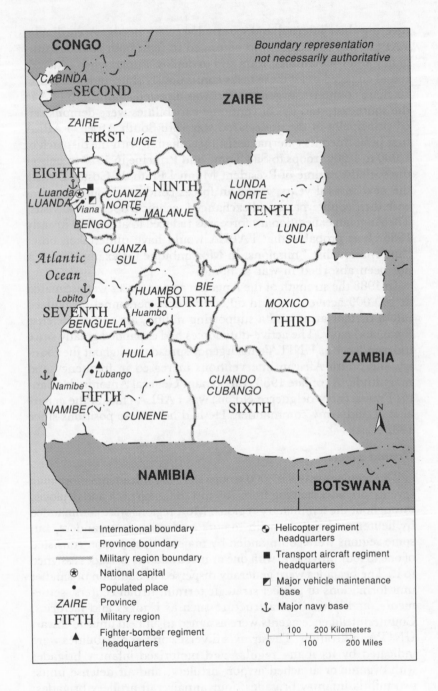

Figure 13. Military Regions and Principal Bases, 1987

recurring conflict: the oil-producing Cabinda Province, the area around the capital, and the southern provinces where UNITA and South African forces operated.

Special commands, military formations, and security arrangements were also created in extraordinary circumstances. Thus, for example, in June 1985 the provincial military authorities in the Tenth Military Region established a unified command to include both FAPLA and the People's Vigilance Brigades (Brigadas Populares de Vigilância—BPV) to confront UNITA's expanding operations in the region (see Internal Security Forces and Organization, this ch.). Similarly, special railroad defense committees were formed in the Ninth Military Region to protect the Luanda Railway between Malanje and Luanda (see fig. 10). These municipal committees were composed of party, government, FAPLA, JMPLA, and BPV units. In 1987 FAPLA was reported to be recruiting regional defense forces to assist the regular army against the UNITA insurgency, but in late 1988 no additional details were available.

FAPLA was equipped almost exclusively by the Soviet Union. In early 1988, it was reported to have at least 550 tanks and 520 armored vehicles, more than 500 artillery pieces and multiple rocket launchers, 500 mortars, at least 900 antitank weapons, and more than 300 air defense guns and surface-to-air missile (SAM) batteries (see table 12, Appendix A). However, in view of continuous losses and the influx of new and replacement matériel, these figures were only approximate. For example, the South African minister of defense reported in late 1988 that Angola's inventory of T–54 and T–55 tanks had increased from 531 to 1,590 between September 1987 and September 1988. Moreover, FAPLA and UNITA exaggerated successes and underestimated losses in military actions. In the major battle of Mavinga in 1986, UNITA claimed to have killed 5,000 FAPLA troops and to have destroyed 41 combat aircraft, 202 tanks and armored vehicles, 351 military transport vehicles, 200 trucks, and 40 SAMs, figures that represented 15 percent to 25 percent of FAPLA's inventory.

In addition to combat troops and equipment, logistical support units, and extensive headquarters organizations, the armed forces established a growing infrastructure to service, repair, and manufacture defense equipment. In 1983 the government created a new company under the Ministry of Defense to rehabilitate and repair armored military vehicles, infantry weapons, and artillery. A maintenance and repair center for Soviet-made light and heavy vehicles, located at Viana near Luanda, was turned over to Angolan authorities by the Soviet Union in 1984 to strengthen Angolan

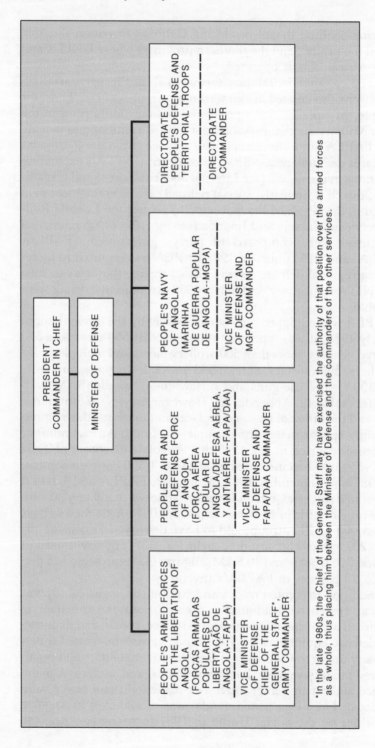

Figure 14. Organization of the Ministry of Defense, 1988

self-sufficiency. This center, reportedly capable of servicing 600 military and commercial vehicles a day, was one of the largest of its kind in Africa. Viana was also the site of an assembly plant for commercial vehicles as well as military trucks and jeeps. In June 1986, the government signed a contract with the Brazilian company Engesa for the purchase of military trucks and construction of a facility with the capacity to repair about 30 percent of the country's heavy trucks, military vehicles foremost.

The regular army was also supported by a 50,000-member citizens' militia, the Directorate of People's Defense and Territorial Troops, an organization under the minister of defense that had both counterinsurgency and police functions. The directorate was established in September 1985 as a successor to the People's Defense Organization (Organização de Defesa Popular—ODP). The ODP had been formed in September 1975 as an adjunct to FAPLA to defend against Portuguese settler resistance and attacks by anti-MPLA insurgents. After the civil war, it retained its territorial defense and counterguerrilla supporting roles but served more as a reserve than as an active paramilitary force. Indeed, some 20,000 ODP militia were inducted into the regular army in the early 1980s, apparently to satisfy an urgent requirement to expand FAPLA. In 1988 the Directorate of People's Defense and Territorial Troops was organized into eleven "Guerrilla Force" brigades, two of which (about 10,000 members) were to be on active duty with FAPLA at any given time. They were deployed in battalion and smaller formations, and they often operated in proximity to or jointly with FAPLA units, defending factories, farms, and villages and maintaining vigilance against insurgents. Although some estimates put the troop strength of the Guerrilla Force as high as 500,000, such figures were probably based on data from the late 1970s or reflected the inclusion of reserve components. Lieutenant Colonel Domingos Paiva da Silva was commander of the Guerrilla Force from 1978 until his death from natural causes in July 1987 (see Internal Security Forces and Organization, this ch.).

Air and Air Defense Force

The People's Air and Air Defense Force of Angola (Força Aérea Popular de Angola/Defesa Aérea y Antiaérea—FAPA/DAA), officially established on January 21, 1976, was the largest air force in sub-Saharan Africa. Colonel Alberto Correia Neto became vice minister of defense and FAPA/DAA commander in September 1986. He succeeded Colonel Carreira, who had held that post since 1983. The 7,000-member FAPA/DAA included about 180 fixed-wing combat attack and interceptor aircraft; an equal number of helicopters; several maritime patrol, reconnaissance, trainer, and transport aircraft; five air defense battalions; and ten SAM battalions (see table 13, Appendix A). Seeking voluntary enlistment was initially the sole form of recruitment, but in the 1980s conscription was increasingly employed until volunteerism was restored in 1988.

Angola's army had about fifteen years to develop an organization and gain combat experience prior to independence. In contrast, FAPA/DAA had to acquire personnel, experience, and equipment immediately, and in the context of a civil war. These unusual circumstances affected both recruitment and force development. FAPA/DAA's pilots, mostly in their mid-twenties, got combat experience immediately. Moreover, given FAPA/DAA's virtually instantaneous creation, its long-term dependence on external assistance was inevitable. Soviet, Cuban, and other communist forces provided pilots and technicians to fly and maintain FAPA/DAA's growing, diversified, and increasingly complex air fleet. The principal tasks of this new branch of the Angolan military were to protect the capital, guard major cities and military installations in the south against South African air raids, and extend the air defense network and combat operations southward to confront UNITA forces and South African invaders.

According to a 1987 press report, FAPA/DAA was reorganized into three regiments: a fighter-bomber regiment headquartered in Lubango, a transport regiment in Luanda, and a helicopter regiment in Huambo. In addition, FAPA/DAA aircraft and air defense units were deployed in strategic locations throughout the country. Of Angola's 229 usable airfields, 25 had permanent-surface runways, 13 of which exceeded 2,440 meters.

The capabilities and effectiveness of FAPA/DAA have increased markedly following its creation. FAPA/DAA's expanded capacity to provide air cover and supplies to forward ground forces, strike at UNITA bases and interdict South African aircraft, evacuate wounded personnel, and perform reconnaissance and liaison missions became particularly apparent during combined offensives after 1985. Like the army, FAPA/DAA developed modern facilities to repair and service both military and civilian aircraft for Angola and other African states.

Navy

The People's Navy of Angola (Marinha de Guerra Popular de Angola—MGPA) remained a relatively unimportant branch of the armed forces because of the exigencies of the ground and air wars in the interior. The navy's fortified headquarters and home port, as well as major ship repair facilities, were at Luanda. Although there were several good harbors along Angola's coastline, the only other ports used regularly were Lobito and Namibe, and these were used only to support temporary southern deployments. The latter two ports were located near railheads and airfields. Lobito had minor repair facilities as well.

The navy's mission was to defend the 1,600-kilometer coastline and territorial waters against South African sabotage, attacks, and resupply operations to UNITA; to protect against unlicensed fishing in Angolan waters; and to interdict smugglers. In early 1985, President dos Santos transferred responsibility for protecting the rich offshore fisheries from the coast guard to the MGPA to provide more effective enforcement of fishing regulations. After Lieutenant Colonel Manuel Augusto Alfredo, vice minister of defense and MGPA commander, was killed in a road accident in June 1985, he was succeeded by Rear Admiral António José Condessa de Carvalho (nom de guerre Toka), who had spent the previous four years in the Soviet Union studying military science.

The MGPA officially dates from July 10, 1976, when late-President Agostinho Neto visited the naval facilities at Luanda. Its senior officers had actually begun training in 1970, during the war of liberation, when the MPLA sent the first cadre of twenty-four naval trainees abroad for a three-year training program. However, there was no navy awaiting their return. The MPLA inherited a small number of Portuguese ships at independence, which were subsequently augmented by various Soviet warships and support craft. In 1988 the MGPA was reported to have 1,500 personnel (thought to be volunteers) and a fleet of about fifty vessels that included guided-missile fast patrol boats, torpedo boats, inland-water and coastal patrol vessels, mine warfare craft, and amphibious landing craft. The independent merchant marine fleet had about 100 vessels that could be impressed into service (see table 14, Appendix A).

Most of the navy's maintenance, repair, and training were provided by Soviet and Cuban technicians and advisers; Portugal and Nigeria also provided training assistance. Despite extensive foreign support, in late 1988 the serviceability of many of the vessels and equipment was in question. Moreover, naval recruitment and the proficiency of MGPA personnel remained problematic; indeed, the MPLA and Ministry of Defense leadership repeatedly appealed to youth (the JMPLA in particular) to join the navy.

Foreign Auxiliary Forces

FAPLA was augmented in the late 1980s by exiled Namibian

and South African black nationalist forces, which enjoyed refuge in Angola. SWAPO had some 9,000 guerrillas encamped primarily in the south. Their location near UNITA's area of operations permitted them to collect intelligence and conduct operations, and about 2,500 SWAPO troops regularly engaged in fighting UNITA. Moreover, about 1,000 ANC guerrillas, exiles from South Africa, also cooperated with FAPLA in action against UNITA and South African forces. Upon implementation of the 1988 regional accords signed by Angola, South Africa, and Cuba, it seemed likely that SWAPO guerrillas would return to Namibia and that the ANC members would be relocated to other African states outside the region.

Troop Strength, Recruitment, and Conscription

FAPLA relied heavily on conscription to meet its staffing requirements. Voluntary enlistments were important, too, especially in FAPA/DAA and MGPA, where greater technical competence was required. Recruitment and conscription were carried out by the General Staff's Directorate for Organization and Mobilization through provincial and local authorities.

Although two-year conscription had been initiated in 1978 pursuant to the Mobilization and Recruitment Law, the First Extraordinary Party Congress held in 1980 decided that increased troop requirements warranted introduction of universal and compulsory military training. Angola thus became the first black-ruled state in sub-Saharan Africa to make its citizens subject to compulsory military service. Of Angola's more than 8.2 million people, males in the fifteen to forty-five age-group numbered almost 2 million, half of whom were considered fit for military service. About 87,000 reached the military recruitment age of eighteen each year, but a sizable proportion, perhaps a majority, were unavailable because of rural dislocation and UNITA's control of at least one-third of the country. The Ministry of Defense issued periodic conscription orders for all men born during a given calendar year. Thus, for example, in February 1988 the Ministry of Defense ordered all male Angolan citizens born during calendar year 1970 to report to local registration centers to be recruited and inducted into active military service as of March 1. Separate days were reserved for teachers and students to report, and officials in charge of workplaces and schools were instructed to deny admission to anyone not properly registered for military service. After military service, all personnel were obliged to enroll in the Directorate of People's Defense and Territorial Troops.

Particularly in the late 1980s, FAPLA apparently resorted to other means besides conscription to satisfy military requirements; political needs were sometimes also met in the process. For instance, in the 1980s several hundred former FNLA rebels were integrated into FAPLA after accepting amnesty. According to UNITA sources, FAPLA also had begun to organize new recruits into battalions formed along ethnic lines, with Mbundu and Bakongo elite forces kept in the rear while Ovimbundu, Kwanhama (also spelled Kwanyama), Chokwe (also spelled Cokwe), and Nganguela (also spelled Ganguela) were sent to the front lines (see Ethnic Groups and Languages, ch. 2). Children of government and party leaders were reported to be exempt from conscription or spared service on the front lines. FAPLA was also reported by UNITA to have forcibly conscripted hospital workers, convicts, youth, and old men after suffering heavy losses in the offensive of late 1987.

Women played a definite but poorly documented role in national defense. They too were subject to conscription, but their numbers and terms of service were not reported. FAPLA included women's units and female officers, whose duties included staffing certain schools, particularly in contested areas. Other details on the size, type, and activities of these units were not available.

Conditions of Service, Ranks, and Military Justice

It was difficult to gauge the conditions of service and morale among FAPLA troops. Little public information was available in the late 1980s, and much of what existed was propagandistic. Nonetheless, service did seem difficult. Conscription was intensive in government-controlled areas, and the spread of the insurgency undermined security everywhere. The constant infusion of raw recruits, the rapid growth of FAPLA, the increasing scope and intensity of military operations, and escalating casualties imposed substantial personal and institutional hardships. The continued dependence on foreign technicians and advisers, many of whom were not deployed in combat zones, had adverse consequences for operations and morale.

Pay and living conditions in garrison were probably adequate but not particularly attractive; in the field, amenities were either sparse or lacking altogether. The expansion of quarters and facilities for troops did not keep pace with the rapid growth of FAPLA, especially in the late 1980s. There were periodic reports of ill-equipped and poorly trained soldiers, as well as breakdowns in administration and services. But given the lack of alternative employment in the war-torn economy, military service at least provided many Angolans with short-term opportunities. UNITA frequently reported incidents of flight to avoid government conscription; demoralization among FAPLA troops from high casualties and deteriorating conditions of service; and battlefield desertions, mutinies, and revolts among FAPLA units. These reports became more frequent during annual FAPLA offensives against UNITA strongholds after 1985.

In early December 1986, the People's Assembly approved new military ranks for the three military services, differentiating those of the army and air force from the navy. FAPLA and FAPA/DAA were authorized to establish the ranks (in descending order) of general, colonel general, major general, and lieutenant general. The MGPA was to have the ranks of admiral, vice admiral, and rear admiral; the ranks of colonel, lieutenant colonel, and major were replaced by captain, commander, and lieutenant commander, respectively. Future navy second lieutenants would be given rank equivalent to that of their counterparts in the army and air force. Later that month, President dos Santos received the rank of general as commander in chief of the armed forces, the minister of defense was appointed colonel general, and ten other senior military officers were promoted to newly established higher ranks (see fig. 15).

Little information was available on the military justice system. Military tribunals were created in each military region, and a higher court, the Armed Forces Military Tribunal, served as a military court of appeal. Some observers inferred from the criminal justice system and the prevalent wartime conditions, however, that Angolan military justice was harsh, if not arbitrary (see Crime and Punishment, this ch.).

Foreign Influences

Communist Nations

The Angolan armed forces were equipped, trained, and supported almost exclusively by communist countries. The Soviet Union provided the bulk of FAPLA's armaments and some advisers, whereas Cuba furnished most of the technical assistance, combat support, and training advisory services. Cubans also participated to a limited extent in ground and air combat. Other communist countries, particularly Czechoslovakia, the German Democratic Republic (East Germany), Hungary, the Democratic People's Republic of Korea (North Korea), Poland, and Yugoslavia, also furnished arms and related aid. In the 1980s, Angola also obtained limited amounts of matériel, military assistance, and training from countries such as Belgium, Brazil, Britain, the Federal Republic of Germany (West Germany), France, Spain, and Switzerland.

*A female member of the People's Armed Forces for the
Liberation of Angola
Courtesy United Nations (Y. Nagata)*

Broadly speaking, there was an international division of labor in which the Soviet Union supplied large quantities of heavy weapons and equipment, other communist states furnished small arms, and the noncommunist suppliers provided mostly nonlethal items.

The MPLA owed its ascendancy in the civil war in large part to the massive Soviet airlift of arms and Cuban troops during 1975 and 1976. Subsequently, Moscow and Havana remained the mainstays of the regime as far as its military needs were concerned. From 1982 to 1986, the Soviet Union delivered military equipment valued at US$4.9 billion, which represented more than 90 percent of Angola's arms imports and one-fourth of all Soviet arms deliveries to Africa. Poland and Czechoslovakia transferred arms valued at US$10 million and US$5 million, respectively, over the same five-year period. During 1987 and 1988, Moscow more than compensated for FAPLA losses with accelerated shipments of heavy armaments. In addition to the tanks noted earlier, dozens of aircraft, heavy weapons, and air defense systems were delivered.

Beyond matériel deliveries, Moscow and its allies continued to provide extensive technical aid. Soviet military, security, and intelligence personnel and advisers helped establish the defense and security forces and served as advisers at all levels, from ministries in Luanda to major field commands. The Soviet Union's civilian

225

and military intelligence services, in coordination with their counterpart organizations from other communist countries, particularly East Germany, Czechoslovakia, and Cuba, assisted in the creation and development of the Angolan state security and intelligence services.

The Soviet Union provided most of the air force pilot and technician training as well as technical assistance in the operation and maintenance of the most advanced equipment: aircraft and warships, major weapons such as missiles, artillery, and rockets, and sophisticated radar and communications equipment. The number of Soviet service members and advisers varied. In 1988 it was estimated by most sources to range between 1,000 and 1,500 personnel, including some fighter pilots. UNITA claimed that the Soviet military presence increased during 1988 to 2,500 or 3,000 and that seven officers were assigned to each FAPLA brigade.

Cuba was the main provider of combat troops, pilots, advisers, engineers, and technicians. As the insurgency war expanded, so did Cuba's military presence. By 1982 there were 35,000 Cubans in Angola, of which about 27,000 were combat troops and the remainder advisers, instructors, and technicians. In 1985 their strength increased to 40,000, in 1986 to 45,000, and in 1988 to nearly 50,000. All told, more than 300,000 Cuban soldiers had served in Angola since 1975. Angola paid for the services of the Cubans at an estimated rate of US$300 million to US$600 million annually.

The Cuban forces, despite their numbers, generally did not engage directly in combat after 1976. Most of the Cubans were organized and deployed in motorized infantry, air defense, and artillery units. Their main missions were to deter and defend against attacks beyond the southern combat zone, protect strategic and economically critical sites and facilities, and provide combat support, such as rear-area security, logistic coordination, air defense, and security for major military installations and Luanda itself. At least 2,000 Cuban troops were stationed in oil-producing Cabinda Province. Cubans also trained Angolan pilots, and flew some combat missions against UNITA and the SADF. In addition, Cuban military personnel provided technical and operational support to SWAPO and the ANC within Angola (see Angola as a Refuge, this ch.).

In mid-1988 Cuba substantially reinforced its military presence in Angola and deployed about one-fifth of its total forces toward the front lines in the south for the first time. This cohort was reported to include commando and SAM units, which raised concerns about direct clashes with South African forces. The move was apparently made to keep UNITA and the SADF at bay and to strengthen the negotiating position of Luanda and Havana in the United States-brokered peace talks.

East Germany and North Korea followed the Soviet Union and Cuba as Angola's most active and influential communist supporters. The East Germans played key roles in the intelligence and security agencies, as well as in the ideology and propaganda organs. They provided communications security services, technicians, mechanics, and instructors to maintain and operate equipment and vehicles and to train artillery crews, radar operators, and combat pilots. The East Germans also reportedly operated a training camp south of Luanda for ANC and SWAPO guerrillas. Estimates of the number of East Germans in Angola ranged from 500 to 5,000, the higher estimates probably including family members and other nonmilitary technicians and advisers.

During the 1980s, North Korea expanded and intensified its diplomatic and military assistance activities in Africa, particularly in the southern part of the continent. After training Zimbabwe's Fifth Brigade in 1981 and 1982 and furnishing arms to that country, North Korea made a major military commitment in Angola. Although denied by Angolan officials, several sources reported that Luanda concluded a military aid agreement with Pyongyang in September 1983 that led to the dispatch of some 3,000 North Korean combat troops and military advisers by May 1984.

The reported activities of the North Koreans included the training of special units, such as hit-and-run forces and sniper squads. North Korean troops also reportedly engaged in combat operations, including FAPLA's early 1986 offensive. North Koreans were also reported to be providing military and ideological instruction to SWAPO and ANC militants in five training camps north and northeast of Luanda.

Other communist states provided more modest military support. Arms deliveries by Poland and Czechoslovakia were noted earlier. A military cooperation agreement was signed in 1982 with Hungary, which was reported to have provided small arms. Yugoslavia furnished grenade launchers, trip-wire grenades, antipersonnel mines, hollow-charge rockets, and air defense artillery; a Yugoslav firm also built a runway and other facilities at Lubango airport. Romania was reported to have given unspecified military aid.

Noncommunist Nations

In the 1980s, Angola diversified its foreign arms acquisitions for political and practical reasons. Politically, Luanda was anxious to gain international legitimacy, counter UNITA's international

Figure 15. *Military Ranks and Insignia, 1988*

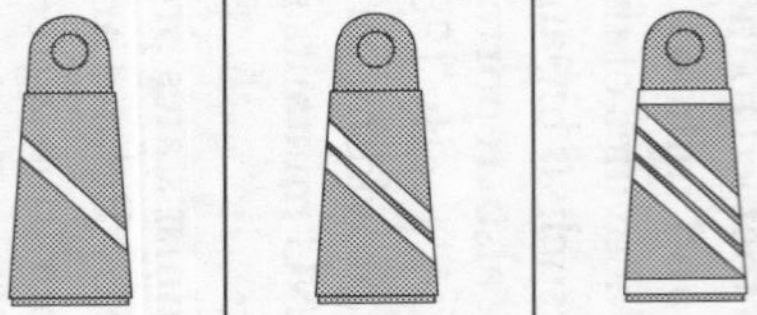

diplomatic offensive, reduce its dependence on its communist allies, and gain leverage in dealing with its traditional arms suppliers. The practical reason was dissatisfaction with the level of support given by the Soviet Union and its allies, the poor quality of some equipment, and the inability to obtain certain military matériel. Perhaps in deference to the Soviet Union and other communist benefactors, most procurements from other sources consisted of relatively inexpensive support equipment. This policy left Moscow with a virtual monopoly on the provision of major weapons systems.

Diversification was evident in FAPLA's purchase of jeeps, Land Rovers, and radios from Britain, trucks and communications equipment from West Germany, small-caliber ammunition and artillery shells from Belgium, uniforms from Japan, and jeeps, trucks, and truck engines from Brazil. The MGPA also discussed the acquisition of corvettes with French, Spanish, and Portuguese shipbuilders. Among the larger purchases made from Western Europe were Swiss Pilatus training aircraft; Spanish CASA C-212 Aviocar transport aircraft; French Dauphin, Gazelle, and Alouette helicopters; French Thomson-CSF tactical military transceivers; and British Racal radio communications equipment.

Ironically, Portugal continued to play a role in the Angolan conflict. Although the Portuguese government did not officially provide arms, military assistance, or troops, private Portuguese "mercenaries" and advisers apparently served with both FAPLA and UNITA. In 1983 retired Portuguese admiral Rosa Coutinho set up a company to hire former military and reserve officers, many of whom had served in Angola during the war of liberation, as contract military advisers and to train FAPLA counterinsurgency units. Twelve were reported to be training FAPLA instructors in early 1984, and a total of thirty-two were reportedly hired in 1986. However, several of these advisers were killed in action against UNITA, and most left by late 1987. UNITA also claimed that some 3,000 Portuguese "communists" were in the country assisting Luanda in late 1986, but this claim may have been either an exaggeration or a reference to civilian technicians. MPLA-PT sources charged that there were more than 2,000 South African-trained Portuguese commandos fighting with UNITA.

Training

Regular and informal training was provided throughout the country at troop recruitment centers, officer candidate schools, specialized technical training centers, and field units. The military regional headquarters were responsible for providing individual training in basic military subjects to troops and noncommissioned officers.

In 1985 the government cited as major accomplishments the establishment of formal training programs for military cadres, the creation of military education centers throughout the country (particularly at the intermediate level for officers and specialists), and the creation of various specialized branches of the armed forces. The Soviet Union and other communist countries provided most of the formal military training. The United States Department of State estimated that 3,260 Angolan military personnel had been trained in the Soviet Union and Eastern Europe through the end of 1986 and that 1,700 Warsaw Pact military technicians were present in Angola that year. Most of the technicians were engaged in maintaining and otherwise servicing military equipment furnished by the Soviet Union and other communist states.

Individual officer candidate training was conducted at the Comandante Zhika Political-Military Academy in Luanda, which opened in 1984. Most of the instruction was originally given by Soviet and Cuban officers and specialists, but since then qualified Angolan instructors reportedly had joined the staff. As the academy's name suggested, the curriculum included training in such military subjects as strategy, tactics, and weapons, as well as political and ideological indoctrination. Another training program at the academy—a condensed version of the officer candidate political-military curriculum—was attended by senior party officials on weekends over a ten-month period.

Senior military officers participated in an eight-month advanced course at the Escola de Oficiais Superiores Gomes Spencer at Huambo, but details on the curriculum were not available. The school's eighth class, which graduated in 1984, included about fifty senior FAPLA officers. Advanced officer training and high-level training for officers and enlisted personnel in armor, artillery, and other specialties was also conducted in Huambo. The Gomes Spencer academy was attacked and extensively damaged by a UNITA commando raid in July 1986.

Although information on unit-level training was not available, battalion-level exercises had been reported in the northern and western provinces, far removed from the war zone. It is likely that such large unit-training exercises immediately preceded deployment to the combat zone. Reserve units also trained, as indicated by the report of a reserve battalion having completed a three-month course that included physical conditioning, hand-to-hand combat, and infantry tactics.

In addition to basic individual and unit-level training, technical training was provided in such specialized functional areas as communications, intelligence, artillery, armor, air defense, motor transport, and logistics. This training was provided at facilities such as the Comandante Econômica Communications School. FAPA/ DAA inaugurated a two-year course for cadets in 1979 at the National Air Force School in Negage. In early 1983, 176 cadets completed the nine-subject course, which was administered by Angolan instructors and "internationalists" (presumably Soviet and Cuban advisers). A course for radio technicians and radar specialists was also offered at the Negage training center.

Some military training was conducted abroad, particularly in the Soviet Union, Eastern Europe, and Cuba. In mid-1985 the commander of the Fifth Military Region's FAPA/DAA reported the arrival in the region of many new pilots and technicians who had recently completed their training program in the Soviet Union. From 1977 to 1981, Soviet specialists trained more than 3,000 motor mechanics and drivers and 100 aircraft technicians in both Angola and the Soviet Union.

FAPLA's Combat Performance

FAPLA's military performance was difficult to gauge, particularly in view of the propagandistic reports issued by the various forces contending in the region. On the one hand, UNITA had extended its range of operations from the remote southeastern extremities throughout the entire country within a few years of Portugal's withdrawal. The SADF had occupied parts of southern Angola for extended periods, virtually without contest, for the purposes of resupplying UNITA, intervening on its behalf, conducting reconnaissance flights and patrols, and attacking SWAPO encampments. UNITA reported low morale among captured FAPLA conscripts, lack of discipline among troops, heavy losses of personnel and equipment in battle, countless ambushes and attacks on FAPLA forces, successful sabotage operations, and desertions by battalion-size FAPLA units. In the late 1980s, Angola's minister of defense publicly called for greater discipline in FAPLA, citing reports of theft, assaults, and drunken military drivers. As late as 1988, in the wake of reports of increased FAPA/DAA effectiveness, the South African Air Force (SAAF) commander dismissed the Angolans as "extremely unprofessional," noting that "50 percent of the threat against us is Cuban."

On the other hand, it could be argued that FAPLA had substantially improved its capabilities and performance. In the first place, FAPLA had begun to develop and acquire the organization, doctrine, and equipment of a conventional army only during the civil war of 1975–76. It was then forced to fight a counterinsurgency war in the most remote and inaccessible parts of the country over extended lines of communications, without the requisite air or ground transport or logistical infrastructure. UNITA also enjoyed the advantages of operating in thinly populated areas along porous borders with Zambia and Zaire, with extensive SADF combat and logistic support, making it impossible for FAPLA to isolate or outflank UNITA. Moreover, military experts believe that counterinsurgency troops must outnumber guerrillas by ten to one in order to win such wars, a ratio FAPLA could never approximate. The air force and navy were even further behind and had required years to acquire the assets and the expertise needed for effective operations. Although the navy was of marginal use in the war, air power was critical. It was only after sufficient aircraft and air defense systems had been deployed in the mid-1980s that Luanda was able to launch and sustain large offensives in the south. Although they suffered heavy losses and perhaps relied too heavily on Soviet military doctrine, FAPLA and FAPA/DAA in the late 1980s showed increased strength, put greater pressure on UNITA, and raised the costs of South Africa's support for UNITA. Luanda's resolve and the improved capabilities and performance of its armed forces were among the essential conditions under which South Africa agreed to negotiate its withdrawal from Angola.

War and the Role of the Armed Forces in Society
The Costs of Endemic Conflict

Persistent internal and external conflict have wrought havoc on Angola. The human cost has been awesome and tragic. It was estimated that as a consequence of war, between 60,000 and 90,000 people had died, and 20,000 to 50,000 persons had become amputees as of 1988 (see Effects of the Insurgency, ch. 2). From 1975 to 1988, almost 700,000 people were forced to flee their rural homes for relative safety in displacement camps or in burgeoning cities and towns, where they suffered gross deprivations in the absence of basic services. About 400,000 Angolans became refugees in neighboring states. Moreover, in 1986 some 600,000 people needed nutritional assistance.

The Angolan economy was also ravaged by wartime destruction and the heavy defense burden. Iron production virtually stopped, diamond mining and timber harvesting were severely curtailed, and smuggling siphoned off needed export earnings. Economic sabotage and attacks on infrastructure by UNITA and South Africa damaged or destroyed hundreds of facilities and made development impossible. The destruction attributed to South African military actions alone was estimated at US$20 billion.

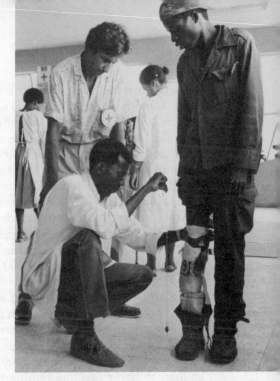

A government soldier is fitted for a prosthesis at a hospital in Huambo.
Courtesy International Committee of the Red Cross (Yannick Müller)

Devastation of the once-prosperous agricultural sector was forcing the government to import about 80 percent of its food requirements in the mid-1980s, at a cost of US$250 million to US$300 million annually. It was only because of oil production in relatively secure Cabinda Province that the country could pay the high cost of defense and keep itself from total economic ruin (see Background to Economic Development; Structure of the Economy, ch. 3).

Military recruitment placed a growing burden on the Angolan population. According to statistics published by the United States Arms Control and Disarmament Agency (ACDA), the number of soldiers per 1,000 people increased from five in 1975 to more than seven in the 1980s, which ranked Angola fifty-seventh among 144 countries in 1985. Any reckoning of the military burden borne by the Angolan people, however, must also take into account UNITA's armed forces. And because both FAPLA and UNITA expanded considerably in the late 1980s as the internal war intensified, the number of combatants per 1,000 people was actually twenty (based on 1988 population and combined armed forces estimates), a figure that moved Angola's global ranking into the top fifteen.

War and the Military in National Perspective

Perpetual war magnified and multiplied the social and economic impact of defense spending. Military expenditures and arms imports were the most obvious indicators of the intensified war effort. Luanda's defense spending nearly quadrupled from US$343 million in 1978 to US$1.3 billion in 1986 (in constant 1980 dollars), the bulk of that increase coming after 1983. In 1986 defense accounted for 40.4 percent of government expenditures. Military expenditure as a percentage of the gross national product (GNP— see Glossary), estimated at 12 percent to 14 percent from 1980 to 1982, rose steadily to 28.5 percent by 1985.

Arms imports also increased dramatically. Measured in constant 1984 dollars, the value of arms imports nearly doubled after 1980. During the late 1970s, arms deliveries remained relatively constant at a bit more than US$500 million per year, but after 1980 they surged to an annual average of more than US$1 billion. Since the 1970s, Angola's arms imports had ranged between 45 percent and 88 percent of total imports. In mid-1988 Angolan government officials estimated the country's external debt at US$4 billion, most of which was owed to the Soviet Union for military purchases, and they were considering the possibility of imposing a compulsory public loan to cover revenue requirements.

Angola's heavy defense burden was evident by comparative standards as well. According to 1985 statistics published by ACDA, Angola ranked sixty-third of 144 countries in both military expenditure and size of its armed forces. These absolute measures of military effort were consistent with Angola's ranking of between sixty-eight and seventy-three in GNP, central government expenditures, and population. However, the militarizing effects were seen more clearly and dramatically in relative measures of defense effort: Angola ranked seventeenth in level of arms imports and sixth in arms imports as a percentage of total imports, twenty-sixth in military expenditure as a percentage of GNP, thirty-second in military expenditure as a percentage of the government's budget, fiftieth in military expenditure per capita, and fifty-seventh in military expenditure relative to the size of the armed forces. The continued growth of the armed forces, military expenditures, and arms imports into the late 1980s further increased the burden of defense and ensured that few resources would be left for social and economic development.

Not only did the armed forces command and consume an enormous share of national wealth and revenue, their increased political power was institutionalized at every level of government. The defense and security forces were heavily represented in the highest organs of the party and government; indeed, the exigencies of war virtually transformed the integrated party-government system into a military machine dedicated to prosecuting war at an increasingly higher price. The reorganization of the territorial administration into military regions and provincial defense councils carried the process even further. It remained to be seen whether the December 1988 regional accords—which excluded UNITA—would result in a reversal of the process.

Civic Action and Veterans' Groups

Like those of many other developing countries, Angola's armed forces were intended to play an important role in nation building through civic-action programs. The Constitution, in fact, specially assigns "production" and "reconstruction" duties to FAPLA. In the late 1970s, FAPLA units were encouraged to grow their own food and to undertake civic action, emergency relief, and public construction projects. However, such tasks were given only nominal attention as the war intensified.

Veterans of the liberation struggle and families of those who died in that protracted conflict enjoyed "special protection" under the Angolan Constitution, but this status was not further defined. The rapidly expanding pool of war veterans in the 1980s could make a substantial contribution to national reconstruction and development if their political, ideological, organizational, social, and technical skills could be mobilized or channeled in such directions. However, the continuation of the war and the absence of information about their postservice occupations and activities precluded observation of veterans' actual roles in society. The MPLA–PT did attend to veterans' interests through party and government organs. As noted earlier, veterans were eligible for party membership, and a high government post, the secretary of state for war veterans, was also dedicated to veterans' affairs. The Angolan War Veterans Committee, with government endorsement, sought aid from the Soviet Union and presumably other potentially sympathetic international donors.

Internal Security

Since independence, the MPLA–PT government had faced several internal opponents and rivals for power. Broadly speaking, one can distinguish between antigovernment and antiregime opposition groups. These groups differed in their goals, methods, and bases of support. On the one hand, antigovernment groups protested or sought to change the incumbent leadership, used conventional means of political opposition ranging from passive resistance to attempted coups, and drew support from constituencies almost entirely within the country. The main source of such political opposition was factionalism within the MPLA–PT. Clandestine opposition groups and religious sects also contributed to antigovernment tensions (see Political Opposition, ch. 4).

On the other hand, antiregime groups sought to transform the political system or overthrow the ruling MPLA–PT, resorted to efforts at secession and armed rebellion, and received substantial external support. The most prominent of these political opponents were FLEC, the FNLA, and UNITA. Whereas the first two had become spent forces by the 1980s, UNITA continued to pose a serious national security challenge.

The MPLA–PT government survived this host of threats by developing an extensive internal security apparatus to supplement the armed forces. This system consisted of a paramilitary territorial militia; a state security ministry with penal functions, political police, and border guards; a national police force; and a nationwide popular vigilance brigade organization.

Antigovernment Opposition

The history of the MPLA party and government is ridden with factional strife based on ideological, political, ethnic, and personal rivalries. In the early 1970s, Daniel Chipenda, a member of the MPLA Central Committee, was thought to have instigated two assassination attempts against President Neto and was expelled from the party in December 1974. As leader of the so-called Eastern Revolt faction, he joined the rival FNLA, based in Kinshasa, Zaire, as assistant secretary general. Former MPLA president Mário de Andrade also opposed Neto's leadership and attempted to rally support for his so-called Active Revolt faction in 1974. In May 1977, Nito Alves, former commander of the first military division and minister of interior, spearheaded an abortive coup with the support of an extremist faction. Many MPLA officials were killed, including seven Central Committee members (see Independence and the Rise of the MPLA Government, ch. 1). And in early 1988, seven military intelligence officers were reported to have been sentenced to imprisonment for fifteen to twenty years and expelled from FAPLA for plotting a coup against President dos Santos.

Other sources of dissent included several small clandestine groups, which, to avoid infiltration, remained anonymous and restricted recruitment mainly to Angolan expatriates and exiles. They reportedly represented a variety of ideological inclinations, were disaffected by the continuing civil war, economic chaos, and political intolerance, and advocated development and a pluralistic political system. In 1987 about two dozen members of one such group, the Independent Democrats, were imprisoned and their leader sentenced to death. These events cast doubt on the group's continued ability to survive.

Religious sects were another source of antigovernment agitation. The Roman Catholic Church was often at odds with the MPLA–PT government but did not openly challenge it. More problematic was the government's clashes with such independent sects as the Jehovah's Witnesses and the Our Lord Jesus Christ Church in the World (Kimbanguist), whose members were popularly called Mtokoists, after the sect's founder, Simon Mtoko (also spelled Simão Toco). After Mtoko's death in 1984, elements of the Mtokoist sect engaged in alleged "antipatriotic activities" that were supposedly responsible for riots that occurred in at least three cities. Angolan security forces were believed to have sponsored rebellious factions within the leadership. During 1986 and 1987, more than 100 Mtokoists were killed in riots and demonstrations, and the sect was banned for one year. Jehovah's Witnesses were banned from practicing their religion for their refusal to perform military service (see Interest Groups, ch. 4).

Erstwhile Opposition: FLEC and the FNLA

FLEC waged an intermittent independence struggle between its establishment in 1963 and its virtual demise by the mid-1980s. Zaire's withdrawal of support and internal dissension in the late 1970s caused FLEC to fragment into five factions, three of which remained marginally active militarily in the late 1980s. A combination of the factions' internal divisions and lack of external support, on the one hand, and the heavy concentration in Cabinda of Cuban troops and FAPLA forces, on the other hand, reduced FLEC to little more than a nuisance. In 1983 Luanda granted an unofficial amnesty to the guerrilla separatists, and more than 8,000 refugees returned home. In February 1985, a cease-fire agreement was signed and talks began, but no formal resolution was reached. In late 1988, FLEC existed in little more than name only.

Holden Roberto's FNLA was also defunct by 1988. After losing to the MPLA in the civil war, the FNLA retreated to its traditional refuge in Zaire and continued to wage a low-level insurgency. However, in 1978 Zaire withdrew its support of the FNLA as part of the Angolan-Zairian accord signed in the wake of the second invasion of Shaba Region. Ousted by his own commanders, Roberto was exiled to Paris in 1979. He emerged again in 1983 in an unsuccessful effort to generate international support and material aid for his 7,000 to 10,000 poorly armed troops, who operated (but did not control territory) in six northern Angolan provinces.

FNLA remnants formed the Military Council of Angolan Resistance (Conselho Militar de Resistência Angolana—Comira) in August 1980 to replace the moribund movement. Comira claimed to have 2,000 troops training in Zaire for an invasion of northern Angola, but it never offered more than sporadic challenges. Its lack of strength was the result of the loss of its major external patron, the broadening of the leadership of the MPLA–PT to include more Bakongo people (the primary source of FNLA support), and more aggressive FAPLA operations. Several Comira leaders defected to the Angolan side, and in 1984 more than 1,500 armed rebels and 20,000 civilian supporters accepted the amnesty originally offered in 1978 and surrendered to Angolan authorities. Hundreds were integrated into FAPLA and the security forces. Luanda reported in October 1988 that 11,000 former FNLA/Comira members had been "reintegrated into national reconstruction tasks," and in November the exiled Roberto was reported to have accepted amnesty.

The Enduring Rival: UNITA

UNITA in the 1980s was a state within a state. Under the leadership of Jonas Savimbi, it survived defeat during the civil war, retreated to the remote southeastern corner of the country, regrouped and made its headquarters at Jamba, and launched a determined campaign to overturn the MPLA–PT regime or at least force it to accept UNITA in a coalition government (see fig. 16). With increasing international support and military aid, particularly from South Africa and, after 1985, the United States, UNITA extended its campaign of destruction throughout the entire country. It enlarged its military forces and scope of operations and withstood several major FAPLA offensives.

Starting with a small army of a few thousand defeated and poorly armed followers at the end of 1976, Savimbi built a credible political organization and fighting force. Unlike what became of the MPLA under its faction-ridden leadership, UNITA remained the creation and vehicle of its founder. Internal opposition occasionally surfaced, but the lack of independent reporting made it difficult to assess its significance. South Africa kept FAPLA and Cuban forces at bay and intervened whenever FAPLA offensives threatened, leaving UNITA comparatively free to consolidate its control throughout the south and to extend its range of operations northward. In February 1988, Savimbi announced the formation of a UNITA government in "Free Angola," the area he controlled. Although his intent was to regularize administration, rather than to secede or seek international recognition, this event marked a new stage in UNITA's organizational development and consolidation, and many Africans states maintained at least informal ties to the movement.

Savimbi's strategy and tactics were designed to raise the costs of foreign "occupation" through maximum disruption and dislocation, while minimizing his own casualties. UNITA's forces infiltrated new areas and contested as much territory as possible, wresting it away from FAPLA control whenever feasible. They rarely seized and held towns, except near their bases in the south. Rather, they sabotaged strategic targets of economic or military value and ambushed FAPLA units when the latter attempted to return to or retake their positions. FAPLA access was also obstructed by extensive mine laying along lines of communication, approaches to settlements, and infrastructure sites. To undermine support for the MPLA–PT, UNITA indiscriminately attacked or took hostage hundreds of expatriate technicians and advisers, and Savimbi repeatedly threatened multinational companies with retaliation for their support of the government. Apparently abandoning hope of military victory, Savimbi sought instead to strengthen UNITA's bargaining position in demanding direct negotiations with Luanda for the establishment of a government of national unity.

UNITA's military progress was remarkable. By 1982 it had declared all but six of the eighteen Angolan provinces to be war zones. In late 1983, with direct air support from South Africa, UNITA took the town of Cangamba, the last FAPLA stronghold in southeastern Angola. This operation marked a shift from guerrilla tactics to conventional warfare, at least in the countryside. In 1984 UNITA announced the beginning of an urban guerrilla campaign and claimed responsibility for acts of sabotage in Luanda itself and even in Cabinda. The movement gained control of the regions bordering Zambia and Zaire, enabling it to develop secure supply lines plus infiltration and escape routes. From 1984 to 1987, UNITA not only continued to advance north and northwest but also repulsed major FAPLA offensives backed by heavy Cuban and Soviet logistic and combat support, in the latter instances relying on SADF air and ground support. In spite of the 1988 regional accords, according to which FAPLA and UNITA were to lose much of their external support, no military solution to the war was expected.

Military Organization and Capability

UNITA's military wing, the Armed Forces for the Liberation of Angola (Forças Armadas de Libertação de Angola—FALA), was under the supreme authority of Savimbi as commander in chief.

Source: Based on information from Jonas Bernstein, "A Freedom Fight Deep in Africa,"
Insight, December 19, 1988, 11.

Figure 16. Territory Claimed by UNITA, 1988

The chief of staff was second in command and controlled the headquarters elements of intelligence, personnel, logistics, and operations. In January 1985, the FALA chief of staff, Brigadier

Demosthenes Amos Chilingutila, who had held that post since 1979, was removed and made chief of operations, possibly because of Savimbi's dissatisfaction with his performance, and replaced by Brigadier Alberto Joaquim Vinama. However, following Vinama's death in an automobile accident in October 1986, Chilingutila was reappointed chief of staff.

By the mid-1980s, FALA had evolved into a well-defined conventional military organization with command and specialized staff organs, a formal hierarchy of ranks, an impressive array of weapons and equipment, and considerable international support. Geographically, UNITA's nationwide area of operations consisted of five fronts commanded by a colonel or brigadier, which were subdivided into twenty-two military regions under a colonel or lieutenant colonel. The regions in turn were divided into sectors (usually three) commanded by a major and further subdivided into zones under captains or lieutenants.

FALA had a four-tiered hierarchical structure. The lowest level, the local defense forces, had six battalions of poorly armed men recruited as guards and local militia in contested areas. The next stratum consisted of dispersed guerrillas who trained in their local areas for about sixty days and then conducted operations there, either in small groups of about twenty or in larger units of up to 150. They were armed with automatic weapons and trained to attack and harass FAPLA convoys, bases, and aircraft. The third level included forty-four semi-regular battalions that received a three-month training course and were sent back to the field in units of up to 600. These forces were capable of attacking and defending small towns and strategic terrain and infrastructure. Finally, FALA regular battalions of about 1,000 troops each completed a six-month to nine-month training period, and about a quarter of them also received specialized training in South Africa or Namibia in artillery, communications, and other technical disciplines. Armed with heavy weapons plus supporting arms such as artillery, rockets, mortars, and antitank and air defense weapons, these FALA regulars had the tasks of taking territory and holding it.

By 1987 UNITA claimed to have 65,000 troops (37,000 guerrilla fighters—those in the first three categories cited above—and 28,000 regulars), but other estimates put FALA's total strength closer to 40,000. Among its specialized forces were sixteen platoons of commandos and other support units, including engineering, medicine, communications, and intelligence. In late 1987, women were integrated into FALA for the first time when a unit of fifty completed training as semi-regulars. Seven members of this group received commissions as officers.

In addition to combat forces, UNITA had an extensive logistical support infrastructure of at least 10,000 people, about 1,000 vehicles (mostly South African trucks), an expanding network of roads and landing strips, schools, hospitals, supply depots, and specialized factories, workshops and other facilities used to manufacture, repair, and refurbish equipment and weapons. The main logistical support center and munitions factory was Licua. Many smaller centers were scattered throughout UNITA-controlled territory. Like Jamba, UNITA's capital, these centers were mobile.

It was difficult to determine the conditions of service with UNITA guerrillas. Military service was voluntary and uncompensated, but soldiers and their families normally received their livelihood, even if it sometimes meant appropriating local food supplies. Moreover, political indoctrination was an essential part of military life and training. Although visitors to UNITA-controlled territory reported that the armed forces were highly motivated, FALA defectors and captives allegedly reported coercive recruiting and low morale.

FALA had a substantial arsenal of weapons and equipment of diverse origin, most of which was captured from FAPLA during attacks on convoys, raids, or pitched battles, or donated by the SADF as war booty. The remainder came from various countries and the international black market. Included in FALA's inventory were captured T–34 and T–55 tanks, armored vehicles, vehicle-mounted rocket launchers, 76mm and 122m field guns, mortars (up to 120mm), RPG–7 and 106mm antitank weapons, heavy and light machine guns, various antiaircraft guns, SA–7 and United States-manufactured Redeye and Stinger SAMs, and G–3 and AK–47 assault rifles.

External Support

FALA, like FAPLA, would not have been able to expand its size, capabilities, and range of operations without extensive external assistance. By supplying UNITA with US$80 million worth of assistance annually during the 1980s, Pretoria remained the group's principal source of arms, training, logistical, and intelligence support. The SAAF made regular air drops of weapons, ammunition, medicine, food, and equipment, sometimes at night to avoid interception, and was reported occasionally to have ferried FALA troops. South African instructors provided training in both Namibia and UNITA-controlled areas of southern Angola. The largest training center in Namibia was at Rundu, where intensive three-month training courses were conducted. In late 1988, amidst regional peace negotiations, there were reports that UNITA was planning to relocate its main external logistical supply lines from South Africa to

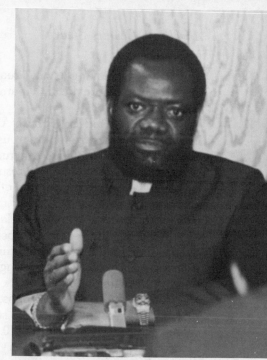

*Jonas Savimbi,
the leader of the National Union
for the Total Independence
of Angola
Courtesy Free Angola
Information Service*

*UNITA troops atop a
Soviet-built BTR-60
captured in Mavinga in 1987
Courtesy Free Angola
Information Service*

243

Zaire and was moving its headquarters and forces into Namibia's Caprivi Strip before the anticipated arrival of a UN peacekeeping force.

In addition to aid from South Africa, UNITA received support in varying degrees from numerous black African and North African states. Zaire provided sanctuary and allowed its territory to be used by others to train and resupply UNITA forces, and Zambia and Malawi were suspected of granting clandestine overflight and landing privileges. During the 1970s, UNITA troops were trained in Senegal, Tanzania, Zambia, and other African countries. Subsequently, Egypt, Morocco, Senegal, Somalia, and Tunisia also furnished financial and military aid. Morocco, which had supplied arms to the MPLA during the liberation struggle, switched sides and became a major source of military training for FALA, especially for officers, paratroops, and artillery personnel. Saudi Arabia, Kuwait, and other Arab states furnished financial support valued at US$60 million to US$70 million annually. Israel was also reported to have provided military aid and training to UNITA soldiers at Kamina in Zaire. Although Savimbi denied that UNITA had ever employed foreign mercenaries or advisers, there had been reports of South African, French, Israeli, and Portuguese combatants among his forces.

Beginning in 1986, the United States had supplied UNITA with US$15 million to US$20 million annually in "covert" military aid funded out of the budget of the Central Intelligence Agency (CIA). The first acknowledged shipments of United States aid consisted of nonlethal items such as trucks, medical equipment, and uniforms, but antitank and air defense weapons soon followed. The bulk of this matériel was reportedly airlifted through Kamina airbase in Zaire's Shaba Region, where a UNITA liaison detachment was stationed and CIA operatives were believed by Luanda to have trained 3,000 UNITA guerrillas. The remainder was thought to have been delivered through South Africa, Gabon, and Central African Republic.

Angola as a Refuge

The MPLA-PT government, conscious of its own revolutionary and anticolonial origins and committed to the liberation of South African-occupied Namibia and of South Africa itself, provided both sanctuary and material support to SWAPO and the ANC. Although FAPLA never made a preemptive attack south of the Namibian border, Pretoria's forces repeatedly invaded or otherwise intervened militarily in Angola. South Africa's regional strategy was to ensure UNITA's success, contain and disrupt SWAPO, prevent the establishment of ANC bases in southern Angola, and halt Cuban and Soviet expansion southward. In addition to SWAPO and the ANC, a large contingent of Katangan gendarmes (remnants of the force that had invaded Zaire's Shaba Region in 1977 and 1978) enjoyed the protection of the Angolan government.

SWAPO was headquartered in Luanda and directed camps primarily in southern Angola from which its militants could infiltrate Namibia in small units. SWAPO's military wing, the People's Liberation Army of Namibia (PLAN), had main command centers in Luanda and Lubango and training camps in Huíla, Benguela, and Cuanza Sul provinces. To avoid identification, infiltration, and attack by the SADF, most of its camps were mobile. SWAPO recruits were trained at Angolan and Cuban military facilities, whence they were dispatched to SWAPO camps and formally organized into battalions of 400 to 800 troops each. PLAN's strength in 1988 was estimated at 9,000 troops, most of whom were engaged in operations in Angola against UNITA, rather than against the SADF in Namibia. It was uncertain whether PLAN's anti-UNITA operations represented a quid pro quo for Angolan sanctuary and material support or reflected limited chances to operate in Namibia because of South African defenses. In the Angolan government's 1986 offensive against UNITA, for example, it was estimated that 6,000 to 8,000 SWAPO guerrillas operated with FAPLA.

In May 1978, South African forces made their first major cross-border raid into Angola, attacking SWAPO's main camp at Cassinga. Other major South African incursions against SWAPO bases and forces occurred in 1981 and 1983. These attacks and the many that followed, coupled with UNITA's territorial expansion, disrupted SWAPO and forced it to disperse and move northward. The Lusaka Accord of February 1984 provided for a cease-fire, South African withdrawal, and relocation of SWAPO under FAPLA control to monitored camps north of a neutral zone along the Namibian border. But Pretoria, alleging that SWAPO's redeployment was incomplete, delayed its own pullout until April 1985. In September 1985, however, South Africa launched another major air and ground attack on SWAPO and later claimed to have killed about 600 guerrillas in 1985 and 1986.

The southern African peace negotiations in 1988 rekindled rumors of debate within the MPLA–PT about continued support for SWAPO. The regional accords required Angola to restrict PLAN to an area north of 16° south latitude, about 150 kilometers from the Namibian border. South Africa accused SWAPO of violating the agreement by remaining in the proscribed area and intensifying its operations from a military command headquarters at Xangongo. Accusations aside, SWAPO intended PLAN to form the nucleus of a future Namibian national army, into which it would integrate the existing territorial forces after a period of reorientation and rehabilitation.

The ANC, banned in South Africa, operated mainly in Angola under the protection and control of Luanda. At least seven major training camps for an estimated 1,000 to 1,400 members of the ANC's military wing, Umkhonto we Sizwe (Zulu for "Spear of the Nation"), were in Angola. Most of the ANC's personnel, which were organized into three battalions, had their encampment at Viana, outside Luanda. This location in northern Angola provided security from South African attacks but restricted the ANC's ability to infiltrate or mount attacks on South Africa. Other major camps were also in the north at Caculama, Pango, and Quibaxe. ANC militants, like those of PLAN, were engaged along with FAPLA forces in fighting UNITA. Some ANC forces may have been integrated into FAPLA units. Such joint training and operations facilitated the ANC's access to weapons and supplies, which came mostly from the Soviet Union and its allies. Sanctuary in Angola became all the more important after the March 1984 Mozambique-South Africa nonaggression and mutual security pact, the Nkomati Accord, which obliged Maputo to control ANC activities. By 1988 a combination of internal and external pressures had considerably weakened the ANC, including assassinations of its leadership, South African infiltration and crackdowns at home, attacks on ANC cadres in Botswana, and the United States-brokered peace accords under which Luanda agreed to terminate its assistance to the ANC. As 1988 ended, the ANC decided to relocate its bases out of Angola; reportedly, Ethiopia, Tanzania, Nigeria, and Uganda had been mentioned as possible destinations.

Finally, Angola was a refuge for some 1,400 Zairian dissidents. Although quiescent since 1978, these former Katangan gendarmes, who formed the National Front for the Liberation of the Congo (Front National pour la Libération du Congo—FNLC), remained Luanda's potential trump card if relations with Zaire became intolerable.

Internal Security Forces and Organization

Internal security responsibilities in Angola were distributed among the ministries of defense, state security, and interior, plus the People's Vigilance Brigades (Brigadas Populares de Vigilância—BPV). This elaborate internal security establishment was another manifestation of endemic crises and the mass mobilization undertaken to cope with them. The Ministry of Defense's

Directorate of People's Defense and Territorial Troops, established as the ODP in late 1975, had 600,000 members, with some of these personnel in virtually every village by 1979. By that time, 50,000 ODP troops were also reported to be fighting alongside the regular army against UNITA and the SADF. Estimates of the size of the ODP militia in the late 1980s varied widely, from an effective strength of 50,000, one-fifth of whom served with FAPLA, to a nominal (possibly reserve) strength of 500,000. This militia had both armed and unarmed units dispersed in villages throughout the country to guard likely UNITA targets such as bridges, power plants, wells, schools, and clinics. The ODP also cooperated with FAPLA, sometimes in joint operations, to thwart infiltration and attacks by small units in areas where UNITA or other insurgent forces were operating.

State security functions were assigned to the Angolan Directorate of Intelligence and Security (Direção de Informação e Segurança de Angola—DISA) in the Ministry of Interior. As the principal internal security organ with intelligence collection and political police functions, the DISA was powerful and feared. Its national security police force had wide-ranging powers and discretion to conduct investigations, make arrests, detain individuals, and determine how they would be treated. Indeed, during Colonel Ludy Kissassunda's tenure as director (1975–79), the agency came into disrepute for excesses that included torture and summary executions. In mid-1979 President Neto announced the dissolution of the DISA, the arrest of Kissassunda and several other top security officials, and the reorganization of the state security apparatus. Although officially abolished, the DISA remained the colloquial term for the state security police. Its agents were trained at a school in Luanda by East German and Soviet instructors. The DISA reportedly also operated out of the Angolan chancery in Portugal to maintain surveillance over expatriate activities and received assistance from counterparts in various communist embassies in Lisbon.

The Ministry of State Security was created in July 1980 as part of a government reorganization by dividing the Ministry of Interior into two separate ministries. The new ministry consolidated the DISA's internal security functions with those relating to counterintelligence, control of foreigners, anti-UNITA operations, and frontier security. Colonel Kundi Paihama, the former minister of interior, became the minister of state security upon creation of the ministry, but in late 1981 Colonel Paulo succeeded Paihama.

In early 1986, after having revitalized the party organs and formed a new Political Bureau, President dos Santos undertook to purge and reorganize the Ministry of State Security. He removed Paulo and Deputy Minister Mendes António de Castro, took over the portfolio himself, and appointed Major Fernando Dias da Piedade dos Santos, deputy minister of interior since mid-1984, as new deputy minister of state security. In March 1986, the president formed the Commission for Reorganization of the Ministry of State Security, composed of all the directors at the ministries of interior and state security, under Piedade dos Santos's leadership. After the arrest and jailing of several senior state security officials for abuse of their positions, corruption, and other irregularities, the commission was disbanded in March 1988. In May 1988, President dos Santos relinquished the state security portfolio to Paihama, who also retained the position of minister of state for inspection and control.

The Angolan Border Guard (Tropa Guarda Fronteira Angolana— TGFA), under the Ministry of State Security, was responsible for maintaining security along more than 5,000 kilometers of land borders with Congo, Zaire, Zambia, and Namibia; maritime border surveillance may also have been included in the TGFA's mission. The TGFA's strength was estimated at 7,000 in 1988. Local training took place under Cuban instructors at several centers, including Omupanda, Saurimo, Negage, and Caota, although some border guards were sent to Cuba, presumably for advanced or specialized training.

After its reorganization in 1980, the Ministry of Interior supervised the national police, provincial administration, and investigation of economic activities. Although the Ministry of State Security was responsible for administering the national prison system, certain prison camps were run by the Ministry of Interior. It was unclear how territorial administration was carried out in relation to the regional military and provincial defense councils. Colonel Manuel Alexandre Rodrigues (nom de guerre Kito), who had been vice minister of interior in charge of internal order and the national police, was promoted to minister in the 1980 reorganization and was still serving in that post in late 1988. At that time, however, in response to reports that "special forces of a commando nature" had been established within the ministry without authorization, President dos Santos ordered an investigation as a prelude to a restructuring and personnel purge.

The national Angolan People's Police evolved from the Portuguese colonial police and the People's Police Corps of Angola, which was set up in 1976 under the Ministry of Defense. Headquartered in Luanda but organized under provincial and local commands, the police numbered about 8,000 men and women and reportedly was supported by a paramilitary force of 10,000 that resembled a national guard. Cuban advisers provided most recruit training at the Kapolo Martyrs Practical Police School in Luanda, but some police training was also given in Cuba and Nigeria. In 1984 Minister of Interior Rodrigues dismissed Fernando da Conceição as police director and named Piedrade dos Santos as his provisional replacement. Rodrigues relieved Major Bartolomeu Feliciano Ferreira Neto as chief of the general staff of the police general command in November 1987, appointing Inspector José Adão de Silva as interim chief of the general staff pending a permanent posting. In December 1988, Armindo Fernandes do Espírito Santo Vieira was appointed commander general of the Angolan People's Police (apparently the top police post, formerly titled director). At the same time, police functions were being reorganized and consolidated within the Ministry of Interior to eliminate unauthorized activities, give the police more autonomy, and make them more responsive to party and government direction.

Finally, President dos Santos created the BPV in August 1983 as a mass public order, law enforcement, and public service force in urban areas. Organizationally, the BPV had ministerial status, and its commander reported directly to the president. In some ways, the BPV was the urban counterpart of the Directorate of People's Defense and Territorial Troops. Unlike this directorate, however, whose members served alongside the army, the BPV was strictly defensive. Some BPV units were armed, but most performed public security and welfare duties and local political and ideological work—including intelligence gathering, surveillance and security patrols, civil defense, crime prevention and detection, and the organization of health, sanitation, recreation, beautification, and other social services—with and through local government and the field offices of central government agencies. The brigades were organized at the provincial level and below, operated in small units of up to 100 members, and expanded rapidly, particularly in areas affected by UNITA insurgency. In late 1984, a large number of FAPLA soldiers were integrated into the BPV to strengthen its numbers and technical military skills. The BPV was also reported to serve as a recruitment pool for FAPLA. By 1987 the BPV's strength was estimated by various sources to be from 800,000 to 1.5 million. A third of its members were said to be women, organized into 30,000 brigades under Colonel Alexandre Lemos de Lucas (nom de guerre Bota Militar).

The rapid growth and diverse social composition of the BPV were illustrated by reports from Namibe and Huambo provinces. In early 1985, there were about 500 vigilantes organized into twenty-six squads in Namibe, capital of Namibe Province. These vigilante units had just been credited with neutralizing a network of "saboteurs" who were stealing and selling large quantities of food and housewares at high prices. Two years later, the Namibe provincial BPV was reported to have 11,885 men and women organized into 6 municipal and 228 intermediary brigades. Among the ranks were 305 MPLA-PT members, 266 members of the Organization of Angolan Women (Organização da Mulher Angolana—OMA), 401 members of the JMPLA, and 448 members of the National Union of Angolan Workers (União Nacional dos Trabalhadores Angolanos—UNTA). In Huambo Province, there were reportedly about 100,000 brigade members in early 1986, one-third of them women, and the authorities planned continued expansion to 300,000 by the end of that year.

As in the case of the armed forces, the Angolan internal security organs were subject to ideological and institutional controls. They were also heavily influenced by Soviet, East German, and Cuban state security doctrines, organizational methods, techniques, and practices. Advisers from these countries were posted throughout the security ministries, where their presence, access, and influence ironically became a security problem for the Angolan government. They reportedly penetrated the internal security apparatus so thoroughly and recruited so many Angolan security officials that President dos Santos removed foreigners from some sensitive areas and dismissed several Angolan security officers for "collaboration" with foreign elements. A security school, staffed entirely by Angolan personnel, also opened in late 1987, thereby reducing the need and attendant risks of sending officers abroad for training.

Crime and Punishment
Criminal Justice System

The Ministry of Justice administered the civil legal and penal systems, although its jurisdictional boundaries with the Ministry of State Security, the Ministry of Interior, the Ministry of Defense, and the regional military councils were unclear. The civilian court system, known as the People's Revolutionary Tribunal (Tribunal Popular Revolucionário), was established in 1976 to deal with capital offenses against national security. These courts had jurisdiction over crimes against the security of the state, mercenary activities, war crimes, and so-called crimes against humanity, and they could unilaterally assume jurisdiction over any criminal case that had a significant impact on national security (see Judicial System, ch. 4). Such tribunals, composed of three to five judges, were established in each provincial capital but administered by a national directorate in Luanda. In late 1988, Fernando José de Franca Dias Van Dúnem had been minster of justice since February 1986, when he had succeeded Diógenes Boavida.

In 1983 military tribunals were set up in each military region and empowered to try crimes against the security of the state, including alleged offenses committed on behalf of UNITA such as terrorism, espionage, treason, sabotage, destabilization, and armed rebellion; "economic crimes" such as speculation, hoarding, and currency violations; disobedience of directives from the regional military council; and other acts that might "damage or endanger the interests of collective defense and security." The independence of the judicial structure and process was severely circumscribed by political control of the court system and the fact that the judges of the military tribunals were military officers whose appointment, reassignment, and removal were controlled by the minister of defense. Military courts frequently handed down death sentences, which were usually carried out by firing squad. Although persons sentenced to death by military courts were legally entitled to automatic appeal to the Armed Forces Military Tribunal, the highest military court, such appeals were not known to have been lodged.

Article 23 of the Constitution provides that citizens shall not be arrested and tried except in accordance with the terms of law and states the right of accused persons to legal defense. However, the extent to which these provisions were observed was uncertain. Amnesty International, a human rights organization, reported the detention without charge or trial of dozens of political prisoners and trials by military tribunals of hundreds who were not given adequate opportunity to prepare their defense or appeal sentences.

Angolan law provided that persons suspected of having committed serious crimes against the security of the state could be detained without charge by the Ministry of State Security for up to three months and that this period could be extended an additional three months. Unlike common criminals, such detainees did not have to be brought before a judge within forty-eight hours of arrest and could not challenge the basis of detention. Political prisoners had to be informed of the accusations against them after six months in detention and then had to be referred to a public prosecutor or released. If charges were pressed, there was no stated time period within which a trial had to be held, and delays of several years were common.

Prison System

Little information was available on the Angolan prison system. Prisons were primitive, and authorities apparently had wide discretion in dealing with prisoners. As in most Third World countries, prisons were designed for custodial and punitive purposes, not for rehabilitation. Detention facilities were overcrowded, diets were substandard, and sanitation and medical facilities were minimal. Intimidation, prolonged interrogations, torture, and maltreatment, especially of political prisoners, were common. Visits by families, friends, and others appeared to be restricted arbitrarily. Prisoners were sometimes held incommunicado or moved from one prison to another without notification of family.

The ministries of state security and interior reportedly administered penal institutions, but their respective jurisdictions were unknown. The principal prisons were located in Luanda, where a maximum security institution was opened in early 1981, and in several provincial and local jurisdictions. The main detention centers for political prisoners were the Estrada de Catete prison in the capital and the Bentiaba detention camp in Namibe Province. The government-run detention center at Tari in Cuanza Sul Province was identified as one of the main rural detention centers. Tari was a former sisal plantation turned into a labor farm, where prisoners lived in barracks or in their own huts while doing forced labor. In 1983 it was reported that Tari's prisoners included those already sentenced, awaiting trial, or detained without trial as security risks. Political reeducation, once an integral element of rehabilitation, was not widely or consistently practiced. Foreign advisers, principally East German and Cuban security specialists, assisted in operating detention centers and in training Angolan state security service personnel. Elsewhere, East Germans were reported to be in charge of a political reeducation camp.

Incidence and Trends in Crime

It is difficult to generalize about the incidence of crime in Angola. Indeed, the government's characterization of UNITA and other insurgent groups as bandits, gangsters, criminals, puppet gangs, rebels, and counterrevolutionaries suggested a complex mixture of civil, criminal, and political criteria. However, it is likely that Angolan society exhibited criminal patterns similar to those of societies in other developing countries experiencing uncontrolled rural-to-urban migration, rapid social change, unemployment and

Migration from rural areas to cities and the consequent creation of slums, such as those pictured above, contributed to a rise in urban crime.
Courtesy United Nations (J. P. Laffont)

underemployment, the spread of urban slums, and the lack or breakdown of urban and social services. It is also likely that such patterns were even more pronounced because of three decades of endemic conflict and massive dislocation. Historical and comparative patterns suggest that crimes against property increased with urban growth and that juveniles accounted for most of the increase.

Available evidence, although fragmentary, indicated that the crime rate was rising. Smuggling, particularly of diamonds and timber, was frequently reported as a major criminal offense, occasionally involving senior government and party officials. Dealing in illegal currency was another common crime. Persons acting as police or state security agents sometimes abused their writs by illegally entering homes and stealing property. Intermittent police crackdowns on black market activities had only short-term effects. Endemic production and distribution problems and shortages gave rise to embezzlement, pilfering, and other forms of criminal misappropriation. The enormous extent of this problem was indicated by an official estimate in 1988 that 40 percent of imported goods did not reach their intended consumers because of the highly organized parallel market system. The government later approved new measures to combat economic crime on a national scale.

Human Rights

Angola was a signatory to several international human rights conventions, including the Convention on the Political Rights of Women of 1953, the Convention on the Elimination of All Forms of Discrimination against Women, the Geneva Conventions of 1949 Relative to the Treatment of Prisoners of War and the Protection of Civilian Persons in Time of War, and the Convention and Protocol Relating to the Status of Refugees of 1967. However, as of 1988 Angola was not a signatory to the Slavery Conventions of 1926 and 1956; the Genocide Convention of 1948; or the International Conventions on Civil and Political Rights and on Economic, Social, and Cultural Rights of 1966.

Although Angola had acceded to such conventions, and its Constitution guarantees most human rights, actual observance was subject to severe abridgments, qualifications, and contrary practices. A human rights organization, Freedom House, consistently gave Angola the lowest ratings on its scale of political rights and civil liberties, and *The Economist World Human Rights Guide* assigned Angola an overall rating of "poor." Amnesty International and the United States Department of State also issued reports highly critical of human rights practices in Angola.

The lack or disregard of international human rights standards in Angola was evident in several respects. Arbitrary arrest and imprisonment without due process were among the most common abuses. Although Angolan law limited the amount of time one could be detained without charge, there did not appear to be a specific period within which a suspect had to be tried, and as many as several hundred political prisoners may have been detained for years without trial. The regional military councils had broad authority to impose restrictions on the movement of people and material, to requisition supplies and labor without compensation, and to try crimes against state security. The BPV also had functions relating to maintenance of public order, the exercise of which was not subject to normal judicial safeguards and due process.

Constitutional protections of the inviolability of the home and privacy of correspondence were routinely ignored by government authorities, who made arbitrary home searches, censored correspondence, and monitored private communications. Arbitrary executions of political prisoners, especially those accused of supporting UNITA or perpetrating "economic crimes," occurred despite international protests and periodic reorganizations of the security services. The government maintained strict censorship, did not tolerate criticism or opposition, and denied freedom of assembly

254

to any group that was not sanctioned or sponsored by the MPLA–PT. UNITA alleged that compulsory military service was meted out as punishment by the Ministry of State Security and the BPV. Furthermore, the government did not permit the International Committee of the Red Cross access to persons arrested for reasons related to internal security or military conflict.

Amnesty International also reported numerous instances of torture during the late 1970s and early 1980s. Ministry of State Security officials were reported to have permitted or sanctioned torture of criminals and political prisoners by such methods as beating, whipping, and electric shock. Political detainees arrested for offenses such as criticizing government policies were deprived of food and water for several days and subjected to frequent and severe beatings during interrogation and confinement. Although allegations of torture and mistreatment remained common in the mid-1980s, such practices did not appear to have been systematic.

* * *

There is voluminous material available on Angola's military history and contemporary national security affairs. The Angolan independence struggle is thoroughly examined in John A. Marcum's two-volume *The Angolan Revolution*. The civil war of 1975–76 is covered by some of the excellent essays in *Southern Africa since the Portuguese Coup*, edited by John Seiler. The external dimension of the civil war is treated in Charles K. Ebinger's *Foreign Intervention in Civil War*, Arthur Jay Klinghoffer's *The Angolan War*, and Ernest Harsch and Tony Thomas's *Angola: The Hidden History of Washington's War*.

The UNITA movement has been extensively studied as well. One sympathetic treatment is Fred Bridgland's *Jonas Savimbi*. Two excellent politico-military analyses of the UNITA insurgency are Donald J. Alberts's "Armed Struggle in Angola" in *Insurgency in the Modern World* and James W. Martin III's unpublished doctoral dissertation, "UNITA Insurgency in Angola."

The human cost of the war—at least in terms of refugees—is well covered by the U.S. Committee for Refugees' *Uprooted Angolans*. The devastating economic impact of the protracted war is most fully and systematically examined in Tony Hodges's *Angola to the 1990s*.

A standard reference work on military forces and order of battle data is *The Military Balance*, issued annually by the International Institute for Strategic Studies. Supplementary information is available in the annual *Defense and Foreign Affairs Handbook*, specialized annuals such as *Jane's Fighting Ships, Jane's Weapon Systems,* and *Jane's All the World's Aircraft,* and *Combat Fleets of the World,* edited by Jean Labayle Couhat and Bernard Prézelin. Other useful reference works are John M. Andrade's *World Police and Paramilitary Forces* and Michael J.H. Taylor's *Encyclopedia of the World's Air Forces.* Statistics and other information on arms transfers, military spending, and armed forces are contained in the United States Arms Control and Disarmament Agency's annual *World Military Expenditures and Arms Transfers* and the Stockholm International Peace Research Institute's annual *SIPRI Yearbook.*

Internal security and human rights conditions are evaluated annually in the *Amnesty International Report* and the United States Department of State's *Country Reports on Human Rights Practices.* Additional worldwide human rights reviews are Charles Humana's *The Economist World Human Rights Guide* and Raymond D. Gastil's *Freedom in the World.*

Finally, specialized current news sources and surveys are indispensable to research on contemporary national security affairs. The most relevant and accessible include the annual *Africa Contemporary Record* and periodicals such as *Africa Research Bulletin, Africa Confidential, Africa Diary, Defense and Foreign Affairs Weekly, Jane's Defence Weekly,* and *International Defense Review.* The most useful sources are *African Defence Journal* and its sister publication, *Afrique Défense.* (For further information and complete citations, see Bibliography.)

Appendix A

Table 1. Metric Conversion Coefficients and Factors

When you know	Multiply by	To find
Millimeters	0.04	inches
Centimeters	0.39	inches
Meters	3.3	feet
Kilometers	0.62	miles
Hectares (10,000 m²)	2.47	acres
Square kilometers	0.39	square miles
Cubic meters	35.3	cubic feet
Liters	0.26	gallons
Kilograms	2.2	pounds
Metric tons	0.98	long tons
....	1.1	short tons
....	2,204	pounds
Degrees Celsius	9	degrees Fahrenheit
(Centigrade)	divide by 5 and add 32	

Table 2. *Urban-Rural Breakdown of Population by Province, 1988*

Province	Urban [1]	Rural [2]	Total
Bengo	18,700	137,400	156,100
Benguela	297,700	308,800	606,500
Bié	201,600	842,400	1,044,000
Cabinda	73,600	73,600	147,200
Cuando Cubango	3,600	122,000	125,600
Cuanza Norte	18,000	347,100	365,100
Cuanza Sul	52,700	576,600	629,300
Cunene	4,600	215,200	219,800
Huambo	214,400	1,201,900	1,416,300
Huíla	250,800	578,200	829,000
Luanda	1,363,900	15,900	1,379,800
Lunda Norte	36,300	243,000	279,300
Lunda Sul	80,000	71,400	151,400
Malanje	174,900	643,400	818,300
Moxico	39,600	255,700	295,300
Namibe	75,200	27,500	102,700
Uíge	211,000	550,100	761,100
Zaire	92,800	63,700	156,500
TOTAL	3,209,400	6,273,900	9,483,300

[1] Includes cities and towns.
[2] Includes villages and open countryside.

Source: Based on information from United States Private Voluntary Agency, United States
Government Assessment Team to Angola, ''Final Report,'' October 25, 1988,
Annex B, B-2.

Table 3. Major Civilian Hospitals by Province, 1988 [1]

Province City	Name	Number of Beds	Services
Bengo			
Caxito	Civilian Hospital	120	General medical, surgical, X-ray, and laboratory.
Benguela			
Benguela	Central Hospital	250	General medical, X-ray, and laboratory; staffed by Cuban personnel.
Lobito	Civilian Hospital	190	General medical, surgical, X-ray, and laboratory.
Bié			
Catabola	Catabola Municipal Hospital	80	General medical.
Chissamba	Civilian Hospital	140	General medical, surgical, X-ray, and laboratory.
Kuito	Regional Hospital	n.a.	General medical, surgical, X-ray, and laboratory.
Cabinda			
Cabinda	Lombe-Lombe Hospital	n.a.	General medical, surgical, and teaching facility for rural workers.
Cuando Cubango			
Menongue	Regional Hospital	130	General medical, surgical, X-ray, and laboratory.
Huambo			
Huambo	Huambo Hospital	600	General medical, orthopedic; depends on UNICEF and International Committee of the Red Cross for equipment and food. [2]
Longonjo	Bongo Mission Hospital	100	General medical Seventh-Day Adventists hospital.
Huíla			
Caluquembe	Missionary Hospital	129	General medical, surgical, and teaching facility for rural workers.
Lubango	Central Hospital	240	General medical, surgical, X-ray, and laboratory.

Table 3.—Continued.

Province City	Name	Number of Beds	Services
Luanda			
Luanda	Americo Boavoia Hospital	600	General medical, surgical, X-ray, and laboratory.
-do-	University Hospital	500	General medical, surgical, X-ray, laboratory, and teaching facility.
-do-	Central Hospital	n.a.	General medical.
Lunda Sul			
Saurimo	Regional Hospital	n.a.	General medical, surgical, X-ray, and laboratory.
Namibe			
Namibe	N'Gola Kimbanda Hospital	120	General medical, X-ray, and laboratory; staffed by 13 specialized physicians.
Uíge			
Uíge	Uíge Regional Hospital	100	General medical, X-ray, and laboratory.

n.a.—not available.

[1] Does not include hospitals in areas claimed by the National Union for the Total Independence of Angola (União Nacional para a Independência Total de Angola—UNITA).

[2] UNICEF—United Nations Children's Fund.

Table 4. Revenues, Expenditures, and Deficits, 1980–86
(in billions of kwanzas) [1]

	1980	1981	1982	1983	1984	1985	1986
Revenues							
State enterprises	10.4	11.1	11.1	10.1	10.4	12.1	18.1
Taxes	41.9	53.3	32.3	38.7	54.4	56.4	35.1
Other	7.9	9.3	7.2	6.8	9.8	10.0	17.3
Total revenues [2]	60.1	73.7	50.7	55.6	74.6	78.5	70.5
Expenditures							
Economic development ....,	28.4	43.4	26.3	17.9	22.0	23.4	14.8
Social services	13.7	13.8	15.1	14.8	17.3	18.7	21.4
Defense and security	15.0	15.0	15.0	23.3	29.4	34.4	34.6
Administration	17.0	11.8	13.7	9.2	9.5	9.9	9.8
Other	13.1	7.7	2.0	2.4	4.2	4.1	4.8
Total expenditures [2]	87.2	91.6	72.1	67.6	82.3	90.4	85.5
Deficits	27.1	17.9	21.4	12.0	7.7	11.9	15.0

[1] For value of the kwanza—see Glossary.
[2] Figures may not add to total because of rounding.

Source: Based on information from Tony Hodges, *Angola to the 1990s,* London, 1987, 42;
and Economist Intelligence Unit, *Country Report: Angola, São Tomé and Príncipe* [London], No. 2, 1987, 12.

Table 5. Agricultural Production Marketed by
State Enterprises, 1982–85
(in tons)

Commodity	1982	1983	1984	1985
Seed cotton	3,130	2,130	290	254
Bananas	11,000	15,290	10,775	21,094
Potatoes	12,790	8,370	3,336	5,309
Coffee	23,470	15,630	10,589	13,686
Citrus fruit	3,320	2,290	2,435	2,291
Vegetables	14,370	16,920	9,866	16,982
Dry cassava	17,610	6,730	4,164	5,522
Maize	32,570	22,700	16,343	11,935
Palm oil	2,500	2,440	1,532	1,190
Rice	4,600	3,140	1,725	285

Source: Based on information from Economist Intelligence Unit, *Country Report: Angola,
São Tomé and Príncipe* [London], No. 1, 1987, 16.

Table 6. Value of Exports, 1980–86
(in millions of United States dollars)

Commodity	1980	1981	1982	1983	1984	1985	1986
Crude oil	1,391	1,345	1,234	1,526	1,748	1,905	1,240
Refined oil and lique-							
fied petroleum gas .	98	101	60	120	122	128	80
Coffee	164	97	95	71	80	55	60
Diamonds	226	179	104	90	64	33	15
Other	9	6	4	3	3	4	5
TOTAL *	1,888	1,727	1,497	1,810	2,018	2,125	1,400

* Figures may not add to total because of rounding.

Source: Based on information from Tony Hodges, *Angola to the 1990s,* London, 1987, 123;
Economist Intelligence Unit, *Country Report: Angola, São Tomé and Príncipe* [London],
No. 1, 1987, 13; and Economist Intelligence Unit, *Country Report: Angola, São Tomé
and Príncipe* [London], No. 4, 1987, 2.

Table 7. Multilateral Development Assistance, 1979–84
(in millions of United States dollars)

Donor	1979	1980	1981	1982	1983	1984
United Nations						
World Food Programme	5.0	3.1	4.8	6.1	8.5	9.5
Office of the United Nations						
High Commissioner for						
Refugees	4.3	4.5	3.8	3.7	5.0	6.0
United Nations Development						
Programme	2.7	4.1.	6.0	4.8	5.3	3.4
United Nations Children's						
Fund	4.7	3.2	2.5	1.7	3.0	3.3
European Community	0.6	1.0	3.2	1.6	2.5	9.7
Arab Organization of						
Petroleum Exporting						
Countries	n.a.	n.a.	n.a.	n.a.	1.8	1.1
TOTAL	17.3	15.9	20.3	17.9	26.1	33.0

n.a.—not available.

Source: Based on information from Tony Hodges, *Angola to the 1990s,* London, 1987, 129.

Table 8. Crude Oil Production by Area, 1981–85
(in thousands of barrels per day)

Area	1981	1982	1983	1984	1985
Cabinda	85.6	80.5	130.3	58.4	165.2
Block 2	5.1	12.7	12.1	9.3	7.2
Block 3	0.0	0.0	0.0	0.0	23.8
Congo River Basin	34.9	32.4	30.7	31.9	31.7
Cuanza River Basin	3.7	4.0	4.9	4.5	4.0
TOTAL*	129.4	129.6	178.0	204.0	231.9

*Figures may not add to total because of rounding.

Source: Based on information from Tony Hodges, *Angola to the 1990s*, London, 1987, 58.

Table 9. Production and Exports of Diamonds, 1977–87

Year	Production		Exports	
	Volume [1]	Value [2]	Volume [1]	Value [2]
1977	333	885	337	847
1978	707	3,512	689	3,325
1979	839	4,365	791	4,225
1980	1,479	6,929	1,460	6,767
1981	1,397	4,959	1,409	5,350
1982	1,221	3,063	1,260	3,099
1983	1,030	2,784	1,002	2,704
1984	920	1,764	954	1,921
1985	714	945	741	977
1986	400	n.a.	n.a.	n.a.
1987	750	n.a.	n.a.	n.a.

n.a.—not available.
[1] In thousands of carats.
[2] In millions of kwanzas (for value of the kwanza—see Glossary).

Source: Based on information from Tony Hodges, *Angola to the 1990s*, London, 1987, 75; and Economist Intelligence Unit, *Country Report: Angola, São Tomé and Príncipe* [London], No. 4, 1987, 17.

Table 10. *Coffee Production, Exports,*
and Closing Stocks, 1971–86
(in thousands of bags)

Year	Production	Exports	Closing Stocks [1]
1971	3,888	3,019	4,785
1972	4,031	3,097	5,619
1973	3,500	4,135	4,942
1974	3,206	2,961	5,147
1975	1,062	2,600	3,574
1976	958	1,123	3,379
1977	951	963	3,342
1978	572	1,245	2,644
1979	289	1,012	1,896
1980	721	661	1,931
1981	344	850	1,399
1982	290	620	1,024
1983	214	440	778
1984	254	370	616
1985	214	333	477
1986 [2]	270	313	414

[1] Coffee held in storage at end of year.
[2] Government forecast.

Source: Based on information from Tony Hodges, *Angola to the 1990s*, London, 1987, 92.

Table 11. *Balance of Payments, 1982–85*
(in billions of kwanzas) [1]

	1982	1983	1984	1985
Exports [2]	44.7	47.5	58.8	59.3
Imports [2]	33.7	29.7	38.0	41.2
Balance [3]	11.0	17.8	20.9	18.0
Invisibles (net)	19.0	19.8	23.6	26.5
Current account balance	-7.2	-1.0	-1.7	-7.0
Medium-term and long-term capital	3.0	1.6	6.1	6.7
Reserves at end of year	3.2	3.3	5.2	6.1

[1] For value of the kwanza—see Glossary.
[2] Free on board.
[3] Figures may not result in balance because of rounding.

Source: Based on information from Tony Hodges, *Angola to the 1990s*, London, 1987, 42–43.

Table 12. Major Army Equipment, 1988

Type	In Inventory
Main battle tanks	
T-34	100
T-54/-55	300
T-62	100 +
T-72	n.a.
Light tanks	
PT-76	50
Armored vehicles	
BRDM-1/-2	200 +
AML-60/-90	n.a.
BTR-40/-50/-60/-152	255
BMP-2	65
Panhard M3	n.a.
Artillery	
Assortment of 76mm, 85mm, 100mm, 122mm, 130mm, and 152mm guns	500
SU-100 (self-propelled)	n.a.
BM-21/-24 multiple rocket launchers	75
120mm mortars	40 +
82mm mortars	460
Antitank weapons	
AT-3	n.a.
75mm, 82mm, and 107mm recoilless rifles	900
Air defense guns	
ZSU-23-4 (self-propelled)	20
ZSU-57-2 (self-propelled)	40
S-60	70
ZPU-1/-2/-4	n.a.
ZU-23-2	n.a.
M-1939	n.a.
M-55	n.a.
Surface-to-air missiles	
SA-7/-4	n.a.

n.a.—not available.

*Table 13. Major Air Force and Air Defense
Force Equipment, 1988*

Type	In Inventory
Attack aircraft	
MiG-23 Flogger	55
MiG-21MF Fishbed	60
Su-22 Fitter	7
Interceptors	
MiG-17F Fresco	20
MiG-19 Farmer	8
MiG-21bis Fishbed	30
Counterinsurgency and reconnaissance	
PC-7 Turbo-Trainer	8
Maritime patrol	
Fokker F-27MPA Friendship	1
EMB-111 Bandeirante	2
Fixed-wing transports	
Douglas C-47 Dakota	3
CASA C-212 Aviocar	11
L-100-30	1 or 2
Do-27	5
Nord 262	4
BN-2A Islander	13
TU-134A Crusty	1
Yak-40 Codling	1
Commander 690A	1
PC-6B Turbo-Porter	4
An-2 Colt	10
An-12 Cub	2
An-26 Curl	33
An-32 Cline	3
Trainers	
MiG-15UTI Midget	3
Yak-11 Moose	6
Cessna 172	3
PC-7	11
PC-9	4
Helicopters	
Mi-8 Hip	50
Mi-17	13
Mi-24 Hind C	27
Mi-25	21
SA-316B Alouette III	24
IAR-316B Alouette III	16
SA-342 Gazelle	5
SA-365N Dauphin	8
SA-315B Lama	1

Table 13.—Continued.

Type	In Inventory
Surface-to-air missiles	
SA-2 Guideline	12
SA-3 Goa	40
SA-6 Gainful	72
SA-8 Gecko	48
SA-9 Gaskin	n.a.
SA-13 Gopher	n.a.

n.a.—not available.

Table 14. Major Navy Equipment, 1988

Type	In Inventory
Fast missile craft	
OSA-II with four SS-N-2	
Styx missiles	6
Fast torpedo craft	
Shershen with four 533mm heavyweight torpedo tubes	4 or 5
Inland-water and coastal patrol boats	
Argos	4
Poluchat-I	2
Zhuk	1 or 2
Jupiter	1 or 2
Bellatrix	4 or 5
Mine warfare craft	
Yevgenya MH1	2
Amphibious vessels	
Polnocny-B	3
Alfrange	1
LCT	1
T-4	4 or 5
LDM-400	9 or 10
Coastal defense equipment	
SS-C1 Sepal radar system at Luanda	1

1988 REGIONAL ACCORDS

Tripartite Agreement, December 22, 1988

AGREEMENT AMONG THE PEOPLE'S REPUBLIC OF ANGOLA, THE REPUBLIC OF CUBA, AND THE REPUBLIC OF SOUTH AFRICA

The Governments of the People's Republic of Angola, the Republic of Cuba, and the Republic of South Africa, hereinafter designated as "the Parties,"

Taking into account the "Principles for a Peaceful Settlement in Southwestern Africa," approved by the Parties on 20 July 1988, and the subsequent negotiations with respect to the implementation of these Principles, each of which is indispensable to a comprehensive settlement,

Considering the acceptance by the Parties of the implementation of United Nations Security Council Resolution 435 (1978), adopted on 29 September 1978, hereinafter designated as "UNSCR 435/78,"

Considering the conclusion of the bilateral agreement between the People's Republic of Angola and the Republic of Cuba providing for the redeployment toward the north and the staged and total withdrawal of Cuban troops from the territory of the People's Republic of Angola,

Recognizing the role of the United Nations Security Council in implementing UNSCR 435/78 and in supporting the implementation of the present agreement,

Affirming the sovereignty, sovereign equality, and independence of all states of southwestern Africa,

Affirming the principle of noninterference in the internal affairs of states,

Affirming the principle of abstention from the threat or use of force against the territorial integrity or political independence of states,

Reaffirming the right of the peoples of the southwestern region of Africa to self-determination, independence, and equality of rights, and of the states of southwestern Africa to peace, development, and social progress,

Urging African and international cooperation for the settlement

271

of the problems of the development of the southwestern region of Africa,

Expressing their appreciation for the mediating role of the Government of the United States of America,

Desiring to contribute to the establishment of peace and security in southwestern Africa,

Agree to the provisions set forth below:

(1) The Parties shall immediately request the Secretary General of the United Nations to seek authority from the Security Council to commence implementation of UNSCR 435/78 on 1 April 1989.

(2) All military forces of the Republic of South Africa shall depart Namibia in accordance with UNSCR 435/78.

(3) Consistent with the provisions of UNSCR 435/78, the Republic of South Africa and People's Republic of Angola shall cooperate with the Secretary General to ensure the independence of Namibia through free and fair elections and shall abstain from any action that could prevent the execution of UNSCR 435/78. The Parties shall respect the territorial integrity and inviolability of borders of Namibia and shall ensure that their territories are not used by any state, organization, or person in connection with acts of war, aggression, or violence against the territorial integrity or inviolability of borders of Namibia or any other action which could prevent the execution of UNSCR 435/78.

(4) The People's Republic of Angola and the Republic of Cuba shall implement the bilateral agreement, signed on the date of signature of this agreement, providing for the redeployment toward the north and the staged and total withdrawal of Cuban troops from the territory of the People's Republic of Angola, and the arrangements made with the Security Council of the United Nations for the on-site verification of that withdrawal.

(5) Consistent with their obligations under the Charter of the United Nations, the Parties shall refrain from the threat or use of force, and shall ensure that their respective territories are not used by any state, organization, or person in connection with any acts of war, aggression, or violence, against the territorial integrity, inviolability of borders, or independence of any state of southwestern Africa.

(6) The Parties shall respect the principle of noninterference in the internal affairs of the states of southwestern Africa.

(7) The Parties shall comply in good faith with all obligations undertaken in this agreement and shall resolve through negotiation and in a spirit of cooperation any disputes with respect to the interpretation or implementation thereof.

(8) This agreement shall enter into force upon signature.

Signed at New York in triplicate in the Portuguese, Spanish, and English languages, each language being equally authentic, this 22nd day of December 1988.

FOR THE PEOPLE'S REPUBLIC OF ANGOLA
Afonso Van Dúnem
FOR THE REPUBLIC OF CUBA
Isidoro Octavio Malmierca
FOR THE REPUBLIC OF SOUTH AFRICA
Roelof F. Botha

Bilateral Agreement, December 22, 1988

Following is the unofficial United States translation of the original Portuguese and Spanish texts of the agreement, with annex.

AGREEMENT BETWEEN THE GOVERNMENTS OF THE PEOPLE'S REPUBLIC OF ANGOLA AND THE REPUBLIC OF CUBA FOR THE TERMINATION OF THE INTERNATIONALIST MISSION OF THE CUBAN MILITARY CONTINGENT

The Governments of the People's Republic of Angola and the Republic of Cuba hereinafter designated as the Parties,
Considering,
That the implementation of Resolution 435 of the Security Council of the United Nations for the independence of Namibia shall commence on the 1st of April,
That the question of the independence of Namibia and the safeguarding of the sovereignty, independence, and territorial integrity of the People's Republic of Angola are closely interrelated with each other and with peace and security in the region of southwestern Africa.
That on the date of signature of this agreement a tripartite agreement among the Governments of the People's Republic of Angola, the Republic of Cuba, and Republic of South Africa shall be signed, containing the essential elements for the achievement of peace in the region of southwestern Africa,
That acceptance of and strict compliance with the foregoing will bring to an end the reasons which compelled the Government of the People's Republic of Angola to request, in the legitimate exercise of its rights under Article 51 of the United Nations Charter, the deployment of Angolan territory of a Cuban internationalist

military contingent to guarantee, in cooperation with the FAPLA [the Angolan Government army], its territorial integrity and sovereignty in view of the invasion and occupation of part of its territory,

Noting,

The agreements signed by the Governments of the People's Republic of Angola and the Republic of Cuba on 4 February 1982 and 19 March 1984, the platform of the Government of the People's Republic of Angola approved in November 1984, and the Protocol of Brazzaville signed by the Governments of the People's Republic of Angola, the Republic of Cuba, and the Republic of South Africa on December 13, 1988,

Taking into account,

That conditions now exist which make possible the repatriation of the Cuban military contingent currently in Angolan territory and the successful accomplishment of their internationalist mission,

The Parties agree as follows:

Article 1

To commence the redeployment by stages to the 15th and 13th parallels and the total withdrawal to Cuba of the 50,000 men who constitute the Cuban troops contingent stationed in the People's Republic of Angola, in accordance with the pace and time frame established in the attached calendar, which is an integral part of this agreement. The total withdrawal shall be completed by the 1st of July, 1991.

Article 2

The Governments of the People's Republic of Angola and the Republic of Cuba reserve the right to modify or alter their obligations deriving from Article 1 of this agreement in the event that flagrant violations of the tripartite agreement are verified.

Article 3

The Parties, through the Secretary General of the United Nations, hereby request that the Security Council verify the redeployment and phased and total withdrawal of Cuban troops from the territory of the People's Republic of Angola, and to this end shall agree on a matching protocol.

Article 4

This agreement shall enter into force upon signature of the tripartite agreement among the People's Republic of Angola, the Republic of Cuba, and the Republic of South Africa.

Signed on 22 December 1988, at the Headquarters of the United

Nations, in two copies, in the Portuguese and Spanish languages, each being equally authentic.

FOR THE PEOPLE'S REPUBLIC OF ANGOLA
Afonso Van Dúnem
FOR THE REPUBLIC OF CUBA
Isidoro Octavio Malmierca

Annex on Troop Withdrawal Schedule

CALENDAR

In compliance with Article 1 of the agreement between the Government of the Republic of Cuba and the Government of the People's Republic of Angola for the termination of the mission of the Cuban internationalist military contingent stationed in Angolan territory, the Parties establish the following calendar for the withdrawal:

Time Frames

Prior to the first of April, 1989 (date of the beginning of implementation of Resolution 435)	3,000 men
Total duration of the calendar Starting from the first of April, 1989	27 months
Redeployment to the north:	
to the 15th parallel by	1 August 1989
to the 13th parallel by	31 October 1989
Total men to be withdrawn:	
by 1 November 1989	25,000 men
by 1 April 1990	33,000 men
by 1 October 1990	38,000 men
by July 1991	50,000 men

Taking as its base a Cuban force of 50,000 men.

Bibliography

Chapter 1

Abshire, David M., and Michael A. Samuels. "The Continuing Crisis in Angola," *Current History*, 82, No. 482, March 1983, 124–25, 128, 138.

Abshire, David M., and Michael A. Samuels (eds.). *Portuguese Africa: A Handbook.* New York: Praeger, 1969.

"Angola." Pages B667–87 in Colin Legum (ed.), *Africa Contemporary Record: Annual Survey and Documents, 1979–80.* New York: Africana, 1981.

"Angola: Post-Neto Reverberations," *Africa Confidential* [London], 20, No. 20, October 3, 1979, 1–4.

"Angola: A State of Flux," *Africa Confidential* [London], 22, No. 9, April 22, 1981, 1–3.

"Angola: Talks about Talks," *Africa Confidential* [London], 23, No. 8, April 14, 1982, 1–3.

Axelson, Eric. *Portugal and the Scramble for Africa, 1875–1891.* Johannesburg: Witwatersrand University Press, 1967.

Bender, Gerald J. *Angola under the Portuguese: The Myth and the Reality.* Berkeley: University of California Press, 1978.

_____. "Planned Rural Settlements in Angola, 1900–1969." Pages 235–79 in Franz-Wilhelm Heimer (ed.), *Social Change in Angola.* Munich: Weltforum Verlag, 1973.

Birmingham, David. "The African Response to Early Portuguese Activities in Angola." Pages 11–28 in Ronald H. Chilcote (ed.), *Protest and Resistance in Angola and Brazil: Comparative Studies.* Berkeley: University of California Press, 1972.

_____. "Central Africa from Cameroun to the Zambezi." Pages 325–83 in Richard Gray (ed.), *The Cambridge History of Africa, c. 1600 to c. 1790,* 4. Cambridge: Cambridge University Press, 1975.

_____. "The Date and Significance of the Imbangala Invasion of Angola," *Journal of African History* [London], 6, No. 2, 1965, 143–52.

_____. *The Portuguese Conquest of Angola.* London: Oxford University Press, 1965.

Boxer, C.R. *The Portuguese Seaborne Empire, 1415–1825.* New York: Alfred A. Knopf, 1969.

_____. *Race Relations in the Portuguese Colonial Empire, 1415–1825.* Oxford: Clarendon Press, 1963.

————. *Salvador de Sá and the Struggle for Angola and Brazil.* London: Athlone, 1952.

Bruce, Neil. *Portugal: The Last Empire.* New York: John Wiley and Sons, 1975.

Centro de Estudos Angolanos. *História de Angola.* Porto, Portugal: Edições Afrontamento, 1965.

Chilcote, Ronald H. (ed.). *Protest and Resistance in Angola and Brazil: Comparative Studies.* Berkeley: University of California Press, 1972.

Clough, Michael. "United States Policy in Southern Africa," *Current History,* 83, No. 491, March 1984, 97–100, 135.

Davidson, Basil. *A History of East and Central Africa to the Late Nineteenth Century.* Garden City, New York: Doubleday, 1969.

————. *In the Eye of the Storm: Angola's People.* Garden City, New York: Doubleday, 1972.

Delgado, Ralph. *História de Angola.* (4 vols.) Benguela: Edição da Tipografia, do Jornal de Benguela, 1948–53.

Dias, Jill R. "Black Chiefs, White Traders, and Colonial Policy near Kwanza: Kabuku Kambilo and the Portuguese, 1873–1896," *Journal of African History* [London], 17, No. 2, 1976, 245–65.

Duffy, James. *Portugal in Africa.* Cambridge: Harvard University Press, 1962.

————. *Portuguese Africa.* Cambridge: Harvard University Press, 1959.

————. "Portuguese Africa, 1930 to 1960." Pages 171–93 in L.H. Gann and Peter Duignan (eds.), *Colonialism in Africa, 1870–1960,* 2. Cambridge: Cambridge University Press, 1970.

Economist Intelligence Unit. *Quarterly Economic Review of Angola, Guinea Bissau, Cape Verde, São Tomé and Príncipe* [London], Second Quarter, 1981, 6–14.

————. *Quarterly Economic Review of Angola, Guinea Bissau, Cape Verde, São Tomé and Príncipe* [London], First Quarter, 1986, 7–14.

Ehnmark, Andres, and Per Wästberg. *Angola and Mozambique: The Case Against Portugal.* New York: Roy, 1963.

Falk, Pamela S. "Cuba in Africa," *Foreign Affairs,* 65, No. 5, Summer 1987, 1077–96.

Gunn, Gillian. "Cuba and Angola." Pages 71–82 in Helen Kitchen (ed.), *Angola, Mozambique, and the West.* New York: Praeger, 1987.

Hammond, Richard J. *Portugal and Africa, 1816–1910: A Study in Uneconomic Imperialism.* Stanford: Stanford University Press, 1966.

————. "Some Economic Aspects of Portuguese Africa in the Nineteenth and Twentieth Centuries." Pages 256–80 in L.H. Gann and Peter Duignan (eds.), *Colonialism in Africa, 1870–1960,* 4. Cambridge: Cambridge University Press, 1975.

———. "Uneconomic Imperialism: Portugal in Africa Before 1910." Pages 352–82 in L.H. Gann and Peter Duignan (eds.), *Colonialism in Africa, 1870–1960,* 1. Cambridge: Cambridge University Press, 1969.

Henderson, Lawrence W. *Angola: Five Centuries of Conflict.* Ithaca: Cornell University Press, 1979.

Hodges, Tony. *Angola to the 1990s: The Potential for Recovery.* (Special Report No. 1079.) London: Economist, 1987.

Humbaraci, Arslan, and Nicole Muchnik. *Portugal's African Wars.* New York: Joseph Okpaku, 1974.

Keefe, Eugene K., David P. Coffin, Sallie M. Hicks, William A. Mussen, Jr., Robert Rinehart, and William J. Simon. *Portugal: A Country Study.* (DA Pam 550–181.) Washington: GPO for Foreign Area Studies, The American University, 1976.

Kitchen, Helen (ed.). *Angola, Mozambique, and the West.* (Washington Papers Series, 130.) New York: Praeger, 1987.

Klinghoffer, Arthur Jay. *The Angolan War: A Study in Soviet Policy in the Third World.* Boulder, Colorado: Westview Press, 1980.

Marcum, John A. "Angola: Twenty-five Years of War," *Current History,* 85, No. 511, May 1986, 193–96, 229–31.

———. *The Angolan Revolution, 1: The Anatomy of an Explosion (1950–1962).* Cambridge: MIT Press, 1969.

———. *The Angolan Revolution, 2: Exile Politics and Guerrilla Warfare (1962–1976).* Cambridge: MIT Press, 1978.

———. "Bipolar Dependency: The People's Republic of Angola." Pages 12–30 in Michael Clough (ed.), *Reassessing the Soviet Challenge in Africa.* Berkeley: Institute of International Studies, University of California, 1986.

———. "Radical Vision Frustrated: Angola and Cuba." (Paper presented to Seminar on Cuban Internationalism in Sub-Saharan Africa sponsored by Radio Martí Program, United States Information Agency, January 23, 1987.) Washington: January 1987.

Martin, Phyllis M. *Historical Dictionary of Angola.* (African Historical Dictionaries, No. 26.) Metuchen, New Jersey: Scarecrow Press, 1980.

Miller, Joseph C. "Cokwe Trade and Conquest in the Nineteenth Century." Pages 175–201 in Richard Gray and David Birmingham (eds.), *Pre-Colonial African Trade.* London: Oxford University Press, 1970.

———. "The Imbangala and the Chronology of Early Central African History," *Journal of African History* [London], 13, No. 4, 1972, 594–674.

———. *Kings and Kinsmen: Early Mbundu States in Angola.* Oxford: Clarendon, Press, 1976.

————. "Nzinga of Matamba in a New Perspective," *Journal of African History* [London], 16, No. 2, 1975, 201–16.

————. "Requiem for the 'Jaga'," *Cahiers d'études africaines* [Paris], 13, No. 1, 1973, 121–49.

————. "Slaves, Slavers, and Social Change in Nineteenth Century Kasanje." Pages 9–29 in Franz-Wilhelm Heimer (ed.), *Social Change in Angola*. Munich: Weltforum Verlag, 1973.

————. *Way of Death: Merchant Capitalism and the Angolan Slave Trade*. Madison: University of Wisconsin Press, 1988.

Newitt, Malyn. *Portugal in Africa: The Last Hundred Years*. London: C. Hurst, 1981.

Oliver, Roland. "The Problem of Bantu Expansion," *Journal of African History* [London], 7, No. 3, 1966, 361–76.

Oliver, Roland, and Brian M. Fagan. *Africa in the Iron Age, c. 500 B.C. to A.D. 1400*. Cambridge: Cambridge University Press, 1975.

Pélissier, René. "Evolution des mouvements ethno-nationalistes Bakongo d'Angola avant la révolte du nord-ouest (1961)," *Revue française d'études politiques africaines* [Paris], 10, No. 111, March 1975, 81–103.

Porter, Bruce D. *The USSR in Third World Conflicts: Soviet Arms and Diplomacy in Local Wars, 1945–1980*. Cambridge: Cambridge University Press, 1984.

Rodney, Walter. "European Activity and African Reaction in Angola." Pages 49–70 in T.O. Ranger (ed.), *Aspects of Central African History*. Evanston: Northwestern University Press, 1968.

Smith, Alan K. "Antonio Salazar and the Reversal of Portuguese Colonial Policy," *Journal of African History* [London], 15, No. 4, 1974, 653–67.

Somerville, Keith. *Angola: Politics, Economics, and Society*. (Marxist Regimes Series.) Boulder, Colorado: Lynne Rienner, 1986.

Sykes, John. *Portugal and Africa*. London: Hutchinson, 1971.

Teixeira, Bernardo. *The Fabric of Terror: Three Days in Angola*. New York: Devin-Adair, 1965.

Thornton, John. "Demography and History in the Kingdom of Kongo, 1550–1750," *Journal of African History* [London], 18, No. 4, 1977, 507–30.

Turner, Victor (ed.). *Profiles of Change: African Society and Colonial Rule*. In L.H. Gann and Peter Duignan (eds.), *Colonialism in Africa. 1870–1960*, 3. Cambridge: Cambridge University Press, 1971.

United States. Department of State. Bureau of Public Affairs. Office of Public Communication. *Background Notes: Angola*. (Department of State Publication No. 7975.) Washington: GPO, June 1987.

Vansina, Jan. *Kingdoms of the Savanna: A History of Central African States until European Occupation.* Madison: University of Wisconsin Press, 1968.

_____. "More on the Invasions of Kongo and Angola by the Jaga and the Lunda," *Journal of African History* [London], 7, No. 3, 1966, 421–29.

Wheeler, Douglas L., and C. Diane Christensen. "To Rise with One Mind: The Bailundu War of 1902." Pages 54–92 in Franz-Wilhelm Heimer (ed.), *Social Change in Angola.* Munich: Weltforum Verlag, 1973.

Wheeler, Douglas L., and René Pélissier. *Angola.* New York: Praeger, 1971.

Young, Thomas. "Angola: Recent History." Pages 224–28 in *Africa South of the Sahara, 1986.* London: Europa, 1985.

Chapter 2

African Statistical Yearbook, 1986, Pt. 3. Addis Ababa: United Nations Economic Commission for Africa, 1986.

"Angola." Pages 219–39 in *Africa South of the Sahara, 1988.* London: Europa, 1987.

"Angola." Pages 231–52 in *Africa South of the Sahara, 1989.* London: Europa, 1988.

"Angola: 'Criminal' Religious Sect," *Africa Research Bulletin* [Oxford], 24, No. 2, March 15, 1987, 8399–8400A.

"Angola: Religious Riot," *Africa Confidential* [London], 28, No. 5, March 4, 1987, 8.

"Angolan Refugees Return Home from Zaire," British Broadcasting Corporation, *Summary of World Broadcasts* [London] (ME/0286/B/1.) October 19, 1988.

Bender, Gerald J. *Angola under the Portuguese: The Myth and the Reality.* Berkeley: University of California Press, 1978.

Bender, Gerald J., and P. Stanley Yoder. "Whites in Angola on the Eve of Independence: The Politics of Numbers," *Africa Today* [London], 21, No. 4, 1974, 23–38.

Brooke, James. "Angolans Strive for Military Victory," *New York Times,* September 9, 1988, Sect. A, 9.

_____. "Angola of 2 Minds on Economic Shift," *New York Times,* June 12, 1988, Sect. I, 15.

_____. "The Yearning of Refugees: Angola Unity," *New York Times,* October 6, 1988, Sect. A, 15.

Carp, Carol, and William J. Bicknell. *Review of Health Care in*

Angola: Issues, Analyses, and Recommendations. Washington: Family Health Care and Africare, 1978.

Childs, Gladwyn Murray. *Umbundu Kinship and Character.* London: Oxford University Press, 1949.

Coxhill, H. Wakelin, and Kenneth Grubb. *World Christian Handbook, 1968.* Nashville: Abingdon Press, 1967.

Dalby, David. *Language Map of Africa and the Adjacent Islands.* (Provisional ed.) London: International African Institute, 1977.

Doyle, Mark. "Christians and Socialists." Pages 202–3 in Jo Sullivan and Jane Martin (eds.), *Global Studies: Africa.* (2d ed.) Guilford, Connecticut: Dushkin, 1987.

Edwards, Adrian C. *The Ovimbundu under Two Sovereignties: A Study of Social Control and Social Change among a People of Angola.* London: Oxford University Press, 1962.

Estermann, Carlos. *The Ethnography of Southwestern Angola.* (3 vols.) (Ed., Gibson Gordon.) New York: Africana, 1976.

Ferreira, Eduardo de Sousa. *Portuguese Colonialism in Africa: The End of an Era.* Paris: UNESCO, 1974.

Garrett, Laurie. "Deadly Virus Spreads Quietly Across Nations," *Newsday,* December 26, 1988, News Section, 18.

Hance, William. *The Geography of Modern Africa.* (2d ed.) New York: Columbia University Press, 1975.

Harden, Blaine. "Angola Reports Hunger Is Widespread," *Washington Post,* August 14, 1987, Sect. A, 1.

"Health, Housing Problems Discussed" (Trans. from Portuguese.), *Jornal de Angola* [Luanda], March 8, 1985, 2–3.

Heimer, Franz-Wilhelm. "Education, Economics, and Social Changes in Rural Angola: The Case of the Cuima Region." Pages 112–43 in Franz-Wilhelm Heimer (ed.), *Social Change in Angola.* Munich: Weltforum Verlag, 1973.

Henderson, Lawrence W. "Ethnolinguistic Worlds: Seeing the People of Angola in Their Language Groupings." Pages 50–60 in Robert T. Parsons (ed.), *Windows on Africa: A Symposium.* Leiden: E.J. Brill, 1971.

―――――. "Protestantism: A Tribal Religion." Pages 61–80 in Robert T. Parsons (ed.), *Windows on Africa: A Symposium.* Leiden: E.J. Brill, 1971.

Heywood, Linda M. "The Dynamics of Ethnic Nationalism in Angola: The Case of UNITA, 1964–1987." (Unpublished paper.) Washington: Howard University, 1988.

Hodges, Tony. *Angola to the 1990s: The Potential for Recovery.* (Special Report No. 1079.) London: Economist, 1987.

Hoover, James Jeffrey. "The Seduction of Ruwej: Reconstructing Ruund History (The Nuclear Lunda: Zaire, Angola, Zambia)."

(Ph.D. dissertation.) New Haven: Yale University, 1978.

Hunter, John M., and Morris O. Thomas. "Hypothesis of Leprosy, Tuberculosis, and Urbanization in Africa," *Social Science and Medicine,* 19, No. 1, 1984, 27–57.

International Committee of the Red Cross. "Special Report: Angola, 1985–1986," *ICRC Bulletin,* January 1986.

Joint Publications Research Service—JPRS (Washington). The following items are from the JPRS series:

Translations on sub-Saharan Africa.

"The Bishops and the Conspiracy," *Jornal de Angola* [Luanda], January 26, 1978. (JPRS 70682, No. 1884, February 24, 1978).

"BPV Activities Praised by National Secretary," *Jornal de Angola* [Luanda], June 16, 1987. (JPRS SSA-87-074, August 21, 1987, 7–9).

"Conditions in Jamba Described," *Tempo* [Lisbon], November 26, 1987. (JPRS SSA-88-009, February 19, 1988, 9–11).

"Doctor Shortages," *Africa Confidencial* [Lisbon], April 22, 1987. (JPRS SSA-87-058, June 23, 1987, 16).

"Essential Objectives, Tasks of Angolan Reconstruction," (Document issued by First Congress of the MPLA, December 4–10, 1977.) [Luanda], December 1977. (JPRS 70891, No. 1905, April 4, 1978).

"Government Seeks to Control Religious Sect; Many Killed," *Africa Confidencial* [Lisbon], April 16, 1987. (JPRS SSA-87-065, July 17, 1987, 14–15).

"Health College Creation Announced," *Jornal de Angola* [Luanda], July 9, 1987. (JPRS SSA-87-076, August 31, 1987, 52).

"Huambo's Orthopedic Center Featured," *Jornal de Angola* [Luanda], March 14, 1987. (JPRS SSA-87-061, July 1, 1987, 24–25).

"Information on Rectification Movement," *Jornal de Angola* [Luanda], January 27, 1978; January 29, 1978; February 1, 1978; and February 2, 1978. (JPRS 70711, No. 1887, March 1, 1978).

"Journalist Describes Sojourn with Unita," *Expresso* [Lisbon], September 26, 1987. (JPRS SSA-87-088, November 20, 1987, 7–8).

"Journalist Describes UNITA School System," *Tempo* [Lisbon], March 26, 1987. (JPRS SSA-87-051, June 2, 1987, 24–26).

"Journalist Describes Visit to UNITA, Interview of Savimbi," *Figaro* [Paris], January 22, 1987. (JPRS SSA-87-037, April 21, 1987, 13–18).

"Lara Discusses MPLA Congress, Scores Petty Bourgeois," *Jornal de Angola* [Luanda], November 17, 1977. (JPRS 70357, No. 1853, December 20, 1977).

"Life of Angolan Students in Cuba Described," *Jornal de Angola* [Luanda], March 26, 1987. (JPRS SSA-87-061, July 1, 1987, 6-13).

"Nascimento Criticizes Bishops at Provincial Commissioners Meeting," *Jornal de Angola* [Luanda], March 7, 1978. (JPRS 70863, No. 1902, March 30, 1978).

"Racism, Tribalism Detrimental to Unity," *Jornal de Angola* [Luanda], February 2, 1978. (JPRS 70755, No. 1892, March 9, 1978).

"Students' Summer Labor, Literacy Programs Reviewed," *Jornal de Angola* [Luanda], September 27, 1987. (JPRS SSA-88-003, January 21, 1988, 17-18).

"Thousands Swell BPV Ranks in Namibe," *Jornal de Angola* [Luanda], January 31, 1987. (JPRS SSA-87-037, April 21, 1987, 21-22).

" 'Tocoist' Sect Criticized," *Jornal de Angola* [Luanda], February 27, 1987. (JPRS SSA-87-061, July 1, 1987, 23).

"UNITA: The Banned Angola," *Expresso* [Lisbon], September 26, 1987. (JPRS SSA-87-088, November 20, 1987, 7-8).

"UNITA Has More Students in Lisbon Than MPLA," *O Diário* [Lisbon], May 3, 1988. (JPRS SSA-88-025, June 3, 1988, 7-8).

McCulloch, Merran. *The Ovimbundu of Angola.* (Ethnographic Survey of Africa.) London: International African Institute, 1952.

Marcum, John A. "Angola: Background to the Conflict," *Mawazo* [Kampala, Uganda], 4, No. 4, 1976, 3-25.

———. "Angola: Twenty-five Years of War," *Current History,* 85, No. 511, May 1986, 193-96, 229-31.

Margarido, Alfredo. "The Tokoist Church and Portuguese Colonialism in Angola." Pages 29-52 in Ronald H. Chilcote (ed.), *Protest and Resistance in Angola and Brazil: Comparative Studies.* Berkeley: University of California Press, 1972.

Martin, Phyllis M. *Historical Dictionary of Angola.* (African Historical Dictionaries, No. 26.) Metuchen, New Jersey: Scarecrow Press, 1980.

Miller, Joseph C. *Angola.* Washington: Agency for International Development, February 1977.

———. "Imbangala Lineage Slavery (Angola)." Pages 205-33 in Suzanne Miers and Igor Kopytoff (eds.), *Slavery in Africa.* Madison: University of Wisconsin Press, 1977.

_____. *Kings and Kinsmen: Early Mbundu States in Angola.* Oxford: Clarendon Press, 1976.

Monteiro, Ramiro Ladeiro. "From Extended to Residual Family: Aspects of Social Change in the Musseques of Luanda." Pages 211–33 in Franz-Wilhelm Heimer (ed.), *Social Change in Angola.* Munich: Weltforum Verlag, 1973.

Murdock, George Peter. *Africa: Its Peoples and Their Culture History.* New York: McGraw-Hill, 1959.

Niddrie, David L. "Changing Settlement Patterns in Angola," *Rural Africana,* No. 23, 1975, 47–78.

Ottaway, David, and Marina Ottaway. *Afrocommunism.* New York: Africana, 1981.

Pössinger, Hermann. "Interrelations Between Economic and Social Change in Rural Africa: The Case of the Ovimbundu of Angola." Pages 32–52 in Franz-Wilhelm Heimer (ed.), *Social Change in Angola.* Munich: Weltforum Verlag, 1973.

Redinha, José. "Carta Etnica da Província de Angola." (Map.) Luanda: Edição Olisipo-Editorial de Publicações, 1973.

"Refugees and Displaced Persons in Southern Africa, 1986," *Review of African Political Economy* [London], 40, December 1987, 67.

Robertson, Claire, and Iris Berger. "Introduction: Analyzing Class and Gender—African Perspectives." Pages 3–24 in Claire Robertson and Iris Berger (eds.), *Women and Class in Africa.* New York: Africana, 1986.

Simmonds, Stephanie P. "Refugee Community Health Care in the Tropics: Refugees, Health, and Development," *Transactions of the Royal Society of Tropical Medicine and Hygiene* [London], 78, 1984, 726–33.

Somerville, Keith. *Angola: Politics, Economics, and Society.* (Marxist Regimes Series.) Boulder, Colorado: Lynne Rienner, 1986.

U.S. Committee for Refugees. *Uprooted Angolans: From Crisis to Catastrophe.* Washington: American Council for Nationalities Service, August 1987.

United Nations Children's Fund. "Country Programme Profile: Angola." (Unpublished document.) UNICEF Programme Committee, April 12, 1983.

United Nations Development Programme. "Living Conditions in the People's Republic of Angola." Luanda: Office of the UNDP Resident Representative in the People's Republic of Angola, February 1984.

United States. Agency for International Development. Bureau for Africa. Office of Southern Africa Affairs. "Development Needs and Opportunities for Cooperation in Southern Africa, Annex A: Angola." Washington: 1979.

_____. Central Intelligence Agency. *The World Factbook, 1988.* Washington, 1988.

United States. Department of State. Bureau of Public Affairs. Office of Public Communication. *Background Notes: Angola.* (Department of State Publication No. 7975.) Washington: GPO, June 1987.

United States Private Voluntary Agency. United States Government Assessment Team to Angola. "Final Report." October 25, 1988.

Warren, Kenneth S., and Adel A. Mahmoud. *Tropical and Geographical Medicine.* New York: McGraw-Hill, 1984.

Westphal, E.O.J. "The Click Languages of Southern and Eastern Africa." Pages 367–420 in Thomas A. Sebeok (ed.), *Current Trends in Linguistics, 1: Linguistics in Sub-Saharan Africa.* The Hague: Mouton, 1971.

Wheeler, Douglas L. "Origins of African Nationalism in Angola: Assimilado Protest Writings, 1859–1929." Pages 67–87 in Ronald H. Chilcote (ed.), *Protest and Resistance in Angola and Brazil: Comparative Studies.* Berkeley: University of California Press, 1972.

Wheeler, Douglas L., and René Pélissier. *Angola.* New York: Praeger, 1971.

World Health Organization. *World Health Statistics Quarterly,* 37, No. 4, 1984.

Yu, Alan K. "The Angola Food Emergency: The Extent of the Problem and Current U.S. Emergency Assistance Policy." (Library of Congress, Congressional Research Service, Report for Congress, 88–653F.) Washington: October 12, 1988.

(Various issues of the following publication were also used in the preparation of this chapter: *Angop News Bulletin* [London]).

Chapter 3

Bender, Gerald J. *Angola under the Portuguese: The Myth and the Reality.* Berkeley: University of California Press, 1978.

"Country's Oil Industry Discussed," *African Business* [London], April 1986, 22–23.

Direction of Trade Statistics Yearbook, 1986. Washington: International Monetary Fund. 1987.

Economist Intelligence Unit. *Country Report: Angola, São Tomé and Príncipe* [London], No. 1, 1987, 13, 16.

_____. *Country Report: Angola, São Tomé and Príncipe* [London], No. 2, 1987, 12.

_____. *Country Report: Angola, São Tomé and Príncipe* [London], No. 4, 1987, 2, 17.

"History of Country's Oil Development," *SADCC Energy* [Luanda], June–August 1984, 11–14.

Hodges, Tony. *Angola to the 1990s: The Potential for Recovery.* (Special Report No. 1079.) London: Economist, 1987.

International Telecommunication Union. *26th Report by the International Telecommunication Union on Telecommunication and the Peaceful Uses of Outer Space.* Geneva: 1987.

International Wheat Council. *World Wheat Statistics.* 1986.

Joint Publications Research Service—JPRS (Washington). The following items are from the JPRS series:
Translations on sub-Saharan Africa.

"Angola-Portugal: Beginning of Rapprochement?" *Africa Hoje* [Lisbon], August 15, 1986. (JPRS SSA-86-105, October 16, 1986, 8-10).

"Benguela Continues Efforts to Eliminate Black Market," *Jornal de Angola* [Luanda], June 25, 1987. (JPRS SSA-87-078, September 8, 1987, 33-34).

"FRG Set to Offer Government Developmental, Economic Aid," *Frankfurter Rundschau* [Frankfurt], May 27, 1987. (JPRS SSA-87-084, October 2, 1987, 3-4).

"KUP Comments on Chevron Partial Withdrawal" (Broadcast.), February 28, 1987. (JPRS SSA-87-025, March 20, 1987, 22).

"Measures Adopted to Improve Trade," *Jornal de Angola* [Luanda], October 17, 1986. (JPRS SSA-87-013, February 19, 1987, 42-43).

"Paper Provides Survey on Nation's Economy," *Africa Hoje* [Lisbon], March 1986. (JPRS SSA-86-062, June 13, 1986, 8-15).

"Petrangol, Sonangol to Sign Strategic Oil Reserve Agreement," *Semanario* [Lisbon], February 21, 1987. (JPRS SSA-87-041, April 29, 1987, 2-4).

Lloyds of London. *Lloyds Ports of the World.* London: 1987.

Newitt, Malyn. *Portugal in Africa: The Last Hundred Years.* London: C. Hurst, 1981.

"Reportage on Sonangol's Evolution," *Afrique-Asie* [Paris], March 9-22, 1987, 36-44.

Sugar Yearbook. London: International Sugar Organization, 1986.

"10 Years of Oil Industry Development Viewed," *SADCC Energy* [Luanda], 3, No. 10, 1985, 11-16, 29.

United Nations. Economic Commission for Europe. *Statistics of World Trade in Steel.* Geneva: 1986.

_____. Food and Agriculture Organization. *Monthly Bulletin of Statistics* [Rome], November 1987, Tables 16 and 20.

United States. Central Intelligence Agency. Directorate of Intelligence. *International Energy Statistical Review.* (DI IESR 84–011.) Washington: November 27, 1984.

_____. Central Intelligence Agency. Directorate of Intelligence. *International Energy Statistical Review.* (DI IESR 88–009.) Washington: September 27, 1988.

United States Private Voluntary Agency. United States Government Assessment Team to Angola. "Final Report." October 25, 1988.

World Bank. *World Development Report, 1987.* New York: Oxford University Press, 1987.

(Various issues of the following publications were also used in the preparation of this chapter: *Africa Economic Digest* [London]; *Africa Hoje* [Lisbon]; *Africa Jornal* [Lisbon]; *Africa Research Bulletin* (Economic Series) [Oxford]; *AfricAsia* [Paris]; *Afrique-Asie* [Paris]; Economist Intelligence Unit, *Country Report: Angola, São Tomé and Príncipe* [London]; Foreign Broadcast Information Service, *Daily Report: Middle East and Africa* (until April 1987) and *Daily Report: Africa sub-Saharan* (since April 1987); *Jeune Afrique* [Paris]; *Marchés tropicaux et méditerranéens* [Paris]; and *West Africa* [London].)

Chapter 4

"Angola." Pages 219–39 in *Africa South of the Sahara, 1988.* London: Europa, 1987.

"Angola." Pages B619–37 in Colin Legum (ed.), *Africa Contemporary Record: Annual Survey and Documents, 1986–1987.* New York: Africana, 1988.

"Angola: The Party and the President," *Africa Confidential* [London], 27, No. 4, February 12, 1986, 3–5.

"Angola: Tenth Anniversary but Little to Celebrate." Pages B617–34 in Colin Legum (ed.), *Africa Contemporary Record: Annual Survey and Documents, 1985–1986.* New York: Africana, 1987.

Banks, Arthur S. (ed.). *Political Handbook of the World, 1984–1985.* Binghamton: State University of New York, 1985.

"The Battle for Angola: Fidel Castro Speaks," *Sechaba* [Lusaka, Zambia], 22, No. 11, 1988, 2–5.

Baumgartner, Jacques. "UNITA: The Imponderable in Angola," *Swiss Review of World Affairs* [Zurich], 38, No. 7, October 1988, 25–26.

Bender, Gerald J. "American Policy Toward Angola: A History of Linkage." Pages 110–28 in Gerald J. Bender, James S. Coleman, and Richard L. Sklar (eds.), *African Crisis Areas and U.S. Foreign Policy.* Los Angeles: University of California Press, 1985.

_____. *Angola under the Portuguese: The Myth and the Reality.* Berkeley: University of California Press, 1978.

_____. "The Continuing Crisis in Angola," *Current History,* 82, No. 482, March 1983, 124–25, 128, 138.

Bhagavan, M.R. *Angola's Political Economy, 1975–1985.* (Research Report No. 75.) Uppsala, Sweden: Scandinavian Institute of African Studies, 1986.

Birmingham, David. "Carnival at Luanda," *Journal of African History* [London], 29, 1988, 93–103.

Bridgland, Fred. "The Future of Angola," *South Africa International* [Johannesburg], 19, No. 1, July 1988, 28–37.

_____. *Jonas Savimbi: A Key to Africa,* New York: Paragon House, 1987.

Clarence-Smith, W.G. "Capital Accumulation and Class Formation in Angola." Pages 163–99 in David Birmingham and Phyllis M. Martin (eds.), *History of Central Africa,* 2. New York: Longman, 1983.

_____. "Class Structure and Class Struggles in Angola in the 1970s," *Journal of Southern African Studies,* 7, No. 1, 1980, 109–26.

Clough, Michael. "Southern Africa: Challenges and Choices," *Foreign Affairs,* 66, No. 4, Summer 1988, 1067–90.

Coker, Christopher. "Pact, Pox, or Proxy: Eastern Europe's Security Relationship with Southern Africa," *Soviet Studies* [Glasgow], 40, No. 4, October 1988, 573–84.

Copson, Raymond W. "Angola-Namibia Peace Prospects: Background, Current Problems, and Chronology." (Library of Congress, Congressional Research Service.) Washington: August 16, 1988.

Falk, Pamela S. "Cuba in Africa," *Foreign Affairs,* 65, No. 5, Summer 1987, 1077–96.

Fukuyama, Francis. "Patterns of Soviet Third World Policy," *Problems of Communism,* 36, No. 5, September–October 1987, 1–13.

Gavshon, Arthur. *Crisis in Africa: Battleground of East and West.* New York: Penguin Books, 1981.

Graham, D.G. "The Prospects for Increased Economic Interaction in Southern Africa," *ISSUP Bulletin* (Institute for Strategic Studies, University of Pretoria) [Pretoria], March 1988, 1–12.

Grundy, Kenneth W. "The Angolan Puzzle: Varied Actors and Complex Issues," *Issue: A Journal of Opinion,* 15, 1987, 35–41.

Harding, Jeremy. "Timetable Troubles," *Africa Report,* 33, No. 6, November–December 1988, 36–38.

Hodges, Tony. *Angola to the 1990s: The Potential for Recovery.* (Special Report No. 1079.) London: Economist, 1987.

Jackson, Denise. "People's Republic of Angola." Pages 19–23 in George E. Delury (ed.), *World Encyclopedia of Political Systems and Parties,* 1. (2d ed.) New York: Facts on File, 1987.

Kerpen, Karen Shaw. "Angola." In Albert P. Blaustein and Gisbert H. Flanz (eds.), *Constitutions of the Countries of the World.* Dobbs Ferry, New York: Oceana, 1981.

Kramer, Mark N. "Soviet Arms Transfers to the Third World," *Problems of Communism,* September-October 1987, 36, No. 5, 52–68.

Liebenow, J. Gus. *Southern Africa: "Not Yet Quiet on the Western Front."* (Universities Field Staff International. UFSI Reports. Africa-Middle East, No. 3.) Indianapolis: 1988–89, 1–15.

McDonald, Steve. "Savimbi Misrepresents UNITA History," *Washington Report on Africa,* 6, No. 13, August 1, 1988, 47, 49.

Marcum, John A. "Angola: Twenty-five Years of War," *Current History,* 85, No. 511, May 1986, 193–96, 229–31.

———. *The Angolan Revolution, 1: The Anatomy of an Explosion (1950–1962).* Cambridge: MIT Press, 1969.

———. *The Angolan Revolution, 2: Exile Politics and Guerrilla Warfare (1962–1976).* Cambridge: MIT Press, 1978.

———. "Bipolar Dependency: The People's Republic of Angola." Pages 12–30 in Michael Clough (ed.), *Reassessing the Soviet Challenge in Africa.* Berkeley: Institute of International Studies, University of California, 1986.

———. "The People's Republic of Angola: A Radical Vision Frustrated." Pages 67–83 in Edmond J. Keller and Donald Rothchild (eds.), *Afro-Marxist Regimes.* Boulder, Colorado: Lynne Rienner, 1987.

———. "Radical Vision Frustrated: Angola and Cuba." (Paper presented to Seminar on Cuban Internationalism in Sub-Saharan Africa sponsored by Radio Martí Program, United States Information Agency, January 23, 1987.) Washington: January 1987.

Martin, James W., III. "Cuban Involvement in the Angolan Civil War: Implications for Lasting Peace in Southern Africa," *ISSUP Bulletin* (Institute for Strategic Studies, University of Pretoria) [Pretoria], October 1988, 1–15.

Martin, Phyllis M. *Historical Dictionary of Angola.* (African Historical Dictionaries, No. 26.) Metuchen, New Jersey: Scarecrow Press, 1980.

Morrison, J. Stephen. "Mr. Savimbi Goes to Washington," *Africa Report,* 33, No. 5, September-October 1988, 55–58.

Ogunbadejo, Oye. "Angola: Ideology and Pragmatism in Foreign

Policy," *International Affairs* [London], 57, Spring 1981, 254–69.
Organização da Mulher Angolana (Organization of Angolan Women). London: Blackmore Press, 1985.
Ottaway, David, and Marina Ottaway. *Afrocommunism*. New York: Africana, 1981.
Popular Movement for the Liberation of Angola-Workers' Party (Movimento Popular de Libertação de Angola-Partido de Trabalho). *Angola: Trabalho e luta*. Paris: Réalisation (Edições DIP), 1985.
Scott, Catherine V. "Political Development in Afro-Marxist Regimes: An Analysis of Angola and Mozambique." (Ph.D. dissertation.) Atlanta: Department of Political Science, Emory University, 1986.
_____. "Socialism and the 'Soft State' in Africa: An Analysis of Angola and Mozambique," *Journal of Modern African Studies* [London], 26, No. 1, March 1988, 23–36.
Sidler, Peter. "South Africa and the Namibia Question," *Swiss Review of World Affairs* [Zurich], 38, No. 4. July 1988, 21–22.
Smith, Wayne S. "A Trap in Angola," *Foreign Policy*, No. 62, Spring 1986, 61–74.
Somerville, Keith. *Angola: Politics, Economics, and Society*. (Marxist Regimes Series.) Boulder, Colorado: Lynne Rienner, 1986.
_____. "Angola: Soviet Client State or State of Socialist Orientation?" *Millennium: Journal of International Studies* [London], 13, No. 3, 1984, 292–310.
Soremekun, Fola. "Angola." Pages 25–59 in Timothy M. Shaw and Olajide Aluko (eds.), *The Political Economy of African Foreign Policy*. New York: St. Martin's Press, 1984.
The Statesman's Year-Book, 1984–1985. London: Macmillan Press, 1984.
Stührenberg, Michael. "Pulling Cuban Soldiers Out of Angola," *World Press Review*, 35, No. 12, December 1988, 30–32.
U.S. Committee for Refugees. *Uprooted Angolans: From Crisis to Catastrophe*. Washington: American Council for Nationalities Service, August 1987.
United States. Department of State. Bureau of Public Affairs. *Agreements for Peace in Southwestern Africa*. (Selected Documents, No. 32.) Washington: December 1988.
Wildschut, Adele. "The Soviet Union's Economic Relations with Southern Africa," *Africa Insight* [Pretoria], 18, No. 2, 1988, 80–91.
Wolfers, Michael, and J. Bergerol. *Angola in the Frontline*. London: Zed Press, 1983.
Young, Thomas. "The Politics of Development in Angola and Mozambique," *African Affairs* [London], 87, No. 347, April 1988, 165–84.

(Various issues of the following publications were also used in the preparation of this chapter: *Africa Confidential* [London]; *Africa Contemporary Record; Africa Report; Africa Research Bulletin* (Political Series) [Oxford]; *Angop News Bulletin* [London], 1987–88; *Boston Globe,* 1987–88; *Financial Mail* [Johannesburg], 1988; Foreign Broadcast Information Service, *Daily Report: Middle East and Africa* (until April 1987) and *Daily Report: Africa sub-Saharan* (since April 1987); *Guardian* [London]; *Jeune Afrique* [Paris], 1988; Joint Publications Research Service, *Report on sub-Saharan Africa; Marchés tropicaux et méditerranéens* [Paris], 1988; *New York Times,* 1988; and *Wall Street Journal,* 1988).

Chapter 5

Air Forces of the World, 1986. Geneva: Interavia, 1986.

Alberts, Donald J. "Armed Struggle in Angola." Pages 235–67 in Bard E. O'Neill et al., *Insurgency in the Modern World.* Boulder, Colorado: Westview Press, 1980.

Amnesty International Report, 1987. London: Amnesty International, 1987.

Andrade, John M. "Angola: República Popular de Angola." Page 5 in John M. Andrade (ed.), *World Police and Paramilitary Forces.* New York: Stockton Press, 1985.

"Angola." Pages 105–6 in *Torture in the Eighties.* London: Amnesty International, 1984.

Bender, Gerald J. *Angola under the Portuguese: The Myth and the Reality.* Berkeley: University of California Press, 1978.

_____. "The Continuing Crisis in Angola," *Current History,* 82, No. 482, March 1983, 124–25, 128, 138.

Bernstein, Jonas. "A Freedom Fight Deep in Africa," *Insight,* December 19, 1988, 11.

Birmingham, David. "The Twenty-seventh of May: An Historical Note on the Abortive 1977 Coup in Angola," *African Affairs* [London], 77, No. 309, October 1978, 554–64.

Bridgland, Fred. *Jonas Savimbi: A Key to Africa.* New York: Paragon House, 1987.

Chilcote, Ronald H. (ed.). *Protest and Resistance in Angola and Brazil: Comparative Studies.* Berkeley: University of California Press, 1972.

Couhat, Jean Labayle, and Bernard Prézelin. *Combat Fleets of the World, 1988–1989.* Annapolis: Naval Institute Press, 1988.

Day, Alan J., and Henry W. Degenhardt (eds.). *Political Parties of the World.* (2d ed.) Detroit: Gale Research, 1984.

Degenhardt, Henry W. *Political Dissent.* Detroit: Gale Research, 1983.

Ebinger, Charles K. *Foreign Intervention in Civil War: The Politics and Diplomacy of the Angolan Conflict.* (Ph.D dissertation.) Medford, Massachusetts: Fletcher School of Law and Diplomacy, Tufts University, 1981.

El-Khawas, Mohamed A. "U.S. Intervention in Angola," *Africa and the World,* 1, No. 2, January 1988, 1–12.

Falk, Pamela S. "Cuba in Africa," *Foreign Affairs,* 65, No. 5, Summer 1987, 1077–96.

Gastil, Raymond D. *Freedom in the World: Political Rights and Civil Liberties, 1986–1987.* Westport, Connecticut: Greenwood Press, 1987.

Grundy, Kenneth W. "The Angolan Puzzle: Varied Actors and Complex Issues," *Issue: A Journal of Opinion,* 15, 1987, 35–41.

Hamalengwa, M., et al. (comp.). *The International Law of Human Rights in Africa.* Dordrecht, The Netherlands: Nijhoff, 1988.

Harsch, Ernest, and Tony Thomas. *Angola: The Hidden History of Washington's War.* New York: Pathfinder Press, 1976.

Henderson, Lawrence W. *Angola: Five Centuries of Conflict.* Ithaca: Cornell University Press, 1979.

Hobday, Charles. *Communist and Marxist Parties of the World.* Santa Barbara: ABC-Clio, 1986.

Hodges, Tony. *Angola to the 1990s: The Potential for Recovery.* (Special Report No. 1079.) London: Economist, 1987.

Holness, Marga. "Angola: The Struggle Continues." Pages 73–109 in Phyllis Martin and David Martin (eds.), *Destructive Engagement: Southern Africa at War.* Harare: Zimbabwe Publishing House, 1986.

Hough, M. "The Angolan Civil War with Special Reference to the UNITA Movement," *ISSUP Strategic Review* (Institute for Strategic Studies, University of Pretoria) [Pretoria], November 1985, 1–11.

Humana, Charles (ed.). *The Economist World Human Rights Guide.* New York: Facts on File, 1986.

Jackson, Denise. "People's Republic of Angola." Pages 19–23 in George E. Delury (ed.), *World Encyclopedia of Political Systems and Parties,* 1. (2d ed.) New York: Facts on File, 1987.

Janke, Peter. *Guerrilla and Terrorist Organizations: A World Directory and Bibliography.* New York: Macmillan, 1983.

Kitchen, Helen (ed.). *Angola, Mozambique, and the West.* (Washington Papers Series, 130.) New York: Praeger, 1987.

Klinghoffer, Arthur Jay. *The Angolan War: A Study in Soviet Policy in the Third World.* Boulder, Colorado: Westview Press, 1980.

Marcum, John A. *The Angolan Revolution, 1: The Anatomy of an Explosion (1950–1962).* Cambridge: MIT Press, 1969.

_____. *The Angolan Revolution, 2: Exile Politics and Guerrilla Warfare (1962-1976)*. Cambridge: MIT Press, 1978.

The Military Balance, 1988-1989. London: International Institute for Strategic Studies, 1988.

"Minister of Defense Explains Creation of Military Fronts," *Angop News Bulletin* [London], No. 101, June 30, 1988, 8-9.

Radu, Michael. "The African National Congress: Cadres and Credo," *Problems of Communism*, 36, No. 4, July–August 1987, 58–74.

Seiler, John (ed.). *Southern Africa since the Portuguese Coup*. Boulder, Colorado: Westview Press, 1980.

Shelly, Louise I. *Crime and Modernization*. Carbondale: Southern Illinois University Press, 1981.

SIPRI Yearbook, 1988: World Armaments and Disarmament. (Stockholm International Peace Research Institute.) New York: Oxford University Press, 1988.

Somerville, Keith. *Angola: Politics, Economics, and Society*. (Marxist Regimes Series.) Boulder, Colorado: Lynne Rienner, 1986.

Taylor, Michael J.H. *Encyclopedia of the World's Air Forces*. New York: Facts on File, 1988.

U.S. Committee for Refugees. *Uprooted Angolans: From Crisis to Catastrophe*. Washington: American Council for Nationalities Service, August 1987.

United States. Arms Control and Disarmament Agency. *World Military Expenditures and Arms Transfers, 1987*. Washington: 1988.

_____. Central Intelligence Agency. *The World Factbook, 1988*. Washington, 1988.

_____. Congress. 94th, 2d Session. Senate. Committee on Foreign Relations. Subcommittee on African Affairs. *Angola*. Washington: GPO, 1976.

_____. Congress. 95th, 1st Session. House of Representatives. Committee on Foreign Affairs. *Angola: Intervention or Negotiation*. Washington: GPO, 1986.

_____. Congress. 95th, 2d Session. House of Representatives. Committee on International Relations. Subcommittee on Africa. *United States-Angolan Relations*. Washington: GPO, 1978.

_____. Congress. 96th, 2d Session. House of Representatives. Committee on Foreign Affairs. Subcommittee on Africa. *United States Policy Toward Angola—Update*. Washington: GPO, 1980.

_____. Congress. 99th, 2d Session. Senate. Committee on Foreign Relations. *Angola: Options for American Foreign Policy*. Washington: GPO, 1986.

_____. Department of State. *Country Reports on Human Rights Practices for 1987*. (Report submitted to United States Congress, 100th, 2d Session, Senate, Committee on Foreign Relations, and House of Representatives, Committee on Foreign Affairs.) Washington: GPO, February 1988.

Wheeler, Douglas L., and René Pélissier. *Angola*. New York: Praeger, 1971.

Wolfers, Michael. "People's Republic of Angola." Pages 62–86 in Bogdan Szajkowski (ed.), *Marxist Governments: A World Survey*, 1. London: Macmillian, 1981.

Wolfers, Michael, and J. Bergerol. *Angola in the Frontline*. London: Zed Press, 1983.

(Various issues of the following publications were also used in the preparation of this chapter: *Africa Confidential* [London]; *Africa Contemporary Record; Africa Diary* [New Delhi]; *Africa Economic Digest* [London]; *African Defence Journal* [Paris]; *Africa Now* [London]; *Africa Report; Africa Research Bulletin* (Political Series) [Oxford]; *AfricAsia* [Paris]; *Afrique Défense* [Paris]; *Air International* [London]; *Atlanta Constitution;* British Broadcasting Corporation, *Summary of World Broadcasts* [London]; *Christian Science Monitor; Defense and Foreign Affairs Handbook; Defense and Foreign Affairs Weekly; Facts and Reports* [Amsterdam]; Foreign Broadcast Information Service, *Daily Report: Middle East and Africa* (until April 1987) and *Daily Report: Africa sub-Saharan* (since April 1987); *Flight International* [London]; *International Defense Review* [Geneva]; *Jane's All the World's Aircraft* [London]; *Jane's Armour and Artillery* [London]; *Jane's Defence Weekly* [London]; *Jane's Fighting Ships* [London]; *Jane's Weapons Systems* [London]; *Jeune Afrique* [Paris]; Joint Publications Research Service, *Report on sub-Saharan Africa; Marchés tropicaux et méditerranéens* [Paris]; *Soldier of Fortune; Washington Post; Washington Times;* and *West Africa* [London].)

Glossary

assimilado(s)—Those Africans and *mestiços (q.v.)* considered by the colonial authorities to have met certain formal standards indicating that they had successfully absorbed (assimilated) the Portuguese language and culture. Individuals legally assigned to the status of *assimilado* assumed (in principle) the privileges and obligations of Portuguese citizens and escaped the burdens, e.g., that of forced labor, imposed on most Africans (*indígenas— q.v.*). The status of *assimilado* and its legal implications were formally abolished in 1961.

barrels per day (bpd)—Production of crude oil and petroleum products is frequently measured in barrels per day. A barrel is a volume measure of forty-two United States gallons. Conversion of barrels to metric tons depends on the density of the special product. About 7.3 barrels of average crude oil weigh one metric ton. Heavy products would be about seven barrels per metric ton. Light products, such as gasoline and kerosene, would average eight barrels per metric ton.

degredado(s)—Exiled convicts; refers to convicted criminals sent from Portugal to Angola. *Degredados* constituted a very substantial part of the Portuguese who came to Angola from the sixteenth century to the early twentieth century.

fiscal year (FY)—January 1 to December 31.

gross domestic product (GDP)—A value measure of the flow of domestic goods and services produced by an economy over a period of time, such as a year. Only output values of goods for final consumption and intermediate production are assumed to be included in final prices. GDP is sometimes aggregated and shown at market prices, meaning that indirect taxes and subsidies are included; when these have been eliminated, the result is GDP at factor cost. The word *gross* indicates that deductions for depreciation of physical assets have not been made. *See also* gross national product.

gross national product (GNP)—Gross domestic product (GDP— *q.v.*) plus the net income or loss stemming from transactions with foreign countries. GNP is the broadest measurement of the output of goods and services by an economy. It can be calculated at market prices, which include indirect taxes and subsidies. Because indirect taxes and subsidies are only transfer payments, GNP is often calculated at factor cost, removing indirect taxes and subsidies.

indígena(s)—An African or *mestiço (q.v.)* without *assimilado (q.v.)* status. In Portuguese terms, it means unassimilated or uncivilized. Before the abolition of the status (and the distinction between it and that of *assimilado)* in 1961, roughly 99 percent of all Africans were *indígenas.*

International Monetary Fund (IMF)—Established along with the World Bank *(q.v.)* in 1945, the IMF is a specialized agency affiliated with the United Nations and is responsible for stabilizing international exchange rates and payments. The main business of the IMF is the provision of loans to its members (including industrialized and developing countries) when they experience balance of payments difficulties. These loans frequently carry conditions that require substantial internal economic adjustments by the recipients, most of which are developing countries.

kwanza—Angolan currency unit that replaced the Angolan escudo after January 8, 1977. The kwanza, named for the Cuanza (Kwanza) River, consists of 100 lwei (lw), named for one of the river's tributaries. The kwanza was a nonconvertible currency, but exchange rates for authorized transactions were established regularly. In late 1988, US$1 officially equaled Kz29.3; reportedly, the kwanza traded on the parallel market for up to Kz2,100 per US$1.

Lomé Convention—An agreement between the European Community (EC) and the African, Caribbean, and Pacific (ACP) states whose provisions call for the EC to extend economic assistance to ACP countries. Much of the aid is for project development or rehabilitation, but a large portion is set aside for the Stabilization of Export Earnings (STABEX) system, designed to help developing countries withstand fluctuations in the prices of their agricultural exports.

mestiço(s)—An individual of mixed white and African ancestry. Several varieties, depending on the nature and degree of mixture, were recognized by the Portuguese and *mestiços* in the colonial era. Before 1961 most *mestiços* had the status of *assimilado (q.v).*

Paris Club—A noninstitutional framework whereby developed nations that make loans or guarantee official or private export credits to lesser developed states meet to discuss borrowers' ability to repay debts. The organization, which met for the first time in 1956, has no formal or institutional existence and no fixed membership. Its secretariat is run by the French treasury, and it has a close relationship with the World Bank *(q.v.),* the International Monetary Fund (IMF—*q.v.),* and the United

Nations Conference on Trade and Development.

World Bank—Informal name used to designate a group of three affiliated international institutions: the International Bank for Reconstruction and Development (IBRD), the International Development Association (IDA), and the International Finance Corporation (IFC). The IBRD, established in 1945, has the primary purpose of providing loans to developing countries for productive projects. The IDA, a legally separate loan fund administered by the staff of the IBRD, was set up in 1960 to furnish credits to the poorest developing countries on much easier terms than those of conventional IBRD loans. The IFC, founded in 1956, supplements the activities of the IBRD through loans and assistance specifically designed to encourage the growth of productive private enterprises in the less developed countries. The president and certain senior officers of the IBRD hold the same positions in the IFC. The three institutions are owned by the governments of the nations that subscribe their capital. To participate in the World Bank group, member states must first belong to the International Monetary Fund (IMF—*q.v.*).

Index

Abako. *See* Alliance of Bakongo (Abako)
accords, regional (1988) (*see also* agreements; Joint Military Monitoring Commission): Angola's probable gains from, 5, 195; for Cuban troop removal, 194–95; effect of, xxv–xxvi, xxvii, 222
ACDA. *See* Arms Control and Disarmament Agency (ACDA)
Action Committee for the National Union of Cabindans (Comité d'Action d'Union Nationale des Cabindais: CAUNC), 33
Active Revolt (1974), 41, 46, 170, 236
administration, government: executive branch in, 165, 167–68; judicial system of, 169; legislative branch of, 168–69; at local level, 169–70
Afonso (Kongo king), 7
African League, 26
African National Congress (ANC), 61, 106; base and activity in Angola of, 191–92, 246; fighting against UNITA by, 222; MPLA-PT support for, 244
African Petroleum Producers' Association, 130
Africans as traders, 19
Africans in Angolan society, 22–24
Africa Têxtil, 144
Agip Oil Company, 131
Agostinho Neto Organization of Pioneers (Organização dos Pioneiros Agostinho Neto: OPA), 181
Agostinho Neto University, 102, 198
agreements, 38, 162; of Angola, Cuba, and South Africa (1988), 205–6; with Comecon, 198; Lomé III Agreement, 121–22; of military cooperation with Hungary, 227; nonaggression pact: Zaire, Zambia, Angola, 207–8; between Portugal and Belgium, 19; related to fishing rights, 140; with Soviet Union, 197
agricultural sector (*see also* associations, farm; cooperatives, farm; farmers as interest group; imports): components of, 88–90; economic crisis of, 121, 138; effect of resettlement on, 35; effect of UNITA insurgency on, 50, 56, 63, 92,

184; free trade policy for, 118; migration from, xxiii; plantations in, 88, 115; population in, 90–91; Portuguese farms of, 114; production of, 135–37; ratio of labor force in, 123; socialism for, 45
AIDS Policy Research Center, United States, 106
air force. *See* People's Air and Air Defense Force of Angola (Força Aérea Popular de Angola/Defesa Aérea y Antiaérea: FAPA/DAA)
air transport industry, 113, 151
Alfredo, Manuel Augusto, 221
Algeria, 29–30, 130
Alliama. *See* Alliance of Mayombe (Alliama)
Alliance of Bakongo (Alliance des Bakongo: Abako), 27, 73
Alliance of Mayombe (Alliance de Mayombe: Alliama), 33, 73
Almeida, Roberto de, 47
Alvaro I (Kongo king), 9
Alvaro II (Kongo king), 9
Alves, Nito (*see also* Nitistas), 42, 164, 170, 180, 212, 236
Alvor Agreement (1975), 38, 162
Ambundu (Akwaluanda) people, 71–72
Amnesty International, 251–55
ANC. *See* African National Congress (ANC)
Andrade, Mário, 27, 41
Angola Airlines (Linhas Aéreas de Angola: TAAG), 151
Angolan Border Guard (Tropa Guarda Fronteira Angolana: TGFA), 248
Angolan Cement Company (Emprêsa de Cimento de Angola: Cimangola), 147
Angolan Directorate of Intelligence and Security (Direção de Informação e Segurança de Angola: DISA), 247
Angolanization law (Decree 20/82) (1982), 124
Angolan Journalists' Union, 190
Angolan People's Police, 248–49
Angolan Red Cross, 105
Angolan War Veterans' Committee, 235
angolar, 22
Angol (SACOR subsidiary), 126

301

Published Country Studies

(Area Handbook Series)

550-65	Afghanistan	550-87	Greece
550-98	Albania	550-78	Guatemala
550-44	Algeria	550-174	Guinea
550-59	Angola	550-82	Guyana and Belize
550-73	Argentina	550-151	Honduras
550-169	Australia	550-165	Hungary
550-176	Austria	550-21	India
550-175	Bangladesh	550-154	Indian Ocean
550-170	Belgium	550-39	Indonesia
550-66	Bolivia	550-68	Iran
550-20	Brazil	550-31	Iraq
550-168	Bulgaria	550-25	Israel
550-61	Burma	550-182	Italy
550-50	Cambodia	550-30	Japan
550-166	Cameroon	550-34	Jordan
550-159	Chad	550-56	Kenya
550-77	Chile	550-81	Korea, North
550-60	China	550-41	Korea, South
550-26	Colombia	550-58	Laos
550-33	Commonwealth Caribbean, Islands of the	550-24	Lebanon
550-91	Congo	550-38	Liberia
550-90	Costa Rica	550-85	Libya
550-69	Côte d'Ivoire (Ivory Coast)	550-172	Malawi
550-152	Cuba	550-45	Malaysia
550-22	Cyprus	550-161	Mauritania
550-158	Czechoslovakia	550-79	Mexico
550-36	Dominican Republic and Haiti	550-76	Mongolia
550-52	Ecuador	550-49	Morocco
550-43	Egypt	550-64	Mozambique
550-150	El Salvador	550-35	Nepal and Bhutan
550-28	Ethiopia	550-88	Nicaragua
550-167	Finland	550-157	Nigeria
550-155	Germany, East	550-94	Oceania
550-173	Germany, Fed. Rep. of	550-48	Pakistan
550-153	Ghana	550-46	Panama

550–156	Paraguay	550–53	Thailand
550–185	Persian Gulf States	550–89	Tunisia
550–42	Peru	550–80	Turkey
550–72	Philippines	550–74	Uganda
550–162	Poland	550–97	Uruguay
550–181	Portugal	550–71	Venezuela
550–160	Romania	550–32	Vietnam
550–37	Rwanda and Burundi	550–183	Yemens, The
550–51	Saudi Arabia	550–99	Yugoslavia
550–70	Senegal	550–67	Zaire
550–180	Sierra Leone	550–75	Zambia
550–184	Singapore	550–171	Zimbabwe
550–86	Somalia		
550–93	South Africa		
550–95	Soviet Union		
550–179	Spain		
550–96	Sri Lanka		
550–27	Sudan		
550–47	Syria		
550–62	Tanzania		